Prevention of Alcohol Abuse

Prevention of Alcohol Abuse

Edited by

Peter M. Miller

Sea Pines Behavioral Institute
Hilton Head Island, South Carolina

and

Ted D. Nirenberg

Veterans Administration Medical Center, and
Brown University
Providence, Rhode Island

Plenum Press • New York and London

Library of Congress Cataloging in Publication Data

Main entry under title:

Prevention of alcohol abuse.

Includes bibliographies and index.
1. Alcoholism — Prevention — Addresses, essays, lectures. I. Miller, Peter Michael, 1942–   . II. Nirenberg, Ted D., 1952–   . [DNLM: 1. Alcoholism — Prevention and control. WM 274 P944]
HV5047.P73   1983   362.2′927   83-19203
ISBN 0-306-41328-0

© 1984 Plenum Press, New York
A Division of Plenum Publishing Corporation
233 Spring Street, New York, N.Y. 10013

Printed in the United States of America

Contributors

AMECHI ANUMONYE, Department of Psychiatry, Lagos University Teaching Hospital, Lagos, Nigeria

HOWARD T. BLANE, Minimizing Alcohol Problems Project, School of Education, University of Pittsburgh, Pittsburgh, Pennsylvania

BARBARA BRAUCHT, Department of Psychology, University of Denver, Denver, Colorado

G. NICHOLAS BRAUCHT, Department of Psychology, University of Denver, Denver, Colorado

C. CAMPILLO-SERRANO, Epidemiological and Social Sciences Department, Instituto Mexicano De Psiquiatria, Antiquo Camino A Xochimilco 101, Mexico

TONY CELLUCCI, Department of Psychology, North Carolina Wesleyan College, Rocky Mount, North Carolina

DONALD W. GOODWIN, Department of Psychiatry, University of Kansas School of Medicine, Kansas City, Kansas

K. GUNNAR GÖTESTAM, The University of Trondheim, Östmarka Hospital, Trondheim, Norway

THOMAS C. HARFORD, National Institute on Alcohol Abuse and Alcoholism, Rockville, Maryland

LINDA E. HEWITT, Department of Psychology, University of Pittsburgh, Pittsburgh, Pennsylvania

RAYMOND J. HODGSON, Whitchurch Hospital, Whitchurch, Cardiff, Wales

SHUJI IDA, Department of Pharmacology, Kyoto Prefectural University of Medicine, Kawaramachi-Hirokoji, Kamikyo-Ku, Kyoto, Japan

LT. COL. JOHN E. KILLEEN, United States Army, Office of Drug and Alcohol Abuse Prevention, Department of Defense, The Pentagon, Washington, D.C.

FELIX KLAJNER, Addiction Research Foundation and University of Toronto, 33 Russell Street, Toronto, Canada

DAVID P. KRAFT, Mental Health Division, University Health Services, University of Massachusetts, Amherst, Massachusetts

KINYA KURIYAMA, Department of Pharmacology, Kyoto Prefectural University of Medicine, Kawaramachi-Hirokoji, Kamikyo-Ku, Kyoto, Japan

STEPHEN R. MANSKE, University of Waterloo, Waterloo, Ontario, Canada

BARBARA S. McCRADY, Butler Hospital and Brown University, Providence, Rhode Island

M. E. MEDINA-MORA, Epidemiological and Social Science Department, Instituto Mexicano de Psiquiatria, Antiquo Camino A Xochimilco 101, Mexico

PETER M. MILLER, Sea Pines Behavioral Institute, Sea Pines Plantation, Hilton Head Island, South Carolina

WILLIAM R. MILLER, Department of Psychology, The University of New Mexico, Albuquerque, New Mexico

PETER E. NATHAN, Rutgers, The State University, New Brunswick, New Jersey

TED D. NIRENBERG, Alcohol Dependence Treatment Program, Veterans Administration Medical Center, Providence, Rhode Island and Section of

Psychiatry and Human Behavior, Brown University, Providence, Rhode Island

NORA E. NOEL, Butler Hospital, Providence, Rhode Island

SEITARO OHKUMA, Department of Pharmacology, Kyoto Prefectural University of Medicine, Kawaramachi-Hirokoji, Kamikyo-Ku, Kyoto, Japan

ANDREA PAGE, University of Waterloo, Waterloo, Ontario, Canada

DOUGLAS A. PARKER, Department of Sociology, California State University, Long Beach, California

OLA RÖSTUM, Blue Cross Alcoholism Treatment Center, Trondheim, Norway

RONALD P. SCHLEGEL, University of Waterloo, Waterloo, Ontario, Canada

REGINALD G. SMART, Addiction Research Foundation, 33 Russell Street, Toronto, Ontario, Canada

LINDA C. SOBELL, Addiction Research Foundation and University of Toronto, 33 Russell Street, Toronto, Ontario, Canada

MARK B. SOBELL, Addiction Research Foundation and University of Toronto, 33 Russell Street, Toronto, Ontario, Canada

I. A. SYTINSKY, Research Group of Neurochemical Basis of Alcoholism, A. A. Ukhtomsky Institute of Physiology, Leningrad University, Leningrad, U.S.S.R.

VIJOY K. VARMA, Department of Psychiatry, Postgraduate Institute of Medical Evaluation and Research, Chandigarh, India

Preface

The abuse of alcohol presents a major health problem throughout the world. Until recently both clinical and research efforts have been geared toward treatment and rehabilitation of alcoholism. With the growing number of problem drinkers entering treatment, the need for a better understanding of the prevention of alcohol abuse has become increasingly evident. Although still in its infancy, the field of alcoholism prevention is growing at a rapid rate. Increasing numbers of behavioral scientists throughout the world are conducting or planning prevention projects. Policy planners, school administrators, military agencies, community groups, state and local alcoholism agencies, and industries are initiating alcohol abuse prevention programs with fervor. Legislators at all levels of government are also developing a keen interest in legislation aimed at reducing the extent of problem drinking.

This book represents one of the first systematic attempts to compile a comprehensive text on the prevention of alcohol abuse. Many of the contributors to *Prevention of Alcohol Abuse* have international reputations that strengthen their understanding of the complex nature of prevention. By providing a critical review of the current knowledge about prevention, the text will serve to stimulate and lay the groundwork for further prevention efforts.

We thank all of the chapter authors for their excellent contributions. It is through their efforts that the field will thrive. Our appreciation also is expressed to Leonard Pace, formerly of Plenum Press, for his encouragement and helpful comments in the development of the text.

PETER. M. MILLER
TED D. NIRENBERG

Contents

PREDICTORS OF PROBLEM DRINKING

APPROACHES TO PREVENTION

PRACTICAL APPLICATIONS OF PREVENTION STRATEGIES

I

History and Issues of Alcohol Abuse Prevention

While the abuse of alcohol has a long history, its prevention is a relatively recent phenomenon. This section focuses on the major historical trends in prevention as well as current issues of concern to researchers and practitioners.

In Chapter 1, Nirenberg and Miller provide a brief introduction to past and present attempts at preventing alcohol abuse. They emphasize the critical needs for the development of effective prevention strategies in light of the growing prevalence of drinking problems. While treatment programs have benefited from intensive efforts at research and evaluation, prevention is only recently receiving the public and professional attention it deserves.

A detailed review of conceptual and methodological issues related to alcohol abuse prevention is presented in Chapter 2 by Cellucci. Unless these basic research issues are identified and addressed, the efficacy of prevention efforts will remain unclear. Cellucci's critical review serves as an excellent forerunner to the research programs to follow by alerting the reader to the important conceptual threads that weave through all aspects of alcoholism prevention.

The identification of populations in need of prevention together with matching groups is an essential prerequisite to effective prevention. Prevention programs will have minimal impact unless specific determinants of alcohol abuse in specific populations are incorporated into the prevention system. Noel and McCrady, in Chapter 3, address prevention in terms of three target groups—American Indians, the elderly, and women. The idiosyncratic drinking patterns and determinants of alcohol abuse in each group are reviewed and prevention strategies suggested.

1

History and Overview of the Prevention of Alcohol Abuse

TED D. NIRENBERG AND PETER M. MILLER

The abuse of alcohol constitutes a significant and ever-increasing health problem in most countries throughout the world. Alcohol is being produced and consumed in larger and larger quantities. Between 1960 and 1972 estimated worldwide production increased by 19% for wine, 68% for beer, and 61% for liquor (Finnish Foundation for Alcohol Studies and World Health Organization, 1977). Concomitantly, availability of alcoholic beverages increased as a result of fewer restrictions on the time, place, and quantity of alcohol sales, as well as the addition of retail outlets. In Germany and Japan alcoholic beverages can even be obtained via automatic vending machines.

With the increase in production and availability came a significant increase in consumption. According to estimates of the Finnish Foundation for Alcohol Studies and the World Health Organization (1977), consumption of alcoholic beverages doubled in Australia and the United States between 1950 and 1972. During the same period the consumption of wine increased eightfold in Finland and twentyfold in the Netherlands. Increases in alcohol use have been particularly spectacular in some countries. For example, during the past 25 years Finland and West Germany have experi-

TED D. NIRENBERG • Alcohol Dependence Treatment Program, Veterans Administration Medical Center, Providence, Rhode Island and Section of Psychiatry and Human Behavior, Brown University, Providence, Rhode Island 02908.   PETER M. MILLER • Sea Pines Behavioral Institute, Sea Pines Plantation, Hilton Head Island, South Carolina 29928.

enced a 276% and 529% increase in per capita alcohol consumption, respectively (Moser, 1980).

Some population groups within countries are increasing consumption dramatically. The young, for example, are drinking much more than previously. The Fourth Special Report to the United States Congress on Alcohol and Health (DeLuca, 1981) reported that in 1978, 32% of 10th- to 12th-graders and over 24% of 15-year-olds were moderate to heavy drinkers. Overall, American adults (14 years of age and older) consume on the average 2.7 gallons of ethanol per person per year (approximately two standard drinks per day), a large amount considering that about one-third of the adult population is abstinent.

As consumption increases, alcohol-related problems are intensified. It is quite evident that level of consumption is related to alcohol dependence and physical and social problems. Adverse effects of drinking are noted in as many as 17% of drinkers who consume on the average as little as one or two drinks per day (Polich & Orvis, 1979). Serious health problems associated with heavy drinking are also on the rise. In several countries cirrhosis now ranks among the five leading causes of adult death (Schmidt, 1977). Turner, Mezey, and Kimball (1977a,b), in two comprehensive reviews, found that daily alcohol consumption of 150 g to 400 g is related to health impairments including damage to the liver, brain, pancreas, and fetus, as well as fragmented sleep, alcohol withdrawal syndrome, and hypertension.

Heavy drinkers are also more prone to injuries. In 1975, traffic accidents in the United States accounted for 45,853 deaths. Of these, one-half involved alcohol (Noble, 1978). The National Institute on Alcohol Abuse and Alcoholism (Noble, 1978) estimated that 25% of drivers in nonfatal accidents and 59% of those in fatal accidents had blood alcohol concentrations of over .10%. Alcohol has also been found to be associated with aviation crashes (Lacefield, 1975), industrial accidents (National Safety Council, 1976), drownings (Giertsen, 1970), and even accidental fires (Haberman & Baden, 1974). In addition, alcohol use is associated with several violent crimes—during the criminal act 13% to 50% of sex offenders, 24% to 72% of assault offenders, and 28% to 86% of homicide offenders are under the influence of alcohol (e.g., Amir, 1971; Hollis, 1974; Pittman & Handy, 1964).

PREVENTION VERSUS TREATMENT

In terms of the growing problem of alcohol abuse, treatment efforts have always fallen short in terms of keeping pace with the number of people who require treatment. The reasons are many and varied. Certainly too few treatment facilities and personnel are available. To adequately cope with the number of problem drinkers and their families would take an all-out effort requiring an unrealistic amount of money and an impractical amount of social support. In addition, the efficacy of the types of alcoholism treatments in current use is still questionable. Clinical researchers continue to grapple with the problem of which treatments are best for which people. The variable effectiveness of treatment results in a high rate of recidivism, which further clogs the alcoholism treatment system.

Although treatment efforts are worthwhile, they cannot constitute the only intervention effort if widespread progress is to be made. The constant flow of alcoholics into the system must be slowed at its source through prevention efforts. Alcoholism prevention has always seemed a rather idealistic concept that receives a great deal of rhetoric but very little action. Historically, prevention has been neglected in terms of professional interest and federal funding with treatment priorities receiving the largest share of incentives.

In recent years the trend has been changing. Alcoholism prevention is being treated more seriously and an increasing number of clinicians and researchers are devoting their efforts to prevention. Advances are being made on both theoretical and practical grounds. As in any relatively new field, information is growing rapidly. This book represents one of the first attempts to compile the current state-of-the-art of this diverse specialty and to point to present trends and future directions.

RESISTANCE TO PREVENTION

Although most people would acknowledge that the prevention of alcohol problems is worthwhile, several fronts of resistance exist. Producers of alcoholic beverages often fear that prevention may lead to less consumption and hence fewer sales. Federal and local governments rely heavily on taxes from alcohol sales as a source of revenue. In the United States public revenue from the sale of alcohol totaled over 9 billion dollars in 1975.

Less production and consumption of alcohol would have drastic effects on employment in areas where distilleries are located. With the current problem of high unemployment throughout the world, social and health policies that might impede employment would not be very popular. The United States government finds itself in a similar bind with the tobacco industry. Although acknowledging that cigarettes constitute a significant health hazard, the federal government also subsidizes tobacco farmers in order to keep the tobacco industry economically stable and to avoid unemployment.

Prohibitions against the excessive use of alcohol are considered by some as restrictions on personal freedom. A heavy drinker, for instance, may say, "If I want to kill myself with alcohol, that's my business." In contrast, others may argue that since their lives are in jeopardy by having the heavy drinker on the highways, and their tax money may eventually be used to hospitalize or incarcerate him or her, restrictions are legitimate.

Basically, there is a lack of a well-organized constituency for the prevention of alcohol misuse. Advocates of alcoholism treatment efforts such as Alcoholics Anonymous are well organized and have shown that such organizations and commitment can pay off.

WHAT IS PREVENTION?

With any health or social problem three basic types of prevention exist. *Primary prevention* attempts to stop problem drinking before it begins. This can be accomplished by efforts to promote complete abstinence among youth (e.g., through legislation) or to promote responsible attitudes and decisions regarding the use or nonuse of alcohol (e.g., through junior high school alcohol education programs). The age at which primary prevention efforts should begin is somewhat questionable. Most programs focus on junior high school students between the ages of 11 and 15 years. However, many investigators argue that the ingredients predisposing a person to problem drinking are formulated much earlier in life. For example, Jahoda and Cramond (1972) found that children as young as three years of age had already developed attitudes and values about alcohol use and abuse. Goodwin, Schulsinger, Hermansen, Guze, and Winokin (1973) would argue that family history of alcoholism and hereditary factors constitute such a high risk for some forms of alcoholism that prevention could begin from the moment of birth in terms of parental education and intervention.

Secondary prevention is aimed at heavy drinkers who are just beginning to develop problems because of their use of alcohol. The problem has already begun and the goal is to control it before it worsens. Secondary prevention efforts are frequently focused at young adults between the ages of 18 and 25 years. This age group experiences more life problems due to alcohol misuse than any other age group (USDHEW, 1974). Many secondary prevention efforts are educational in nature and take the form of media campaigns, military and college programs, and driver-safety courses. Early identification of problems related to alcohol is an important key together with insuring that the prevention program is delivered to and accepted by the potential client. Removing the social stigma often attached to individual alcohol problems is essential. For example, industrial-based programs that stress the nonproductive employee as opposed to the problem-drinking employee have proven to be especially acceptable to participants and effective in the early detection of problem drinkers.

Tertiary prevention is aimed at people who have already been diagnosed as alcoholics. The goal is to prevent further deterioration and prevent chronicity. Thus, tertiary prevention and treatment are essentially the same. For the most part, alcoholism prevention is usually thought of in terms of primary and secondary approaches.

THE TARGETS OF PREVENTION

The targets of alcoholism prevention projects usually vary in age from junior high school level to young adulthood. It is during these periods that initial experimentation with alcohol and peer pressure to drink often begin. Some investigators (Jessor & Jessor, 1977; Zucker & Barron, 1973) argue that certain behavioral characteristics (e.g., antisocial behavior) during the junior high school periods help to predict later problem drinking. These characteristics may help to better delineate subpopulations in need of the most intensive prevention efforts.

Other investigators insist that primary prevention must begin earlier in life, since attitudes regarding alcohol and drinking are formulated during early childhood (Jahoda & Cramond, 1972). Prevention efforts aimed at very young children (e.g., in the form of comic books) are increasing. Other special populations such as women, blacks, American Indians, and the elderly historically have been ignored by both treatment and prevention projects. Although alcoholism treatment resources for these populations have increased at a rapid rate, prevention programs are more recent and are developing at a slower pace.

Special "captive" populations such as college students, military personnel, and drunken-driving offenders are also the targets of intervention. Such interventions point up the necessity for specialized prevention programs designed to meet the needs of specified groups. An ultimate goal of prevention may be to match strategies to populations in order to produce maximum effectiveness. Global, "shotgun" approaches to prevention are often not appropriate. Even though they may seem cost-effective since one message or intervention can be given to everyone, their efficacy is questionable.

HISTORY OF ALCOHOL ABUSE PREVENTION

The need for prevention of alcohol abuse probably existed very soon after alcoholic beverages were introduced for human consumption. Even the Old Testament warns of the negative consequences of the overindulgence of alcohol; its tenets regarding the use of alcohol can be considered one of the early attempts at prevention.

Cultural restrictions on the use of alcohol have been varied, ranging from complete prohibition to liberalization. Controls have been inconsistent and frequently have been relaxed or tightened to meet the philosophy of current thinking. For instance, around the end of the 19th century and the beginning of the 20th century, a conservative shift in several countries (e.g., certain Canadian provinces, Nordic countries, and the United States) led to periods of prohibition. This conservative trend lasted until the end of World War II, at which time a gradual liberalization of controls occurred. During the past decade there has again been a worldwide tendency toward stricter alcohol controls.

Probably the most notable attempt at prevention in the United States was the temperance movement that pioneered the notion that alcohol use was socially, morally, and physically corrupt and should be abolished. Temperance ideas were frequently tied in closely with strong fundamentalist religious beliefs. These sentiments eventually led to social legislation in the form of prohibition. Although national prohibition was not popular and eventually was ended, forms of legislated abstinence still exist in some states or counties. The underlying theme of prohibitionist movements has been that *alcohol* is evil, not the person abusing it. The philosophy is "Eradicate the alcohol, eradicate the problem."

Gradually, the notion that alcohol abuse is both a people problem and a substance problem developed. Alcoholism was labeled as a disease partly in an effort to remove social stigma barriers to treatment. The disease concept has taken on various meanings over the years with the nature of prevention efforts varying with these meanings. Alcoholics Anonymous, for example, historically has viewed "disease" literally in the medical sense: Alcoholism is akin to diabetes. The view is based on the idea that something is physically different about the alcoholic and results in his or her loss of control over alcohol. The shortcoming of this belief is that the "something" different about alcoholics has never been identified. In terms of prevention, this results in only one viable approach, that is, abstinence for everyone. Since prohibition is unpopular, those espousing this notion of alcoholism as a physical disease have put most of their prevention efforts into media and educational campaigns designed to identify problem drinkers early. Symptoms of alcoholism are listed for the intended audience to diagnose themselves, a friend, or a relative. This approach is essentially secondary prevention.

MODELS OF PREVENTION

It is apparent, then, that the philosophy or theory behind the etiology of alcoholism greatly influences the nature of the prevention approach that is established. There are three major concepts regarding the development of alcoholism that influence prevention programs. These include (1) the distribution-of-consumption model, (2) the sociocultural model, and (3) the social-psychological model.

DISTRIBUTION-OF-CONSUMPTION MODEL

The distribution-of-consumption, or single-distribution, model assumes a direct relationship between per capita consumption and alcohol abuse. The main premise is that a reduction in per capita consumption by reducing the availability of alcoholic beverages will reduce the number and severity of alcohol-related problems (Bruun, Edwards, Lumio, Makela, Pan, Popham, Room, Schmidt, Skog, Sulkunen, & Oesterberg, 1975; Popham, Schmidt, & de Lint, 1976; Schmidt, 1977).

Evidence in support of this approach demonstrates that changes in per capita consumption of alcohol are related to similar changes in the number of heavy drinkers. In addition, since excessive use of alcohol results in physical and social problems, average consumption should be directly related to these problems. Data directly relating per capita consumption to the incidence of cirrhosis are also supportive of this model.

Parker and Harmon (1978), however, note that the model relies too heavily on cirrhosis data. Correlations between per capita consumption and other alcohol-related problems such as traffic accidents, child abuse, mental illness, and cancer are needed. In addition, they cite data to indicate that several studies do not demonstrate a significant correlation between per capita consumption and incidence of alcohol abuse.

A more damaging argument against the distribution-of-consumption model relates to the fact that "normal" drinkers and alcohol abusers may react differentially to changes in availability. That is, attempts to reduce availability may reduce the per capita consumption of social drinkers but not influence the drinking of heavy drinkers. This has often been referred to as the bimodal model. Preliminary evidence exists to indicate that problem drinkers are not as responsive to external manipulations as light and moderate drinkers. To analyze this differential responsivity, Miller, Hersen, Eisler, Epstein, and Wooten (1974) examined the relationship between visual alcohol cues and alcohol consumption in alcoholics and social drinkers. All subjects performed an operant drinking task in which lever presses on a console earned an alcoholic beverage. The drinking task was administered under two conditions. During Condition 1, a variety of visual alcohol cues (bottles of alcohol; pictures of people consuming alcohol) were in full view of the subject. In Condition 2, the room was bare, with no alcohol cues in sight. Social drinkers were strongly influenced by the alcohol cues, drinking significantly less when they were absent. Alcoholics, on the other hand, were totally unresponsive to the presence or absence of these cues. They drank a great deal in both conditions. These results suggest that individual social-psychological factors may take precedence over external factors in determining alcohol consumption of alcoholics. Basically the reasoning is that if an individual is prone to drink heavily, he or she will find a way to do so regardless of alcohol cues or availability.

The major variables that those espousing the distribution-of-consumption model manipulate are availability, price, and age limitations. Restricting hours of sales and increasing prices have been shown to decrease alcohol consumption. Age limitations have led to mixed results. Lowering the age limit seems to result in increased consumption initially, but this trend is modified the longer the age limitations have been in effect. Barsby and Marshall (1977), on the other hand, found that such initial increases in consumption were small and not statistically significant.

Thus, although there is general interest in this model, the results of intervention strategies have been mixed. Reducing per capita consumption is a complex goal that requires extensive investigation in different settings and with different populations.

Sociocultural Model

Proponents of the sociocultural approach argue that in order to solve the problem of alcohol abuse, social norms about drinking must be changed (Room, 1974; Wilkinson, 1970). In contrast to the distribution-of-consumption model, it is believed that per capita alcohol consumption does not increase rates of alcoholism. Those espousing the sociocultural model argue that alcohol problems result from insufficient social norms regarding the safe use of alcoholic beverages. The prevention goal, therefore, would include the establishment of a new morality about drinking to promote safe, responsible drinking. This would be achieved by (1) clearly distinguishing between responsible drinking and alcohol abuse, (2) establishing a "safe" drinking level in terms of quantity and frequency, (3) reducing the social importance and mystique of drinking, and (4) emphasizing the use of alcohol in a social-recreational context rather than solitary drinking for the purpose of intoxication.

Using this sociocultural approach, Wilkinson (1970) devised specific suggestions regarding a prevention program that would include:

1. Reducing the minimum drinking age to 18 years
2. Allowing those under 18 years of age to drink alcohol at home under the supervision of parents

3. Providing for community education programs aimed at teaching responsible drinking
4. Encouraging colleges and universities to establish supervised drinking environments for students

Those who oppose this sociocultural approach find difficulty with the vague and varied ways in which the phrase *responsible drinking norm* is used. In this regard, if one is to teach responsible, safe drinking, some consensus is necessary on exactly what *is* safe drinking. In spite of the mass amount of alcohol research, scientists still disagree.

In addition, the sociocultural model implies a homogeneity within and across cultures that simply does not exist. Drinking and alcohol abuse norms differ widely. The model is frequently supported by the fact that Jews drink but have low rates of alcoholism. The implication is that they have well-delineated norms regarding the use of alcohol. However, Popham *et al.* (1976) note that the low rate of alcoholism among Jews is probably due to their low per capita consumption and not their morality regarding drinking.

Bruun *et al.* (1975) seriously question the validity of this approach. They argue that if one were to teach and encourage responsible drinking skills, per capita consumption would increase and then lead to a concomitant rise in alcohol abuse problems.

SOCIAL-PSYCHOLOGICAL MODEL

The social-psychological model proposes that problem drinking results from the interaction between personality and social factors. The major variables assumed to influence drinking include peers, family, sociocultural and environmental factors, and personality. Of all these factors, peer and parental influences (e.g., parent–child relationships and broken homes) are considered the most crucial.

Personality factors that increase the likelihood of heavy drinking include feelings of alienation from others, personal dissatisfaction, and a liberal attitude toward personal and social deviations. Also at risk for future alcohol problems are youngsters who drink heavily and frequently, tend to do poorly in school, and show a general tendency toward antisocial behavior. In contrast, regular church attendance, religious commitment, and academic achievement seem to predispose against alcohol abuse.

The major proponents of this model have been Jessor and Jessor (1975) and Zucker (1979). Alcohol use and abuse are seen as developmental phenomena related to relationships, attitudes, and personality traits. Zucker summarizes the main conclusions of this model as follows:

1. There is evidence of the early childhood appearance of behavioral markers that show developmental stability into adulthood and that relate to the later emergence of problem drinking.
2. Mainstream educational efforts about alcohol directed at middle childhood and adolescence generally miss their focus because the cognitive capacity of children at these ages and their earlier learning are at odds with both the content and the timing of the educational messages offered.
3. Significant internal restructuring of peer and family influences goes on, to the extent that efforts to predict drinking behavior on the sole basis of environmental influences will lead to inadequate and statistically less substantial predictive models.
4. Conversely, attempts at predicting the developmental peak age for learning to drink and the peak age for problem-drinking behavior not only need to take account of individual, transition-related attitudes and behaviors, but also need to focus on the social-structure demand characteristics of the normative structure into which the individual is moving in a developmentally appropriate way.
5. Multiple-level influence theories are best utilized not by contrasting which type of influence is most predictively powerful at any specific developmental time point (cross-sectional analysis), but rather by asking which influences are either directly or interactively salient at specified developmental times, and in what way they contribute. (pp. 139–140)

The social-psychological model emphasizes the need to modify attitudes, peer relationships, and parent–child relationships. The focus of prevention is on intervention geared toward improving these relationships and providing both parent and child with better coping skills. Adolescents and young adults would be taught social-emotional skills such as assertiveness to better deal with peer pressure. Values clarification discussion groups would be used to help youngsters examine their belief systems both in general and specifically as they apply to drinking.

Attitudes toward drinking can be modified through such discussions or through the mass media. Television, radio, newspapers, and magazines have all been used to change attitudes toward alcohol. Initially, such efforts were geared simply toward the identification of problem drinkers. More recently efforts have focused on fostering more responsible attitudes toward decisions regarding the use of alcohol. Unfortunately, the effects of these direct public service announcements have been mixed. Most have simply increased the public's knowledge without substantially changing attitudes or behavior. Part of the reason for these disappointing results may lie in the fact that television programming, for example, is inundated with portrayals of alcohol use and abuse. Very often alcohol consumption is shown as a way to alleviate stress and cope with problems. The Fourth Special Report to the United States Congress on Alcohol and Health (DeLuca, 1981) notes that an advisory group of influential television producers has been formed to explore industry-wide standards for the portrayal of alcohol. Mosher and Wallack (1979) have studied this issue and have established the Mass Media Project. Among others, this program is designed to consult on television scripts and to propose programs regarding the responsible use of alcohol.

Although alcohol abuse is clearly a significant worldwide health problem with a long and devastating history, the field of prevention is in its infancy. The present volume attempts to synthesize currently available empirical information in such a manner as to stimulate further investigation of prevention. The remainder of this section includes an examination of the methodological problems involved in evaluating prevention programs and a review of the need to differentially target the delivery of prevention programs to certain high-risk populations.

REFERENCES

Amir, M. *Patterns in forcible rape.* Chicago: University of Chicago Press, 1971.

Barsby, S. L., & Marshall, G. L. Short-term consumption effects of a lower minimum alcohol-purchasing age. *Journal of Studies on Alcohol,* 1977, *38*(9), 1665–1679.

Bruun, K., Edwards, G., Lumio, M., Makela, K., Pan, L., Popham, R. E., Room, R., Schmidt, W., Skog, O. J., Sulkunen, P., & Oesterberg, E. *Alcohol control policies in public health perspective.* Helsinki: Finnish Foundation for Alcohol Studies, 1975.

DeLuca, J. R. (Ed.). *Fourth special report to the U.S. Congress on alcohol and health.* (DHEW Publ. No. ADM 81–1080.) Washington, D.C.: U.S. Government Printing Office, 1981.

Finnish Foundation for Alcohol Studies and World Health Organization European Office. *International statistics on alcoholic beverages: Production, trade, and consumption 1950–1972* (Vol. 27). Helsinki: Author, 1977.

Giertsen, J. C. Drowning while under the influence of alcohol. *Medical Science Law,* 1970, *10,* 216–219.

Goodwin, D. W., Schulsinger, F., Hermansen, L., Guze, S. B., & Winokin, G. Alcohol problems in adoptees raised apart from alcoholic biological parents. *Archives of General Psychiatry,* 1973, *28,* 238–243.

Haberman, P., & Baden, M. Alcoholism and violent death. *Quarterly Journal Studies on Alcohol,* 1974, *35,* 221–231.

Hollis, W. S. On the etiology of criminal homicides—The alcohol factor. *Journal of Political Science Administration,* 1974, *2,* 50–53.

Jahoda, G., & Cramond, J. *Children and alcohol.* London: HMSO, 1972.

Jessor, R., & Jessor, S. L. Adolescent development and the onset of drinking. *Journal of Studies on Alcohol,* 1975, *36,* 27–51.

Jessor, R., & Jessor, S. L. *Problem behavior and psychosocial development: A longitudinal study of youth.* New York: Academic Press, 1977.

Keller, M. (Ed.). *Second special report to the U.S. Congress on alcohol and health.* (DHEW Publ. No. ADM 75–212.) Washington, D.C.: U.S. Government Printing Office, 1974.

Lacefield, D. J. Alcohol continues to play a big part in plane crashes. *Journal of American Medical Association,* 1975, *233,* 405.

Miller, P. M., Hersen, M., Eisler, R. M., Epstein, L., & Wooten, L. S. Relationship of alcohol cues to the drinking of alcoholics and social drinkers: An analogue study. *Psychological Record,* 1974, *24,* 61–66.

Moser, J. *Prevention of alcohol-related problems: An international review of preventive measures, policies, and programmes.* Toronto, Canada: Alcoholism and Drug Addiction Research Foundation, 1980.

Mosher, J. F., & Wallack, L. M. *The DUI project: Description of an experimental program conducted by the California Department of Alcoholic Beverage Control.* Sacramento: California Department of Alcoholic Beverage Control, June 1979.

National Safety Council. *Accident facts:* 1976 edition. Chicago: National Safety Council, 1976.

Noble, E. P. (Ed.). *Third special report to the U.S. Congress on alcohol and health.* (DHEW Publ. No. ADM 79–832.) Washington, D.C.: U.S. Government Printing Office, 1978.

Parker, D. A., & Harmon, M. S. The distribution of consumption model of prevention of alcohol problems: A critical assessment. *Journal of Studies on Alcohol,* 1978, *39,* 377–399.

Pittman, D., & Handy, W. Patterns in criminal aggravated assault. *Journal of Criminal Law and Criminal Police Science,* 1964, *55*(4), 462–470.

Polich, J. M., & Orvis, B. R. *Alcohol problems: Patterns and prevalence in the U.S. Air Force* (R–2308–AF). Santa Monica, Calif.: Rand Corporation, 1979.

Popham, R. E., Schmidt, W., & de Lint, J. The effects of legal restraint on drinking. In B. Kissin & H. Begleiter (Eds.), *The biology of alcoholism* (Vol. 4). New York: Plenum Press, 1976.

Room, R. Governing images and the prevention of alcohol problems. *Preventive Medicine,* 1974, *3,* 11–23.

Schmidt, W. Cirrhosis and alcohol consumption: An epidemiological perspective. In G. Edwards & M. Grant (Eds.), *Alcoholism: New knowledge and new responses.* London: Croom Hall, 1977.

Turner, T. B., Mezey, E., & Kimball, A. W. Measurement of alcohol-related effects in man: Chronic effects in relation to levels of consumption, Part A. *John Hopkins Medical Journal,* 1977, *141,* 235–248. (a)

Turner, T. B., Mezey, E., & Kimball, A. W. Measurement of alcohol-related effects in man: Chronic effects in relation to levels of consumption, Part B. *John Hopkins Medical Journal,* 1977, *141,* 273–286. (b)

Wilkinson, R. *The prevention of drinking problems:* Alcohol control and cultural influences. New York: Oxford University Press, 1970.

Zucker, R. A. Developmental aspects of drinking through the young adult years. In H. T. Blane & M. E. Chafetz (Eds.), *Youth, alcohol, and social policy.* New York: Plenum Press, 1979.

Zucker, R. A., & Barron, F. H. Parental behaviors associated with problem drinking and antisocial behavior among adolescent males. In M. E. Chafetz (Ed.), *Research on alcoholism I: Clinical problems and special populations* (DHEW Publ. No. HSM 74–675.) Washington, D.C.: U.S. Government Printing Office, 1973.

2

The Prevention of Alcohol Problems
Conceptual and Methodological Issues

TONY CELLUCCI

> Prevention attempts . . . require rational specification both of goals and of procedures as well as measurement of the relationship of procedures to any relevant change. (Bacon, 1978, p. 1129)

> Answers to alcohol problems are not be found solely in the study of alcohol and its use, but are intimately and inextricably linked to the human condition. (Blane, 1976, p. 526)

Although concern over the prevention of alcohol problems has a long history, evaluative research regarding such effects is of more recent vintage. In effect, the post-prohibition era shifted the focus of social concern from alcohol *per se* to the individual with alcohol problems, individuals said to be predisposed and afflicted with the disease of alcoholism. Consequently, the major emphasis in the alcohol field became treatment. The formation and subsequent reports of the Cooperative Commission on the Study of Alcoholism (Plaut, 1967; Wilkinson, 1970) emerged later as a major prevention landmark. The members of this commission, who represented various professions and disciplines, examined the many social and developmental influences on alcohol problems from a broad perspective. The commission's

TONY CELLUCCI • Department of Psychology, North Carolina Wesleyan College, Rocky Mount, North Carolina 27801.

observations and resultant recommendations essentially constituted a programmatic social plan for reducing the country's drinking problems. It is no small tribute that many of their specific proposals for prevention found their way into the early activities of the then newly formed National Institute on Alcohol Abuse and Alcoholism (NIAAA). The overriding theme of a need for change in alcohol-related attitudes and social norms, with a particular emphasis on the preventive value of education, characterizes the literature of the late 1960s and early 1970s. Changes in distribution and licensing were seen as important ways of modifying key social attitudes. More recently the possibility of employing the regulatory system to directly influence alcohol problems has been recognized. An important review by Blane (1976) provides an overview of these early developments. His characterization of the prevention literature as extensive, scattered, and of uneven quality remains true today, but that it is becoming less so is evidenced by the present volume.

By all accounts, the magnitude and extent of problems related to or complicated by alcohol is astounding. Associated costs involve not only health problems, but also lost production, accidents, crime, and interpersonal violence (Third Special Report to Congress, Noble, 1978). The finding that emphasizing treatment alone has been a relatively ineffective response to the many alcohol-related problems in our society is perhaps the most persuasive argument in favor of researching prevention.

As is widely recognized, the alcohol field itself is currently undergoing a period of conceptual questioning and change, with data from epidemiological research, laboratory studies, and outcome evaluative projects challenging traditional notions regarding alcohol abuse (Pattison, Sobell, & Sobell, 1977). This changing context is significant in that the conceptual framework from which one views alcohol problems surely will influence resultant thinking about prevention. Room (1974) highlighted this very point discussing what he termed continuing "governing images." For example, perceiving alcohol as a dangerous substance leads to regulation. Theorizing that alcohol-related disruptive and compulsive behavior arises from society's ambivalence about alcohol suggests the need for educational efforts aimed at modifying attitudes and norms. The belief that alcohol problems are manifestations of a specific disease process logically requires an emphasis on early case finding. As Room (1974) noted, these existing images have all operated within the traditional framework of a general disease formulation, a perspective that at least has required revision (Keller, 1976).

Current reviews summarize the prevention literature in terms of two overall models. The social science or sociocultural model (Chafetz, 1970; Plaut, 1972; Wilkinson, 1970) was based on observations regarding dissimilar rates of alcohol problems among various ethnic groups. Variations in drinking practices and problems are seen as reflecting differences in cultural beliefs and attitudes, the group's normative structure, and the specific socialization experiences provided. As an individual's pattern of drinking is learned, it is suggested that a reduction in drinking problems might be brought about by (1) teaching young people responsible and particularly *integrated* drinking in which the use of alcohol is tied to family and recreational activities and (2) educational and social reforms directed at changing social attitudes. The second conceptual perspective, called the distribution-of-consumption model (Bruun, Edwards, Lumio, Mäkelä, Pan, Popham, Room, Schmidt, Skog, Sulkunen, & Oesterberg, 1975; Popham, Schmidt, & de Lint, 1976a) has a more limited focus. The model is based on the finding that the distribution of alcohol consumption appears constant across populations conforming to a logarithmic normal curve in which the proportion of heavy or excessive drinkers is dependent on the mean level of general consumption. In that alcohol abuse, specifically cirrhosis, is related to per capita consumption, the latter becomes the logical target of prevention efforts. Decreases in overall consumption brought about through restrictive changes in availability and increases in relative price of alcohol are thus hypothesized to reduce social morbidity and mortality due to alcohol. It is evident that these models may lead to conflicting strategies of prevention, for example, the practice of encouraging responsible drinking may increase overall consumption. Such contradictions, however, are hardly surprising in that both models are clearly myopic in terms of what research finding they chose to consider. In a thought-provoking paper, Whitehead (1975b) has suggested some lines along which reconciliatory proposals might be designed. What are clearly necessary, though, are expanded and more integrative conceptual models.

There have been many critical comments regarding the logic and feasibility of prevention (Bacon, 1978; Kalb, 1975; Roman & Trice, 1974). It is often stated that widespread use of a largely public-health model of prevention is inappropriate. To begin, there are of course definitional problems surrounding the concepts of alcoholism and alcohol abuse with no strictly agreed-on criteria. It also may be argued that not enough is known regarding the etiology, antecedent conditions, or continuity of alcohol problems to meaningfully discuss prevention. The specifics of prevention and a rationale for adopting particular procedures often are lacking. For example, within the sociocultural perspective, neither the means nor the consequences of changing social normative structures have been considered in detail. Other social functions that problem-related patterns may be serving have remained unexamined, as have possible side effects and social-ethical questions involved in proposed interventions. There has also been a general absence of evaluative research to suggest that prevention efforts, particularly education, are effective. Stressing the negative consequences of excessive drinking have not been shown to change behavior. Although seemingly overstated at times, these issues remain alive and are reflected below. Perhaps as a result of such criticisms, there has been a needed shift from general discussions of sociocultural change to environmental and prevention programs targeted at selected groups with specific alcohol-related problems. This is not to imply encouraging examination of drinking-related attitudes and emphasing responsible drinking has been ineffective. Rather, the success of such proposals (Plaut, 1967; Wilkinson, 1970) no doubt has made possible present prevention efforts.

This chapter summarizes the currently available research literature on alcohol prevention and focuses specifically on conceptual issues and methodological concerns. Four major areas and related studies are reviewed: secondary prevention, legal regulation and public control measures, alcohol education, and the developmental context of alcohol abuse. Such a review is possible because of the many investigators whose work and writings are herein discussed. Their concern with evaluation allows the field to be productively self-conscious about prevention efforts.

SECONDARY PREVENTION PROGRAMS

In public-health models of prevention, primary prevention refers to removing the causes of a disorder and secondary prevention to early identification and treatment. Several arguments might be advanced for favoring secondary prevention efforts. Given that existing knowledge relating to the causes of alcoholism is incomplete, earlier and increased use of known intervention or treatment strategies might be more effective (Cross, 1967). Such an emphasis also seems to fit well with the reasonable strategy of focusing on specific problems (Room, 1981). Relatedly, since secondary prevention techniques and programs would be designed to affect the presently occurring behavior of target groups, they would appear to lend themselves more readily to objective evaluation. Although these sentiments are not without merit, programmatic planning of secondary prevention programs must address several difficult pragmatic concerns: (1) Who or what population to serve, (2) how this group may best be reached, (3) what information, treatment services, and so forth, are to be provided for what specific aims, and (4) how the program might be successfully evaluated.

Epidemiological research findings have been clear in documenting that in addition to traditionally defined alcoholics there exists a large population of frequent heavy drinkers with problem rates as high or higher than alcoholics, and of equally great social costs (Blane, 1979; Cahalan & Cisin, 1976). Although heavy in terms of consumption, drinking patterns among this group are episodic with associated acute problems occurring regularly. Beyond the direct physical and behavioral effects of intoxication, problems to which heavy drinkers are especially prone include disrupted relationships and families, job difficulties, fights, impaired driving, accidents, and arrests for assaults and other serious crimes against persons. To a large extent these are the problems that secondary prevention aspires to address. To date, secondary prevention efforts have involved DWI offenders, occupational programs, and recent behavioral programs for problem drinkers. Illustrations of programs, evaluation data, and the problems presented might be drawn from these areas.

Given legislation and existing programs directed at apprehending DWI offenders, tying prevention efforts to this target group would appear to be an effective way of reaching frequent heavy drinkers. Indeed, research on the characteristics of the drunk-driver population suggests that rather than reflecting a mixture of alcoholics and social drinkers, men arrested for driving while intoxicated represent a distinct group characterized by heavy and problematic drinking, as well as self-reported depression, aggressive and paranoid feelings, and low self-esteem (Selzer, Vinokur, & Wilson, 1977). As a consequence of the programmatic difficulties alluded to above, however, the strategy of focusing on DWI offenders has been less than successful in clearly documenting effective secondary prevention.

Although targeting DWI offenders for prevention programs is supported by the available data, it is limited in terms of the population reached. In a thought-provoking critique of efforts in this area, Whitehead (1975a) pointed out that the extremely low risk of apprehension assures that at best only a small portion (i.e., "the tip of the iceberg") of those who drink and drive will be influenced; relatedly, he challenges the idea that those arrested are a representative group. Even more significantly, there is neither sufficient evidence nor compelling reasons for believing in the effectiveness of current program contents. Although purported to have secondary prevention goals, most programs for offenders (often called Phoenix programs after the prototype) consist largely of presenting basic educational information (e.g., about alcohol, its physical effects, DWI laws, and penalties) in four to six weekly sessions. This reliance on education almost alone to reduce problems and problem proneness is questionable. As Whitehead (1975a) indicated, is it really possible that DWI offenders do not know *intellectually* that driving after drinking exposes themselves and others to serious risk or that it is illegal? Research simply has not supported a strong relationship between knowledge regarding alcohol or drugs and significant attitudes and behavior (Kinder, 1975). Rather it would seem, as Selzer *et al.*

(1977) reasoned, that the aforementioned findings regarding the psychosocial characteristics of drunk drivers indicate the need for sophisticated psychological intervention programs.

In keeping with these criticisms, existing evaluations of prevention programs for drunk drivers have been disappointing. Most studies have been restrictive in their selection of outcome measures, focusing only on recidivism. Some reduction in the recidivism measure was suggested in a preliminary evaluation of the original Phoenix program (Crabb, Gettys, Malfetti, & Steward, 1971). In a recent review, Alden (1980) reported small and sometimes inconsistent reductions, with few studies incorporating controls. In addition, DWI recidivism is probably a particularly poor evaluation measure in that the recidivism rate is relatively low. By far the largest number of DWI arrestees are first-time offenders.

From the citizen–taxpayer's perspective, the most desired payoff for funding prevention programs for DWI offenders would appear to be a reduced risk of being involved in a serious automotive accident. Seemingly with this concern, the federal government initiated the so-called Alcohol Safety Action Projects (ASAPs) in the early 1970s. Conducted in a number of states, such programs included public education and legal sanctions and referral to existing treatment resources (secondary prevention). Evaluation of such a large-scale social program is of course replete with difficulties; it is of interest, however, that although some slight effects may have occurred in some ASAP areas, overall there was no evidence of a resulting reduction in crash fatalities (Zador, 1976). Secondary prevention programs for DWI offenders often are advocated on the basis of the alarming proportion of accidents that appear to be alcohol related. The reality, however, is that it is as yet unclear to what degree the problem of fatal crashes can be prevented by focusing on heavy drinkers in general, the majority of whom have enviable driving records (Zylman, 1975). Those charged with the task of designing and evaluating programs for drunk drivers should begin attempting to identify those offenders with additional characteristics (e.g., "aggressive irresponsibility") that place them at high risk for accident involvement.

Only one reported study has examined the effectiveness of a DWI educational program in directly reducing alcohol consumption and behavioral impairment. Employing a modified Solomon-four groups design, Scoles and Fine (1977) found that program participants did not reduce their alcohol intake more than controls. Interestingly, there was an interaction between the pretest and the information presented, suggesting pretest sensitization (Lana, 1969) may be a methodological problem in this area. The investigators surmised that the reduced consumption found in their evaluation was most likely the result of the aversiveness of the arrest itself. Clearly, more research is needed, including follow-up data. If targeting DWI offenders is to be an effective prevention strategy, programs must take more seriously the heterogeneity in this population, tailoring interventions accordingly to the type and degree of disturbance, and employing more sensitive measures of program effects.

Beyond projects directed at DWI offenders, occupational programs (Roman & Trice, 1970, 1976) probably constitute the most widespread attempt at secondary prevention (Blane, 1976; Roman, 1975). The impetus for focusing on employees who abuse alcohol arises from (1) the relatively high levels of drinking among specific occupational groups, and (2) the associated costs to work organizations in terms of impaired performance, absenteeism, and accidents. For example, a recent study of railroad employees (Mannello & Seaman, 1979) found that between 11% and 15% of the workers were problem drinkers, and further estimated that such employees had a 20% lower production pattern than the other workers. In keeping with other data, these problem drinkers missed 4 times as much work as other employees and had $3\frac{1}{2}$ times as many accidents. To a large degree, practical problems of management rather than a sense of social responsibility usually have been the basis for employers adopting alcohol intervention programs (Roman, 1975). As highlighted by Roman, the unique promise of these programs for prevention is that such intervention efforts are directly tied to important social institutions with existing norms and roles within work organizations (e.g., appraisal and supervision) legitimizing prevention activities.

During the 1970s, there was a dramatic rise in the number of occupational alcoholism programs and an increase in the availability of health insurance coverage through major carriers and employee health plans (Third Special Report to Congress, Noble, 1978). One survey of Fortune 500 company executives reported that within half of the sampled companies (up from 25% in 1972), there existed some type of program directed at identifying and providing assistance to problem-drinking employees. Traditionally, occupational programming has involved training supervisors to recognize and constructively confront the employee with a drinking problem on the basis of impaired performance. Through a company liaison, referral to outside treatment agencies may be offered. More recently, there has been an apparent shift to broadly conceptualized employee assistance programs with a greater emphasis on providing counseling services, although this development has not gone without critical comment (Roman, 1981). Perhaps most surprising and of greater immediate concern, both the increase in occupational efforts and associated developments in the field have unfortunately occurred in the almost complete absence of guidance from research findings (Roman & Trice, 1976). The lack of published evaluative research appears to be related to the real difficulties (e.g., access and confidentiality) involved when working within private corporations. The result, however, is clear: Although testimony to the success of occupational programs abounds, it is difficult to evaluate adequately their outcomes or effectiveness at secondary prevention.

Two frequently cited studies are illustrative. Hilker, Asma, and Eggert (1972) reported on a 10-year evaluation of their program at Illinois Bell Telephone Company. The records of 402 referred employees were examined for the 5 years prior to and subsequent to their entering the program. Case findings generally were followed by referral to Alcoholics Anonymous singularly or in combination with psychiatric care, depending on assessed needs. The reported findings were impressive: 57% of the employees were judged to be abstinent and another 15% considered improved. Increased ratings of job performance also were documented, as were significant reductions in absences and accidents. Although suggestive of clear benefits, the lack of controls and possibility of evaluator bias unfortunately limit the strength of the conclusions.

In terms of prevention, it is noteworthy that 63% of those referred were diagnosed as chronic alcoholics mostly in their middle-adult years. The investigators interpret this statistic as indicating that the program was missing employees in the early stages of alcoholism, and by implication today, heavy problem drinkers. In a second type of evaluation, Smart (1974) compared the outcome of employed alcoholics who were either mandated to treatment or sought help voluntarily for their drinking. Improvement on supervisory ratings (e.g., sobriety, dependability, job performance, and absenteeism) was found for both groups with no difference in one treatment center and only a slightly higher rate of improvement among the self-referred clients in a second. Assuming preexisting differences in motivation, it has been argued (Trice, 1980) that such findings attest to some degree to the efficacy of occupational prevention.

The existing program outcome evaluations have not progressed beyond simple case demonstrations and these preliminary studies (Trice, 1980). A major methodological shortcoming that has not been addressed is the possibility of unknown selection biases (see B. Miller, Pokorny, Valles, & Cleveland, 1970) in terms of who is referred and accepted into such programs. Randomized field experiments in which identified problem drinkers are assigned to distinct prevention treatments are overdue. Specifically, there is a need to examine the effects of confrontation and the organizational application of contingent consequences, alone and together with various types of counseling programs. To date, it would appear that occupational programming has focused largely on the chronic alcoholic employee and overrelied on traditional forms of therapy. If it is to realize its potential for secondary prevention, experimentation with innovative program contents is vital. Truly moving in the direction of prevention may be difficult, for as Roman (1975) suggests, the evolution of current occupational programming has led to the development of vested political and economic interests. As an excellent example, many company programs now make extensive use of inpatient services even though there is little evidence for the increased effectiveness of long-term hospitalization (Stein, Newton, & Bowman, 1975). In addition, a practical difficulty has hindered the acceptability and potential influence of occupational prevention, specifically the differential use of such intervention measures among lower status levels. The autonomy and unique job province of executives (or, for that matter, college professors) presents real and unsolved obstacles to accessing these populations. To add to the dilemma, little is known about the possible negative consequences (personal and professional) incurred by an individual identified as having a drinking-related problem. Finally, Roman (1975) has suggested the need for further research and theory on the etiological contribution of job factors and the desirability of more closely aligning occupational programming to the emergent fields of management science and organizational behavior.

The advent of behavioral treatment programs (Nirenberg, Ersner-Hershfield, Sobell, & Sobell, 1981) and their extension to problem drinkers is clearly the most current and exciting development in secondary prevention. Such programs are innovative and distinct from more general educational and counseling efforts in that they are explicit *teaching* programs (i.e., a skills curriculum), theoretically based in social learning theory (Bandura, 1974), specifically directed at behavior change (although with presumed concurrent or secondary effects on attitudes and self-concept), and importantly, characterized by an integral concern for evaluating program outcomes. Commonly employed behavioral principles and techniques are organized and presented to clients within a self-management framework (Williams & Long, 1975). Problem drinkers thus are asked to be active participants, assimilating new skills with the unique treatment goal of learning how to drink without incurring problems. Although experimental and controversial with alcoholics, this option of modifying drinking patterns (especially for individuals in young adulthood who are typically unwilling and unlikely to remain abstinent for more than a temporary period) holds substantial promise for prevention.

Frequently employed strategies and components of behavioral treatment with relevance for preventive programs include: (1) self-monitoring and functional analysis of drinking behavior, (2) teaching new skills and perspectives to eliminate problem antecedents (e.g., drink refusal, rearranging cues, and cognitive restructuring), (3) learning to discriminate blood alcohol concentration, (4) modifying drinking behavior directly, (5) building alternative responses (e.g., relaxation and recreational pursuits), and (6) programming contingencies (i.e., the interpersonal environment) to support moderate drinking. (See P. Miller & Mastria, 1977, and P. Miller, 1979 for a more extensive discussion.) Although more basic research is needed, P. Miller (1979) has reviewed the available evidence supporting the general effectiveness and contribution of many of these components. For example, within a multiple baseline design, P. Miller, Becker, Foy, and Wooten (1976) found that instructions and practice could be used to modify such topographical features of drinking as sip magnitude and rate. Moderate drinkers also have been successfully taught to estimate their blood alcohol concentrations using both internal and external cues (Huber, Karlin, & Nathan, 1976; Ogurzsoff & Vogel-Sprott, 1976). Additional data suggest that meditation and relaxation may reduce consumption in young adults. In a correlational study, Shafii, Lavely, and Jaffe (1975) reported a high rate of discontinuation of beer, wine, and especially liquor use among individuals who had maintained the practice of meditating for more than 2 years. Controlled evaluation of short-term training programs in relaxation and meditation techniques also have found decreases in consumption relative to no-treatment controls, although similar decreases in attentional-placebo subjects indicate the involvement of nonspecific factors (Marlatt & Marques, 1977). Extrapolating from research conducted with alcoholics (e.g., Chaney, O'Leary, & Marlatt, 1978; Foy, Miller, Eisler, & O'Toole, 1976), short-term training in drink refusal, assertiveness, and problem-solving skills is likely to be effective in producing specific behavior changes and increased control over drinking. Such skill training not only appears to be the direction in which treatment programs increasingly are moving, but also has certain application in prevention.

Clinically, these treatment components are combined to form an effective intervention or prevention package, which is then hopefully tailored to individuals. A recent chapter describing a program for outpatient problem drinkers (Noel, Sobell, Cellucci, Nirenberg, & Sobell, 1982) is noteworthy for its account of assessment procedures, listing of individual treatment plans, and strategic application to the client's situation of such counseling techniques as problem solving, contracting, assertive and skills training, and cognitive restructuring. Evaluation of comprehensive behavioral programs for problem drinkers, however, is just beginning.

In an initial project, W. Miller (1978) described a comparative study of three behavioral treatment strategies. Self- and court-referred problem drinkers were evaluated for their appropriateness for participation in a controlled drinking treatment program and then randomly assigned to either an aversive counterconditioning group, behavioral self-control training, or an alcohol discrimination and self-control training condition. Forty-six clients (approximately 70%) successfully completed the 10 weekly treatment sessions. Across all groups, weekly alcohol consumption and peak blood alcohol concentration were reduced; relatively, the aversion conditioning therapy produced the least initial improvement, and training in self-control skills alone appeared to be the most cost-effective. Behavioral self-control training (including self-monitoring, functional analysis, rate control, and identification and practice of alternatives) decreased collateral estimates of consumption from an average of 48 to 19 standard ethanol units (.5 oz. ethanol), with these reductions maintained over 3-month and 1-year follow-ups. Subsequent investigation (W. Miller & Taylor, 1980; W. Miller, Taylor, & West, 1980) has replicated significant, albeit somewhat smaller decreases in consumption and suggested that for some heavy drinkers provision of a detailed self-control manual alone may constitute an effective secondary prevention strategy. Improvements on other measures of life health generally have accompanied changes in drinking disposition data.

Pomerleau and Adkins (1980) also have summarized their evaluation of a multicomponent behavioral program for middle-income problem drinkers. Of 39 accepted clients, 32 entered treatment and were assigned to either the behavioral program or a traditional psychotherapy comparison group. Weekly 90-minute sessions involving small groups were held for 3 months, with five follow-up sessions extending through the year. The behavioral therapy group included (1) use of a refundable compliance deposit, (2) keeping detailed records, (3) shaping and contingency management approaches to establish a reduced drinking pattern (at least 3 days of abstinence per week with no more than 3 oz. of ethanol per day or 10 oz. per week), (4) assigned nondrinking activities, and (5) applying behavior therapy procedures (e.g., relaxation, marital contracting) to emotional situations that might precipitate excessive drinking. The traditional comparison treatment was provided by a psychiatrist experienced in alcohol problems who focused on abstinence and led participants in recognizing and confronting denial patterns. Unfortunately, the investigators reported considerable differential attrition, with perhaps the major finding being that more clients assigned to the behavioral program completed treatment (89% vs. 57%). The small sample sizes with a seemingly greater proportion of females in the experimental group actually makes any comparisons tenuous. However, at the 1-year follow-up, 72% of the behaviorally treated clients were either abstinent (6%) or had reduced their drinking below pretreatment levels (66%).

Alden (1980) has described a pilot study of a behavioral secondary prevention program for problem drinkers that was conducted in a public health setting. As in earlier studies, clients were carefully screened prior to participation. It is noteworthy that 27 contacts (approximately 40%) had to be referred elsewhere because of psychiatric problems, severe alcoholism, or medical contraindications to continued drinking. Of the 36 (86%) entering clients, 31 completed 10 weekly scheduled treatment sessions. In this evaluation, individual training in basic self-management skills was compared to an enriched condition. The former consisted of self-monitoring, training in the parameters of social drinking, practicing drink refusal, and efforts to modify reactions to the settings and feeling accompanying overdrinking, while the latter additionally included some training in stress and anxiety management techniques. A number of drinking indices (e.g., total consumption, peak blood alcohol, and collateral estimates of drinking) as well as life-style measures (job and marital satisfaction, feelings of depression, anxiety) were used to gauge program effectiveness. The data suggested that program involvement was associated with beneficial pre- to posttreatment changes across subjects with relatively little difference between the groups. Considering the related drinking measures, 70% of the clients completing the program had reduced consumption and were drinking in a nonhazardous fashion (12.5 oz. of ethanol per week), with these results maintained over a 6-month follow-up. The reductions in problem-drinking measures were somewhat greater for the enriched condition, but the difference failed to reach statistical significance levels. Marital satisfaction similarly improved, with clients in the basic self-management group reporting somewhat greater increases. Delayed positive effects on job satisfaction and depression also were found at the 6-month assessment.

The preliminary evidence on the effects of behavioral prevention programs has been very encouraging. This conclusion must be tempered, however, both because of the small number of individuals involved and the general absence of controls for nonspecific factors. Such prevention programs may have difficulty as well accessing the relevant population. Alden (1980) received only about a fourth of the usual public response using traditional recruitment methods. P. Miller (1979) has suggested that alcohol prevention efforts be tied to the theme of health prevention broadly conceived. This would appear to have several strategic advantages, including (1) increasing public acceptability, (2) highlighting often overlooked alternatives to drinking such as physical exercise, and (3) focusing more clinical and research attention on the interaction of health-related habits (e.g., drinking and dieting). Another concern is how problem drinking is to be defined (P. Miller, 1979). One approach is to set drinking limits based on research investigating the effects of blood alcohol concentration on hepatic functioning and/or acute cognitive impairments. Clinically, however, one would consider possible detrimental effects on an individual's job or marriage, and importantly, the functions drinking serves in a person's life. Behavioral programs now include a number of procedural components whose value and relative contribution to treatment outcome is unknown. Experimentation with program contents needs to consider the time frame available for treatment (Alden, 1980), cost-effectiveness (W. Miller, 1978), and the possible interactive effects of treatment techniques (Nirenberg *et al.*, 1981). Although an exciting development, behavioral programs for problem drinkers have involved demonstration projects by only a small cadre of clinicians well trained in behavior therapy. At present, it is too early to evaluate if such programming efforts will be more successful and have a greater impact than earlier DWI and occupational programs in achieving secondary prevention goals.

Methodological issues and needed improvements related to evaluating secondary prevention programs essentially correspond to those found at large in the alcohol treatment evaluation literature. It is of interest that the emergence of a multivariate, biosocial view of alcohol abuse has led to increased sophistication in evaluation efforts. Although past reviews (Crawford & Chalupsky, 1977; Hill & Blane, 1967) have emphasized the serious and continued limitations in existing outcome research, recent advances (Sobell, Sobell, & Ward, 1980) reflect considerable progress. Indeed, in many ways, assessing alcohol treatment effectiveness has evolved beyond evaluation in other areas of mental health. Methodological concerns and typical problems have been reviewed in a number of excellent papers (Caddy, 1980; Nathan & Lansky, 1978; Schuckit & Cahalan, 1976; Sobell, 1978). The major recommendations include the following:

- Evaluation planning should precede the implementation of secondary prevention rather than be attempted retrospectively.
- The program participants or clients should be adequately described in terms of relevant diagnostic and social-demographic variables as well as entering behavior. This concern would extend to considering possible sources of bias and unrepresentativeness in sampling, and to accounting for any attrition from the program.
- Some subjects must be randomly assigned to an appropriate control or comparison condition if the specific effects of the prevention program are to be determined. This is particularly important as the rate of nonspecific improvement and spontaneous remission known to occur in alcohol populations might be expected to be greater among problem drinkers.
- A more detailed description of the intervention itself should be included.
- In comparing secondary prevention packages as in behavior therapy, efforts should be entertained to equate them in terms of length, scope of problems addressed, therapist commitment, and the expectations for improvement they generate.

- In the selection of assessment measures, multiple measures of life health (Maisto & MaCollam, 1980) need to be included, with information sought from converging data sources.
- Outcome measures such as drinking should be represented as continuous and quantifiable.
- Greater effort in demonstrating the reliability of the measures obtained must be exerted.
- It is necessary to collect follow-up data (generally, at about 18 months) through the use of established tracking procedures, trained interviewers, and frequent assessment intervals.
- Evaluation data should be reported for individuals (i.e., compared to pretest baseline) as well as for the group. In this way, attention may be directed to results of clinical and practical significance.

LEGAL REGULATION AND PUBLIC CONTROL MEASURES

With the repeal of prohibition and the later passage of the Federal Alcohol Administration Act, government concern over alcoholic beverages shifted to the regulation of the industry (i.e., manufacture and sales) and the collection of tax revenues. It is within this context that the existing and complicated Alcohol Beverage Commission (ABC) systems and related legislation evolved. Although many of the original temperance motives behind these laws were lost over the years, increased recognition of alcohol misuse as a major public health problem has rekindled interest in whether regulation might function more effectively to prevent alcohol problems. Consequently, with a view toward prevention, the NIAAA commissioned the Medicine in the Public Interest group to study the relationship between current ABC laws and the incidence and patterns of alcohol consumption (Medicine in the Public Interest, 1979). Their report provides a sound starting place for examining the potential effectiveness of public control measures.

Current state regulations lack coherence and consistency. In addition, policy research on the effects of ABC laws in the United States is sorely absent. A number of barriers to prevention-oriented changes currently exist. The ABC unit personnel perceive their function as administrative in character, and are currently most influenced by the industry's position of regulated maximum availability. To date, economic and political considerations, rather than public health, have had more impact on the creation and reformulation of regulations. There are thus legitimate but vested interests in the system that must be understood and addressed in approaching change. In part, these arise from the widely recognized built-in conflict within legislation both aimed at raising revenue and restricting the inappropriate use of alcohol. Even if the decision were to be made to give greater emphasis to the public health objectives of regulation, ABC units and staff have little training in or contact with health service providers and alcohol specialists and therefore lack the professional resources to address such issues. Although it is therefore naive to expect rapid developments in this area, the Medicine in the Public Interest report concludes that it is necessary to take several first steps including better articulation of the goals of specific regulations and a clearer recognition that the regulatory system does in myriad ways affect consumption. Rather than forsake the reorganization or reform of the regulatory system as a means of prevention, judicious changes need to be proposed, well presented, and carefully evaluated.

The existing literature on public control measures has developed largely within the framework of the distribution-of-consumption model (Bruun *et al.*, 1975; Popham *et al.*, 1976a). Unfortunately, the available supporting data are limited since they are largely correlational in nature. Essentially, heavy consumption and alcohol morbidity statistics appear related to per capita consumption, and the latter, to availability. Economic studies have demonstrated that alcohol consumption is responsive or elastic to variations in price and disposable income (Lau, 1975; Ornstein, 1980). For example, an early study by Seeley (1960) found the ratio of price to disposable income (i.e., relative price) negatively related to per capita sales. Based on such data, Popham *et al.* (1976a) have argued for stabilizing accessibility by tying the cost of beverage alcohol to disposable income.

Although alcohol may act as a commodity, it is also evident that its elasticity values vary appreciably in different times, geographic areas, and even across beverage types. For example, beer has been reported to be inelastic (Lau, 1975). Such differences make difficult the derivation of widely applicable but specific price policy recommendations (Bruun *et al.*, 1975). Critics of the distribution-of-consumption model (Parker & Harman, 1978; Room, 1978) have also pointed out its overreliance on cirrohosis as the consequence of alcohol abuse. The relationship between consumption levels and the more acute negative social consequences of drinking (e.g., drunk driving and marital problems) is less clear (Mäkelä, 1978). The proposed lognormal distribution based on an aggregate of consumers is also said to obscure critical variations in drinking among important subgroups, for whom the proposed relationship may not apply. Breakdowns by such variables as age, sex, and income would appear to be warranted, as well as information on how price changes would affect heavy drinkers. Perhaps most significantly, Room (1978) has cautioned against inferring probable future changes in consumption from static distributional data. The effect of price changes and regulations regarding availability must eventually be determined experimentally.

Unfortunately, only a few reported studies focus on specific evaluations of social policy changes. Popham *et al.* (1976a) noted how Kuusi (1957) successfully evaluated the effects of opening beer and wine stores in selected towns in rural Finland. Through careful study and monitoring of the drinking habits of experimental and control populations, an increase in consumption, attributable to the introduction of the outlets, was documented. There was no increase in the frequency of intoxication, a finding that, interestingly, the investigator was able to interpret through ancillary data as reflecting a secondary decline in the use of illicit alcohol. Bruun *et al.* (1975) also have discussed at length the effect of Finland's marked increase in retail outlets in 1969. Per capita consumption, particularly of beer, but also of spirits, increased significantly, along with a greater proportion of heavy drinkers. Although such reports are suggestive, as others have pointed out (e.g., Room, 1978), it is problematic as to whether the changes resulted from the relaxation of legal restrictions *per se* or from the underlying change in public sentiment that necessarily accompanies such legislative reforms. Moreover, there remains the question of the generalizability of the Finnish findings to other nations.

There is also evidence that price changes and regulations affect beverage choice and drinking patterns. In this connection, Denmark's experience during World War I is often cited (Bruun *et al.*, 1975; Popham *et al.*, 1976a). Presumably on account of food shortages, a heavy tax was introduced on liquors with beer relatively unaffected. Within several years, the country's alcohol consumption was largely converted to beer. Raymond (1969) found that extending the closing time for on-premise sales in an Australian city affected the peak hourly pattern of motor vehicle accidents, although the overall rate remained unchanged. It would seem that further study of the effect of regulations on drinking patterns and their consequences is warranted. Room (1978) has made the point that the intent of regulations (i.e., whether they are meant to affect drinking behavior, a target group, drinking circumstances, or consequences) often is unclear, with the further possibility that controls that appear preventative on some dimensions might negatively affect other dimensions.

A somewhat singular study is the Popham, Schmidt, and de Lint, (1976b) evaluation of Ontario's 1947 liberalization of on-premise outlets. Cocktail and dining lounges with higher standards of decor, entertainment, and dancing were introduced, in contrast to older beverage rooms in which social interaction among patrons was more restricted. Such changes might be seen as being in keeping with arguments to demystify alcohol and encourage integrated drinking. Analysis of alcohol statistics for 8-year periods before and after the change and comparison with the adjacent province of Manitoba suggested a slight increase in sales but with drunkenness convictions and cirrhosis mortality actually rising at a somewhat lower rate in Ontario. In discussing this study, however, Popham *et al.* (1976a) pointed out the pragmatic problem raised in selecting an adequate control for an entire province or state. Moreover, specific interpretation of documented effects is tenuous, since multiple legal changes were introduced simultaneously. A very sound recommendation is made that regulations concerning the type and activity of outlets and their effects on drinking behavior might be elucidated further through ethnographic studies.

Most recently, interest and research activity has focused on evaluating the effects of changes in drinking-age laws. With the passage of the Federal Voting Rights Act, granting the right of ballot to 18-year-olds, many states also lowered the legal drinking age; there were concurrent age reductions in the Canadian provinces. This trend was questioned, however, as a number of reports indicated a correlated increase in alcohol-related auto accidents. In what is now a seminal study, Schmidt and Kornaczewski (1975) found a marked increase in consumption for 18- to 21-year-olds and a distinct additive effect on their involvement in alcohol-related accidents. In his review and discussion of the age issue, Smart (1979) related that the short-term effects of the age reductions have actually been variable in the states. Such effects may also be temporary. Later, more inclusive longitudinal studies (e.g., Douglass & Freedman, 1977) have suggested a less significant impact on drinking accidents which unfortunately have shown an overall rising trend. Nevertheless, it is significant that since 1976, 14 states have reversed their legislation, again favoring higher legal drinking ages. Moreover, recent data from Michigan and Maine indicate a decline in road accidents among the affected age group, which was not evident in control states. The current evidence thus supports age regulations as effective countermeasures, albeit further and especially long-term research is needed. Unfortunately, the effects of drinking-age law changes on behavior patterns, public disturbances, family life, and the incidence of alcohol in the schools has not been examined.

Designing and conducting evaluative research directed at detecting the effects of legal change presents formidable difficulties. Diamond (1981) recently listed factors often implicated in evaluations of sociolegal innovations showing no effects. Frequently, proposed changes may never be enacted or are modified in implementation. For example, public conformity to regulations and their enforcement may depend respectively on the perceived legitimacy of policy changes and a perception of "real intent" on the part of law enforcement and court officials. Changes that are seen by influential groups as impractical or increasing health or community problems may be resisted, resulting in a diluted treatment. The effectiveness of proposed control measures may be lessened further by a failure to reach their intended target. A telephone survey by Shover and Bankston (1973) found that less than half the sampled population in Tennessee were aware of a state change in the DWI law, with only 12.5% mentioning the critical provision of a mandatory jail stay. Regulatory changes also may be compensated for by homeostatic processes within the legal or regulatory system, such as shifting adjustments in arrest charges or sentencing practices. Investigators interested in evaluating legal and public control measures must concurrently study how the existing system operates and monitor the implementation of changes. Perhaps most critically, given some of these inherent difficulties, evaluators should not expect to find strikingly large changes; rather, evaluations should be designed with the power to detect moderate effects.

In that much of the research in this area employs a variant of the interrupted-time-series design, special comment is warranted. Such studies examine a data series for a change corresponding to the point at which a new regulation or modification is introduced. Although well suited for examining social policy changes, it must be emphasized that unambiguous interpretation of time series is not without problems. Cook and Campbell (1979) have provided an excellent discussion of factors bearing on the design's interpretability. First, as a result of serial dependency among observations in a time series, a special form of analysis employing the use of so-called ARIMA models is required (Hartmann, Gottman, Jones, Gardner, Kazdin, & Vaught, 1980; McCain & McCleary, 1979). Improper statistical procedures (e.g., covariance) have sometimes been employed. Even more fundamentally, reliance on archival data requires increased sensitivity to the many problems and possible biases statistical data may present (Walsh & Walsh, 1973). The results may be influenced by (1) incomplete data sets, (2) instrumentation changes, (3) shifting definitions of constructs such as drunkenness, (4) changing attitudes or awareness on the part of those collecting the relevant information, and (4) differential attrition or selection in the population on which the statistics are gathered (e.g., a change in the proportion of drinkers). The analysis must also take into account long-term maturational and regularly occurring cyclic trends.

The possibility that other outside events, usually termed history, might account for any changes is a major threat to validity and is not always easily ruled out. For this reason a control series (i.e., from as similar as possible a location or population) is usually necessary. A conceptually related but presumably unaffected dependent variable also may be used for comparisons. In a study of the British breathalyzer crackdowns, Ross, Campbell, and Glass (1970) showed a selective decline in traffic fatalities mainly during those hours in which English pubs were open, and therefore were able to make a strong argument for causal efficacy. Unfortunately, this use of a more sensitive indicator is not always possible, as routinely collected data are not always flexible enough to allow for such breakdowns. Unexpected changes in proportional categories such as nighttime crashes may also be misinterpreted as effects (Zador, 1976). Finally, the impact of certain regulations and policy changes may be gradual or delayed. Again, it would be helpful to monitor the diffusion of a change in some cases. Largely, however, more background theory and experience are required to predict such outcomes (Cook & Campbell, 1979).

In summarizing, further analytically and conceptually sophisticated research is needed. Although the evidence suggests that alcohol control measures may have a role in prevention efforts, data on availability are not conclusive. As Parker and Harman (1978) pointed out, existing studies primarily have involved changes in the direction of increased liberalization. There is also a need to broaden the dependent measures studied and to examine specific subgroups. How do policy changes and regulations affect drinking patterns? Smart (1979) has argued, for example, that the manner in which young people drink, rather than their level of consumption, may be more important in predicting problems in this group. Research on the distribution-of-consumption model clearly has provided some important insights and has served to regenerate scholarly interest in the preventive potential of alcohol control measures; future work, however, would no doubt be enhanced by adopting a broader conceptual framework. In addition, public attitudes and perceptions of existing and proposed control measures should be assessed. Cahalan, Roizen, and Room (1974) found that although two-thirds of the respondents would support measures aimed at protecting individuals from the problematic consequences of excess drinking (e.g., devices preventing intoxicated persons from starting cars), substantially fewer would endorse such policies as closing bars earlier or increasing taxes.

It should be evident that prevention efforts involving public regulation and controls involve important value issues. It might legitimately be argued that increasing alcohol taxes in keeping with the discretionary income level of the population would be an unfair burden on the poor, who, even with reduced consumption, are likely to lose more of the family budget (Room, 1978). Similarly, the question of the minimum drinking age cannot easily be separated from the issue of the younger citizen's social–political rights. Investigators in the alcohol field have no special wisdom or mandate to resolve such questions. Rather, as in other areas of behavioral science (Bandura, 1969), the social researcher's goal in a democratic system must be to study and present to society the consequences of such value decisions.

ALCOHOL EDUCATION

The major prevention activity directed toward youth has been alcohol education. Until very recently such efforts were aimed exclusively at adolescents. As a result of social forces and change, concern over teenage drinking and associated problems has been increasing. It is interesting to note, however, that the actual prevalence of alcohol use and the frequency of intoxication among teenagers apparently has been fairly stable (Blane & Hewitt, 1977). In their comprehensive review, Blane and Hewitt found that 70% of teenagers report drinking, with their first drink (as distinct from tasting) usually occurring at about the age of 13. More problematically, 19% admit to monthly intoxication. Although teenage alcoholism is rare, teenage problem drinkers clearly suffer a variety of negative consequences (e.g., impaired school performance, disturbed interpersonal relations with parents or friends, drunk driving, and police involvement). Not surprisingly, there is considerable correspondence between adolescent drinking patterns and the practices of their parents and peers. Although drinking to conform to peers is rarely acknowledged, adolescents who report such motives tend to drink more. Also of concern, frequent drinking is positively associated with negative perceptions of the quality of family relationships, general feelings of alienation, and personal dissatisfaction.

Findings such as those cited above have accrued from population surveys. It is also important to point out that heavy alcohol involvement is further noted in clinical reports as part of a more generalized pattern of social, family, and psychological disorganization. In this context, it is accompanied by such indicators as poverty, broken homes, delinquency, and parental psychopathology. Use of the syndrome concept to separate those adolescents whose problem drinking exists as part of a severely disturbed life-style appears both conceptually and clinically appropriate. This point will be returned to in the next section. For now, it is sufficient to point out that it would be folly to think that providing alcohol education is an effective response to children who have such intensive and largely unmet needs.

Public schools are required by state law to provide alcohol education. However, the implementation of such laws into actual instructional programs has been inconsistent and superficial (Blane, 1976; Milgram, 1975, 1976). Milgram (1976) has provided a thorough review of the history and changes in the field. A major point is that alcohol education with its roots in the temperance movement has reflected historical and continued ambivalence toward drinking in our society. Blane's (1976) proscriptive model emphasizing the evils of drinking and dangers of alcoholism only gave way in the 1950s to advocates of more objective education as surveys revealed that the majority of high school students used alcohol, most of these being introduced to it in their homes. Despite acceptance of a more social-science-oriented philosophy, surveys from the late 1960s and early 1970s still indicated the following problems: (1) there is a consistent lack of meaningful education from the school, home, or community, with the most frequent source of information being the peer group; (2) that most teachers avoid the area due to discomfort with their lack of training and perceived community attitudes; and (3) that curriculum materials have largely emphasized such topics as the physiology of alcohol and the problem of alcoholism, devoting scant attention to the sociology of drinking patterns and particularly teenage drinking. Milgram (1976) pessimistically summarized the field by characterizing alcohol education as inadequate, ambivalent, and vague.

Although more is being written about alcohol education, little is being done about it. Blane (1976) noted an increase in objective curriculum materials. The serious issues raised by his incisive analysis (i.e., definition of goals and objectives, nature of materials, teaching methods and training, and lack of evaluation) remain to be addressed. The molar analysis of drinking problems and associated evidence provided by proponents of the distribution-of-consumption model has also had little influence on educational efforts, but increasing discussion of regulations affecting young people and the possible health justification for regulation suggest a clear need. Proposals for alcohol education rest on a strong societal belief in the value of health education, an assumption that whether justified or not resists evaluation. In this respect, it is of interest that Blane (1976) questions whether the adversary relationship and the low credibility of high school teachers to many students limit the effectiveness of the school setting in providing alcohol education.

There have been recent suggestions that educational programming begin earlier in elementary school (e.g., Blom & Snoddy, 1980). The impetus for this direction is grounded in well-designed research indicating that children form alcohol-related concepts (i.e., being drunk, motives for drinking, and its effects) at a relatively early age (e.g., Jahoda & Cramond, 1972). Developmental findings thus suggest the possible effectiveness of such an approach, but it is uncertain whether professional groups and the community will provide the necessary support. In describing their program for teacher training, Blom and Snoddy (1980) have also proposed integrating alcohol education within a broad psychosocial curriculum focusing on responses to human problems. Prevention would thus constitute education for competence and effective living. Cognitive-behavioral teaching modules would be designed to enhance such attributes as social competence, self-concept, sense of identity, appropriate autonomy, social responsibility, future perspective, internal locus of control, and ability to delay gratification. Spoth and Rosenthal (1980) have argued for a developmental skills curriculum in providing alcohol education to adolescents. In addition to alcohol information, they would include such components as values clarification, decision-making skills, communication and assertiveness training, responding to peer pressures, discussions of parent relationship issues, and career planning. Teaching problem solving and competencies to children is clearly an exciting idea. Originating in the psychological literature, it is also a distinct departure from historical alcohol education efforts, and traditionalists may object to its nonspecific nature. Although promising to engage the attention of professionals interested in children over the next decade, such strategies are currently in need of further research and trial.

Perhaps most distressing is the dearth of quality evaluation research on the effects of alcohol education, let alone its long-term potential for preventing later alcohol problems. A frequently noted report by Williams, DiCicco, and Unterberger (1968) appears to be the only adequate attempt at evaluation through the early 1970s. These investigators examined the impact of a week of five small-group discussion sessions on the knowledge, attitudes, and drinking behavior of third-year high school students. Random assignment to experimental or control groups was employed, with both 1-month and 1-year follow-ups. The results indicated that knowledge of alcohol facts among the experimental students was increased relative to controls. Attitudes also were affected; there was a shift in the direction of moderate attitudes with a significant between-group difference at 1 month, although not at 1 year. Interestingly, the behavioral data were mixed. There was a trend for more of the experimental students to have become intoxicated during the following year; however, of all those students who had been intoxicated (64% of the experimental subjects and 57% of controls), considerably more control subjects (60% vs. 30% of experimental subjects) became intoxicated frequently (five or more times). Granting that adolescents are moving into adult social roles, including drinking (Jessor & Jessor, 1975), the decrease in intoxication incidents is certainly encouraging.

It is not implausible that alcohol education might increase student experimentation with drinking over the short term. It is now widely known that evidence from evaluations of more general drug education programs (often including alcohol information) support this conclusion (Kalb, 1975; Zarraro, 1973). For example, Stuart (1974) reported a sophisticated attempt to evaluate variations in a drug education program for seventh- and ninth-grade students. The major finding was that across experimental groups there was an increase in knowledge, greater alcohol, marijuana, and LSD use, and less worry about drugs. Of the students in the experimental groups, 13% reported escalating drug use at the 4-month follow-up versus 4% of the controls. The author cautiously cited limits to the generalizability of these results, especially to programs that also include exploring values and building alternative skills. Others have argued that given the limited number of studies and their various methodological problems, extrapolating these concerns from the drug literature may be premature and particularly unfair to alcohol education (Cooper & Sobell, 1979). Conceptually, an increase in use or proportion of users among adolescents does not necessarily indicate abuse.

Increased concern over prevention has resulted in several major initiatives in the area. Noteworthy among those targeting younger-aged children is the CASPAR Alcohol Education Program. This program operates through teacher training and use of peer educators in attempting to better equip youngsters to make responsible decisions about drinking. An initial evaluation of program effects (Carifio, Biron, & Sullivan, 1978) suggested that those junior and senior high school students exposed to the full CASPAR curriculum, as opposed to a less comprehensive educational program, showed the greatest gains both in alcohol knowledge and attitude change. In support of the increasing attention given to earlier grades, the most marked changes in attitudes occurred in younger children with less prior exposure to alcohol education.

As a result of positive reactions to the program, CASPAR was selected by NIAAA for replication in several states. Unfortunately, little evaluation data from the replication sites are contained in the final report (Urban and Rural Systems Associates, 1980). This document might be profitably studied by those interested in the practical problems of model program dissemination and replication. Some of the difficulties encountered included: (1) a perceived incompleteness in documentation needed to implement the program with some curriculum materials not readily adaptable (e.g., reading difficulty) to the new target group, (2) a lack of needed social-community support as reflected in problems recruiting teachers and denied access to schools wishing to "return to basics," (3) specific restrictions and opposition to the use of peer educators, for example denying them use of school time or payment, with students themselves in some areas ill-equipped to deal with this role, and (4) a noted lack of resources allocated for evaluation. The little evaluation data collected emphasized process measures, for example, the number of students exposed to the program. One site, Wheeler Clinic, did manage to obtain some outcome data. On a 1-year posttest, ninth-through twelfth-grade students receiving the curriculum demonstrated greater increases in knowledge and attitudes on a student alcohol inventory than control subjects. Drinking data collected on peers involved in the program were reminiscent of the early study by Williams *et al.* (1968). These students reported drinking somewhat more, but with fewer episodes of drunkenness.

To date, the most comprehensive evaluation appears to be a report by Goodstadt, Sheppard, and Crawford (1978) on an alcohol education curriculum used in the Toronto schools. Lesson plans for grades 7 and 8 and grades 9 and 10 were developed by staff of the Addiction Research Foundation, with informal evaluations and feedback from teachers. These plans were designed as a series of separate units including such topics as alcohol and myths, advertising and/or TV portrayal of alcohol, effects of drinking, why people drink, drinking and driving, teenagers and alcohol, alcohol and the family, and alcohol and fitness. The evaluation employed a pre-post control-group design, and involved 16 schools with 1,351 and 684 students (both experimental and controls) participating at the elementary and secondary grade levels, respectively. In actuality, some teachers only implemented a small subset of the lessons. The findings were complicated but are described as being positive overall. At both levels, experimental subjects increased their knowledge relating to alcohol. Some existing attitudes appeared to be reinforced, with male drinkers becoming more pro-alcohol in their attitudes, and male abstainers in the elementary school becoming less pro-alcohol. Significantly, elementary school nondrinkers and secondary school drinkers reported less alcohol use in the week prior to the posttest, with female nondrinkers and male drinkers at the secondary level expecting to drink less in the next 12 months. Limitations of this study include a lack of follow-up (in the majority of schools the posttest was given a week after program completion) and the possibility that demand characteristics of the evaluation itself appreciably influenced the students' responses. Nevertheless, these results suggest that alcohol education may have beneficial effects.

Mention should be made of evaluations of college programs. Kraft (1979) has provided an overview of activities and efforts in this area. Generally, studies have demonstrated an increase in alcohol knowledge but seldom behavioral effects (Engs, 1977; Portnoy, 1980). Concerned about the possible detrimental effects of educational prevention, Engs (1977) first reported on a pilot study of an alcohol presentation developed for use with small groups in residential living areas. The program included a film, discussion of such topics as misconceptions about drinking and the negative consequences of excessive drinking, and a number of related values clarification exercises. As a control condition, some students went through a similar program format focusing on human sexuality. Administration of a student alcohol questionnaire before and after the program and at a 3-month follow-up revealed that the participants had increased their alcohol knowledge; however, there were no significant effects on any of 23 drinking-behavior items either between or within the groups. In evaluating an alcohol education program designed on a Health Belief Model, Portnoy (1980) similarly reported increased knowledge levels along with positive changes in intentions toward responsible drinking, but little or no effect on consumption. Subject selection itself may be a limitation of such studies. In Portnoy's (1980) evaluation the students were enrolled in a health education class and their drinking practices were judged to be in the responsible-use range. More comprehensive programs also have been undertaken. The multifaceted campus program at the University of Massachusetts (Kraft, Dustin, & Mellor, 1977) is of particular significance, in that, like CASPAR, it has served as a sort of prototype, with NIAAA sponsored replications at four additional sites. This project is explained in detail in Chapter 9 in the present text.

In summary, efforts to evaluate alcohol education objectively have been severely limited. Other reviewers (Braucht, Follingstad, Brakarsh, & Berry, 1973; Cooper & Sobell, 1979) have already noted methodological requirements for future research in the area. Their recommendations are not unlike those previously discussed under secondary prevention. Currently, all that can be said with confidence is that alcohol education has been demonstrated to increase knowledge about alcohol (Engs, 1977; Goodstadt *et al.*, 1978). From the available evidence, it would be unwarranted to conclude that preventive alcohol education is ineffective or detrimental. Positive effects on attitudes and especially behavior, however, often appear to be indirectly related to program exposure (Portnoy, 1980; Stuart, 1974). Without further evaluation, the really important questions, such as the relation of observed posttest changes in attitudes and behavioral intentions to long-term drinking patterns, will remain unanswered.

A considerable proportion of teenagers now experience alcohol-related problems similar to those of young adults. In the Research Triangle's national study of adolescent drinking behavior (Rachal, Hubbard, Williams, & Tuchfeld, 1976), problem drinking was operationally defined by frequency of drunkenness and/or negative consequences. Employing the most stringent definition (i.e., drunk at least 6 to 10 times in the past year or negative consequences in at least three areas) resulted in roughly 18% of the sample being classified as problem drinkers. These statistics notwithstanding, many of the reported problems experienced by youth no doubt result in part from adolescents being less experienced drinkers. Those discussing the problem of teenage alcohol use would do well to remember that generally the youthful population is merely adopting in a reasonably controlled fashion the pattern of drinking shown by young adults (Mandell & Ginzburg, 1976). A related conceptual point has to do with the perceived relevance of alcohol education to most students. In the curriculum evaluation by Goodstadt *et al.* (1978) the lessons were well received by the participating children; however, these students felt that they learned more about other people than about themselves. They did not perceive the course material as having impact on their own behavior. Portnoy (1980) similarly discusses how perceived susceptibility might influence the effectiveness of educational efforts. Educators charged with the development and implementation of alcohol prevention have the responsibility of continued evaluation to assure that it is as effective as possible. Health education no doubt will and should be continued. Possible inherent limitations and the lessons of evaluative research must be considered, however, lest the delusion be created that education alone constitutes an effective response to the problems presented by alcohol in our society. It may be that greater long-term gains will be achieved by focusing on developmental studies of children at high risk for severe problems.

THE DEVELOPMENTAL CONTEXT OF ALCOHOL ABUSE

Conceptual knowledge regarding the development of alcohol problems places an upper limit on the sophistication of primary prevention efforts. Several surveys over short periods (Cahalan, 1978; Polich, Armor, & Braiker, 1980) and one long-term study (Fillmore, 1974) have established a general lack of continuity in drinking patterns and specific problems over time. Understandably, these data have been used to question the traditional disease formulation of alcohol abuse and to highlight the importance of situational and contextual factors as determinants of drinking patterns. Many individuals tend to move in and out of drinking problems with a pattern of increased moderation in later years. Nevertheless, from a prevention perspective, it needs to be emphasized that these same data reaffirm in other problem drinkers a sense of underlying stability. Cahalan (1978) thus concluded that although the continuity for specific problems is low, if an individual developed alcohol-related difficulties, there was an increased probability of future involvement in alcohol problems. Similar results were borne out in Fillmore's (1974) 20-year follow-up study of college students. It is apparent that behavioral data alone, such as consumption indices, cannot adequately reflect continuities in development. Rather, as Fillmore suggested, in studies over time, variables more closely tied to an individual's experience in terms of attitudes and the inner context of drinking will no doubt be more productive.

Drinking patterns and the place of alcohol in a person's life are learned via the important developmental process referred to as socialization (Barnes, 1977; Plant, 1979). At different life stages, both beliefs about alcohol and its usage change in conjunction with social forces. Unfortunately, only a general outline of the developmental changes underlying drinking and alcohol abuse is available. Zucker (1976, 1979) has taken the most significant steps toward outlining developmental influences on eventual drinking behavior. In his proposed model there are four classes of relevant variables: sociocultural and community, parent personality and family interactions, secondary groups (peers), and intraindividual factors. In a study of a tri-ethnic community, for example, Jessor, Graves, Hanson, and Jessor (1968) related sociocultural factors to parental socialization and personality attributes conducive to deviance, including excess alcohol consumption. Thus, depending on parental beliefs and controls, decreased access to the social opportunity structure might be expected to lead to alienation and personal disjunction, predisposing an adolescent to alcohol abuse. Direct family and parental influences may be drinking or nondrinking specific in character (Zucker, 1976). In support of modeling theories, the best single predictor of adolescent drinking habits appears to be the attitudes and behaviors of parents regarding alcohol (Barnes, 1977). Such effects remain influential through the high school years, even though peer influences and pressure become increasingly important (Alexander & Campbell, 1967; Margulies, Kessler, & Kandel, 1977). A role for nondrinking specific family factors is suggested by evidence that heavy teenage drinkers generally share a perception of inadequate family relations. In reviewing such research, Barnes (1977) noted that excessive users were less likely to feel close to their families, felt loosely controlled, and experienced tension and rejection in their relationships with their fathers. Finally, in addition to biologically mediated influences, intraindividual factors would include the development of particular cognitive and personality structures. In this regard and in keeping with the previously mentioned Glasgow project (Jahoda & Cramond, 1972), there is a need for greater study of the development of children's alcohol-related social cognitions (Higgins, 1980). Intraindividual personality variables, such as aggressive and impulse-related behavior in problem-drinking adolescents, may also be viewed as reciprocally interacting with family factors.

At least two groups are significantly at risk for the development of severe alcohol problems in later life. First are the offspring of alcoholic parents. There is presently persuasive evidence that some biologically mediated characteristic is implicated in chronic forms of alcoholism (Goodwin, Schulsinger, Hermansen, Guze, & Winokin, 1973; Johnson & Leeman, 1977). Such biological predictors are reviewed in detail in Chapter 4.

It is apparent that children in such families may suffer a number of adverse consequences including neglect, inconsistency, and often divorce (Blane & Hewitt, 1977; Wilson & Oxford, 1978). Existing studies of behavioral problems and psychopathology in these children are limited methodologically by problems in sampling, lack of adequate comparison groups, and questions as to the appropriateness of the measures employed. Tentatively, however, it seems reasonable from a number of studies involving clinic records and parental reports (e.g., Chafetz, Blane, & Hill, 1971; El-Guebaly, Offord, Sullivan, & Lynch, 1978; Fine, Yudin, Holmes, & Heinemann, 1976) to conclude that, similar to children of psychiatric patients, many children of alcoholics exhibit emotional problems, school difficulties, and behavioral disturbances primarily of an externalizing nature. Clinically, there is perhaps some danger of overemphasizing pathology in these children; many have very good social competence and usually appear to be reacting to situational influences. Interestingly, the little data available (reviewed in Blane & Hewitt, 1977) suggest few effects on adolescent drinking behavior, although the finding in one study of a greater proportion of abstainers among adolescents with unrecovered parents perhaps hints of subtle impacts in this area. Wilson and Orford (1978) have highlighted significant themes or factors needing further investigation. These included the effects of variations in parental drinking patterns and exposure, sex differences in heavy parental drinking and correlated impacts on family roles and tasks, the child's perception and feelings toward both parents, shifting moods and the atmosphere in the family, changes in family coalitions and communication patterns, effects in the educational and social spheres, especially the process of forming friendships, and the possible supportive impact of extended family or neighbors along with observed patterns of coping.

Longitudinal and cross-sectional studies strongly indicate that antisocial and aggressive children also are likely to develop alcohol problems (Robins, Bates, & O'Neal, 1962; Zucker, 1976; Zucker & DeVoe, 1975). In the classic 30-year follow-up study conducted by Robins et al. (1962) of children who had been seen previously at a child psychiatric clinic, later alcoholism was positively related to the number and variety of antisocial activities present in childhood. These included such delinquent behaviors as running away, theft, and assault, and particularly was true if these problems were severe enough to warrant a juvenile court appearance. As pointed out earlier, delinquents have high rates of heavy drinking (Barnes, 1977), and there is strong evidence in support of a general deviance theory for understanding much of adolescent problem drinking (Jessor et al., 1968; Zucker, 1976). In illustration, the Middle Atlantic States community study (Zucker, 1976; Zucker & DeVoe, 1975) found clear associations between children's drinking, antisocial behavior, and negative family climates and disturbed childrearing practices. Heavy alcohol consumption among both girls and boys was related to intraindividual measures of impulsive and aggressive behavior, earlier and more sexual activity, and delinquent role involvement. Although there were sex differences among parental behaviors and practices predictive of drinking, nonspecific family influences on adolescent problem drinking included perceived family tension, parental absence and lack of involvement, deprivation of privileges, and little affectional support or nurturance. Children with aggressive behavior and inadequate socialization, along with the children of alcoholics, would appear to provide the best empirically defined target populations for prevention efforts.

Currently, there is considerable interest in providing preventive educational and psychological services to the children of alcoholics (Homonoff & Stephen, 1979; Kern, Tippman, Fortgang, & Paul, 1977). These programs generally are associated with alcohol treatment agencies. In addition to recruitment problems, a possible concern is whether the counselors in most such agencies have the relevant developmental and clinical training to assess and work with children. Significantly, although some program descriptions and honest attempts to determine progress exist (Kern *et al.,* 1977), there are as yet virtually no real evaluative data on primary alcohol prevention to review. In an uncontrolled study, Hughes (1977) did report that adolescent children of alcoholic parents who were also members of Alateen did not experience the negative emotional moods, low self-esteem, and social adjustment difficulties evident in comparing nonmember adolescents of alcoholic parents to normal controls. What clearly is needed, however, in intensive, long-term monitoring and further life-history studies of such children.

In the last decade there have been some solid beginnings in prospective research of children at high risk for serious pathology, particularly schizophrenia (Garmezy, 1975). These groundbreaking efforts might serve as a foundation and model for confronting unaddressed developmental questions in the primary prevention of alcohol problems. Since many children of alcoholics and deviancy-prone adolescents show adaptive adjustment in later life, the study of vulnerability highlights the individual and his or her specific experiences in life. Behavior and personality variation within classes of sociocultural influences has suggested the need to focus more narrowly psychologically on the perceptual and cognitive styles, attitudes, and values that are derived from a given socialization experience. Following the lead of ego psychologists, behavioral workers now must investigate the development of reciprocal influence processes involved in the problem drinker or alcoholic's family and social learning history. In discussing this area and specifically the Minnesota Project on vulnerable children, Garmezy (1975) outlined four phases of risk research: (1) defining and measuring age-related indices of competence, (2) identifying response parameters distinguishing individuals at risk, (3) short-term prospective studies of later adaption, and (4) intervention aimed at modifying response parameters and assessing effects on competence. Many of the noted measures of competence such as effectiveness in school, self-esteem, delay of gratification, internal locus of control, a reflective cognitive style, and social role taking would also appear to have relevance for children at risk for alcohol problems. Peer judgments have provided sensitive indicators of later maladjustment (Cowen, Pederson, Babigian, Izzo, & Trost, 1973), but have not yet been used in predicting alcohol problems. Family influences on transmission (Schneiderman, 1975; Steinglass, 1980) should be studied; for example, the finding of Wolin, Bennett, and Noonan (1979) that the generational recurrence of alcohol problems is associated with the disruption of family rituals needs further replication. In addition, examination of the adaptive behavior, use of social supports, and the coping style of children in high-risk families who remain invulnerable will suggest fruitful lines of research.

The findings that children of alcoholics exhibit similar problems to the children of adults with other psychiatric disorders and that children characterized by antisocial behavior are at risk generally for adult maladjustment including alcoholism, suggest that nonspecific primary mental health prevention programs for children also might be useful. Tableman (1981) has provided an overview of this area, including infant stimulation programs, interventions for high-risk preschool children, and community services for children of disordered adults. For example, a model project for at-risk children might include monitoring of a child's functioning at school and at home, coordination with the parent's therapist, parent education, counseling with the child to enhance coping, advocacy for the child, and referral to tutoring and recreational programs. Unfortunately, it appears that prevention efforts directed at antisocial, delinquent children have been discouraged prematurely due to earlier negative findings as evident in the famous Cambridge-Sommerville youth study (McCord, 1978; McCord & McCord, 1959). A recent analysis of the drinking habits of men seen 30 years earlier by counselors as part of this community project to deter delinquent behavior actually suggested a possible detrimental effect (McCord, 1978). Although lessons from this period regarding the need for evaluation should not be lost, knowledge currently available concerning preventive interventions with acting-out children (Cowen, Orgel, Gesten, & Wilson, 1979; Patterson, Reid, Jones, & Conger, 1975; Wiltz & Patterson, 1974) and skill approaches to treating delinquents (Shore & Massimo, 1972, 1973) provide reason for greater optimism and increased effort. In fact, such successes raise serious questions as to whether investigators might not have an ethical obligation to provide services to identified high-risk children (Golann, 1969).

Research on the development of drinking and drinking-related problems has involved either cross-sectional or longitudinal designs. Cross-sectional designs in which different age groups are tested at a single point necessarily confound maturational and cohort effects. Time also might have a selective influence in that problem-prone individuals are often lost from older groups. On the other hand, findings from longitudinal research are not only more costly to obtain, but are limited by reactive effects and possible historical influences. Developmental researchers have advocated the use of combined cross-sectional and longitudinal procedures that might be employed in alcohol studies (Schaie & Baltes, 1975). These sequential strategies involve sampling at least two cohort groups and testing them sequentially. The validity of the resultant observations might be additionally strengthened by checking the pretest representativeness of subjects lost and, if warranted, by selecting some subjects to receive only the post-test to examine the data for sensitization effects.

SUMMARY

Within the last decade, concern for the prevention of alcohol problems has come of age. The need for a greater balance between treatment and prevention activities is increasingly expressed. However, review of the available literature indicates that if prevention is to fulfill its promise, both further conceptual development and systematic, controlled research will be necessary. Secondary prevention efforts directed toward the needs and problems of young-adult, heavy drinkers suggest the beginnings of authentic progress. Although further evaluation and refinement are needed, behavioral teaching programs conducted within a self-management framework would seem to offer considerable advantage. Occupational programming also has proliferated, but without the benefit of evaluative research. The application of organizational contingencies as well as the conjoint provision of counseling should be assessed. With regard to DWI offenders, the extent of the problem must be recognized and difficulties related to preventing serious accidents more clearly understood. Within such programs, attention must focus on the heterogeneity and psychological characteristics of this population in designing appropriate program contents.

The realization that public control and legal measures regulating alcohol use have health consequences also has advanced the field. Concern over increasing per capita consumption is empirically justified. Studies regarding price should be expanded in order to examine effects on different groups and on a broad range of consequences. Significantly, current research indicates that lower drinking-age laws negatively affect the accident involvement of young people. The long-term effects of such changes are still unclear.

Despite a long history, alcohol education has neither escaped social ambivalence regarding drinking, nor been shown effective in preventing alcohol problems. Hopefully, such efforts will be reexamined in light of the developing child's social cognitions regarding alcohol use. The practical problems surrounding implementation might be addressed through programmatic research. Recent evidence (Carifio *et al.*, 1978; Goodstadt *et al.*, 1978) supports the proposition that well-planned programs have beneficial effects. Proposed curricula in life-skills and psychological competencies are promising but await further evaluation.

Finally, research on primary prevention involving high-risk children is underdeveloped. This is unfortunate since such studies may have the greatest potential for preventing problem drinking and alcoholism. Investigators interested in alcohol prevention are encouraged to pursue a developmental view not only of drinking, but of its inner context and possible entanglement with social-emotional growth and identity formation. Both the children of alcoholics and overly aggressive children are appropriate target groups for needed prospective studies. Such life-history research may be organized around the related themes of competence and individual differences in vulnerability.

REFERENCES

Alden, L. Preventive strategies in the treatment of alcohol abuse: A review and proposal. In P. Davidson & S. M. Davidson (Eds.), *Behavioral medicine: Changing health lifestyles.* New York: Brunner/Mazel, 1980.

Alexander, C. N., & Campbell, E. O. Peer influences on adolescent drinking. *Quarterly Journal of Studies on Alcohol,* 1967, *28,* 444–453.

Bacon, S. D. On the prevention of alcohol problems and alcoholism. *Journal of Studies on Alcohol,* 1978, *39,* 1125–1147.

Bandura, A. *Principles of behavior modification.* New York: Holt, Rinehart, & Winston, 1969.

Bandura, A. Behavior theory and the models of man. *American Psychologist,* 1974, *29,* 859–869.

Barnes, G. M. The development of adolescent drinking behavior: An evaluative review of the impact of the socialization process within the family. *Adolescence,* 1977, *12,* 571–591.

Blane, H. T. Education and the prevention of alcoholism. In B. Kissin & H. Begleiter (Eds.), *Biology of alcoholism: Social apsects of alcoholism.* New York: Plenum Press, 1976.

Blane, H. T. Middle-aged alcoholics and young drinkers. In H. T. Blane & M. E. Chafetz (Eds.), *Youth, alcohol, and social policy.* New York: Plenum Press, 1979.

Blane, H. T., & Hewitt, L. E. *Alcohol and youth: An analysis of the literature* (Report No. PB–268–698). Rockville, Md.: National Institute on Alcohol Abuse and Alcoholism, 1977.

Blom, G. E., & Snoddy, J. E. Child, the teacher, and the drinking society: A conceptual framework for alcohol education in the elementary school. In W. J. Filstead & J. E. Mayer (Eds.), *Adolescence and alcohol.* East Lansing, Mich.: Michigan State University Press, 1980.

Braucht, G. N., Follingstad, D., Brakarsh, D., & Berry, K. L. Drug education: A review of goals, approaches, and effectiveness, and a paradigm for evaluation. *Quarterly Journal of Studies on Alcohol,* 1973, *34,* 1279–1292.

Bruun, L., Edwards, G., Lumio, M., Mäkelä, K., Pan, L., Popham, R. E., Room, R., Schmidt,

W., Skog, O., Sulkunen, P., & Oesterberg, E. *Alcohol control policies in public health perspective.* Helsinki: Finnish Foundation for Alcohol Studies, 1975.

Caddy, G. R. A review of problems in conducting alcohol treatment outcome studies. In L. C. Sobell, M. B. Sobell, & E. Ward (Eds.), *Evaluating alcohol and drug abuse treatment effectiveness.* New York: Pergamon Press, 1980.

Cahalan, D. Implications of American drinking practices and attitudes for prevention and treatment of alcoholism. In G. A. Marlatt & P. E. Nathan (Eds.), *Behavioral approaches to alcoholism.* New Brunswick, N. J.: Rutgers Center of Alcohol Studies, 1978.

Cahalan, D., & Cisin, I. H. Epidemiological and social factors associated with drinking problems. In R. E. Tartar & A. A. Sugarman (Ed.), *Alcoholism: Interdisciplinary approaches to an enduring problem.* Reading, Mass.: Addison-Wesley, 1976.

Cahalan, D., Roizen, R., & Room, R. *Attitudes on alcohol problem prevention measures.* Paper presented at the North American Congress on Alcohol and Drug Problems, San Francisco, 1974.

Carifio, J., Biron, R. M., & Sullivan, D. *Selected findings on the impact of CASPAR alcohol education program on teacher training and curriculum implementation* (Evaluation Report No. 8). Sommerville, Mass.: CASPAR, Inc., 1978.

Chafetz, M. E. The prevention of alcoholism. *International Journal of Psychiatry,* 1970, *9,* 329–348.

Chafetz, M. E., Blane, H. T., & Hill, M. J. Children of alcoholics: Observations in a child guidance clinic. *Quarterly Journal of Studies on Alcohol,* 1971, *32,* 687–697.

Chaney, E. F., O'Leary, M. R., & Marlatt, G. A. Shill training with alcoholics. *Journal of Consulting and Clinical Psychology,* 1978, *46,* 1092–1104.

Cook, T. D., & Campbell, D. T. *Quasi-experimentation: Design and analysis issues for field settings.* Chicago: Rand McNally, 1979.

Cooper, A. M., & Sobell, M. B. Does alcohol education prevent alcohol problems? Need for evaluation. *Journal of Alcohol and Drug Education,* 1979, *25,* 54–63.

Cowen, E. L., Orgel, A. R., Gesten, E. L., & Wilson, A. B. The evaluation of an intervention program for young school children with acting-out problems. *Journal of Abnormal Child Psychology,* 1979, *7,* 381–396.

Cowen, E. L., Pederson, A., Babigian, H., Izzo, L. D., & Trost, M. A. Long-term followup of early detected vulnerable children. *Journal of Consulting and Clinical Psychology,* 1973, *41,* 438–446.

Crabb, D., Gettys, J., Malfetti, J., & Steward, E. Development and preliminary tryout and evaluation measures for Phoenix driving-while-intoxicated reeducation program (Tempe, Arizona: Arizona State University, 1971). Cited in G. J. Driessen & J. A. Bryk, Alcohol countermeasures: Solid rock and shifting sands. *Journal of Safety Research,* 1973, *5,* 108–129.

Crawford, J. K., & Chalupsky, A. B. The reported evaluation of alcoholism treatments, 1968–1971: A methodological review. *Addictive Behaviors,* 1977, *2,* 63–74.

Cross, J. N. Epidemiological studies and control programs in alcoholism. Public health approaches to alcoholism control. *American Journal of Public Health,* 1967, *57,* 955–964.

Diamond, S. S. Detecting legal change and its impact. In L. Bickman (Ed.), *Applied social psychology.* Beverly Hills, Calif.: Sage, 1981.

Douglass, R. L., & Freedman, J. A. A study of alcohol-related casualties and alcohol beverage market response to alcohol availability policies in Michigan (Ann Arbor, Mich.: Highway Safety Research Institute, 1977). Cited in Smart, R. G. Priorities in minimizing alcohol problems among young people. In H. T. Blane & M. E. Chafetz (Eds.), *Youth, alcohol, and social policy.* New York: Plenum Press, 1979.

El-Guebaly, N., Offord, D. R., Sullivan, K. T., & Lynch, G. W. Psychosocial adjustment of the offspring of psychiatric inpatients. *Canadian Psychiatric Association Journal*, 1978, *23*, 281–289.

Engs, R. C. Let's look before we leap: The cognitive and behavioral evaluation of an university alcohol education program. *Journal of Alcohol and Drug Education*, 1977, *22*, 39–48.

Fillmore, K. M. Drinking and problem drinking in early adulthood and middle age. *Quarterly Journal of Studies on Alcohol*, 1974, *35*, 819–840.

Fine, E. W., Yudin, L. W., Holmes, J., & Heinemann, S. Behavioral disorders in children with parental alcoholism. *Annals of the New York Academy of Sciences*, 1976, *273*, 507–517.

Foy, D. W., Miller, P. M., Eisler, R. M., & O'Toole, D. H. Social skills training to teach alcoholics to refuse drinks effectively. *Journal of Studies on Alcohol*, 1976, *37*, 1340–1345.

Garmezy, N. The experimental study of children vulnerable to psychopathology. In A. Davids (Ed.), *Child personality and psychopathology: Current topics* (Vol. 2). New York: Wiley, 1975.

Golann, S. E. Emerging areas of ethical concern. *American Psychologist*, 1969, *24*, 454–459.

Goodstadt, M. S., Sheppard, M. A., & Crawford, S. H. *Development and evaluation of two alcohol education programs for the Toronto Board of Education* (Substudy No. 941). Toronto: Addiction Research Foundation, 1978.

Goodwin, D. W., Schulsinger, F., Hermansen, L., Guze, S. G., & Winokin, G. Alcohol problems in adoptees raised apart from alcoholic biological parents. *Archives of General Psychiatry*, 1973, *28*, 238–243.

Hartmann, D. P., Gottman, J. N., Jones, R. R., Gardner, W., Kazdin, A., & Vaught, R. Interrupted time-series analysis and its application to behavioral data. *Journal of Applied Behavioral Analysis*, 1980, *13*, 543–559.

Higgins, E. T. *Social cognition: The Ontario symposium* (Vol. 1). Hillsdale, N. J.: Lawrence Erlbaum, 1980.

Hilker, R. R. J., Asma, R. E., & Eggert, R. L. A company sponsored alcoholic rehabilitation program. *Journal of Occupational Medicine*, 1972, *14*, 769–772.

Hill, M. J., & Blane, H. T. Evaluation of psychotherapy with alcoholics: A critical review. *Quarterly Journal of Studies on Alcohol*, 1967, *28*, 76–104.

Homonoff, E., & Stephen, A. Alcohol education for children of alcoholics in a Boston neighborhood. *Journal of Studies on Alcohol*, 1979, *40*, 923–926.

Huber, H., Karlin, R., & Nathan, P. Blood alcohol level discrimination by nonalcoholics: The role of internal and external cues. *Journal of Studies on Alcohol*, 1976, *37*, 27–39.

Hughes, J. M. Adolescent children of alcoholic parents and the relationship of Alateen to these children. *Journal of Consulting and Clinical Psychology*, 1977, *45*, 946–947.

Jahoda, G., & Cramond, J. *Children and alcohol*. London: HMSO, 1972.

Jessor, R., Graves, T. D., Hanson, R. L., & Jessor, S. L. *Society, personality, and deviant behavior: A study of a tri-ethnic community*. New York: Holt, Rinehart, & Winston, 1968.

Jessor, R., & Jessor, S. L. Adolescent development and the onset of drinking. *Journal of Studies on Alcohol*, 1975, *36*, 27–51.

Johnson, G. F. S., & Leeman, M. M. Analysis of family factors in bipolar affective illness. *Archives of General Psychiatry*, 1977, *34*, 1074–1083.

Kalb, M. The myth of alcoholism prevention. *Preventive Medicine*, 1975, *4*, 404–416.

Keller, M. The disease concept of alcoholism revisited. *Journal of Studies on Alcohol*, 1976, *37*, 1694–1717.

Kern, J. C., Tippman, J., Fortgang, J., & Paul, S. A treatment approach for children of alcoholics. *Journal of Drug Education*, 1977, *7*, 207–218.

Kinder, B. N. Attitudes toward alcohol and drug abuse: II. Experimental data, mass media research, and methodological considerations. *International Journal of the Addictions*, 1975, *10*, 1035–1054.

Kraft, D. P. Strategies for reducing drinking problems among youth: College programs. In H. T. Blane & M. E. Chafetz (Eds.), *Youth, alcohol and social policy*. New York: Plenum Press, 1979.

Kraft, D. P., Dustin, E., & Mellor, E. T. *Alcohol education programming at the University of Massachusetts and evaluation of results to date*. Amherst: University of Massachusetts Demonstration Alcohol Education Project, 1977.

Kuusi, P. Alcohol sales experiment in rural Finland (Helsinki: Finnish Foundation for Alcohol Studies, 1957). Cited in Popham, R. E., Schmidt, W., & de Lint, J. R. The effects of legal restraint on drinking. In B. Kissin & H. Begleiter (Eds.), *The biology of alcoholism: Social aspects of alcoholism* (Vol. 4). New York: Plenum Press, 1976.

Lana, R. E. Pretest sensitization. In R. Rosenthal & R. L. Rosnow (Eds.), *Artifact in behavioral research*. New York: Academic Press, 1969.

Lau, H. H. Cost of alcoholic beverages as a determinant of alcohol consumption. In R. J. Gibbins, Y. Israel, H. Kalant, R. E. Popham, W. Schmidt, & R. G. Smart (Eds.), *Research advances in alcohol and drug problems* (Vol. 2). New York: Wiley, 1975.

Maisto, S. A., & McCollam, J. B. The use of multiple measures of life health to assess alcohol treatment outcome: A review and critique. In L. C. Sobell, M. S. Sobell, & E. Ward (Eds.), *Evaluating alcohol and drug abuse treatment effectiveness*. New York: Pergammon Press, 1980.

Mäkelä, K. Levels of consumption and social consequences of drinking. In Y. Israel, F. Glaser, H. Kalant, R. E. Popham, W. Schmidt, & R. G. Smart (Eds.), *Research advances in alcohol and drug problems* (Vol. 4). New York: Plenum Press, 1978.

Mandell, W., & Ginzburg, H. M. Youthful alcohol use, abuse, and alcoholism. In B. Kissin & H. Begleiter (Eds.), *Biology of alcoholism: Social aspects of alcoholism*. New York: Plenum Press, 1976.

Mannello, T. A., & Seaman, F. J. Prevalence, costs, and handling of drinking problems on seven railroads: Final report (Washington, D. C.: University Research Corporation, 1979). Cited in Trice, H. M. Job based alcoholism and employee assistance programs. *Alcohol Health and Research World*, 1980, *4*, 4–16.

Margulies, R. Z., Kessler, R. C., & Kandel, D. B. A longitudinal study of onset of drinking among high-school students. *Journal of Studies on Alcohol*, 1977, *38*, 897–911.

Marlatt, G. A., & Marques, J. K. Mediation, self-control and alcohol use. In R. B. Stuart (Ed.), *Behavioral self-management: Strategies, techniques outcome*. New York: Brunner/Mazel, 1977.

McCain, L. J., & McCleary, R. The statistical analysis of the simple interrupted time-series quasi-experiment. In T. D. Cook & D. T. Campbell (Eds.), *Quasi-experimentation: Design and analysis issues for field settings*. Chicago: Rand McNally, 1979.

McCord, J. A thirty-year follow-up study of treatment effects. *American Psychologist*, 1978, *33*, 284–289.

McCord, J., & McCord, W. A. A follow-up report on the Cambridge-Somerville youth study. *Annals of the American Academy of Political and Social Science*, 1959, *322*, 89–96.

Medicine in the public interest. A study in the actual effects of alcoholic beverage control laws. Washington, D. C.: Medicine in the Public Interest, Inc., 1979.

Milgram, G. Current status and problems of alcohol education in the schools. *Journal of School Health*, 1975, *46*, 317–320.

Milgram, G. A historical review of alcohol education research and comments. *Journal of Alcohol and Drug Education*, 1976, *21*, 1–16.

Miller, B. A., Pokorny, A. D., Valles, J., & Cleveland, S. E. Biased sampling in alcoholism treatment research. *Quarterly Journal of Studies on Alcohol*, 1970, *31*, 97–107.

Miller, P. M. Behavioral strategies for reducing drinking among young adults. In H. T. Blane & M. E. Chafetz (Eds.), *Youth, alcohol, and social policy*. New York: Plenum Press, 1979.

Miller, P. M., & Mastria, M. A. *Alternatives to alcohol abuse.* Champaign, Ill.: Research Press, 1977.

Miller, P. M., Becker, J. V., Foy, D. W., & Wooten, L. S. Instructional control of the components of alcoholic drinking behavior. *Behavior Therapy*, 1976, *1*, 472–480.

Miller, W. R. Behavioral treatment of problem drinkers: A comparative outcome study of three controlled drinking therapies. *Journal of Consulting and Clinical Psychology*, 1978, *46*, 74–86.

Miller, W. R., & Taylor, C. A. Relative effectiveness of bibliotherapy, individual, and group self-control training in the treatment of problem drinkers. *Addictive Behaviors*, 1980, *5*, 13–24.

Miller, W. R., Taylor, C. A., & West, J. C. Focused versus broad-spectrum behavior therapy for problem drinkers. *Journal of Consulting and Clinical Psychology*, 1980, *48*, 590–601.

Nathan, P. E., & Lansky, D. Common methodological problems in research on the addictions. *Journal of Consulting and Clinical Psychology*, 1978, *46*, 713–726.

Nirenberg, T. D., Ersner-Hershfield, S., Sobell, M. B., & Sobell, L. C. Behavioral treatment of alcohol problems. In C. K. Prokop & L. Bradley (Eds.), *Medical psychology: A new perspective.* New York: Academic Press, 1981.

Noble, E. P. (Ed.). *Third special report to the U.S. Congress on alcohol and health.* (DHEW Publ. No. ADM 79–832.) Washington, D.C.: U.S. Government Printing Office, 1978.

Noel, N. E., Sobell, L. C., Cellucci, T., Nirenberg, T. D., & Sobell, M. B. Behavioral treatment of outpatient problem drinkers: Five clinical case studies. In W. M. Hay & P. E. Nathan (Eds.), *Clinical case studies in the behavioral treatment of alcoholism.* New York: Plenum Press, 1982.

Ogurzsoff, S., & Vogel-Sprott, M. Low blood alcohol discrimination and self-titration skills of social drinkers with widely varied drinking habits. *Canadian Journal of Behavioral Science*, 1976, *8*, 232–242.

Ornstein, S. I. Control of alcohol consumption through price increases. *Journal of Studies on Alcohol*, 1980, *41*, 807–817.

Parker, D. A., & Harman, M. S. The distribution of consumption model of prevention of alcohol problems. *Journal of Studies on Alcohol*, 1978, *39*, 377–399.

Patterson, G. R., Reid, J. B., Jones, R. R., & Conger, R. E. *A social learning approach to family intervention.* Eugene, Ore.: Castalia Publishing Co., 1975.

Pattison, E. M., Sobell, M. B., & Sobell, L. C. *Emerging concepts of alcohol dependence.* New York: Springer, 1977.

Plant, M. A. Learning to drink. In M. Grant & P. Gwinner (Eds.), *Alcoholism in perspective.* Baltimore: University Park Press, 1979.

Plaut, T. F. A. *Alcohol problems: A report to the nation.* New York: Oxford University Press, 1967.

Plaut, T. F. A. Prevention of alcoholism. In S. E. Golann & C. Eisdorfer, *Handbook of community mental health.* New York: Appleton-Century Crofts, 1972.

Polich, J. M., Armor, D. J., & Braiker, H. B. *Patterns of alcoholism over four years.* Santa Monica, Calif.: Rand Corporation, 1980.

Pomerleau, D., & Adkins, D. Evaluating behavioral and traditional treatment for problem drinkers. In L. C. Sobell, M. B. Sobell, & E. Ward (Eds.), *Evaluating alcohol and drug abuse treatment effectiveness.* New York: Pergamon Press, 1980.

Popham, R. E., Schmidt, W., & de Lint, J. R. The effects of legal restraint on drinking. In B. Kissin & H. Begleiter (Eds.), *The biology of alcoholism Social aspects of alcoholism* (Vol. 4). New York: Plenum Press, 1976. (a)

Popham, R. E., Schmidt, W., & de Lint, J. The prevention of hazardous drinking: Implications for research on the effects of government control measures. In J. A. Ewing & B. A. Rouse (Eds.), *Drinking.* Chicago: Nelson-Hall, 1976. (b)

Portnoy, B. Effects of a controlled-usage alcohol education program. *Journal of Drug Education*, 1980, *10*, 181–195.

Rachal, J. V., Hubbard, R. L., Williams, J. R., & Tuchfeld, B. S. Drinking levels and problem drinking among junior and senior high-school students. *Journal of Studies on Alcohol*, 1976, *37*, 1751–1761.

Raymond, A. Ten o'clock closing—The effect of the change in hotel bar closing time on road accidents in the metropolitan area of Victoria. *Australian Road Research*, 1969, *3*, 3–17.

Robins, L. W., Bates, W. M., & O'Neal, P. Adult drinking patterns of former problem children. In D. Pittman & C. R. Snyder (Eds.), *Society, culture, and drinking patterns*. New York: Wiley, 1962.

Roman, P. M. Secondary prevention of alcoholism: Problems and prospects in occupational programming. *Journal of Drug Issues*, 1975, *5*, 327–343.

Roman, P. M. From employee alcoholism to employee assistance. Deemphases on prevention and alcohol problems in work-based programs. *Journal of Studies on Alcohol*, 1981, *42*, 244–272.

Roman, P. M., & Trice, H. M. The development of deviant drinking behavior: Occupational risk factors. *Archives on Environmental Health*, 1970, *20*, 424–435.

Roman, P. M., & Trice, H. M. Strategies of preventive psychiatry and social reality: The case of alcoholism. In P. M. Roman & H. M. Trice (Eds.), *Sociological perspectives on community mental health*. Santa Cruz, Calif.: Davis Publishing Co., 1974.

Roman, P. M., & Trice, H. W. Alcohol abuse and work organization. In B. Kissin & H. Begleiter (Eds.), *The biology of alcoholism* (Vol. 4). New York: Plenum Press, 1976.

Room, R. Governing images and the prevention of alcohol problems. *Preventive Medicine*, 1974, *3*, 11–23.

Room, R. Evaluating the effects of drinking laws on drinking. In J. A. Ewing & B. A. Rouse (Eds.), *Drinking alcohol in American society: Issues and current research*. Chicago: Nelson-Hall, 1978.

Room, R. Case for a problem prevention approach to alcohol, drug, and mental problems. *Public Health Reports*, 1981, *96*, 26–33.

Ross, H. L., Campbell, D. T., & Glass, G. V. Determining the social effects of a legal reform: The British "Breathalyzer" crackdown of 1967. *American Behavioral Scientist*, 1970, *13*, 493–509.

Schaie, K. W., & Baltes, P. B. On sequential strategies in developmental research and the Schaie-Baltes controversy: Description or explanation? *Human Development*, 1975, *18*, 384–390.

Schmidt, W., & Kornaczewski, A. The effect of lowering the legal drinking age in Ontario on alcohol-related vehicle accidents. In S. Israelstom & S. Lambert (Eds.), *Alcohol, drugs, and traffic Safety*. Proceedings of the Sixth International Conference on Alcohol, Drugs, and Traffic Safety. Toronto: Addiction Research Foundation, 1975.

Schneiderman, I. Family thinking in the prevention of alcoholism. *Preventive Medicine*, 1975, *4*, 296–309.

Schuckit, M. A., & Cahalan, D. Evaluation of alcoholism treatment programs. In W. J. Filstead, J. J. Rossi, & M. Keller (Eds.), *Alcohol and alcohol problems: New thinking and new directions*. Cambridge, Mass.: Ballinger, 1976.

Scoles, P., & Fine, E. Short-term effects of an educational program for drinking drivers. *Journal of Studies on Alcohol*, 1977, *38*, 633–637.

Seeley, J. R. Death by liver cirrhoses and the price of beverage alcohol. *Canadian Medical Association Journal*, 1960, *83*, 1361–1366.

Selzer, M. L., Vinokur, A., & Wilson, T. D. A psychosocial comparison of drunken drivers and alcoholics. *Journal of Studies on Alcohol*, 1977, *35*, 1294–1312.

Shafii, M., Lavely, R., & Jaffe, R. Meditation and the prevention of alcohol abuse. *American Journal of Psychiatry,* 1975, *132,* 942–945.

Shore, M. F., & Massimo, J. L. An innovative approach to the treatment of adolescent delinquent boys within a suburban community. In S. E. Golann & C. Eisdorfer (Eds.), *Handbook of community mental health.* New York: Appleton-Century-Crofts, 1972.

Shore, M. F., & Massimo, J. L. After ten years: A follow-up study of comprehensive vocationally oriented psychotherapy. *American Journal of Orthopsychiatry,* 1973, *43,* 128–132.

Shover, N., & Bankston, W. Some behavioral effects on new legislation (University of Tennessee, 1973). Cited in Diamond, S. S. Detecting legal change and its impact. In L. Bickman (Ed.), *Applied social psychology.* Beverly Hills, Calif.: Sage, 1981.

Smart, R. Employed alcoholics treated voluntarily and under constructive coercion: A follow-up study. *Quarterly Journal of Studies on Alcohol,* 1974, *35,* 196–209.

Smart, R. Priorities in minimizing alcohol problems among young people. In H. T. Blane & M. E. Chafetz (Eds.), *Youth, alcohol, and social policy.* New York: Plenum Press, 1979.

Sobel, L. C. Critique of alcoholism treatment evaluation. In G. A. Marlatt & P. E. Nathan (Eds.), *Behavioral approaches to alcoholism.* New Brunswick, N. J.: Rutgers Center of Alcohol Studies, 1978.

Sobell, L. C., Sobell, M. B., & Ward, E. (Eds.). *Evaluating alcohol and drug abuse treatment effectiveness.* New York: Pergamon Press, 1980.

Spoth, R., & Rosenthal, D. Wanted: A developmentally oriented alcohol prevention program. *Personnel and Guidance Journal,* 1980, *59,* 212–216.

Stein, L., Newton, J. R., & Bowman, R. S. Duration of hospitalization for alcoholism. *Archives of General Psychiatry,* 1975, *32,* 247–252.

Steinglass, P. A life history model of the alcoholic family. *Family Process,* 1980, *19,* 211–226.

Stuart, R. B. Teaching facts about drugs: Pushing or preventing. *Journal of Educational Psychology,* 1974, *66,* 189–201.

Tableman, B. Overview of programs to prevent mental health problems of children. *Public Health Reports,* 1981, *96,* 38–44.

Trice, H. M. Applied research studies; job based alcoholism and employee assistance programs. *Alcohol, Health, and Research World,* 1980, *4,* 4–16.

Urban and Rural Systems Associates. *Final report on the NIAAA replication program (1978–1980)* (Report No. PB–81–197212). Rockville, Md.: National Institute on Alcohol Abuse and Alcoholism, 1980.

Walsh, B. M., & Walsh, D. Validity of indices of alcoholism. *British Journal of Preventive Social Medicine,* 1973, *27,* 18–26.

Whitehead, P. C. DWI programs: Doing what's in or dodging what's indicated? *Journal of Safety Research,* 1975, *7,* 127–134. (a)

Whitehead, P. C. Prevention of alcoholism: Divergence and convergences of two approaches. *Addictive Diseases,* 1975, *1,* 431–443. (b)

Wilkinson, R. *The prevention of drinking problems: Alcohol control and cultural influences.* New York: Oxford University Press, 1970.

Williams, A. F., DiCicco, L., & Unterberger, H. Philosophy and evaluation of an alcohol education program. *Quarterly Journal of Studies on Alcohol,* 1968, *29,* 685–702.

Williams, R. L., & Long, J. D. *Toward a self-managed life style.* Boston: Houghton Mifflin, 1975.

Wilson, C., & Orford, J. Children of alcoholics. *Journal of Studies on Alcohol,* 1978, *39,* 121–142.

Wiltz, N. A., & Patterson, G. R. An evaluation of parent training procedures designed to alter inappropriate aggressive behavior of boys. *Behavior Therapy,* 1974, *5,* 515–521.

Wolin, S. J., Bennett, L. A., & Noonan, D. L. Family rituals and the recurrence of alcoholism over generations. *American Journal of Psychiatry,* 1979, *136,* 589–593.

Zador, P. Statistical evaluation of the effectiveness of "alcohol safety action projects." *Accident Analysis and Prevention,* 1976, *8,* 51–66.

Zarraro, J. Drug education: Is ignorance bliss? *Nations Schools,* 1973, *11,* 29–33.

Zucker, R. A. Parental influences upon drinking patterns of their children. In M. Greenblatt & M. A. Schuckit (Eds.), *Alcoholism problems in women and children.* New York: Grune & Stratton, 1976.

Zucker, R. A. Developmental aspects of drinking through the young adult years. In H. T. Blane & M. E. Chafetz, (Eds.), *Youth, alcohol, and social policy.* New York: Plenum Press, 1979.

Zucker, R. A., & DeVoe, C. I. Life history characteristics associated with problem drinking and antisocial behavior in adolescent girls: A comparison with male findings. In R. D. Wirt, G. Winokur, & M. Roff (Eds.), *Life history research in psychopathology* (Vol. 4). Minneapolis: University of Minnesota Press, 1975.

Zylman, R. DWI enforcement programs: Why are they not more effective? *Accident Analysis and Prevention,* 1975, *7,* 179–190.

3

Target Populations for Alcohol Abuse Prevention

NORA E. NOEL AND BARBARA S. McCRADY

Historically, there has been a division of labor between professionals regarding rehabilitation and prevention of alcohol abuse. Clinicians tend to concentrate their efforts on rehabilitation of individual problem drinkers. To clinicians, prevention of alcohol problems may seem like an ideal but not very realistic goal, and many view prevention as beyond their realm. Conversely, those who work in the prevention area may believe that clinicians are ranging too far afield when they show an interest in prevention. These professionals (e.g., sociologists, anthropologists, demographers, and social psychologists) could resent what they might see as "interference" by clinicians.

Clinicians usually are trained to deal with the problems of the individual or the individual within a group. *Prevention* of alcohol problems involves groups of people and measures success in group, rather than individual terms. Competition between prevention and rehabilitation programs for money, personnel, and political support has also fostered an emotional division. For example, success rates for rehabilitation programs are often easier to "see" than those of prevention efforts. Success for prevention programs is often measured in terms of group change, such as a long-term, decreased rate of some event (drinking), or the increased occurrence of

NORA E. NOEL • Butler Hospital, Providence, Rhode Island 02906.   BARBARA S. McCRADY • Butler Hospital and Brown University, Providence, Rhode Island 02906.

some behavior indirectly or hypothetically related to sobriety. Since individuals within the group have no marker for change (i.e., the drinking problems *did not* occur) and the success rates can only be measured over long periods of time, prevention efforts do not have the immediate, highly visible successes that treatments may claim. Indeed, individuals may resent and resist prevention efforts because they do not expect to develop alcohol problems in the first place. Rehabilitation programs are more popular because they remove an already existing set of problems. Successful rehabilitation of an individual with alcohol problems will incur the support of the individual, family, and friends. In addition, since the changes can be perceived on a short-term basis, the rehabilitation program success is easier to see.

Competition between rehabilitation and prevention has not been functional. Prevention efforts need to be viewed on a continuum with rehabilitation efforts. There needs to be agreement among the personnel in the whole alcohol-problem field on the aims and goals of programs. As clinicians, the present authors contend that the clinical (rehabilitation) viewpoint can help in forming valid guidelines for future prevention programs. Thus, the goals of the present chapter are (1) to provide a fresh perspective on prevention of alcohol problems and (2) to use this new view to suggest practical, more specific problem-oriented directions in prevention.

Three main questions will form the core of the chapter: What behaviors should we work to prevent? What behaviors are problems? and What is the meaning of these questions for different target populations?

Several writers have answered these questions in terms of general notions about alcohol problems. Some discuss drunken-driving statistics and launch an effort to prevent people from driving while intoxicated. Unfortunately, such a nationwide program may be a waste of time and money. The general application of techniques for prevention of drunken driving may not reach the *correct* audience (i.e., populations at high risk for drunken driving, such as young males). Efforts may be wasted by applying the intervention to a population already at fairly low risk for drunk driving (e.g., housewives). Measurement of success also becomes a problem with such a general program. For example, the nationwide program aimed at prevention of driving while intoxicated may reach one or two populations at high risk for drunken driving and may even appreciably reduce rates of drunken driving in those groups. However, a survey of nationwide statistics before and after the program may not show any overall change and may lead to abandonment of the program.

These examples may be somewhat exaggerated, but they illustrate an important point: Prevention efforts need to be specific not only in terms of goals and aims (what to prevent), but also in terms of the target populations for the prevention efforts (what to prevent with whom).

This chapter is divided into five parts. In the first section, the question of identifying *special* populations and their unique configurations of antecedents to and consequences of problem drinking is explored. A model of excessive drinking is presented to help illustrate when and at what stage decisions must be made regarding intervention. The second section contains a more theoretical discussion of guidelines for the "ideal" prevention effort, with examples of how these guidelines may be applied to specific populations. The third section reviews selected existing prevention programs directed at special populations. In the fourth section, some of the current impediments to developing ideal prevention programs for special populations are presented. The last section discusses the implications and conclusions of the "clinician's eye view" of the prevention of alcohol problems with special populations.

Throughout the chapter illustrations are drawn from three special populations: American Indians, women, and the elderly. The theme of the three populations is carried throughout the chapter to provide cohesive examples of applications of ideal guidelines and existing programs.

IDENTIFYING SPECIAL POPULATIONS AND NEEDED PREVENTION EFFORTS

How does one define a *special* population? Groups are often defined on the basis of ethnic or racial identity, for example Blacks, American Indians, or Irish. A second common division is based on sex. For example, women or pregnant women may be seen as special populations. A third basis for division is age. Adolescents or senior citizens are two categories illustrating this type of division. Less common bases for defining special groups are occupation (e.g., police, military, and bartenders); physical, intellectual, or emotional handicaps (e.g., mental retardation); or familial and/or genetic factors (e.g., children of alcoholics).

In this chapter, discussion focuses on three groups, one from each of the most common divisional categories—racial-ethnic, sex, and age. The groups are American Indians, women, and the elderly, and were chosen because they are not often the focus of prevention literature.

PROBLEMS OF VARIABILITY IN CAUSES AND PROBLEMS

One view of preventing alcohol problems refers primarily to preventing the breakup of families and societal structures due to excessive drinking. Another view conceptualizes alcohol problems in terms of the destruction of the alcoholic as an individual (e.g., liver and heart complications, depression, and death resulting from alcohol). Still another focus is on

preventing the negative effects of drinking from being inflicted upon innocent victims (e.g., Fetal Alcohol Syndrome, and deaths and injuries in
drunken-driving accidents). In his analysis of prevention goals, Room
(1980) suggests that alcohol problems can be divided into six major categories: problems of chronic illness; acute health problems related to specific
drinking bouts; problems of demeanor during and after drinking; casualties
(injuries, death, and property loss); default in major social roles; and mental
or existential problems related to drinking.

A multifactorial causation model is most often assumed with alcohol
problems. Room (1980) makes the point that alcohol by itself may have
varied degrees of involvement in the causes of drinking problems. For
example, drinking may be intrinsic to, or a precondition of, some problems
or merely be associated with others. In cases where excessive alcohol consumption is intrinsic to a problem, changing the causes of the drinking may
be addressed by a prevention program. Since both presumed causes of an
individual's alcohol abuse and the consequent problems are multifactorial, a
prevention program could be left with a huge array of target behaviors to
address.

A program designed to prevent all six categories of causes and consequences of excessive drinking would be a monumental undertaking due to
the scope of interventions required. Assessment of the effects of the program interventions on all these variables would be a nightmare. Thus, the
sheer multitude of problems caused by, and factors leading to, excessive
drinking dictates the need for specification of goals and interventions for
prevention of particular problems. A lack of specific goals may be a reason
for the failure of a number of prevention programs.

Another variable in designing prevention programs is the level of intervention to use. A primary level of intervention is aimed at prevention of
drinking, or at least of excessive drinking. A secondary level of intervention
is geared toward preventing some of the negative consequences of excessive drinking. An example of an intervention at a primary level is laws
prohibiting liquor sales during certain hours. There is, however, a prevailing attitude in the United States that one should be allowed to "go to hell in
one's own handbasket" (Room, 1980, p. 41). Such an attitude can lead to
interventions at a more secondary level or a policy of preventing only
alcohol problems that directly or obviously affect others. Thus, for example, assuming that some people will continue to get drunk on Saturday
night, the aim of the anti-DUI campaign is to keep these drinkers out of
their cars. Another example of this secondary level of intervention would
be to add doses of Thiamine and other B vitamins to alcoholic beverages to
inhibit the development of cognitive organic deficits in chronic heavy
drinkers.

STAGE I ▬ ▬ ▬ ▬ ▬ ▶	EXCESSIVE DRINKING ▬ ▬ ▬ ▬ ▬ ▶	STAGE II

ANTECEDENTS OR PRESUMED CAUSES
OF EXCESSIVE DRINKING

ALCOHOL PROBLEMS

Life stresses
Lack of alternative behaviors
Peer group encouragement and
  modeling of excessive drink-
  ing
Ready availability of alcohol
Family history of alcoholism

Car accidents
Liver damage
Fetal alcohol
  syndrome
Marital problems
Cognitive impairment

Figure 1. Simplified model of excessive drinking.

A shorthand method of conceptualizing the issues of level of involvement can be found in the following simplified model of excessive drinking (Figure 1). Various antecedents or presumed causes of excessive drinking lead to abuse of alcohol (acute and/or chronic), which in turn leads to long-term negative consequences. The antecedents may not necessarily have a direct causal link to the particular alcohol problem.

A prevention program designed to intervene at Stage 1 could be considered a *primary prevention* effort. For example, state laws limiting the availability of alcohol could be construed as primary prevention efforts. Their goals are to limit the occurrence of excessive drinking and thus, indirectly, to limit the occurrence of alcohol problems. Programs designed to intervene at the excessive drinking level or at Stage 2 can be classified as *secondary prevention*. Laws and penalties against drunken driving are examples of this type of prevention.

If prevention is conceptualized along a continuum with treatment, primary prevention could be seen as addressing causes of excessive drinking. Secondary prevention would involve dealing with prevention of the negative consequences of drinking with certain "high-risk" populations, and tertiary intervention (i.e., clinical) would involve rehabilitation of problem drinkers from those negative consequences.

Thus, prevention programs can address many alcohol issues and problems at several different levels. Since not all of these factors can be addressed simultaneously, priorities must be assigned and decisions made. The model of excessive drinking presented above provides a framework within which to make decisions about which problems to prevent and how. The model is only the beginning, however. Other important factors, especially those related to target populations, must also become part of the decisional considerations regarding prevention efforts.

DECISIONAL CONSIDERATIONS: WHICH PROBLEMS? WHICH CAUSES? WHICH POPULATIONS?

This section focuses on the specific causes and problems more associated with one population than another and the issues involved in deciding which problems to prevent at what stages with what populations.

Specific Causes and Consequences of Excessive Drinking

One of the most important considerations in setting priorities for targets and goals of alcohol abuse prevention is that specific or presumed causes for excessive drinking or alcohol problems are more often associated with one population than another. This idea is best illustrated by comparisons of antecedents and problems across the three target populations: American Indians, women, and the elderly. Table 1 compares and contrasts antecedents or presumed causes of excessive drinking in each population and Table 2 compares and contrasts their alcohol problems.

Table 1 presents commonly assumed antecedents or causes of excessive drinking in each population. These antecedents are divided into three major categories: biological, individual, and interpersonal (social). Classification of these antecedents can facilitate decision making about the most effective type of intervention for prevention of alcohol problems. In Table 2, alcohol problems are categorized according to Room's (1980) six classifications. The typical manifestations of each type of problem for each population are then detailed.

Issues Involved in Targeting Problems.   Given this array of causes, consequences, and populations, how should priorities be established for prevention targets? Room (1977) listed several preliminary suggestions to aid in choosing targets. These suggestions are expanded here and adapted to the special populations perspective.

First, the *impact of the problem* must be assessed. How severe is the problem in terms of its effects on the drinker, the individual associated with the drinker (e.g., family and friends), the particular subgroups to which the drinker belongs, and/or on society as a whole? The extent of the impact on others is seen by many people as a major criterion in determining the severity, and thus the importance, of the problem, but this may be a limited perspective. For example, cirrhosis of the liver in a mother of three children could have a devastating effect on the woman herself and on her family, who will either lose her or need to support her through a long illness. Public intoxication, on the other hand, although a problem, would have less individual or interpersonal consequences, so it may not be as important a target for change.

Table 1.

Commonly Assumed Causes or Antecedents of Excessive Drinking in Three Populations

	Women	Indians	Elderly
Biological antecedents	Gynecological problems as a cause? for example, premenstrual tension, menopausal problems	"Firewater myths"; very controversial, metabolism difference?	Physical illness or aging can magnify alcohol effects: 1. Decrease alcohol metabolism 2. Increase vulnerability of impaired organs to alcohol effects 3. Toxic interactions between alcohol and medications
Individual antecedents	Presumed greater psychopathology: Increase guilt, anxiety, and decrease self-esteem (cause or consequence or both?) Increase reported incidence of "blow to self-esteem" or "object loss" as reasons for drinking	Devaluation of self as Indian; depression and decrease self-esteem Mood and mind-altering part of culture	With late onset psychopathology plays decrease role than "life stresses" Depression due to life stresses (for example, social isolation, bereavement)
Interpersonal (social) antecedents	Sex role conflicts; women's changing roles Marital conflict Co-alcoholism Fewer outside home opportunities; lack of independent control of finances, etc. Lowered social contacts and support	Conflicts between white and Indian culture Devaluation of Indian culture and consequently of self Increase unemployment and poverty Lack of cultural norms for drinking Historical effects of Prohibition on reservations and encouragement of alcohol by fur traders Drinking as group phenomenon	Retirement self-esteem Diminished social network (friends die, restricted ability to get around, etc.) Loss of spouse Marital discord Reduced income

Table 2.
Examples of Alcohol Problems in Three Populations

Type of alcohol problem	Women	Indians	Elderly
Chronic illness	Telescoping into chronic illness: cirrhosis, pancreatitis, ulcers, cardiovascular diseases Gynecological problems frequent in women alcoholics	Cirrhosis fourth ranked cause of Indian death; 6% of all Indian death vs. 1.7% with population as a whole Indian women especially have higher cirrhosis rate than whites or blacks	High level of chronic health problems exacerbated by alcohol
Acute health problems—specific drinking bouts	Abuse of other medications; likely to experience interaction effects. Corrigan (1980) found 71% abused other drugs (e.g., 43% sleeping pills, 21% stimulants)	High incidence of withdrawal symptoms because liquor still prohibited on some reservations, so drinkers cannot "taper off" like even skid row alcoholics	Sexual problems—impotence Medication and alcohol mix, synergistic or interfering effect
Problems of demeanor during and after drinking	Social stigma attached to female drunkenness Low level of DUIs; question of "afternoon" DUI however Intoxication in public is a very low-level problem for women	Fighting while drinking often excused and tolerated as "the liquor talking." Fighting or antagonizing at other times may cause ostracism. Binge drinking intoxication and violence is norm for many tribes High level of DUIs	Frequent intoxication Problems with police

Casualties	Fetal Alcohol Syndrome (FAS)	High level of FAS among Indian women Accidents first ranked cause of death among Indians; at least 75% are alcohol related Suicides twice national level and 80% of all Indian suicides are alcohol related High level of homicides related to alcohol	Elderly are more prone than population at large to have personal injury accidents. Alcohol use may further increase the probability of having an accident.
Default in major social roles	Women less likely than men to have financial, vocational, legal problems Marital disruption more likely with women, also children taken away more often than with men	Child abuse or neglect related to both parents drinking is higher	Problems with spouses and retaining social network Work problems not common
Mental-emotional problems related to drinking	High level of psychological dependence	Suicides and violence (above) highly related to alcohol consumption	Not known; alcohol may cause depression Psychological dependence

Another consideration related to impact is the frequency with which the problem occurs. A prevention program aimed at reducing public intoxication with women is not very important, because it occurs so infrequently. However, trends over time in frequency of occurrence must also be considered. For example, at present, women do not often experience vocational problems as a result of drinking. However, as time goes by and more women spend more time in the work force, vocational problems among women may occur to a greater extent. Current work programs designed to prevent women's occupational alcohol problems may actually be timely and worthwhile.

A final consideration in terms of problem impact is the particular population's needs and demands. In other words, the standards or judgments of problem severity imposed by those outside the target group often have little similarity to the standards of the group itself. This is an especially important concept when considering Indian populations, since for decades whites (outsiders) have dictated the policies and practices of Indian problem-drinking prevention programs. An Indian tribe as a whole may consider any drinking on the part of tribal members as anathema. Thus, the tribe may identify alcohol consumption itself rather than any particular problem as the most important target for prevention.

Beyond establishing the impact of the drinking problem, the *centrality of alcohol consumption* in the problem must also be considered. This consideration is important not only to the selection of a target but also to the choice of intervention. For example, drunk-driving accidents are a result of both drinking and driving. A program designed to keep people from driving after they have been drinking might be an efficient and effective prevention program. However, assessing the centrality of alcohol consumption to a particular problem is sometimes quite difficult. This is especially true with elderly populations. How much of a role does drinking play in sexual impotence or chronic neurological deficits? In these cases primary prevention might be the intervention level of choice.

Related to establishing the centrality of alcohol's role in the problem is consideration of the effectiveness of currently available prevention strategies to deal with the problem. Although it may be difficult to establish the centrality of alcohol to the problem, almost no data base exists for estimating the effectiveness of most prevention strategies. Research is needed both to determine the relative roles of excessive drinking and other factors in alcohol problems and to assess the level of effectiveness of various prevention strategies. Currently, only estimates and "best guesses" can be used for these considerations.

The final consideration in establishing the priority of targets for prevention is the *ethical factors* involved. Ethical factors need to be considered from two perspectives: (1) What would be the ethical impact and implications of the prevention strategies used to intervene in the problem? and (2) What would the implications of leaving the problem alone be? Too often the second question is not given much consideration by those who object to prevention strategies on the basis of the first question. "Freedom" and "liberty" are important to most United States citizens. From that perspective many prevention programs that are directed at a specific target group may seem like a manifestation of "Big Brotherism." Difficult value judgments are required to discriminate between programs that restrict personal freedom and those that do not. For instance, do laws and sanctions against public intoxication help prevent or attenuate the level of public intoxication? Are the possibly beneficial impacts of laws against public intoxication outweighed by the drawbacks (e.g., fine, police record, and lowered respect for the law)? These questions require careful thought.

GUIDELINES FOR IDEAL PREVENTION PROGRAMS

GENERAL GUIDELINES

In order to implement any prevention program, several problems must be surmounted. To be effective, prevention programs must take into account (1) data on *typical* and *excessive* drinking patterns, (2) data on antecedents and causes of alcohol abuse, (3) clear goals and interventions, (4) access to the target population, (5) support, and (6) methods of self-perpetuating effective components of prevention programs.

Data on Typical and Excessive Drinking Patterns

A solid data base is needed regarding the drinking patterns, patterns of excessive drinking, and the frequency and dimensions of negative consequences or problems and characteristics of those at risk for excessive drinking within the target population. Currently, few such data are available, especially for special populations. Cahalan and his colleagues (e.g., Cahalan, Cisin, & Crossley, 1969) have attempted to provide such information through their national surveys, but most of their studies report on the drinking habits of white males between the ages of 18 and 60. Although Cahalan's data on women drinkers are the most complete data presently available on women's typical drinking patterns, the many changes women have experienced in the last 15 years may make such data outdated. Other investigators (e.g., Corrigan, 1980) have focused only on patterns and consequences of excessive drinking in women. Since even less is known about typical drinking patterns of the elderly and American Indians, the solid data base on which to build a prevention program is lacking.

Data on Antecedents and Causes of Alcohol Abuse

A stronger data base is needed regarding antecedents and causes of excessive drinking within specific populations. All too often alcoholics and problem drinkers within a group are asked why they started drinking excessively, and their self-reports are taken as accurate accounts of the causes of their drinking problems. Until such data are shown to have predictive validity, they are of limited value in understanding the causes and contributing factors of alcohol abuse. Longitudinal studies of drinking, the development of heavy drinking, and the development of problems and alcohol dependence within special populations are needed. In addition, findings from laboratory research on the acute effects of alcohol and on nonalcoholics' reasons for drinking should be incorporated into prevention planning. For example, expectations about alcohol's effects on depression may lead to increased drinking by women, but not necessarily by men (Noel & Lisman, 1980). Such data are needed in order to better predict who is at risk for abusive drinking and what factors, other than access to alcohol, can be manipulated to control alcohol abuse.

Clear Goals and Interventions

A third requirement for the ideal prevention effort is agreement on what to prevent. Goals and methods of intervention must be clearly stated, including details of what behaviors and institutions need to be modified. Decisions must be made about whether to implement a primary or secondary prevention effort.

Access to the Target Population

Channels of access to the population in question must be available. Access involves reaching the population and then being accepted by it. To achieve acceptance of a prevention program, the people in charge of the program should not be perceived as outsiders imposing regulations or restrictions. This is especially important for programs directed at specific racial or ethnic groups. In fact, Edwards (1977) has commented that all too often white Anglo-Saxons are off consulting to other groups about alcohol abuse prevention with little reciprocity. "We" are out there trying to show others how to prevent alcohol problems that "we" do not know much about ourselves. "We" also are not studying the other cultures to understand and learn from *their* prevention–rehabilitation efforts.

Once the barriers of political access are overcome, the problem of reaching the targeted population in some effective manner remains. Among American Indians, women, and the elderly, for example, unemployment is high and contact through work is therefore ineffective. How does one gain access to a hidden population (e.g., women who do not work outside the home)? One method is to consider what kind of public agencies or services the people in the target group may use regularly. For example, in order to involve homemakers in a Fetal Alcohol Syndrome or child abuse prevention program, materials might be distributed through physicians' offices (e.g., pediatricians, gynecologists), women and infants' programs in hospitals, and health maintenance organizations (HMOs). Personnel in these agencies could also be trained to funnel at-risk clients into the prevention program. Women could be contacted through afternoon radio and television announcements or grocery store bulletins. Senior citizens could be reached through active organizations for retirees such as the American Association of Retired Persons (AARP) or other senior citizens' groups. Activist groups (e.g., Gray Panthers) could also become involved. Longer-range planning for prevention of alcohol abuse by the elderly could be done at the work place as an active part of retirement planning. Gaining access to target populations may require effort, imagination, and creativity, but it is an integral part of any prevention program and cannot be neglected.

Support

Finding financial and political support for prevention efforts is the single most political requirement of any program. Any concerted prevention effort requires an enormous amount of time, materials, and personnel to complete and assess. Support, in terms of money and power, is essential.

It is in this arena that the treatment versus prevention issue unfortunately seems most clearly defined. Both public agencies and the private sector seem willing to spend on rehabilitation efforts but tend to shy away from prevention. Some of the reasons for this have been discussed above. For example, success rates are often easier for the public to "see" in a shorter amount of time in treatment rather than in prevention. It is time, however, for the public to begin to understand that rehabilitation programs without complementary prevention programs are akin to "closing the barn door after the horse is out." In the long run, rehabilitation without prevention is an enormous waste of time, lives, and money. Most people, however, do not directly bear the costs of rehabilitation programs, as many are financed through third party insurance company payments. It is rare for insurance companies to fund prevention efforts, although there is a trend in that direction (e.g., through health maintenance organizations or well-baby clinics).

One way to garner more support for prevention programs and to use available support more effectively is through small-scale demonstration projects. Such projects fit into the theme of this chapter because a major component would be a clearly restricted and well-defined population with specific short-term and long-term goals. For example, a program involving assertion and social skills training for women entering the work force could measure behaviors related to drinking immediately after the training program (short-term goal assessment) with continued measurement of drinking levels during the next year or so (intermediate-term goal assessment). An interim indication of success could be produced quickly by such a project, and the intervention could be credited with reducing or preventing excessive drinking.

Projects such as the above could help gain support for prevention efforts in at least two ways. They would establish that prevention efforts can be effective and would emphasize the link between prevention and rehabilitation efforts. These points might be enough to win some support from the private sector. Unfortunately, because of the prevailing political climate, support from the public sector does not appear forthcoming in the near future.

Methods of Self-Perpetuating Effective Components of Prevention Programs

This requirement is complementary to the need for support. No prevention program should be conceived without some method of assessment. No matter how promising a program seems, a clear demonstration of effectiveness is needed. However, once certain components of a program have been shown to reduce the rate or severity of specific drinking problems within a population, some method should be found to continue those components of the program. These methods should be planned into the program from the beginning. The problem of maintaining a program involves both gaining support from the target group and effecting a permanent change in some societal role or expectation regarding drinking or drinking problems.

GUIDELINES SPECIFIC TO PRIMARY PREVENTION

Reference to the previously presented excessive-drinking model (see Table 1) helps to emphasize the distinctions between primary and secondary prevention. Primary prevention programs intervene in the presumed causes of excessive drinking itself, while secondary programs, presuming that some excessive drinking will continue, seek to attenuate specific negative consequences. These distinctions present some unique advantages and problems for primary prevention programs.

An "ideal" program for primary prevention of excessive drinking can be conceived of as part of a more global movement toward health maintenance programs. In recent years, the United States has seen an increase in emphasis on "wellness" philosophies and *healthy living* (see Ng, Davis, & Mandersheid, 1978). This movement has produced programs such as Well-Baby Clinics, Comprehensive Health Maintenance Organizations (HMOs), and large-scale heart-problem-prevention projects (e.g., Pawtucket Memorial Heart Health Program; for a comprehensive review of recent developments in this area, see Matarazzo, 1980). These programs and projects may provide a vehicle for primary prevention of alcohol problems. Certainly, such a goal would be within the health philosophy, and target populations could be readily accessible. In fact, some of these programs already do target changes in alcohol consumption. A more specialized population emphasis and assessment of those at high risk could probably increase the potential for positive change in drinking habits.

It should also be emphasized that primary prevention interventions do not even have to pertain directly to alcohol consumption. For example, if employment stresses lead to (among other problems) excessive drinking, a program to help employers change the stresses or to help employees cope with those stresses may reduce alcohol consumption without ever specifically addressing drinking habits. A Heart Health Project emphasizing changes toward a more positive life-style (e.g., relaxation training, healthy eating habits, and exercise programs) may also lead to concurrent decreases in drinking. As such, even without directly addressing alcohol consumption, the project could constitute an effective effort for primary prevention of alcohol problems.

A stronger data base is needed regarding causes and antecedents of excessive drinking within a given population. Conceivably, if some of the causes of excessive drinking can be alleviated or alternative means of coping can be provided, excessive drinking can be indirectly attenuated. Thus, for example, if devaluation of American Indian tribal customs and culture is shown to be a cause of excessive drinking by members of the tribe, an emphasis on reviving American Indian culture could result in a downward trend in drinking.

Similarly, if certain specific behaviors are found to be directly related to excessive drinking in a given group, modification of these behaviors could also be used to reduce drinking levels. For example, alcohol abuse in some women is attributed to the woman's response to her husband's drinking. That is, an alcoholic husband may request, cajole, or insist that his wife join him in drinking. A primary prevention program aimed at this high-risk group (i.e., wives of alcoholics) may teach wives alternatives for dealing with husbands' drinking behavior. Assessment of success with this program would include measurements of wives' changed behavior toward their husbands and measurement of wives' drinking levels.

Accurate assessment of results can be tricky for some programs. Because some factors may influence drinking in indirect but important ways, it may be quite difficult to assess when and how changes in that factor lead to changes in drinking level. In the Fourth Special Report to Congress, it has been suggested (DeLuca, 1981) that the impact of a primary prevention program may be best understood in terms of a chain of events. A successful program produces changes in the regulatory, social, or physical environment that, in turn, lead to a new set of drinking norms that eventually have an impact on individuals. Unfortunately, in assessing the effects of a program, the individual impact may not occur for a relatively long period of time, and may be manifest with individuals who were not directly related to or studied by the project. For example, a program aimed at wives of alcoholics may actually have its greatest impact on the drinking habits of the children in those families. Thus, a thorough assessment of indirect measures of success is important to determine the impact of a program directed at primary prevention of alcohol problems.

GUIDELINES SPECIFIC TO SECONDARY PREVENTION

Establishment of Appropriately Limited Goals

Room (1977) suggests that every alcoholism prevention program must be based on the premise that drinking will continue. This premise is especially appropriate to assume in the case of secondary prevention efforts. Some programs may even begin with the assumption that excessive drinking may continue with many individuals, so that the purpose of the program would be to reduce the frequency and severity of negative consequences of the excessive drinking. If concurrent factors and behaviors can be changed to prevent drinking problems per se, then why not target those behaviors for intervention?

Establishing such limited goals may appear to be a negative restriction on prevention programs, but in many ways these limitations can be assets. The requirement that a program have clear goals and interventions is certainly much easier to fulfill when those goals do not need to be global and the interventions can be directly related to the specific problem. Results can be seen more quickly and more clearly.

Achievement of Experimental Control

With a smaller, more specific prevention project, research into the most effective of several types of procedures could more easily be conducted. Instead of various "horse-race" studies (e.g., "this procedure, as a package, works better than nothing"), more specific examination of effects of, and interactions among, various components of prevention packages could be achieved. Thus, a recommended guideline for the ideal secondary prevention effort is the inclusion of a strong research component involving the control and active manipulation of various prevention techniques. This would mean, as noted above, that the program planners would have to decide on various preplanned stopping points for assessment and refinement of the program and would have to be flexible enough to incorporate changes necessary to achieve adequate research control.

APPLICATION OF GUIDELINES IN SPECIFIC POPULATIONS

In this section, the three selected special populations (women, American Indians, and the elderly) are briefly described in terms of (a) available data about typical drinking behavior, (b) information about presumed causes or antecedents of abusive drinking, (c) suggestions for primary prevention programs, (d) drinking problems specific to the population, and (e) specific secondary prevention programs designed to reduce the risk of these problems. The reader is referred back to Tables 1 and 2 for a summary of this data.

Women

Typical Drinking Patterns. With any group as diverse as one-half the population, typical drinking habits are difficult to describe. However, some general group findings can be discussed. The most recent detailed survey of United States drinking patterns was a 1979 NIAAA-sponsored survey (Clark & Midanik, 1981). The results of this survey indicate that women typically either do not drink or drink very infrequently or lightly (an average of .01 to .21 oz. ethanol per day). Women report drinking less volume per drinking incident and less frequently, and report fewer problems with drinking than men.

In contrast, women can have severe drinking problems, and these problems can have a devastating effect not only on the woman herself, but on her family and co-workers. Denial of drinking problems, possibly because of societal stigmas regarding alcoholic women and protection of many women from the consequences of alcohol abuse (e.g., fewer DUI convictions) may contribute to the underreporting of alcohol problems.

Historically, drinking by women in the United States has been politically connected with the women's rights movement (Gomberg, 1976). After the late nineteenth century, Frances Willard, leader of the Women's Christian Temperance Union, maintained that alcohol abuse was largely responsible for many problems, especially of lower-class women. Excessive drinking by men was seen as contributing to wife abuse and neglect of family duties (e.g., earning a living), and women's drinking was thought to lead to child neglect. Bars, which were largely male dominated, thus became the target of people like Carrie Nation, and drinking was viewed as "anti-woman." This political movement, in fact, eventually led to the Prohibition Amendment to the Constitution, probably the largest full-scale prevention effort ever mounted.

Several historians (Kobler, 1974) believe that Prohibition indirectly led to the increase in women's drinking since World War I. Instead of being generally scorned, drinking by women in illegal night clubs ("speakeasies") was viewed as glamorous, exciting, and daring. It was during this period that more American women began to drink in public.

In 1969, Cahalan et al. reported that 60% of the adult females in the United States drank on occasion. On the average, black women reported drinking greater amounts of alcohol than did white women (although blacks tended toward either abstinence or heavy drinking). Women of blue-collar status or married to men in blue-collar jobs tended to drink more than those who were college educated. Single women (divorced, separated, or never married) drank more, and more often, than married women. In a more recent national survey, Clark and Midanik (1981) reported that, in the United States, the percentage of women who drink is highest in the 21 to 34 age range, with a steady linear decrease above age 35. (This finding may, in fact, represent current generational increments in the number of drinkers.) In contrast, the percentage of heavy drinkers among women tends to peak at ages 35 to 49 (in contrast to men at ages 21 to 34) and then shows a sharp decrease. Finally, surveys of women reveal that drinking levels may be somewhat related to reproductive cycles. During pregnancy, women tend to drink much less (Little, Schultz, & Mandell, 1976). Women often report higher levels of drinking during premenstrual distress.

Presumed Causes or Antecedents of Womens' Alcohol Abuse. Both the Cahalan et al. (1969) and Clark and Midanik (1981) surveys of American drinking practices suggest that women heavy drinkers usually are found in the lower socioeconomic groups, living in poverty in urban settings and lacking social supports for remaining abstinent. These women also tend to be divorced or never-married mothers. Thus, although sex-role conflict (Wilsnack & Wilsnack, 1978) is often cited as a presumed cause of women's heavy drinking, a majority of women alcohol abusers seem to be locked into traditional female roles. With these women, frustration and disenchantment may be a more likely cause of drinking than sex-role conflicts.

Sex-role conflicts or rejection of traditionally feminine roles (Wilsnack & Wilsnack, 1978) would seem more likely among women who are of higher socioeconomic status and more career oriented. This is probably the reason why such a high percentage of women who are employed and married are problem drinkers (Schuckit & Morrisey, 1976). However, there may be important commonalities between these two groups of women that contribute to their alcohol abuse. For example, for both groups, role overload, or having too much to do, may be a contributing factor. Also, Wilsnack and Wilsnack (1978) note that rejecting traditional female roles could also indicate rejection of traditional female values—such as the admonition "ladies don't drink." The discussion above about the changing drinking patterns of women brought about by Prohibition, combined with these data, suggests that some women's heavy drinking may result from lack of clear values and sanctions regarding alcohol. Abstinence is rejected, but what guidelines take its place?

Besides lack of clear guidelines and sanctions for drinking among women, other presumed causes of alcohol abuse have been cited, especially in the clinical literature (see Table 1). Married women (or "hidden housewife") drinkers may abuse alcohol because of loneliness, lack of social contacts or support, fewer opportunities outside the home, and lack of independent control in their lives (over finances, for example). For other married women, marital conflict is seen as leading to alcohol abuse (Corrigan, 1980; Mulford, 1977). However, this marital conflict may serve as an antecedent and a result of abusive drinking, with the order of events difficult to determine. Another possible antecedent related to marital status is *co-alcoholism.* A husband may begin to drink heavily, and his wife, in turn, begins to drink more frequently to "keep him company." The wife is actually more at risk than the husband in these situations because her smaller size and lower tolerance for alcohol make her more likely to become addicted to it. In addition, physical problems are often seen more quickly with women than with men (see discussion of *telescoping* below). Thus, co-alcoholism is a separate cause with separate, severe alcohol problems resulting.

Other presumed causes of abusive drinking among women (as described in Table 1) include gynecological problems (Gomberg, 1976), blows to self-esteem (Beckman, 1975), or some forms of psychopathology (e.g., depression). This category includes drinking to alleviate premenstrual tension or to cope with menopausal symptoms. It also includes drinking in response to the guilt and anxiety often reported by women drinkers (Beckman, 1975) or from loss of self-esteem. A frequently cited example is the "empty-nest syndrome" (Curlee, 1967), which commonly occurs about the time of menopause and may precipitate a late-life drinking problem.

There are many suggested causes of women's alcohol abuse. Unfortunately, these speculations regarding causes are often derived from studies of women who already are problem drinkers. In this population, it is difficult to obtain accurate information about the order of events that led to drinking problems or to discriminate between causes and consequences. For example, increased gynecological problems may lead to increased drinking or vice versa. Perhaps women who drink heavily become more likely to abandon traditional feminine roles rather than such role conflicts being a cause of heavy drinking. However, until a better data base is available, surveys and clinical suggestions need to be used to direct prevention programs for women.

Primary Prevention Programs with Women. The major assumption of any primary prevention program is that drinking will continue. The aim of the program is to lessen the frequency of heavy drinking (see Room, 1980). Of all of the presumed causes of excessive drinking by women, the lack of drinking norms or values about moderate drinking appears to be one of the most prevalent. One type of primary prevention effort for women may thus consist of an ambitious plan to attempt establishing new drinking norms. With small, circumscribed groups of women this goal may be achievable. For example, women at a university or in particular dorms may be trained in moderate drinking and would then model responsible drinking habits for other women on the campus or in their community. Recent research by Leid and Marlatt (1979) suggests that even women who normally drink heavily will drink lightly if exposed to a female light-drinking peer, which is not true for males. Combining education about women's drinking and modeling of responsible drinking could be initiated to lower the level of alcohol consumption within a particular group. Such a program is grounded in the idea of establishing new drinking norms to replace the rejected traditional feminine ideal of abstinence.

A problem with such a plan involves what constitutes a "safe" level of drinking or responsible drinking habits. Research by the Sobells and their colleagues (e.g., Sobell, Schaeffer, & Mills, 1972) suggests how problem drinkers can be taught to drink like normal drinkers (e.g., to sip, not gulp), but most of the drinkers in their studies are males. Observations of women's drinking have found that the form of alcoholic women's drinking is indistinguishable from that of normal drinking males (e.g., Tracey & Nathan, 1976). Should women's drinking, because of the weight differential, for example, be different? Popham and Schmidt (1978) have also questioned the "biomedical definition of a 'safe' level of drinking" (p. 233). For women, the safe level may vary considerably depending even on the time of the menstrual cycle. Current research (e.g., Jones & Jones, 1976) suggests that given a constant dose of alcohol, women's peak blood alcohol levels often fluctuate with changing hormonal levels at different points in the menstrual cycle. In addition, if a woman is pregnant, a lower-than-usual level of drinking is usually suggested to prevent Fetal Alcohol Syndrome or other birth defects. Thus, decisions about how to establish norms and habits await a solid data base before anything but suggested information can be given.

Another type of primary prevention program for women may not even be directly related to alcohol consumption. For example, if frustration with a "dead-end" life-style contributes to heavy drinking, then programs designed to alleviate these problems should also have an indirect impact on drinking. For example, programs designed to provide more job training and education for lower SES women (while providing child care and shelter) may help alleviate feelings of powerlessness and anger and allow the woman coping responses that are more constructive than drinking.

Attempts to deal more directly with the woman herself may also help alleviate some reasons for drinking. As suggested above, assertion training for women may help them to deal directly with pressures to drink (e.g., from an alcoholic husband) and with indirect causes of drinking (e.g., managing two full-time jobs, such as housewife–mother and outside-the-home worker).

One of the most difficult problems in this area is gaining access to the population. The lower-class urban mother at risk for heavy drinking may be located through child-care, welfare, or other governmental agencies. Perhaps some assessment of where the target populations spend time is important. Grocery stores and beauty shops, for example, may provide important access to the hidden housewife population. Emphasis on home visits by prevention program workers may also alleviate the difficulty of trying to get the woman out of the house. Well-Baby Clinics and "Housewife Hotlines" could also be tried, and contact through employers of large numbers of women may also be useful.

Women's Alcohol Problems. Problems experienced by women who drink heavily are many and varied. Table 2 illustrates the range and complexity of these problems.

One frequently cited problem seen with women more than men is called *telescoping.* Often women with shorter and less severe drinking histories than men suffer more devastating physical and emotional consequences of their drinking (the course of their drinking problem is telescoped). Thus, heavy-drinking women are more likely than men to have liver dysfunction, chronic heart problems, and diabetes. They also seem to acquire a psychological dependence on alcohol more quickly than do men.

Often gynecological problems are also prevalent with heavy-drinking women, but whether caused by, or a result of, alcohol abuse is unclear. There is some recent evidence suggesting that alcohol does affect female hormone production (Russell, 1981) but, as noted above, hormones also affect the level of alcohol in the blood of a woman drinker (e.g., Jones & Jones, 1976).

Abuse of other drugs in addition to alcohol is quite common with women alcoholics and the interactions of these drugs with alcohol is often unpredictable and life threatening. Corrigan (1980) found that 71% of all problem-drinking women abused other drugs (e.g., sleeping pills and stimulants), usually prescribed by the women's doctors. Presumably, the doctors did not realize the women had a drinking problem or felt the pills would "help."

Another set of problem consequences often seen with women alcohol abusers involves the family. Corrigan (1980) reported that women who abuse alcohol are twice as likely as their male counterparts to have been divorced and remarried. Alcoholic women are also likely to have their children taken away by social welfare agencies or relatives. Fetal Alcohol Syndrome (FAS) and other birth defects are thought to result from heavy drinking during pregnancy. Although there is some controversy regarding the frequency with which FAS occurs, it is clear that alcohol and other drugs can have a detrimental effect on the developing fetus. The amount of alcohol in the woman's blood passes directly through the placenta into the fetus. In fact, the danger does not stop at birth, since a nursing mother's milk has the same alcohol concentration as her blood (Binkiewicz, Robinson, & Senior, 1978). Thus, the infant may continue to be exposed to alcohol throughout its early development.

The vocational and legal areas are other settings where women may experience drinking problems. Research suggests that alcohol-abusing women often experience a low frequency of financial, vocational, or legal problems consequent to drinking. However, clinical lore attributes this low level of problems to denial and protection of the woman alcoholic by society. Clinicians believe that a woman is less likely than a male employee to be referred for help when a supervisor notices she has work problems resulting from intoxication. The police also may be less likely to arrest a woman for drunken driving because they may be inclined to feel that they are protecting her by giving her a warning (Wilsnack, 1978).

Contrary to clinical lore, however, Chatham, Anderson, Person, and Keyes (1979) have found that, at least in the work situation, women are just as likely to be referred as men for their work-related drinking problems.

Also, research reported by Argeriou and Paulino (1976) suggests that, although women are less likely to be arrested for driving while intoxicated (DWI), several other factors in addition to "protection" are involved. Most DWI patrols take place in the evening and night hours when women are less likely to be driving. Most arrests of married women occur in late afternoon or early evening, and usually on weekdays, not weekends. There is some evidence, however, that denial is operating in regard to these arrests, because the police would not usually test a woman for alcohol or arrest her for DWI except when other factors, such as an automobile accident, mandated the arrest. Argeriou and Paulino conclude that although the unequal treatment is apparently favorable to women, in the long run it aids in keeping their alcohol problems hidden.

Women's Programs for Secondary Prevention. As with primary prevention programs, secondary programs for women need to pay careful attention to accessing the target populations (e.g., pregnant and nursing mothers and hidden housewife alcoholics). One major method of access that immediately presents itself is through physicians or the medical community. Such a program could be two-pronged, involving education of medical personnel as well as the alcohol abuser herself.

Since physicians often prescribe other mood-altering drugs to alcohol-abusing women, some research is needed into the reasons for this. Prescriptions may be given in a misguided attempt to help the woman stop abusing alcohol (e.g., use of Valium instead of alcohol to calm down), or because the physician and the medical staff are unaware of the alcohol abuse (or do not look for such symptoms in women). Thus, education for physicians, nurses, and other medical personnel who have contact with a patient may help increase identification and referral of alcohol abusers into treatment. Most importantly, such education could decrease the number of minor tranquilizers, barbiturates, and other addictive drugs available to the woman alcohol abuser and thus decrease the frequency of drug interactions. Recent reports suggest that physicians are responsive to such informational campaigns, as evidenced by the marked decrease in prescribing barbiturates and amphetamines in recent years.

Educating medical personnel may help in disseminating information to women about the many effects a woman's alcohol abuse can have on her children. Thus, obstetricians may help the pregnant woman decide to cut down her alcohol intake. Parent-training classes in Well-Baby Clinics could include some sections directly related to alcohol's effects and help mothers establish some safe level of alcohol consumption.

More general information regarding the effects of women's heavy drinking should also be made available to the general public. Campaigns to encourage women who both smoke and use birth control pills to have regular physical checkups have apparently been successful. Why not work with the general public to increase awareness of the need for frequent physical examinations and caution because of the problem of telescoping? Such information, for example, could appear in newspapers, on television and radio and be available through grocery stores and areas where working women tend to congregate (e.g., employee lunchrooms). Part of the job of such a program would seemingly be to help remove the "stigma" associated with women's drinking and acknowledge that although drinking is going to continue, protection of one's health can still be accomplished.

American Indians

Typical Drinking Patterns. As with women, describing typical drinking patterns among Indians can be very difficult. The sheer number of tribes and tribal customs suggests much diversity in the use of alcohol. Some tribes, for example, tend to be agriculturally based, while others have (or had) a more nomadic life-style (e.g., Plains Indian tribes). Because of the cultural differences among tribes and varying amounts of exposure to alcohol, very different norms for drinking may have developed.

American Indians generally were not exposed to alcohol until the coming of white Europeans to America in the 1600s. Thus, Indians had no cultural experience to limit or guide their use of alcohol. Historians have suggested that whites took advantage of this problem by encouraging Indians to get intoxicated and then trading with them. Intoxicated, the Indians would be more likely to give up land and possessions at bargain rates. In addition, because they tended to consume the alcohol they could obtain quickly, they would then be more willing to trade valuable possessions to obtain needed alcohol.

At least partially motivated by the desire to help end these disadvantages for the Indians, the United States passed a law in 1832 prohibiting liquor sales to them. Since this law, as well as others restricting Indian behavior, was imposed from outside, it was generally ignored or resented by most tribes. Since alcohol consumption was illegal for Indians, no norms or guidelines for limiting its use evolved. In general, Indian drinking continued, but National Prohibition for Indians was not lifted until 1953. Prohibition of alcohol on many reservations continues to the present day.

As a result of this emphasis on heavy illegal drinking, alternating with abstinence when no alcohol was available, "typical" drinking patterns among Indians are not easily described. Most studies of Indian drinking instead have emphasized the extremely high incidence of alcohol problems among Indians. Additional studies of nonproblem drinking are sorely needed.

Presumed Causes and Antecedents of Indians' Drinking. As with women, a major contributor to heavy drinking among Indians seems to be the lack of norms, guidelines, or cultural controls on alcohol consumption. The lack of norms appears to have resulted from the combined effects of Indian Prohibition laws and the encouragement of heavy drinking by white fur traders. In addition, the effects of 300 years of oppression have devalued Indian culture and until recently, made the development of cultural guidelines unlikely.

This devaluation of Indian culture is also seen as a direct cause of heavy drinking. If a person does not regard his or her cultural or racial group highly, a devaluation of self can take place. The resultant low self-esteem, depression, and resentment may lead to drinking heavily. This devaluation of one's Indian cultural background is most strongly experienced by the urban-dwelling Indian. In a conflict between white and Indian culture, Indian beliefs are often ignored. Jilek-Aall (1981), for example, points out that an Indian man of status traditionally kept track of his geneology and extended family, often including hundreds of scattered relatives. For those who track their geneology, there is strong family pressure to travel even to distant relatives' marriages, funerals, and other family events. An Indian who holds a job is confronted with the choice between losing the job or facing severe disapproval from his family. Either choice can produce considerable negative consequences and lead to depression, tension, and heavy drinking.

As with women, frustration and poverty also seem connected with Indians' drinking level. Unemployment and poverty are rampant among American Indians. These problems are further emphasized by crowding, either on reservations or in highly populated urban areas. Having no job and feeling frustrated, poor, and powerless can lead to heavy drinking. In addition, especially for urban Indians, heavy drinking has become a group experience, a reason to get together, and an opportunity for social interaction. This seems especially true for young men, whose group norms encourage alcohol abuse (drinking each other "under the table," or passing around the bottle to friends).

Another presumed cause of heavy drinking among Indians is a biological-genetic difference hypothesized to exist between Indians and whites. Although research in this area is inconclusive (see Bennion & Li, 1976; Farris & Jones, 1978), this theory ("the firewater myth") suggests that Indians metabolize alcohol at a different rate than do whites, resulting in Indians becoming more intoxicated and remaining intoxicated longer (MacAndrew & Edgerton, 1969). As noted, there is a raging controversy in this area that appears to be as politically based as it is research based. The "firewater myth" and possible metabolic differences may exist and *may* account for the frequent intoxication seen among Indians, but supporting evidence is lacking.

Primary Prevention Programs for Indians. There are many similarities between ideal primary prevention programs for Indians and for women. For both, a major problem involves accessing the population and effectively disseminating information. A second major problem is the lack of moderate drinking values and guidelines and the question of how to help establish these norms for drinking.

The differences in prevention programs for Indians versus women illustrates a major theme of this chapter—the need for specialized programs for targeted populations. For example, it may seem easier to gain access to the population of Indians than with women. Groups of Indians tend to live together and congregate socially on a frequent basis, either on a reservation or in urban settings. There are, of course, exceptions, such as Indians who live in scattered rural settings or who lack contact with other Indians. However, the large majority of the population can be found living together. Unfortunately, so many white-governed programs have been forced on Indians that government-sponsored programs in *any* area (including alcohol abuse prevention) tend to be regarded suspiciously. In addition, lack of understanding of Indian culture and traditions can be the downfall of many programs. Developing Indian alcohol abuse prevention programs first requires a thorough understanding of beliefs, traditions, needs, and culture. Indians themselves need to decide what they want from a primary prevention program. The aims and goals need to be established within the culture. This is not to say that non-Indians should not participate, only that the guiding values need to be provided by the targeted ethnic group.

In recent years, Indians have begun to become more visibly active in alcohol abuse work with their people. Such actions are encouraging for two reasons: (1) They provide a cultural basis for decisions, programs, and so on, and (2) They promote increased public awareness of Indian culture and conflicts. Thus, the cultural values and traditions of Indians are accorded status, and awareness of conflicts between Indian and white culture can be understood by significant whites, such as employers.

The increased visibility of Indian values is reflected in the political Indian movements of recent years, for example, Rights for American Indians Now (RAIN). Alcohol abuse prevention is not promoted as a direct aim of these programs; nevertheless, if devaluation of Indian culture contributes to alcohol abuse, promotion of Indian power may indirectly cut down the level of alcohol abuse. Perhaps primary prevention programs could be mounted through such organizations.

Although other issues and problems exist in designing primary prevention programs for Indians, the problems of access and cultural values remain major. In addition, more research is needed in several areas, including: (1) studies of the hypothesized alcohol metabolism factor and (2) studies of nonproblem drinking styles of Indians.

Problems of Alcohol Abuse Specific to Indians. As can be seen in Table 2, many problems accrue to Indians as a result of excessive drinking. A few will be examined here. First, because of prohibition laws on many reservations, Indians have a high frequency of alcohol withdrawal symptoms. The Indian "binge drinker" on the reservation, because of the unavailability of alcohol, cannot "taper off" as the urban dweller can. Second, violence resulting from alcohol abuse, in which the Indian is either aggressor or victim, is rampant. Alcohol-related suicide, homicide, fighting, and accidents are common. DWI arrests are frequent. Third, child abuse and neglect are common concomitants of alcohol problems among Indians. This is especially true when both parents are drinking heavily and often results in children being taken away from their parents. Finally, the very high level of liver cirrhosis (higher than for whites or blacks) is the fourth leading cause of death for Indians.

Programs for Secondary Prevention. A few examples will be presented here. For the most part, the problem of access remains as discussed in the previous section.

Withdrawal symptoms, currently so prevalent on reservations, could be dealt with through the provision of detoxification centers and medical care on the reservation. In spite of the fact that liquor sales are prohibited on reservations, potentially life-threatening consequences of major alcohol withdrawal syndrome need to be acknowledged and dealt with. Specific education regarding withdrawal and its management may be of use to both the drinker and the drinker's family. Ways to avoid withdrawal and to change drinking patterns could also be included in educational materials. Finally, the logic and value of the existing alcohol laws should be questioned.

The high level of DWI arrests could be addressed and minimized in a number of ways. More emphasis could be placed on avoiding driving after drinking, including DWI classes, easily accessible for all drivers on reservations or in urban areas heavily populated by Indians. Classes and information at tribal centers may also be of help. Portable breath testers could be provided and their use before driving emphasized (Sobell, VanderSpek, & Saltman, 1970). Identification of those at risk (e.g., second offenders) for more intensive intervention (e.g., treatment for alcohol problems) or greater legal restrictions may also promote the decline of Indian DWIs. The child abuse and neglect problem could be dealt with as suggested in the previous section on women. Political action groups may also be able to emphasize directly traditional family values as well as to work with children.

The Elderly

Typical Drinking Patterns.   Clark and Midanik (1981) have suggested, based on their survey, that the elderly as a group display a very low level of drinking, and many are abstinent. The results suggest that about 40% of all American women and 65% of all American men over 65 drink on occasion. However, only 2% and 8%, respectively, are heavy drinkers. However, this conclusion is complicated by a number of problems: (1) only a very small number of elderly persons (over age 65) were interviewed in the survey, (2) the survey methodology may have led to missing some isolated elderly who might be most likely to be drinking, (3) less alcohol consumption is probably needed to constitute heavy drinking in the elderly (because of slower alcohol metabolism rates, alcohol–medication interactions, etc.), and (4) drinking levels may not decrease with age, but instead the older, chronic alcoholics may have died by 65, resulting in a lower mean alcohol consumption than for younger groups which may include higher rates of chronic alcoholism.

Presumed Causes of Heavy Drinking in the Elderly.   The major cause of elderly persons' heavy drinking is presumed to be related to loss: loss of spouse, loss of job, lowered income level, loss of physical health, or loss of independence. A related contributing factor is the isolation often suffered by the elderly. Reduced income, lack of transportation, fear of getting hurt, and a smaller social network (as friends and relatives die) lead to isolation, depression, and boredom. Frequently an elderly person has "nothing to do" but sit and drink. Literature in the area describes a common phenomenon called *nesting.* The person will spend the day in a favorite chair, facing the television, with a table close at hand for cigarettes, snacks, and drinks (Dunlop, 1981).

Another probable cause of "heavy" drinking among the elderly is related to physical changes. Aged and diseased organs, physical illness, and medications exacerbate the effects of alcohol. What formerly constituted a moderate level of drinking now has the same effects as heavy drinking. Unfortunately, drinking by elderly persons is often viewed by younger relatives as the "last pleasure" of the person, and so they are left alone with the bottle and television.

Primary Prevention.   With this population the most difficult problem is access. Isolation, especially among those most at risk for alcohol problems, is common, and distrust of younger people "trying to run my life" can also impede prevention efforts.

One way to avoid the problem of isolation is to plan ahead, even in retirement plans, to keep up a social network. Retirement programs at work can include some components on social-life planning and alcohol–drug-abuse prevention. Once the person has retired, or is already isolated, home visits and access through telephone hotlines may become necessary. Access through agencies and political activist groups that deal with the elderly (e.g., Social Security and Gray Panthers) may be useful. Planned group activities not centered around alcohol may also be of use. Effort would have to focus on locating isolated elderly persons, building trust between them and the program staff, and finally, involving the person in some meaningful daily activity.

Physicians who treat the elderly may be educated and trained to recognize the signs of beginning alcohol abuse or isolation and depression. Patients referred to alcoholism prevention programs may be helped to adjust to new social and vocational expectations, keep up social support and community involvement, and feel useful.

Problems Specific to the Elderly. Examination of Table 2 will show the breadth and extent of problems the elderly may suffer as a result of abusive drinking. In general, these problems are difficult to separate from the problems of aging itself (e.g., chronic health problems, neurological deficits, and impotence). Similarly, accidents are common among the elderly and may be increased by alcohol consumption.

Other problems experienced by the elderly are frequent intoxication and trouble with the police. The intoxication may be a result of lowered tolerance level and interactions with medications. In general, problems of alcohol abuse among the elderly are largely unresearched, unknown, and ignored.

Secondary Prevention Programs for the Elderly. Even though not much is known about the problems created by excessive drinking among the elderly, programs can be suggested to help alleviate some of the more obvious problems. For example, as noted above, accidents are generally a frequent occurrence among the elderly. Alcohol tends to increase the occurrence of accidents and may thus increase the chances of severe injury or death. Incapacitating accidents are especially dangerous for elderly, isolated alcohol abusers. If a person with no regular contact with others falls and breaks a hip, his or her absence may not be noted for several days, or even weeks. A system of establishing minimal contacts with such persons may help to reduce the severest consequences of home accidents. Daily home visits from a "Meals on Wheels" volunteer, for example, may provide both a checkup and good nutrition each day. Daily telephone contacts may also be feasible if the person lives in a remote section or does not want daily visitors. Arrangements can be made, for example, for the elderly person to contact a volunteer or relative by phone by a certain time each day. If no call comes through, the contact person may then attempt to call, or failing that, visit the elderly person.

This type of program may require enormous amounts of effort to access the population (finding the isolated elderly), but after that the effort required would be minimal. It is possible, in fact, that such an effort could be organized and conducted through groups of elderly volunteers and could contribute to facilitating their building up a new social network (see Primary Prevention section of this chapter).

Memory problems, especially among elderly chronic alcoholics, present a special obstacle for working with this population. Secondary prevention programs to alleviate this problem could be patterned after programs designed by Goodwin (1977) to help prevent memory blackouts due to alcohol. For example, Goodwin suggests that, to facilitate recall during drinking (not during blackouts), prompts should be provided no more than 30 minutes after the event. Thus, later on, if the person does not remember the event, he or she may remember it after the prompt. Elderly persons who drink often may need to have prompts and other aids to help them remember information about alcohol and its effects, how to get help, and basic survival skills, such as getting enough to eat or heat in the house.

EXISTING PREVENTION PROGRAMS

The last section discussed ideal programs for preventing alcohol abuse and negative consequences of alcohol abuse. This section briefly describes existing prevention programs. Since empirical support of these programs is not available, the section will focus on how existing programs have been applied to special populations.

EDUCATION/MASS MEDIA APPROACHES

Education and mass media approaches include newspaper, radio and television campaigns, distribution of posters, pamphlets, and related materials, and additionally, incorporate specific educational efforts (e.g., classes on alcohol and drugs for school children) directed at particular groups. All these approaches are based on the idea that information about the negative consequences of drinking leads to changes in drinking behavior.

These types of programs have many drawbacks that have been discussed above, the biggest being the model on which they are based. Generally, educational programs and pamphlets are distributed based on the assumption that proper information will lead to predictable behavior change. This assumption has yet to be well supported by data. Applying educational or mass media approaches to special populations raises the additional questions (1) How can the target group be reached? and (2) What can and should be communicated to them? These questions have been dealt with differently in programs specific to each population.

Women

Educational approaches to prevention of alcohol problems in women are seen in public clinics and doctor's offices. These include pamphlets and booklets from the National Institute of Alcohol Abuse and Alcoholism (NIAAA), such as *Alcohol and Your Unborn Baby,*[1] which suggests only light drinking during pregnancy and describes the effects alcohol can have on a developing fetus. Various women's organizations and alcohol treatment groups occasionally put out informational posters about women's alcohol abuse, the effects alcohol can have on women, or where women can get help. In general, these pamphlets, posters, and books are directed toward getting the woman who already abuses alcohol into treatment. There is little emphasis on prevention of alcohol problems in women.

What emphasis there is toward prevention has focused on Fetal Alcohol Syndrome (FAS). One program, the FAS Prevention Program (DeLuca, 1981) is sponsored by the California Women's Commission on Alcoholism and supported by a grant from the NIAAA. A public information campaign, through newspapers, radio, television, and other media, will be used to reach women of childbearing age in Los Angeles County and will give warnings about the dangers of drinking during pregnancy. A research component is also included in the study. Outcome evaluations will be based on mail surveys and reviews of birth records.

American Indians

In general, mass media approaches for prevention of alcohol problems among Indians is an underdeveloped area. For the most part, the emphasis of Indian alcohol programs is on treatment, not prevention.

What limited efforts exist for prevention are directed primarily at children. Educational campaigns are directed at Indian children and administered through schools and organizations on reservations or in tribal centers. The emphasis of these alcohol abuse prevention programs is (1) to teach about alcohol, (2) to raise ethnic pride, and (3) to provide alternative group activities besides alcohol consumption.

A recent NIAAA report on alcohol and American Indians notes only

---

[1]This booklet and others are available from the NIAAA at this address: National Clearinghouse for Alcohol Information, Box 2345, Rockville, Maryland 20852.

one study of alcohol-problem prevention programs among Indians. This study (Moss, 1979) indicated that adult Indians are generally poorly informed about alcohol and alcoholism, with most of their information coming from television shows, newspapers, and other media. Meetings and workshops on alcohol with Indian leaders in their communities seemed to be more effective in changing tribal attitudes about alcohol than exposure to media programs. However, most Indians interviewed in the study did not appear interested in formal educational programs about alcohol. The NIAAA report suggests, then, the use of "counselling" type meetings to teach about alcohol and help prevent alcohol abuse among Indians.

The Elderly

In general, alcohol services for the elderly are quite new. Although some interesting and fairly comprehensive treatment programs for elderly problem drinkers have come into existence recently, they generally do not have a well-developed prevention component. There are some exceptions, however. For example, the Clark County, Washington, Senior Alcohol Services provides a pamphlet for physicians to help them recognize and distinguish alcohol abuse problems from aging problems.[2] In addition, the pamphlet provides information about alcohol's effects on the elderly that physicians can give to their elderly patients.

PROVISION OF ALTERNATIVES TO DRINKING

In general, the aim of these programs is to provide some healthy, competitive alternatives to drinking. Thus, if drinking is functioning as a "social lubricant" and as an excuse to get together, some nondrinking activity (e.g., organized sports) may be provided to serve the same purpose.

These programs can be general or specific to alcohol. For the most part, there are few programs devoted to providing alternatives to alcohol use, but they do exist (e.g., "coffeehouses" for adolescents). The most difficult problem faced by such prevention programs is how to "compete" with alcohol, that is, what are *attractive* and *viable* alternatives to alcohol-oriented activities? A second, more subtle problem faced by these programs is whether such alternatives will necessarily exclude or discourage heavy drinking.

Such programs should take very different forms, depending on empha-

---

[2]This pamphlet is available from Senior Alcohol Services, P.O. Box 425, Vancouver, WA.

sis needed in the particular target population. For example, the idea of the coffeehouse or other nonalcohol-oriented activities for adolescents reflects the need for social activities among teenagers. A program to help provide full employment for Indians reflects the need for work, financial gain, and time structuring in this often unemployed group. The programs are organized differently, but the aim remains the same—to provide something else to do besides drink.

Women

There has been little effort to develop prevention programs that provide alternatives for women. As noted above, however, the aim and content of alternatives programs does not have to be related directly to alcohol to make them effective. Thus, the upsurge of women's activist and social-political groups may reflect a natural movement away from drinking. Many such organizations tend to discourage heavy drinking among women, but do not espouse the radical abstinence–prohibition approach of the past. Self-help and support groups for women also tend to discourage drinking by providing other outlets for dealing with stress and role conflicts (e.g., assertion training support from other women and organized physical activities).

Increasing emphasis on women's problems in some of the older, established alcoholism self-help organizations (e.g., Alcoholics Anonymous) is probably of help to women who already have alcohol problems. However, groups such as Women for Sobriety can sometimes help a heavy drinker early, before severe alcohol problems develop, and thus prevent some of the severe problems associated with drinking.

American Indians

In general, organized alternatives–prevention programs for American Indians' alcohol problems focus on children. Reservation youth are most often the target group, and the alternatives program is built into the reservation's educational system. For example, Indian children in King County, Washington, are encouraged to participate in an NIAAA-sponsored program in which they are taught traditional tribal rituals and outdoors skills at a summer camp. A major message of the program is that these gatherings and tribal traditions can later function for the adult Indian as an alternative to alcohol-oriented group activities.

A less direct alternative method of prevention may be seen in the increasing popularity of "Indian Pride" groups (e.g., American Indian Movement, AIM), whose aims are often political, but also may eventually help relieve the frustration, boredom, and feelings of powerlessness that are believed to lead to Indians' alcohol abuse. In this way, these organizations may promote less abuse of alcohol, even though that is not their direct goal.

The Elderly

With the recent upsurge in treatment efforts for alcohol problems of the elderly, there may eventually come a similar emphasis on prevention. Currently, alternatives–prevention programs specifically for the elderly are indirect and related to other group efforts.

As noted above, alcohol abuse by the elderly appears to be associated with physical and transportation restrictions and the breakdown of the elderly person's social network. Social programs for senior citizens emphasizing group activities and providing transportation may be of help in preventing alcohol problems. The effectiveness of these programs, however, is unknown.

Providing new roles for the elderly may also be effective in preventing alcohol problems. Organizations such as Foster Grandparents may be effective prevention efforts. Similar efforts, with a more direct emphasis on alcohol, are also occasionally seen. For example, an alcohol–drug-abuse prevention program in Rhode Island involves elderly citizens as counselors for youth; the Florida Citizens Commission on Alcohol Abuse trains elderly volunteers as alcohol educators and counselors for other elderly persons.

More alternatives–prevention programs may develop out of elderly alcohol treatment programs. For example, the Geriatric Alcohol Program at the Visiting Nurse Association in Albany, New York, emphasizes home visits and referrals for treatment and is developing programs for senior citizen's groups to heighten their awareness of problems of alcohol abuse.

LIMITING ACCESS TO ALCOHOL

Generally, limiting access to alcohol involves legal restrictions and, as such, cannot be directed specifically at any one ethnic group or sex (although there are, of course, age restrictions on the use of alcohol). Probably the most ambitious and well-known effort to limit access to alcohol was the Prohibition Amendment to the United States Constitution. The effects of Prohibition in the United States, especially in regard to women's drinking patterns, have been discussed above. Current efforts in this vein include control of alcohol sales through alcohol beverage control laws, high taxation of alcoholic beverages in some states, and "dram shop" laws which make persons who serve alcoholic beverages legally responsible for those who consume them. Decisions for these controls are generally made on a state-by-state or regional basis. For example, some states still have "dry" counties where alcohol sales are prohibited.

A variation on such efforts to prevent alcohol problems involves laws against abuses resulting from excessive alcohol consumption, including laws against public intoxication and drunken driving. Although strong arguments can be made for keeping the drunken-driving laws, those against public intoxication have been increasingly challenged. Some authors have contended that making public drunkenness an offense makes those with alcohol problems criminals, which in essence, unnecessarily adds to their problems. Others argue that arrest for public intoxication leads to treatment, but such a result is rare. In many cases, a person can be arrested for the same offense hundreds of times, and, after spending a night in jail and paying a fine, return to the streets again with the alcohol problem unaddressed. For some groups, the laws may even give excessive drinking a certain attractiveness. "Getting away with it," for example, may be seen by some teenagers as an attractive inducement to drink heavily. Also, a warm place to sleep and a hot meal may make jail appealing to the homeless person.

Women

Some of the historical effects of Prohibition on women's drinking have been discussed above. In general, Prohibition seems to have led to an attitude of rebellion against restrictions. Drinking in speakeasies was seen as daring and sophisticated and women drank in public to appear exciting. Thus, in the long run, laws against alcohol consumption have had a negative effect on women's drinking.

Current laws limiting alcohol consumption and alcohol-related behavior may have little effect on women. Limited hours of sale, for example, may not hinder the purchase of alcohol by the hidden-housewife alcoholic who does not work outside of her home. Laws against DWI may not affect her much, because most special patrols for DWI are at night when women are less likely to be drinking and driving and are less likely to be breath-tested for alcohol even when stopped. Laws against public intoxication also do not have much effect on women, because women for the most part do not drink to intoxication in public.

In general, it seems that women have as much or more access to alcohol than men, and the laws have little effect on this. Since liquor stores are often located in shopping malls, and wine and beer are often sold in grocery stores; bottled alcohol may be more available to women than to men.

American Indians

As noted above, prohibition may indirectly encourage alcohol consumption. This has been seen with American Indians as well as with women.
Prohibition is still enforced on some reservations and alcohol problems
(e.g., withdrawal symptoms) result. Laws against drunken driving and public
intoxication have a major impact on Indians. Many are arrested repeatedly
for these offenses. However, the effectiveness of these laws is questionable.
Wholesale arrests encourage active disregard for the law and agents of the
law. Contempt for police and the courts results, especially if Indians view
these laws as imposed by whites.

In addition, other restrictions on alcohol accessibility (e.g., high taxation) generally have little or a very negative effect on Indians. Limiting
hours of sale does not seem to limit purchases of liquor by unemployed
people. High taxation may have some effect on the very poor, but many
people spend money on alcohol that was needed for food and shelter for
their families. Parker and Harman (1978) have suggested that heavy drinkers, in particular, have "inelastic" demands for alcohol and that increases in
price are not likely to decrease consumption.

The Elderly

The elderly seem to be affected particularly adversely by laws against
drunkenness. Among the most frequent alcohol problems experienced by
the elderly alcohol abuser are problems with police. The elderly person,
perhaps because of his lowered tolerance, is particularly susceptible to becoming publicly intoxicated and, thus, to being arrested. These arrests do
not very often lead to treatment (e.g., Sobell & Sobell, 1974).

Legal restrictions on access to alcohol are probably not very helpful in
prevention efforts directed at the elderly. Even passive restrictions, such as
limiting hours of sale, will not necessarily cut down on the accessibility of
alcohol to these people. Only occasionally will lowered fixed-income levels
and difficulty in transportation limit the amount of alcohol an elderly person can obtain.

RESTRAINTS ON DEVELOPING IDEAL PROGRAMS FOR
SPECIAL POPULATIONS

Why is there a discrepancy between what has been suggested here as
ideal prevention efforts for each group and the reality of what now exists?
The blocks to developing ideal programs fall into two categories: (1) lack of
data base and (2) political limitations.

The former category has been discussed above and is relatively easy (although time consuming and costly) to correct. More data are needed to gain an understanding of what programs are needed and whether they can be effective for particular target groups. The political problems, in contrast, are more difficult.

An important reason for the lack of prevention aimed at special populations is the lack of visibility. Women, for example, are not often seen as having a high frequency of drinking problems. Why should money and effort be expended to prevent alcoholism among women when they do not drink as much as men in the first place? Also, their problems may not be seen as readily. Men are more likely than women to be seen intoxicated in public or be arrested for DWI. The woman's less visible problems (e.g., cirrhosis) may not attract attention from the general public. The elderly and American Indians do not constitute a large part of the population, so their alcohol problems may not be viewed as important enough to warrant large expenditures of money on programs for them.

A second political block to developing ideal prevention programs is the problem of polemics with no data base. For example, it has yet to be established that Indians' metabolism of alcohol is any different than whites'. The myth that "Indians can't hold their liquor" is nonetheless rampant and encourages the belief that prevention programs among Indians would fail.

A third problem involves the desire of most Americans for individual freedom and resentment of prevention efforts that impose external controls on their lives. This desire for freedom, sometimes at the expense of a common goal, is reflected in data collected and reported by Cahalan, Roizen, and Room (1978). In a statewide California survey they found that 88% of the population sample would favor laws and courts "being tough" on drunken drivers. However, prevention measures designed *a priori* to limit the number of drunken drivers were favored by much smaller groups: Only 41% wanted to limit the number of hours that bars could be open, and only 38% favored higher taxes on alcohol.

A fourth problem is that of costs versus return. Alcohol problems among minorities and special populations occur infrequently when compared to the population as a whole. Thus, the population targeted may not be seen as worth the substantial time, effort, and money required to mount an effective prevention program. In addition, the cost-versus-return issue is reflected in the viewpoint that alcoholism is an individual, not a group problem, and that a "clinical" rehabilitative approach is more cost effective than a prevention approach.

The impediment to mounting a good prevention program is that clinical and prevention approaches are often pitted against one another for money and personnel. They are seen as mutually exclusive, with one taking away resources from the other. Thus, clinical efforts are favored at the expense of prevention without recognition that both are needed in a good program of alcohol services. As a corollary, many treatment personnel view alcoholism as a disease with a biological basis and believe that the only way to prevent alcoholism is to prevent drinking. Thus, many of the prevention ideas presented here would be viewed as irrelevant and a waste of resources needed for treatment.

CONCLUSIONS

Several conclusions can be drawn regarding special populations and prevention efforts. The most effective prevention programs (primary or secondary) will result from data-based population–problem–program matches. To approach this ideal, several kinds of actions are needed.

First, data-based judgments must be made regarding the most likely effective components of *package* programs. Demonstration projects could be used to test intervention components. Second, recognition must be given to the fact that effective programs (especially in regard to primary prevention) do not necessarily need to relate specifically to drinking or drinking problems.

Third, communication must be recognized as an important tool in developing these programs. Communication between clinical researchers and prevention researchers is especially needed. Communication should also increase between researchers concentrating on the basic alcohol processes and their effects on emotion, cognition, and social systems and prevention researchers. Communication between special groups and the programmers is needed. Edwards (1977) comments that "we" always try to teach "others" how to deal with alcohol. Moss's (1979) study, for example, suggests that, even though alcohol education is directed mostly to Indian children, parents of these children would prefer that their children *not* be taught about alcohol in the schools. The parents would rather learn about alcohol themselves and then teach the children, but they were not asked their preference.

Finally, empirical judgments aside, value judgments must be made regarding time, effort, limited amounts of money, and the worth of various programs. Room (1980) points out that, like it or not, prevention efforts are essentially political, and society as a whole needs to make decisions about which populations most need help and to what degree society wants to invest in clinical versus prevention efforts. These questions often are decided by elected officials and not by scientists. The public as a whole should recognize that they are electing officials to make such decisions. Prevention efforts should not be seen as imposed, but as decided by the majority, which consists of many special populations.

REFERENCES

Argeriou, M., & Paulino, D. Women arrested for drunken driving in Boston: Social characteristics and circumstances of arrest. *Journal of Studies on Alcohol,* 1976, *37,* 648–658.

Beckman, L. Women alcoholics: A review of social and psychological studies. *Journal of Studies on Alcohol,* 1975, *36,* 797–824.

Binkiewicz, A., Robinson, M., & Senior, B. Pseudo-cushing syndrome caused by alcohol in breast milk. *Journal of Pediatrics,* 1978, *93,* 965–967.

Bennion, L., & Li, T. Alcohol metabolism in American Indians and whites: Lack of racial differences in metabolic rate and liver alcohol dehydrogenase. *New England Journal of Medicine,* 1976, *294,* 9–13.

Cahalan, D., Cisin, I., & Crossley, H. *American drinking practices: A national survey of behavior and attitudes* (Monograph No. 6). New Brunswick, N.J.: Rutgers Center of Alcohol Studies, 1969.

Cahalan, D., Roizen, R., & Room, R. Alcohol problems and their prevention: Public attitudes in California. In R. Room & S. Sheffield (Eds.), *The prevention of alcohol problems.* Sacramento: California State Office of Alcohol Program Management, 1978.

Chatham, L., Anderson, M., Person, P., & Keyes, J. *Employed alcoholic women: The right to be the same or different.* Paper presented at the National Alcoholism Form of the National Council on Alcoholism, 1979.

Clark, W., & Midanik, L. Alcohol use and alcohol problems among U.S. adults. In *Alcohol consumption and related problems* (NIAAA Alcohol & Health Monograph No. 1). Rockville, Md.: National Institute of Alcohol Abuse and Alcoholism, 1981.

Corrigan, E. *Alcoholic women in treatment.* New York: Oxford University Press, 1980.

Curlee, J. Alcoholic women: Some considerations for further research. *Bulletin of the Menninger Clinic,* 1967, *31,* 154–163.

DeLuca, J. R. (Ed.). *Fourth special report to the U.S. Congress on alcohol and health.* (DHEW Publ. No. ADM 81–1080.) Washington, D.C.: U.S. Government Printing Office, 1981.

Dunlop, J. *Pathophysiological interactions; Aging and alcohol.* Mimeographed handout from Senior Alcohol Services, P.O. Box 425, Vancouver, Wash., 1981.

Edwards, G. Theoretical synthesis: Discussion. In T. Harford, D. Parker, & L. Light (Eds.), *Normative approaches to the prevention of alcohol abuse and alcoholism* (NIAAA Research Monograph No. 3). Rockville, Md.: National Institute of Alcohol Abuse and Alcoholism, 1977.

Farris, J., & Jones, B. Ethanol metabolism and memory impairment in Indian women and white women social drinkers. *Journal of Studies on Alcohol,* 1978, *39,* 1975–1979.

Gomberg, E. Alcoholism in women. In B. Kissin & H. Begleiter (Eds.), *The biology of alcoholism: Social aspects of alcoholism,* (Vol. 4). New York: Plenum Press, 1976.

Goodwin, D. The alcoholic blackout and how to prevent it. In I. Birnbaum & E. Parker (Eds.), *Alcohol and human memory.* New York: Wiley, 1977.

Jilek-Aall, L. Acculturation, alcoholism and Indian-style Alcoholics Anonymous. In D. Heath (Ed.), *Cultural factors in alcohol research and treatment of drinking problems. Journal of Studies on Alcohol,* Supplement No. 9, 1981.

Jones, B., & Jones, M. Alcohol effects in women during the menstrual cycle. *Annals of the New York Academy of Sciences,* 1976, *273,* 576–587.

Kobler, J. How prohibition failed in New York. In R. T. Shoenstein (Ed.), *The booze book: The joy of drink.* Chicago: Playboy Press, 1974.

Leid, E., & Marlatt, G. A. Modelling as a determinant of alcohol consumption: Effect of subject sex and prior drinking history. *Addictive Behaviors,* 1979, *4,* 47–54.

Little, R., Schultz, F., & Mandell, W. Drinking during pregnancy. *Journal of Studies on Alcohol,* 1976, *37,* 375–379.

MacAndrew, C., & Edgerton, R. *Drunken comportment.* Chicago: Aldine Publishing Company, 1969.

Matarazzo, J. Behavioral health and behavioral medicine: Frontiers for a new health psychology. *American Psychologist,* 1980, *35,* 807–817.

Moss, F. Drinking attitudes and practices in twenty Indian communities. University of Utah, Salt Lake City: Western Regional Alcoholism Training Center, 1979.

Mulford, H. Women and men problem drinking: Sex differences in patients served by Iowa's Community Alcoholism Centers. *Journal of Studies on Alcohol,* 1977, *38,* 1627–1639.

Ng, L., Davis, D., & Mandersheid, R. The health promotion organization: A practical intervention designed to promote healthy living. *Public Health Reports, Washington, D.C.,* 1978, *93,* 446–455.

Noel, N., & Lisman, S. Alcohol consumption by college women following exposure to unsolvable problems: Learned helplessness or stress-induced drinking? *Behaviour Research and Therapy,* 1980, *18,* 429–440.

Parker, D., & Harman, M. A critique of the distribution of consumption model of prevention. *Journal of Studies on Alcohol,* 1978, *39,* 377–399.

Popham, R., & Schmidt, W. The biomedical definition of safe alcohol consumption: A crucial issue for the researcher and the drinker. *British Journal of Addiction,* 1978, *73,* 233–235.

Room, R. *The prevention of alcohol problems.* Berkeley, Calif.: Social Research Group, School of Public Health, University of California, 1977.

Room, R. Concepts and strategies in the prevention of alcohol-related problems. *Contemporary Drug Problems,* 1980, *9,* 9–48.

Russell, M. Personal communication. December, 1981.

Schuckit, M., & Morrisey, E. Alcoholism in women: Some clinical and social perspectives. In M. Greenblatt & M. Schuckit (Eds.), *Alcoholism problems in women and children.* New York: Grune & Stratton, 1976.

Sobell, L., & Sobell, M. The erudite transient. *The International Journal of Social Psychiatry,* 1974, *20,* 242–256.

Sobell, L., VanderSpek, R., & Saltman, P. Utility of portable breath alcohol testers for drunken driving offenders. *Journal of Studies on Alcohol,* 1980, *41,* 930–934.

Sobell, M., Schaeffer, H., & Mills, K. Differences in baseline drinking behavior between alcoholics and normal drinkers. *Behaviour Research and Therapy,* 1972, *10,* 257–268.

Tracey, D., & Nathan, P. Behavioral analysis of chronic alcoholism in four women. *Journal of Consulting and Clinical Psychology,* 1976, *44,* 832–842.

Wilsnack, R., & Wilsnack, S. Sex roles and drinking among adolescent girls. *Journal of Studies on Alcohol,* 1978, *39,* 1855–1874.

Wilsnack, S. Prevention of alcohol problems in women: Current status. *Alcohol Health and Research World,* 1978, *3,* 23–31.

II

Predictors of Problem Drinking

One of the most important areas of prevention research lies in the identification of early precursors of alcoholism problems. If specific physiological, situational, and behavioral factors early in life can predict later abusive drinking patterns, intervention may begin prior to the onset of drinking. In the field of attitude and behavior change, the earlier the intervention, the more likely the chances of success. Such predictors also will enable prevention efforts to be targeted toward specific groups that have the greatest propensity toward future problems. Such an approach would be highly cost-effective in terms of both time and money. Since early predictors have not as yet been defined with a sufficient degree of accuracy, prevention programs are aimed at heterogeneous population groups.

As Goodwin points out in Chapter 4, the strongest predictor of alcoholism is family history. Alcoholism tends to run in families although the method of transmission from one generation to another is not known.

Genetic markers must be identified and future research must analyze the influence of both heredity and environment. Enough evidence does exist, however, to demonstrate that children of alcoholic parents are at high risk for the development of alcoholism. Until this familial alcoholism factor can be refined further, children of alcoholics would seem to be a prime target for alcoholism prevention approaches. Such approaches could begin even in early childhood since the significant predictive factor is known even before birth. Care must be taken to avoid further stigmatizing these children who often must grow up in emotionally and possibly financially unstable homes.

Couples in which one or both parents are alcoholic also must be apprised of the potential influence of their drinking problem on the future development of their children. Such information should be included as part of family planning and counseling sessions.

In Chapter 5 Harford describes the importance of situational predictors of problem drinking within a developmental perspective. Drinking behavior varies within different drinking contexts, but some are more conducive to excessive drinking and problem drinking. For example, the presence of parents or adults in drinking settings represents an important dimension of control. The absence of parents is related to more drinking and more problems related to alcohol. Drinking in cars and drinking at unsupervised parties are risk factors for youth. Alcohol availability is also an important factor with drinking problems increasing in direct relation to availability.

Situational predictors of problem drinking, however, must be viewed in terms of their interaction with individual predictors. What, for example, makes an adolescent seek out a particular drinking setting that results in heavy drinking? Perhaps the best predictors are multiple ones in which hereditary, behavioral, and situational factors are combined to provide an index of proneness toward alcohol abuse. Unfortunately, researchers in this field often work in relative isolation. There is, however, a growing trend for more coordinated efforts.

The utilization of predictors also raises an issue related to human rights. Targeting alcoholism-prone individuals places a stigma on them which may have negative social or psychological influences. Researchers and alcoholism educators who implement these findings must proceed with due caution. All issues must be considered, including the costs versus benefits of singling out these individuals and providing alcoholism prevention strategies.

4

Biological Predictors of Problem Drinking

DONALD W. GOODWIN

FAMILIAL SUSCEPTIBILITY TO ALCOHOLISM

The strongest known predictor of alcoholism occurring in a particular individual is the presence of alcoholism in his or her family. It is, in fact, the only *known* predictor. The way alcoholism is transmitted from generation to generation in families is not known, but there is growing evidence that biological factors (i.e., heredity) influence the transmission. The first section of this chapter reviews this evidence in detail.

FAMILY STUDIES

The first systematic studies of the families of alcoholics came in the late nineteenth century. One of the earliest was conducted by Long (1879) who questioned 200 Michigan doctors regarding the offspring of alcoholics. They attributed about 21% of "inherited disease" to alcohol, without specifying the disease. Shuttleworth and Beach (1900) found alcoholic parentage in 19% of the idiots at a paupers' home and in 13% at a charitable institution. MacNicholl (1905) surveyed the school children of New York

DONALD W. GOODWIN • Department of Psychiatry, University of Kansas School of Medicine, Kansas City, Kansas 66502.

City in one of the largest studies of alcohol as a cause of mental retardation ever attempted. He found that of 6,624 children of drinking parents, 53% were retarded whereas among 13,000 children of abstainers, only 10% were retarded.

In 1909 Crothers reported that of 4,400 inebriates he treated over 35 years in practice, 70% had predecessors who drank moderately or excessively. In the first two decades of the century, several other investigators reported similar findings, with only one exception occurring when Elderton and Pearson (1910) reported that children of alcoholics were as normal as children of nonalcoholics. As Warner and Rosett (1975) commented in their excellent review, this led to heated controversy with opponents criticizing the investigators for using moderate drinkers rather than abstainers as a control group and for failing to determine whether the parent's drinking began before or after the birth of the children studied.

With this one exception, every family study of alcoholism, irrespective of country of origin, has shown much higher rates of alcoholism among the relatives of alcoholics as compared to the general population. The lifelong expectancy rate for alcoholism among males appears to be about 3% to 5%; the rate for females ranges from .1% to 1% (Goodwin, 1971).

Boss (1929), examining the siblings and parents of 909 male and 166 female alcoholics, found that alcoholism occurred in 53% of the fathers, 6% of the mothers, 30% of the brothers, and 3% of the sisters. Pohlisch (1933) compared the siblings and parents of chronic alcoholics with the siblings and parents of opiate addicts with respect to alcoholism and morphinism. Alcoholism was found in 22% of the brothers of alcoholics and 6% of the brothers of opiate addicts. Alcoholism occurred in 47% of the fathers of alcoholics and 6% of the fathers of opiate addicts. Conversely, among the parents and siblings of opiate addicts, opiate addiction occurred more frequently than did alcoholism. Studying a large sample of alcoholics and their families, Brugger (1934) found that about 25% of the fathers were alcoholic. Åmark (1953), Gregory (1960), and Winokur and Clayton (1968) reported similar figures. Viewing the situation from another aspect, Dahlberg and Stenberg (1934) reported that 25% of hospitalized alcoholics come from families where one of the parents abused alcohol.

A more recent study by Winokur, Reich, Rimmer, and Pitts (1970) showed a particularly high prevalence of alcoholism among the full siblings of alcoholics. Among the full siblings of male alcoholics, there was a lifetime expectancy of excessive drinking in 46% of the brothers and 5% of the sisters; the lifetime expectancy of alcoholism among the full siblings of female alcoholics was 50% in the brothers and 8% in the sisters. These expectancy rates are higher than those reported in most other studies, possibly because the investigators studied family members rather than relying solely on information from alcoholic probands. A study by Rimmer and Chambers (1969) has shown that "family studies" in which family members are interviewed show higher rates of alcoholism than occur in "family history studies" where only alcoholic probands are interviewed.

In all, according to a recent review by Cotton (1979), upwards to 140 estimates of the familial incidence of alcoholism are now in the literature. Of these, Cotton eliminated about 50 because they were in journals published in languages other than English. Of the remainder, 39 insufficiently describe the source of subjects, sample size, sex of subjects, geographical scope of study, source of information, definition of alcoholism, and relationship of family member to the alcoholic to be even roughly useful for comparative purposes. Only eight had controls, that is, data on the incidence of alcoholism in the families of both alcoholics and nonalcoholics. Nonalcoholics include populations of nonpsychiatric patients from surgical and medical wards, nonalcoholics having a variety of psychiatric diagnoses, and persons who were neither patients nor problem drinkers.

Two-thirds of the studies found that at least 25% of alcoholics had fathers who were alcoholics. Fathers and brothers of alcoholics were more likely than mothers and sisters to be alcoholics. According to half of the estimates, maternal alcoholism occurred in fewer than 5% of the alcoholics' families. In the remaining studies, it was reported to occur in 6% to 20% of the alcoholics' families. Many studies reporting data on fathers failed to report comparable data on mothers.

Most of the studies reviewed by Cotton reported only the instance of alcoholism in subjects' parents. However, 18 also reported high rates of alcoholism in siblings and 8 reported high rates among other relatives. Rates of sibling alcoholism were reported as the number of alcoholics in the total number of siblings or as the number of patients having one or more siblings who was an alcoholic. In either case, rates of sibling alcoholism were consistently higher in samples of alcoholics than in all types of nonalcoholics studied. Naturally, rates of parents are not comparable with those of siblings, since the parents have passed through a much longer period of risk. As many as 62% of one sample of alcoholics had one or more relatives in the preceeding two generations who had "problems with alcohol." Three-quarters of another sample of hospitalized alcoholics reported alcoholism in first degree relatives. In most studies the incidence of alcoholism in first degree relatives was higher than that of more distant relatives of alcoholics.

In nine studies comparing rates of alcoholism in families of male versus families of female alcoholics, seven showed higher rates in the families of women than of men. In one study, for example, approximately one-half of the female and one-third of the male alcoholics came from families in which at least one parent was an alcoholic; only 9% of the siblings of male alcoholics compared with 24% of the siblings of female alcoholics were alcoholics. Cotton (1979) interpreted the finding that female alcoholics are more likely than male alcoholics to come from families in which pathological drinking has occurred as indicating that women are more vulnerable than men to the impact of familial alcoholism. Another explanation is that still existent social barriers to heavy drinking in women requires a heavier "genetic load" for alcoholism to emerge in female members of the family.

All comparisons of samples of alcoholics and nonalcoholics reveal lower frequencies of parental alcoholism in the families of nonalcoholics. Even when the nonalcoholics were psychiatric patients, the rates of familial alcoholism were low. Winokur and Clayton (1968), for example, were able to find only a 9.5% incidence of parental and a 1.1% incidence of maternal alcoholism in the parents of 366 patients having affective disorders. Thus, as Cotton (1979) points out, a high rate of parental alcoholism is perhaps uniquely a characteristic of populations of alcoholics. Parental alcoholism usually ranges from 1% to 2% in the nonpsychiatric samples reviewed and maternal alcoholism never exceeds 1% of the mothers of any of the samples of nonalcoholics. These rates are similar to the rates of alcoholism expected in general populations, based on five studies of nonalcoholics in the general population (Goodwin, 1971).

Several authors have attempted to analyze their data in a way to control for environmental factors. Dahlberg and Stenberg (1934) established that one of the parents of their alcoholics was in 25% of the cases an alcoholic, and that both parents were abstainers in 12% of the cases. The severity of alcoholism was the same if the parents were alcoholics or abstainers. The authors interpreted this finding as indicating a hereditary influence in alcoholism. Åmark (1953) reported that "periodic" and "compulsive" alcoholics more frequently had alcoholic children than did alcoholics whose illnesses presumably were less severe. Home environments were found to be equally "good" or "bad" in both groups, again suggesting that alcoholism had a hereditary component. Utilizing a pedigree approach to an investigation of a single large family, Kroon (1924) concluded that alcoholism was influenced by a sex-linked hereditary trait—a subject that will come up again under the section about genetic markers.

Alcoholism also has been studied with regard to its possible association with other psychiatric illnesses. On the basis of several studies (Åmark, 1953; Bleuler, 1932; Brugger, 1934; Guze, Wolfgram, McKinney, & Cantwell, 1967; Winokur, Reich, Rimmer, & Pitts, 1970), it appears there is an excess of depression, criminality, sociopathy, and "abnormal personality" in the families of alcoholics. Typically, depression occurs most often in the female relatives and alcoholism or sociopathy in the male relatives. Rela tives of alcoholics were no more often schizophrenic, mentally defective, manic, or epileptic than were relatives of nonalcoholics.

Familial is not, of course, synonymous with *hereditary.* Speaking French may also be familial but not because of genes. Nevertheless, in studying familial disorders, it is important to determine whether the illness is influenced by heredity. Unless the illness follows a precise Mendelian mode of inheritance, such as Huntington's chorea, separating "nature" from "nurture" is difficult. The temptation, however, to attempt to disentangle the two is apparently strong; nature–nurture studies are still popular, despite widespread skepticism about their feasibility.

The main problem in assessing the relative importance of heredity and environment is that both are usually provided by an individual's progenitors, at least early in life. Through the years, a number of strategies have been developed to circumvent the nature–nurture problem with regard to alcoholism. In general, these can be grouped into three types: (1) twin studies, (2) adoption and half-sibling studies, and (3) genetic marker studies.

TWIN STUDIES

One method for evaluating whether genetic factors may predispose individuals to a particular disease is to compare identical with fraternal twins where at least one member of each pair has the illness. Originally proposed by Galton, this approach assumes that monozygotic and dizygotic twins differ only with respect to genetic makeup and that environment is as similar for members of a monozygotic pair as for a dizygotic pair. Given these assumptions, the prediction is that genetic disorders will be concordant more often among identical twins than among fraternal twins.

The twin approach has been applied to alcoholism in two large-scale studies, one Swedish, the other Finnish. In the Swedish study, Kaij (1960) located 174 male twin pairs where at least one partner was registered at a temperance board because of a conviction for drunkenness or another indication of alcohol abuse. He personally interviewed 90% of the subjects and established zygosity by anthropometric measurements and blood type. The concordance rate for alcohol abuse in the monozygotic group was 54%; in the dizygotic group it was 28%, a statistically significant difference. Moreover, by dividing alcohol abusers into subgroups based on severity, the largest contrast occurred when individuals with most extensive use of alcohol were considered.

Kaij also found that social and intellectual "deterioration" was more correlated with zygosity than with extent of drinking; that is, a "deteriorated" heavy-drinking monozygotic twin was more likely to have a light-drinking partner showing signs of deterioration than was true of dizygotic twins where one partner was deteriorated. He interpreted this as indicating that "alcoholic deterioration" occurred more or less independently of alcohol consumption and may be a genetically determined contributor to the illness rather than a consequence.

In the Finnish study Partanen, Bruun, and Markkanen (1966) found more equivocal evidence of a genetic predisposition to alcoholism. They studied 902 male twins 28 to 37 years of age, a substantial proportion of all such twins born in Finland between 1920 and 1929. Zygosity diagnosis was based on anthropometric measures and serological analysis. The authors also studied a sample of brothers of the same age as the twins. Little difference in within-pair variation was found between dizygotic twins and the nontwin brothers. Subjects were personally interviewed and evaluated by personality and intelligence tests.

In contrast to Kaij (1960), Partanen et al. (1966) found no difference between monozygotic and dizygotic twins with regard to consequences of drinking (perhaps the most widely accepted basis today for diagnosing alcoholism). More or less normal patterns of drinking, however, did appear to reflect genetic factors. Frequency and amount of drinking were significantly more concordant among monozygotic twins than among dizygotic twins. Abstinence also was more concordant among identical twins. However, the authors found no signs of heritability for the presence of "additive" symptoms, arrests for drunkenness, or various social complications of drinking.

A third twin study was conducted in the United States, utilizing questionnaire data. Leohlin (1972) studied 850 pairs of like-sex twins chosen from a group of some 600,000 high school juniors who took the National Merit Scholarship Questionnaire Test. Included in the questionnaire were 13 items related to attitudes toward alcohol and drinking practices. Also included were items permitting a rough approximation of zygosity. Leohlin found that putative monozygotic twins were more concordant for "heavy drinking" than were putative dizygotic twins. Drinking customs and attitudes toward drinking appeared to be uninfluenced by zygosity. Leohlin conceded that his data were "somewhat fragile" but suggestive.

Jonsson and Nilsson (1968) reported findings based on questionnaire data obtained from 7,500 twin pairs in Sweden. Zygosity diagnoses were known for about 1,500 pairs. Monozygotic twins were significantly more concordant with regard to quantity of alcohol consumed than were dizygotic twins. Social-environmental factors, on the other hand, seemed to explain much of the variation in consequences from drinking, a result corresponding closely to that reported in the Partanen et al. (1966) study.

Using the twin method, Perry (1973) examined the relative effect of heredity and environment on attitudes towards alcohol drinking, cigarette smoking, and coffee drinking. The results supported a significant genetic factor in the attitude toward alcohol drinking, but not in attitudes toward cigarette smoking and coffee drinking.

Of six twin studies of alcoholism, only one fails to show a significant difference between MZ twins and DZ twins with respect to concordance for alcoholism. Gurling and Murray (unpublished communication, 1981) used the Maudsley Hospital Twin Register to identify a consecutive series of 78 same-sexed alcoholic probands. Preliminary results after investigation of 56 of these and their co-twins showed concordance rates for alcoholic dependence of 21% for MZ twins and 25% for DZ twins. In short, the concordance for both DZ and MZ twins was similar to the prevalence of alcohol dependence in first-degree family members.

The authors speculated about reasons for their findings. Many of the twins were still relatively young, and alcohol dependence may yet occur in more subjects. Their eventual findings for the total cohort may also show higher concordance rates for the MZ twins, although the authors felt it was unlikely. Gurling and Murray (1981) also studied both women and men, whereas most studies include only men. Finally, different criteria for alcohol dependence were used in the Gurling and Murray study than in other twin studies. Still, the study is a sound one and must be addressed in any consideration of evidence for a genetic factor in alcoholism.

Vesell, Page, and Passanti (1971) studied the elimination rates of alcohol in 14 pairs of twins. The subjects were given 1 ml/kg of 95% ethanol solution orally and the ethanol elimination rate was followed by taking blood samples over a 4-hour period. They found that the heritability value for the ethanol elimination rate was .98. In short, the rate was almost totally controlled by genetic factors. Forsander and Eriksson (1974) compared six monozygotic and eight dizygotic male twin pairs in Finland. A heritability value of 80% was found for ethanol elimination rates and a heritability value of 60% to 80% for acetaldehyde in venous blood. On the basis of these two studies, it would appear that the alcohol elimination rate is under a high degree of genetic control. This was confirmed in twin studies by Kopun and Propping (1977), who found, however, that genetic control was not total, being modified by such environmental factors as smoking and frequency of alcohol intake.

Like all approaches to the nature–nurture problem, twin studies have a number of weaknesses. For example, the assumption that identical and fraternal twins have equally similar environments is open to question. In the Partanen *et al.* (1966) study, identical twins differed from fraternal twins in that they lived longer together, were more concordant with respect to marital status, and were more equal in social, intellectual, and physical dominance relationships. Even in rare instances where monozygotic twins are reared apart, zygosity may influence environmental effects; a person's appearance, for example, influences people's behavior toward him or her—individuals who look alike may be treated alike. In this and other ways, the interaction between physical characteristics and the environment may tend to reduce intrapair differences in identical twins and increase differences in fraternal twins.

ADOPTION AND HALF-SIBLING STUDIES

Another approach to separating nature from nurture is to study individuals separated from their biological relatives soon after birth and raised by nonrelative adoptive parents. Beginning in 1970, my colleagues and I began a series of adoption studies in Denmark supported by the National Institute of Alcohol Abuse and Alcoholism investigating further the possibility that alcoholism in part had genetic roots. The studies have gone through three phases.

Phase One

Because men are more likely to develop drinking problems than are women, the first phase of the study involved analyzing a sample of Danish males who had a biological parent with a hospital diagnosis of alcoholism and who had been adopted in the first few weeks of life by nonrelatives. The control group, consisting of age-matched men without, as far as was known, alcoholism in their biological parents, was selected from a large pool of adoptees. A psychiatrist interviewed the total sample of 133 men (average age 30), 55 who had a biological parent who was alcoholic and a matched sample of 78 controls with no known alcoholism in their parents. (It was possible some did have alcoholic parents, but there was no record of this in the central registries maintained in Denmark.) The interviewer did not know whether the interviewees were sons of alcoholics or sons of presumed nonalcoholics and the study was "blind" from its inception until the data were analyzed. Experimenter bias therefore could not have been a factor in the study.

The results of the study can be summarized as follows:

1. Of the 55 probands (sons of alcoholics), 10 were alcoholic, using both specific criteria and a history of treatment for alcoholism. Of the 78 controls, 4 met the criteria for alcoholism but none had received treatment. The difference was significant at the .02 level.

2. The probands were no more likely to be heavy drinkers or drinkers with occasional problems from drinking than were the controls. About 40% of each group were heavy drinkers, defined as daily drinkers who drank six or more drinks at least several times a month. Having a biological parent who was alcoholic increased the likelihood of the son being alcoholic but did not increase the chance of his being classified as a heavy drinker.

3. The interviewer, a trained psychiatrist, obtained a complete history and performed a mental status examination. The probands were no more likely to receive a diagnosis of depression, sociopathy, drug abuse, or other diagnosable psychiatric conditions than were the controls. Both groups had sizable numbers of individuals diagnosed as having various personality disturbances, but these vaguely described traits were as common in the control group as in the probands.

From these data it could be concluded that sons of alcoholics were about four times more likely to be alcoholic than were sons of nonalcoholics, despite having no exposure to the alcoholic biological parent after the first few weeks of life. Moreover, they were likely to be alcoholic at a relatively early age (in their 20s) and have a form of alcoholism serious enough to warrant treatment. Having a biological parent who was alcoholic apparently did not increase their risk of developing psychiatric disorders other than alcoholism and did not predispose them to heavy drinking in the absence of alcoholism. The familial predisposition to alcoholism in this group was *specific* for alcoholism and *not on a continuum* with heavy drinking (Goodwin, Schulsinger, Hermansen, Guze, & Winokur, 1973).

Phase Two

Some of the probands had brothers who had been raised by their alcoholic biological parents (most of the alcoholic parents, by the way, were fathers). The sons of alcoholics raised by their alcoholic biological parents also had a high rate of alcoholism, compared to controls consisting of non-adopted men raised by nonalcoholic parents. Their rate of alcoholism, however, was no greater than was the rate observed in their brothers raised by nonalcoholic foster parents (about 18% in both groups; Goodwin, Schulsinger, Moller, Hermansen, Winokur, & Guze, 1974).

The conclusions from the first two phases were (1) alcoholism was transmitted in families and (2) increased susceptibility to alcoholism occurred about equally in men raised by their alcoholic biological parents and men raised by nonalcoholic foster parents. In other words, if there were a genetic predisposition to alcoholism, exposure to the alcoholic parent did not appear to augment this increased susceptibility.

Phase Three

The final phase of the study involved studying daughters of alcoholics, both those raised by foster parents and those raised by their alcoholic biological parents. The sample consisted of 49 proband women (adopted-out daughters of alcoholics) and 48 controls (adopted-out daughters of presumed nonalcoholics). As was the case of the former studies, the interviews were conducted blindly, to reduce the chance of experimenter bias. The subjects were between the ages of 30 and 41, with a mean age of 35. The major findings were as follows:

1. One of the probands was clearly alcoholic and another was a serious problem drinker who failed to meet completely the criteria for alcoholism. Two of the controls were alcoholic. The three women diagnosed as being alcoholic had all received treatment for their alcoholism. Hence, 4% of the women in both groups were either alcoholic or serious problem drinkers. The sample was too small to draw definite conclusions from this, but since there is an estimated prevalence of alcoholism among Danish women of about .1% to 1%, the data suggest that there may indeed be an increased prevalence of alcoholism in the two groups. Since nothing is known about the parents of the control women other than that none had a biological parent with a hospital diagnosis of alcoholism, possibly the two alcoholic controls had parents who had alcohol problems. The parents could not be located, and there was no way of determining whether this was the case. It was, however, interesting that both the alcoholic controls had foster parents who were described as alcoholic, suggesting environmental exposure to alcoholism may contribute to alcoholism in women but not to alcoholism in men.

2. More than 90% of the women in both groups were abstainers or very light drinkers. This contrasted with the Danish male adoptees; about 40% of the latter were heavy drinkers.

3. Family history studies have suggested that alcoholics often have male relatives who are alcoholic or sociopathic and female relatives who are depressed (Winokur *et al.* 1970). In this study, complete psychiatric histories were obtained and mental status examinations performed. Among the adopted women, there was a low rate of depression in both groups, with no more depression in the daughters of the alcoholics than in the controls. Among daughters of

alcoholics raised by their alcoholic parents, depression was significantly more present than in controls. There was no evidence of increased susceptibility to other psychiatric disorders in the daughters of alcoholics, whether raised by foster parents or their own alcoholic biological parents. (Goodwin, 1976)

It appears, therefore, that alcoholism in women may have a partial genetic basis, but that sample size in the present study precluded definitive conclusions. Since the majority of the women were very mild drinkers, it is possible that social factors discouraging heavy drinking may suppress a genetic tendency, if one exists. There was no evidence of a genetic predisposition to depression in the daughters of alcoholics. At any rate, if such a predisposition exists, environmental factors are apparently required to make the depression clinically manifest. Regarding the daughters raised by their alcoholic parents, it is not possible to determine whether their increased rate of depression was due to environmental factors precipitating a genetic predisposition or entirely to environmental factors.

It should be noted that some evidence indicates that women develop alcoholism at a later age than do men, and possibly these 35-year-old women had not all entered the age of risk for alcoholism. Further follow-up studies are needed to explore this possibility.

Four similar studies have been conducted. Roe and Barks (1944) obtained information about 49 foster children in the 20 to 40 year age group, 22 of normal parentage and 27 with a biological parent described as a "heavy drinker." Among children with heavy-drinking parents, 70% were users of alcohol, compared to 64% in the control parentage group. In adolescence, two children of "alcohol-parentage" got into trouble because of drinking too much as compared to one in the "normal-parentage" group. The authors found that adopted children of heavy drinkers had more adjustment problems in adolescence and adulthood than did adopted children of nonalcoholics, but the differences were not significant and neither group had adult drinking problems. They concluded there was no evidence of hereditary influences on drinking.

This conclusion, however, can be questioned on several grounds. First, the sample was small. There were only 21 men of alcoholic parentage and 11 of normal parentage. Since women, particularly at the time of the study, were at very low risk for alcoholism, discovering they had no problem with alcohol was expected. Second, although the biological parents of the proband group were described as "heavy drinkers," it is unclear how many would justify a diagnosis of alcoholism. Most had a history of antisocial behavior, and apparently none had been treated for a drinking problem. All of the biological parents of the proband group in the Danish study received a hospital diagnosis of alcoholism at a time when this diagnosis was rarely employed in Denmark.

Schuckit, Goodwin, and Winokur (1972) also studied a group of individuals reared apart from their biological parents where either a biological parent or a "surrogate" parent had a drinking problem. The subjects were significantly more likely to have a drinking problem if their biological parent were considered alcoholic than if their surrogate parent were alcoholic. Studying 32 alcoholics and 132 nonalcoholics, most of whom came from broken homes, it was found that 62% of the alcoholics had an alcoholic biological parent compared to 20% of the nonalcoholics. This association occurred irrespective of personal contact with the alcoholic biological parent. Simply living with an alcoholic parent appeared to have no relationship to the development of alcoholism.

Bohman (1978) studied 2,000 adoptees born between 1930 and 1949 by inspecting official registers in Sweden for notations about alcohol abuse and criminal offenses in the adoptees and their biological and adoptive parents. There was a significant correlation between registrations for abuse of alcohol among biological parents and their adopted sons. Registered criminality in the biological parents did not predict criminality or alcoholism in the adopted sons. The higher the number of registrations for alcoholism in the biological parents, the greater the incidence of registration for alcohol abuse in the adopted children.

Cadoret and Gath (1978) studied 84 adult adoptees (18 years of age or older) separated at birth, and having no further contact with their biological relatives. Alcoholism occurred more frequently in the adoptees whose biological background included an individual with alcoholism than it did in adoptees without this biological background. Alcoholism did not correlate with other biological parental diagnoses. Childhood conduct disorder was significantly higher in those adoptees who later received a diagnosis of alcoholism or problem drinking.

Both of the above adoption studies produced results closely similar to those found in the Danish adoption studies (Goodwin *et al.,* 1973). In other words, alcoholism in the biological parents predicted alcoholism in their male offspring raised by unrelated adoptive parents but did not predict other psychiatric illness (such as criminality). In both the Danish studies (Goodwin, Schulsinger, Hermansen, Guze, & Winokur, 1975) and the Cadoret and Gath study (1978), alcoholics had an increased incidence of childhood conduct disorder but no higher incidence of other psychopathology.

Several studies bear on possible genetic modes of transmission. Kaij and Dock (1975) tested the hypothesis of a sex-linked factor influencing the occurrence of alcoholism by comparing alcohol abuse rates in 136 sons of the sons versus 134 sons of the daughters of 75 alcoholics. No substantial difference between the groups of grandsons was found in frequency of alcoholism, suggesting a sex-linked factor was not involved. The total sample was also used to calculate the risk of registration for alcohol abuse among the grandsons; rate of registration by the grandsons' fifth decade of life was 43%, approximately three times that of the general male population. This result is incompatible with an assumption of a recessive gene being involved in the occurrence of alcoholism, though it fits with the assumption of a dominant gene. The section on genetic markers later in this chapter will discuss this possibility further.

FAMILIAL ALCOHOLISM

Over 40 years ago, Jellinek and Jolliffe (1940) proposed a diagnostic category called *familial alcoholism.* The Danish studies, in particular, seem to support this concept. Familial alcoholism, as described by Jellinek and supported by the Danish data, consists of the following features:

1. A family history of severe, unequivocal alcoholism
2. Early onset
3. Bender-type alcoholism requiring treatment at a relatively young age
4. No increased susceptibility to other types of substance abuse or diagnosable psychiatric illness

From a research standpoint, separating familial from nonfamilial alcoholism may reveal some interesting and useful correlations. About half of alcoholic patients on many alcoholism wards give a family history of alcoholism. Hence, separating alcoholic patients into these groups would yield similarly sized cells for comparison purposes.

One study (Lucerno, Jensen, & Ramsey, 1971) found that if an alcoholic had one family member who was alcoholic, 82% reported having two or more family members who were alcoholic, further strengthening the concept of familial alcoholism.

Another study (Parker, 1972) found that 69% of women alcoholics who were "spree" drinkers, as opposed to 22% of women alcoholics who were "nonspree" drinkers, had fathers who were heavy drinkers. As Cotton (1979) points out, many additional variables, such as age of onset of heavy drinking, the interval between the first drink and heavy drinking, the efficacy of different treatment modalities or the frequency of marriage to an alcoholic spouse, may differentiate alcoholics who have a family history of alcoholism from those who do not.

BIOLOGICAL CONCOMITANTS OF ALCOHOLISM

The first section of this chapter dealt with the familial susceptibility to alcoholism and the evidence that it may be genetic in origin. Although no one can doubt the concentration of alcoholism in families, the evidence for a hereditary basis remains less conclusive. If alcoholism—or some alcoholism—does have a hereditary basis, this has important implications for prevention as well as research.

The second section of this chapter deals with more equivocal predictors. First, the rather large and inconsistent literature on genetic marker studies in alcoholism is surveyed. Next, the truly enormous literature comparing alcoholics to nonalcoholics on a multitude of biological variables (and always finding differences: Keller's Law) is scanned for recent, potentially important entries, pointing out the obvious: it is impossible to know if the difference is a cause of the alcoholism, a consequence, or happenstance.

Finally, tolerance for alcohol and how much is innate and how much acquired will be discussed as a predictor of alcoholism, concluding with evidence that intolerance may be a better predictor than tolerance.

GENETIC MARKERS

An association of alcoholism with known inherited characteristics would afford support for a biological factor in the etiology of alcoholism. The following is a review of studies exploring this possibility.

Nine studies have compared ABO blood group types in alcoholics versus nonalcoholics. Two found that blood Group A predominated in alcoholics and cirrhotics. Seven studies failed to confirm the association. Other serological markers (e.g., proteins) have also been studied, with conflicting results (Swinson, 1970).

In three studies, alcoholics were compared to controls with regard to secretion of ABH blood group substances in saliva (Swinson & Madden, 1973). All three found a remarkable increase in nonsecretors among alcoholics, but *only* in those with blood Group A. This is the most consistent finding in the genetic marker literature and warrants further study. Although the high rate of nonsecretors may represent an acquired change rather than genetic marker, it is difficult to understand why this only occurs in Group A alcoholics.

One investigator (Peeples, 1962) reported an increased percentage of nontasters of phenylthiocarbamide (PTC) among alcoholics (PTC taste response being inherited as an autosomal dominant trait), but others (Swinson, 1972) fail to find the difference, and loss of taste sensitivity in alcoholics may explain the original finding.

At least nine studies (Cruz-Coke, 1964; Swinson, 1972) report an association between color blindness and alcoholism. Usually the color blindness disappears after the acute alcohol symptoms subside, suggesting a toxic or nutritional rather than a genetic etiology. A pedigree study, however, suggests the issue is not closed (Cruz-Coke & Varela, 1966). Color vision was studied in relatives of alcoholics and it was found that male nonalcoholic relatives did not differ from male controls, but that female relatives differed significantly, indicating transmission by sex-linked recessive genes. Like the ABH finding, this warrants further study.

Pharmacogenetic markers have drawn attention recently. The pharmacokinetics and metabolism of many drugs, including alcohol, appears to be under a high degree of genetic control. The best evidence for this comes from twin studies (reviewed earlier), in which it has been shown repeatedly that identical twins metabolize specific drugs at a similar rate and fraternal twins metabolize specific drugs at different rates.

In the case of alcoholism, an interesting pharmacogenetic finding was reported by Schuckit and Rayses (1979), who found higher levels of acetaldehyde in the blood of moderate-drinking family members of alcoholics after drinking alcohol than in moderate-drinking relatives of nonalcoholics. If replicated, this finding not only would help identify individuals at high risk for alcoholism but also have theoretical implications for the addictive process itself.

Family members of alcoholics do *not* differ from family members of nonalcoholics in the rate of ethanol elimination (Schuckit & Rayses, 1979; Utne, Hansen, Winkler, & Schulsinger, 1977). This suggests the possibility of an "atypical" isoenzyme of alcohol dehydrogenase producing a more rapid buildup of acetaldehyde, and/or differences in aldehyde dehydrogenase activity in families of alcoholics.

Another type of "marker" study involves platelet monoamine oxidase (MAO) activity (believed to correspond closely to MAO activity in brain synaptosomes). In two studies of the relatives of alcoholic individuals (Major & Murphy, 1978; Sullivan, Stanfield, Schanberg, & Cavenar, 1978), highly consistent results were obtained. Both investigations involved a large number of subjects and demonstrated higher incidences of alcoholism in the relatives of low-MAO alcoholics compared to high-MAO alcoholics. There is a large, albeit inconsistent, literature relating variations in central monoamine metabolism with alcoholism; the MAO studies are important and deserve replication. Based on twin studies, platelet MAO activity is also under a high degree of genetic control.

Twin studies have also shown that electroencephalographic (EEG) patterns are highly influenced by genetic factors and that EEG responses to alcohol are also in large part genetically controlled (Propping, 1978). Several studies report that alcoholics have a smaller percentage of alpha activity

on their EEG record than do nonalcoholics, although this could be attributable to effects of chronic drinking on the brain. However, recent
unpublished data of my associates and myself indicate that nonalcoholic
sons of alcoholics also have an decreased percentage of alpha. On receiving
alcohol, they show an *increase* of alpha, so their EEGs resemble those of
sons of nonalcoholics receiving the same amount of alcohol. In short, alcohol appears to have a "normalizing" effect on the EEG of sons of alcoholics—a provocative finding, if replicable. It suggests that low alpha may
predict future alcoholism in young people and may even relate to etiology.

   Genetic marker studies have also been conducted in a search for predictors of cirrhosis in alcoholics. Although epidemiological data suggest that
the development of cirrhosis in alcohol abusers is related to the duration
and amount of ethanol intake, the fact that only a small percentage of
alcohol abusers develop cirrhosis remains unexplained and suggests a possible predisposing genetic factor. Several previous studies have reported an
association between various human leucocyte antigens (HLA) and alcoholic
cirrhosis (Rada, Knodell, Troup, Kellner, Hermanson, & Richards, 1981).
In the most recent study, HLA frequencies were determined in cirrhotic
and noncirrhotic alcoholics and in a control group of nonalcoholic patients
without liver disease. No statistically significant differences in HLA frequencies among the groups were found. Since HLA is only one class of
marker, it is possible other markers will be found that will help predict
which alcoholics are most likely to get cirrhosis (a very useful predictor to
have, and worth searching for).[1]

---

[1]Some recent evidence from a large twin study suggests a genetic influence in alcoholic
cirrhosis, despite the inconsistent HLA reports (Hrubec & Omenn, 1981). Medical histories
of 15,924 male twin pairs in the National Academy of Sciences—National Research Council
Twin Registry were examined to determine, within pairs, concordances for alcoholism and its
medical end points. Prevalences per 1,000 among individual twin subjects were 29.6 for
alcoholism, 4.1 for alcoholic psychosis, 14.2 for liver cirrhosis, and 2.1 for pancreatitis.
Prevalences were similar for monozygotic (MZ) and dizygotic (DZ) twins. Prevalences in
percent among co-twins of diagnosed subjects, that is casewise twin concordance rates, were,
respectively, by diagnosis: alcoholism: 26.3 (MZ), 11.9 (DZ); alcoholic psychosis: 21.1 (MZ),
6.0 (DZ); and liver cirrhosis: 14.6 (MZ), 5.4 (DZ). No twin pairs concordant for pancreatitis
were found.
   The greater concordance for alcoholic psychosis and for liver cirrhosis among MZ than
DZ twins could not be explained by the difference in alcoholism concordance between them.
The difference in concordance between MZ and DZ twins persisted when, in addition, it was
assumed that only half the actually occurring cases of alcoholism and half of each of the end
points have been ascertained. These results provide evidence in favor of genetic predisposition to organ-specific complications of alcoholism.

BIOCHEMICAL AND HEMATOLOGICAL CORRELATES

In almost every study conducted, alcoholics are found to differ from nonalcoholics in one way or another. The problem is that alcoholics *drink more* than nonalcoholics; the difference may be due to the alcohol and not the alcoholism.

Here, nevertheless, are some differences reported between alcoholics and nonalcoholics reviewed because (1) they are new and interesting, and (2) because the differences are sometimes referred to as "markers" and may be confused with genetic markers (which they almost certainly are not).

Ryback and associates at the National Institute of Alcohol Abuse and Alcoholism found that alcoholics could be distinguished from nonalcoholics using the routine chemistry tests and hematograms patients ordinarily receive on entering a hospital (Ryback, Eckardt, & Pautler, 1980). No one test or small group of tests were very helpful, but the tests *in toto*, analyzed with a computer program, identifed 85% of alcoholic inpatients and 100% of nonalcoholic inpatients.

The alcoholics had all been drinking shortly before hospitalization, and their chemical-hematological "fingerprints" may reflect physical changes from drinking rather than constitute a predictor (antecedent) of the alcoholism. The latter possibility could be tested by studying relatives of alcoholics, or partly resolved by studying dry alcoholics, but this has not been done.

One proposed biologic marker of alcoholism is the ratio of alpha amino-n-butyric acid to leucine in blood. In 1978, Shaw and Lieber measured this ratio in four groups: 40 hospitalized alcoholics, 20 control subjects, 19 patients with liver disease unrelated to alcohol, and 25 patients in a methadone maintenance program. They concluded that the ratio increased in relation to long-term alcohol consumption, correlated positively with the degree of alcoholism assessed by separate criteria, and could be used to identify the majority of alcoholics within a population.

These findings were not substantiated in three subsequent studies. Two of them (Dienstag, Carter, & Wands, 1977; Morgan, Milsom, & Sherlock, 1977) reported that ratios of alpha amino-n-butyric acid to leucine are not an index of or a marker for the diagnosis of alcoholism but, rather, that elevated ratios are a nonspecific indicator of liver disease. The third (Ellingboe, Mendelson, & Varanelli, 1978) found that ratios in alcoholic patients with no or minimal evidence of liver disease were virtually identical to those in controls.

Literally thousands of alcoholics have undergone neuropsychological testing, almost all as inpatients within a short period after heavy drinking. Many of the studies report some "deficit" in the test performance. In general, the deficits are scattered across the range of neuropsychological tests with little consistency. Also, in a number of studies the deficits are diminished or disappear when retesting occurs after the patient has been abstinent for a longer period, suggesting the impairment was reversible. The deficits may reflect the depressed mood experienced by many hospitalized alcoholics or short-lived toxic effects from prolonged inebriation. In any case, they apparently are not indicative of permanent brain damage. There has been one exception to this lack of consistency: the Categories test of the Halstead Battery has rather consistently shown deficits in alcoholic patients. The Categories test measures what is sometimes called "conceptual shifting."

Recent unpublished work by myself and my associates found that nonalcoholic sons of alcoholics also do poorly on the Categories test. If substantiated in other studies, it would suggest that, once again, apparent consequences of heavy drinking may actually precede heavy drinking and even cause heavy drinking. This is reminiscent of Kaij's (1960) finding (reviewed earlier) that identical twins were concordant for alcoholic deterioration even when one twin had never been alcoholic.

TOLERANCE AND INTOLERANCE

Tolerance to alcohol has been overrated. Compared to tolerance to morphine, for example, tolerance to alcohol is nugatory. In animals only a modest amount of tolerance can be produced by repeated administration of alcohol, and recent evidence indicates that learning may be as important as "adaptive changes" in cell membranes in the development of tolerance.

Consider the recent experiment in which rats were trained to walk on a treadmill to avoid shock (Wenger, Tiffany, Bombardier, Nicholls, & Woods, 1981). The animals developed tolerance for ethanol if given subsequent practice *while ethanol-intoxicated*. Rats given equivalent doses of ethanol *after practice* did not develop tolerance. These results challenge the idea that mere repeated doses of ethanol are sufficient to induce tolerance. It seems that tolerance does not develop *unless the response used to measure tolerance is performed while the subject is intoxicated.*

In addition, differences in tolerance may be largely innate rather than acquired. Young men given large amounts of alcohol vary strikingly in their behavioral tolerance to alcohol, despite having comparable previous experience with alcohol (Goodwin, Powell, Bremer, Hoine, & Stern, 1969). A seasoned alcoholic at peak tolerance can still only consume about double what an inexperienced drinker can consume, assuming the inexperienced drinker is not *intolerant* of alcohol.

Only recently has much attention been given to intolerance for alcohol.

It turns out that millions of people have a genetically determined physiological intolerance for alcohol that permits them to drink only a small amount without experiencing discomfort. Among Orientals, perhaps two-thirds are severely intolerant of alcohol (Wolff, 1972). After a drink or two, they develop a cutaneous flush accompanied by unpleasant feelings such as nausea and headache. This profoundly discourages them from further drinking. The response is genetic in origin: Oriental infants, given a small amount of alcohol in their milk, also flush.

There is a low rate of alcoholism in the Orient and this is usually attributed to family or cultural factors. This partly may be the explanation, but almost certainly another explanation is the now well-documented fact that most Orientals are "protected" from alcoholism by a genetically determined physiological intolerance for alcohol.

The basis for the intolerance is not known. There is some evidence that Oriental "flushers" have higher levels of acetaldehyde after drinking than do nonflushers. It was recently reported that 85% of Japanese carry an atypical liver alcohol dehydrogenase which may be more active than the ADH found in most Caucasians (Stamatoyannopoulos, Chen, & Fukui, 1975). The flush seen in the Oriental flushing reaction resembles that seen with an alcohol-disulfiram reaction. Thus, an elevated acetaldehyde level in susceptible Orientals may be the physiological explanation.

On the other hand, my colleagues and I have found that the Oriental flush can be inhibited by a combination of H^1 and H^2 antihistamine antagonists (unpublished data). In short, the chemical basis for the flushing response has still not been determined to everyone's satisfaction, but the flush nevertheless is real and affords potent protection against the development of alcoholism.

Women are alcoholic less often than men. Again, cultural factors usually are given the credit. This may be only partly true. It appears that more women than men are physiologically intolerant of alcohol. After a drink or two, they lose their desire to drink for a variety of reasons: a "full" feeling, headache, nausea, dizziness. During pregnancy most women spontaneously reduce their drinking because of discomfort from small amounts. There is also some evidence that drinking by women fluctuates somewhat in accordance with the menstrual cycle. In other words, hormonal differences between the sexes may account for the differences in physiological intolerance.

Physiological intolerance may also partly explain the low rate of alcoholism in certain groups (e.g., Jews). Only in Orientals has physiological intolerance been studied systematically, but among biological predictors of alcoholism, intolerance for alcohol must rank very high as a negative predictor.

REFERENCES

Åmark, C. A study in alcoholism: Clinical, social-psychiatric and genetic investigations. *Acta Psychiatrica Neurologica Scandinavica,* Supplementum 70, 1953.

Bleuler, M. Psychotische Belastung von körperlich Kranken. *Z. Gesamte. Neurol. Psychiatr.,* 1932, *142,* 780–782.

Bohman, M. Some genetic aspects of alcoholism and criminality. A population of adoptees. *Archives of General Psychiatry,* 1978, *35* (3), 269–276.

Boss, M. Zur Frage der erbbiologischen Bedeutung des Alkohols. *Mschr. Psychiatr. Neurol.,* 1929, *72,* 264–268.

Brugger, C. Familienuntersuchungen bei Alkoholdeliranten. *Z. Gesamte. Neurol. Psychiatr.,* 1934, *151,* 740–741.

Cadoret, R. J., & Gath, A. Inheritance of alcoholism in adoptees. *British Journal of Psychiatry,* 1978, *132,* 252–258.

Cotton, N. S. The familial incidence of alcoholism: A review. *Journal of Studies on Alcohol,* 1979, *40*(1), 89–116.

Crothers, T. D. Heredity in the causation of inebriety. *British Medical Journal,* 1909, *2,* 659–661.

Cruz-Coke, R. Colour blindness and cirrhosis of the liver. *Lancet,* 1964, *2,* 1064–1065.

Cruz-Coke, R., & Varela, A. Inheritance of alcoholism: Its association with colour blindness. *Lancet,* 1966, *2,* 1282–1284.

Dahlberg, G., & Stenberg, S. *Alkoholismen som Samhallsproblem.* Stockholm: Oskar Eklunds, 1934.

Dienstag, J., Carter, E., & Wands, J. Plasma alpha amino-n-butyric acid to leucine (A/L) ratio; nonspecificity as a marker for alcoholism. *Gastroenterology,* 1977, *73,* 1217.

Elderton, E., & Pearson, K. A first study of the influence of parent's alcoholism on the physique and ability of the offspring. *Eugeni Laboratory Memoir X.* London: Cambridge University Press, 1910.

Ellingboe, J., Mendelson, J. H., & Varanelli, C. C. Plasma alpha amino-n butyric acid: Leucine ratio: Normal values in alcoholics. *Journal of Studies on Alcohol,* 1978, *39,* 1467–1476.

Forsander, O., & Eriksson, K. Forekommer det etnologiska skillnader i alkoholens amnesomsattningen. *Alkoholpolitik,* 1974, *37,* 315.

Goodwin, D. W. Is alcoholism hereditary? A review and critique. *Archives of General Psychiatry,* 1971, *25*(12), 545–549.

Goodwin, D. W. *Is alcoholism hereditary?* New York: Oxford University Press, 1976.

Goodwin, D. W., Powell, B., Bremer, D., Hoine, H., & Stern, J. Alcohol and recall: State-dependent effects in man. *Science* 1969, *163,* 1358–1360.

Goodwin, D. W., Schulsinger, F., Hermansen, L., Guze, S. B., & Winokur, G. Alcohol problems in adoptees raised apart from alcoholic biological parents. *Archives of General Psychiatry,* 1973, *28*(2), 238–243.

Goodwin, D. W., Schulsinger, F., Moller, N., Hermansen, L., Winokur, G., & Guze, S. B. Drinking problems in adopted and nonadopted sons of alcoholics. *Archives of General Psychiatry,* 1974, *31*(2), 164–169.

Goodwin, D. W., Schulsinger, F., Hermansen, L., Guze, S. B., & Winokur, G. Alcoholism and the hyperactive child syndrome. *Journal of Nervous and Mental Disorders,* 1975, *160*(5), 349–353.

Gregory, I. Family data concerning the hypothesis of hereditary predisposition toward alcoholism. *Journal of Mental Science,* 1960, *106*(444), 1068–1072.

Gurling, H. M. D., & Murray, R. M. *Investigations into the genetics of alcohol dependence and into its effects on brain function.* Unpublished communication, 1981.

Guze, S. B., Wolfgram, E. D., McKinney, J. K., & Cantwell, D. P. Psychiatric illness in the families of convicted criminals: A study of 519 first degree relatives. *Diseases of the Nervous System,* 1967, *28*(10), 651.

Hrubec, Z., & Omenn, G. S. Evidence of genetic predisposition to alcoholic cirrhosis and psychosis: Twin concordances for alcoholism and its biological end points by zygosity among male veterans. *Alcoholism: Clinical and Experimental Research,* 1981, *5* (2), 207–215.

Jellinek, E. M., & Jolliffe, N. Effect of alcohol on the individual: Review of the literature of 1939. *Quarterly Journal of Studies on Alcohol,* 1940, *1*(1), 110–181.

Jonsson, E., & Nilsson, T. Alkoholkonsumption ho s monozygota och dizygota tvillingar. *Nordisk Hygienisk Tidskrift,* 1968, *49,* 21.

Kaij, L. *Studies on the etiology and sequels of abuse of alcohol.* Lund, Sweden: Department of Psychiatry, University of Lund, 1960.

Kaij, L., & Dock, J. Grandsons of alcoholics. *Archives of General Psychiatry,* 1975, *32,* 1379–1381.

Kopun, A., & Propping, P. The kinetics of ethanol absorption and elimination in twins and supplementary repetitive experiments in singleton subjects. *European Journal of Clinical Pharmacology,* 1977, *11,* 337–344.

Kroon, H. M. Die Erblichkeit der Trunksucht in der Familie X. *Genetica,* 1924, *6,* 319.

Leohlin, J. C. An analysis of alcohol-related questionnaire items from the National Merit Twin Study. *Annals of the New York Academy of Science,* 1972, *197,* 117–120.

Long, J. F. Use and abuse of alcohol. *Transactions of the Medical Society of North Carolina,* 1879, *26,* 87–100.

Lucerno, R. J., Jensen, K. F., & Ramsey, C. Alcoholism and teetotalism in blood relatives of abstaining alcoholics. *Quarterly Journal of Studies on Alcohol,* 1971, *32*(1), 183–185.

MacNicholl, T. A. A study of the effects of alcohol on school children. *Quarterly Journal of Inebriatism,* 1905, *27,* 113–117.

Major, L. F., & Murphy, D. L. Platelet and plasma amine oxidase activity in alcoholic individuals. *British Journal of Psychiatry,* 1978, *132,* 548–554.

Morgan, M. Y., Milsom, J. P., & Sherlock, S. Ratio of plasma amino-n-butyric acid to leucine as an empirical marker of alcoholism: Diagnostic value. *Science,* 1977, *197,* 1183–1185.

Parker, F. B. Sex-role adjustment in women alcoholics. *Quarterly Journal of Studies on Alcohol,* 1972, *33*(3), 647–657.

Partanen, J., Bruun, K., & Markkanen, T. Inheritance of drinking behavior. New Brunswick, N. J.: Rutgers University Center of Alcohol Studies, 1966.

Peeples, E. E. *Taste sensitivity to phenylthiocarbamide in alcoholics.* Master's thesis, Stetson University, De Land, Florida, 1962.

Perry, A. The effect of heredity on attitudes toward alcohol, cigarettes, and coffee. *Journal of Applied Psychology,* 1973, *58*(2), 275–277.

Pohlisch, K. Soziale und personliche Bedingungen des chronischen Alcoholismus. In *Sammlung psychiatrischer und neurologischer Einzeldarstellungen.* Leipzig, Germany: G. Thieme, Verlag, 1933.

Propping, P. Alcohol and alcoholism. *Human Genetics, Supplement 1,* 1978, 91–99.

Rada, R. T., Knodell, R. G., Troup, G. M., Kellner, R., Hermanson, S., & Richards, M. HLA antigen frequencies in cirrhotic and noncirrhotic male alcoholics: A controlled study. *Alcoholism: Clinical and Experimental Research,* 1981, *5*(2), 188–191.

Rimmer, J., & Chambers, D. S. Alcoholism: Methodological considerations in the study of family illness. *American Journal of Orthopsychiatry,* 1969, *39,* 760.

Roe, A., & Burks, B. Adult adjustment of foster children of alcoholic and psychotic parentage and the influence of the foster home. Memoirs of the Section on Alcohol Studies, Yale University, No. 3. *Quarterly Journal of Studies on Alcohol,* 1945.

Ryback, R. S., Eckardt, M. J., & Pautler, C. P. Biochemical and hematological correlates of alcoholism. *Research Communications in Chemical Pathology and Pharmacology,* 1980, *27*(3), 533–549.

Schuckit, M. A., & Rayses, V. Ethanol ingestion: Differences in blood acetaldehyde concentrations in relatives of alcoholics and controls. *Science,* 1979, *203,* 54–55.

Schuckit, M. A., Goodwin, D. W., & Winokur, G. A study of alcoholism in half-siblings. *American Journal of Psychiatry,* 1972, *128*(9), 1132–1136.

Shaw, S., & Lieber, C. S. Plasma amino acid abnormalities in the alcoholic: Respective role of alcohol, nutrition, and liver injury. *Gastroenterology,* 1978, *74,* 677–682.

Shuttleworth, G. E., & Beach, F. Idiocy and imbecility. In T. C. Allbutt (Ed.), *A system of medicine by many writers.* New York: Macmillan, 1900.

Stamatoyannopoulos, G., Chen, S. H., & Fukui, M. Liver alcohol dehydrogenase in Japanese: High population frequency of atypical form and its possible role in alcohol sensitivity. *American Journal of Human Genetics,* 1975, *27,* 789–796.

Sullivan, J. L., Stanfield, C. N., Schanberg, S., & Cavenar, Jr., J. O. Platelet monoamine oxidase and serum dopamine-b-hydroxylase activity in chronic alcoholics. *Archives of General Psychiatry,* 1978, *35,* 1209–1212.

Swinson, R. P. *A study of genetic polymorphism in an alcoholic population.* Unpublished M. D. thesis, University of Liverpool, Liverpool, England, 1970.

Swinson, R. P. Genetic polymorphism and alcoholism. *Annals of the New York Academy of Science,* 1972, *197,* 129–133.

Swinson, R. P., & Madden, J. S. ABO blood groups and ABH substance secretion in alcoholics. *Quarterly Journal of Studies on Alcohol,* 1973, *34,* 64–70.

Utne, H. E., Hansen, F. V., Winkler, K., & Schulsinger, F. Ethanol elimination rate in adoptees with and without parental disposition towards alcoholism. *Journal of Studies on Alcohol,* 1977, *38*(7), 1219–1223.

Vesell, E. S., Page, J. G., & Passanti, G. T. Genetic and environmental factors affecting ethanol metabolism in man. *Clinical Pharmacology Therapy,* 1971, *12,* 192–198.

Warner, R. H., & Rosett, H. L. The effects of drinking on offspring. An historical survey of the American and British literature. *Journal of Studies on Alcohol,* 1975, *36*(11), 1395–1420.

Wenger, J. R., Tiffany, T. M., Bombardier, C., Nicholls, K., & Woods, S. Ethanol tolerance in the rat is learned. *Science,* 1981, *213,* 575–577.

Winokur, G., & Clayton, P. J. Family history studies IV: Comparison of male and female alcoholics. *Quarterly Journal of Studies on Alcohol,* 1968, *29*(4), 885–891.

Winokur, G., Reich, T., Rimmer, J., & Pitts, F. Alcoholism III: Diagnosis and familial psychiatric illness in 259 alcoholic probands. *Archives of General Psychiatry,* 1970, *23,* 104–111.

Wolff, P. H. Ethnic differences in alcohol sensitivity. *Science,* 1972, *175,* 449–450.

5

Situational Factors in Drinking

A Developmental Perspective on Drinking Contexts

THOMAS C. HARFORD

An important characteristic in adolescent development is the disengagement of the adolescent from parental objects. Coleman (1961) has shown the increasing influence of age peers and the decreasing role of parents as models from whom adolescents acquire many values and behaviors. In their longitudinal study of problem behavior and psychosocial development, Jessor and Jessor (1977) state that "there is a decline in parental controls and an increase in friends' support and approval for models of problem behavior" (p. 162). Although the Jessors have reported an increase with age in problem behaviors such as problem drinking, sexual experience, general deviance, and drug use, they are careful to subsume the development of problem behavior under the broad context of psychosocial development. They note that many of the changes observed over the four-year period of the study were changes in a direction that may be defined as socially more mature. This even applies to the increase in problem drinking since this behavior is usually age graded (pp. 162–163). What is evident in the research of Jessor and Jessor (1977) is that the conception of alcohol use among youth is not an isolated activity but a basic part of their overall psychosocial development in contemporary society.

THOMAS C. HARFORD • National Institute on Alcohol Abuse and Alcoholism, Rockville, Maryland 20857.

It is important to note that psychosocial changes in adolescent development are not isolated from the overall changes occurring in society and in adult behaviors. Normative changes in sexual conduct over the past two decades, for example, are reflected in sexual behaviors of both adults and adolescents and care must be taken in labeling the sexual behavior of youth as reflective of problem behavior in general. This is not to minimize the seriousness of potential consequences stemming from sexual precocity or alcohol consumption but rather to place such behavior in a more general perspective. Within this perspective it becomes very clear that a determination of what constitutes problem drinking among adolescents is no easy task, either conceptually or empirically.

The intent of this chapter is to identify environmental factors that contribute to the onset of drinking and to examine situational variables in drinking contexts that influence the level of alcohol consumption among populations at different age levels. It is argued that a delineation of the environmental components in the development of drinking will provide a needed normative perspective for the determination of problem drinking.

The importance of viewing drinking among youth in a broad environmental perspective is evident in the powerful associations of adolescent drinking prevalence and that of adult drinking prevalence, on the one hand, and between the availability of alcohol and the level of per capital consumption, on the other.

Despite the fact that the legal age for the purchase and consumption of alcoholic beverages is 18 years of age and older in the United States, it is not uncommon to find that the vast majority of teenagers have experienced the effects of alcohol. Moreover, a significant proportion of youth have established a stable pattern of consumption prior to attaining the legal age (Rachal, Williams, Brehm, Cavanaugh, Moore, & Eckerman, 1975). This discrepancy stems, in part, from the observations that the use of alcohol by youth is symbolically associated with adult status and that the United States is not homogeneous with respect to adult disapproval of teenage drinking (Blane & Hewitt, 1977). On special occasions that include the use of alcohol, parents may allow children to drink. They sanction its use under special conditions of control.

An important variable, then, in the use of alcohol by youth is the use of alcohol by adults. Teenagers tend to follow adult models in their drinking patterns. Adult drinking patterns in any community are important predictors of teenage drinking patterns in the same community. Abstinence on the part of parents often corresponds to abstinence by their children and, similarly, between drinking by parents and adolescents.

Explanations of the association between adult and adolescent drinking practices may be found in two approaches to alcohol studies: sociocultural models and the distribution-of-consumption, lognormal model (Harford, Parker, & Light, 1980). The former would argue that the correspondence between adult and adolescent drinking practices relates to the regulatory function of drinking norms that characterize population subgroups with different traditions of the use of alcohol. The distribution-of-consumption model would argue that the level of average consumption in society is related to the proportion of heavy drinkers, and a shift in the level of alcohol consumption would be accompanied by a shift in the same direction in the proportion of heavy drinkers. Policies that influence the overall availability of alcohol would affect the overall consumption levels of both adult and adolescent drinkers. Both of these models contain variables that define the social contexts in which alcohol is consumed (Harford, 1979a). Variations in legal drinking age, for example, serve to structure the place where adolescent drinking occurs and the source from which alcohol is obtained. Similarly, the drinking practices of parents and other adults influence the social control structure associated with the onset of drinking in the adolescent period.

The prevalence of drinking increases with increasing age among teenagers. Concomitant with this is an increase in the problems associated with alcohol use. Again, it is important, to view these age-related changes in drinking behavior not as isolated bits of experience but as integrated into the broader social fabric of contemporary society. This is not meant to minimize the seriousness of the negative consequences of alcohol misuse but rather to direct attention to the relevant variables in society and in the circumstances of drinking. In so doing, in untangling the complexity of this network, more effective programs can be implemented for prevention planning.

This chapter examines (1) environmental and situational factors in adolescent drinking; (2) age-related data for the frequency of drinking in adult supervised and nonsupervised contexts; (3) the influences of geographic region and alcohol availability on teenage drinking contexts; (4) age-related data for the frequency of adult supervised and nonsupervised teenage parties, the availability of alcohol at parties, and the drinking behavior of teenagers; (5) the patterns and correlates of drinking contexts among college students by year in school; and (6) the transition from adolescent drinking to adult drinking.

ENVIRONMENTAL INFLUENCES IN ADOLESCENT DRINKING

Jessor and his colleagues (Donovan & Jessor, 1978; Jessor & Jessor, 1977) have shown that when adolescents report similar interests and common expectations between parents and friends and when the views and opinions of parents are more influential than that of friends, drinking behavior is less problematic. When adolescents report their parents to have a more tolerant attitude toward teenage drinking, alcohol is more likely to be used by adolescents. The relationship between parental attitudes and adolescent drinking practices is not a simple one, however, and not of a linear relationship. Davies and Stacey (1972) noted that abstainers, occasional drinkers, and heavy drinkers perceived their parents' attitudes toward drinking as being negative, whereas light and moderate drinkers perceived their parents' attitudes as being positive.

Although studies generally indicate that peer influences have more of an impact on adolescent drinking than parental influences do, parents nevertheless play a very significant role. Wechsler and Thum (1973) found that heavier teenage drinkers were less likely than moderate drinkers to report being "very close" to their families. Prendergast and Schaefer (1974) reported that perceived parental attitudes and behaviors toward the child, particularly maternal control, correlated more strongly with adolescent drinking behavior than either parent's drinking behavior or attitudes toward drinking. However, Smart, Gray, and Bennett (1978) found that parental rejection and control had very little association with adolescent drinking behavior. Margulies, Kessler, and Kandel (1977) found that neither the closeness of relationship to their families nor the perception of parental control significantly influenced the onset of drinking. However, the relative closeness of parents and peers did predict onset of drinking, with adolescents closer to peers more likely to start drinking.

Jessor and his colleagues obtained data pertaining to social support for drinking in a longitudinal study of high school students. Perceived support for drinking from peers was the most important variable accounting for a subject's change in drinking status from abstainer to drinker during a one-year period (Jessor, Collins, & Jessor, 1972). They also indicated that adolescent drinking became more frequent and heavier as the extent of perceived drinking among peers increased.

Taken together, these studies indicate that when the youth is parent-oriented, as reflected in measures of parental compatibility and in conventional behaviors in harmony with parental expectations and normatively approved by society, then there is continued abstinence, a delay in the onset of drinking, or a tendency to adopt patterns of alcohol use characterized as light or moderate in consumption levels. To state, however, that the adolescent drinks excessively and/or engages in problem drinking behavior because he or she moves toward peers and away from parents does not explain the phenomenon of such behavior. In a survey of high school students in Ontario, Canada, it was found that heavier drinking and reported frequency of getting high and drunk were more strongly correlated with situational factors (drinking away from home and drinking in cars) than other types of peer or parental influences (Smart, Gray, & Bennett, 1978). The authors concluded that social influences from parents' and friends' drinking may have more impact on whether a student drinks or not than amounts of alcohol consumed. Thus modeling may be more important for the onset of drinking, whereas place and extent of drinking are more important in predicting the signs of heavy drinking.

It is clear from the studies reviewed in this chapter that several environmental factors are implicated in the drinking behavior of adolescents. Recently, Harford and Spiegler (1982) examined the interrelationships between parental and peer drinking models, perceived access to alcohol, and selected drinking contexts (at teen parties when parents were not present and at home on special occasions). The data were drawn from the recent national survey of senior high school students in the United States (Rachal, Maisto, Guess, & Hubbard, 1980).

The environmental measures were related to estimates of the frequency of alcohol consumption, the number of drinks consumed on a typical occasion, and the number of times over the past year that teenagers reported being drunk or very, very high. Each of the drinking measures was regressed on grade in school and several environmental variables. These variables were entered into a step-wise regression model in the following order: school grade, parental drinking, peer drinking, access to alcohol, teen parties, and home drinking contexts. The ordering was based on the assumption that age and parental drinking are antecedent to peer networks and drinking contexts while the latter are more proximal to drinking behavior. This order also allowed an assessment of the relationship of context to drinking behavior when other variables, known to relate to adolescent drinking, were entered first into the regression equation as covariates.

Although grade in school related significantly to the three drinking measures, it accounted for only a small proportion of the variance. Parental drinking models were not significant in any of the regression equations. Peer models, however, related significantly to reported drinking behavior for both sexes. The number of drinking peers was related directly to increased drinking frequency, level of consumption, and reported number of times drunk in the past year.

Perceived access to alcohol was significant in each of the regression equations. The reported ease of obtaining alcohol was related directly to the three drinking measures for both sexes. The inclusion of access to alcohol appreciably increased the overall variance of the drinking measures that were accounted for by peer models.

Of the two remaining variables, teen parties were significantly related to drinking behavior in each of the regression models and substantially increased the overall level of variance accounted for by these environmental variables. The frequency of drinking at home on special occasions was related significantly to drinking frequency, especially for boys. Home contexts were not significantly related to average quantities or times drunk.

The inclusion of these measures in a regression equation accounted for a significant proportion of the variance in selected drinking measures (35% of the variance in times drunk for boys and 29% for girls). Peer drinking models, when compared to parental models, were more powerful predictors of drinking levels. Measure of perceived access to alcohol made independent contributions to the drinking measures. Although access may relate both to the level of alcohol availability and to social networks of access to alcohol, not all of its variance is shared by the peer group. This finding directs attention to the influence of the general level of alcohol availability in society as a contributing factor to drinking levels among teenagers.

Peer parties and, to a lesser extent, home drinking contexts contributed significantly to drinking behaviors when other factors such as peer models and access to alcohol were controlled. The frequency of peer parties when parents or other adults are not present was related to higher levels of overall consumption and reported frequency of times drunk. These data enable specification of contexts that place the adolescent at risk with respect to negative consequences.

DEVELOPMENTAL TRENDS IN ADOLESCENT DRINKING CONTEXTS

The disengagement of the adolescent from parents is reflected in shifts in the settings in which alcohol is consumed. Studies have indicated that most teenagers are introduced to alcohol at home and in the presence of their parents (Davies & Stacey, 1972; Maddox & McCall, 1964). The most commonly reported occasions on which teenagers are likely to drink, however, are at parties attended by peers with no adult supervision (Maddox & McCall, 1964; Sower, 1959). Studies also have indicated that heavier or more frequent drinkers are more likely to report using alcohol in peer settings than in the context of the family. Maddox and McCall (1964) reported that for users, the most likely occasion for drinking was at a party attended by peers and not supervised by adults, whereas the drinking occasions of infrequent users were most likely to be special events celebrated in the home and with adults present. Similarly, the 1974 Research Triangle Institute national survey (Rachal *et al.*, 1975) indicated that the great majority of heavy drinkers drank mostly with peers whereas only a small proportion of the infrequent drinkers reported drinking mostly with peers. As the drinking level increased, the proportions of students drinking most of the time with peers also increased.

Although these studies have attempted to determine the percentages of teenagers who drink in various situations and to relate contexts of drinking to patterns of consumption, there are very few data on the frequency and amount of drinking that occurs in specific contexts and on the identities of drinking companions and sources of alcohol in each of these settings. In a survey of 1,321 students from 14 to 17 years old in Glasgow, Scotland, Davies and Stacey (1972) examined in detail the drinking behavior of adolescents in three types of settings: the home of parents or an adult relative, the home of a friend of the same age, and somewhere other than a home (e.g., at a dance, in a hotel or pub, outdoors, or somewhere else). Most of the teenagers reported drinking at home (92%) but the amounts of alcohol consumed there were relatively small. Fewer teenagers, but nevertheless a substantial proportion (71%), reported drinking in the home of a friend but consumed more alcohol than in the home setting. Fewer still (66%) reported drinking outside the home but consumed more alcohol than in either of the other two settings. The findings therefore indicated that although more students drank in the parental home than in other settings, drinking in the home was characterized by consumption of significantly less quantities of alcohol than in other drinking contexts.

In home settings parents usually were present (68%) and more likely to be the persons serving drinks (45%) than not (23%). Drinking in this setting appeared to be mostly confined to "special occasions" for the younger teenagers. In the home of a friend, parents were less likely to be present (15%) while other adults were more likely to be present (40%) and serving drinks (32%). The major difference between this setting and that of the home was the predominance of teenage peers, 47% of whom served drinks. In settings other than a home, a pattern similar to that in the home of a friend was reported. Parents were least likely to be present (13%) whereas teenage peers predominated (67%).

These data provide support for the hypothesis that social controls for teenage drinking are most likely to be exercised in the home of parents where access to alcohol generally is under the supervision of parents or other adult relatives. Outside the parental home, drinking appears to be largely under the control of teenagers themselves. There is clearly a shift with age from drinking under parental control to drinking under peer control.

Information on the frequency of drinking in selected contexts was included in the 1974 national survey of junior and senior high school students (Rachal *et al.*, 1975). This survey included a nationwide probability sample of all junior and senior high schools students in the contiguous 48 states and the District of Columbia. A self-administered questionnaire was completed by the students during regular school hours at the end of the school year in 1974. Usable questionnaires were completed by 13,122 students with a 73% response rate. These data permit an assessment of the circumstances of drinking most frequently related to teenage drinking, an indication of variation in frequency as a function of age and sex, and finally, information on the extent to which unsupervised drinking occurs. Information on drinking contexts also was contained in the more recent 1979 survey of senior high school students. The present section focuses on the earlier survey since it included a broader age range for assessing age-related changes. Analyses have shown that the pattern of drinking among adolescent school children in senior high has remained stable between the 1974 and the 1979 surveys (Rachal, Maisto, Guess, & Hubbard, 1980). Included in the 1974 survey were the following items on drinking contexts:

Contexts Supervised by Adults
- At home on special occasions, such as birthdays, or holidays, such as Thanksgiving
- At dinner at home with the family
- Teenage parties when others are drinking and parents or other adults are present

Contexts Unsupervised by Adults
- Teenage parties when others are drinking and parents or other adults are not present
- Driving around or sitting in a car at night
- At places where teenagers hang around when their parents or other adults are not present
- During or after a school activity, such as a dance or football game, when parents or other adults are not present or cannot see the respondent
- Alone

Respondents were asked to indicate how often they drank beer, wine, or liquor in each of the above settings. The response categories included never drink or do not drink in this setting, sometimes, frequently, most of the time. It is well established that the frequency of drinking increases with increasing age at each age level. These items, however, do not provide estimates of the frequency with which adolescents report drinking in these contexts. For example, students who report that they drink most of the time at unsupervised parties may vary in the frequency of drinking in this context from one or more times a week to less than once a month. Thus care must be exercised in interpretation. Nevertheless, an examination of the distributions provides an indication of the use of various settings for the consumption of alcohol by teenagers.

The distributions of the drinking context items are present in Table 1 by school grade and sex for the 1974 survey of junior and senior high school students. Abstainers and former drinkers (respondents defined as drinker but not drinking in the past year) were excluded from this table. The items are organized to distinguish between drinking contexts in which adults are present from those in which adults are not present. The response categories were combined to distinguish between nondrinkers and drinkers in a particular context and, among the drinkers, those that reported frequent consumption in that context.

With respect to adult contexts, *drinking at home on special occasions* is the most frequently reported context: 78% for boys and 85% for girls. Among both sexes, there is a slight decline in the overall frequency of drinking in this setting with increasing age. Among 7th graders (average age 13 years) the proportions are highest and begin to diminish in the senior high school years. The proportions are lowest for boys and girls in the 10th grade (the first year of senior high school). These findings are consistent with the existing literature and reveal that the vast majority of teenage drinkers have consumed alcohol in this setting. Although the items do not permit an assessment of how often they drink in this context, the wording *special occasions* suggests that the exposures are not very frequent, perhaps several times a year. This interpretation and evidence from other studies that indicate that consumption levels are low when parents are present suggests that this setting is not a significant contributor to overall consumption level among teenagers and would not necessarily be at risk to negative consequences, other than as a way of introducing alcohol to youth. The influence of parental drinking and drinking at home in the early years of youth as possible variables of etiological significance for problem drinking for older youth and in the adult years are addressed later. The fact that the proportion of drinkers remains fairly high throughout the school grades suggests it to be a fairly stable setting in which teenagers consume alcohol. The proportions, however, who report drinking frequently or most of the time in this setting decline more sharply than do those for total drinkers. It should be noted that girls drink more frequently in this setting than do boys.

The second item, *at dinner at home with the family,* might suggest a more frequent basis of participation in this context than simply dinner to celebrate special occasions. It could vary, however, from Sunday dinner to almost daily use of alcohol with meals as in the case of various ethnic groups (Lolli, Serianni, Golder, & Luzzatto-Fegiz, 1958). The proportions of boys and girls are much less than in the former context and show a decline with

Table 1.
Distribution of Drinking Contexts in a Sample of Junior and Senior High School Students by School Grade and Sex, in Percentage[a]

Supervised contexts	Boys							Girls						
	7	8	9	10	11	12	Total	7	8	9	10	11	12	Total
Home on special occasions														
Do not drink	15	18	20	28	24	24	22	10	9	15	20	16	16	15
Drink	85	82	80	72	76	76	78	90	91	85	80	84	84	85
Drink frequently	47	43	43	34	39	39	40	56	57	48	44	45	46	49
Dinner at home														
Do not drink	45	53	57	61	58	57	56	39	44	52	55	56	52	51
Drink	57	47	43	39	42	43	44	61	56	48	45	44	48	49
Drink frequently	15	12	9	9	8	8	10	21	16	13	12	11	13	13
Teenage parties														
Do not drink	49	48	45	44	39	30	42	44	47	44	41	37	25	39
Drink	51	52	55	56	61	70	58	56	53	56	59	63	75	61
Drink frequently	19	20	21	21	24	30	23	20	20	18	21	25	32	23

Unsupervised contexts

							Total							Total
Teenage parties														
Do not drink	34	26	19	13	9	6	16	36	28	18	15	15	13	19
Drink	66	74	81	87	91	94	84	64	72	82	85	85	87	81
Drink frequently	26	41	53	59	64	70	54	29	40	49	53	58	52	49
In cars														
Do not drink	64	51	38	33	29	23	38	61	57	45	39	38	45	46
Drink	36	49	62	67	71	77	62	39	43	55	61	62	55	54
Drink frequently	12	23	29	31	37	37	30	14	18	24	28	28	21	23
At school														
Do not drink	55	43	34	29	26	23	34	54	51	37	37	37	43	42
Drink	45	57	66	71	74	77	66	46	49	63	63	63	57	58
Drink frequently	17	26	35	37	42	43	35	21	21	30	32	32	25	28
At hangouts														
Do not drink	48	35	28	22	20	17	27	48	39	29	31	31	31	33
Drink	52	65	72	78	80	83	73	52	61	71	69	69	69	67
Drink frequently	23	32	39	44	46	47	39	24	33	37	37	38	34	35
Alone														
Do not drink	49	40	37	42	41	40	41	55	53	54	59	64	68	59
Drink	51	60	63	58	59	60	59	45	47	46	41	36	32	41
Drink frequently	14	22	19	14	14	12	16	14	13	11	7	5	6	9
Total sample	444	633	652	653	758	705	3845	326	582	726	609	777	703	3223

ᵃThe "do not drink" and "drink" categories sum to 100%. The "drink frequently" category is drawn from the "drink" category.

increasing school grade. Again, the lower proportion of users in this context is to be expected since (1) it suggests a more routine and frequent basis of exposure, and (2) it reflects a more integrated use of alcohol in the family setting, a sanctioning of use on a more routine basis that is particular to small population subgroups and not reflective of the population in general.

The third and final item dealing with adults present relates to *teenage parties when parents and other adults are present.* Among both boys and girls, the age trends reverse those of the other two contexts in which adults are present. With increasing age there is increased frequency of drinking in this context. The increase is gradual during the junior high school years and is highest among 12th graders. Again, it is difficult to estimate the frequency with which this occurs but it may reflect infrequent special occasions, particularly among younger teenagers. The fact that parents are present on this occasion may also draw on a greater age range of teenagers in attendance, notably siblings. Thus, the higher proportions during the senior year of high school may relate to graduations, and younger teenagers may be present and drinking on these occasions as well. Estimates of the frequency of this occurence, as well as comparisons with parties when adults are not present, are presented in the section on situational factors. It is clear that as teenagers grow older more of them are likely to drink in this context. It is also fair to assume that the frequency of drinking in this context also would increase with increasing age, though the amount consumed should not be excessive (Davies & Stacey, 1972). The increase in drinking frequency with age for this setting is also reflected in the increase in proportions of boys and girls who report drinking most of the time in this context. The proportions are similar for both.

The fourth item in Table 1 relates to *teenage parties when adults are not present.* Among boys, this is the most prevalent context, in which 84% report drinking and 54% report drinking frequently or most of the time. Among girls, this context is also high, 81%, and is surpassed in numbers only by drinking at home on special occasions. For both groups, the number of teenagers who report drinking in this context increases with increasing age at each age level and stabilizes at the senior high level. These increases are also present among those who drink frequently in this setting. The levels are comparable for boys and girls and may relate to the fact that the preferred composition of youth on these occasions is that of "mixed-sex groups." When compared to previous contexts, in which adults are present at teen parties, it is clear that unsupervised parties are more popular and draw the largest number of teenagers. Based on previously cited studies, unsupervised parties tend to be associated with higher levels of aclohol consumption.

Comparisons of supervised and nonsupervised contexts yield some conclusions regarding the social behavior of adolescents. As expected, home contexts (special occasions and with meals) tend to decrease with increasing age whereas both supervised and nonsupervised party contexts increase with age. This reflects the general social and outgoing behaviors characteristic of teenagers during their development.

The next item relates to contexts of drinking *while driving around or sitting in cars at night*. This context has been implicated in problem drinking in several studies (Babor & Berglas, 1981; Smart *et al.*, 1978) and, in view of the high risk attendant in drinking and driving, and epidemiologic fatalities report statistics among young drivers, this context may also be subsumed under contexts at risk. Among both sexes, the frequency of this context increases with age. Although it is slightly lower in number than nonsupervised parties, it approaches parties in frequency, particularly among boys. Approximately one-third of senior high school boys report drinking frequently or most of the time in this context. During the junior high school years the differences between boys and girls are slight but are more pronounced during the senior high school years.

The next item examines *nonsupervised contexts related to school activities such as dances or sports events*. Although often cited as a particularly attractive occasion for the use of alcohol among teenagers, this context draws lower numbers of youth when compared to teenage parties. Although the proportions of boys who report drinking frequently in this setting increase with age, age trends are less pronounced for girls and even decrease at the 12th grade. It is not clear why this is the case. It might relate to access networks to alcohol at events where adults are nearby and present at such activities, even though they are reported not to be around when the youth are drinking.

The next item relates to *nonsupervised teenage hangouts*. Compared to school events this context draws more youth especially at the senior high school level for both boys and girls. Age trends are less evident for girls.

The final item deals with *drinking alone*. Despite the fact that adults report alcohol use to be a social occasion and not frequently consumed alone, a large proportion of youth report drinking in this context, although the number is lower than all of the other contexts, except dinner at home. There are no age trends among boys and, for girls, frequency decreases with age. For both boys and girls, the proportions who drink frequently in this setting decrease with age and are lowest among girls.

Overall, these data suggest trends by age in the adolescent years in which there is a slight decrease in drinking in home settings, other than on special occasions and in party contexts with adults present, and an increase in settings in which adults are not present to supervise. The context data examined thus far, however, do not treat the items as mutually exclusive. It is unclear what proportions of students who drink at home also drink in peer settings. Harford and Spiegler (in press) developed a drinking typology based on the 1974 context items (Rachal *et al.,* 1975) to address just this issue. The typology differentiated students into the following categories:

1. Exclusive drinking at home (home only)
2. Exclusive drinking in peer settings (peer only)
3. Drinking both at home and in peer settings (home-peer)

This analysis enabled some assessment of the interrelationship between supervised and nonsupervised contexts by age. It was found that the majority of students, 51%, drank both at home and in peer settings. A large proportion, 36%, drank exclusively at home and a smaller proportion, 13%, drank exclusively in peer settings. Although the proportion of students who drank exclusively at home decreased with age, the proportions who drank both at home and in peer settings, as well as those who drank exclusively with peers, increased with age. The frequency and the amount of alcohol typically consumed by students who drank in both settings (home-peer) also increased with age. There were no age-related trends in the frequency and quantity of consumption among students who drank exclusively at home. Students who drank exclusively in peer settings, however, drank less frequently than home-peer students but the amounts consumed per occasion were similar to home-peer students. This finding addresses an issue raised earlier: The influence of the introduction of alcohol to youth in the home setting on subsequent drinking. Since the two categories, home-peer and peer-only, did not differ in average consumption, there is little evidence in this data of a carry-over effect between drinking at home in supervised settings and drinking behavior in unsupervised settings. The differences in the frequency of drinking in these two groups may be attributed to less access to alcohol among the peer-only students than home-peer students.

ENVIRONMENTAL INFLUENCES IN ADOLESCENT DRINKING CONTEXTS

National surveys of adult drinking patterns typically reveal differences in drinking patterns by geographic region. There are proportionately more drinkers in the East, North, and West, and fewer in the South. Rural areas tend to have larger proportions of abstainers than do the more urbanized areas. National surveys of teenage alcohol use reflect regional patterns similar to those of adults (Rachal *et al.,* 1975, 1980). These differences have been shown to relate to variations in religious affiliation, race, and other demographic characteristics of population groups (Cahalan, Cisin, & Crossley, 1969).

A noted source of regional impact upon drinking, particularly in the South, is the presence of a large number of fundamentalist religious groups that proscribe drinking. Thus, regional variation encompasses a variety of normative influences associated with geographic areas.

Harford and Spiegler (in press), in an analysis of the 1979 national survey of senior high school students, report that among boys and girls the frequency of teenage parties when adults are not present is higher in the Northeast and North Central regions and lower in the South and West. The regional pattern for parties when adults are present revealed a similar pattern for boys, but, among girls, it is much weaker and is highest in the South. The frequency of drinking at home on special occasions was highest in the Northeast for boys and girls and slightly lower in the South and West.

Geographic variables, however, accounted for only a small proportion of the variance in drinking patterns and context frequency in this study. The absence of a strong relationship is due, in part, to the various other factors that are associated with geographic region. Regional variations are conceptually more remote from drinking behavior, and whatever influence they exert is more likely to be mediated by other variables.

Geographic regions often differ on the degree to which teenagers have access to alcohol. Legal restrictions in the availability of alcohol have been found to influence not only the prevalence of adolescent drinking (Maisto & Rachal, 1980) but also the contexts for drinking (Globetti, 1972, 1973).

Maisto and Rachal (1980) investigated differences in drinking practices among senior high school students residing in states with different minimum drinking age laws. It was found that teenagers living in states with a minimum legal drinking age of 21 had lower incidences of drinking, heavy drinking, and drinking and driving, and less frequent reports of intoxication compared with students living in states with 18 to 20 or "mixed" drinking age laws.

The drinking habits of high school students in a rural southern abstinence community were found to be markedly different from the patterns reported in studies of teenage drinking in other less restricted locations (Globetti, 1969, 1973). One study (Globetti, 1973) reported that 25% of the students used alcohol, and another (Globetti, 1972) that 32% used alcohol, both percentages being considerably lower than the 60% to 90% cited in other investigations. The events and circumstances surrounding the act of drinking also were found to be somewhat different. Rather than being introduced to alcohol in the home with parents or relatives present, drinkers in abstinent communities usually were introduced to alcohol outside the home and very few drank with parents or adults. Most respondents drank with peers in secretive situations, without parental knowledge or approval. There is some evidence to suggest that these students may experience more problems with alcohol than those who drink with parents or relatives (Globetti, 1969, 1972). It also has been found that in a permissive community alcohol is usually obtained illegally (under age) from a legal merchant, whereas in a restrictive community it is usually obtained illegally from an illegal merchant (Globetti, Harrison, & Oetinger, 1967; Windham, Preston, & Armstrong, 1967).

These findings from the southern communities help to clarify the regional differences noted earlier in the national youth surveys. Variations in the patterns of legal availability and sources of access differentiate peer-only contexts from those including adults and reflect the overall normative patterns of community alcohol use and the correspondence between adult and adolescent drinking practices.

It has been suggested that legal restrictions may have more impact on the places where drinking occurs and the source from which alcohol is obtained than on actual amounts consumed (Stacey & Davies, 1970). Davies and Stacey (1972) explain their finding that younger teenagers (age 14) drink more often in parks and streets than do older teenagers on the basis that younger teenagers cannot purchase drinks in a public establishment. In a study of the drinking behavior of boys aged 14 to 18 in Helsinki, Copenhagen, Oslo, and Stockholm, it was concluded that the main effect of more rigid control was an increase in the amount of liquor bought illegally by underage drinkers (Bruun & Hauge, 1963).

A recent study focused on the issue of availability by surveying the drinking patterns of teenagers in three counties in the United States (Santangelo & McCartney, 1980). This study was based on a probability sample of all adolescents aged 12 to 18 years residing in Allegheny County, Pennsylvania (Pittsburgh and its suburbs), Pima County, Arizona (Tuscon and its suburbs), and Spartanburg County, South Carolina. Completed interviews were obtained for 662 teenagers in Allegheny (80% response rate), 601 in Pima (79% response rate), and 567 in Spartanburg (87% response rate). The data were collected between October 1979 and March 1980. These counties reflected variations in the level of alcohol availability. Availability was based on several dimensions but overall reflected differences in terms of per capita consumption for each county. A measure of perceived access to alcohol ("Can you get alcoholic beverages when you want them?") was related to per capita consumption. In the lowest alcohol availability site, 58% of the teenagers said they could not get alcohol compared to 44% in the highest availability site.

Pima County, Arizona is a medium size urban county in the Southwest and had the highest availability of alcohol. Allegheny County, Pennsylvania is a large urban county in the Northeast and was moderate in the level of availability. Spartanburg County, South Carolina is a small rural county in the Southeast and had the lowest availability of the three selected sites. The final sample consisted of 1,805 teenagers. Age and sex were distributed similarly by county, but the percentage of Blacks varied, being highest in Allegheny (53%), lower in Spartanburg (30%), and lowest in Pima (13%).

It was hypothesized that the proportion of drinkers would be higher over all age and sex groups in locations where the availability of alcohol was greater. Of particular interest to the present chapter is the fact that this survey included a set of items dealing with drinking contexts similar to those used in the national surveys of junior and senior high school students (Rachal *et al.*, 1975, 1980). These data serve to complement the national findings in this regard by focusing on the drinking behavior of a representative sample of teenagers in three specific areas. In view of the findings reviewed earlier (Globetti, 1969, 1973), it might be expected that the frequency and type of context would vary as a function of availability.

Table 2 presents the distribution-of-drinker status by type of county, sex, and age. The distributions of the total sample of teenagers reveals that the proportion of abstainers is highly related to availability. In the county of lower availability (Spartanburg) approximately 61% were abstainers as compared to 37% in the higher availability county (Pima). This, of course, is not simply a function of legislation but reflects a myriad of social variables. However, the impact of availability can be observed, and is more in evidence in variations in drinking contexts.

Table 2.
Distribution of Abstainers and Drinkers in a Sample of Teenagers by County and Sex

	Spartanburg (percentage)	Allegheny (percentage)	Pima (percentage)
Boys			
Abstainers	57	39	35
Drinkers	43	61	65
Total	275	321	270
Girls			
Abstainers	64	47	39
Drinkers	36	53	61
Total	286	332	324
Total sample			
Abstainers	61	43	37
Drinkers	39	57	63
Total	561	653	594

The results from this survey are consistent with national data in terms of the high prevalence of drinking at teenage parties when adults are not present. Table 3 clearly indicates that the prevalence of drinking in this context increases with increased availability (32% to 50% for the total sample). Also, within each of the communities this context is the most prevalent, attracting the majority of drinkers. In Spartanburg, 32% of the sample drank in this context, and the next most prevalent context was drinking at home on special occasions (22%). A similar pattern is obtained in each of the other communities.

It is of interest to compare this context to parties in which adults and parents are present. There is a corresponding increase in the proportion of teenagers in this context across the three counties (16% to 42%). There

Table 3.
Distribution of Drinking Contexts in a Sample of
Teenagers by County and Sex, in Percentage[a]

Drinking contexts	Boys			Girls			Total		
	Spart.	Alleg.	Pima	Spart.	Alleg.	Pima	Spart.	Alleg.	Pima
Supervised									
Teen parties									
Do not drink	23	27	20	23	20	20	23	23	20
Drink	19	34	44	13	33	41	16	34	42
Special occasions									
Do not drink	17	14	16	17	7	11	17	11	13
Drink	26	47	49	19	46	51	22	46	50
At dinner									
Do not drink	32	39	39	28	31	38	30	35	38
Drink	8	22	25	7	22	23	8	22	24
Unsupervised									
Teen parties									
Do not drink	9	15	12	6	15	13	7	15	13
Drink	34	46	52	29	38	47	32	42	50
In bars									
Do not drink	24	45	46	22	37	33	23	41	39
Drink	17	16	19	13	16	28	15	16	24
In cars									
Do not drink	19	39	36	18	36	40	18	38	38
Drink	22	22	29	18	17	22	20	19	25
Out-of-doors									
Do not drink	24	30	31	22	33	32	23	31	31
Drink	18	30	33	13	21	29	15	26	31
Total sample	275	321	270	286	332	324	561	653	594

[a]Selected percentages from the total sample of teenagers.

also is greater convergence between the proportion who drink in these two contexts in counties of moderate (Allegheny) to high (Pima) availability as compared to low availability (Spartanburg). The percentage differences of drinkers in these two counties (8%) is half that of the difference in Spartanburg (16%). Although teen parties attract more teenagers than adult parties in Allegheny and Pima counties, the differences are not as great as in Spartanburg where availability is lower. This, no doubt, reflects the proportion of nondrinking adults and the parental sanction against drinking in this region.

For this reason, it would be expected that drinking at home on special occasions would follow a similar pattern as adult parties. In this regard, it may be noted that the proportion of drinkers at home on special occasions is similar to the proportion of drinkers at teen parties in Allegheny and Pima counties, areas of moderate to high availability. The item on the context of alcohol at home with meals is interpreted to reflect a more integrated use of alcohol in the family setting and, for this reason, one would expect low proportions in Spartanburg County.

In view of the age of the sample, 12 to 18 years, the context item on bars is of interest and predictably low. The minimum age for the purchase of alcohol at the time of the survey was 21 years in Allegheny County, 21 years for liquor (distilled spirits) and 18 years for beer and wine in Spartanburg County, and 19 years in Pima County. These limitations are reflected in the proportions of teenagers who report drinking in bars and taverns and clubs. They are higher in Pima County than in the other two counties. Despite the fact that the minimum age in Pima is 19 years, one-fourth of the sample report drinking in that context at least occasionally if not frequently. This serves to illustrate the complexity of factors associated with monitoring access to public settings despite legal sanctions.

In view of the sanctions against drinking that are intensified in areas of low availability, one also might expect settings of a more secretive nature (cars, out-of-doors) to be more prevalent in this region. Although the prevalence of drinking in these contexts increases as the availability of alcohol across counties increases, the differences are not as marked as in the case of teen parties when adults are not present. Drinking in cars, for example, involves similar proportions of teenagers in each of the three counties.

In order to adjust for differences in abstinence rates in the three counties, percentages were recalculated based on the sample of drinkers only (Table 4). This has the effect of highlighting drinker preference in choice of context compared across the three counties. Among drinkers, there is little difference in the proportions who drink at teen parties when adults are not present. This is clearly the most prevalent context even in areas of low availability. Among drinkers in Spartanburg, the prevalence of contexts in

Table 4.
Distribution of Drinking Contexts in a Sample of
Teenager Drinkers by County and Sex, in Percentage

Drinking contexts	Boys			Girls			Total		
	Spart.	Alleg.	Pima	Spart.	Alleg.	Pima	Spart.	Alleg.	Pima
Supervised									
Teen parties									
Do not drink	57	44	32	65	37	32	60	40	32
Drink	43	56	68	35	63	68	40	60	68
Special occasions									
Do not drink	40	23	25	49	13	16	44	18	20
Drink	60	77	75	51	87	84	56	82	80
At dinner									
Do not drink	81	65	61	80	58	61	80	62	61
Drink	19	35	39	20	42	39	20	38	39
Unsupervised									
Teen parties									
Do not drink	21	25	19	18	28	22	19	27	21
Drink	79	75	81	82	72	78	81	73	79
In bars									
Do not drink	60	74	71	63	70	54	61	72	62
Drink	40	26	29	37	30	46	39	28	38
In cars									
Do not drink	48	65	55	51	68	64	49	66	60
Drink	52	35	45	49	32	36	51	34	40
Out-of-doors									
Do not drink	59	50	48	65	61	52	62	55	50
Drink	41	50	52	35	39	48	38	45	50
Total sample	117	195	174	102	176	196	219	371	370

which adults are present (adult parties, at home on special occasions, etc.) is considerably lower than in areas of moderate to high availability.

With respect to the other peer contexts, the proportion of teenagers who drink in cars tends to be higher in counties of low availability and lower in counties of high availability; that is, it reverses the previous pattern. This is also true for bar contexts among boys. The "out-of-doors" contexts tend to be lower in Spartanburg.

These findings yield some variation in drinking contexts as a result of variations in alcohol availability. These data, of course, do not necessarily implicate the level of availability as the causal factor since the counties also differ in ecology and social drinking norms. Adult contexts are much lower in prevalence in counties of low availability while more secretive contexts, such as cars, are higher. In counties of lower alcohol availability, teenagers manage to obtain access to alcohol but do so on occasions when adults are not present. Santangelo and McCartney (1980) report that the access patterns for alcohol are very similar between the three counties. The most important source for obtaining alcohol is "an acquaintance would get it for me." The next most likely source is "a friend would give it to me" or "I'd buy it myself." Again, there is little variation between counties. The only exception is that a slightly higher proportion checked "from home" in Pima County, where availability is high. This is consistent with adult drinking patterns in that region and the higher prevalence of adults being present in teenage drinking contexts.

An examination of sex differences reveals some expected results. The abstinence rates are higher for girls than boys in all three counties (Table 2) and slightly higher proportions of boys than girls drink at teenage parties when adults are not present. There is little difference between boys and girls in the proportion who drink in adult settings, but the proportion of boys is slightly higher than for girls when the drinking context is in cars or "out-of-doors." There is little variation between the sexes in public settings such as bars and restaurants. The only exception is a higher proportion of girls (28%) than boys (19%) in Pima County. This may reflect more a restaurant activity than actual bar patronage. Except for differences in abstinence rates, there are more similarities than differences in the drinking contexts of boys and girls in the three counties.

SITUATIONAL FACTORS IN ADOLESCENT DRINKING CONTEXTS

The studies reviewed in the earlier sections of this chapter clearly indicate that the presence and absence of parents and other adults is a critical dimension in teenage drinking behavior. The results suggest that the absence of adults in drinking settings is related to higher consumption levels and problems associated with alcohol.

Although drinking "in cars" has been identified as a context at risk for youth (Babor & Berglas, 1981; Smart *et al.,* 1978), drinking at parties with peers when adults are not present is also implicated in higher levels of alcohol consumption. As indicated in Table 1, this context represents the most prevalent context among youth aged 13 to 18 years.

Teenage parties, however, vary considerably with respect to several dimensions—the composition of the drinking group, the physical location of the parties, and the access to alcohol. In order to examine this context in more detail, data were obtained from the 1980 Gallup Youth Survey. The Gallup Youth Survey is conducted by telephone on a periodic basis among a representative sample of 1,000 teenagers, aged 13 to 18 years, living in private households in the United States and excluding institutions and military bases. The 1980 survey included 1,003 teenagers who were interviewed by telephone in April 1980. Of the total sample, 599 reported drinking alcohol once a year or more (60%), 98 reported drinking less than once a year (10%), 291 reported no drinking at all (29%), and data were not obtained for 15 respondents (1%). The data to be reported in this section draw on the total sample regardless of drinker status.

Information was obtained on the frequency of party attendance for parties when parents are present and when they are absent, whether alcohol is served or not, and whether the respondents drink on these occasions. Table 5 examines the frequency of party attendance by type of party, sex, and age for the total sample of 1,003 teenagers.

Among boys, a majority attend parties when adults are present (69%) more than once a year. Thirty-eight percent attend once a month or more frequently. A similar proportion (62%) attends parties when adults are not present more than once a year. Among girls, 69% attend parties more than once a year when adults are present but slightly lower proportions attend parties when adults are not present (53%).

Among boys the frequency of party attendance increases with age. For parties where adults are present, the proportion who report attending this context once a month or more increases from 27% at age 13 to 46% at age 18 years. A similar pattern occurs for boys at parties when adults are not present, increasing from 13% among 13-year-olds to 64% among 18-year-olds. Age interacts with type of party. Slightly higher proportions of younger boys attend parties when parents are present and much higher proportions of older boys attend parties when parents are not present.

Among girls, age interacts more dramatically with type of party. The frequency of party attendance when adults are present decreases with increasing age, while the frequency of party attendance when adults are not present increases with increasing age.

The comparison between the sexes underscores the interaction of age by type of party. At parties when adults are present, younger girls (13 to 16) report higher proportions of frequent attendance (once a month or more) than is the case for boys age 13 to 16. Among older teenagers (17 to 18) the proportion of boys at these parties is higher than for girls age 17 to 18 years.

Comparisons between boys and girls at parties when adults are not present reveals higher proportions of older boys (17 to 18) than girls (17 to 18). The proportions of the other age groups (13 to 16) are similar for boys and girls. The only exception is among 13-year-old girls who report higher frequencies than 13-year-old boys. This may reflect the fact that the majority of parties are of mixed sex and thereby indicate different social networks

Table 5.

Distribution of Party Frequency in a Sample of Teenagers by Type of Party, Age, and Sex

	Parents are present (percentage)							Parents are not present (percentage)						
Age	13	14	15	16	17	18	Total	13	14	15	16	17	18	Total
Boys														
Once a month or more	27	34	38	32	48	46	38	13	32	35	44	57	64	42
More than once a year	36	34	32	32	27	29	31	20	21	13	24	20	19	20
Once a year or less	35	30	27	32	17	21	27	52	40	40	30	16	14	31
Total N	75	73	82	97	86	90	503	75	73	82	97	86	90	503
Girls														
Once a month or more	42	49	32	42	30	36	38	24	21	33	44	39	50	35
More than once a year	35	30	30	26	35	29	31	13	12	19	21	22	23	18
Once a year or less	18	18	32	27	24	24	24	37	53	37	28	30	16	33
Total N	78	78	89	86	83	86	500	78	78	89	86	83	86	500

of access to parties among the sexes. Santangelo and McCartney (1980) report that the predominant context among teenagers is mixed-sex companions rather than members of the same sex.

These data serve to provide a normative framework for the study of drinking behavior among teenagers. In general, there is more frequent exposure to parties with increasing age, especially in contexts in which parents and adults are not present. This reflects the normative development of youth and movement away from parental objects and into the world of peers. As noted earlier, the absence of parental and adult controls on these occasions are associated with higher risks of negative consequences with respect to alcohol use. Before examining this issue, it is necessary to consider the other component in such behavior, namely, the availability of alcohol.

For each of the two party-context items, respondents were asked to indicate whether or not alcohol was served at these parties. Table 6 presents the distribution for this question by type of party, age, and sex.

Among boys, a slightly higher proportion of respondents indicated that alcohol was more likely to be served at parties when adults were not present (51%) than when they were (46%). A similar pattern occurs among girls. Alcohol was more likely to be served when adults were not present (49%) than when they were present (39%). Comparisons between boys and girls reveal that alcohol is less likely to be served for girls and boys when adults are present, though the differences are not large. There is little difference between the sexes when adults are not present. Among both sexes and for both types of parties, the probability of alcohol being served increases with increasing age.

Among younger boys (13 to 15) the proportions who report that alcohol is served are similar whether parents are present or not. Thereafter, among older boys, the proportions who report alcohol is served are higher when adults are not present. However, even in the case of contexts in which adults are present, the probability of alcohol being served is high. Among girls, the proportions who report that alcohol is served is consistently higher when adults are not present, except at age 13, and increases consistently with increasing age. The comparison between the sexes indicates that when parents are present, slightly higher proportions of boys compared to girls report that alcohol is served. These differences are less pronounced for parties when adults are not present.

These data, in contrast to the frequency of party behaviors, reveal more similarities between the sexes than differences. Although the social networks leading to exposure to party contexts may differ for boys and girls, the probability of alcohol being served by type of context is more similar. Since the majority of teenage contexts involve opposite-sex composition, the absence of sex differences in the probability of alcohol being

Table 6.

Presence/Absence of Alcohol in a Sample of Teenagers by Type of Party, Age and Sex

		Parents are present (percentage)							Parents are not present (percentage)						
Age	13	14	15	16	17	18	Total	13	14	15	16	17	18	Total
Boys														
Alcohol served														
Yes	21	22	37	46	57	82	46	15	32	38	58	65	87	51
No	72	74	54	49	41	13	49	63	62	45	38	21	12	39
Do not know	7	4	9	5	2	5	5	21	6	16	3	14	1	10
Total N	75	73	82	97	86	90	503	75	73	82	97	86	90	503
Girls														
Alcohol served														
Yes	10	19	37	53	49	61	39	9	28	48	66	64	71	49
No	83	71	56	38	42	31	53	76	58	43	24	27	20	40
Do not know	7	10	7	8	8	8	7	15	13	8	9	9	9	10
Total N	78	78	89	86	83	86	500	78	78	89	86	83	86	500

served is not unexpected. In view of the mixed-sex composition for these contexts, the variables affecting the presence of alcohol would be similar for boys and girls.

Despite the fact that variables relating to the presence of alcohol in party contexts would be similarly distributed for boys and girls, one might expect differences in whether or not alcohol actually is consumed on these occasions. Table 7 reproduces the total percentages from Table 5 and provides a breakdown of those respondents who drink.

Among boys at parties when adults are present, 49% indicated that alcohol was not served. Of the 46% who reported it was served, 30% drank and 16% did not. When this distribution was compared to parties when adults are not present, 38% indicated that alcohol was not served, and of the 39% who indicated it was served, 38% drank. In summary, alcohol is more likely to be served and consumed at parties in which adults are not present. The differences, however, are not that dramatic. It seems that even at parties when adults are present, if alcohol is served, it is likely to be consumed. This is better illustrated by the subpercentages for boys at parties when alcohol is served. Of these, 64% drank when adults are present and 75% drank when adults are not present. The presence or absence of parents and adults is not a critical factor in the decision to drink at parties. Unfortunately, data on amount of consumption was not obtained and the adult dimension may be more significantly implicated in amount of consumption.

Among girls at parties when adults are present, 53% indicated that alcohol was not served. Of the 39% who reported it was served, 22% drank and 17% did not. When this distribution is compared to parties at which adults are not present, 41% indicated that alcohol was not served and of the 48% who indicated that it was served, 30% drank. As was the case for boys, the absence of adults yielded slightly higher proportions of drinkers. Among girls who reported that alcohol was served, 57% drank at parties when adults were present and 62% drank when adults were not present.

With increasing age, there is increased exposure to settings in which alcohol is present and, as has been shown, its presence on these occasions is highly related to its being consumed by youth, even when parents and other adults are present. Further work needs to be directed at some of the situational variables that relate to drinking levels on these occasions and to identify the major antecedent variables relating to the frequency of exposure to these contexts.

DEVELOPMENTAL TRENDS IN COLLEGE DRINKING CONTEXTS

This section presents data from a survey of New England college students (Wechsler & McFadden, 1979). The survey draws on a sample of

Table 7.

Distribution of Teenagers by Alcohol Served, Alcohol Consumed, Type of Party, and Sex

Alcohol served	No	Do not know	Yes			Total
Alcohol consumed	n/a	n/a	Yes	No	Do not know	
Boys						
Parents are present						
Total N	245	24	147	79	2	497
Total percentage	49	5	30	16	0	100
Subpercentage			64	36		228
Parents are not present						
Total N	194	50	189	64	0	497
Total percentage	39	10	38	13	0	100
Subpercentage			75	25		253
Girls						
Parents are present						
Total N	262	36	110	82	1	491
Total percentage	53	7	22	17	0	99
Subpercentage			57	43		193
Parents are not present						
Total N	200	51	148	89	3	491
Total percentage	41	10	30	18	1	100
Subpercentage			62	38		240

students attending four-year colleges in the New England area. A random sample of full-time undergraduates was selected at each of the 34 colleges participating in the study. The final sample consisted of 10,500 students. Questionnaires were sent out by mail in the spring of 1977 and follow-up mailings were sent to nonresponders. Questionnaires were returned by 7,170 students in response to the initial and first follow-up mailing. There are several reasons for addressing this group in particular. First, they represent a group of young adults characterized by a high prevalence of drinking. Second, they define a group of younger adult drinkers in which the continuity from high school to young adulthood is not interrupted. And third, the four years of college experience provide an encapsulated period of development in which alcohol consumption patterns change.

In developing a drinking typology among the college students, Wechsler and McFadden (1979) noted that frequent light drinking increased with years in school for both men and women whereas frequent heavy drinking decreased with years in school for women, but not for men. In this regard it is instructive to examine the contextual drinking patterns of these students with special attention to their variation with year in school.

Table 8 summarizes the distribution of drinking context frequency by type of companion and settings. As was the case in the national school survey, these items do not assess the frequency with which students drink in these settings. Rather, they define what proportions of students drink in different settings. Inspection of the distributions for companion status indicates that for both men and women drinking among college students is primarily a social activity. Few report drinking alone, though 33% of the men and 21% of the women report drinking alone once in a while. Among men, the majority report drinking most of the time or some of the time in group settings and some of the time in dyads. Among women, the majority report drinking most of the time in mixed-sex groups and in dyads with a member of the opposite sex. Women, it would appear, are more likely then men to drink with members of the opposite sex. This finding has been reported for adult drinkers as well (Harford, 1978).

Examination of the distributions of setting indicates that the most popular settings for both men and women are nightclubs and bars. Among men, dormitories and their own apartments attract the next higher proportions. Among women, dormitories and restaurants are the next most popular settings in terms of number of drinkers. Both men and women, however, report drinking at least some of the time in all of the settings included in the questionnaire. Less frequented contexts among men and women include drinking at home with parents, at special events such as concerts and athletic events, and in out-of-doors settings.

Table 9 summarizes the distributions of students who report drinking

Table 8.

Distribution of the Frequency of Drinking Contexts in a Sample of College Students (2,997 men and 3,649 women) by Sex, in Percentage

Drinking contexts	Men				Women			
	Most of the time	Some of the time	Once in a while	Never	Most of the time	Some of the time	Once in a while	Never
Companions								
Alone	1.5	6.5	32.8	59.2	0.7	3.2	21.1	75.0
One person, same sex	8.0	36.0	45.8	10.2	4.7	24.4	52.3	18.6
One person, opposite sex	9.8	40.5	39.1	10.6	19.0	38.6	34.0	8.4
Small group, same sex	21.2	38.8	28.7	11.2	10.2	27.3	38.9	23.6
Small group, mixed sex	21.7	47.4	26.6	4.3	28.3	41.3	26.7	3.7
Large, mixed group	17.2	38.0	36.5	8.3	20.7	32.9	36.3	10.2
Setting								
Dormitories	15.4	26.8	29.4	28.4	12.0	25.5	31.6	30.9
Own apartment	10.6	25.4	40.4	23.6	8.3	22.6	41.5	27.6
Friend's apartment	5.2	32.3	48.8	13.6	6.9	30.9	47.8	14.4
Nightclubs and bars	29.3	37.5	27.5	5.7	33.8	33.5	25.5	7.3
Restaurants	6.5	28.1	52.4	13.0	11.7	37.9	43.3	7.0
At home with parents	2.6	17.2	51.5	28.7	4.6	21.0	48.9	25.5
Special events	7.6	20.0	37.6	34.8	2.6	11.2	31.8	54.5
Out-of-doors	2.9	16.0	42.6	38.5	1.3	7.7	32.0	59.1

Table 9.
Distribution of Drinking Contexts in a Sample of College Students
(2,997 men and 3,649 women) by Year in School and Sex, in Percentage[a]

Drinking contexts	Men				Women			
	Freshman	Sophomore	Junior	Senior	Freshman	Sophomore	Junior	Senior
Companions								
Alone	4.6	8.7	8.1	10.3	2.8	3.4	4.0	5.3
One person, same sex	37.3	43.4	44.6	50.1	26.8	29.0	27.8	32.9
One person, opposite sex	40.6	47.2	53.1	59.2	51.2	55.9	61.9	62.2
Small group, same sex	62.0	60.5	57.6	60.1	43.0	36.2	35.4	34.7
Small group, mixed sex	69.8	68.5	68.2	69.9	72.6	69.1	68.7	67.4
Large, mixed group	58.3	59.2	51.7	52.1	60.0	54.6	47.6	50.9
Setting								
Dormitories	50.9	47.3	38.9	32.8	43.0	42.1	34.8	29.2
Own apartment	22.5	30.4	40.3	49.7	20.2	27.7	34.7	42.4
Friend's apartment	32.5	30.0	40.8	45.6	32.7	35.9	37.8	45.4
Nightclubs and bars	64.7	65.6	67.5	69.0	68.6	70.4	64.9	64.7
Restaurants	29.5	33.5	37.4	37.7	45.9	50.9	50.6	51.8
At home with parents	17.5	18.4	22.0	21.1	24.1	24.4	27.5	26.6
Special events	33.3	27.1	25.0	25.4	20.2	14.1	10.7	9.0
Out-of-doors	21.9	17.3	19.4	17.2	12.0	9.7	5.9	7.7
Total sample	745	711	718	823	944	903	855	897

[a]For students who report drinking most of the time or some of the time in specific contexts.

most of the time or some of the time in drinking contexts by year in school. Among men there are consistent increases in the proportions who report drinking in dyadic contexts with increasing year of school. Drinking in small group settings, both same and mixed sex, remains stable over the four years of school and there is a slight decline among the upper classes in terms of proportions who report drinking in large mixed-sex groups. There is a slight increase with year in school in proportions reporting drinking alone.

Among women, there is a consistent increase with each year of school in the proportions who report drinking in opposite sex-dyads. There are also slight increases in same-sex dyads and drinking alone. In contrast to men, the proportions of women who report drinking in group settings decreases with year in school.

It is clear in these data that college students experience changes in the drinking settings defined by companion status. Although these trends undoubtedly reflect changes in social networks and friendship patterns, the antecedents and specific correlates of these changes need to be examined. The contextual trends in companion status, however, do suggest a transition from group setting to more intimate relations with one other person and to solitary drinking. These trends are suggestive of more general patterns of social change during the college years and may reflect the transition from large networks of contacts during the earlier years of college to greater selectivity and intimacy in choice of friends in the later years of college, years preparatory to the transition to adult society.

How might these contextual trends relate to changes in drinking behaviors? Harford, Weschler, and Rohman (1981) examined the relationship between typical companion status and level of alcohol consumption among New England college students. Typical companion status was related to the average number of drinks consumed. Average consumption was lower in dyads than in groups, but small and large groups did not differ. Among men and women, the presence of members of the opposite sex in both small groups and dyads was related to lower average consumption.

These results yielded significant relationships between social contexts of drinking and amount of consumption among college students. The findings are consistent with other studies that have reported consumption to be higher among groups than dyads or solitary drinkers. The findings also extended previous studies, which were restricted to bars and taverns, in that the relationship between typical companions and consumption was similar for each of three locations (dormitories, apartments, and bars) despite differences in average consumption between locations.

Based on this evidence, the correlation or association between drinking contexts and alcohol consumption becomes more apparent, particularly among women. It will be recalled that Wechsler and McFadden (1979) reported that frequent light drinking increased with year in school while frequent heavy drinking decreased. This is very consistent with the changes in companion status during the college years in which dyadic settings increased in frequency, while group settings decreased. Among men, the increase in the proportions who report dyadic settings is also consistent with the increase in frequent light drinking cited by Wechsler and McFadden (1979). The association between level of consumption and group size supports this interpretation. It is not clear as to the direction of influence. A contextual hypothesis would indicate that shifts in drinking contexts reflect the broader influences of the college experience and that the shifts in contexts relate to changes in the level of alcohol consumption. Alternatively, individual experience with alcohol may determine the selection of settings in which to drink, with the heavier drinkers preferring the company of groups and lighter drinkers preferring the quiet intimacy of dyads. The nature of this person–situation interaction needs to be studied in a longitudinal design.

The second part of Table 9 examines the distributions of locations by year in school. Among men, there are consistent decreases with year in school in the proportions who report drinking in dormitories, at special events, and in out-of-doors settings. Wechsler and Rohman (1981) have shown that these settings are more likely to be populated by the heavier drinking male students. The trends for decreased frequency in these heavier drinking contexts, however, are offset by the slight increase in bar patronage, which attracts the highest proportion of male students. There is ample evidence in the literature that these settings are associated with heavier levels of alcohol consumption and also attract the heavier drinkers in the drinking population. This contextual trend is congruent with the fact that frequent heavy drinking tends to remain stable during the college years among men (Wechsler & McFadden, 1979).

Among men, there are consistent increases with year in school in the proportions who report drinking in apartments (friends' and own) and in restaurants. These trends are consistent with the increase in dyadic settings and with the reported increases in patterns of frequent light drinking during the college years. Apartments and restaurants tend to be settings associated with lower levels of alcohol consumption or settings that attract lighter drinkers.

Among women, the context trends with respect to location are entirely consistent with those of men. There are consistent decreases with year in school in the proportions who report drinking in dormitories, at special events, and out-of-doors. There is a slight decline in the frequency of bar patronage but this context attracts the largest proportion of female students. There are consistent increases with year in school in the proportions who report drinking in apartments and restaurants. As with the men, these contextual changes during the college years are compatible with changes in drinking patterns.

To summarize, during the college years frequent light drinking increased for both sexes and frequent heavy drinking decreased among women. These trends are compatible with shifts in drinking contexts, contexts which have been related to differential levels of alcohol consumption. The major distinctions between men and women appear to be that among men heavier drinking settings (particularly groups and bars) tend to be retained during the college years while other lighter drinking settings (restaurants, dyads, apartments) are incorporated into the larger variety of context repertoire. Among women, heavier drinking contexts tend to be replaced with lighter drinking contexts during the college years.

SITUATIONAL FACTORS IN ADULT DRINKING CONTEXTS

The previous sections of this paper have focused on drinking patterns and contextual aspects of drinking during the adolescent years of development. This emphasis is related to the fact that these formative years, both with respect to psychosocial developmental processes and with the onset of drinking, are of critical importance in generating sound empirical basis for the formation of preventive strategies. Within this framework it is only logical that the period of development be extended into the adult period and even through the stages of the aging process.

In a previous paper, Harford (1979b) examined the distribution of a contextual typology of drinking events in an adult sample from metropolitan Boston. Two major trends emerged from this analysis with respect to age-related drinking contexts. First, drinking in contexts of shorter duration (one hour or less), in private settings, with two or fewer relatives present, on both weekdays and weekends, increased with age. Second, the frequency of drinking in settings of longer durations (more than one hour) with three or more friends decreased with age. These two trends are suggestive of the types of occasions that characterize adults on either end of the age spectrum. Among young adults, drinking contexts are difficult to typologize since young adults drink in a variety of settings, a heterogeneity that reflects and extends the experiences with alcohol during the senior high school years. These drinking patterns and contexts reflect the formative processes of changing and developing social networks, career opportunities, and mate selection. In sharp contrast, elderly adults tend to drink in relatively few contexts.

Although there is a certain amount of arbitrariness in contrasting developmental processes in different age groups, the trends are instructive with respect to drinking structures. They command a broader perspective for interpretation and one that removes some of the mystery from the addiction process. That is, the shifts in drinking patterns and in the circumstances of drinking with increasing age are part of the normative structure of society and are reflective of deeper movements in the stream of social change and development. Such a normative perspective is essential in defining deviant patterns and focusing attention on their antecedents.

In view of the findings from several national surveys that average consumption per occasion tends to decrease with increasing age, it is tempting to ascribe a causal relationship to the association between the reduction in average consumption with increasing age and the contextual age differentiations described above for adult drinkers. That is, changing social networks, occupational conditions, and patterns of residence may serve to circumscribe or narrow the range of settings in which older adults drink, settings that are conducive to lower levels of alcohol consumption.

Studies of adult contexts of drinking also provide another perspective. The study of contextual drinking trends in adolescence when compared to those of the adult years provides a conceptual bridge to the drinking contexts of adults. With the exception of a small proportion of teenage drinkers, the majority are initiated into the use of alcohol in the home setting with parents and other adults present. During the course of adolescent development, it was shown that there is more frequent exposure to away-from-home settings in which peers occupy a more prominent role. These trends, it was noted, are accompanied by increased levels of alcohol consumption. The heterogeneity of drinking contexts among younger adults serves to expose the continuity of drinking between these periods. On a broader developmental level, these trends suggest a curvilinear relationship between age and context. The onset of drinking begins at home with family members, extends to away-from-home settings with peers and friends, and returns, in the later years, to the home setting.

SUMMARY AND CONCLUSIONS

This chapter has reviewed the developmental nature of drinking contexts among adolescents and adults. It was shown initially that a range of environmental variables, including parental and peer models, perceived access to alcohol, and type of drinking situation related significantly to selected drinking measures. Of the environmental variables selected for analysis, the frequency of drinking in certain contexts was the most powerful predictor of drinking amounts and frequency of times drunk. Jessor and

Jessor (1977) organized the environment on a distal-proximal dimension and reported that the more proximal features of the perceived environment are more powerful predictors of behavior in general. The fact that drinking behavior varies by type of drinking contexts comes as no surprise. The type of drinking context serves as an indicator of those situational variables that are significantly associated with variations in drinking levels. Although research in this area is fairly recent, studies indicate that the presence/absence of parents and other adults is one strong dimension in these settings.

Data from the 1974 national school survey were presented in order to assess the frequency of drinking in selected contexts and the variation by year in school (age). It was found that there was a slight decrease with increasing age in the frequency of drinking in supervised contexts. Non-supervised contexts were shown to increase with increasing age. These results place in sharp focus some developmental trends among youthful drinkers.

In general, there was more frequent exposure to parties with increasing age, especially in contexts in which parents and other adults were not present. These age trends in party behavior provide a broader orientation to the behavior of adolescents during this phase of social development. The consumption of alcohol in such circumstances must be viewed as part of the broader social behavior characteristic of adolescent growth and its societal contexts. With increasing age, there is increased exposure to settings in which alcohol is present and its presence is strongly related to its being consumed, even when parents are present.

It was shown that the frequency of drinking in supervised contexts varied directly with the level of alcohol availability. There was little variation across counties, however, with respect to the frequency of drinking in nonsupervised peer parties. Nonsupervised, more secretive, or seclusive contexts, were inversely related to the level of alcohol availability. These data, of course, do not necessarily implicate the level of availability as the causal factor. The counties differed considerably with respect to ecological and normative structures. The fact that adolescents maintain access to alcohol despite the presence of these structures and that the level of availability influences, in part, access to different contexts needs to be emphasized for the conduct of subsequent studies.

The examination of the contextual drinking patterns among adults serves to reinforce the continuity between adolescence and adulthood drinking practices and the fact of the influence of general life-style variables on drinking behaviors. This was illustrated in greater detail with the change in drinking contexts during the college years. It was noted that the four years of college were associated with changes in both the location of drinking and in the type of drinking companions. Although these trends were not directly related to drinking practices, the associations noted are consistent with other studies that have related contextual variables to the amount of consumption. These surveys reported in this chapter were based on cross-sectional studies of independent samples of youth and adults. A discussion of these findings within a longitudinal perspective has obvious limitations and constitutes only a partial view of development. The findings, however, offer some empirical guidelines that future longitudinal studies can address.

The identification of relevant drinking contexts yield two areas of needed inquiry in subsequent studies. The first relates to the identification of relevant structural variables in the drinking settings that initiate and maintain variations in drinking levels and consequences associated with drinking. Thus far, the focus has been on the presence and absence of adult models in these settings. Other structures that may make independent contributions may include the age and sex composition of participants in the setting, the formality or spontaneity of the occasion, the physical location, and the network of access to alcohol, to mention a few. It should be obvious that a determination of the relevant structures in the drinking setting that relate to consumption level and negative consequences would better inform intervention strategies.

The second agenda for subsequent study relates to the antecedent networks of access to these contexts. This area would include both an identification of the types of drinkers who seek out certain settings (demographic status and personality factors) as well as a broader range of environmental variables. It is clear from the results of several studies that adult drinking practices correlate with adolescent drinking practices, generally speaking, and that the overall level of alcohol availability also relates to the drinking practices of both adults and adolescents.

ACKNOWLEDGMENTS

I would like to thank Cherry Lowman, Danielle Spiegler, and Jeanette Bell for their help in the preparation of this chapter.

REFERENCES

Babor, T. F., & Berglas, S. Toward a system-ecological primary approach to the prevention of adolescent alcohol abuse. *Journal of Prevention*, 1981, *2*, 25–39.
Blane, H. T., & Hewitt, L. E. Alcohol and youth: An analysis of the literature 1960–75. Final report submitted to the National Institute on Alcohol Abuse and Alcoholism, Contract NO. (ADM) 281–75–0026, 1977.
Bruun, K., & Hauge, R. *Drinking habits among northern youth*. Helsinki: Finnish Foundation for Alcohol Studies, 1963.

Cahalan, D., Cisin, I. H., & Crossley, H. M. *American drinking practices.* New Brunswick, N. J.: Rutgers Center for Alcohol Studies, 1969.

Coleman, J. *The adolescent society.* New York: Free Press, 1961.

Davies, J., & Stacey, B. *Teenagers and alcohol* (Vol. 2). London: Her Majesty's Stationery Office, 1972.

Donovan, J. E., & Jessor, R. Adolescent problem drinking: Psychosocial correlates in a national sample study. *Journal of Studies on Alcohol,* 1978, *39,* 1506–1524.

Gallup Youth Survey. N. J.: Gallup Organization, 1980.

Globetti, G. The use of alcohol among high school students in an abstinence setting. *Pacific Sociological Review,* 1969, *12,* 105–108.

Globetti, G. Problem and non-problem drinking among high school students in abstinence communities. *The International Journal of the Addictions,* 1972, *7,* 511–523.

Globetti, G. Teenage drinking in a community characterized by prohibition norms. *British Journal of Addiction,* 1973, *68,* 275–279.

Globetti, G., Harrison, D. E., & Oetinger, G. Sociology Anthropology Series, No. 10. State College, Miss.: Mississippi State University, 1967.

Harford, T. C. Contextual drinking patterns among men and women. In F. A. Sexias (Ed.), *Currents in alcoholism* (Vol. 4). New York: Grune & Stratton, 1978.

Harford, T. C. The social contexts of alcohol consumption. In P. Avogaro, C. R. Sirtori, & E. Tremoli (Eds.), *Metabolic effects of alcohol.* Amsterdam: Elsevier/North-Holland Biomedical Press, 1979. (a)

Harford, T. C. Ecological factors in drinking. In H. T. Blane & M. E. Chafetz (Eds.), *Youth, alcohol and society.* New York: Plenum Press, 1979. (b)

Harford, T. C., & Spiegler, D. L. *Environmental influences in adolescent drinking. Alcohol and Health Monograph 4. Special Population Issues.* DHSS Publication No. (ADM) 82–1193, 1982, 167–193.

Harford, T. C., & Spiegler, D. L. Developmental trends of adolescent drinking. *Journal of Studies on Alcohol,* in press.

Harford, T. C., Parker, D. A., & Light, L. (Eds.). *Normative approaches to the prevention of alcohol abuse and alcoholism.* Washington, D. C.: Research Monograph No. 3, DHEW No. (ADM) 79–847, 1980.

Harford, T. C., Wechsler, H., & Rohman, M. Contextual drinking patterns of college students: The relationship between typical companion status and consumption level. In M. Galanter (Ed.), *Currents in alcoholism* (Vol. 7). New York: Grune & Stratton, 1981.

Harford, T. C., Zucker, R. A., & O'Leary, J. *The 1980 Gallup Youth Survey: Age specific frequency of party attendance.* Unpublished paper, 1981.

Jessor, R., Collins, M. J., & Jessor, S. L. On becoming a drinker: Social-psychological aspects of an adolescent transition. In F. E. Seixas (Ed.), *Nature and nurture in alcoholism. Annals of New York Academy of Science,* 1972, *197,* 199–213.

Jessor, R., & Jessor, S. L. *Problem behavior and psychosocial development: A longitudinal study of youth.* New York: Academic Press, 1977.

Lolli, G., Serianni, E., Golder, G. M., & Luzzatto-Fegiz, P. *Alcohol in Italian culture: Food and wine in relation to sobriety among Italians and Italian-Americans.* New Brunswick, N.J.: Monograph of the Rutgers Center of Alcohol Studies, 1958.

Maddox, G. L., & McCall, B. C. *Drinking among teenagers: A sociological interpretation of alcohol use by high school students.* New Brunswick, N.J.: Rutgers Center for Alcohol Studies, 1964.

Maisto, S. A., & Rachal, J. V. Indications of the relationship between adolescent drinking practices, related behaviors, and drinking age laws. In H. Wechsler (Ed.), *Minimum-drinking-age laws.* Lexington, Mass.: Lexington Books, 1980.

Margulies, R. Z., Kessler, R. C., & Kandel, D. B. A longitudinal study of onset of drinking among high-school students. *Journal of Studies on Alcohol,* 1977, *38,* 897–912.

Prendergast, T. J., Jr., & Schaefer, E. S. Correlates of drinking and drunkenness among high school students. *Quarterly Journal of Studies on Alcohol,* 1974, *35,* 232–242.

Rachal, J. V., Maisto, S. A., Guess, L. L., & Hubbard, R. L. *A National study of adolescent drinking behavior—1978.* Final Report prepared for the National Institute on Alcohol Abuse and Alcoholism under Contract No. (ADM) 281–76–0019. Research Triangle Park, N.C.: Research Triangle Institute, 1980.

Rachal, J. V., Williams, J. R., Brehm, M. L., Cavanaugh, B., Moore, R. P., & Eckerman, W. C. *A national study of adolescent drinking behavior, attitudes, and correlates.* Final report prepared for National Institute on Alcohol Abuse and Alcoholism under Contract No. (ADM) 281–76–0019 Research Triangle Park, N.C.: Research Triangle Institute, 1975.

Santangelo, N., & McCartney, D. *A tri-community study of adolescent drinking.* Final report prepared for National Institute on Alcohol Abuse and Alcoholism under Contract ADM–281–77–0020. Pittsburgh, Pa.: Consad Research Corp., 1980.

Smart, R. G., Gray, G., & Bennett, C. Predictors of drinking and signs of heavy drinking among high school students. *The International Journal of the Addictions,* 1978, *13,* 1079–1094.

Sower, C. Teen-age drinking as group behavior. *Quarterly Journal of Studies on Alcohol,* 1959, *20,* 655–668.

Stacey, B., & Davies, J. Drinking behavior in childhood and adolescence: An evaluative review. *British Journal of Addiction,* 1970, *65,* 203–212.

Wechsler, H., & McFadden, M. Drinking among college students in New England: Extent, social correlates and consequences of alcohol use. *Journal of Studies on Alcohol,* 1979, *40,* 969–996.

Wechsler, H., & Rochman, M. Extensive use of alcohol among college students. *Journal of Studies on Alcohol,* 1981, *42,* 149–155.

Wechsler, H., & Thum, D. Teenage drinking, drug use, and social correlates. *Quarterly Journal of Studies of Studies on Alcohol,* 1973, *34,* 1220–1227.

Windham, G. O., Preston, J. D., & Armstrong, H. B. High school students in Mississippi and beverage alcohol. *Journal of Alcohol Education,* 1967, *13,* 1–12.

III

Approaches to Prevention

There are four major approaches toward alcohol abuse prevention. First, legislative rules and regulations can be established to outlaw alcohol use totally (i.e., prohibition) or, at least, to limit its use. Second, alcohol education can be used to change knowledge, attitudes, and behavior in a manner that will reduce the future likelihood of alcohol abuse. Third, intervention strategies aimed at the developmental antecedents to alcohol abuse can be implemented. Instead of focusing on alcohol use directly, alcohol misuse is viewed as the ultimate result of problems in a person's life history (e.g., inadequate parent–child relationship, broken homes, poor peer models). It is assumed, therefore, that prevention should be directed to these early experiences. Fourth, no intervention may be better than some intervention. That is, if one ignores the problem of alcohol abuse, the problem may eventually disappear. Proponents of this approach suggest that by placing restrictions on the use of alcohol or paying attention to alcohol through education, alcohol will derive a "mystic" quality that will actually increase its use. One aspect of this approach has been the "forbidden fruit" hypothesis which suggests an increased use of substances that are prohibited; for example, individuals under the legal drinking age may drink abusively simply because they are not allowed to drink. Although highlighting alcohol through education and/or restrictions may lead to increase of alcohol use, prevention through absentia appears to be far too simplistic and naive.

The first chapters of this section contain short reviews of legislative attempts to deal with the problem of alcohol abuse. To provide an understanding of the complex nature of alcohol control policies throughout the world, prominent investigators from several countries summarize the legislative attempts of their governments.

Although the existing programs of these countries differ widely, it is clear that alcohol abuse is a priority national health concern. Moreover, prevention is viewed as a viable solution. Legislative rules and regulations are clearly not always directed toward prevention. Historically, such legislation has attempted (1) to establish a social morality for drinking; (2) to protect the community from alcohol abusers; (3) to protect alcohol abusers from themselves; and (4) to establish a source of government income in the form of taxation. Only during the past 20 years have legislative attempts been formally used as a preventive tool.

In terms of prevention, alcohol legislation involves either efforts to limit the availability of alcohol or criminalization and punishment of alcohol-related behaviors. Efforts to limit availability include (1) prohibition; (2) limits on alcohol importation; (3) price setting and taxation; (4) restricting sales to certain segments of the population (e.g., individuals under the legal drinking age, intoxicated patrons); (5) advertising bans; (6) alcohol content limits; and (7) controls on alcohol sales establishments, such as licensing of alcohol beverage businesses, guidelines on the location, number and types of alcohol sale outlets, hours of liquor sales, and availability of food at sale outlets. If efforts to reduce availability fail, the alcohol abuser is also faced with the threat of negative consequences outlined in various international, national, and local criminal codes. The criminal statutes range in severity from minor reprimands for public drunk offenses to possible execution for vehicular homicide while under the influence of alcohol.

Legislative efforts to prevent alcohol abuse are complex and difficult to evaluate. These efforts also interact with national and international policy. For instance, Amechi Anumonye notes that international trade agreements (i.e., guaranteeing free trade) not only restrict prevention attempts (limits on importation) but in fact sustain and potentiate alcohol abuse in African countries. In addition, a tightening of a regulation may lead to a concomitant change in another variable that will ultimately reduce the intended effect of the regulation. For instance, as Igor Sytinsky, Gunnar Götestam, and Ola Röstum separately note, attempts to reduce availability through price increases and/or taxation lead to illegal importation and increased home distillation. Unless such variables are addressed, the effect of these legislative attempts is limited.

The two remaining chapters of this section examine educational approaches to prevention. Braucht and Braucht provide a review of educational strategies presented to school-age children. Their review not only pinpoints the significant deficiencies in available research but provides cogent guidelines for future research efforts. They stress the need to extrapolate specific types of educational strategies that are useful with particular segments of the population.

Hewitt and Blane examine the utility of mass media in prevention. Their analysis describes several methodological problems in the current literature and provide useful advice to future investigators. Mass media messages regarding the responsible use of alcohol appear to have minimal impact. However, mass media messages as a starting point followed by community mobilization and interpersonal communication programs regarding alcohol use offer a viable prevention approach. The author's discussion of the utility of mass media messages in terms of market segmentation and audience penetration is also noteworthy.

6A

Alcohol Control Policy in Canada

REGINALD G. SMART

Alcohol controls have been a controversial and rapidly changing aspect of public policy in Canada. In the past, the temperance sentiment was so important in Ontario that elections of government were won or lost because of it. As alcohol policies become liberalized, they also become much less important politically. However, public controversy still surrounds the minimal drinking age, alcohol advertising, and whether beer and wine should be sold in grocery stores. Alcohol control policies are complex in Canada, with laws and regulations varying by province and over time in the same province. This chapter describes the background of controls in Canada, their current status and rationale, and the controversy surrounding them.

ALCOHOL CONTROL IN CANADA: AN OVERVIEW

The constitution in Canada is currently a combination of the new Canadian Constitution and remnants of the British North America Act (B.N.A. Act), which together define the powers of the various levels of government and the courts. The B.N.A. Act of 1867 set out the most important rules for the establishment of institutions and the use of political power in the country, and these have not yet been changed by the new Constitution. It describes the powers held by the federal and provincial governments. Although alcohol control policies, alcohol sales, and alcohol distribution are

REGINALD G. SMART • Addiction Research Foundation, 33 Russell Street, Toronto, Ontario, Canada M5S/ 251.

not specifically mentioned in the Act, it is stated that "in each province the legislature may exclusively make laws in relation to . . . Shop, Saloon, Tavern, Auctioneer, and other licenses . . . [and] . . . generally all matters of a merely local or private nature in the province." Also, trade within provinces is regulated by the provinces themselves. In practice, most aspects of alcohol control policies, such as ages of access to alcohol, numbers and types of outlets, distribution networks, types of beverages, and hours of sale are governed by the provinces.

Limited federal powers control some aspects of how alcoholic beverages are marketed. For example, the federal government controls customs and hence most aspects of importation. It can also tax alcoholic beverages in all provinces. Because broadcasting is federally controlled, the types of alcohol advertisements are limited by federal regulations. Alcohol sales on airplanes, in airports, and to Eskimos and Indians are also federally regulated. Both federal and provincial regulations govern packaging, labeling, and the purity of the ingredients of alcoholic beverages. In practice, however, the alcohol control system is chiefly a provincial one and is seen to be so by citizens and politicians.

Because alcohol control policies are mostly a provincial matter, there is no one unified system of controls. There are 10 provincial systems plus one for the Yukon and another for the North West Territories, or 12 in all, plus many local variations on Indian reservations and in Eskimo communities. There is little effort to harmonize these systems or to provide central control or management. Each is operated independently.

ALCOHOL CONSUMPTION IN CANADA

Per capita, alcohol consumption in Canada increased by about 50% between 1950 and 1975. In 1975 the average consumption was 2.47 gallons of absolute alcohol per person (15 and over). Since 1975 there has been virtually no change in average consumption. Speculations about the reasons for the recent stabilization of consumption include changes in life-style and attitudes, increased prices, concern about alcohol problems, and personal austerity created by the stabilization of real income. Currently, the actual importance of these reasons is unclear.

Alcohol use is not uniform across the country (Addiction Research Foundation, 1978). The highest consumption is in the Yukon and the North West Territories—about twice as high as in New Brunswick. Indians and those living in the north are especially high consumers. Currently, about 80% of the adult population drinks, with higher proportions of drinkers among men, those aged 18 to 55, and those living in large cities. About 50% drink once a week or more and 10% to 15% drink almost daily.

Canada is a predominantly beer- and spirits-drinking country. About 53% of alcohol is consumed as beer with about 38% as spirits and about 9% as wine. Spirits contribute a larger proportion to overall consumption in the provinces of Ontario, Manitoba, Alberta, British Columbia, and the Yukon. Beer predominates in the other provinces. Although wine has made the largest proportionate increase in sales over the past 25 years, it remains a small part of all alcohol sold. Single and Giesbrecht (1979) have estimated that the contribution of home production of beverages results in an underestimation of real consumption by about 4% to 6%. Home production has never been a substantial contributor to consumption in Canada.

CURRENT STATUS OF MAJOR ALCOHOL CONTROLS

In Canada, alcoholic beverages are made available chiefly through government monopoly systems. Each province has a "liquor control" board, commission, or corporation. These boards, or commissions, have virtually total control over what alcoholic beverages can be sold, how and when they are sold, and to whom. They also set prices for alcoholic beverages (along with the federal government) and govern the number of outlets of all types. This differs considerably from some states in the United States and many European countries in which prices and availability are set by market forces rather than government regulation.

Sales Outlets

Various alcohol monopolies exert strong control over the distribution of alcoholic beverages. None of the monopolies actually produces alcoholic beverages of their own. However, some do import them in bulk and rebottle them with their own labels and thus appear to the consumer to be the manufacturer. In fact, all production of alcohol in Canada is in the hands of private companies.

The relative proportions of different types of outlets vary somewhat from one province to another within a rather narrow range. In no province do monopolies operate restaurants or bars, and their retail activities are limited to package stores of different types. The most usual situation is that spirits and wine are sold only through the monopoly's own stores, whereas beer is more freely available. However, in Ontario there are a small number of privately owned wine stores operated by the wineries.

A few provinces allow the sale of alcoholic beverages in grocery stores. Quebec allows the sale of beer and wine in small grocery stores, as well as in the liquor corporation's own stores. Ontario does not technically allow the sale of wine in grocery stores, but a few large stores have small booths for wine sales operated by the wineries themselves. However, wine purchases must be paid for separately and cannot be part of the food sales. Beer is sold in food stores in Newfoundland. No other provinces allow the sale of alcoholic beverages in food stores.

Packaged beer is made available in Canada in a number of ways. Typically, imported beer is available only through monopoly stores. Local beer is sold only through such stores in several Maritime provinces. In Ontario, however, it is sold not only through monopoly stores, but also at breweries and at stores owned by the brewery consortium. Western provinces have sales through board stores but also sales through hotels with off-premise licences. The Canadian drinking public has far better access to beer than to wine or spirits, except perhaps for the Quebec drinker who can purchase beer and wine at grocery stores.

On-premise consumption is allowed at a variety of places, including the following:

1. Taverns, or public houses, or beer parlors typically sell only beer (with or without food). Restrictions have been raised in some provinces to sell wine as well. Western provinces recently have allowed the sale of spirits in these previously "beer only" places.
2. Restaurants can sell alcoholic beverages only with meals. The majority can sell all three types of beverages, but some are limited to beer and wine.
3. Lounges sell all beverages without any food requirement.
4. Clubs may have the right to sell any or all beverages on a permanent basis.
5. For special events, churches, clubs, or other institutions may get licenses to sell beverages, usually only wine or beer, for a particular event (e.g., a wedding or party).

Local option laws in most provinces allow voting on the introduction of different types of outlets. In most parts of Canada such votes have been won by liberal forces and consequently alcoholic beverages are available nearly everywhere. However, some anomalies exist. For example, local option has kept alcoholic beverages from being sold in any form in an area of Toronto, and several communities in the North West Territories have voted to have prohibition introduced (Smart, 1979).

Visitors to Canada usually find availability of alcoholic beverages low compared to most European countries or most parts of the United States and about comparable to most Scandinavian countries.

HOURS OF SALE

The hours of sale in Canada are difficult to summarize. They change frequently. Most package stores are open for business for 8 to 12 hours per day with no sales on Sundays or holidays. On-premise consumption is typically allowed from noon until midnight or 1 A.M., with a break for the dinner hour in some provinces. Formerly, on-premise consumption on Sundays was not generally allowed, but now some provinces allow Sunday drinking especially when a meal is also ordered.

ADVERTISING OF ALCOHOLIC BEVERAGES

There is a wide range of laws and regulations affecting advertising in Canada. Prince Edward Island permits virtually no advertising of any kind while in Saskatchewan and in New Brunswick only public service advertisements in newspapers are allowed. Ontario and Quebec are the most liberal about advertising, but neither allows exterior signs, billboards, or posters. All Canadian provinces have far less alcohol advertising than do European countries and most states in the United States.

The advertising of alcoholic beverages is limited by both federal and provincial regulations. Although federal regulations forbid the advertising of spirits on radio or television, magazine and newspaper advertising is allowed for spirits in several provinces. In most provinces beer and wine can be advertised in any media but wine is not frequently advertised on radio and television because of the high costs. Even where advertising is permitted, there are numerous regulations as to types of advertisements allowed, who can be in them (no children), what they can portray (fun but no problem-solving effect of alcohol), and where they can be presented (e.g., not on children's television programs). Manitoba has recently banned beer advertising in electronic media as did British Columbia, but there seems to have been no effect on sales (Ogborne & Smart, 1980; Smart & Cutler, 1976).

LEGAL DRINKING AGE

The legal drinking age for alcoholic beverages is either 18 (Prince Edward Island, Quebec, Manitoba, Alberta) or more frequently 19. It changed in all areas from 20 or 21 in the period between 1970 and 1975. This was part of a general movement toward lowering and standardizing the age of majority. Recent findings by several provinces that these age reductions led to increases in drinking and drinking problems among young people (Smart & Goodstadt, 1977) have led to debate about the age law in many provincial legislatures. Consequently, Saskatchewan and Ontario increased their drinking ages from 18 to 19 in the late 1970s.

SOME HISTORY AND CURRENT POLICY ISSUES

Alcohol control policies have been public and political issues in Canada. In the early 1900s politicians could not be elected in many areas without a clear temperance plank to their platform. Temperance issues were frequently debated in legislatures. Most provinces voted for prohibition in the early part of the century. The temperance movement seems to have lost its political base and now holds little influence over political life in Canada.

Much of the current availability of alcohol in Canada is recent and follows a change in public attitudes concerning it. Prior to conclusion of World War II, many provinces had no on-premise consumption of spirits in bars or lounges and few restaurants where any alcohol could be purchased. "Beer parlors" and "hotels" were common where only beer was sold, frequently only to men, although some had "women's sections." With the end of the World War II there were many social and attitudinal changes. A clear need was seen by politicians (apparently without actual surveys) for bringing liquor laws into step with more liberal public attitudes. The period from 1948 to 1975 was one in which physical availability of alcohol to Canadians greatly increased. The number of changes is too great to document fully here but the list for Ontario, which is similar to most provinces, includes the following:

> 1948—Drinking in bars—spirits by the drink for the first time
> 1951—Votes of local option nature could be held before a license was issued rather than only afterward
> —Liquor could be consumed in a trailer or tent for the first time
> 1953—Food could be sold in taverns
> 1956—Local option votes were allowed in areas with populations of 50,000 or over
> 1957—Liquor permit books discontinued in favor of permit cards
> 1960—Allowance was made for carrying liquor bottles from the store to a residence
> —Liquor could be given as a gift
> 1962—Liquor permits were discontinued altogether
> —Private clubs could have licenses in otherwise dry areas

—Hours of sale for on-premise consumption were extended up to 12 hours per day

1962—Liquor could be served through room-service in hotels

—Motels and summer resorts were allowed to apply for licenses for the first time

1965—"Wine" could be made from all fruits as well as grapes

—No cancellation of licenses allowed without a hearing

—Right to appeal interdiction proceedings introduced

—Allowed hotels in small towns to apply for licenses

—Allowed sale of liquor on airplanes

—Allowed sale of liquor in theatres

—Allowed opening of public houses between 6:30 and 8:00 P.M.

—Approved open-air drinking on patios, in backyards, etc.

—Allowed drinking in hotel rooms for those who were not actual residents

1969—Introduction of self-service stores

1970—Allowed unsegregated seating of males and females in licensed establishments

—Licenses could be granted to resort centers in dry areas of the provinces

1971—It was no longer necessary to order a meal in order to have a drink in a dining lounge

—Drinking was allowed with meals on Sunday in licensed restaurants

—Relaxed permits for special events, for example, fairs, festivals, winter carnivals, Oktoberfests, etc.

—40 oz. bottles of spirits allowed for sale (26 oz. was the largest before)

—Package stores were allowed to stay open until midnight

—Duty free stores at airports were allowed to sell alcoholic beverages

—Drinking establishments were allowed to open after polls had closed on voting days

1971—Licenses were issued to new premises without a waiting period

—Lowering of the legal drinking age from 21 to 18

1973—Broadening of definitions of recreational facilities and theatres eligible for licenses

—Licenses allowed for canteens on campuses of colleges and universities

1975—Minors could be served alcohol by parents in their own houses

—Opened bottles could be transported to any destination

None of these changes is significant in isolation. However, their combined impact was to change a temperance-oriented, rather dry province into one in which alcohol was readily available and the majority of people were drinking. Similar changes were enacted throughout the country.

At present, availability has stabilized or even slightly decreased in several parts of the country. Two provinces have *increased* the legal drinking age (Ontario in 1979, Saskatchewan in 1976). Several communities in the north have introduced prohibition (Smart, 1979) and others are considering it. Also, some provinces have introduced limited alcohol advertising bans for electronic media. In addition, some provinces (e.g., Ontario and Saskatchewan) recently have strengthened advertising codes to limit "lifestyle" advertisements. Several provinces have debated the issue of introducing wine and beer into grocery stores at the request of local merchants and tourist agencies. In Ontario and Manitoba, however, these plans have been clearly rejected, at least for the present. Overall, there seems to be a tendency for governments to hold physical availability at its present level and in some areas, for example, age laws and advertising, to even decrease it slightly. Whether this tendency can and should continue is a matter for speculation and debate.

REFERENCES

Addiction Research Foundation. Statistical supplement to the annual report, 1977–78. Toronto, 1978.

Ogborne, A. C., & Smart, R. G. Will restrictions on alcohol advertising reduce alcohol consumption? *British Journal of Addiction,* 1980, *75,* 293–296.

Single, E., & Giesbrecht, N. The 16 percent solution and other mysteries concerning the accuracy of alcohol consumption estimates based on sales data. *British Journal of Addiction,* 1979, 165–173.

Smart, R. G. A note on the effects of changes in alcohol control policies in the Canadian North. *Journal of Studies on Alcohol,* 1979, *40,* 908–913.

Smart, R. G., & Cutler, R. E. The alcohol advertising ban in British Columbia: Problems and effects on beverage consumption. *British Journal of Addiction,* 1976, *71,* 13–21.

Smart, R. G., & Goodstadt, M. Effects of reducing the legal alcoholic purchasing age on drinking and drinking problems: A review of empirical studies. *Journal of Studies on Alcohol,* 1977, *38,* 1313–1323.

6B

Alcohol Control Policy in England and Wales

RAYMOND J. HODGSON

Buying and consuming alcohol are certainly influenced by their consequences. Even the chronic drunken offender will moderate his drinking if enough positive incentives are provided (Miller, 1975). Future societies will no doubt attempt to reward sobriety instead of punishing drunkenness by providing inexpensive life, automobile, and health insurance, as well as a range of other benefits to moderate drinkers. Until now, however, most governments have made greater use of penalties and controls. This section, therefore, reviews the restrictive controls that have been or are being imposed in England and Wales. These controls include liquor licensing laws, the drunken offender, drink and driving, fiscal policies, and advertising controls.

HISTORICAL ASSOCIATIONS BETWEEN LICENSING AND CONSUMPTION TRENDS

Britain is, by tradition, a predominantly beer-drinking country. The Celts made and consumed ale prior to the Roman conquest in 55 B.C. and hop-flavored beers date back to the fifteenth century. In those days, it was much safer to drink beer than water and, toward the end of the seventeenth century, most liquid refreshment had a "head" on it. In the 1680s, for

RAYMOND J. HODGSON • Whitchurch Hospital, Whitchurch, Cardiff, CF4 7XB, Wales.

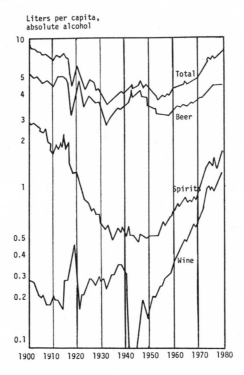

Figure 1. Alcohol consumption by type, 1900–1979 (Office of Health Economics).

example, more than two pints of beer were consumed per person per day; four times the present level (Spring & Buss, 1977). Spirit drinking did not increase until controls on gin sales were relaxed in the 1720s. Thereafter, there was a 14-fold per capita increase in alcohol consumption over a period of 30 years. More restrictive legislation was eventually passed in 1752 and, by the end of the century, the consumption of spirits had gradually declined to about 2 million gallons per annum.

The next major fluctuation occurred early in the nineteenth century, when beer drinking was encouraged as a way of counteracting the consumption of spirits. There was also growing sympathy for the philosophy of free trade and, in 1830, the Beer House Act lifted controls on the licensing of beer sales. The Beer House Act was a disaster and has been called one of the most notable events in the history of licensing (Williams & Brake, 1980). A gradual increase in consumption followed until the Act was revoked in the late 1860s and new licensing laws were passed in 1872 and

1904. Following this restrictive legislation, consumption gradually declined. This trend was enhanced by the licensing and other controls that were imposed during the First World War. During the last 30 years, however, there has been a clear upward trend toward the relatively high consumption levels at the start of the century, as shown in Figure 1. Wine sales in particular are now higher than at any time in the past and still rising steeply. The annual figure for drunkenness arrests rose from 47,717 to 103,203 between 1950 and 1974, with the most dramatic changes being observed in the young (Figure 2). Factors involved in this steep rise in consumption include a reduction in the real price of liquor, an increase in real wages, and some relaxation in the way in which the licensing system actually has been applied.

Although it appears that there are associations between legal controls on availability and per capita consumption, dogmatic assertions about causal relationships are historically unwarranted. Per capita consumption is deter-

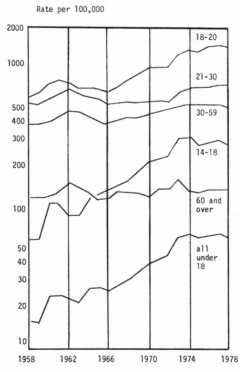

Figure 2. Findings of guilt for offenses of drunkenness, males, by age, 1958–1978 (Office of Health Economics).

mined by a network of causes and the importance of licensing controls in isolation is difficult to estimate. For example, the restrictive controls imposed during World War I were followed by a 55% drop in the consumption of spirits and a 56% drop in beer consumption. Concurrently, however, other factors were also changing, including the war itself, the diversion of raw materials away from the brewing industry, men being called up to serve in the military, and a social climate in which habitual heavy drinking was not condoned. There also have been attempts to impose controls that have *failed* to produce the intended effect. A good example was the Gin Act of 1736 which prohibited the sale of spirits in quantities of less than two gallons without a license. The license cost £50 ($100) per year and the duty per gallon was raised to £20 ($40). This was prohibition in all but name. Despite 12,000 convictions in two years for breaking the law, an illicit trade flourished and consumption rose from 11 million to 20 million gallons over a 10-year period (Williams & Brake, 1980).

Current licensing laws in England and Wales are more restrictive than those of many continental countries and, 10 years ago, the Erroll Committee (Home Office, 1971) encouraged more flexible hours for the sale of spirits and advised that families with children should be given access to licensed premises. Against the backdrop of rapidly escalating consumption figures and a powerful medical lobby, successive governments have decided to ignore this report. It is unlikely that the current laws will be relaxed in the near future.

THE CURRENT LICENSING SYSTEM

Justices of the Peace have always been the licensing authority in England and Wales. They were given this responsibility in 1552, when licensing was first introduced. The present system involves district licensing committees (popularly known as the Brewster Sessions) which must meet in the first half of February and then four to eight times during the ensuing year. The licensing committee is guided by two statutory requirements: (1) The applicant is a fit and proper person, and (2) The premises are structurally adapted to the type of license required. The justices' responsibility to consider the needs of the neighborhood has always been implicit but is nowhere written into the Act itself.

For practical purposes, the various licenses are best considered under the following headings:

1. *Full on-license.* Most frequently held by the owner of premises (such as public houses) that sell drink for consumption on or off the premises by members of the public.

2. *Off-license.* Held by an "off-license shop" or a supermarket to sell liquor that will be consumed off the premises.
3. *Restaurant license.* Granted for premises that provide main meals at midday and/or in the evenings. The premises have to be structurally adapted for the purpose, and the license is subject to the condition that drink has to be sold to a person taking a meal in the restaurant and for consumption as an ancillary to the meal.
4. *Residential license.* Granted to hotels. Board must include breakfast and at least one other main meal. Liquor cannot be sold other than to persons living there for consumption by them or their guests.

PERMITTED HOURS

On weekdays, other than Good Friday and Christmas Day, the permitted hours for on-license premises are from 11 A.M. to 10:30 P.M., with a break of 2½ hours beginning at 3 P.M. On Sundays, Good Friday, and Christmas Day, the hours range from 12 noon till 10:30 P.M., with a break of five hours from 2 P.M. In the inner London area, the weekday hours are extended to 11 P.M. Elsewhere in England and Wales, the Licensing Justices have the discretion to extend the hours to 11 P.M. The Licensing Justices also have the power to vary the permitted hours to suit particular circumstances, provided that: (1) they do not begin before 10 A.M., (2) there is an afternoon break of at least 2 hours, and (3) the overall total hours and the terminal hour remain unchanged. A drinking-up period of 10 minutes is allowed, or 30 minutes when drink is consumed with a meal. Residents in licensed premises (such as hotel guests) can buy and consume liquor at any time and also buy drinks for their guests.

Premises licensed only for off-sales are permitted to sell liquor from 8:30 A.M. and there is no afternoon break. These hours also apply to the off-sales departments of on-licensed premises, such as a public house, as long as that department is not connected by any internal communication with the rest of the premises that is open to customers.

THE LAW AND YOUNG PEOPLE

The legal position regarding *access* to licensed premises and the age at which young people are allowed to *consume* drink in them gives rise to considerable misunderstanding.

Regarding *access,* children under 14 years of age are not allowed in the bar of licensed premises during permitted hours. A bar is defined as a place used exclusively or mainly for the sale and consumption of intoxicating liquor. The only children exempt from this prohibition are the children of license holders, children residents on the premises, and children passing through the bar.

Regarding *drinking,* young people under the age of 18 cannot buy a drink in licensed premises. The only exceptions are children over the age of 16 who can buy beer, porter, and cider for consumption with a meal, if it is not served in a bar. Persons under 18 cannot drink in a bar, but are allowed to drink elsewhere in licensed premises. It is an offence for anyone to buy drink in a bar for a young person under the age of 18 and it is also an offence for a licensee to sell drink to under 18-year-olds or to allow them to drink in a bar.

One very common confusion, experienced by families with children under the age of 14, revolves around the definition of a bar. Some public houses have a separate room in which parents can drink in the presence of their children. It is not a bar, since drinks are *bought* in an adjacent room. But even a separate family room can upset the Licensing Justices if the connection with the bar is too open, as for example, when children were recently and suddenly banned from the family room of a local country pub. At a stroke, a long tradition of family country walks and pub lunches came to an end. The reply from the Clerk to the Licensing Justices regarding this act demonstrated how much discretion the justices are permitted and also the reasons why the law is interpreted so strictly in this particular respect (although not in other respects).

> The problem on the occasion of the Licensing Justices carrying out their triennial inspection of licensed premises. The purpose of this inspection is not to investigate or criticize the operation of the licenses, but is concerned almost entirely with the structure and amenities of the individual house. The visiting Justices reported that there was a room adjoining the main saloon bar which was used by children and parents. The room was directly connected with the main bar by a door which was never closed, and parents intermittently brought their children through the main bar into the children's room, which was also used as access to the main male and female toilets. Unfortunately, Section 168 of the Licensing Act 1964 prohibits children under 14 years of age from being in a bar of a licensed premises during permitted hours.
>
> The Law affecting children has altered little over the last four or five decades. Certainly, there have been moves to amend the law admitting children into licensed premises, but this is a highly controversial subject and so far no progress has been made. The licensees themselves, I feel, are against it and there is much public opinion on their side. Perhaps the problem is symptomatic of human nature, insofar as parents with children would wish to take them into a licensed premise, but adults whose children have attained the age of 14 years or over, and do not have family responsibilities, would feel that the presence of children would inhibit bar atmosphere and be such a pronounced change, that the British public house as it is known today, would lose some of its identity.

The licensing laws do allow for the provision of a room in which children can sit with their parents, "provided the rooms are not bars within the meaning of the Act." Clearly, however, what is and what is not a bar is somewhat ambiguous and is left to the discretion of the Licensing Justices.

THE QUESTION OF NEED

Restricting the number of outlets has been one of the functions of the licensing authority ever since the early statutes in the fifteenth and sixteenth centuries. For long periods, however, especially during the seventeenth and eighteenth centuries, the administration of the licensing law has been notoriously lax and, under the Beer Houses Act of 1830, the Justices lost any power to refuse licenses to beer houses. Toward the end of the nineteenth century, drunkenness was seen to be such an escalating social problem that drastic steps had to be taken. These steps resulted in the Licensing Act of 1904 which restored to the Justices their wide powers to refuse licenses when they thought the *needs* of the locality were adequately or more than adequately catered for. This change led to a decline in the number of licensed premises and the number of drunkenness arrests (Robinson, Day, Edwards, Hawks, Hershon, MacCafferty, Oppenheimer, Orford, Otto, & Taylor, 1973).

Justices also have absolute discretion in determining whether a particular area actually needs another outlet for liquor sales. From the health and prevention point of view, this question of need is a crucial issue.

The current law continues to be based on the assumption that the criterion of *need* is at the center of the licensing system, an assumption that turns out to be totally false. In practice, today's licensing committees, which have absolute discretion in these matters, are not concerned about the question of need. Erroll (Home Office, 1971) noted:

> In more than one area, the Justice took the view that the mere fact of an application for a new on-license was a reasonable ground for assuming that a 'need' existed—on the basis that no reasonable businessman would consider selling intoxicating liquor unless there was some evidence of public demand. (p. 82)

During the last 20 years, the greatest change in licensing procedures has been the relaxation of this need criterion for off-license premises. The Licensing Act of 1961 reintroduced an appeal procedure and it soon became apparent that the courts would not usually uphold a licensing committee's decision if a license was refused simply on the grounds that the need did not exist. For example, Judge David Q. C., Chairman of the Chester Quarter Sessions, in October 1969, stated the prevailing view as follows:

> If it be accepted that the principle object of licensing legislation is the preserva-
> tion of public order, it is difficult to see what restrictions there should be on the
> grant of off-licenses provided that the premises are suitable, and the applicant is
> suitable. Public disorder arising from the manner in which off-licensed premises
> are conducted is almost unheard of. The test of "need" applied so vigorously in
> the past has no doubt been of inestimable value to the trade, restricting competi-
> tion as it did without any apparent advantage to the public.

Judge David and licensing committees throughout the land appear to have
turned a blind eye to the issue of public health and prevention.

The 1961 Act also relaxed the permitted sale hours of off-licenses,
enabling them to remain open during normal shop hours. Prior to this Act,
supermarkets did not open an off-license department, since it had to be
closed most of the time. When supermarkets were permitted to sell liquor
all day long, however, many supermarket off-license departments were
opened, especially when the abolition of resale price maintenance in 1964
gave them the chance to sell alcholic drinks at a discount.

The result of all these changes has been a dramatic increase in the
number of off-license premises. Between 1950 and 1960, there was an
increase of 138 (0.5%), but in the 10 years following the 1961 Act, there
was an increase of 4,232 (17%).

According to McGuinness (1980), a 1% decrease in the number of
licensed premises might reduce the total amount of alcohol consumed by
about 2%. If we accept this argument that availability is one important
factor in the equation that determines per capita consumption, then the
demise of the need criterion should be seen as an event with far-reaching
consequences for public health and public order.

PUBLIC ORDER AND PUBLIC SAFETY

There has been a long history of legislation in this area resulting in a set
of laws that are sometimes difficult to interpret. Some of the laws on the
Statute Book have fallen into total disuse and the current position has been
described as unsatisfactory, illogical, and confusing. The statutory provisions covering drunkenness offenses are listed in Table 1.

"Simple drunkenness," which is nearly always the equivalent of "drunk
and incapable," refers to public drunkenness not associated with unlawful
behavior, whereas "drunkenness with aggravations" refers to drunkenness
that occurs together with antisocial behavior, the most frequent example
being "drunk and disorderly." There is a provision for the courts to administer a fine for simple drunkenness and either a fine or a prison sentence for
"drunkenness with aggravations." Alternatively, the court can make a pro-

Table 1.
Drunkenness Offenses and Statutes

Simple drunkenness	
Being found drunk in a highway or other public place, whether a building or not, or on licensed premises	Licensing Act 1872
Drunkenness with aggravations	
Being guilty while drunk of riotous or disorderly behavior in a highway or other place, whether a building or not	Licensing Act 1892
Being drunk while in charge, on any highway or other public place, of any carriage, horse, cattle, or steam engine.	Licensing Act 1872
Being drunk while in possession of any loaded firearms.	Licensing Act 1872
Refusing or failing when drunk to quit licensed premises when requested	Licensing Act 1964
Refusing or failing when drunk to quit any premises or place licensed under the Late Night Refreshment Houses Act 1969, when requested	Late Night Refreshment Houses Act 1969
Being found drunk in any street or public throughfare within the Metropolitan Police District, and being guilty while drunk of any riotous or indecent behavior	Metropolitan Police Act 1839
Being drunk in any street, and being guilty of riotous or indecent behavior therein	Town Police Clauses Act 1847
Being intoxicated while driving a hackney carriage	Town Police Clauses Act 1847
Being drunk during employment as a driver of a hackney carriage or as a driver or conductor of a stage carriage in the Metropolitan Police District	London Hackney Carriages Act 1843
Being drunk and persisting, after being refused admission on that account, in attempting to enter a passenger steamer	Merchant Shipping Act 1894
Being drunk on board a passenger steamer and refusing to leave such steamer when requested.	Merchant Shipping Act 1894
Being found drunk in a highway or other public place, whether a building or not, or on any licensed premises while having the charge of a child under the age of 7 years	Licensing Act 1902

bation order of from one to three years so that the problem is then the concern of the social services. A conditional discharge, for any period up to three years, allows the court to impose a delayed sentence if a further offence should occur. A probation order can include the provision that the defendant submit for up to 12 months of treatment under the direction of a duly qualified medical practitioner (Criminal Justice Act, 1948) and offenses that carry the penalty of imprisonment can lead alternatively to compulsory treatment if the defendant is suffering from "mental illness," "psychopathic disorder" or "subnormality" (Mental Health Act, 1959). This possibility is, infrequently used to deal with drunkenness offenders.

One example of a statute that has fallen into disrepute is Section 1 of the Inebriates Act 1898 which states that

> Any person convicted on indictment of an offence punishable by imprisonment, if the offence was committed when the defendant was under the influence of drink; or if drunkenness was a contributory cause, and the defendant either admits or is found by the jury to be an habitual drunkard, can be sentenced to be detained for up to 3 years in a state or certified inebriate reformatory.

There is one problem with this liberal piece of legislation. No "inebriate reformatories" are to be found anywhere in England or Wales.

DRINK AND DRIVING

In England and Wales, the Road Safety Act of 1967 had an immediate impact. Highway traffic deaths were reduced by 1,000.

> In no other country have laws against drinking and driving led to such large demonstrable savings. The effect on public attitudes was equally marked and more lasting; opposition to strong and effective measures against the drinking driver has virtually disappeared. (Department of the Environment, 1976)

Unfortunately, in recent years, the drinking and driving problem has started to escalate (Figure 3). The proportion of drivers killed in accidents who have a blood alcohol concentration above 80 mg per 100 ml, the legal limit, is now higher than it has ever been and the social cost of road accidents involving alcohol exceeds £100 million ($200 million) per year. This increasing problem appears to result from three factors: (1) there has been a continuing growth in personal transport and alcohol consumption during the last 10 years; (2) the powerful effect of publicity generated in 1967 is continuing to decay and, of course, many young people who are now driving were not exposed to this publicity; and (3) there is a growing appreciation by drinking drivers that the risks of being detected on any particular occasion are actually quite low.

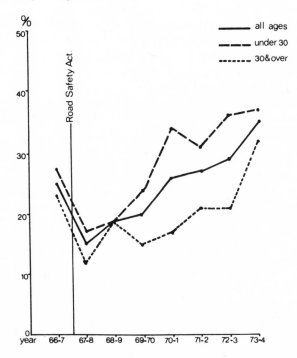

Figure 3. Drivers killed in accidents. Percentage over legal limit (England and Wales).

In an attempt to counteract this escalating social problem, the Blen-nerhassett Committee (1976) devised a number of proposals designed to close the loopholes in the 1967 Road Safety Act and to simplify the procedures for estimating blood alcohol concentrations and deal with the "high-risk" cases (i.e. those with very high BACs and repeat offenders). At the time of writing, these very sensible proposals remain before Parliament and are making slow progress.

RESTRICTIONS ON ADVERTISING

In 1933, the Director of the Brewer's Society, Sir Edgar Sanders, suggested a large-scale advertising campaign "to get the beer drinking habit instilled into thousands, almost millions of young men, who do not at present know the taste of beer." Today, we now have a very large and escalating health problem and the advertising of liquor that Sir Edgar Sanders promoted enthusiastically has become a matter of widespread concern.

The first official response to this concern came from the Advertising

Standards Authority in 1975. It incorporated the following controls into a
new code of practice: (1) children should not be portrayed in drink advertisements, except, for example, in a family situation where they would
normally be present but would not be consuming alcohol and (2) advertisements should not encourage young people to drink.

There is also a list of constraints on advertising alcohol on the radio and
television in Great Britain that was drawn up by the Independent Broadcasting Authority in 1975 and amended in 1978 for television and radio
advertising. They include the following:

1. No spirits can be advertised on television.
2. Liquor advertising should not be addressed to the young.
3. No one associated with drinking in an advertisement should seem
    to be younger than 25.
4. Personalities who command the loyalties of the young must not be
    used.
5. The advertisement should not imply that drinking is essential to
    social success or acceptance or that refusal is a sign of weakness.
6. Immoderate drinking and the buying of rounds should not be
    encouraged.
7. It should not be claimed that alcohol has therapeutic qualities or
    can improve physical performance nor should it be offered as a
    stimulant, sedative, or tranquilizer.
8. Undue emphasis should not be placed on the strength of alcoholic
    drinks.
9. Drink should not be linked with driving or the use of potentially
    dangerous machinery.
10. No liquor advertisement may publicize competition.
11. Advertisers must neither claim nor suggest that drink can contrib-
    ute to sexual prowess.
12. Advertisers must not suggest that solitary drinking is acceptable,
    nor associate drinking with masculinity.

These new codes provide clear evidence that the advertising authorities are taking seriously the ground swell of concern about the increasing levels of consumption in recent years, especially among the young.

FISCAL POLICY

When health professionals and government officials come to blows
over preventive measures, it is usually in the area of fiscal policy. Table 2
shows that the total amount of taxation from excise duties and value-added

Table 2.
Tax as a Percentage of Consumers' Expenditure on Alcoholic Drink

	1968	1969	1970	1971	1972	1973	1974	1975	1976	1977	1978	1979
Beer	36.6	36.9	33.4	30.9	29.1	28.6	28.5	29.9	30.5	30.0	28.7	29.2
Spirits	56.3	57.9	56.2	54.6	53.5	52.2	53.5	52.8	58.1	53.5	53.7	52.7
Wines and cider	23.2	26.3	26.4	28.2	24.4	22.9	24.2	29.1	31.0	31.0	30.7	31.5
All alcoholic drink	40.0	40.7	38.5	36.6	34.8	34.5	34.9	36.1	38.0	36.1	35.6	36.1

tax accounts for a high proportion of most alcoholic drinks in the United Kingdom. The proportion varies from about one-third of the expenditure on beer and wine to over half in the case of spirits. Taxation on alcoholic drinks raised approximately £4,000 million ($8,000 million) from 1980 to 1981, accounting for 6% of central government revenue.

During the last 10 years, the real price of alcoholic drinks has been falling fairly steadily, as has the level of taxation on beer and spirits (Table 2). It is not surprising, therefore, that there has been a plea for increased taxation in the interests of public health and public order. Both the House of Commons Expenditure Committee and the Advisory Committee on Alcoholism published reports in 1977 recommending the maintenance of the price of alcohol in relation to incomes. The Special Committee of the Royal College of Psychiatrists in its 1979 report on "Alcohol and Alcoholism" recommended that "public revenue policies of Government should be intentionally employed in the interests of health, so as to ensure that per capita alcohol consumption does not increase beyond the present level, and is, by stages, brought to an agreed lower level" (p. 139).

It is now apparent that this advice has fallen on stony ground. A recent publication by the Department of Health and Social Security (DHSS 1981) concluded that

> Taking account of the economic as well as the health and social considerations, and bearing in mind the practical difficulties involved, the Government cannot accept recommendations that have been made for the systematic use of tax rates as a means of regulating consumption. Health and social implications are, however, clearly of great importance, and the Government intends, within the context of its overall economic strategy, to continue to take these into account when changes in duty and wider taxation policy are considered. (p. 58)

The three main arguments put forward to support this conclusion can be summarized in the following quotations:

> Maintaining or increasing the real price of alcohol is not likely to influence many problem drinkers who will probably maintain their consumption by switching to a cheaper drink or reducing their expenditure on other items—perhaps to the detriment of their family. (p. 53)

> Ceasing to vary the level of the duties primarily in accordance with the need for revenue or with the needs of the economy would mean that the revenue from a significant source might be either more or less than if the judgement were made on the ground of economic policy . . . this could have consequences for the Government's ability to take other factors (such as energy policy) into account in setting other indirect taxes. (p. 56)

> Any social, legal or fiscal measures to contain or reduce consumption could have adverse effects on the output, employment and investment of the drinks industry, on the activities of associated industries and, overall, on the economy generally. (p. 57)

This is an honest and unambiguous set of statements. The first is almost certainly false, especially if future problem drinkers are included in the equation. The other two confirm the impression that public health has a very low priority when a government is struggling to keep a grip on inflation and unemployment.

The fate of a recent "think tank" report on alcohol policies produced by the government's Central Policy Review staff in 1979 is somewhat more mysterious. This report presented an excellent account of the alcohol problem in the United Kingdom and the options open to the Government. It clearly noted that economic and social concerns must be balanced, but nevertheless, a number of steps could be taken immediately, including fiscal measures to prevent per capita alcohol consumption from rising above current levels. The suppression of this report angered many people who are concerned with the escalating alcohol problem in the United Kingdom. A recent editorial in the *British Journal of Addiction* comments that: "Continuing suppression must have about it a sick smell of scandal with the stench worse each month that follows" (*British Journal of Addiction* editorial, March, 1982).

It is apparent that alcohol control policies in England and Wales have evolved over a period of 500 years into a loosely stretched patchwork of measures. The recent government "think tank" managed to identify the weak spots in present alcohol control policies and produce a number of sensible proposals. Unfortunately, the report was suppressed and disappeared with hardly a trace. The philosophy of the present government precludes tightening up of control policies if this would interfere with market forces. The economy is now center stage, and the health of the nation must wait in the wings.

ACKNOWLEDGMENT

Many thanks are due to Professor Griffith Edwards for his advice and comments on the original manuscript.

REFERENCES

Department of the Environment. Drinking and Driving (Report of the Blennerhassett Committee). London: H.M.S.O., 1976.

Department of Health and Social Security. Drinking sensibly. London: H.M.S.O., 1981.

Home Office. *Report of the Departmental Committee on Liquor Licensing* (Erroll Report). London: H.M.S.O., CMND. 5154, 1971.

McGuinness, T. An econometric analysis of total demand for alcoholic beverages in the U.K. 1956–75. *Journal of Industrial Economics*, 1980, *39*, 85–109.

Miller, P. M. A behavioral intervention program for chronic public drunkenness offenders. *Archives of General Psychiatry*, 1975, *32*, 915–18.

Robinson, D., Day, I., Edwards, G., Hawks, D., Hershon, H., MacCafferty, M., Oppenheimer, E., Orford, J., Otto, S., & Taylor C. *Where Erroll went wrong on liquor licensing* (Critique). London: Camberwell Council on Alcoholism, 1973.

Royal College of Psychiatrists. The Report of a Special Committee. *Alcohol and alcoholism.* London: Tavistock, 1979.

Spring, J. A., & Buss, D. G. Three centuries of alcohol in Britain. *Nature,* 1977, *270,* 567.

Williams, G. P., & Brake, G. T. *Drink in Great Britain 1900–1979.* London: Edsall, 1980.

6C
Alcohol Control Policy in India

VIJOY K. VARMA

BACKGROUND

With a land area of approximately 3.3 million square km, India covers some 2.4% of the world's land area. Its present population of some 680 million (1981 census) represents 15% of the world's population. There is reason to believe that the use of alcoholic beverages has skyrocketed in the last three to four decades. Many recent studies in North India have put the percentage of current users as high as 50% to 70% among adult males (Deb & Jindal, 1974; Lal & Singh, 1978; Varma, Singh, Singh, & Malhotra, 1980). The available data give some credence to the concept of increasing consumption among the rural population, beneficiary of recent affluence as a consequence of advanced technology and among students and nonstudent youth (Varma & Dang, 1979, 1980; Varma et al., 1980).

HISTORICAL PERSPECTIVE

ANCIENT INDIA

The available evidence suggests that the processes of fermentation and distillation were known to the Hindus in ancient times. The early Aryans

VIJOY K. VARMA • Department of Psychiatry, Postgraduate Institute of Medical Education and Research, Chandigarh-160 012, India.

who migrated to India around 1500 B.C. were given to drinking spirituous beverages and a *soma* and *sura* (a distilled potent spirit manufactured from rice meal) was a common drink of high alcoholic strength. In ancient Indian literature distinction is made between *soma* and *sura*. "The *soma* is truth, prosperity, light; and the *sura* untruth, misery, and darkness" (cited in Chand, 1972). There is some doubt if *soma* was an alcoholic beverage at all (Prohibition Study Team Report, 1964, pp. 390–91), whereas *sura* was admittedly an alcoholic beverage. The drinking of *soma* is not mentioned as a vice in the Vedic literature; however, the drinking of *sura* is severely condemned (Chand, 1972). An ancient author, *Pulastya,* enumerated 12 kinds of liquors in addition to *soma* that were made from different ingredients. Drinking prevailed in all ages of India's ancient history, Vedic and post-Vedic. Reference to alcoholic beverages and the practice of consumption finds place in such epics and scriptures as Sutras, Mahabharata, Jatakas, Shakuntala, and Kumar Sambhav. In ancient medical works, the use of liquor is suggested as an aphrodisiac and for other medical purposes.

The ancient Indians were not, however, totally oblivious of the unpleasant and deleterious effects of alcohol ingestion. This led to severe condemnation of alcohol use. The *Puranas* have condemned the use of wine. According to the *Smriti* of *Manu,* the lawgiver, drinking of *Sura (Arrack)* was considered to be one of the five *mahapatakas* (mortal sins) meriting severe punishment. "A man who steals gold, who drinks spirits, who dishonors his preceptor's bed, who kills a Brahmana, these four, fall, and as fifth, he who associates with them. These are the five most deadly sins of the 'twice-born'" (cited in Chand, 1972). Drinking by women was deprecated and was considered a cause of their ruin. "She who drinks spirituous liquor is of bad conduct, rebellious, diseased, mischievous, or wasteful, may at any time be superseded [by another wife]" (Manu, IX, 80). Severe punishments were prescribed and indicate that the Hindu society looked upon drinking with abhorrence.

MIDDLE AGES

The history of social control over alcohol since the advent of the Christian era until the onset of Western contact and especially of British supremacy is very sketchy. During the Muslim period, as the Islamic culture has been abstinential and the alcohol taboo has had a religious basis, the early Muslim rulers were very strict and forbade the use of intoxicating beverages. It is said that "during the flight from Mecca, Mohammed's lieutenants had been gambling and drinking and were unable to function. As a result Mohammed forbade both drinking and gambling" (cited in Prohibition Study Team Report, 1964, Vol. II, p. 392). Ibn Batuta who visited India in the time of Ala-ud-Din Khilji, reported of the use of alcoholic beverages in India: "Spirituous liquor was strictly forbidden; and the Sultan himself set an example by giving up the habit of drink. . . . The nobles were permitted to drink individually at their houses but all social intercourse was strictly prohibited" (cited in Prohibition Study Team Report, 1964, Vol. II, p. 392). The Muslims did not consider dealing in alcohol as a source of revenue to the state. Subsequent foreign travelers including Vasco de Gama, Bernier, and Tavernier also observed that people generally were free from the evil of drink. Alcohol was never considered a legitimate source of state revenue and at no time is there any evidence of the state undertaking the manufacture and distribution of liquor (Prohibition Study Team Report, 1964, Vol. II, p. 392).

BRITISH RULE

Organized governmental control over production and sale of alcoholic beverages has had a very short history in India. It came with the advent of the British rule. In 1790, the East Indian Company, for the first time, introduced excise duty on liquor as a regular source of revenue. The Bengal Excise Commission of 1884 addressed itself to improving the system of excise administration and in 1892 the government laid down objectives to discourage alcohol use. In the pre-Independence India, however, the government decided against direct interference in the habits of the people as to alcohol use. This finds lucid expression in the resolution on the report of the Indian Excise Committee of 1905:

> The Government of India has no desire to interfere with the habits of those who use alcohol in moderation and it is necessary in their opinion to make the provision for the needs of such persons. Their settled policy, however, is to minimise temptation to those who do not drink and to discourage excess among those who do, and to a furtherance of this policy all considerations of revenue must be absolutely subordinated. The most effective method of furthering this policy is to make the tax on liquor as high as it is possible to raise it without stimulating illicit consumption to a degree, which would increase, instead of diminishing the total consumption and without driving people to substitute deleterious drugs for alcohol or a more or less harmful form of liquor. Subject to the same considerations, the number of liquor shops should be restricted as far as possible and their location should be periodically subject to strict examination with a view to minimise the temptation to drink and to conform as far as is reasonable to public opinion. It is also important to secure that the liquor which is offered for sale is of good quality and not necessarily injurious to health. (cited in *Prohibition: Policy and Programmes,* 1977, p. 12)

It is obvious that the British government was interested in levying excise duty simply as a means of revenue and not to deter alcohol consumption.

INDEPENDENCE MOVEMENT AND POST-INDEPENDENCE ERA

Prohibition formed one of the major planks of the Indian National Congress which spearheaded the movement toward self-rule or independence ever since its foundation in 1885. As early as its fourth session, held in 1888, it recognised the serious increase in the consumption of intoxicants under the prevailing excise system and "respectfully urged [the Government] to adopt some such improved system as shall tend to discourage insobriety." At its fourteenth session in 1900, it viewed "with grave alarm and deep regret the rapid increase in the consumption of intoxicants, specially liquor," and expressed its firm conviction that moral, material, and physical deterioration of the people would result unless the government took immediate practical steps. It gave great importance to this question and protested against the cheap supply of liquor.

In 1907, *Madyapan Nisedha Sabha* was organized to denounce the drinking habit. Stalwarts of the Indian National Congress in the beginning of this century, including G. K. Gokhale and B. G. Tilak, were arch prohibitionists and often expressed themselves on this point. In 1921, a vigorous campaign was launched against the use of intoxicating drinks under the leadership of Mahatma Gandhi and peaceful picketing of liquor shops started. The President of Indian National Congress at its 1926 session emphasized that "we must devise effective ways of removing the drink evil," and at its 1928 session the Congress finally adopted in its Bill of Rights that "intoxicating drinks and drugs shall be totally prohibited except for medicinal purposes," which subsequently was to be incorporated in the Constitution of India. In the same year, the All-Parties' Convention, which met for drafting the Constitution for an independent India, resolved that "it shall be the duty of the Commonwealth to save its citizens from . . . alcoholic liquor," and that as soon as possible after the establishment of a government, it shall "make laws for the total prohibition of the manufacture, import, possession, or sale of alcoholic liquor and intoxicating drugs, except for medicinal or industrial purposes." Total prohibition figured as the first condition in the 11 terms Mahatma Gandhi stated to the Viceroy in 1930. The 1931 resolution of the Congress hoped that "the women of the country will redouble their efforts in weaning the drunkard and drug addict from a habit that ruins both body and soul and desolates happy homes."

Consequent to the Government of India Act of 1935, general elections were held in 1937 in which Congress won in a majority of provinces where Congress ministries were installed. The Working Committee of the Congress in 1937 directed the Congress ministries to bring about total prohibition, expecting them to accomplish it within three years.

Prohibition was first introduced in 1937 in parts of Madras, Bombay, United Provinces, Bihar, and Central Provinces and launched in Bombay on August 1, 1939, with great fanfare. Unfortunately, the Congress ministries resigned in 1939 to protest India's participation in World War II, and from 1940 to 1946, when the Congress was out of office, the prohibition policy was watered down and virtually reversed. Following fresh elections in 1946 and installation of Congress ministries in a number of provinces, there was gradual introduction of prohibition and by October 1948, Madras, and in April 1950, Bombay became wholly dry.

Since Independence, the government has instituted a number of committees to inquire into the effect of alcohol on the society and to examine the desirability of prohibition.

Prohibition Enquiry Committee, 1954

This committee was formed on December 16, 1954, under the chairmanship of Shri Shriman Narayan to make recommendations for a program on prohibition on a national basis, indicating the manner and stages in which, and the machinery through which it should be carried out. The committee submitted its report on September 10, 1955, with a set of 15 recommendations.

Central Prohibition Committee, 1960

For introducing prohibition in a phased manner in the country, the Ministry of Home Affairs, which was previously in charge of the subject, set up in consultation with the state governments a Central Prohibition Committee in 1960. Its purpose was to advise the government on the measures to be taken to achieve this objective under the chairmanship of Minister of State in the Ministry of Home Affairs.

Study Team on Prohibition, 1963

To study the working of prohibition in different states, the planning commission appointed a study team on prohibition in April 1963, headed by Justice Tek Chand, retired judge of the Punjab High Court. The committee submitted its report in April 1964.

Expert Committee, 1972

In order to objectively assess the effects of human consumption of alcohol on health and nutrition, an expert committee, under the chairmanship of Dr. V. Ramalingaswami, was constituted by the goverment of India in 1972. The Expert Committee submitted its report on March 21, 1974, and concluded that alcohol causes many diseases and affects the normal resistance of the human body to diseases. Another important point brought out by the committee was that the ill effects of alcohol are more marked in those who are exposed to nutritional deficiencies.

Drug Addiction Committee, 1976

This committee was constituted under the chairmanship of Dr. C. Gopalan. The Committee submitted its report on October 1, 1977.

The history of prohibition in the post-Independence period (since 1947) has had a checkered record. Various states have formulated prohibition policies at some time or other. Regarding the situation then prevailing, the Prohibition Study Team in its 1964 report stated:

> Today, about one-third of the total area and a quarter of the total population are under prohibition. At present, total prohibition is in operation in the States of Madras, Maharashtra and Gujarat and in eleven districts of Andhra region of the Andhra Pradesh. In Assam, Madhya Pradesh, Orissa, Mysore and Kerala, there are certain areas which have been brought under prohibition. (Vol. 2, p. 402)

At present, only the State of Gujarat (with a population of 4.9% of the national total) is totally dry and it has been so continuously. The Union Territory of Lakshadeep, which is almost totally Muslim, with 1971 population of approximately 32,000, is also and has been totally dry. Of the other states, Maharashtra (part of the erstwhile Bombay province) and Tamil Nadu (earlier called Madras) have had prohibition for a considerable length of time since Independence. At present, however, prohibition is not in force in either of these two states.

There have been several ups and downs concerning the governmental control of alcohol over the last decade. During Emergency (June 1975 to March 1977), the Government declared a policy of gradual enforcement of total prohibition and in view of that brought out a minimum 12-point program to reduce the consumption of alcoholic beverages and prepared the ground for introduction of total prohibition. This program consisted of the following measures:

1. Discontinuance of advertisements and public inducements relating to drink
2. Stoppage of drinking in public places such as hostels, hotels, restaurants, and clubs and at public receptions

3. Banning of liquor shops near industrial, irrigation, and other development projects in order to keep the workers from drinking
4. No liquor shops to be allowed along highways and in residential areas in towns and villages nor anywhere near educational institutions, religious places, and colonies of laborers
5. Pay days in different areas to be uniformly "dry" days
6. Strict restrictions to be enforced on motor vehicle drivers and pilots; any infringement of rules to be punished with the cancellation of their licences for a sufficiently long period
7. Government servants of all categories, including employees of public undertakings, to abstain from drinking in public; drunkenness while on duty to be severely punished
8. No new liquor shops to be opened in any part of the country merely to earn more excise revenue
9. No licence for creation of additional capacity or expansion of existing capacity for distillation or brewing of alcoholic drinks to be granted save in 100% export-oriented cases
10. The existing legislation to be tightened up with a view to punishing the guilty more effectively; special mobile police squads to be organised for the purpose where necessary
11. Widespread and concerted propaganda by offical as well as non-official agencies against the evil of drinking
12. Leaders of public opinion to set the tone by their personal example (cited in *Prohibition: Policy and Programmes,* 1977, pp. 43–44)

The period of Emergency was followed by installation of the Janata government at the Centre in March 1977 headed by Morarji Desai as Prime Minister. Mr. Desai, a teetotaller and a strong prohibitionist, attempted to strengthen the movement toward prohibition. During the Janata regime, many other states also experimented with various degrees of prohibition. Part or whole of many states that had been traditionally wet went dry. The number of dry days was increased and the serving of alcoholic beverages in bars, restaurants, and clubs was mostly stopped. With the emergence of the Congress rule headed by Mrs. Indira Gandhi after the January 1980 elections, there has been a considerable relaxation with regard to control on alcoholic beverages. On each of the points mentioned, the state governments have vied with each other in trying to follow the central policy. The recent relaxation has been in terms of reduction of number of dry days; grant of licenses to bars, restaurants, and clubs to serve alcoholic beverages; and so forth.

As is apparent from the foregoing, governmental control policies regarding alcohol in India have been characterized by lack of uniformity, contradictions, and frequent changes. In this regard, it may be of interest to point out that the response to a WHO questionnaire on "preventive policies and programs" pertaining to India prepared by a colleague (Mohan, 1979) as recently as 1978–1979 already makes rather curious reading as if the description given by him pertains to a different country or to an entirely different era. A great deal of ambivalence toward the substance ethanol seems apparent. The ambivalence and conflict may be enamating from, among others, the following:

1. It is possible that in a rapidly changing, industrializing, and urbanizing non-Western society use of alcohol and other dependence-producing drugs may have a connotation different from that traditionally ascribed in the West. In a recent study, we have found (Agarwal, Varma, & Dang, 1980) that among university students there was an inverse correlation between drug use and scores on alienation, which implies that drug users may not be alienated as is traditionally considered, but actually more integrated with the society. Drug use, in this respect, may be viewed as consistent with modernity, that is, integration with changing social values. It also may be that as opposed to traditional drugs in India, cannabis and opium, alcohol may be more highly equated with modernity.

2. It has been pointed out by some workers, especially anthropologists, that perhaps Hindus are more concerned about what to eat and what not to eat. "One is always likely to become what he eats" (Marriott & Inden, 1977). This may be related to the conceptualization of Hindu adult personality as an open system, very much dependent upon what physically goes in and comes out of the person. In contrast to the generally closed, homogeneous, and enduring mental integrations attributable to adults in the West, Hindu adults are posited as persons "who are open, composed to exogenous elements, substantially fluid . . . and thus necessarily changing and interchanging in their nature. . . . Given the vulnerability of open Hindu persons to a cosmos of interpersonal flow, persons as wholes cannot be thought of as enduring or bounded 'egos' in any Western sense" (Marriott, 1979). In this way, conflict toward alcohol is understandable.

3. The legacy of British rule has also had its consequences. As opposed to the cannabis and opium traditionally used in India, the use of drugs by Europeans in the heyday of the British Raj was limited to alcoholic beverages. It is possible that the identification of alcoholic beverages with the British overlords may have generated negative affects toward it; in the same way as equating it with the West in general is now causing a positive emotion, its use represents modernity.

CURRENT STATUS OF CONTROL POLICIES AND PRACTICES

It was only natural that on achieving independence in 1947, pro-prohibition policies were put into effect in India. Article 47 of the Constitution of India which came into force in 1950 enjoins the state as a part of the Directive Principles: "The State shall regard the raising of the level of nutrition and the standard of living of its people and the improvement of public health as among its primary duties and, in particular, the State shall endeavor to bring about prohibition of the consumption except for medicinal purposes of intoxicating drinks and drugs which are injurious to health."

The Constitution of India makes fairly sharp divisions between the prerogatives of the Centre and of the states. Article 246 provides for separate "union list," "state list," and "concurrent list" as given in its Seventh Schedule. The "lists" enumerate subjects on which the Union (Centre) or the state or both exercise control. Government control over alcohol is primarily a state subject. It is covered under entries 8 and 51 of the state list as follows:

List II—State List
   8. Intoxicating liquors, that is to say, the production, manufacture, possession, transport, purchase and sale of intoxicating liquors.
  51. Duties of excise on the following goods manufactured or produced in the State and counterveiling duties at the same or lower rates on similar goods manufactured or produced elsewhere in India:
     (a) Alcoholic liquors for human consumption
     (b) Opium, Indian hemp and other narcotic drugs and narcotics; but not including medicinal and toilet preparations containing alcohol or any substance included in sub-paragraph (b) of this entry.

The only sphere pertaining to the control of alcoholic beverages that comes under the purview of the Centre is "medicinal and toilet preparations including alcohol" (Union list, Item 84).

India, at present consists of 23 states in addition to 8 federally administered union territories. Each may have a separate policy regarding control over alcohol. In addition, there have been examples, too numerous to mention in detail, of one part of a state being declared "dry" and the other part continuing to be "wet."

A state exercises its control over alcohol in two principal ways, namely, by regulating production, manufacture, possession, transport, purchase, and sale (List 2, Item 8), and by levying excise duty on alcoholic liquors for human consumption (List 2, Item 51).

In addition to Article 47 of the Constitution of India, which forms a part of the Directive Principles of the State, and the Excise Acts and rules of various states, which control and regulate manufacture, transport, sale, possession, and use of alcoholic beverages, social control over alcohol is also indirectly enforced through a number of other laws. The principal ones are the following:

> *Section 510 of the Indian Penal Code (I.P.C.) of 1860: Misconduct in public by a drunken person:*
> Whoever, in a state of intoxication, appears in any public place, or in any place which it is a trespass in him to enter and there conducts himself in such a manner as to cause annoyance to any person, shall be punished with simple imprisonment for a term which may extend to twenty-four hours, or with fine which may extend to ten rupees, or with both.
>
> *Section 34 of the Police Act 1861: Punishment for certain offences on roads, etc.:*
> Any person who, on any road or in any open place or street or thoroughfare within the limits of any town to which this section shall be specially extended by the State Government, commits any of the following offences, to the obstruction, inconvenience, annoyance, risk, danger or damage of the residents or passengers shall, on conviction before a Magistrate, be liable to a fine not exceeding fifty rupees, or imprisonment with or without hard labour not exceeding eight days. . . . Being found drunk or riotous or incapable of taking care of himself.
>
> *Section 17 of the Motor Vehicles Act, 1939:*
> A court shall order the disqualification of an offender convicted of an offence punishable under section 117 and such disqualification shall be for a period of not less than six months.
>
> *Section 117 of the Motor Vehicles (Amendment) Act, 1977: Driving by a drunken person or by a person under the influence of drugs:*
> Whoever, while driving, or attempting to drive, a motor vehicle or riding or attempting to ride a motor cycle (a) has, in his blood, alcohol in any quantity however small the quantity may be, or (b) is under the influence of a drug to such an extent as to be incapable of exercising proper control over the vehicle, shall be punishable for the first offence with imprisonment for a term which may extend to six months or with a fine which may extend to two thousand rupees, or with both; and for a second or subsequent offence, if committed within three years of the commission of the previous similar offence, with imprisonment for a term which may extend to two years, or with a fine which may extend to three thousand rupees, or with both.
>
> *Section 128–A of the Motor Vehicles (Amendment) Act, 1977: Breath tests:*
> A police officer in uniform may require any person driving or attempting to drive a motor vehicle in a public place to provide one or more specimens of breath for breath test there or nearby, if the police officer has any reasonable cause: (a) to suspect him of having alcohol in any quantity in his body, (b) to suspect him of having committed an offence punishable under section 117.

Being under the influence of alcohol does not, however, absolve a person from the responsibility for having committed an offense unless the thing that intoxicated him was administered without his knowledge or against his will (Sections 85 and 86 of the Indian Penal Code).

The laws relating to drunkenness are relatively mild. The Prohibition Study Team Report (1964) expressed the opinion that "the statutes relating to intoxicating beverages in the United Kingdom and in the United States of America are far more stringent and comprehensive than the laws in our country" (Vol. 1, p. 305). With regard to the actual implementation of the law, the same report states that, "Our experience of different states has been that a large number of liquor offences remain undetected and unreported" (Vol. 1, p. 297), and that "the sentences in a large number of cases are hardly deterrent. The records which we have had an occasion to see showed that where sentences of imprisonment was compulsory, the court paid lip homage to that provision and awarded imprisonment till rising of the court" (Vol. 1, p. 300). With regard to drunk driving, the report felt that "although driving under the influence of drink is frequent, cases of prosecution of such drivers are very few" (Vol. 1, p. 313). Our own figures for arrests for alcohol-related crimes also support the belief that the number of such arrests is quite meager considering the country's population.

Our survey conducted in 1978 inquiring from the various states and union territories with regard to the statistics pertaining to criminal acts

Table 1.
Data Concerning Certain Criminal Acts Committed under the Influence of Alcohol in India, 1972–1976

	1976	1975	1974	1973	1972
1. For being drunk in a public place, causing rowdyism and obstruction (Section 34, Police Act)					
Arrests	55,362	44,199	42,531	43,858	41,699
Prosecutions	54,289	47,792	41,627	41,175	38,795
Convictions	43,707	39,978	34,439	34,599	33,999
2. For rioting/quarreling under the influence of alcohol (Section 510, IPC)					
Arrests	3,073	2,765	2,788	2,693	2,632
Prosecutions	2,859	2,618	2,653	2,430	2,602
Convictions	2,430	2,287	2,057	2,013	2,177
3. Alcohol-related traffic accidents (e.g., driver being under the influence of alcohol)					
Total number	648	592	588	520	683
Number of convictions for the above	433	384	406	367	518
4. Driving under the influence of alcohol					
Arrests	956	757	582	521	505
Prosecutions	906	708	517	463	450
Convictions	554	544	400	364	359

committed under the influence of alcohol yielded the data presented in Table 1 (all of the states and union territories responded to the questionnaire except for the states of Assam, Manipur, Madhya Pradesh, and Uttar Pradesh, which together account for 26.6% of the national population).

With regard to the regulations regarding dry days and the limits on the maximum quantity that a person could buy or stock at a time, wide variability was found from state to state. The data gave a range of 5 to 27 bottles (of 650 ml each) of beer, 2 to 12 bottles (of 750 ml each) of spirits and 1 bottle of country liquor. As to the strength of various beverages, the strength of beer varied from 3% to 11%, the usual strength of the spirits (whisky, rum, gin, brandy, or what is generally referred to as "Indian made foreign liquor" or IMFL) is 25° underproof or approximately 42% by volume and of country liquor 15 to 35% by volume.

There also has been a wide variability across states and over time with regard to the number of dry days. At the height of the Janata regime, in some situations the dry days numbered as many as 100 to 150 days a year. At present, most states observe one or two dry days per month (usually the first or the seventh of the month, or both) in addition to the three national holidays, namely, Republic Day (January 26), Independence Day (August 15), and the birthday of Mahatma Gandhi (October 2).

A word also should be said concerning the system of liquor permits for medical reasons that has been followed in many dry states. This has been in vogue in states including Gujarat, Maharashtra, and Tamil Nadu where, on medical certification, a certain amount of liquor could be sold to a person. There does not seem to be much doubt that this system has been widely abused. Also, strangely, a distinction is made between Indians and foreigners in terms of the permissible quantity, it being greater in case of the latter. This and other anomalies, such as the serving of alcoholic beverages to foreigners and not to Indians in bars and restaurants (which has been practiced at certain times and places), have been resented by many.

Although prohibition forms a part of the Directive Principles of the State as enshrined in the Constitution of India, the total approach of the government toward it has been haphazard and contradictory. Many state governments are directly involved in production of alcohol beverages. There are numerous things that can be done by the state short of total prohibition toward which the approach has been not very effective. There is no reason why the government cannot effectively ban sale of alcoholic beverages on or near highways. In the same way, the hours of sale, sale to minors, and so forth can be controlled more effectively. If the state is at all serious concerning the bringing about of gradual prohibition, the present anachronism exemplified by its participation in production and sale of alcoholic beverages must be removed.

ACKNOWLEDGMENTS

I wish to acknowledge gratefully the valuable help received from Justice Tek Chand, retired judge, Punjab High Court, a past president of the International Commission for the Prevention of Alcoholism, and chairman of the Prohibition Study Team whose 1964 report was most useful in preparation of this paper. Mr. S. C. Nagpal, advocate, Chandigarh, was most helpful in checking the legal references.

REFERENCES

Agarwal, R. K., Varma, V. K., & Dang, R. Interrelationship between drug use, anomie, alienation and authoritarianism amongst University students. *Indian Journal of Psychiatry,* 1980, *22,* 103–107.

Chand, T. *Hindu scriptures and intoxicating drugs.* Paper presented at the First World Congress of the International Commission for the Prevention of Alcoholism, Kabul, Afaghanistan, 1972.

Deb, P. C., & Jindal, R. B. *Drinking in rural areas—A study in selected villages of Punjab.* Ludhiana: Punjab Agricultural University, 1974.

Lal, B., & Singh, G. Alcohol consumption in Punjab. *Indian Journal of Psychiatry,* 1978, *20,* 212–216.

Marriott, M. *The open Hindu person and humane sciences.* Unpublished paper, 1979.

Marriott, M., & Inden, R. B. Toward an ethnosociology of South Asian caste system. In K. David (Ed.), *The new wind: Changing identities in South Asia,* The Hague: Mouton, 1977.

Mohan, D. Response to Questionnaire of the WHO Project "Prevention of Alcohol-related Disabilities." 1979, pp. 25–1 to 25–9.

Prohibition Enquiry Committee Report, New Delhi: Planning Commission, 1955.

Prohibition Study Team Report. New Delhi: Planning Commission, 1964.

Prohibition: Policy and Programmes. Government of India, Ministry of Education and Social Welfare, 1977.

Varma, V. K., & Dang, R. Non-medical use of drugs amongst school and college students. *Indian Journal of Psychiatry,* 1979, *21,* 228–234.

Varma, V. K., & Dang, R. Non-medical drug use amongst non-student youth in India. *Drug and Alcohol Dependence,* 1980, *5,* 457–465.

Varma, V. K., Singh, A., Singh, S., & Malhotra, A. Extent and pattern of alcohol use and alcohol-related problems in North India. *Indian Journal of Psychiatry,* 1980, *22,* 331–337.

6D

Alcohol Control Policy in Japan

KINYA KURIYAMA, SHUJI IDA, AND SEITARO OHKUMA

INTRODUCTION

In modern society, the amount of alcohol consumed has become one of the resources used to reduce psychic stress arising from the complexity of social circumstances. It has increased in proportion to the amount of alcohol produced. As a consequence, the incidence of alcoholism has increased (Ewing & Rouse, 1978; Hayman, 1965).

The drinking of alcohol became popular in Japan after the 1880s when modern industries developed remarkably. Since alcohol had been an expensive drug prior to that time, the general public in Japan could not purchase alcohol and thus few alcoholics were found before the 1880s. Some problems caused by alcohol drinking, however, were raised after the industrial developments in Japan.

Until quite recently, Japan was a so-called paradise for drunken men because it had been thought for a long time that excess drinking of alcohol was a heroic deed and that even criminal acts committed by drunken men were considered innocent. However, some groups, including the Japanese Medical Society of Alcohol Studies, began to study the problems caused by alcohol drinking and to make an effort to reduce alcohol consumption. At the present time, most of the civilized nations in the world have laws

KINYA KURIYAMA, SHUJI IDA, and SEITARO OHKUMA • Department of Pharmacology, Kyoto Prefectural University of Medicine, Kawaramachi-Hirokoji, Kamikyo-Ku, Kyoto 602, Japan.

relating to the production, sale, and drinking of alcohol. In Japan, the production and sale of alcohol are regulated by the Liquor Tax Law (Law Bulletin Series, Japan).

LAW FOR PROHIBITING LIQUOR TO MINORS

This law was legislated in 1922 to protect youth, who were still developing mentally and physically, from the evil effects of alcohol drinking. Article 1 prohibits minors (younger than 20 years old) from drinking alcohol and prohibits dealers from selling alcohol to minors. It also instructs parents and guardians to direct minors to avoid alcoholic beverages (Law Bulletin Series, Japan).

According to the recent report by Yokoyama, Sakurai, and Noda (1969), in Japan the percentage of alcoholics who start to drink alcohol at an age younger than 20 is 64.7%. It also has been reported that 13.7% and

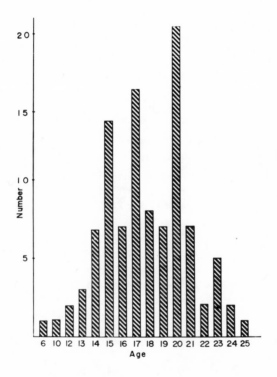

Figure 1. Age of onset of alcohol drinking in alcoholics in Japan (from the report by Yokoyama *et al.*, 1969).

15.6% of alcoholics started to drink alcohol at an age younger than 15 and 17 years old, respectively. These facts suggest that the early initiation of alcohol drinking in youth increases the chances of alcoholism. This law, therefore, is considered to be appropriate for postponing the age initiating alcohol drinking and for decreasing the incidence of alcoholics, especially in boyhood.

PROVISION FOR PROHIBITING DRUNKEN DRIVING

The number of traffic accidents caused by drunken drinkers in Japan in 1973 was 21,124. This constitutes a total of 6% of all traffic accidents that occurred in 1973. Needless to say, precise and safe driving requires one to recognize and judge situations correctly and to operate a vehicle properly.

Since decreases in the capacity to recognize and judge situations in addition to impairments in vision and reaction time are observed in drunkenness, it is obvious that drinking alcohol before driving may be one of the causes of traffic accidents. Driving after drinking, therefore, is considered to be a punishable offense.

The provision for prohibiting drunken driving in the Japanese Road Traffic Law consists of the following articles: (1) No one under the influence of alcohol may drive a vehicle and (2) No one may offer alcohol to a person who may possibly drive a vehicle in violation of the provision of Article 1 (Law Bulletin Series, Japan). The first article prohibits a drinker from driving primarily as a means of preventing traffic accidents. The second article, on the other hand, was legislated to prohibit the offering of alcohol to anyone who may drive a vehicle shortly after the alcohol intake. It is noteworthy that this article applies to anyone, not only managers of bars or drive-ins.

This law requires that a driver who has a blood alcohol concentration of more than 0.5 mg per ml or 0.25 mg per liter of expiratory air must be considered to be a drunken driver. In Japan, the methods to detect intoxication mainly consist of the examination of the concentration of alcohol in a driver's expiratory air and the observation of the appearance of the driver. The latter is subdivided in two ways. First, the driver is questioned. The questions are composed of 12 items such as name, age, address of the driver, and time when the driver is interrogated. Various procedures to examine the certainty of memory and the existence of speech disturbances are also included. Second, the driver's behavior and appearance are observed. These observations focus on his ability to walk straightly, to stand upright, the odor of liquor in expiratory air, and facial color. From the results of these examinations, drivers are divided into two classes. One is a slightly drunken driver whose appearance seems to be normal and whose concentration of alcohol in expiratory air is lower than 0.25 mg. The other is a heavily drunken driver whose appearance is not normal and whose concentration of alcohol in expired air is higher than 0.25 mg. However, the driver who appears abnormal is also classified into the latter class, even though the concentration of alcohol in expiratory air is lower than 0.25 mg. A penalty for driving after drinking is graver in a heavily drunken driver than in a slightly drunken one.

The Provision for the Restriction of Public Drunkenness

The purpose of the Law for the Prevention of Troublesome Actions by Drunkards to the Public legislated in 1961, is to contribute to the public welfare and to protect Japanese people and society from evil actions by problematic drinkers (Law Bulletin Series, Japan). This provision also provides a means of supplying medical care to public drunkenness offenders. Some articles described in this law are as follows: (1) Everyone must refrain from pressuring others to drink alcohol and must limit themselves to moderate, responsible drinking. (2) Intoxicated persons must be isolated from the public and observed for a certain period under a policeman's control in a relief or police station. This applies particularly to drunken men who act in an unruly manner or cry in public places (e.g., roads, parks, stations) or in the public traffic facilities (e.g., trains, ships, and airplanes). (3) Policemen also can enter the house of a drunken man who becomes violent to relatives or friends. Originally, this law was unpopular, since public opinion in Japan was tolerant toward drunken men. However, public understanding of the purpose of this law has been gradually deepened as evidenced by the public concept that drunken men are social evils and that criminal acts by drunken men should be prevented by the law. This law clearly applies to the protection of the drunken man only in public places or in public traffic facilities. Accordingly, its application in the home is difficult without infringing on citizen rights. Moreover, the penalty for habitual drunkenness is so light that this law is considered to be practically ineffective.

COUNTERMEASURES FOR ALCOHOLICS

The necessity for taking measures to prevent problems associated with drinking has recently increased because of the increase in the number of alcoholics. Therefore, The Outline for Performing Consultations and Directions on the Evil Effects of Drinking in the Center for Mental Hygiene was legislated in 1979. This law was also legislated for the purpose of preventing alcoholism and for returning alcoholics to social life (Law Bulletin Series, Japan).

This law consists of the following articles: (1) Drinkers must be directed not to drink to excess and the detrimental effects of drinking alcohol must be advertised publically. (2) An alcoholic and his family must be consulted medically and the results of these medical consultations must be provided to a health center. These results must also be referred to a medical center such as a hospital if medical treatment is considered necessary. (3) Official systems to reduce the evil effects of drinking alcohol must be organized by each governmental office concerned. (4) The actions of private groups aiming to reduce the evil effects of drinking alcohol must be directed and supported to be effectively performed. (5) Technical and methodological supports must be given to each governmental office concerned with the enforcement of this law.

The Provision of Systems for Forcing Alcoholics to be Treated

According to The Law for Mental Hygiene, alcoholics can be forcibly committed to a hospital if more than two psychiatrists consider the patient to be an alcoholic having severe mental distortions. In other words, serious alcoholics may be admitted indefinitely to hospitals based solely on the diagnosis of at least two psychiatrists. Since the term for the admission is not defined in this provision, it is entirely dependent on the judgment of psychiatrists. Although the intended purpose of this provision will be upheld if it is appropriately applied, it is possible to raise the question of infringing on the people's rights when this provision is used as a precautionary measure.

The Provision for a System for Restriction of the Mentally Ill

A draft to deal with the mentally ill and drug addicts, who are regarded as subjects for treatment and restriction of behavior, was proposed and legislated in 1972 (Law Bulletin Series, Japan). In order to enhance the reliability of the law in terms of protecting fundamental human rights by the legal authority, the measures chiefly consisted of methods to protect the human rights of the general population from those who were mentally ill.

This provision applies to: (1) people who are sentenced to more severe punishment than imprisonment due to habits such as alcoholism, (2) people who must be sentenced again to more severe punishments than imprisonment in the near future, and (3) those who require restriction.

People unable to discharge their duties completely or partially due to alcohol intoxication have often been exempt from criminal penalties.

Therefore, this provision was legislated to maintain public safety and to treat these individuals in medical facilities. One of the important problems in this provision is that the term of restriction is clearly expressed, although no description of the term of enforced hospitalization is given. Although the term of hospitalization is dependent on the judgment of psychiatrists, the term for incarceration is generally from one to three years. The renewal of the term of restriction should be decided by a law court. These differences in handling of the term for hospitalization and incarceration occasionally result in disagreements between the opinions of psychiatrists and those of law.

The Provision for the System of Restriction is considered to be a part of the criminal code, and trends in criminal penalties in many nations include treatment and education for these incarcerated people. These trends are partially opposed in Japan for the following reasons: (1) This system is considered to be ineffective in the reduction of the crimes by alcoholics. (2) The anticipation of a second offense is considered to be impossible. (3) The drug abuser is regarded as a criminal by the general public. (4) The determination of drug addiction is considered to be difficult and it is possible that this system is utilized as an oppressive measure.

CONCLUSION

Generally speaking, drinking alcohol is closely related to the occurrence of crimes. Crimes such as violence, injury, homicide, arson, sex offense, and fraud are closely related to acute alcohol intoxication. On the other hand, crimes such as shameless action, vagrancy, and mendicancy are closely related to chronic alcoholism. Accidental homicide or accidental infliction of injury while driving after drinking alcohol also pose serious social problems. In Japan, the laws especially for crimes by the drunken man were legislated only recently. Accordingly, it can be said that the legal regulation for alcoholics has been gradually established in Japan. Controversy and debate continue to exist regarding the relationship between legal restrictions and the protection of human rights.

REFERENCES

Ewing, J. A., & Rouse, B. A. *Drinking.* Chicago: Nelson-Hall, 1978.
Hayman, M. *Alcoholism.* Springfield, Ill.: Charles C Thomas, 1965.
Law Bulletin Series. Japan: Eibun-Horei-Sha, Tokyo (Japan).
Yokoyama, T., Sakurai, M., & Noda, H. Clinico-static observation of alcoholics accommodated in the psychiatric department of our hospitals. *Kyushu Neuro-psychiatry,* 1969, *5,* 270–279.

6E

Alcohol Control Policies in Mexico

M. E. MEDINA-MORA AND C. CAMPILLO-SERRANO

Alcohol intake and its adverse individual and social consequences is a problem widely recognized by many countries of the world. Mexico has not been an exception. This concern is reflected in the creation of official bodies oriented to the control of the problem and in the considerable number of legal measures that regulate the production and distribution of alcohol (including some efforts oriented to the reduction of demand). The National Constitution of 1917 specifies that it is the obligation of the State to promote campaigns to control alcoholism. In spite of the existence of these measures, alcohol consumption and associated problems have increased. The present chapter will discuss different prevention measures utilized in Mexico.

OVERVIEW OF THE PROBLEM

In Mexico the availability of alcoholic beverages has increased considerably in the last decade. Most beverages consumed are domestic (Silva Martinez, 1972) and include in order of decending use: spirits, *pulque*[1], and wine. The actual amount of production and estimations of per capital intake are difficult to obtain mainly due to illegal production.

In spite of these disadvantages, it is known that the legal production of beer and *pulque* remained relatively constant between 1968 and 1977, while

---

[1]*Pulque* is a product that results from the mixed fermentation essentially alcoholic of the *aguamiel,* that is, a juice extracted from the *maguey* (Mexican agave).

M. E. MEDINA-MORA and C. CAMPILLO-SERRANO • Epidemiological and Social Science Department, Instituto Mexicano De Psiquiatria, Antiquo Camino A Xochimilco 101, Mexico, D.F. 14 370.

brandy showed an increase of 3.9 times between 1968 (16 million liters) and 1978 (63 million liters) (Rosovsky de Ripstein, 1981). Authorized premises for the selling of alcoholic beverages increased by 7.5% from 1955 to 1970 (Bustamante, 1974).

Mexico is the leading beer producer in Latin America and is ninth in the world. This industry is among the four most important of the country (Rosovsky de Ripstein, 1981). The government income from alcohol in the form of taxes increased from 3.67 in 1968 to 1,352.1 million pesos in 1972 (Fuente & Campillo-Serrano, 1978). In spite of this, prices of alcoholic beverages have not increased in the same proportion as other products such as milk or meat (Rosovsky de Ripstein, 1981).

Per capita alcohol intake per year in the Mexican Republic, among the population 15 years and over, has been estimated to be 47.2 liters of beer, 5.0 liters of distilled drinks, and 0.4 liters of wine; total equal to 5 liters of absolute alcohol per year (Finish Foundation and World Health Organization, 1977).

Based on mortality resulting from hepatic cirrhosis and using Jellinek's formula (1960), it has been estimated that among the population 20 years and over of both sexes, the percentage of alcoholism varied in 1971 from 5.7% (derived from a modification of the original values of the Jellinek formula adapting them to the difference in nutritional levels of the Mexican population; Bustamante, 1974) to 7.0% (utilizing the original values of the formula; Ibarra, Alarcon, & Pedroza, 1973).

Patterns of alcohol use have been investigated through four different types of surveys. In the first, the definition of alcohol abuse was very strict and included only the severe cases, resulting in low indexes, estimated to be 9.8 per 1,000 inhabitants in a national sample in 1960 (Direction de Salud Mental, SSA, 1960). The second group of surveys utilized the Marconi (1967) operational definitions of alcohol abuse. Two such surveys indicated that in 1969 in a sector of Mexico City there were 30% nondrinkers, 11.7% pathological drinkers, and 12.5% excessive drinkers (Cabildo, Martinez, & Juarez, 1969). In 1965 in a rural area there were 16% nondrinkers, 14% pathological drinkers, and 13% excessive drinkers (Maccoby, 1965). The third group comprises household surveys of the population (14 years and over) in different cities of the Mexican Republic, which use quantity indices of alcohol (Cahalan, Cisin, & Corssely, 1969). Estimations for regular drinking varied between 21% and 37% and for heavy drinking from 6% to 20%. These rates are low due to the rate of females that are heavy drinkers. For instance, in the Federal District there was one female for each 12 male heavy drinkers. The rate of heavy drinking among the male population varied from 10% to 35% (Medina-Mora, Parra, & Terroba, 1980a,b; Natera & Terroba, 1975; Parra, Terroba, & Medina-Mora, 1976, 1980; Terroba, Saltijeral, & Medina-Mora, 1978).

A more recent survey undertaken in collaboration with the World Health Organization (WHO) in the two communities within Mexico City (Calderon, Campillo-Serrano, & Suarez, 1981) showed that (1) regular alcohol use was relatively low, while intoxication was quite frequent along with problems associated with its use and (2) sex was an important determinant of alcohol use. Although the male population age was important, in the female population no important differences were observed in the different age groups. Alcohol intake was more frequent among the rural males, while in the urban community more females reported drinking, in comparison with those from the rural area. Attitudes toward drinking and intoxication did not vary. In general, it was more acceptable for men to drink; females and minors were more restricted. It seems that there is no norm oriented toward moderation in drinking. Instead, regulation apparently is directed toward those who may drink. These patterns of drinking may vary from other socioeconomic groups where more moderated regular drinking is observed. If, however, the patterns reported by the WHO project to similar communities, one can expect a high rate of adverse consequences or social problems associated with alcohol use.

Death resulting from hepatic cirrhosis has been constant during the last 10 years, with an average of 20 for each 100,000 inhabitants (Fuente & Campillo-Serrano, 1978). This rate exceeds the rates reported in the United States, Italy, Canada, and Latin America. Only the rate in Chile is higher (Rice, 1970). Hepatic cirrhosis was the leading cause of death among the male population between 40 and 50 years in 1970 (Atlas de Salud, SSA, 1973). Deaths resulting from alcoholism and alcohol psychosis have been estimated at 4.5 per 100,000 inhabitants (Atlas de Salud, SSA, 1973). Alcohol has been present in 51% of the cases of lesions (Cabildo, 1972) and 18% of the traffic accidents reported in 1973 were due to alcohol (Silva Martinez, 1972). It also was estimated that in 1972, 2% of the workers per day were absent from their jobs due to alcohol (Cabildo, 1972).

Although the problem of alcohol abuse has not been neglected by the Mexican authorities reflected in the existence of different regulations and bodies that have been created for the control of the problem, the increase in the availability and in the adverse consequences of intake may reflect the inadequacy of some of these measures.

PREVENTION STRATEGIES, ALCOHOL CONTROL POLICIES, NATIONAL LEGISLATION

Several codes regulate the production, distribution, and demand of alcoholic beverages in Mexico. The Sanitary Code regulates the activities related to the conservation and improvement of health of the population of the Mexican Republic. It establishes matters of general salubrity as the following: (1) The promotion of physical and mental health of the population; (2) The sanitary control of alcoholic beverages; (3) The national campaign against alcoholism, including the measures related to the limitation and prohibition of alcohol intake.

In addition to the Sanitary Code, complementary regulations include the Sanitary Regulation of Alcoholic Beverages and General Regulation for Commercial Premises and Public Spectacles, which regulates the distribution of alcoholic beverages. This regulation is specific for the different regions of the Mexican Republic. Specifications for the Federal District are included in this chapter paper. In addition, there are specific laws in the Labor Legislation and in the Code for Mass Media. These regulations which are related primarily to the Ministry of Health had little or no repercussions in related sectors. A general integrated policy thus was difficult to develop.

Mexico has experienced accelerated industrial development. Its economic and political system favors free enterprise. Government policy favors investments, generation of employment, and the development of certain areas through industry. Thus, the fiscal policy favors the establishment and growth of these industries, one of them being the alcohol industry. The general criteria is economic more than health oriented. As a consequence, despite the existence of regulations, a nonintegrated policy is followed.

In April of 1982, a General Anti-Alcoholic Council was created which integrates the different sectors involved (health, education, industry, and commerce, among others) with the purpose of developing policies considering all the different interests.

REDUCTION OF SUPPLY

Government control policies of production and trade and their support of industry favor production of alcoholic beverages. This is reflected in the increased availability of these substances. This increase in availability does not always equal demand but rather results from agricultural and industrial development. The only restriction that exists in this matter is the sanitary control of the process and of the different operations that are undertaken from the manufacture to the distribution to the public. In relation to trade, policies are orientated to the protection of alcoholic beverages that are of national production.

Policies of control of distribution include times of sales, number, types, and location of premises permitted to sell. The Sanitary Code stipulates that new premises designated for consumption of alcoholic beverages that exceed 5% of alcohol will not be authorized with the exception of those that, according to the Ministry of Tourism, due to their locations and characteristics may be considered centers of touristic quality. These premises cannot be located in close proximity to schools or sporting centers or other meeting places for children or youth.

In addition, a regulation for the distribution of alcoholic beverages, revoked in February of 1982, limited the location of premises permitted to sell "closed bottles." These specifications were not always followed; thus, a new regulation was enacted. It reflects the present situation better but leaves to the discretion of the different government offices the permission for opening new premises, the stipulation of the times, and the location.

The general regulations are oriented to sanitary control, type of construction, and protection from public disturbances. It stipulates that restaurants are authorized to sell table wine that does not exceed 15° G.L., and beer, both of national production without an additional license, if they are consumed with the food. In order to sell other beverages the corresponding license is required. Alcoholic beverages can be sold in closed bottles in special premises and in food stores, including supermarkets. Beer can be sold for consumption at sporting events. Beer and *pulque* can be sold at other popular festivities with a special corresponding license.

It seems that this regulation is oriented to the protection of beverages of national production and to the restriction of alcoholic beverages with a high concentration of alcohol.

Policies for the Control of Prices, Purchase, and the Promotion of Sales

Price control is regulated by the relationship between supply and demand more than by health reasons. Prices of some beverages have not increased to the same level as other basic products. Taxation policies reflect the interest of the government in developing some specific geographical areas of the country. Age is a restriction for consuming alcohol in specific places but not for buying it in closed bottles.

More specific measures exist in relation to advertising. Advertising and publicity of alcoholic beverages must be limited to providing information about the characteristics of the product's quality and manufacturing techniques, and not to its effect. Advertising should not promote consumption for health reasons, associate consumption with sports, home, or labor activities, include children or adolescents in advertising, or direct publicity toward them.

Alcohol advertising and publicity is authorized by the Ministry of Health. This disposition is aimed at protecting the public against deception regarding alcohol quality, origin, purity, conservation, and properties, or induction of practices harmful to health. All publicity materials are subject to this control including those used at demonstrations, exhibitions, and expositions.

Broadcasting agencies must combine or alternate advertising and publicity of alcoholic beverages with messages of health, education, and improvement of nutrition as well as with those formative messages oriented to the improvement of mental health and the causes of alcoholism (these dispositions are mandatory in the National Territory). Despite these measures, the criteria of the governmental officer prevails. Beer, for instance, is less restricted. Beer advertising is allowed in day hours and beer is associated with sporting events.

REDUCTION OF DEMAND

The Ministry of Health is sponsoring a national campaign against alcoholism. At present, the most significant efforts have been oriented to the training of professionals and paraprofessionals (i.e., medical doctors, psychologists, social workers, school teachers, police corps). In relation to alcohol-oriented education in schools, general aspects of health education are included in the official textbooks but specific programs have not been undertaken. Perhaps the most active group for high-risk populations is Alcoholics Anonymous and the integration of family members through its associated groups.

CONCLUSIONS

Alcohol-related problems represent an important problem in Mexico, which probably will increase due to various factors. These include (1) the replacement of national and local beverages by international beverages such as beer and brandy; (2) the relaxation of traditional norms that limit frequency and quantity of alcohol intake; and (3) the development of alcohol industries.

Despite this, administrative and legal measures tend to increase, rather than limit, the problem. It is hoped that in the near future an integrated policy may be developed that will reduce availability of alcoholic beverages. The most promising measures seems to be the increase in prices due to taxes and educational campaigns oriented to the limitation of demand.

REFERENCES

Atlas de Salud de las República Mexicana. Secretaría de Salubridad y Asistencia. Mexico City: 1973.

Bustamante, M. E. El alcoholismo y sus consecuencias socio-médicas: aspectos sociomédicos. *Gaceta Médica de México,* 1974, *107,* 227–254.

Cabildo, H. M. Panormaa epidermiogógico del alcoholismo. *Revista de la Facultad de Medicina,* 1972, *15.*

Cabildo H. M., Martínez, M. J., & Juárez, J. M. Encuesta sobre hábitos de ingestión de bebidas alcoholicas. *Salud Pública Mex* Epoca, 1969, *2,* 759–769.

Cahalan, D., Cisin, I. H., & Corssely, H. M. American drinking practices: A national study of drinking behaviour and' attitudes. New Brunswick, N.J.: Monograph No. 6, Rutgers Center of Alcohol Studies, 1969.

Calderón, G., Campillo-Serrano, C., & Suárez, C. Respuestas de la Comunidad ante los problemas relacionados con el alcohol. *Reporte Especial,* Instituto Mexicano de Psiquiatría/Organización Mundial de la Salud, 1981.

Dirección de Salud Mental y Dirección de Bioestadística. Secretaría de Salubridad y Asistencia. Primera investigación Nacional de Enfermos Neurológicos y Psiquiátricos. Mexico: Publication de la SSA, 1960.

Finnish Foundation for Alcohol Studies, 1977. International Statistics on alcohol beverages: Production, trade and consumption. 1977.

Fuente, R. de la, & Campillo-Serrano, C. Alcoholism and drug abuse in Mexico. World Health Organization/Addiction Research Foundation. Canada: ARF Books, 1978.

Ibarra I. G., Alarcón, M. A., & Pedroza, H. J. La participación de la comunidad en la lucha contra el alcoholismo. 1a. Convencion Nacional de Salud en México, 1973.

Jellinek, E. M. *The disease concept of alcoholism.* New Haven: Hillhouse Press, 1960.

Maccoby, M. El alcoholismo en una comunidad campesina. *Revista Psicoanálisis, Psiquiatría, Psicología,* Fondo de Cultura Económica, 1965, *1,* 63–64.

Marconi, J. Definiciones Básicas. In M. Horwitz & J. Marconi (Eds.), *Epidemiología del alcoholismo en América Latina.* 1967.

Medina-Mora, M. E., Parra, A. de la, & Terroba G. G. El consumo de alcohol en la población del Distrito Federal. *Salud Pub Mex* Epoca 5, 1980, *22,* 281–288. (a)

Medina-Mora, M. E., Parra, H. de la, & Terroba, G. G. Extensión del consumo de alcohol en la población de la Paz, B. C. (Encuesta de Hogares). *Cuadernos Científicos Centro Mexicano de Estudios en Salud Mental,* 1980, *12,* 193–204. (b)

Natera, G. & Terroba, G. Consumo de fármacos in la ciudad de Monterrey, N. L. (a través de encuestas de hogares). *Cuadernos Científicos Centro Mexicano de Estudios in Salud Mental,* 1979, *11,* 101–122.

Parra, A de la, Terroba G. G., & Medina-Mora, M. E. Estudio epidemiológico sobre el consumo de fármacos en la cuidad de Puebla, Pue. Report Especial Centro Mexicano de Estudios en Farmacodependencia, 1976.

Parra, A de la, Terroba G. G., & Medina-Mora, M. E. Prevalencia del consumo de alcohol en la cuidad de San Luis Potosí, S. L. P." *Enseñanza e Investigación en Psicología,* 1980, *2,* 236–245.

Rice, M. Estudio sobre la mortalidad urbana. Organizacíon Mundial de la Salud, 1960.

Rosovsky de Pirpstein, H. R. Panormaa del impacto del consumo de alcohol en Mexico". Conferencia presentada en la Reunión Internacional "Las estrategias preventivas ante los problemas relacionados con el alcohol." Instituto Mexicano de Psiquiatría. Mexico, D. F., julio 1981.

Silva Martínez, M. Alcoholismo y accidentes de tránsito. *Salud Pub Mex,* 1972, *14,* 809.

Terroba, G. G., Saltijeral, M. T., & Medina-Mora, M. E. Estudio epidemiológico sobre consumo de farmacos in la ciudad de Mexicali, B. C. Reportes Especiales Centro Mexicano de Estudios en Salud Mental, 1978.

6F

Alcohol Control Policy in the Nordic Countries (Denmark, Finland, Norway, Sweden, Iceland)

K. GUNNAR GÖTESTAM AND OLA RÖSTUM

There are interesting similarities and differences in the alcohol control policies in the Nordic countries, which include the three Scandinavian countries, Denmark, Norway, and Sweden, plus Finland and Iceland. This opens up the possibility of a comparative analysis of regulatory policies in these countries, which in other respects have rather similar cultural settings.

Finland, Norway, Sweden, and Iceland have similar types of alcohol legislation. Denmark has no special alcohol legislation, but has tried to include alcohol regulations in other laws. In addition, alcohol regulations in Denmark are more liberal as compared to the other countries.

Several factors affect alcohol consumption. One of these, which has been considered very important, is legislation. Others include price policy, increased urbanization, increased leisure time, spread of prosperity, facilitated communications, enlarged youth populations, and augmented tourist traffic bringing more contact with drinking patterns in other cultures (Kommittébetänkande, 1978).

High levels of alcohol consumption also increase the number of alcoholics (Skog, 1980–81). Recent research has shown that an increase in the

K. GUNNAR GÖTESTAM • University of Trondheim, Östmarka Hospital, Trondheim, Norway.   OLA RÖSTUM • Blue Cross Alcoholism Treatment Center, Trondheim, Norway.

total consumption by a factor of two increases the number of alcoholics by a factor of four (Bruun, Edwards, Lumio, Mäkelä, Pan, Popham, Room, Schmidt, Skog, Sulkunen, & Österberg, 1975; Skog, 1980–81). With an individual increase in alcohol consumption, the probability of liver cirrhosis is also increased (Skog, 1980, 1980–81) and, in several countries, a relation between increased alcohol consumption and higher death rates from liver cirrhosis has been shown (Bruun *et al.*, 1975; Skog, 1980). Other chronic health damages caused by alcohol also seem to follow increases in alcohol consumption (Skog, 1980–81).

Although it seems appropriate to assume a causal relationship between the amount of alcohol consumed and the occurrence of other damages caused by alcohol (i.e., acute health damages and social defects), such a relationship has been difficult to document since factors other than alcohol consumption affect such damage. Cancer in the proximal part of tractus gastrointestinalis is dependent both on the amount and type of liquor consumed, with the highest risk for strong spirits (Tuyuns, Pequignot, & Abbatucci, 1979; Skog, 1980–81). Much harm occurs from drinking in connection with driving or working. There are also clear correlations between total alcohol consumption and injuries, such as damages in traffic accidents, criminality under alcohol influence, social damages at work and in the family, and death by acute alcohol intoxication (Kommittébetänkande, 1978).

A natural hypothesis from present knowledge is that alcohol legislation affects the consumption of alcohol and this in turn affects the total damage caused by alcohol. Although this may be a feasible starting point for lawmakers, the causal relationship has been difficult to pinpoint.

In this chapter, alcohol control policies in the Nordic countries are described from 1900 to 1980 for Finland and Iceland and from 1945 to 1980 for Norway, Sweden, and Denmark. Total consumption is then presented for these countries, from 1950 to 1980. Finally, available statistics for liver cirrhosis are discussed.

Reports from national boards and committees were studied to provide a description of current legislation and changes in legislation during the last three decades. The findings are described for each country. From the same sources, the consumption pattern from 1950 to 1980 was also extracted, together with data on the occurrence of liver cirrhosis.

Table 1 shows the current 1980 alcohol control policies in the Nordic countries. Although they are quite similar, Denmark has the most liberal policies.

The different countries, however, have had rather different histories, part of which are revealed in Table 2, where changes in legislation from 1950 to 1980 are shown.

In Figure 1 the total alcohol consumption, expressed as 100% alcohol

Table 1.
Comparison between the Current Alcohol Control Policies
(1980) for the Different Nordic Countries (Except for Iceland)

Item	Denmark	Finland	Norway	Sweden	Iceland
Drinking age	18	18	18[a]/20	18	21[b]
Sale age	—	20	18[a]/20	18[a]/20	21[b]
State monopoly	no	yes	yes	yes	yes
Restrictions of sale	few	yes	yes	yes	yes
Taxation	yes	yes	yes	yes	yes
Advertisement	reduced	banned	banned	banned	banned
Alcohol driving prohibited	yes	yes	yes	yes	yes

[a]The lower figure indicates wine and beer, whereas the higher indicates strong spirits.
[b]For strong liquors and wine (more than 2.25 vol. % alcohol).

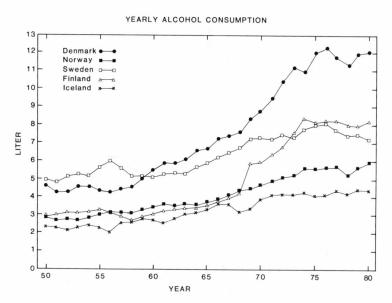

YEARLY ALCOHOL CONSUMPTION

Figure 1. Mean yearly consumption of alcohol (calculated as pure alcohol) per inhabitant over 15 years in the Nordic countries in the period 1950 to 1980 (data from Om alkoholpolitikken, 1980–81, reprinted with permission). In the data from Iceland, an approximation of the data for a population above 15 years has been made for 1950–63, as only figures for the total population were available.

Table 2.

Comparisons between the Different Legal Systems and Changes in Them in the Period
1950 to 1980 in the Five Nordic Countries

Year	Denmark	Finland	Norway	Sweden	Iceland
1954				The Bratt system abolished; establishment of state monopoly	Spirit monopoly; advertisement ban
1957	Liberalization of restrictions on restaurants				
1958			Liberalization for hotels		
1965				Introduction of medium beer	
1967			Liberalization of retail sale		
1968		New alcohol act (medium beer, rural prohibition abolished)			
1971		Individual purchase control abolished			
1973	Spirit monopoly abolished (EEC)		Liberalization of sale		
1975			Advertisement ban		
1977		Advertisement ban		Medium beer withdrawn; advertisement ban	
1978	Increased local control				

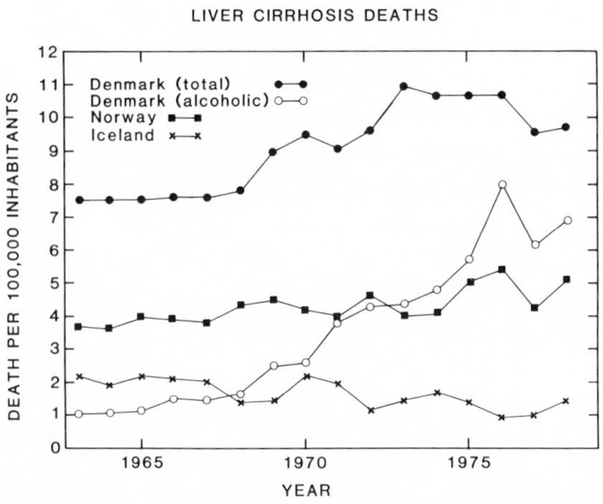

LIVER CIRRHOSIS DEATHS

Figure 2. Annual mortality rate per 100,000 inhabitants from liver cirrhosis in Denmark, Norway, and Iceland in the period 1963 to 1978 (data partially from Prytz and Skinhøj, Alcoholic and nonalcoholic cirrhosis of the liver, reprinted with permission from Ugeskrift for Laeger, copyright 1981). The data from Iceland have a great variability (from 0 to 7 deaths per year), and therefore are presented as floating means per three-year period. For Finland, see text.

per inhabitant above 15 years of age, in the period 1950 to 1980, is shown. Both Table 2 and Figure 1 are discussed in relation to the descriptions provided for each country below.

In Figure 2, the death rate in liver cirrhosis per 100,000 inhabitants is shown for Denmark, Norway, and Iceland for the period 1963 to 1978. These and other aspects of damages also are discussed under each section below.

DENMARK

LEGISLATION

In Denmark, there is no special alcohol law, since regulations regarding alcohol have been covered in laws governing taxation, hotels and restaurants, traffic, and primary schools. In 1917, a high alcohol tax was introduced. It has been gradually increased, but not as rapidly as wages. When Denmark was admitted to the European Common Market (EEC) in 1973, the Danish spirit monopoly was abandoned. Danish and foreign products became equal with regard to price regulation and taxes, and the real price since has been reduced, especially for wine. There are no special regulations on the sale of alcohol, apart from the rule that it must only be sold during regular opening hours of stores.

Hotel and restaurant laws include regulations regarding the serving of alcohol, prohibiting service to drunken persons and persons under the age of 18. Traffic laws prohibit drunken driving and determine sanctions when the law is violated. The primary school law requires that information on alcohol use and abuse be given in the first nine school grades.

Some increase in alcohol taxes is foreseen, as well as some restrictions on alcohol advertisement, although it will not be totally banned, as in the other Nordic countries.

PROPHYLAXIS AND ATTITUDES TOWARD ALCOHOL

The use of price policy and taxes has been regarded in Denmark as the main means of restricting total alcohol consumption. In 1917 such steps resulted in an abrupt decrease in total consumption and cases of delirium tremens. However, illegal import and home distillation tend to increase when price is increased. In general, there has been a relatively liberal attitude regarding the use of alcohol in Denmark (Kontaktutvalget, 1980).

CONSUMPTION

In the period between 1950 and 1980, consumption has increased by three times, with a continuous development during the period (see Figure 1). After liberalization of the legislation in 1958 (see Table 2) the sharpest increase has been seen. Denmark also has the highest consumption among the Nordic countries. This may depend not only on relatively liberal legislation, but also on liberal attitudes toward alcohol use in the population (Danmarks Statistik, 1980; Stortingsmelding, 1980–81).

DAMAGES CAUSED BY ALCOHOL

The death rate from liver cirrhosis increased 29% in the period between 1963 and 1978. Alcohol-dependent liver cirrhosis has been responsible for most of this increase (see Figure 2). It is evident that the death rate from alcohol-dependent liver cirrhosis increased seven times during the period (Danmarks Statistik, 1980; Prytz & Skinhøj, 1981).

FINLAND

LEGISLATION

Prohibition of home distillation was introduced in Finland in 1866. Until the end of the nineteenth century, the local communes determined production and distribution of alcohol. In 1919, production, sale, and import of all substance with more than 2% (vol. %) alcohol was prohibited, with the exception of alcohol for medical, technical, or scientific purposes. This law was abolished when a new alcohol law was introduced in 1932. This law was intended to restrict the use of alcohol and prevent alcoholism and alcohol problems. A state monopoly took charge of production and sale, and local communes were responsible for retail sales. Permits to serve alcohol had to be approved by the country councils. Age to buy alcohol was 21 years, whereas the age to be served was 18.

In 1968 there were great changes in the legislation. Age to buy alcohol was reduced to 20 years (for strong spirits), and medium beer (2.25 to 3.7%) was introduced in stores and coffee shops. Restrictions in advertisements were introduced in 1977.

PROPHYLAXIS

Parallel to these legal changes, efforts were made to intensify the preventions of alcohol problems through (1) price increases, (2) the establishment of special temperance boards in the communes (1944), (3) the education of youth leaders in temperance work (in 1950), and (4) the establishment of an alcohol policy research institute. Campaigns to reduce the strength of alcohol beverages (light wine, light beer) were also held.

ATTITUDES TOWARD ALCOHOL

Attitudes toward alcohol policy were changed from a restrictive attitude in the 1940s and 1950s to a more liberal attitude in about 1960. This was reflected in more liberal legislation in 1968. Penalties for drunkenness in public were removed in 1969. From 1970 to the present, attitudes have no longer been so liberal. This coincides with increased problems caused by alcohol on productivity, family life, and national health.

Consumption

Alcohol statistics have been registered since 1933. They show an abrupt increase in consumption when the prohibition law was abolished in 1932 (from 1933 to 1934 there was a 71% increase). Consumption then remained relatively constant until 1945, except for a fall of 22% from 1938 to 1939. This decrease may be related to the outbreak of World War II in Finland (in 1939). In 1945 the consumption increased by 56% from the year before (1944), which similarly may be related to the end of the war. Until about 1958 the consumption was relatively constant, followed by an increase from 1958 to 1974. This presumably is related to urbanization, increased incomes, and a more positive attitude toward alcohol. The increase after 1969 should be noted, since it followed the liberalization of the alcohol laws. As seen in Figure 1, the increase in this period represents a much higher percent increase than the comparable increases in Sweden, Norway, and Iceland. One possible explanation is that the real price of alcohol in Finland was reduced about 20% in the years from 1970 to 1974, whereas the real income increased about 20% in the same period.

Damages Caused by Alcohol

In the period from 1958 to 1974 there was a four-fold increase in drunken driving, a three-fold increase in traffic accidents related to alcohol, and a clear increase in deaths caused by acute alcohol intoxication. In the same period, liver cirrhosis death rates increased by about 50% (Kommit-tébetänkande, 1978).

NORWAY

Legislation

Since the Prohibition Act of 1919 was abolished in 1927, the goal in Norwegian alcohol legislation has been to prevent alcohol damage but at the same time to ensure the citizen's right to choose to use alcohol. Only the state monopoly can produce and sell alcohol, although retail sales are determined locally by the commune board. Since 1956, local polls have played an important role in retail sales and serving restrictions (Horverak, 1979). Since 1967, communes with less than 400 inhabitants have had the authorization to sell alcohol.

Advertisement was banned in 1976 (Kommitébetänkande, 1978). The price control policy has included rather high prices on liquors (since 1972 there have been four tax classes of beer, with Class 0 on 0.7% alcohol or below, and Class 3 on 4.75 to 7% alcohol). In 1973, the sale age for alcohol was reduced from 21 to 20 years for strong spirits and 18 years for wine and beers. Beginning in 1973, regulations regarding serving and hours of sales of alcohol could be determined locally (Horverak, 1979).

CONSUMPTION

The alcohol statistics show a clear and nearly continuous increase in the consumption from 1953 to 1977 (see Figure 1). During this period the increase has been 109%. Recent investigations have also shown that the number of alcohol users has increased, especially among youth and women (Stortingsmelding, 1980–81). The largest increase in consumption is associated with legal changes in 1967 and 1973 (see Table 2 and Figure 1). In 1978, the fall in consumption was related to a lengthy strike in the state monopoly sales chain.

DAMAGES CAUSED BY ALCOHOL

In Norway some increase in the liver cirrhosis mortality rate is shown, although this increase is much smaller than that shown for Denmark (see Figure 2).

SWEDEN

LEGISLATION

Alcohol legislation in Sweden was thoroughly reformed in 1954, when the ransom system introduced by Bratt in 1917 was abolished. A state monopoly was established, which now is responsible for retail sale and restaurant sale of strong spirits, wine, and strong beer (above 2.8% alcohol). Until 1955, only beer below 2.8% alcohol was allowed, but in 1965 this limit was elevated to 3.6% with the introduction of medium beer in stores and coffee shops. The age for sale was set at 18 in 1972.

In 1977 the alcohol legislation again was reformed. The medium beer disappeared and regulations similar to those functioning from 1955 to 1965 were reintroduced. Age for sale remained at 20 years for strong spirits and 18 for wine and beer. There were also regulations with regard to where alcohol could be served and the price policy, in an attempt to direct use from stronger to lighter liquors. Prevention and information campaigns as well as leisure activity among youth, alcohol-free restaurants, temperance organizations, and education of leaders and support persons were supported by the state. Alcohol advertisement was also banned.

CONSUMPTION

In Figure 1 a small increase is shown in 1954 to 1956, which coincides with the reform in legislation in 1954 (abolishment of ransom system). The total consumption increased from 5.64 in 1964 to 7.32 in 1970 and 8.11 in 1976. Sweden had an increase in total consumption during the period 1965 to 1977 when medium beer was on the market. It is unclear if the medium beer reform really affected the total consumption, since the change is smaller than the comparable changes in Norway and Iceland (Kommittébetänkande, 1978; Stortingsmelding, 1980–81; Sveriges officiella statistik, 1979).

ICELAND

LEGISLATION

After a national poll in 1915, there was a total prohibition against import and sale of alcohol. However, as early as 1917, physicians were allowed to prescribe alcohol, and in 1922 Iceland had to import and sell wine containing up to 21% (because of economical pressure from Spain). A state monopoly was established in 1922, limiting retail sale stores to seven and places where alcohol could be served to one. The prohibition law was abolished and replaced by an alcohol law in 1935 (with smaller changes in 1940 and 1954 still in function). The goal of this law was to prevent abuse of alcohol and prevent accidents caused by alcohol (Den Islandske alkohollov, 1954). Commune polls determine retail sale places, and home distillation and advertisements are prohibited.

PROPHYLAXIS

The Parliament (Alltinget) established a special temperance board which should facilitate temperance and prevent damage caused by alcohol. This board has supervising and controlling functions in relation to commune boards, and has responsibility for doing research and spreading information about alcohol. Alcohol education is mandatory in the primary school.

ATTITUDES TOWARD ALCOHOL

Since 1884 the Independent Order of Good Templars (IOGT) has been working on influencing alcohol laws in Iceland. This movement, which has been implanting a restrictive attitude toward alcohol, had a significant influence on lawmaking until about 1930. At that time the legislation became more liberal, reflecting the attitudes of the population (Arnason, 1980).

CONSUMPTION

Statistics show a decrease in consumption from 1881 to 1885 (2.38 liter) to about 1916 to 1920, where a minimum was achieved. At this time, there was a continuous increase until approximately 1950, with the exception of lower consumption during the war from 1940 to 1945. From 1950 to 1980, there was a steady increase to a level twice as high as 1950 (see Figure 1). There was no change in legislation after 1954, so changes in consumption must be attributed to other factors. A rather low level may be attributed to the fact that the figures do not include beer (*Yearbook of Nordic Statistics,* 1982).

DAMAGES CAUSED BY ALCOHOL

Liver cirrhosis mortality for the 10-year period 1960–69 was about 70% higher than for 1950–59. In the next 10 years, 1970–79, it again returned to the 1950–59 level (see Figure 2).

CONCLUSIONS

It is difficult to draw any clear conclusions from the data presented. Apart from legislation, several other factors may affect the alcohol consumption. These factors, however, all contribute to increases in the alcohol consumption in Western society. Although it is difficult to draw any causal conclusions, some coinciding temporal patterns are striking. In Table 3,

Table 3.
Comparison of Changes in Legislation, Consumption, and
Damages (Liver Cirrhosis) for the Nordic Countries

Country	Year	Law	Consumption	Damages
Denmark	58	+	+	?
	73	+	+	+
	78	−	−	−
Finland	68	+	+	
	70	+	+	+
	77	−	−	?
Norway	57	+	+	?
	67	+	+	+
	73	+	+	+
	76	−	−	−
Sweden	54	+	+	?
	65	+	+	?
	77	−	−	?
Iceland	54	−	−	?

Liberalized legislation (+), restrictive legislation (−), consumption increase (+), and decrease (−), and increase (+) and decrease (−) in liver cirrhosis. Data not available (?).

comparisons of changes in the legislation, consumption, and damage (liver cirrhosis) patterns are presented. When data are available, the consumption changes temporally follow the changes in legislation, and the changes in liver cirrhosis mortality rate in turn follow the consumption changes. Phi correlations were computed between the three sets of data, showing significant correlations between changes in legislation and alcohol consumption ($\Phi = 0.99$, $p < .001$), between alcohol consumption and alcohol-induced damages (liver cirrhosis) ($\Phi = 0.99$, $p < .01$), and between legislation and damages ($\Phi = 0.99$, $p < .01$). Although the phi correlation is not comparable to other correlation measures, these data strongly indicate that the legislation may affect consumption and damages and may thus be used as an instrument (among other factors) to regulate consumption.

REFERENCES

Arnason, O. H. Den alkoholpolitiske situation i Island (The alcohol political situation on Iceland). *Tidsskrift om edruskaps-spørsmål*, 1980, *2*, 18–19.
Bruun, K., Edwards, G., Lumio, M., Mäkelä, K., Pan, L., Popham, R. E., Room, R., Schmidt, W., Skog, O.-J., Sulkunen, P., & Österberg, E. *Alcohol control policies in public health perspective*. Helsinki: The Finnish Foundation for Alcohol Studies, 1975.
Danmarks Statistik. *Færdselsuheldsstatistik* (Traffic accident statistics). København, 1980.

Den Islandske alkohollov, Nr. 58 (Alcohol legislation of Iceland). Reykjavik, 1954.

Horverak, Ø. *Norsk alkoholpolitikk 1960–75* (Norwegian alcohol policy 1960 to 1975). Oslo: Statens institutt for alkohol-forskning, 1979.

Kommittébetänkande 1978:33. *Alkoholkommitténs betänkande* (Report of the Finnish alcohol committee). Helsinki, 1978.

Kontaktutvalget vedrørende alkohol og narkotikaspørgsmål. *Dansk alkohollovgivning* (Danish alcohol legislation). København, 1980.

Norges offisielle statistikk. *Alkohol og andre rusmidler* (Alcohol and other euphoria-producing substances). Oslo: Statistisk Sentralbyrå, 1981.

Nyhus, P., & Gullbrand, A. *Spesiallover for elever ved Politiskolen* (Special legislation for students at the Police School). Oslo: Politiskolen, 1977.

Prytz, H., & Skinhøj, P. Alkoholisk og ikke-alkoholisk cirrose (Liver cirrhosis of alcohol and other ethiology in Denmark). *Ugeskrift for Læger,* 1981, *110,* 1175–1179.

Skog, O.-J. Sammenhengen mellom totalforbruk og omfanget av skadevirkninger (Relation between total alcohol consumption and alcohol-induced damages). In Stortingsmelding Nr. 24: *Om alkoholpolitikken* (About the alcohol policy). Oslo, 1980–81.

Skog, O.-J. Liver cirrhosis epidemiology: Some methodological problems. *British Journal of Addiction,* 1980, *75,* 227–243.

Stortingsmelding Nr. 24 *Om alkoholpolitikken* (About the alcohol policy). Oslo, 1980–81.

Sveriges officiella statistik: *Alkoholstatistik 1979* (Alcohol statistics in Sweden 1979). Stockholm: Socialstyrelsen, 1980.

Tuyns, A., Pequignot, G., & Abbatucci, J. S. Oesophagal cancer and alcohol consumption: Importance of type of beverage. *International Journal of Cancer,* 1979, *23,* 443–447.

Yearbook of Nordic Statistics 1981 (Vol. 19). Copenhagen: Nordic Council and Nordic Statistical Secretariat, 1982.

6G

Alcohol Control Policy in Nigeria

AMECHI ANUMONYE

To determine the aims of alcohol control policies in Nigeria, it is necessary to clarify the topic and to present some basic information on relevant features of the country. Alcohol control policies refer to the legal, economic, and physical factors that bear on the availability of alcohol to the individual. The word *policies* relates to all relevant strategies that government may apply to influence availability. It will also be necessary to describe other factors of importance, including informal controls, range of attitudes and values, and relevant sociological and anthropological data.

COUNTRY FEATURES

Nigeria is between 4 and 14 degrees north of the equator, a feature of considerable cultural, medical, economic, historical, and political importance. It is the largest geographical unit on the West African coast, with a climate and vegetation ranging from the tropical through the savanna to the temperate in the hills and plateaus.

The population of Nigeria has been a controversial issue since 1953 because of the economic and political significance in revenue allocation. Population figures in this report refer to the United Nations estimation of 77 million for 1980.

AMECHI ANUMONYE • Department of Psychiatry, Lagos University Teaching Hospital, Lagos, Nigeria.

More than 80% of Nigerians live in rural areas. Industrialization and urbanization have led to considerable in-migration from villages into overcrowded industrial cities. The problems (the stresses produced by rapid change) are remarkably similar in both the cities and the villages, especially in relation to housing, electricity, and water shortage. Overpopulation, poor sanitation, inadequate food supply, unemployment, and underemployment afflict the cities. The traditional extended family is rapidly disappearing in the cities. A good percentage exists in the rural areas.

The Nigerian economy is predominantly agricultural even with the present small-scale industrialization related to the country's diverse natural resources: natural oil and gas, coal, tin, iron, timber, water, and fisheries. The total labor force is small, with employed males numbering nearly four times the females. Women engage in trading and are powerful factors in the distribution of alcoholic drinks. The average per capita income is about 141 Naira ($211) per annum.

The Federal Republic of Nigeria has 19 states. Once a British colony, Nigeria became independent in October 1960 and a republic in 1963. Originally, there were a federal parliament, a ceremonial president, and a prime minister, with four self-governing states. This was followed by military rule for 13 years. The present political structure, an executive presidential system, started in October 1979. It has a three-tier system (federal, state, and local) of government with the functions and powers clearly defined. By the United Nations estimation, the yearly average increase in population is 1.7 million. The Nigerian Federal Office of Statistics puts it at an average annual growth rate of 2.8% to 3.4%. Within the next 20 years Nigeria would double her population, thereby setting a world record. This is ominous considering that her land mass is not undergoing a similar change. The United Nations 1980 estimate of sex distribution is 49% males; it also is estimated that in 1980, people below 15 years of age constituted 23% of the population and the percentage of those over 65.only 2%.

SOCIOCULTURAL FEATURES

There is a great diversity of ethnic groups, language, religion, and culture in Nigeria, and many traditions have been retained to the present. There currently are over 250 ethnic groups. Many of the apparently homogeneous groups have smaller language subgroups. The major ethnic groups are Hausa, Ibo, and Yoruba. Other major language groups include Edo, Efik, Ijaw, Fofode, and Tiv. Nigeria and other West African groups share similar characteristics as well as basic beliefs in animism, superstition, and rituals.

Although the working language in Nigeria is English, Arabic is also used in the north. Three major types of religion exist and have great influence on the life of Nigerians: (1) the traditional, basic, and fundamental animism; (2) Islam, primarily in the north, southwestern, and midwestern areas and less so in the southeast; (3) Christianity in the remaining parts of the east, midwest, and southwest. The north has few Christians. A number of syncretic Christian sects have recently sprung up all over the country. This political structure makes planning and execution of national policies very difficult. Such diversity is a problem for alcohol control since the states are competing with each other for the establishment of beer breweries.

TYPES OF ALCOHOLIC BEVERAGES

Traditional or indigenous alcoholic drinks consist of: (1) Palm wine, which is the sap of the palm tree has two types. the old palm tree and the raphia palm tree. At the early unfermented stage both are sweet and are said to contain no alcohol. The alcohol content increases with storage and fermentation. (2) cereal-based alcoholic drinks which are called *Burukutu* and *Pito* are made from millet. Palm trees flourish in the southern rain forest areas, while the millet grows mostly in the northern savanna lands; (3) Some types of alcoholic beverages are also made from maize and cocoa pods. (4) Locally made gin has several names, the most common being *Ogogoro*. It is distilled from palm wine predominantly in the southern riverine areas but by no means restricted to those places. This was formally illicit but has recently been legalized; (5) There also is locally brewed beer and stout, for which imported barley and wheat are used. Many state governments in collaboration with indigenous and foreign partners own breweries. The urge to build breweries is great, and one state is known to have not less than four breweries. (6) Whiskey is bottled locally by some pharmacists who import both the alcohol for dilution, standard bottles, and registered patented brand names on labels. (7) Wines are not yet made in Nigeria. Great potential exists for wines in the large varieties of fruits in the country. (8) Imported alcohol includes beverages imported into Nigeria before 1978 including beer, stout, spirits, and wine. Importation of beers, stout, champagne, and sparkling wines was banned in the 1978/79 budgetary exercise to safeguard local breweries (beer and stout) and to protect public morality (champagne). Importation continues for spirits (whiskey, gin, brandy) and for other wines.

Factors Affecting Alcohol Control Policies

Certain factors need consideration in devising alcohol control policies for Nigeria: (1) historical background of alcohol control policies; (2) sociocultural significance of alcoholic beverages; (3) economic and political role of alcohol manufacture and distribution; and (4) concept of alcoholism and statistics relating to alcohol-related problems.

Historical Background of Alcohol Control Policies

An account of the control policies during the colonial days is provided by Pam (1975). The following series of events are noteworthy. Fifteenth-century European trade relied very heavily on liquor (especially spirits) as articles of commerce (in exchange for Nigerian products) in spite of protests from missionaries, explorers, and colonial administrators. The dangerous effect of cheap spirits exported to Africa by European traders and the association of alcohol with slave trade generated opposition to alcohol and slave trade in both Europe and Africa. Although the British at the Berlin Conference of 1884 (for the partitioning of Africa) were trying to introduce measures against the hazards of liquor trade, the Germans and the Dutch were strongly opposed to this move. At the Brussels Conference of 1889–1890 (for suppression of slave trade) liquor trade and alcoholism were treated as aspects of the slave trade; the importation and indigenous production of liquor therefore were forbidden in some areas of Africa while taxation was instituted in other areas not affected by the prohibition. However, this Brussel General Act was ineffective.

Protest resolutions (signed by Africans at meetings in 1895 in Nigeria) condemning liquor trade in West Africa yielded no results. Nigerian Anglican bishops protested at the International Congress on Alcohol Abuse in Brussels (1897) that, apart from being harmful morally, physically, mentally, and spiritually, liquor traffic was destroying the trade in other less harmful but more useful articles. Other conferences, in 1899, 1906, and 1912 tried in vain to bring about a change in alcohol policies of the colonial powers.

In 1913, a publication was issued by the German colonial office related to alcohol and native policy. Distinguished German, French, and English men formed an international federation for the protection of natives against alcohol. Trade interests, however, supervened. The Native Races and the Liquor Trade Committee of 1909 investigated the liquor trade in Southern Nigeria and expressed concern over the excessive use of alcohol. The focus on Southern Nigeria indicates the protective role of the Islamic religion and law in the north during this period. This control has broken down.

The International Convention of St. Germain-en-Laye in September

1919 (following the end of World War I), involving the United States, Belgium, Britain, France, Portugal, Italy, and Japan, was the first treaty to concern itself with alcohol. It prohibited the importation, distribution, sale, and possession of every kind of trade on spirits and beverages as well as the manufacture and access to distilling apparatus. All Africa was included in this treaty except the northern countries of Algeria, Tunisia, Libya, Morroco, Egypt, and the Union of South Africa. The treaty was supervised by the League of Nations.

Following the failure of legal prohibition as a measure against alcohol in the United States and Finland, by the year 1932 little interest was shown in the 1919 St. Germain-en-Laye Treaty. The International Bureau Against Alcoholism convened a conference in Geneva in 1925 to increase interest in alcoholism as a health problem. However, trade interest (of France and Portugal) again blocked this.

In 1947 the WHO included alcoholism in its health program. In the 1950s the industrialized countries cooperated by developing treatment and preventive services for alcoholism as a disease. After World War II, in 1949, the Nigerian Brewery Company was set up marking the beginning of a new era in the Nigerian alcohol scene and national control policies.

In 1956, following France's change of heart, a French government committee convened the first All-African Congress on Alcoholism on the Ivory Coast and dealt with alcoholism as a disease. As the country neared independence, alcoholism became the concern of the Department (and later Ministry) of Health. However, since the alcohol-related problems were to compete with other priorities, interest declined. Ekundare (1973) noted that, in 1960, the governor general of Nigeria suggested the replacement of foreign imports of spirits with more useful and less harmful articles. No action followed his speech. Ever since the formation of the Nigerian Brewery Company in 1949, Nigerian alcohol control policy has seen only few changes.

Current national control policies include taxation of alcoholic beverages and licensing laws embodying the inspection of the places of alcohol sales and consumption.

SOCIOCULTURAL SIGNIFICANCE OF ALCOHOLIC BEVERAGES

Alcohol has been in use among the southern ethnic groups for a long time for several purposes:

- Traditional religions' ceremonies and rituals
- Merrymaking at festive occasions and social events such as marriages, burials, title initiations

- Young children (boys more than girls) are allowed to drink in moderation under the supervision of adults during social occasions
- Certain traditional medications are prepared with alcohol

Social structures of importance in alcohol use in Nigeria include

- Insecurity associated with rapid environmental changes in urbanization, industrialization, and acculturation
- Scarcity of living spaces related to rapid population growth
- Decreasing opportunity for self-fulfillment, attendant on the current political and economic states
- Use of alcohol as a means of reducing tension associated with stresses of life in urban centers
- For some people, alcohol use is a status symbol; this led to the ban on champagne
- For the southern riverine areas alcohol drinking is a normal way of living

Governments cannot prohibit distribution without creating a black market.

Alcohol control policy in Nigeria should take cognizance of information available in the industrialized countries:

1. Many alcoholics do not want their illness cured.
2. In many countries prevention is merely an utopian aim.
3. Some reduction can be achieved by the application of certain basic strategies of persuasion and compulsion

In persuasion, attempts are made to obtain changes of behavior through direct information (such as in alcohol education programs) or through indirect information (campaigns and news media advertising). In compulsion, behavior is modified by control and pricing policies. Thought must be given to:

1. Ethical problems as to why and by whom an individual's behavior pattern should be interfered with
2. The observation that changing the price of alcohol affects maximally the poorer members of the community
3. The fact that increasing taxes beyond a certain limit will create the use of other substances of dependence
4. The fact that there is need for widespread community support arising out of health education.

At present, it is unlikely that Nigeria will enter into international agreements about alcohol control policies.

REFERENCES

Anumonye, A., Omoniwa, N., & Adaranijo, H. Excessive alcohol use and related problems in Nigeria. *Drug and Alcohol Dependence,* 1977, *2,* 23.

Asuni, T. *Pattern of alcohol problems as seen in the Neuro-Psychiatric Hospital, Aro, Abeokuta, 1964–1973.* Proceedings on the 1974 Workshop of the Association of Psychiatrists in Africa on Alcohol and Drug Dependence, Kenya, September 1974. International Council on Alcohol and Addiction Publication, 1973.

Ekundare, R. O. An economic history of Nigeria 1860–1960. New York: Africana, 1973.

Federal Office of Statistics *Digest of Statistics* (Vol. 24). April, July, October, 1975.

Lambo, T. A. Socio-economic changes and mental health in Man and Africa. In G. Wolstenholme and M. O'Connor, Ciba Foundation Symposium. London: J. & A. Churchill, 1965.

Marinho, A. A. *Problems of alcohol and drug dependence in Nigeria—A response to WHO enquiry.* Mimeograph, 1972.

Pam, L. Alcohol in colonial Africa. *The Finnish Foundation for Alcohol Studies* (Vol. 22). Helsinki, 1975.

6H

Alcohol Control Policy in the United States

DOUGLAS A. PARKER

Few policies of governments have aroused as much interest and generated as much debate as those controlling alcohol use and misuse. In the nineteenth century, social reformers such as Dr. Benjamin Rush urged support for a campaign against spirits in order to "save our fellow men from being destroyed by the great destroyer of their lives and souls" (quoted in Levine, 1978). The Temperance Movement which evolved from that period regarded liquor as a powerful substance that needed to be controlled, if not eliminated altogether by governmental regulations. Support for the prohibition of alcohol production and sales increased during the first two decades of the twentieth century and resulted in the passage of the Eighteenth Amendment. The subsequent repeal of national prohibition in 1933 because of problems of enforcement and changes in the attitudes of the population did not end government alcohol control policies or the controversy over them.

STATE AND FEDERAL RESPONSIBILITIES

The Twenty-first Amendment to the Constitution of the United States assigned the states the right and responsibility for the regulation of the manufacture, distribution, sale, and consumption of alcoholic beverages

DOUGLAS A. PARKER • Department of Sociology, California State University, Long Beach, California 90840.

within their borders. In response, states either continued prohibition (e.g., Oklahoma and Mississippi), assumed monopoly control over distribution and sales (e.g., Ohio and Michigan), gave priority to local control over alcohol (e.g., Deleware and Massachusetts), and/or established state boards and commissions to administer control policies (e.g., California and Colorado). Increasing opposition to prohibition eventually led to its repeal by the few states that had continued it (Morgan, 1978).

By the 1970s, 18 states were using a monopoly system of control and the other 32 states and the District of Columbia were using a license system (Licensed Beverage Industries, 1973a). Under the monopoly system distilled spirits (and sometimes beer and wine as well) are purchased only from a state bureau or department. All sales in off-premise outlets (establishments that sell alcohol in packaged form for consumption away from the sales outlets) are conducted in stores owned and operated by the state. Sales in on-premise outlets (establishments that sell alcohol by the drink for consumption within the establishments) are conducted in licensed businesses that are privately owned and operated but which obtain their alcoholic beverages from the state. Under the license system, the states and, in some places, counties and cities, issue licenses to some privately owned businesses for either off-premise sales, on-premise sales, or for both off-premise and on-premise sales.

Both monopoly and license states place restrictions on the type of off-premise outlet that can sell wine and beer. For example, 8 of the 18 monopoly states and 12 of the 32 license states prohibit the sale of wine in grocery stores. Beer, however, is more readily available. Only one of the monopoly states and 4 of the license states prohibit the sale of beer in grocery stores (Licensed Beverage Industries, 1973a). The monopoly and license states also place restrictions on the sale of food in off-premise outlets. Seventeen of the monopoly states and 13 of the license states prohibit the sale of food in package stores (Licensed Beverage Industries, 1973b).

Both monopoly and license states impose regulatory limitations on the number of alcohol sales outlets that can be licensed. Twenty-four of the 50 states place restrictions on the number of outlets per unit of population (Licensed Beverage Industries, 1973c). For example, Pennsylvania, a monopoly state, issues one on-premise license for each 1,500 persons (Pennsylvania also issues licenses to separate parts of a municipality and to resort areas without regard to population). New Jersey, a license state, issues one off-premise license for each 3,000 persons and one on-premise license for each 7,500 persons. Most of the states and the District of Columbia also impose regulatory limitations on the hours and days of sale of these outlets.

All of the states have minimum age requirements for individuals who consume or sell alcoholic beverages. Twenty-three of the states and the

District of Columbia have a minimum drinking age of 21; although six of these states and the District of Columbia permit consumption of either light wine or beer or both at the age of 18. The minimum drinking age in the other states ranges from 18 to 20. Most states also require that persons employed in selling, handling, and serving alcoholic beverages meet the age requirements for the purchase of these beverages (Licensed Beverage Industries, 1972a; Smart, 1980).

In many of the states, persons who sell alcoholic beverages to minors (Licensed Beverage Industries, 1972b) and minors who purchase alcoholic beverages may be fined and/or jailed (Licensed Beverage Industries, 1972c). The states also impose penalties for public intoxication and for operating an automobile under the influence of alcohol. Although it is a misdemeanor to be drunk in public, in many states detoxification centers are offered rather than imprisonment ("drunk tanks") to deal with this behavior.

The Comprehensive Alcohol Abuse and Alcoholism Prevention, Treatment, and Rehabilitation Act of 1970 established the National Institute on Alcohol Abuse and Alcoholism (NIAAA) to assume responsibility for federal activities oriented toward (1) the accumulation and dissemination of knowledge concerning the health hazards associated with the misuse of alcohol and (2) the enhancement and promotion of the capacity of individual states and communities for sustaining programs of alcoholism prevention, treatment, and rehabilitation. The NIAAA was also established to assume responsibility for the formulation of federal prevention policies. In the first decade of its existence, NIAAA developed policies that have provoked considerable discussion and criticism.

RESPONSIBLE DRINKING NORMS

During the first five years of its existence, the NIAAA policy on the prevention of alcohol misuse was the promotion of norms of "responsible drinking." NIAAA contended that Americans could be taught to drink in moderation and in contexts in which peers, family members, and others would encourage moderation. The NIAAA policy implied that the experiences of Jews and other groups whose ethnic heritage proscribed heavy drinking, prescribed moderate drinking, and had low rates of alcohol problems could be translated into a national program of prevention through educational tactics and mass persuasion. Others were skeptical, however. As Howard Blane put it, "to expect that a particular practice, rooted in cultural-religious tradition, can be transplanted and flourish in secular, pragmatic America is naive" (1976).

Underlying the NIAAA policy was the assumption that the United States had a high rate of alcoholism and alcohol-related problems because of a culturally induced ambivalence about alcohol use. As the first NIAAA director, Dr. Morris E. Chafetz argued in a report to Congress:

> The rate of alcoholism . . . has been shown to be low in groups whose drinking-related customs, values and sanctions are widely known, established, and congruent with other cultural values. On the other hand, alcoholism rates are higher in those populations where ambivalence is marked. Apparently, in cultures which use alcohol but have a low incidence of alcoholism, people drink in a definite pattern. The beverage is sipped slowly, consumed with food, taken in the company of others—all in relaxing, comfortable circumstances. Drinking is taken for granted. No emotional rewards are reaped by the man who shows prowess of consumption. Intoxication is abhorred. Other cultures with a high incidence of alcohol-related problems usually assign a special significance to drinking. Alcohol use is surrounded with attitudes of ambivalence and guilt. Maladaptive drinking, drinking without food, and intoxication are common. . . . The guilt that so many families feel about their own drinking behavior is reflected in society's attitudes. Ours is a nation that is ambivalent about its alcohol use. This confusion has deterred us from creating a national climate that encourages responsible attitudes toward drinking for those who choose to drink; that is, using alcohol in a way which does not harm oneself or society. (Chafetz, 1971, pp. 1–4)

The NIAAA prevention policy was derived from the federally funded Cooperative Commission on the Study of Alcoholism (Plaut, 1967; Wilkinson, 1970) which had reviewed and evaluated numerous studies of alcohol use and misuse among different ethnic groups and social classes. The commission had found that persons at risk for alcohol problems were those that had been subjected to anti-alcohol sentiments and attitudes from parents, schools, and other sources of religious and secular authority. As one of the members, Robert Straus, recalled: "What we saw was that problems were associated with a high consumption that took place in the face of negative sanctions" (Harford, Parker, & Light, 1980). Commission members, according to Straus, "talked about Mississippi and how much conspicuous consumption took place when people drove down to the Gulf Coast, bought carloads of liquor, brought it back, and were preoccupied with procurement, supply, and consumption" (Harford, Parker, & Light, 1980).

The social genesis of alcoholism was thought to reside in the inconsistency between drinking behavior and abstinent sentiments which coexisted in many communities (Pittman, 1967; Straus & Bacon, 1953). In such communities, the use of alcohol was accompanied by feelings of guilt and ambivalence. Excessive consumption and intoxication were people's resolution, though temporary, of the ambivalence and constituted a kind of reaction formation. Seen in these terms, alcoholism in the United States was to some extent the legacy of the Temperance Movement which had created a climate of opinion unsympathetic to the use of alcohol (Room, 1976). For the commission members and subsequently for the NIAAA policymakers, an appropriate intervention was to remove one of the sources of the ambivalence—the negative sanctions applied to the moderate use of alcohol.

Not everyone accepted the basic argument about inconsistency and ambivalence, however. In a criticism of the concepts in explanations of alcohol problems, Room (1976) maintained that an inconsistency would not explain anything unless it reached the level of cognitive appropriation: "Even if congruity is the 'natural' state of mind, an incongruity implies strain only to the extent that the incongruous elements are brought together to interact and are subjectively—rather than in the opinion of the observer—incongruous." However, as stated by Parker (1979), this issue should be settled empirically. Clinical research has shown that alcoholics underperceive the impact of stressful life events such as marital difficulties and job changes. Not perceiving that life events have strong effects on their lives, they fail to protect themselves against their occurrence (Mules, Hague, & Dudley, 1977).

The responsible drinking prevention policy was intended to gain acceptance for moderate drinking and thereby make it unnecessary for drinkers to engage in compulsive behavior such as episodic heavy drinking. This required that alcohol not be viewed as a "forbidden fruit" to be used excessively but as a substance that could be consumed responsibly during most leisure activities. Proposals were advanced to lift restrictions on the availability of alcohol in restaurants, grocery stores, theaters, and other settings and to introduce lighter proof liquors in these settings (Wilkinson, 1970). The goal was to substitute responsible drinking practices for less responsible ones.

However, empirical data from other countries concerning the short-term effects of such policies were less than encouraging. A study of the liberalization of the number and location of alcohol outlets and the type of beverages marketed during 1968–1969 in Finland revealed that new drinking practices emerged, but these did not moderate previously established habits. Total alcohol consumption actually increased. Liberalization of control policies promoted an additive, not a substitutive, effect (Mäkelä, 1975). Sulkunen (1976) suggested that the diffusion of drinking cultures encouraged the convergence of consumption levels both in terms of quality (specific beverage consumed) and in terms of quantity (total alcohol consumed).

Perhaps the major problem with the responsible drinking policy was that it was not based on carefully designed analytical studies and clinical trials. The policymakers had not undertaken the research necessary to specify the conditions under which responsible drinking norms could be activated and mobilized in a manner that would influence drinking behavior. As others put it, "The relationship between norms and behavior needs to be seen as problematic, and the issue is not simply the content of norms but *the factors that influence the hold that norms have over conduct* (Jessor & Jessor, 1980).

STABILIZATION OF CONSUMPTION

During the second five years of its existence, NIAAA made a complete change in its approach to prevention. The "responsible drinking" policy was replaced by a plan to halt the increasing use of alcohol. In 1977, under its second director, Dr. Ernest P. Noble, the NIAAA circulated a draft of a "National Plan to Combat Alcohol Abuse and Alcoholism." The stabilization of alcohol consumption was one of the major objectives of the plan: "Since the trend in this country during the last decade has been towards ever-increasing total consumption, a major effort is required to stabilize this increase which, in view of the population increase, will in reality result in a reduction of the per capita consumption" (NIAAA, 1977). Claiming that consumption rates "are strongly related to availability and such factors as advertising and distribution," the NIAAA document indicated that "the beverage industry's market, strategies, production, and advertising will be analyzed, and efforts will be made to develop alternative policies in the reduction of alcohol consumption" (NIAAA, 1977). The NIAAA plan proposed to "establish and implement a national code of standards on beverage alcohol advertising and the portrayal of alcoholic beverages in all public media" (NIAAA, 1977).

The response from other government agencies was generally favorable. The Health Services Administration of the federal government, for example, commented that

> alcohol prices have not escalated [as] steeply as have other products caught in our economic inflationary trend. In effect, beverage alcohol is, therefore, now commensurately cheaper than it was a decade ago. In order to stabilize the average per capita consumption at the present rate it may be appropriate to artificially raise the price of beverage alcohol by adding further taxes to the existing tax load so it becomes more expensive. . . . The increased incidence of teenage and subteenage alcoholics may be due to the erroneous message which the public received, during the first five years of NIAAA's existence, that children should be taught to drink responsibly. Perhaps [a] goal should be to provide educational opportunities to children to learn about the dangers of use and/or misuse of alcohol. Heavy emphasis should be given to undo the damage of "teaching children to drink responsibly." (Health Services Administration, 1977, p. 1)

The response from groups outside government was critical, however, and the NIAAA director, Dr. Noble, indicated that the stabilization of consumption would not be a goal in itself but rather an index of the success of treatment and prevention efforts to reduce drinking among groups at high risk for alcohol problems. At the same time, Dr. Noble stated that

> we need to study the competition. We need to take a look at the alcoholic beverage industry—how it markets, distributes and advertises. Naturally enough, its goal is to increase consumption, and it stands to reason they're working full time on that goal. (quoted in Lewis, 1977, p. 2)

A former president of the Alcohol and Drug Problems Association, H. Leonard Boche, suggested that the NIAAA Director was "ill advised to describe prevention in terms antagonistic to the beverage alcohol production and distribution industry" (quoted in Lewis, 1977). However, by 1978, NIAAA was funding several groups to evaluate policies that would stabilize alcohol consumption and alcohol problems. The most prominent of these groups, the National Research Council of the National Academy of Sciences, issued a report in September 1981, which argued that

> prices affect the quantity of consumption and the quantity of consumption affects the health and safety of drinkers.
> An increased tax on alcoholic beverages has the particular effect of improving the chronic health picture (as indexed by liver failure) of the heavier drinkers—who are, it can be added, paying most of the tax increase. Therefore we see good grounds for incorporating an interest in the prevention of alcohol problems into the setting of tax rates on alcohol. (quoted in Lewis, 1981)

The argument had been made earlier by an international group of scientists (Bruun *et al.,* 1976), two of whom, Robin Room and Wolfgang Schmidt, subsequently served on the National Research Council panel. In what was apparently the basis for the 1977 NIAAA draft plan, Bruun *et al.* contended that (1) there is a direct relationship between the prevalence of heavy drinking and rates of morbidity and mortality, (2) there is a direct relationship between per capita consumption of alcohol and the prevalence of heavy drinking, and (3) there is an inverse relationship between the prices of alcoholic beverages and per capita consumption. From these relationships, it was concluded that raising or maintaining the prices of alcohol relative to disposable income would reduce per capita consumption or at least stabilize it. This would be followed by a reduction in or stabilization of the prevalence of heavy drinking which, in turn, would be followed by a reduction in or stabilization of the rates of alcohol-related morbidity and mortality.

The argument by Bruun *et al.* has been criticized for both methodological and theoretical shortcomings (Parker & Harman, 1978). Perhaps the most fundamental criticism is that there is no evidence that price and nonprice elasticities of demand for alcoholic beverages are uniform throughout the population. It might be the case that elasticity is much lower among those in the heavy drinking part of the consumption distribution. As others put it, "attempts to reduce overall consumption by limiting availability via a tax or price policy *could well be least effective with precisely those who are abusing alcohol*" (Jessor & Jessor, 1980).

Other criticisms that have been made include the following:

1. That aspects of alcohol availability other than the prices of alcoholic beverages are associated with per capita consumption, rates of alcoholism, and rates of drinking problems. Recent studies (Harford, Parker, Pautler, & Wolz, 1979; Parker & Wolz, 1979; Parker, Wolz, & Harford, 1978) have found that the number of sales outlets and the number of employees who work in these outlets per unit of population predict alcohol consumption and alcohol problems and probably signify the presence of a heavy drinking subpopulation.
2. That liver cirrhosis is usually employed as the only index of alcohol problems although the correlation between liver cirrhosis mortality and other measures of alcohol-related problems is extremely weak (Parker & Wolz, 1979). The use of several measures of alcohol problems would also seem to be warranted by the distributions of these problems among different age, sex, and socioeconomic groups (Parker & Harman, 1978).
3. That the relationship between per capita consumption and alcohol-related mortality rates disappears when ethnicity is controlled (Longnecker, Wolz, & Parker, 1981). This finding suggests that a prevention approach should be tailored to groups at high risk for alcoholism and alcohol abuse.

Responsible drinking norms and stabilization of consumption have been the dominant prevention approaches of the national government during the past decade. The stabilization approach through a taxing mechanism may be utilized in the 1980s by an administration that is concerned with increasing budgetary deficits. If alcohol use and misuse is influenced by stress factors such as unemployment, low income, status inconsistency, time pressures, and job uncertainties and by nonstress factors such as parental modeling, peer group contacts, cultural sanctions to drink, and personality, then there is a need for a more comprehensive model of prevention. Whether or not such a model will be developed will depend on the fiscal policies of federal and state governments and on the funding priorities of the private sector of the economy.

REFERENCES

Blane, H. T. Issues in preventing alcohol problems. *Preventive Medicine,* 1976, 5, 176–186.

Bruun, K., Edwards, G., Lumio, M., Makela, K., Pan, L., Popham, R. E., Room, R., Schmidt, W., Skog, O. J., Sulkunen, P., & Osterberg, E. *Alcohol control policies in public health perspective.* Helsinki: Finnish Foundation for Alcohol Studies, 1976.

Chafetz, M. E. Introduction. *First Special Report to the U.S. Congress on Alcohol and Health.* Washington, D.C.: National Institute on Alcohol Abuse and Alcoholism, U.S. Government Printing Office, 1971.

Harford, T. C., Parker, D. A., Pautler, C., & Wolz, M. Relationship between the number of on-premise outlets and alcoholism. *Journal of Studies on Alcohol,* 1979, 40, 1053–1057.

Harford, T. C., Parker, D. A., & Light, L. (Eds.). *Normative approaches to the prevention of alcohol abuse and alcoholism.* Research Monograph No. 3, National Institute on Alcohol Abuse and Alcoholism. Washington, D.C.: U.S. Government Printing Office, 1980.

Health Services Administration. Comments of the Health Services Administration on the NIAAA National Plan to Combat Alcohol Abuse and Alcoholism. Memorandum, September 1977.

Jessor, R., & Jessor, S. L. Toward a social-psychological perspective on the prevention of alcohol abuse. In T. C. Harford, D. A. Parker, & L. Light (Eds.), Normative approaches to the prevention of alcohol abuse and alcoholism. Research Monograph No. 3, National Institute on Alcohol Abuse and Alcoholism. Washington, D.C.: U.S. Government Printing Office, 1980, 27–46.

Levine, H. G. The discovery of addiction. *Journal of studies on Alcohol,* 1978, 39, 143–174.

Lewis, J. S. The Alcoholism Report, 1977, 5, 1–10.

Lewis, J. S. The Alcoholism Report, 1981, 9, 1–8.

Licensed Beverage Industries. Alcoholic beverage control laws concerning minimum age requirements. Report 2201, 1972. (a)

Licensed Beverage Industries. Penalties invoked for the sale of alcoholic beverages to a minor. Report 2203, 1972. (b)

Licensed Beverage Industries. Penalties invoked for the purchase of alcoholic beverages by a minor. Report 2204, 1972. (c)

Licensed Beverage Industries. Retail stores permitting sale of beer and wine. Report 2103, 1973. (a)

Licensed Beverage Industries. Commodities other than liquor sold in package stores. Report 2104, 1973. (b)

Licensed Beverage Industries. Distilled spirits—License restrictions by states; restrictions on number of retail licenses; statutory and regulatory limitations by population. Report 2101, 1973c.

Longnecker, M. P., Wolz, M., & Parker, D. A. Ethnicity, distilled spirits consumption and mortality in Pennsylvania. *Journal of Studies on Alcohol,* 1981, 42, 791–796.

Mäkelä, K. Consumption level and cultural drinking patterns as determinants of alcohol problems. *Journal of Drug Issues,* 1975, 5, 344–357.

Morgan, P. A. *Examining United States alcohol policy: Alcohol control and the interests of the state.* Paper presented at the Ninth World Congress of Sociology. Uppsala, Sweden, 1978.

Mules, J. E., Hague, W. H., & Dudley, D. L. Life change, its perception and alcohol addiction. *Journal of Studies on Alcohol,* 1977, 38, 487–493.

National Institute on Alcohol Abuse and Alcoholism. National Plan to Combat Alcohol Abuse and Alcoholism: FY 1979–1983. Document, August 1977.

Parker, D. A. Status inconsistency and drinking behavior. *Pacific Sociological Review*, 1979, *22*, 77–95.

Parker, D. A., & Harman, M. S. The distribution of consumption model of prevention: A critical assessment. *Journal of Studies on Alcohol*, 1978, *39*, 377–399.

Parker, D. A., Wolz, M., & Harford, T. C. The prevention of alcoholism: An empirical report on the effects of outlet availability. *Alcoholism: Clinical and Experimental Research*, 1978, *2*, 339–343.

Parker, D. A., & Wolz, M. Alcohol problems and the availability of alcohol. *Alcoholism: Clinical and Experimental Research*, 1979, *3*, 309–312.

Pittman, D. J. International overview: Social and cultural factors in drinking patterns, pathological and non-pathological. In D. J. Pittman (Ed.), *Alcoholism*. New York: Harper, 1967.

Plaut, T. F. A. *Alcohol problems: A report to the nation*. Cooperative Commission on the Study of Alcoholism. New York: Oxford University Press, 1967.

Room, R. Ambivalence as a sociological explanation: The case of cultural explanations of alcohol problems. *American Sociological Review*, 1976, *41*, 1047–1065.

Smart, R. G. Availability and the prevention of alcohol-related problems. In T. C. Harford, D. A. Parker, & L. Light (Eds.), Normative approaches to the prevention of alcohol abuse and alcoholism. Research Monograph No. 3, National Institute on Alcohol Abuse and Alcoholism. Washington, D.C.: U.S. Government Printing Office, 1980.

Straus, R., & Bacon, S. *Drinking in college*. New Haven: Yale University Press, 1953.

Sulkunen, P. Drinking patterns and the level of consumption; an international overview. In R. J. Gibbins, Y. Israel, H. Kalant, R. E. Popham, W. Schmidt, & R. G. Smart (Eds.), *Research advances in alcohol and drug problems* (Vol. 3) New York: Wiley, 1976.

Wilkinson, R. *The prevention of drinking problems; Alcohol control and cultural influences*. New York: Oxford University Press, 1970.

61

Alcohol Control Policy in the USSR

I. A. SYTINSKY

The first decrees of the Soviet government addressing the problems of drunkenness and home brewing were spread widely in 1916–1917 in connection with a ban imposed on sales of alcoholic beverages. On December 19, 1919, the Soviet People's Commissars adopted a decree "on banning the production and selling of alcohol, strong drinks, and alcohol-containing substances not dealing with drinks." The prohibition remained in force until 1925.

The struggle for abstinence was reflected in the Russian Communist party (Bolsheviks) program developed by V. I. Lenin and adopted at the congress of the party in 1919. In this program alcoholism as a social phenomenon was put in the same category as tuberculosis and venereal disease. V. I. Lenin decisively came out against hard drinking and against any attempts to receive profits from the sales of alcoholic beverages.

The campaign against alcoholism which in the 1920s was mainly expressed in administrative measures against home brewing, was relatively ineffective. The failure of prohibition was evident in the gradual increase of home brewing. In 1922, 94,000 cases of home-made beverages were discovered. In 1924, 275,000 cases were discovered. In the same year, home brewing resulted in damages (i.e., waste of grain and fuel) worth over 235 million rubles (approximately $340 billion). In this regard the People's Commissar of Health, N. A. Semashko, underlined that a habit of hard

I. A. SYTINSKY • Research Group of Neurochemical Basis of Alcoholism, A. A. Ukhtomsky Institute of Physiology, Leningrad University, Leningrad, USSR.

drinking could not be averted by simple banning the production and sale of alcoholic beverages.

The apparent failure of prohibition forced the Soviet government to place the responsibility for the production and sale of vodka on the state. The sale of alcoholic beverages to a maximum of 80 proof, including vodka, was permitted by the decision of the Central Executive Committee and Soviet People's Commissariat of the USSR in August 1925. After the repeal of national prohibition the number of distilleries increased by more than three times and the production of alcoholic beverages also increased. In 1927 the consumption of absolute alcohol per capita increased more than four times in comparison with 1925. This increase in consumption was accompanied by an intensified struggle against excessive drinking and alcoholism. In September 1926, the Soviet People's Commissariat of the Russian SFSR adopted a decision "on the nearest measures in the field of treatment-and-compulsory therapy and cultural and educational work in the struggle against alcoholism." In April 1927, instructions were issued regarding compulsory treatment of alcoholics. According to the decision of the Soviet People's Commissariat of the Russian SFSR in March 1927, "on measures of limitation of alcoholic beverages sale," sales of alcoholic drinks to minors and intoxicated persons was prohibited.

Social organization also began to be involved in the struggle against alcoholism and drunkenness. In May 1927, the decision of the All-Union Central Executive Committee and Soviet People's Commissariat of the USSR, signed by M. I. Kalinin, adopted an "arrangement of local special commissions dealing with the problems of alcoholism." An All-Union Society to Prevent Alcoholism, set up in 1928, played a great role in the establishment and development of an anti-alcoholic movement. Leaders of society and employees of the People's Commissariat of Health of the Russian SFSR spoke before the community and inhabitants of some towns. Many new forms and methods were used during this anti-alcoholic movement, including week- and month-long campaigns regarding the prevention of alcoholism, anti-alcoholic talks in schools, and inclusion of anti-alcoholic struggle indices into the socialist pledges of the industrial enterprises.

World War II led to marked growth of heavy drinking and alcohol diseases in the majority of the developed industrial countries of the world. In the USSR a tendency toward increased consumption of alcohol per capita is also traced to the postwar period. In comparison to 1940, per capita alcoholic beverage sales (which indicate alcohol consumption) doubled in 1960, quadrupled in 1970, and was 7.7 times as great in 1980.

In the post-World War II period the main work in the field of alcoholism was done by the institutions of the Ministry of the Interior Affairs and the Ministry of Health. To cure alcoholics municipal medical sobering-up stations (*medvytrezviteli*), narcologic[1] consulting rooms, and hospitals were organized. Radical changes in these institutions and their expansion were accomplished by the decision of the Central Committee of the Communist Party of the Soviet Union (CPSU) and the Council of Ministers of the USSR in December 1958 "on reinforcement of the struggle against drunkenness and on strict order in the selling of strong alcoholic beverages." As a result of this decision an order of the Minister of Health of the USSR was issued in December 1958 "on measures to prophylaxis and treatment of alcoholism." This order envisages the establishment of narcologic consulting rooms at psychoneurologic dispensaries, in the general somatic polyclinics, and especially in the medical posts at industrial enterprises (Levertov, 1977; Lisitsyn & Kopyt, 1978).

Under the conditions of the developed socialist society the struggle against hard drinking and alcoholism has been one of the ideological and educative tasks of the Communist party and the Soviet state. The decision "on measures to enhance the fight against drunkenness and alcoholism" (1972) adopted by the Central Committee of the Communist Party of the Soviet Union and the Council of Ministers of the USSR attempted to mobilize the public against drunkenness and alcoholism. This decision and other republican legislative acts adopted in accordance with it, namely, the Decree of the Presidium of the Supreme Soviet of the RSFSR "on measures to enhance the fight against drunkenness and alcoholism" (1972) was a new step in the struggle against alcoholism. These documents foresaw the utility of mass political, cultural, and educative work in labor communities and residences and in the disposition of economic and medical measures. In accordance with the decision of the Council of Ministers of the USSR (1978) "on additional measures for reinforcement of the struggle against drunkenness and alcoholism," several measures were taken that intensified both the anti-alcoholic propaganda efficiency and the treatment of alcoholic patients. All these decisions and legislative acts created a firm organizational and legal foundation to eradicate alcoholism.

Social, political, and legislative measures that attempt to prevent the development of alcoholism are the basis of the struggle against this disease. The legislative acts which include both medical and social-legal sections can be summarized into four groups: (1) acts that determine regulation of alcoholic beverage production and sale; (2) acts that address the criminal and administrative laws dealing with the questions of alcoholism and alcoholic drinks consumption; (3) acts that determine the role of the public in the struggle against alcoholism, the tasks of public, party, and soviet bodies in

---

[1]In Russian, narcology is a part of psychiatry that studies the problem of drug dependence (alcoholism, drug addiction, smoking).

this direction; and (4) acts that regulate the problems of treatment organization and medical help to alcoholic patients (e.g., laws foresee compulsory treatment under court decision according to doctors' resolution if an alcoholic patient refuses to be treated and violates the public order).

The efficacy of the alcoholic person's treatment depends to a considerable degree on the timeliness of their admitting to the problem. In this regard, a special narcological service whose main section is narcological dispensary has been established in the USSR. The close interaction among medical-prophylactic, narcologic, and psychiatric institutions and public organizations, a special feature of this service, adds to its effectiveness. The narcologic service is a specialized system of medical-prophylactic aid to those who suffer chronic alcoholism (Babayan & Pyator, 1981). It gives a narcologist the possibility to individualize the organization of treatment and prevention. The narcologic dispensary is obliged to fulfill in its territory the following tasks:

- Detection and registration of people with alcoholism and provision of specialized help (stationary and ambulatory) to them
- The study of the prevalence of alcoholism and the analysis of the effectiveness of medical and prophylactic help
- Psychohygienic and prophylactic work both inside dispensary area and outside (e.g., industrial enterprises, educational institutions)
- Medical examinations of persons sent for compulsory treatment for alcoholics, labor preventorium, and examination of temporary invalidity and alcohol intoxication
- Consultative and organizational–methodical help to narcologic consulting rooms that are a part of the ambulatory polyclinic, psychoneurologic institutions and medicosanitary units, and to narcologic posts attached to industrial enterprises
- Organization and conducting of measures on specialization and improvement of qualifications of physicians and medium-level medical personnel
- Participation in preventive measures against alcoholism together with other organizations and institutions

Ambulatory narcologic treatment, the most common treatment method, is directed to those who do not require admission to a hospital, those discharged from narcologic hospitals, and those who finished their cure in treatment-and-labor preventorium. The course of ambulatory treatment of alcoholics includes four obligatory stages: (1) detoxification therapy is carried out in a minimum time period (to 8 to 10 days); (2) the course of active anti-alcoholic therapy applying the methods of hypnosuggestive therapy, conditioned-reflex therapy, or sensitizing therapy, as well as the combination of these methods with purposeful psychotherapeutic action lasting from 1 to 2.5 months; (3) supportive treatment, including the use of alcohol-sensitizing agents, symptomatic treatment, different forms of psychotherapeutic action, and rehabilitating measures as well as anti-recurring courses of active treatment, is conducted for 3 years; and (4) a patient is transferred to a passive register and dispensary supervision for the next 2 years under condition of stable remission (Entin, 1979).

During the treatment of alcoholism relations with a patient's family and with public organizations are of great importance. It is the complex and successive influence of a physician, the alcoholic's family, and community that guarantees the success of alcoholic patient treatment.

Methods of collective psychotherapy applied by "the Club of Soberness" (Club of Abstainers) play an important role in increasing the effectiveness of anti-alcoholic therapy. The first members of the club (which was organized in Riga) were former chronic alcoholics who looked to establish contacts with other former alcoholics who deliberately refused the use of alcoholic drinks. The representatives of the public and the members of the patients' families took part in the club's activities and they in turn tried to help their relatives, and so they themselves did not drink alcohol. Remission of one to three years duration was found in 42% of club members, but only 8% of nonclub members who were treated in the psychoneurologic dispensary. The absolute majority (about 90%) of the club's members work according to their speciality and take an active part in social activities. Recently persons considering the use of alcohol to be incompatible with the demands of contemporary labor conditions, mode of life, rest, and the moral demands of the society have entered such clubs more often.

The establishment of narcologic departments at the industrial enterprises is a new organizational form of treatment of alcoholic patients which involves them in productive work in the plant. The treatment of patients in such narcologic departments is conducted on a voluntary basis for three to four months. All patients are obligatorily involved in labor for the entire working day. The participation of the patients in industrial production requires radical changes in routine organization of the curative process in such narcologic departments. The main therapeutic measures must be applied when patients are not working. In the day-care program the same methods of active anti-alcoholic therapy that are applied under ambulatory conditions are used. The combination of psychotherapy and medicamentous therapy with the productive labor in the plant is a condition that maximizes the value of treatment. Its effectiveness is twice as great as that of ambulatory treatment and 1.5 times greater than ordinary treatment offered by narcologic departments in psychiatric hospitals. The organization of narcologic departments in industrial enterprises (day narcologic stationaries and night dispensaries) allows a considerable expansion, both quantitatively and qualitatively, of possibilities in social-labor readaptation of alcoholic patients by helping them to stop hard drinking and return them to the normal social-productive life (Boyko & Sytinsky, 1980).

Persons with alcoholic illness who do not want to be treated and disturb the social order are sent to special treatment-and-labor preventoriums for compulsory treatment and labor re-education for a period of one to two years. At present, the idea of compulsory treatment serves not only for medical treatment and labor re-education of alcoholics, but it is also a reliable form of isolation of the alcoholic patients with the most severe forms of antisocial behavior.

The problem of referral of an alcoholic to a treatment-and-labor preventorium is decided by the people's court in accordance with the application of public organization, working-people communities, state bodies, and medical institutions (if there is a medical resolution about the need and the fixed time of the compulsory treatment of the alcoholic in the treatment-and-labor preventorium).

The main problem in the organization of the medical process lies in the fact that the great majority of patients in the treatment-and-labor preventorium do not consider themselves to have alcoholic illness. They thus look upon their stay in the treatment-and-labor preventorium and the compulsory treatment of alcoholism as a punishment. In this connection the organization of an anti-alcoholic education system and psychotherapeutic work has a great importance. The majority of patients subjected to compulsory treatment follow this course of treatment: (1) disintoxicative, general tonic, symptomatic therapy; (2) active anti-alcoholic therapy with application of conditioned-reflex and sensitizing methods; (3) supportive sensitizing therapy, labor therapy, psychotherapy, and so forth; (4) repeated active anti-alcoholic therapy immediately before the discharge from the treatment-and-labor preventorium; and (5) ambulatory supporting therapy for three to four years after the discharge from the treatment-and-labor preventorium (Filatov & Tabachnikov, 1976).

All the administrative measures mentioned above that could be applied to patients with chronic alcoholism are used supplementary to the medical treatment (Sytinsky & Gurevitch, 1976). They attempt to achieve the complete stopping of alcoholic drink consumption, helping the patients to cease hard drinking and bring them back to the full value of social–industrial activity. The chief component of success for them lies in uniting the efforts of the narcologic service and public health institutions with administrative and public organizations.

REFERENCES

Babayan, E. A., & Pyatov, M. D. Prophylaxis of alcoholism. Moscow: *Meditsyna,* 1981.

Boyko, V. V., & Sytinsky, I. A. The study of socio-psychological aspects of drunkenness and alcoholism. *Addictive Behaviors,* 1980, *5,* 159–170.

Entin, G. M. Treatment of alcoholism and organization of narcologic service. Moscow. Meditsyna, 1979.

Filatov, A. T., & Tabachnikov, S. I. Compulsory treatment of alcoholism. Kiev: Zdorov'e, 1976.

Levertov, S. A. Social-hygienic aspects of chronic alcoholism. Kishinev: Shtiintsa, 1977.

Lisitsyn, Yu. P., & Kopyt, H. Ya. Alcoholism. Moscow: Meditsyna, 1978.

Sytinsky, I. A., & Gurevitch, Z. P. Modern methods in treatment of chronic alcoholism: A review of the soviet literature. *Addictive Behaviors,* 1976, *1,* 269–279.

7

Prevention of Problem Drinking among Youth
Evaluation of Educational Strategies

G. NICHOLAS BRAUCHT AND BARBARA BRAUCHT

EDUCATIONAL STRATEGIES

The search for effective means of preventing problem drinking among young people is an extremely important endeavor. There are two major reasons why prevention is essential. First, a massive body of evidence in the public health field has shown that both physical and mental health problems are relatively difficult to control by treating problem cases after the problems have appeared and become established. Problem drinking and/or alcoholism cases are generally the most intractable of all clinical problems. Despite the fact that the prevalence of alcoholism among adults has not been stemmed by treatment, tremendous expenditures of public resources have been devoted to treatment efforts. In comparison with attempts to prevent the development of these problems, such treatment efforts have had a long and expensive history. Second, identifying effective prevention strategies is vitally important because drinking is a problem of progressively dismaying magnitude among the youth of this country. Some perspectives

G. NICHOLAS BRAUCHT and BARBARA BRAUCHT • Department of Psychology, University of Denver, Denver, Colorado 80210. The preparation of this paper was in part supported by Research Scientist Development Award KO2-AA-00018 from the National Institute on Alcohol Abuse and Alcoholism.

on the dimensions of this problem are afforded by recent reviews on the epidemiology and psychosocial correlates of teenage drinking (Braucht, 1980) and adolescent problem drinking (Braucht, 1981). In these reviews, substantial and converging evidence was found that:

1. Alcohol is the most widely used "drug" among youth aged 12 to 17 in terms of lifetime, annual, or monthly prevalence rates.
2. Prevalence rates of teenage drinking have continued to increase slowly up to the present.
3. More and more young people are having their first drink and starting to drink regularly at progressively younger ages.
4. Drinking not only seems to be a prerequisite for marijuana use, but problem drinking seems to be prerequisite to the use of other illicit drugs such as psychedelics, amphetamines, barbiturates, cocaine, and heroin.
5. The rate of problem drinking among youth aged 12 to 17 now stands at about the 20% level (defined by a self-report criterion involving having been drunk at least six times during the past year or having experienced significant drinking-related negative consequences at least six times during the past year).
6. Among these young problem drinkers, alcohol use seems to be part of a general syndrome of progressive involvement in problem behaviors—a syndrome in which marijuana use, other illicit drug use, precocious sexual behavior, delinquent behavior, and other forms of antisocial behavior are component parts.

Over the past two decades, growing awareness and social concern regarding youthful drinking problems has led to a proliferation of strategies aimed at dealing with various aspects of this problem. First, many public health organizations have developed tertiary prevention (treatment) programs aimed at rehabilitating young problem drinkers. Second, a variety of prevention strategies have been developed that are oriented toward early identification and intervention with young drinkers who are just beginning to experience drinking-related difficulties (secondary prevention). Third, various governmental strategies have been implemented at the state, county, and municipal levels that have taken the form of legislation or law enforcement programs designed to reduce the supply of alcohol to young people. These primary prevention strategies at the societal/legal level are implicitly based on what has been termed the control-of-consumption or the distribution-of-consumption model of prevention (see Bruun, Edwards, Lumio, Makela, Pan, Popham, Room, Schmidt, Skog, Sulkunen, & Osterberg, 1975; de Lint, 1974; Popham & Schmidt, 1976; Popham, Schmidt, & de Lint, 1976; Smart, 1980; Whitehead, 1975). In addition, a variety of educational programs have been developed aimed at inculcating knowledge, values, beliefs, and attitudes that are not conducive to problem drinking. These primary prevention strategies at the individual/educational level are based on what has variously been called a sociocultural, social-psychological, or socialization model of prevention (see Blane, 1976; Jessor & Jessor, 1980; and Whitehead, 1975).

This chapter summarizes the body of published research bearing on school-based approaches within the fourth program category above: educational strategies at the individual level that are aimed at preventing the development of problem drinking among youth. The chapter includes (1) a discussion of the fundamental problem with this body of research; (2) a review of the diversity in such programs, examining their goals and rationale and outlining the variety of evaluation criteria that have been used to assess goal attainment or effectiveness; (3) a review of the empirical evidence regarding program effectiveness; (4) a summary of the general deficiencies in this existing body of evaluation research and guidelines that would facilitate more fruitful research in the future.

GENERAL PROBLEM AND CAVEAT

At the outset, it should be noted that many of the published papers in this area are ambiguous or vague with respect to whether the central topic is educational with regard to the programs' effects on (1) drinking problems; (2) drinking problems *and* problems associated with the use of other drugs; or (3) the use of illicit drug problems only (and not drinking problems). In any given analysis of papers entitled "The effectiveness of drug education," one most often finds that the effects of drinking are lumped together with effects involving other substances. Only rarely are the effects on drinking and drug use systematically identified, independently measured, compared, and contrasted.

This pervasive problem can be dealt with by simply considering any finding regarding program effectiveness as being relevant to drinking problems and to problems involving other drugs. Several cogent reasons could be marshalled in favor of this stance. They include (1) alcohol is a drug; (2) alcohol is an illicit drug for young people just as are the other "more illicit" drugs; (3) few school districts have two separate and distinct educational programs, one aimed at preventing drinking problems and one aimed at preventing problems related to the use of other drugs; (4) in a recent review of 127 primary prevention programs (Schaps, DiBartolo, Palley, & Churgin, 1978), alcohol was found to be assessed in more studies than any other drug except for marijuana (an equal number of studies involved marijuana);

(5) there is a very great degree of communality in the personality, sociocultural, and behavioral correlates of youthful problem drinking and the use of other "more illicit" drugs (see Braucht, 1974; Braucht, 1980; Braucht, 1981; Braucht, Brakarsh, Follingstad, & Berry, 1973; Donovan & Jessor, 1978a; Jessor, 1979; and Jessor & Jessor, 1977); and (6) there is a growing body of evidence that drinking, problem drinking, and the use of other illicit drugs may be considered as progressive stages in a single unidimensional progression of substance abuse (e.g., Braucht, 1980, 1981; Donovan & Jessor, 1978b; Kandel, 1975, 1978; Kandel, Kessler, & Margulies, 1978).

On the other hand, one could adopt a stricter view—that generalizations from "drug-use problems" to drinking-related problems cannot safely be made unless findings of prevention programs' effectiveness are specifically and unambiguously reported in terms of prevention of *alcohol-related* problems. There are several arguments in support of this view including: (1) Alcohol is unlike illicit drugs in that its use in our society is proscribed only for youth, whereas its use by adults is not only legal, but also widespread and even expected; (2) Most youth are surrounded by completely respectable adult models of alcohol use (but not illicit drug use); (3) Although alcohol and other drugs may have similar physiological effects, pervasive social forces such as the mass media of communication reflect very different social definitions of the two classes of substances (Breed & DeFoe, 1980); (4) Personal experience with alcohol, much of it in the home and with parents, is nearly universal by the high school years (this level of socialization into use is not true of other drugs); and (5) The question of generalizing prevention programs' findings of effectiveness from drinking problems to other drug problems (or vice-versa) is an empirical matter that cannot safely be made without additional specific and unambiguous empirical evidence.

GOALS AND APPROACHES

In a review of alcohol education programs for adolescents, Freeman and Scott (1966) noted that the status of such programs as of the mid-1960s was "dismaying" in the sense that most of them were operating without any clear philosophy or consensus regarding goals. For example, Freeman and Scott stated:

> The health educator strains to avoid offending religious groups whose abstinence doctrines are in opposition to teaching persons to drink moderately; on the other hand, the educator must take into account community members—particularly parents—who object to socializing youth to standards that place the parents in a negative light. (1966, p. 222)

This lack of consensus regarding the goals of educational programs—whether abstinence or moderation is the goal—continues to plague the field today (Blom & Snoddy, 1980; Chng, 1981; Fors, 1980). After reviewing current educational approaches, both Blom and Snoddy (1980) and Chng (1981) concluded that the goal of abstinence is often the real but hidden goal, even in programs whose stated goal appears to be moderation. Chng pointed out that abstinence is often concealed or camouflaged in vaguely stated goal statements such as "healthy attitudes," "rational choice," "positive self-concept," "proper behavior toward drugs," and "values-clarified individual" (p. 15). He further listed a variety of approaches that he felt have abstinence as their hidden agenda and ultimate goal. These not only include approaches based on fear tactics, but also informational, values clarification, decision-making, skills development, self-concept development, cognitive dissonance, and social alternatives approaches (1981, p. 14).

Although the latter charge is certainly debatable, it is clearly true that the goals of alcohol/drug educational programs are notoriously unclear (see Braucht, 1971; Smart & Fejer, 1974) and that clearer goal statements and associated outcome measures are a primary and fundamental need (e.g., Hewitt, 1981; for a contrary view about the desirability of goal-directed evaluation, see Salasin, 1974, and Scriven, 1974). As Wittman (1981) noted, "The establishment of appropriate outcome measures depends primarily upon the clarity and purposefulness of the project's objectives. Precise objectives [would] invite precise and informative outcome evaluations" (p. 42).

Although there is no consensus as to whether moderation or abstinence is the ultimate goal of these educational strategies, all of them aim in some way at decreasing (or at least slowing the rate of increase in) rates of problem drinking. In pursuit of this ultimate behavioral goal, a nearly bewildering number of educational strategies have been developed and implemented. The approaches differ in the short-term goals around which they are centered. For example, the informational ("facts only") strategies invariably focus on the short-term goal of bringing about increases in students' knowledge base regarding alcohol. Typically, the implicit hypothesis underlying this approach is that cognitive changes will somehow lead to attitudinal/affective shifts and that these together will ultimately prove personally incompatible with immoderate or problem drinking.

On the other hand, what are known as values clarification and/or decision-making strategies have a different underlying theory that increased cognitive knowledge is not likely to lead to attitudinal, affective, dispositional, or behavioral changes unless concerted and systematic efforts are made in a more directly affective vein. The short-term goals of these strategies are to facilitate young peoples' self-examination of their own value systems and the role(s) they decide alcohol should play in their own lives. This rationale leads to very different educational strategies. Rather than traditional didactic and primarily factual presentations, these strategies involve a variety of small group-process techniques with emphases on affect, self-disclosure, and peer relationships (see Garfield & Jones, 1980, for a descriptive characterization of desirable features within these approaches, and Chng, 1980, for a brief review and ethical critique).

Unfortunately, there is no consensually accepted system for classifying the various educational strategies/approaches, partly because the boundaries separating them are ill defined. Richards (1971) categorized the then extant methods into eight types of education approaches: (1) dogmatic presentations by medical authorities or experienced drinkers/addicts; (b) "scare tactics"; (3) logical exhortatory arguments; (4) two-sided factual approaches; (5) self-examination and attitude confrontation; (6) role/status enhancement vis-à-vis peers; (7) role playing; and (8) other "unusual means" involving stimulation through novelty, humor, drama, and art.

In the past decade, there has been a proliferation in the number and variety of educational approaches. There seems to have been a natural evolutionary process within the field which has resulted in a number of more or less distinct kinds of educational strategies or approaches, each with its own group of adherents. In the empirical literature, the educational approaches involved are very often poorly described or even totally undescribed and their classification is therefore sometimes uncertain. Despite this uncertainty, in the next section several published reports are classified within a scheme of educational approaches/strategies that appear to reflect the natural order within the field.

Scare Tactics

As Richards (1971) noted, strategies featuring scare tactics, typically involving presentations or recall of the negative consequences of drinking and/or drug use, were apparent a decade ago. At about that same time, a large survey of over 10,000 students in grades 7 through 14 (Fejer, Smart, Whitehead, & LaForest, 1971) found that the mass media of communication were one of their most important sources of information about drugs. Kinder (1975) summarized several critiques that were sharply critical of the mass media's use of scare tactics during that era. Although strategies emphasizing scare tactics are still present in some informational approaches, particularly those prominently featuring outside "authorities," they are not explicitly featured in the contemporary literature.

Cognitively Oriented Informational Strategies

These strategies emphasize factual information from the teacher to the student, with a lack of emphasis on discussion. Examples of this approach include those reported by Degnan (1971), Hewitt and Nutter (1979), Mason (1973), Korn and Goldstein (1973), Vogt (1977), Stuart (1974), O'Rourke (1973), O'Rourke and Barr (1974), and Simon and Moyer (1976). Portnoy (1980) described an evaluation of an informational approach for college students with clearly identified ultimate goals: to encourage moderate use of alcohol, rather than abstinence from alcohol. An informational approach is often included as a second approach in evaluation studies that compare its effectiveness with another approach (e.g., Blum, Garfield, Johnstone, & Magistad, 1978; Morgan & Hayward, 1976; Sadler & Dillard, 1978; Smith, 1973; Weaver & Tennant, 1973).

Some strategies that appear to be cognitively oriented informational approaches also include group discussions of course material and/or individual or group research and discussion components (e.g., Daniels, 1970; Eisman, 1971; Johnson, 1968; Jordan, 1968). Some include presentations by outside experts such as psychiatrists, ex-alcoholics or ex-addicts (Swisher & Crawford, 1971), pharmacologists (Tommasello, 1977), psychiatric social workers, attorneys, and pharmacists (Barresi & Gigliotti, 1975; Swisher & Horman, 1970). Perhaps to a greater extent than in other strategies, these approaches are often extremely short, one-shot programs (e.g., Barresi & Gigliotti, 1975; Haskins, 1979; Hewitt & Nutter, 1979; Tennant, Weaver, & Lewis, 1973).

Affective Approaches Featuring Group Process Techniques

Early papers reported promising results based primarily on informational methods (relying mostly on anecdotal evidence, case studies, and/or theoretical analyses), but also suggested the promise of strategies involving a greater degree of active student participation, leadership, and affective involvement in the program (e.g., Kline, 1972; Swisher, Warner, & Herr, 1972; Williams, DiCicco, & Unterberger, 1968). Since that time, several approaches of this type have evolved, including values clarification, decision-making, ombudsmen, self-concept, and alternatives strategies. Each of these involves slightly different techniques, formats, and/or short-term goals. Some of these strategies are cognitively oriented, while others are primarily oriented toward building behavioral competencies.

As compared to informational approaches, however, these strategies share general characteristics (see Blum *et al.,* 1978; Garfield & Jones,

1980). In all of these approaches, the use of alcohol and other drugs is treated as a personal issue to be decided on by each student. All attempts to provide group settings in which the meaning and function of alcohol/drug use in the lives of the students may be discussed freely. Typical topics in these groups include individual value development and clarification, problem solving, decision making, feelings and attitudes toward peers and authorities, and feelings of self-competence. As summarized by Garfield and Jones, "Whatever the program's components, the goal is to affect student attitudes and drug-taking behavior by promoting self-understanding and responsible decision-making" (1980, p. 102).

Values-clarification type educational strategies include those reported by Aubrey (1971), Friedman (1973), Corder (1975), Blum et al. (1978), Sadler and Dillard (1978), Evans, Steer, and Fine (1979), Dennison (1977), and Bry and George (1979). Chng (1980) also has provided a brief review and ethical critique of the values clarification approach.

There have been many programs emphasizing problem-solving, decision-making, and/or personal skills development as goals (e.g., Calmes & Alexander, 1977; DiCicco, 1978; DiCicco, Deutsch, Levine, Mills, & Unterberger, 1977; Fullerton, 1979; Gonzales, 1978; Gonzales & Kouba, 1979; Hoyt, 1976; Kearney & Hines, 1980; Mooney, Roberts, Fitzmahan, & Gregory, 1979; Pearce, 1971; Rose & Duer, 1978; Stephan & DiMella, 1978; and the classic early report by Williams, DiCicco, & Unterberger, 1968). Some of these are reports of strategies that are aimed at elementary age children (e.g., Kearney & Hines, 1980); some are very indirect strategies that do not concern themselves directly with alcohol or other drugs (Hoyt, 1976).

Another type of peer group strategy called the ombudsman approach is described in a recent report by Kim (1981). This is an example of a strategy combining several techniques oriented toward values clarification, learning about oneself, and developing improved communications, decision-making, and helping skills. All of these involve instructors or group leaders who are not regular teachers or otherwise part of the established school structure.

Based on the results of an earlier controlled analogue study (Smart, 1972) and a survey (Smart & Fejer, 1972) in which the credibility of various sources of information were studied, Smart, Bennett, and Fejer (1976) developed an approach based on sources of information thought to be highly credible—the students themselves. In this particular kind of strategy, peer leaders, models, and sources of information are all key elements (see also Fitzwater, 1971). Some such peer group programs are very short in duration and the reports describing them are sparse in detail (e.g., Lewis, Gossett, & Phillips, 1972).

Although some strategies based on a group process model aim to influence drug use, they do not mention drugs. Rather, they focus exclusively on other factors, such as enhancing the students' self-concepts (e.g., Kurzman, 1974). King (1980) also suggests the worth of indirect approaches focusing on development of "self-esteem, a sense of internal control, and effective coping skills" (p. 234). She cites a number of (unpublished) illustrative programs of this type that have been implemented in this country and in Canada.

Finally, what are loosely termed "alternatives" programs have been reported by Brooks (1971), Cohen (1973), Deardon and Jekel (1971), and Bry and George (1979), and an alternatives program featuring behavioral techniques has been reported by Warner, Swisher, and Horan (1973). McClellan (1975) also described an alternatives program that included cognitive, affective, and group process elements. Some of these programs have utilized encounter group and/or sensitivity training groups (e.g., Dearden & Jekel, 1971; Hecklinger, 1971).

EMPIRICAL EVALUATIONS OF EDUCATIONAL PROGRAMS

How successful have these strategies been in bringing about changes in young peoples' alcohol-related knowledge, attitudes, and behavior? Prior to 1977, there were a number of review papers on this topic that were more or less optimistic in tone (e.g., Berberian, Gross, Lovejoy, & Paparella, 1976; Boldt, Reilly, & Haberman, 1976; Braucht, Follingstad, Brakarsh, & Berry, 1973; Goodstadt, 1974; Milgram, 1976a,b; Randall & Wong, 1976; Richards, 1971; Warner, 1975). Since 1978, a number of distinctly less sanguine reviews of the empirical evidence bearing on the effectiveness of educational programs have appeared (e.g., Bry, 1978; Goodstadt, 1980; Hanson, 1980; Hewitt, 1981; Kinder, Pape, & Walfish, 1980; Schaps, DiBartolo, Palley, & Churgin, 1978; Staulcup, Kenward, & Frigo, 1979; Wittman, 1981). In addition to these reviews of evaluation studies, a number of equally critical theoretical and/or conceptual analyses of issues involved in the primary prevention of alcohol misuse by educational means also have appeared recently (e.g., Bacon, 1978; Dembo, 1979; Huba, Wingard, & Bentler, 1980; Jessor & Jessor, 1980; Swisher, 1979).

Among several recent reviews of the empirical evaluation research literature, a remarkable degree of consensus has emerged. As time has passed, points of disagreement have grown fewer and there are more and more points on which there is substantial agreement or on which reviewers have reached complementary conclusions. These papers have reached a degree of consensus that (1) some evaluation studies have shown effects on students' knowledge about alcohol; (2) fewer studies have been able to demonstrate impact on attitudes and these results have been mixed (some positive and some negative effects); (3) very few studies have even attempted to show influences on drinking/drug use behaviors and even fewer have observed significant effects on these behaviors (again, some of these have found negative effects); and (4) severe and pervasive methodological flaws in the extant evaluation studies make *any* conclusions regarding the effectiveness of alcohol/drug-use educational strategies more a matter of reliance on faith than on credible empirical evidence. The purpose of the following section is to detail these points of consensus.

In one of the earliest of these analyses, Bry (1978) reviewed seven evaluation studies that had been conducted between 1971 and 1977. She found that although these evaluation studies generally demonstrated changes in students' knowledge, they were less successful in demonstrating effects on their attitudes toward alcohol and other drug use and that the evaluation studies were usually unable to demonstrate effects on drug-use behaviors. When they did do so, the effects were mixed. For example, the results of one reviewed study on five types of programs with seventh through tenth graders suggested that all the programs prevented large increases in drug use among older students but that all the programs also led to increased drug use among younger students.

Bry's analysis of the deficiencies exhibited by this small group of studies led her to identify five features that future evaluation studies should have: (1) a follow-up period longer than two years (which would afford an opportunity for behavioral effects to appear); (2) sampling procedures that would allow for examination of effects on high-risk students, particularly those who were often absent or who had dropped out of school subsequent to their exposure to the program; (3) natural settings and programs conducted by school personnel who had been trained for long-term service as educators not researchers; (4) random assignment of students or classrooms to program and nonprogram comparison groups; and (5) greater use of interviews conducted by persons who were not connected with the educational program and greater use of unobtrusive measurement techniques, rather than relying exclusively on pencil and paper questionnaires.

Schaps *et al.* (1978) presented perhaps the most exhaustive review of both published and unpublished evaluation studies. It examined 75 empirical studies in which evaluations of a total of 127 primary prevention programs were reported. Eighty-one percent of these programs were based in schools and, as noted earlier, more of these studies dealt with alcohol than with any other drug except for marijuana (an equal number assessed marijuana use). Schaps and his colleagues excluded studies from their review that measured only knowledge and/or nondrug-specific effects (e.g., effects on self-esteem).

In general, Schaps *et al.* found that, "Taken together, the 127 programs were judged to be only slightly effective on the average in influencing drug use behavior and attitudes" (p. 2). Their review suggests that even this weak statement is perhaps somewhat generous with regard to behavioral effects, although it does appear to accurately summarize the evaluations' findings as to attitudinal effects.

Schaps *et al.* also reported analyses of the methodological features of the 75 evaluation studies. These analyses corroborated Bry's list of five deficiencies and recommendations. Specifically, Schaps *et al.* found that (1) only 13% of the evaluations included a follow-up posttest; (2) 86% served general target populations and did not differentiate their target group on any basis such as risk level or drug use levels; (3) 57% of the programs were short-term, brief, or temporary one-shot experimental programs; (4) in only 31% were there nonprogram comparison group(s) that were equivalent to the program group by virtue of random assignment and only 9% more had a nonrandom assignment (quasi-experimental) control group free of confounds that would undermine confidence in obtained results; and (5) 85% of the 127 programs relied exclusively on a single measurement method, only 12% used interview procedures to collect data, only 9% used archival measures (e.g., school records of drug-related disturbances), and none used unobtrusive trace measurement techniques (e.g., counting discarded beer cans and other alcohol containers on the school grounds).

Schaps and his colleagues rated each of the 127 prevention programs in terms of the overall strength of their evaluation methodology. Rating components included the quality of instruments, statistical techniques, experimental design, sampling, and other methodological factors. They also rated each prevention program itself as to its intensity in terms of scope, duration, and quality. Juxtaposition of these two sets of ratings proved illuminating; a strong inverse relationship between evaluation rigor and program intensity was revealed. For example, only 26 of the 127 programs were rated as strong in evaluation methodology. Of these 26, 22 were rated in the *weakest* category on program intensity/quality. Only 1 of the 127 was rated strong in both program intensity and evaluation methodology. These sobering findings, particularly when the relatively exhaustive sample of evaluation studies is considered, clearly indicate that the apparently extensive body of evaluation knowledge regarding effectiveness of educational strategies is largely if not almost entirely illusory.

Using somewhat less stringent criteria, Schaps *et al.* also examined the patterns of effects that were found in eight studies they called "the 'cream of the crop,' in that they coupled high-quality programming with high-quality evaluation" (p. 66). One of these eight (a program involving a combination of group process, counseling, and alternative strategies) showed no effect on any of the outcome criteria and one program (an information-only type program) showed only a negative effect on attitudes toward drug use. The other six programs were comprised of affective/group process strategies alone or in combination with other strategies. Four of these evaluations yielded positive effects on knowledge, attitudes, affective, and/or performance criteria, but *not* on drug use. Only 2 of the 8 showed slight positive effects on alcohol/drug use behavior; and none of the 8 showed substantial positive effects on alcohol/drug use behaviors.

In 1979, a review was published of 21 primary prevention demonstration projects that had been supported by funds from the National Institute on Alcohol Abuse and Alcoholism (Staulcup, Kenward, & Frigo, 1979). Of the 21 projects, 2 were exclusively school-based and 5 operated in both the community at large and in school settings. Staulcup *et al.* found that, "None of the projects offering alcohol education clearly demonstrated a link between knowledge or attitude change and subsequent drinking behavior, a crucial point to be considered in future prevention programming" (p. 962).

In their discussion, Staulcup *et al.* detailed three major deficiencies that they had found to characterize the projects and made three corresponding recommendations for future research: (1) Evaluation designs and procedures should be more explicitly elaborated and should include equivalent control group(s) by virtues of random assignment procedures; (2) Measurement instruments and procedures should be more carefully developed to assure better reliability, validity, and comparability. This would afford opportunities to evaluate the *relative* effectiveness of various approaches; and (3) Evaluation projects should be supported for longer than three years for follow-up purposes so that long-term effects could be assessed. Interested readers should also consult a reply to Staulcup *et al.*'s paper by Maloney (1980).

In 1980, three additional reviews of evaluation studies in the area of alcohol/drug education were published (Goodstadt, 1980; Hanson, 1980; and Kinder, Pape, & Walfish, 1980). In general, these reviews reached the same or compatible conclusions as the earlier analyses regarding the state of knowledge and the prevailing quality of evaluation research. They also began to explicitly question the underlying premises regarding the theoretical linkages between knowledge, attitudinal, and behavioral changes.

Goodstadt's (1980) analysis focused on the available studies that had reported negative effects (15 in number). He found that many of these "negative" findings were based on nonexperimental evidence—surveys and correlational studies—in which the data were often suspect because of the plausible role(s) played by selective attention and/or recall factors. With regard to *experimental* evidence, Goodstadt found that all of the reported negative findings were associated with positive findings in the same study, in the form of either (1) negative findings for one target subgroup and positive findings for another target subgroup on the same criterion variable or (2) negative findings on one criterion variable and positive findings on other variables. The majority of these latter types of mixed findings involved positive effects on knowledge and negative effects on attitudes and/or use behaviors. Goodstadt was unable to detect any program characteristics that were common to these negative effects studies and stated, "The fifteen programs included the full range of program styles from the most completely factual to the most purely affective" (p. 94).

With regard to the quality of research in the evaluation studies, Goodstadt found that, "Few of the studies from which negative findings have been reported have been free from major experimental design problems" (p. 93). He recited a (by now familiar) litany of ills found in these studies, including nonrandom assignment of subjects into experimental groups, small sample sizes, high levels of attrition in samples, unknown validity and reliability of outcome measures, absence of follow-up other than immediate postprogram assessment, and low intensity/quality programs. Thus, as others had called for methodologically sounder research before accepting the verdict that alcohol/drug education is merely ineffective, Goodstadt pointed to the need for better research before accepting the verdict that alcohol/drug education is harmful.

Kinder, Pape, and Walfish (1980) reviewed 8 studies that had evaluated the effects of substance abuse education programs among student samples and 10 additional studies that had focused on adult samples. They concluded that, "drug and/or alcohol education programs have for the most part been ineffective in obtaining the goals of decreasing substance abuse or preventing future abuse. Studies of student populations have obtained contradictory results, but with repeated implications that such programs may lead to increased usage in some instances" (p. 1051).

Kinder and his colleagues also provided a list of methodological flaws and recommendations. Desirable features that were too often missing from evaluation studies included (1) adequate descriptions of the target samples and educational methods; (2) adequate comparison groups by way of random assignment; (3) collection of follow-up data; (4) more appropriate statistical procedures; (5) experimental designs which would allow for the detection of potential interaction effects (e.g., type of educational strategy by type of student); (6) assessment of use behaviors at multiple points in time in addition to assessment of knowledge, attitude, and other intermediate variables; and (7) "the greatest need and challenge for all research in the area is the development and use of measures of attitudes, knowledge, and behavior that are psychometrically adequate" (p. 1052).

In a very extensive and careful review of both published and unpublished evaluations of educational programs, Hanson (1980) concluded that although it is relatively easy to increase alcohol/drug knowledge, it is more difficult to modify attitudes. He noted that many studies have found greater impact on knowledge than on attitudes or have found significant increases in knowledge that were unaccompanied by changes in attitudes. He also concluded that, while a few studies have been able to bring about reductions in alcohol/drug use and a few have found use to be increased, "by far the largest number of studies have found no effects of drug education upon use" (p. 273). Unlike most reviewers, Hanson provided no critique of the methodology of the studies reviewed—which could have accounted for the findings of those studies.

Most recently, two major review papers have been prepared as technical monograph contributions to the Fourth Special Report to the United States Congress on Alcohol and Health (Hewitt, 1981; Wittman, 1981). Wittman's (1981) analysis covered much of the same ground as Staulcup *et al.*'s (1980) review—prevention demonstration projects supported by the National Institute on Alcohol Abuse and Alcoholism, many reports of which were unpublished. In Wittman's review of projects for youth in educational and service organizations, he concluded that most of the early program evaluations were so seriously flawed technically that they are of dubious value in assessing effectiveness. As for the more recent evaluations of educational programs, Wittman concluded that their impact on knowledge and attitudes have been mildly positive but disappointing and, "their impact on alcohol-related problems remains obscure. It is not clear what changes in attitudes toward alcohol use imply for changes in alcohol-related behavior" (Wittman, 1981, preprint, p. 22).

Wittman did specifically note one fairly consistent interaction effect—projects have been able to bring about more significant attitude changes among younger students than among older students (beyond the upper primary grades). For older youth, whose attitudes toward drinking are relatively well formed, Wittman suggested the promise of multicomponent programs aimed at changing behavior directly through use of specialized settings and groups.

In general, Wittman's review provided a critique of the assumptions underlying most extant programs: that changes in knowledge will lead to changes in attitudes, and these in turn will lead to changes in behavior. He clearly differentiated this knowledge–attitude–behavior model (based on cognitive theories from education and psychology) from the model of personal development and training. He noted they are very different models of change in that the former emphasizes relatively passive and brief exposure to cognitive material while the latter emphasizes more active, long-term practice of both cognitive and behavioral competences. In his view, more direct attacks on skills and behaviors via multicomponent programs involving special settings and groups clearly hold greater promise for affecting behavior.

Wittman also noted that the various approaches' effects on behavior have not been adequately evaluated. Specifically, he stated that, "Generally, the projects' quantitative evaluations suffer from absence of standard instruments for reporting drinking behavior, from absence of validity and reliability testing, and from difficulties in making newly developed instruments compatible with each other and with standardized instruments" (preprint, p. 21).

Hewitt (1981) also provided an extensive review of both published and unpublished alcohol education programs for youth under the age of 18, based largely on evaluations that had appeared since 1977. With regard to programs' effects on knowledge, she concluded that (1) several programs had positive pre-post effects on knowledge (but some of these had no control group) and (2) several programs had no effect on alcohol-related knowledge as compared to their control groups.

She found that several studies either had no effect on attitudes toward drinking or unfavorable effects on attitudes. While some programs were able to bring about desired changes in attitudes toward alcohol use, one such evaluation, for example, assessed attitude change by merely asking youth (after they had been exposed to the educational programs) whether they *felt* their attitudes had been affected in a beneficial way—rather than actually measuring pre- and postprogram attitudes toward alcohol use. Hewitt also identified several programs which reported various (positive) nonalcohol-specific attitude changes (e.g., changes in self-esteem, perception of self-responsibility, etc.).

Hewitt's conclusions regarding programs' effects on drinking behaviors were that (1) few of the educational programs even attempted to evaluate effects on behavior; (2) of those that did, some reported positive impact and some reported negative impact; but (3) a variety of methodological flaws and problems made any general conclusions tentative at best. In summary, Hewitt stated that "evaluation of the effectiveness of alcohol education programs have found limited effects on knowledge, attitudes, and behavior" (preprint, p. 21) and in the future, "the use of more sophisticated (evaluation) techniques may become the norm rather than the exception" (preprint, p. 22).

In addition to the usual list of methodological features that she found to be the exception rather than the norm (e.g., valid, reliable, and nonreactive measures, multigroup designs with comparable control groups, long-term follow-up, and adequate statistical techniques), Hewitt also provided some additional guidelines for future programming that were clearly oriented toward differential programming and potential interactive effects. For example, she called for strategies tailored to the different needs of different groups and programs geared more carefully to the developmental level of the students involved. In general, she indicated the need to "tailor alcohol education methods to the characteristics of target populations" (preprint, p. 24)—characteristics such as cultural background, age/developmental level, sex, and level of alcohol use.

Along with differential programming, Hewitt made an important point in explicitly calling for systematic analyses of interactions between target group subcategories and educational strategies. She noted that, "conclusions concerning what constitutes an effective alcohol education program for a particular target group await further evaluation results, as well as the refinement and more widespread use of effective evaluation methods" (preprint, p. 23).

In summary, these recent major review papers all have concluded that very little is now known about the effectiveness of educational strategies that are aimed at preventing young peoples' misuse of alcohol (and/or other drugs). Because of very fundamental and widespread methodological deficiencies, essentially all of the mixed bag of results (positive, negative, or "no difference" effects) that have been found to date are subject to alternative interpretations. Despite the very substantial number of published and unpublished evaluations, the state of knowledge regarding program effectiveness is unfortunately inadequate.

GUIDELINES FOR FUTURE EVALUATION RESEARCH

In addition to the difficulties that have stemmed from the lack of normative consensus as to whether abstinence or moderation is the appropriate goal of prevention programs, an insidious and pervasive deleterious effect has come about as a result of posing the simplistic and inadequate question: "Is alcohol education effective?" (Braucht, 1971; Braucht, 1975; Braucht, Follingstad, Brakarsh, & Berry, 1973). This paradigm question ignores at least three basic and interwoven considerations. First, there are many different educational strategies, based on different theories and rationales, conducted in different sociocultural contexts in various historical eras. Second, it is not only possible but plausible that these various strategies can have different effects. For example, they may differentially influence knowledge, attitudes, skills, and/or patterns of drinking and drug use; may have immediate but transient effects on some or all of these criteria; and they may have delayed but long-lasting effects. Third, different kinds of young people—in terms of their age, developmental level, sex, psychosocial characteristics, and/or level of alcohol/drug use—may react differently to any given type of educational strategy or program.

If one accepts the plausibility of the above three points, then the inadequacy of the question "Is alcohol education effective?" is highlighted. In fact, a great many "evaluations" have apparently posed this simple question. In many cases, they have then proceeded to examine the *average* effect of a *single* educational program (with no control/comparison group) on a *single* outcome variable across a single and *undifferentiated* group of young people. The typical finding has been "no result." In many reviews, this common failure to find a significant effect has been accounted for by inadequate measurement procedures, poor design, and assorted other methodological flaws.

Although these methodological problems are certainly present, it is possible and even plausible that many of the programs in even the most methodologically deficient studies actually resulted in very orderly and significant effects which were *not detected.* Why? Because an overly simplistic question was asked—a question that implicitly assumed that a given program would have the *same* effect on all of the students who were exposed to it. Having posed this simplistic question, the evaluation involved (only) an examination of the average pre- and postprogram levels on a criterion (e.g., attitudes toward drinking). Because the average level of attitude was not observed to change, the program was judged to have had no effect. The unchanged *average* level, however, may well have been composed of a significant positive effect on the attitudes of one kind of student and a comparable negative effect on another kind of student.

In some of the better recent empirical studies (e.g., Blum *et al.,* 1978; Goodstadt, Sheppard, & Crawford, 1978; Moskowitz, Malvin, Schaeffer, Condon, & Schaps, 1981; Moskowitz, Schaps, & Malvin, 1980; and Schaps, Moskowitz, Condon, & Malvin, 1980a,b) and reviews (e.g., Goodstadt, 1980; Wittman, 1981), these kinds of interactive effects have, in fact, been detected or significant effects have been obtained for one kind of student but not for another. For example, Moskowitz *et al.* (1980) found that while a "Magic Circle" primary prevention program had significant positive effects on third-grade *boys'* self-esteem and discipline problem levels, the program had no detectable effects on third-grade *girls'* self-esteem or discipline problem levels. Goodstadt, Sheppard, and Crawford (1978) have provided another example of a complex interactive effect. In their evaluation of the attitudinal effects that were produced by comparable educational programs implemented at both the elementary and secondary school levels in Toronto, they concluded that

> (a) The [elementary and secondary] programs had no effect on the attitudes of female students; (b) Among male students who typically *did not drink* at all, the

elementary school's program resulted in attitudes *less favorable* toward alcohol
and its use; (c) Among male students who *did drink,* both programs produced
attitudes *more favorable* towards alcohol. (p. 72)

In other contexts, important moderators of program impact have included
sex (e.g., Schaps *et al.,* 1980a,b) and initial (preprogram) level of alco-
hol/drug use (Blum *et al.,* 1978; Wittman, 1981). Thus, the complex effects
found by Moskowitz and his colleagues and by Goodstadt and his colleagues do not appear to be isolated or idiosyncratic phenomena peculiar to
certain contexts or samples.

To observe these kinds of patterned effects one must first admit the
possibility that they might exist and then put a more sophisticated research
question to an adequate test. Several investigators have explicitly called for
tailoring different programs to different kinds of youth and examining their
effects on different types of young people. They have specifically recommended that program effects on target groups be differentiated on variables
such as (1) developmental level or age (e.g., Hewitt, 1981; Huba, Wingard,
& Bentler, 1980; Wittman, 1981); (2) current levels of alcohol/drug use or
"risk levels" (e.g., Blum *et al.,* 1978; Bry, 1978; Goodstadt, 1980; Hewitt,
1981; Kinder *et al.,* 1980); and (3) psychosocial characteristics (e.g.,
Braucht, 1971; Braucht, 1974, 1975; Braucht, Follingstad, Brakarsh, &
Berry, 1973; Jessor & Jessor, 1980).

In general, both educational programming and evaluations of the effectiveness of educational programming would benefit from a greater degree
of rapprochement with the extensive body of theory and research on the
psychosocial correlates of youthful drinking. With respect to the development of educational strategies, both Iverson (1978) and Jessor and Jessor
(1980) have recently lamented the fact that most prevention activities seem
to take place with little, if any, reference to any theory of drinking. In
particular, the Jessors have decried the lack of any systematic, theory-based
"conceptualization of persons or of variables to represent individual differences; what seems to be assumed is that one individual can be substituted
for another without significant loss of information" (1980, p. 37). In their
discussion, they provide a compelling illustration of how an analysis of such
individual differences variables within an explicit theoretical framework can
suggest novel prevention strategies.

Both Braucht (1975) and Jessor and Jessor (1980) have also raised the
question of whether developers of prevention approaches can afford to
overlook the growing body of psychosocial research that shows that alcohol
use and abuse among youth are intricately interwoven with other problem
behaviors such as drug use, precocious sexual behavior, and delinquency. In
light of research evidence for this syndromic constellation of problem behaviors among the youthful population (in which alcohol-related problems
are one component), it would seem that the search for prevention strategies

would profit from a more catholic perspective on youthful problem behavior than is now evident. The same comment could also be made in regard to developing a corpus of less parochial educational materials (see Milgram, 1980). In general, it should be clear that the development of prevention approaches and materials should not be restricted to alcohol-specific (only) approaches; what are needed are strategies and materials that address the social and personal conditions that have been found to be common to a fairly wide spectrum of social deviance.

Existing psychosocial research could also be of considerable value in providing theory-based means of differentiating subclasses of total target populations in order for differential program effectiveness to be investigated. As a specific example, existing psychosocial typologies of adolescent abstainers, moderate drinkers, and problem drinkers might form a useful basis for differentiating targets of educational programs. In their typological analyses, both Braucht (1974) and Donovan and Jessor (1978b) have shown that there is no single type of young problem drinker and that different types have distinct patterns of psychosocial characteristics. It is theoretically very likely that these different types of young people (both problem drinkers and nonproblem drinkers) have become involved with alcohol via distinct lines of development and they may be differentially susceptible to different sorts of educational and other influences toward or away from further involvement with alcohol and other drugs. Gorsuch and Butler (1976) have articulated similar theoretical views regarding the multiplicity of factors that can bear (differentially) upon the transition from naive nonuse to initial drug use for different sorts of young people.

In addition to differentiating and describing educational programs and differentiating subclasses of student target groups, future evaluation research should provide for the examination of *patterns* of effects—both over different kinds of criterion variables and over time. Programs have often been found to be relatively successful on one kind of criterion variable (e.g., knowledge), but relatively unsuccessful on another (e.g., behaviors). In addition, a number of the better extant studies have already reported significant target subgroups by type of effect interactions. For example, Moskowitz *et al.* (1981) reported that several sex-by-effect interactions occurred in their analysis of 20 outcome criteria. For males, positive effects were found on five outcome variables and negative effects were found on two variables. In contrast, only two positive effects were found for females. Blum *et al.* (1978) found that the impact of educational programs varied with the kind of program presented and the particular outcome criteria examined and that these effects were significantly related to the initial level of the students' drug use. Wittman (1981) found that a number of the programs he reviewed appeared to have had different effects on knowledge, attitudes, and behaviors, depending on the age of the youth who participated in them.

In this regard, the often-noted need for valid and reliable measurement procedures for a variety of dependent variables is a paramount requirement. Although measures that are tailored specifically to the objectives of particular programs have some significant advantages (Cook, 1974), standardized measures of important outcome variables would be of significant value for comparing program effectiveness (across studies). Program evaluators would benefit from consulting a number of existing sources for measures of knowledge, attitudes, skills, and behaviors (e.g., French, Kaufman, & Burns, 1981; Hater & Simpson, 1981; Nehemkis, Macari, & Lettieri, 1978).

As noted by many investigators (e.g., Schlegel, 1977; Swisher, 1979), it would be desirable to support research for longer periods of time in order to follow the development and/or deterioration of program effects. It will also be necessary to utilize data analysis techniques with more sophistication in order to deal with these longitudinal data. For example, in these data, there are many problems of differential sample attrition which may involve nonequivalence among study groups. The analytic difficulties introduced by nonequivalent groups (even if the groups were initially equivalent by virtue of random assignment procedures) are many and profound. Therefore, in addition to consulting recent works on general methodological issues (e.g., Atkisson, Hargreaves, Horowitz, & Sorensen, 1978), those attempting to deal with these problems would also benefit from recent work conducted in the field of the design and statistical analysis of quasi-experimental studies (e.g., Aiken, 1981; Cook & Campbell, 1979; Reichardt, 1979; Reichardt, Minton, & Schellenger, 1981).

In sum, it is suggested that future programming and evaluation research should be guided by the question, "What kinds of educational strategies have what kinds of effects on what kinds of young people?" Very few existing evaluation studies have seriously attempted to reflect the complexity implied in this question. When they have, they have often been rewarded with glimpses of understandable and sensible interactions among types of programs, students, and effects. In light of the consistent failure to find simple answers to simple questions in this field, the richer conceptualization that underlies this question would appear to hold greater promise. As Bacon (1978, p. 1143) concluded in his recent essay on the prevention of alcohol-related problems, "since we are currently at a position of absolute zero, there is nowhere to go except up."

REFERENCES

Aiken, L. (Ed.). *Prevention evaluation research monograph II: Outcome.* Final report to the National Institute on Drug Abuse, Contract No. 271–78–4627, 1981.

Atkisson, C. C., Hargreaves, W. A., Horowitz, M. J., & Sorensen, J. E. (Eds.). *Evaluation of human service programs.* New York: Academic, 1978.

Aubrey, R. F. Drug education: Can teachers do the job? *Teachers' College Record,* 1971, *72,* 417–422.

Bacon, S. D. On the prevention of alcohol problems and alcoholism. *Journal of Studies on Alcohol,* 1978, *39* (7), 1125–1147.

Barresi, C. M., & Gigliotti, R. J. Are drug education programs effective? *Journal of Drug Education,* 1975, *5* (4), 301–316.

Berberian, R. M., Gross, C., Lovejoy, J., & Papanella, S. The effectiveness of drug education programs: A critical review. *Health Education Monographs,* 1976, (Winter), 377–398.

Blane, H. T. Education and the prevention of alcoholism. In B. Kissin & H. Begleiter (Eds.), *Biology of alcoholism: Social aspects of alcoholism* (Vol. 4). New York: Plenum Press, 1976.

Blom, G. E., & Snoddy, J. E. The child, the teacher, and the drinking society: A conceptual framework for alcohol education in the elementary school. *Adolescence and alcohol.* Cambridge, Mass.: Ballinger, 1980.

Blum, R. H., Garfield, E. F., Johnstone, J. L., & Magistad, J. G. Drug education: Further results and recommendations. *Journal of Drug Issues,* 1978, *8* (4), 379–426.

Boldt, R. F., Reilly, R. P., & Haberman, P. W. A survey and assessment of drug-related programs and policies in elementary and secondary schools. In R. E. Ostman (Ed.), *Communication research and drug education.* Beverly Hills: Sage, 1976.

Braucht, G. N. *Educational approaches to alcohol and drug abuse.* Paper presented to the Silver Anniversary Conference of the National Mental Health Act, June 28–29, 1971, Washington, D.C.

Braucht, G. N. A psychosocial typology of adolescent alcohol and drug users. In M. L. Chafetz (Ed.), *Psychological and social factors in drinking: Proceedings, Third Annual Alcoholism Conference.* Washington, D.C.: U.S. Government Printing Office, 1974.

Braucht, G. N. Preventing teenage problem drinking: An enticing prospect, tried but unproven. *Psychiatric Opinion,* 1975, *12* (3), 22–25.

Braucht, G. N. Problem drinking among adolescents: A review and analysis of psychosocial research. In National Institute on Alcohol Abuse and Alcoholism. *Special Population Issues. Alcohol and Health Monograph No. 4.* Rockville, Md., 1981.

Braucht, G. N. Psychosocial research on teenage drinking: Past and future. In F. R. Scarpitti & S. K. Datesman (Eds.), *Drugs and the youth culture: Sage annual reviews of drug and alcohol abuse* (Vol. 4). Beverly Hills: Sage, 1980.

Braucht, G. N., Brakarsh, W. D., Follingstad, D., & Berry, K. L. Deviant drug use in adolescence: A review of psychosocial correlates. *Psychological Bulletin,* 1973, *79,* 92–106.

Braucht, G. N., Follingstad, D., Brakarsh, D., & Berry, K. L. Drug education: A review of goals, approaches, and effectiveness, and a paradigm for evaluation. *Quarterly Journal of Studies on Alcohol,* 1973, *34* (4), 1279–1292.

Breed, W., & DeFoe, J. R. Mass media, alcohol and drugs: A new trend. *Journal of Drug Education,* 1980, *10* (2), 135–143.

Brooks, H. B. Teaching teachers to teach about drugs. *National Association of Secondary School Principals' Bulletin,* 1971, *55,* 127–134.

Bruun, K., Edwards, G., Lumio, M., Makela, K., Pan, L., Popham, R. E., Room, R., Schmidt, W., Skog, O. J., Sulkunen, P., & Osterberg, E. *Alcohol control policies in public health perspective.* Helsinki: Finnish Foundation for Alcohol Studies, Vol. 25, 1975.

Bry, B. H. Research design in drug abuse prevention: Review and recommendations. *The International Journal of the Addictions,* 1978, *13* (7), 1157–1168.

Bry, B. H., & George, F. E. Evaluating and improving prevention programs: A strategy from drug abuse. *Evaluation and Program Planning,* 1979, *2,* 127–136.

Calmes, R. E., & Alexander, S. D. PAL, a plan for prevention of alcohol abuse: Some evaluative afterthoughts. *Journal of Alcohol and Drug Education,* 1977, *23* (1), 2–7.

Chng, C. L. A critique of values: Clarification in drug education. *Journal of Drug Education,* 1980, *10* (2), 119–125.

Chng, C. L. The goal of abstinence: Implications for drug education. *Journal of Drug Education,* 1981, *11* (1), 13–18.

Cohen, A. *Alternatives to drug abuse: Steps toward prevention.* Washington, D.C.: U.S. Government Printing Office, 1973.

Cook, T. D. "Sesame Street" and the medical and tailored models of summative evaluation research. In J. Abert & M. Kamrass (Eds.), *Social experiments and social program evaluation.* Cambridge, Mass.: Ballinger, 1974.

Cook, T. D., & Campbell, D. J. *Quasi-experimentation: Design and analysis issues for field settings.* Chicago: Rand McNally, 1979.

Corder, B. Value clarification in drug abuse programs. In B. Corder, R. A. Smith, & J. D. Swisher, (Eds.). *Drug abuse prevention: Perspectives and approaches for educators.* Dubuque, Iowa: W. C. Brown, 1975.

Daniels, R. M. Drug education begins before kindergarten: The Glen Cove, New York, pilot program. *Journal of School Health,* 1970, *40,* 242–248.

Dearden, M. H., & Jekel, J. F. Pilot program in high school drug education utilizing non-directive techniques and sensitivity training. *Journal of School Health,* 1971, *41,* 265–272.

Degnan, E. J. An exploration into the relationship between depression and a positive attitude toward drugs in young adolescents and an evaluation of a drug education program. *Dissertation Abstracts,* 1972, *32* (11-B), 6614–6615.

de Lint, J. The prevention of alcoholism. *Preventive Medicine,* 1974, *3,* 24–25.

Dembo, R. Substance abuse prevention programming and research: A partnership in need of improvement. *Journal of Drug Education,* 1979, 9 (3), 189–208.

Dennison, D., Prevet, T., & Affleck, M. Does alcohol instruction affect student drinking behavior? *Health Education,* 1977, *8,* 28–30.

DiCicco, L. Evaluation the impact of alcohol education. *Alcohol Health and Research World,* 1978, (Winter), 14–20.

DiCicco, L., Deutsch, C., Levine, G., Mills, D. J., & Unterberger, H. A school-community approach to alcohol education. *Health Education,* 1977, *8,* 11–13.

Donovan, J. E., & Jessor, R. Adolescent problem drinking: Psychosocial correlates in a national sample study. *Journal of Studies on Alcohol,* 1978, *39,* 1506–1524. (a)

Donovan, J. E., & Jessor, R. *Drinking, problem drinking, and illicit drug use among American adolescents: A psychosocial study of a nationwide sample.* Final report to the National Institute on Alcohol Abuse and Alcoholism, Contract No. ADM 281–75–0026, 1978. (b)

Eiseman, S. Teaching about narcotics and dangerous drugs: Further findings about the student research approach. *International Journal of Health Education,* 1971, *38* (1), 139–144.

Evans, G. B., Steer, R. A., & Fine, E. W. Alcohol value clarification in sixth graders: A film-making project. *Journal of Alcohol and Drug Education,* 1979, *24* (2), 1–10.

Fitzwater, J. W. How to beat the drug problem. *School Management,* 1971, *15,* 8.

Fors, S. W. On the ethics of selective omission and/or inclusion of relevant information in school drug education programs. *Journal of Drug Education,* 1980, *10* (2), 111–117.

Freeman, W. E., & Scott, J. F. A critical review of alcohol education for adolescents. *Community Mental Health Journal,* 1966, *2,* 222–230.

French, J. F., Kaufman, N. J., & Burns, L. S. (Eds.). *Prevention evaluation guidelines.* Final report to the National Institute on Drug Abuse, Contract No. 271–78–4607, 1981.

Friedman, S. M. *A drug education program emphasizing effective approaches and its influence upon intermediate school student and teacher attitudes.* Unpublished doctoral dissertation, Fordham University, 1973.

Fullerton, M. A program in alcohol education designed for rural youth. *Journal of Alcohol and Drug Education,* 1979, *24* (2), 58–62.

Garfield, E. F., & Jones, D. R. Drug education group process: Considerations for the classroom. *Journal of Drug Education,* 1980, *10* (2), 101–110.

Gonzalez, G. M. What do you mean—prevention? *Journal of Alcohol and Drug Education,* 1978, *23* (3), 14–23.

Gonzalez, G. M., & Kouba, J. M. Comprehensive alcohol education: A new approach to an old problem. *National Association of School Principals and Administrators Journal,* 1979, *16* (4), 7–14.

Goodstadt, M. Myths and methodology in drug education. In M. S. Goodstadt (Ed.), *Research on methods and programs of drug education.* Toronto: Addication Research Foundation, 1974.

Goodstadt, M. S. Drug education—a turn on or a turn off? *Journal of Drug Education,* 1980, *10* (2), 89–99.

Goodstadt, M. S., Sheppard, M. A., & Crawford, S. H. *Development and evaluation of two alcohol education programs for the Toronto Board of Education* (Substudy No. 941). Toronto: Addiction Research Foundation, 1978.

Gorsuch, R. L., & Butler, M. C. Initial drug abuse: A review of predisposing social psychological factors. *Psychological Bulletin,* 1976, *83* (1), 120–137.

Hanson, D. J. Drug education. Does it work? In F. R. Scarpitti & S. K. Datesman (Eds.), *Drugs and the youth culture: Sage annual reviews of drug and alcohol abuse* (Vol. 4). Beverly Hills: Sage, 1980.

Haskins, J. B. Evaluating the effect of a one-day drug education program on high school journalists. *Journal of Drug Education,* 1979, *9* (3), 263–271.

Hater, J. J., & Simpson, D. D. *Annotated bibliography of drug abuse prevention evaluation instruments.* Final report to the Texas Department of Community Affairs, Drug Abuse Prevention Division, Contract No. 7330 3979. Fort Worth, Texas: Institute of Behavioral Research, Texas Christian University, 1981.

Hecklinger, F. J. How to deal with the drug problem on campus. *National Association of School Principals and Administrators Journal,* 1971, *9,* 37–42.

Fejer, D., Smart, R. G., Whitehead, P. C., & La Forest, L. Sources of information about drugs among high school students. *Public Opinion Quarterly,* 1971, *35,* 235–241.

Hewitt, D., & Nutter, R. W. A comparison of three drug information presentations. *Journal of Drug Education,* 1979, *9* (1), 79–90.

Hewitt, L. E. Current status of alcohol education programs for youth. In National Institute on Alcohol Abuse and Alcoholism. *Special Population Issues. Alcohol and Health Monograph No. 4.* Rockville, Md.: The Institute, 1981.

Hoyt, J. H. Playing against drugs. *American Education,* 1976, *12* (19), 21–25.

Huba, G. J., Wingard, J. A., & Bentler, P. M. Applications of a theory of drug use to prevention programs. *Journal of Drug Education,* 1980, *10* (1), 25–37.

Iverson, D. C. Utilizing a health behavior model to design drug education/prevention programs. *Journal of Drug Education,* 1978, *8* (1), 279–287.

Jessor, R. Marijuana: A review of recent psychosocial research. In R. L. DuPont, A. Goldstein, & J. O'Donnell, (Eds.). *Handbook on drug abuse.* Washington, D.C.: U.S. Government Printing Office, 1979.

Jessor, R., & Jessor, S. L. *Problem behavior and psychosocial development: A longitudinal study of youth.* New York: Academic, 1977.

Jessor, R., & Jessor, S. L. Toward a social psychological perspective on the prevention of alcohol abuse. In T. C. Harford, D. A. Parker, & L. Light (Eds.), *Normative approaches to the prevention of alcohol abuse and alcoholism. Research Monograph No. 3.* DHEW Publication No. (ADM) 79–847. National Institute on Alcohol Abuse and Alcoholism, 1980.

Johnson, B. B. A junior high school seminar on dangerous drugs and narcotics. *Journal of School Health,* 1968, *38,* 84–87.

Jordan, C. W. A drug abuse project. *Journal of School Health,* 1968, *38,* 84–87.

Kandel, D. B. Convergences in prospective longitudinal surveys of drug use in normal populations. In B. Kandel (Ed.), *Longitudinal research on drug use: Empirical findings and methodological issues.* New York: Wiley, 1978.

Kandel, D. B. Stages in adolescent involvement in drug use. *Science,* 1975, *190,* 912–914.

Kandel, D. B., Kessler, R. C., & Margulies, R. Z. Antecedents of adolescent initiation into stages of drug use: A developmental analysis. In D. B. Kandel (Ed.), *Longitudinal research on drug use: Empirical findings and methodological issues.* New York: Wiley, 1978.

Kearney, A. L., & Hines, M. H. Evaluation of the effectiveness of a drug prevention education program. *Journal of Drug Education,* 1980, *10* (2), 127–134.

Kim, S. An evaluation of ombudsman primary prevention program on student drug abuse. *Journal of Drug Education,* 1981, *11* (1), 27–36.

Kinder, B. N. Attitudes toward alcohol and drug abuse. II. Experimental data, mass media research, and methodological considerations. *International Journal of the Addictions,* 1975, *10* (6), 1035–1054.

Kinder, B. N., Pape, N. E., & Walfish, S. Drug and alcohol education programs: A review of outcome studies. *The International Journal of the Addictions,* 1980, *15* (7), 1035–1054.

King, S. E. Young alcohol abusers: The challenge of prevention. *Journal of Drug Education,* 1980, *10* (3), 233–238.

Kline, J. A. Evaluation of a multimedia drug education program. *Journal of Drug Education,* 1972, *2* (3), 229–239.

Korn, J. H., & Goldstein, J. W. Psychoactive drugs: A course evaluation. *Journal of Drug Education,* 1973, *3* (4), 353–367.

Kurzman, T. A non-drug approach to drug education. *Addictions,* 1974, (Summer), 50–63.

Lewis, J. M., Gosset, J. T., & Phillips, U. A. Evaluation of a drug prevention program. *Hospital and Community Psychiatry,* 1972, April, 36–38.

McClellan, P. P. The Pulaski Project: An innovative drug abuse prevention program in an urban high school. *Journal of Psychedelic Drugs,* 1975, *7* (4), 355–362.

Maloney, S. K. Comment of "A review of federal primary alcoholism projects" by Herbert Staulcup, Kevin Kenward and Donald Frigo. *Journal of Studies on Alcohol,* 1980, *41* (3), 377–380.

Mason, M. L. Drug education effects. *Dissertation Abstracts,* 1973, *34* (4–B), 418.

Milgram, G. G. A descriptive analysis of alcohol education materials, 1973–1979. *Journal of Studies on Alcohol,* 1980, *41* (11), 1209–1216.

Milgram, G. G. A historical review of alcohol education research and comments. *Journal of Alcohol and Drug Education,* 1976, *21* (2), 1–16. (a)

Milgram, G. G. Current status and problems of alcohol education in the schools. *Journal of School Health,* 1976, *46,* 317–320. (b)

Mooney, C., Roberts, C., Fitzmahan, D., & Gregory, L. Here's looking at you—a school-based alcohol education project. *Health Education,* 1979 (Nov./Dec.), 38–41.

Morgan, H. G., & Hayward, A. The effects of drug talks to school children. *British Journal of Addiction,* 1976, *71* (3), 285–288.

Moskowitz, J. M., Malvin, J. H., Schaeffer, G. A., Condon, J. W., & Schaps, E. *The effects of a* classroom management teacher training primary prevention program on fifth-grade students. Napa project report to the National Institute on Drug Abuse, Prevention Branch, March 1981.

Moskowitz, J. M., Schaps, E., & Malvin, J. *A process and outcome evaluation of a magic circle primary prevention program.* Napa project report to the National Institute on Drug Abuse, Prevention Branch, August 1980.

Nehemkis, A., Macari, M. A., & Lettieri, D. J. (Eds.). *Drug abuse instrument handbook* (National Institute on Drug Abuse Research Issues Monograph No. 12). Washington, D.C.: U.S. Government Printing Office, 1978.

O'Rourke, T. W. Assessment of the effectiveness of the New York State Drug Curriculum Guide with respect to drug knowledge. *Journal of Drug Education,* 1973, *3,* 57–66.

O'Rourke, T. W., & Barr, S. L. Assessment of the effectiveness of the New York State Drug Curriculum Guide with respect to drug attitudes. *Journal of Drug Education,* 1974, *4,* 347–356.

Pearce, J. The role of education in combating drug abuse. *Journal of School Health,* 1971, *41,* 83–88.

Popham, R. E., & Schmidt, W. The effectiveness of legal measures in the prevention of alcohol problems. *Addictive Diseases,* 1976, *2,* 497–513.

Popham, R. E., Schmidt, W., & De Lint, J. The effects of legal restraint on drinking. In B. Kissin & H. Begleiter (Eds.), *The biology of alcoholism: Social aspects of alcoholism* (Vol. 4). New York: Plenum Press, 1976.

Portnoy, B. Effects of a controlled-usage alcohol education program based on the health belief model. *Journal of Drug Education,* 1980, *10* (3), 181–195.

Randall, D., & Wong, M. R. Drug education to date: A review. *Journal of Drug Education,* 1976, *6* (1), 1–21.

Reichardt, C. S. The statistical analysis of data from nonequivalent group designs. In T. D. Cook & D. T. Campbell (Eds.), *Quasi-experimentation: Design and analysis issues for field settings.* Chicago: Rand-McNally, 1979.

Reichardt, C. S., Minton, B. A., & Schellenger, J. D. The analysis of covariance (ANCOVA) and the assessment of treatment effects. In L. Aiken (Ed.), *Prevention evaluation research monograph II: Outcome.* Final report to the National Institute on Drug Abuse, Contract No. 271–78–4627, 1981.

Richards, L. Evaluation in drug education. *School Health Review,* 1971, *2,* 22–27.

Rose, S. E., & Duer, W. F. Drug/alcohol education: A new approach for schools. *Education,* 1978, *99,* 198–202.

Sadler, O. W., & Dillard, N. R. A description and evaluation of TRENDS: A substance abuse education program for sixth graders. *Journal of Educational Research,* 1978, *78* (3), 171–175.

Salisin, S. Exploring goal-free evaluation: An interview with Michael Scriven. *Evaluation,* 1974, *1* (2), 9–16.

Schaps, E., DiBartolo, R., Palley, C. S., & Churgin, S. *Primary prevention evaluation research: A review of 127 program evaluations.* Walnut Creek, Calif.: Pacific Institute for Research and Evaluation, 1978.

Schaps, E., Moskowitz, J. M., Condon, J. W., & Malvin, J. *An evaluation of an innovative drug education program.* Napa project report to the National Institute on Drug Abuse, Prevention Branch, August, 1980. (a)

Schaps, E., Moskowitz, J. M., Condon, J. W., & Malvin, J. *A process and outcome evaluation of an affective teacher training primary prevention program.* Napa project report to the National Institute on Drug Abuse, Prevention Branch, November, 1980. (b)

Schlegel, R. P. Some methodological procedures for the evaluation of educational programs for prevention of adolescent alcohol use and abuse. *Evaluation Quarterly,* 1977, *1* (4), 657–672.

Scriven, M. Evaluation perspectives and procedures. In W. J. Popham (Ed.), *Evaluation in education: Current applications.* Berkeley, Calif.: McCutchen, 1974.

Simon, R. K., & Moyer, D. H. A preliminary assessment of a cooperative drug education pilot project in the middle school. *Journal of School Health,* 1976, *46* (6), 325–328.

Smart, R. G. Availability and the prevention of alcohol-related problems. In T. C. Harford, D. A. Parker, & L. Light (Eds.), *Normative approaches to the prevention of alcohol abuse and alcoholism. Research Monograph No. 3.* DHEW Publication No. (ADM) 79–847. National Institute on Alcohol Abuse and Alcoholism, 1980.

Smart, R. G. Rejection of the source in drug education. *Journal of Drug Issues,* 1972, *2,* 55–60.

Smart, R. G., Bennett, C., & Fejer, D. A controlled study of the peer group approach to drug education. *Journal of Drug Education,* 1976, *6* (4), 305–311.

Smart, R. G., & Fejer, D. Credibility of sources of drug information for high school students. *Journal of Drug Issues,* 1972, *2,* 8–18.

Smart, R. G., & Fejer, D. *Drug education: Current issues, future directions.* Toronto: Addiction Research Foundation, 1974.

Smith, B. C. Values clarification in drug education: A comparative study. *Journal of Drug Education,* 1973, *3,* 369–376.

Staulcup, H., Kenward, K., & Frigo, D. A review of federal primary alcoholism prevention projects. *Journal of Studies on Alcohol,* 1979, *40* (11), 943–968.

Stephen, A. I., & DiMella, N. C. Thinking about drinking: Teaching tomorrow's drinkers. *Independent School,* 1978, *38* (1), 11–13.

Stuart, R. Teaching facts about drugs: Pushing or preventing. *Journal of Educational Psychology,* 1974, *66,* 189–201.

Swisher, J. D. Prevention issues. In R. I. DuPont, A. Goldstein, & J. O'Donnell (Eds.), *Handbook of drug abuse.* (National Institute on Drug Abuse Contract Report No. 271–7–6001). Washington, D.C.: U.S. Government Printing Office, 1979.

Swisher, J. D., & Crawford, J. L. Evaluation of a short-term drug education program. *School Counselor,* 1971, *18,* 265–272.

Swisher, J. D., & Horman, R. T. Drug abuse prevention. *Journal of College Student Personnel,* 1970, *18,* 337–341.

Swisher, J. D., Warner, R. W., & Herr, E. L. Experimental comparison of four approaches to drug abuse prevention among ninth and eleventh graders. *Journal of Counseling Psychology,* 1972, *19,* 328–332.

Tennant, F. S., Weaver, S. C., & Lewis, C. E. Outcomes of drug education: Four case studies. *Pediatrics,* 1973, *52* (2), 246–251.

Tommasello, T. *Drug abuse programs in the public schools: A comprehensive pharmacology presentation.* Paper presented at the First International Action Conference on Substance Abuse, Phoenix, 1977.

Vogt, A. T. Will classroom instruction change attitudes toward drug abuse? *Psychological Reports,* 1977, *41,* 973–974.

Warner, R. W. Evaluations of drug abuse prevention programs. In B. Corder, R. A. Smith, & J. D. Swisher (Eds.), *Drug abuse prevention: Perspectives and approaches for educators.* Dubuque, Iowa: W. C. Brown, 1975.

Warner, R. W., Swisher, J. D., & Horan, J. J. Drug abuse prevention: A behavioral approach. *National Association of Secondary School Principals' Bulletin,* 1973, *57,* 49–54.

Weaver, S. C., & Tennant, F. S. Effectiveness of drug education programs for secondary school students. *American Journal of Psychiatry,* 1973, *130* (7), 812–814.

Whitehead, P. C. The prevention of alcoholism; divergencies and convergences of two approaches. *Addictive Diseases,* 1975, *1,* 431–443.

Williams, A. F., DiCicco, L. M., & Unterberger, H. Philosophy and evaluation of an alcohol education program. *Quarterly Journal of Studies on Alcohol,* 1968, *29,* 685–702.

Wittman, F. Current status of research and demonstration programs in the primary prevention of alcohol problems. In National Institute on Alcohol Abuse and Alcoholism. *Prevention, intervention, and treatment: Concerns and models. Alcohol and Health Monograph No. 3.* Rockville, Md., 1981.

8

Prevention through Mass Media Communication

LINDA E. HEWITT AND HOWARD T. BLANE

The widespread belief that mass communications is a potent tool for reducing alcohol problems obscures practical, conceptual, methodological, and sociopolitical difficulties in evaluating its effectiveness and identifying controllable factors that distinguish more successful from less successful campaigns. Reviews of evaluated mass media campaigns to reduce alcohol problems have been uniformly cautious concerning the presence of positive effects and justifiably critical of the state of the art (Blane, 1976; Blane & Hewitt, 1977; Cameron, 1979; Douglas, 1976; Driessen & Byrk, 1972; Haskins, 1969; Wallack, 1980; Whitehead, 1979; Wilde, 1975). These reviews were based on relatively few studies dealing primarily with reducing drunken driving, and programs were often unclear about their objectives, the means for reaching them, and their measurement. Recent developments indicate that more evaluations are occurring and deal with a broader range of content and use stronger evaluation design.

This chapter reviews mass media programming in the alcohol area and the status of evaluative efforts. Alcohol-specific mass media campaigns are viewed in light of current knowledge about the effects of mass media in

LINDA E. HEWITT • Department of Psychology, University of Pittsburgh, Pittsburgh, Pennsylvania 15260.   HOWARD T. BLANE • Minimizing Alcohol Problems Project, School of Education, University of Pittsburgh, Forbes Quadrangle 5K26, Pittsburgh, Pennsylvania 15260. The preparation of this chapter was supported in part by Grant AA-02536 from the National Institute on Alcohol Abuse and Alcoholism.

general. For purposes of this chapter, *mass media* refers to communication through television, radio, newspapers, billboards, films, and printed materials designed for widespread distribution. In practice, television and radio are the most heavily utilized media and the ones that most often are the subjects of evaluation.

GENERAL MASS COMMUNICATION EFFECTS

Three stages of theory and opinion concerning the potential impact of mass communication can be discerned since the turn of the century. Between 1900 and 1940, media were considered powerful, direct shapers of attitudes and behavior (McQuail, 1977). Between 1940 and 1960, opinion reversed and the media were viewed as relatively powerless and only a minor contributor to individual or societal change. Since the 1960s, new evidence on the potential effects of the media has emerged, causing a reexamination of research and theoretical questions about the true impact of mass communication.

The consensus of current thinking about mass communication found in the psychological, communications, and sociological literature is that mass media can be an effective tool for social change under optimal conditions. However, the potential for effectiveness of any particular program is affected by a number of factors and the identification and achievement of optimal conditions is a difficult and complex task. Opinion is least divided over the question of whether mass communication can affect knowledge and awareness levels; there is considerable evidence that it can. The effects of mass communication on attitudes and behavior are much less clear. The following sections summarize findings concerning the general effects of mass communication on knowledge, attitudes, agenda setting, and behavior and the factors that influence these effects.

KNOWLEDGE

Mass communication is generally considered to have the greatest potential for effectiveness at the cognitive level (Atkin, 1979; McQuail, 1977; Roberts & Bachen, 1981). The mass media are viewed as increasingly effective in achieving public awareness of social problems (Shoemaker, 1981). They are also seen as important influences on people's perceptions of social reality (Comstock, Chaffee, Katzman, McCombs, & Roberts, 1978; Holz & Wright, 1979; McQuail, 1977; Withey, 1980a). This influence may especially be felt by children and adolescents (Tudor, 1979). The media provide and reinforce images of the culture through both direct and indirect messages that suggest how things are and how they might be (Withey, 1980b). The media also help define social and cultural reality through what they do not portray (Tudor, 1979). This effect may be particularly strong for television (Comstock *et al.*, 1978; Withey, 1980a) and movies (Jowett & Linton, 1980), due to the homogeneity and popularity of these media.

One complicating factor in the media's effects on knowledge is the concept of "knowledge gap" (Chaffee, 1977). *Knowledge gap* refers to the fact that people who are better informed tend to have more exposure to mass media messages. Thus, those who begin at higher information levels tend to become still better informed, further widening the gap between themselves and less informed people. In this way, mass media may have the greatest effect on those persons least in need of information. However, problems associated with the knowledge gap may be offset by the tendency for "early adopters" of knowledge or ideas to influence those who are more resistant to or less aware of messages (Shoemaker, 1981). If opinion leaders are affected by the message, then others will benefit through their influence. Once knowledge reaches a certain threshold in the population, there will be added pressures on "late adopters" to accept the information (Shoemaker, 1981).

ATTITUDES

Most research on the effects of mass media has focused on attitude change at the individual level (Chaffee, 1977). It has been assumed in the past that attitudes act as a mediator between knowledge and behavior and that knowledge change leads to attitude change, which in turn leads to behavior change. Thus, many mass media campaigns have focused on attitude change, assuming that behavior change would follow. However, this assumption is being replaced by the more sophisticated view that other relationships between knowledge, attitudes, and behavior may exist (e.g., behavior may affect attitudes; attitudes and behavior may each be the result of other causal factors) (Chaffee, 1977; Comstock *et al.*, 1978; McLeod & Reeves, 1980; Wallack, 1980). Research on attitudinal and other effects of the media has also been criticized for failing to distinguish between individual and societal effects (McLeod & Reeves, 1980).

Despite recent moves toward more complex models of attitudinal effects and the attitude–behavior relationship, attitudes may predict behavior under some circumstances, notably when the measures used for each match in specificity on action, target, context, and time dimensions (Ajzen & Fishbein, 1977; Cialdini, Petty, & Cacioppo, 1981). In addition, if current attitudes are based on past behavior, they can be good predictors of future behavior (Zanna, Olson, & Fazio, 1980). Direct or vicarious experience with the attitude object among the target audience may also increase the correlation between attitudes and behavior (Cialdini *et al.,* 1981). However, there is contradictory evidence that more distant, novel messages are more successful, especially when no competing messages are available and the audience has no personal stake in resisting the message (McQuail, 1977).

Repetition of the message increases the likelihood of its acceptance (Brown, 1981). The effects of repeated exposure to a message decline after a point, however, and additional exposure beyond this point may lead to rejection of the message (Chaffee, 1977; Cialdini *et al.,* 1981). A major problem is the difficulty of determining beforehand how much repetition will be too much.

Even with repeated exposure, knowledge of a new idea embedded in a mass media message is likely to be more prevalent (and reach that level of prevalence faster) than acceptance of that idea (Shoemaker, 1981). This is not surprising, considering the fact that of eight sequential requirements postulated for achievement of behavioral change as a result of a mass media message, acceptance of the idea being promoted is the fifth stage. These stages are (1) opportunity for exposure to the message, (2) actual exposure, (3) attention to the message, (4) learning of the message (knowledge), (5) acceptance of the message (attitude change), (6) motivation to act, (7) recall of the message at the time of action, and (8) opportunity for action (behavior change) (Swinehart, 1981).

AGENDA SETTING

It frequently is asserted that mass communication is more effective in persuading people what to think *about* than in persuading them *what* to think (Comstock *et al.,* 1978; Holz & Wright, 1979; Roberts & Bachen, 1981). This is known as an "agenda-setting" effect. Through this effect, mass media messages can influence people's ideas about what constitute important social problems or personal concerns. For example, people may be persuaded to think that alcoholism is a significant social problem or that weight maintenance is an important personal goal. Print media are considered more influential than television in this area (Roberts & Bachen, 1981). Some researchers feel that evidence for the causal influence of the media on agenda setting is accumulating (Roberts & Bachen, 1981). It has been pointed out, however, that the agenda-setting effect may be strong only among those who are seeking guidance (Chaffee, 1977).

Behavior

It is generally conceded that behavioral effects are the most difficult to achieve using mass communication techniques alone. Many researchers stress the "limited" role of mass media (e.g., Atkin, 1979). Mass media campaigns may have had limited effects in the past in part due to their overly ambitious goals of changing behavior in a majority of the population (Atkin, 1979). Concentrating on smaller units of behavior and on segments of the population might result in greater success.

In order to adopt new behaviors, and especially to maintain them over time, people need social reinforcement (Shoemaker, 1981). This is best achieved by combining interpersonal communication with mass media communication (Roberts & Bachen, 1981; Rogers & Shoemaker, 1971; Shoemaker, 1981). Interpersonal sources of information and persuasion interact with mass media messages to produce a greater effect than that achieved by media alone and may also be more effective in themselves than mass media messages (Holz & Wright, 1979). Little information is available, however, concerning under what conditions and with what types of persons interpersonal communications will be more effective.

Factors Influencing Effectiveness

A variety of factors have been identified that influence the effectiveness of mass media communication. In many cases, a clear advantage of one approach over another has yet to be established. However, the accumulated evidence from mass communication campaigns and psychological research points to a number of aspects that must be considered and offers guidance for decision making in campaign development. These factors include source characteristics, message exposure, types of appeals, medium, and audience characteristics.

Source Characteristics

Credibility has been the most studied source characteristic and is viewed as the most crucial source attribute for effectiveness. The critical dimensions of credibility are trustworthiness, expertise, and attractiveness. Both celebrities, because they gain attention, and "ordinary" people, because the audience relates to them, have been found to be effective message sources (Atkin, 1979). However, older celebrities may have little attractiveness to young adult and adolescent audiences (Hochheimer, 1981). The effects of the source's degree of expertise in the subject matter of the message remain unclear (Cialdini *et al.,* 1981). However, sources that have status or authority with the audience tend to be more effective (McQuail, 1977). Prior affective attachment to a source among audience members also increases the potential for media influence (McQuail, 1977).

Message Exposure

As noted above, message repetition tends to increase effectiveness up to a point of diminishing returns (Atkin, 1979; Brown, 1981; Hirsch, 1980; McQuail, 1977). However, mere frequency of messages does not insure that the audience will be exposed to them, much less that it will pay attention to them (Atkin, 1979). Any message confronts a variety of barriers (social, political, psychological) that may prevent the audience from ever attending to the message (Brown, 1981). Thus, appropriate timing of messages so that they reach the desired target group is more crucial than achieving high frequency of messages (Atkin, 1979).

Types of Appeals

The nature of the appeal used in mass media may be the most significant factor in terms of achieving attitude and behavior change (Atkin, 1979). Choice of appeal remains complex, however, since several different approaches have been found to be effective. Both rational and emotional appeals have been successful, with indications that rational appeals are more effective with more sophisticated audiences and that emotional appeals are appropriate with indifferent or "already convinced" audiences (Atkin, 1979).

Fear appeals have had mixed results, but inducing higher fear levels has been found more effective than inducing mild fear, except with adolescents (Atkin, 1979). A recent experiment in which high school students in Ontario were exposed to high, medium, and low threat films about drinking and driving found that those in the high and low threat conditions had more positive attitudes toward impaired driving on the immediate posttest, but no attitudinal differences were found six months later (Kohn, Goodstadt, Cook, Sheppard, & Chan, 1981). None of the films affected self-reported drinking and driving at the six-month interval. A major risk in the use of fear appeals is that they may be too strong and thus counterproductive. The problem is finding the optimum level of anxiety arousal for a particular audience. Fear appeals seem to work best when the source is credible, the appeal includes a concrete solution to the problem, and the audience is characterized by either low anxiety or feelings of invulnerability (Atkin, 1979).

Two-sided appeals, in which both sides of the issue are presented in the same message, also have attendant risks, since the audience may be persuaded to the "wrong" side (Atkin, 1979). Two-sided appeals have been found most effective when the audience is resistant, sophisticated, or likely to be exposed to the opposing viewpoint. Regardless of the approach chosen, mass media messages tend to be most successful when they are readily understandable by the target audience, entertaining, and involving (Atkin, 1979). The message should also be unambiguous and relevant to the target audience (McQuail, 1977). Finally, messages should include explicit conclusions and suggestions for implementing the desired action (Hochheimer, 1981).

Medium

In general, television is the most effective medium for mass communication (Atkin, 1979). Television use and reliance on television over other media as a news source have increased with each succeeding generation (Roberts & Bachen, 1981). By 1974, television had replaced the newspaper as the most frequently mentioned source of national news, even among the college-educated (Comstock *et al.,* 1978). Both adolescents and adults prefer television as a source of information, and adolescents consider television the most believable news source (Roberts & Bachen, 1981). There is, however, a sharp decline in television use among late adolescents, an age group that is often a target for prevention programs (Roberts & Bachen, 1981).

Print media may be more useful than other media for achieving agenda-setting effects (Roberts & Bachen, 1981). They are also more appropriate for detailed and lengthy messages, rational appeals, and "impersonal, competent sources" (Atkin, 1979). Radio is the second best medium for reaching young adolescents, while print media receive little attention from adolescents (Atkin, 1979). Radio may be the most important medium among college students (Hochheimer, 1981).

Audience Characteristics

More focus is being placed on the effects of audience characteristics on mass communication outcomes. The audience is viewed as an interactive social system, rather than merely a passive recipient of messages (Holz & Wright, 1979). Thus, the process of communication is seen as being two-way. The characteristics of the target audience act as a filter through which

messages must pass (Brown, 1981). Some of the more significant characteristics, which affect both mass media usage and responses to particular
messages, are age, sex, race, education, social class, self-esteem, and intelligence (Hochheimer, 1981; Holz & Wright, 1979).

The "uses and gratifications" model of media use focuses on the audience's motivations for using the media and the ways in which media fulfill
audience needs (Gans, 1980; Morrison, Kline, & Miller, 1976). This model
assumes that members of the audience are active choosers of messages that
will offer the desired gratifications rather than passive recipients of messages (Watt, 1979). Through its active role, the audience may modify the
message it receives in ways that the message's creators could not predict.

Some theorists contend that although the uses and gratifications model
may apply to audience choice of news and information supplied by the
media, its applicability to choice of entertainment in the media is less certain (Gans, 1980). A number of researchers have noted that media use is
consummatory rather than functional and therefore characterized by low
involvement (Gans, 1980; Grunig, 1979; Hirsch, 1980; McLeod & Reeves,
1980). Choice of television programming, for example, is seen as being
largely nonpurposeful. The audience may be more attracted to the medium
than to its content, and thus watch television for the sake of watching,
regardless of the program (Hirsch, 1980).

Low audience involvement may or may not mean that media effects are
likely to be equally low (Gans, 1980). A condition of low involvement may
actually lead to greater media influence due to lack of screening and coun-
terargument (Gans, 1980). In addition, effects may be cumulatively strong
and there may be effects from mere exposure to the medium or from
underlying themes and symbolism rather than manifest content (Gans,
1980; Hirsch, 1980; Withey, 1980a). However, low involvement may limit
media effects to those that are short-term and attitudinal (Gans, 1980).

Because of the importance of audience characteristics, mass media
campaigns are generally considered to have the greatest effectiveness when
they are designed for specific segments of the population rather than for the
general public (Atkin, 1979; Shoemaker, 1981). Targets should be defined
in terms of psychological as well as demographic attributes and messages
should be tailored to and pretested with these groups (Atkin, 1979; Shoemaker, 1981). The media habits of the target group should also be taken
into account in selecting the medium and the timing of exposure. In addition, the stage in the adoption process at which the target group is located
(i.e., do they need basic information, persuasion to change attitudes, reinforcement to maintain desired behaviors, or are they at some other stage?)
should also be considered.

SUMMARY

Review of recent psychological, communications, and sociological literature indicates that mass communication's greatest potential for affecting individuals lies in its ability to impart knowledge or create awareness of ideas. Effects on attitudes may occur under certain conditions, but such effects do not necessarily lead to behavioral change. Behavioral effects are the most difficult to achieve through mass communication, although combining interpersonal methods of communication with mass media messages may increase the likelihood that behavioral change will occur. A number of aspects of mass communication must be considered when developing mass media programs for optimal effectiveness. The most important of these are source characteristics, message exposure, types of appeals, medium, and audience characteristics. These factors are interrelated and decisions about each area will ultimately depend on the specific nature of the program being planned, its goals and target audience, and a number of other variables, including constraints on time and resources.

PROGRAM CHARACTERISTICS OF ALCOHOL-RELATED MASS MEDIA CAMPAIGNS

Alcohol-related mass media campaigns conducted and evaluated between 1971 and 1982 were selected for review and analysis. Evaluation was loosely defined to include any systematic collection of outcome data on at least a postcampaign basis. This criterion excluded some studies (e.g., Goodstadt & Kronitz, 1977; Morrison, Kline, & Miller, 1976) that examined campaign-related variables but did not address outcome. Every attempt was made to cover all evaluations that have been reported, but since many reports do not reach published literature channels, it is quite possible that some studies are not reviewed. Of the 17 campaigns reviewed, for example, only 5 were reported in professional journals or books. Five previously reviewed campaigns (Blane & Hewitt, 1977) are reconsidered here because they included a pretest–posttest control group design. Even though the evaluation criterion for inclusion is fairly generous, a relatively large number of reports did not meet it and are therefore not considered here. Although many of these excluded reports contain material useful to practitioners, several of the evaluated programs are superior in this regard (see, e.g., Mielke & Swinehart, 1976; URSA/Pacificon, 1981a,b; Wallack & Barrows, 1981; Worden, Waller, & Riley, 1975).

Table 1 shows program characteristics for each of 17 programs re-

Table 1.

Program Characteristics of Evaluated Alcohol-Related Mass Media Campaigns, 1971–1982

Campaign number	Title, location, reference	Length, dates of implementation	Objectives	Messages	Audience	Media mix	Community mobilization
1	Edmonton study; Alberta (Farmer 1975)	1 month, 1971–72	1. Reduce driving after drinking 2. Eliminate drunk driving	1. "If You Drive After Drinking" 2. Consequences (legal, health) of driving after drinking 3. Drink less than one drink/hour	Social drinkers	1. TV 2. Radio 3. Billboards 4. Other print	Yes[a]
2	Project CRASH; Vermont (Worden et al., 1975)	2 years, 1972–74	Prevent drunk driving	1. "Beer and Consequences" 2. Legal consequences of drunk driving	Male drivers 16–29	1. TV 2. Radio 3. Films at drive-ins	Yes[a]
3	Drinking-driving campaign; Ontario (Pierce et al., 1975)	1 month, 1973	Prevent drunk driving	1. Alternative transportation 2. Limit drinking	General population	1. Radio 2. Newspaper 3. Other print	No
4	NIAAA advertising campaign; United States (Harris, 1974; Rappeport et al., 1975)	3 years, 1973–75	1. Promote responsible use 2. Increase awareness	Twelve responsible-use themes; e.g., alcoholism's effect on family, equivalence of alcoholic beverages, intoxication unacceptable	General population	1. TV 2. Radio	No

	Program	Duration	Objectives	Content	Target population	Media	
5	Children's Television Workshop series; United States (Mielke & Swinehart, 1976)	8 months, 1974–75	1. Prevent drunk driving 2. Responsible drinking	1. "Feeling Good" 2. Consequences of an alternatives to drunk driving 3. Self-recognition of drinking problems 4. Help-seeking by relatives of problem drinkers	General population	1. Public TV Network 2. Newspaper 3. Other print	No
6	"When To Say When"; Pennsylvania (Dickman & Keil, 1977)	5 weeks, 1975	1. Increase awareness of alcoholism 2. Motivate community action	1. "When to Say When" 2. Alcoholism among poor, young, old, and in different occupations	1. Alcoholics 2. Relatives, friends, and employers	1. Public TV Network 2. Other PSAs (media unspecified)	Yes
7	Ontario alcohol education program (Goodstadt, 1977)	1 year, 1975–76	Increase awareness	1. "You Are Your Own Liquor Control Board" 2. Consequences and hazards of alcohol	1. General population 2. Youth 3. Business/industry	1. TV 2. Radio 3. Other print 4. Other audiovisual	No
8	Scottish Health Education Unit campaign; Scotland (Plant et al., 1979)	1 year, 1976	Education on drinking, drunkenness, and alcoholism	1. Help seeking 2. Alcoholic symptoms 3. Consequences of alcoholism	1. General population 2. Problem drinkers	1. TV 2. Newspaper	No

(continued)

Table 1. (Continued)

Campaign number	Title, location, reference	Length, dates of implementation	Objectives	Messages	Audience	Media mix	Community mobilization
9	Drug abuse TV campaign; Florida (Wotring et al., 1979)	3 months, 1976–77	Counter pro-drug use social norm	"Think about drug habits—if you don't it'll cost you"	Middle and upper class adults	TV	No
10	Demonstration alcohol education project; University of Massachusetts (Amherst) (Duston, Hornik, & Kraft, 1980; Kraft, 1980)	4 years, 1976–80 (periods of media exposure vary; different media introduced at different times)	Promote responsible use	1. Equivalence of alcoholic beverages 2. Drinking consequences 3. BAC information 4. Helping problem drinkers 5. Asking for nonalcoholic beverages	College students	1. Radio 2. Newspaper 3. Displays 4. Other print	Yes
11	California Medicine Show; California (Hanneman et al., 1977, 1978)	2 months, 1977	1. Promote safe use of prescriptions, over-the-counter drugs 2. Compare mass media vs. mass media plus community development	1. Mixing drugs (including alcohol) 2. Trading drugs 3. Multiple effects of drugs 4. Consumer–professional communication	Women, 18–49	1. TV 2. Radio 3. Newspaper 4. Mass transit cards 5. Billboards 6. Other print	Yes

No.	Program (reference)	Duration	Objectives	Messages	Target audience	Media channels	Evaluated
12	Reduced Impaired Driving in Etobicoke (RIDE); Ontario (Vingilis et al., 1979)	1½ years, 1977–79	1. Prevent drunk driving 2. Increase arrest of drunk drivers 3. Compare paid vs. nonpaid mass media delivery	1. Negative effects of drunk driving 2. Information on laws and penalties	Potential and actual drunk drivers	1. TV 2. Radio 3. Newspaper 4. Other print	Yes[a]
13	Alcohol Abuse Prevention Project; Florida (Alcohol abuse, 1978; Florida study, 1981; King & Anderson, 1981)	2 years, 1978–80	1. Primary prevention 2. Compare mass media vs. mass media plus community development	Unclear; designed to change undesirable attitudes (e.g., a drink has to be alcoholic to be good)	General population	1. TV 2. Radio 3. Newspaper 4. Magazines	Yes
14	"Winners Quit While They're Ahead" Program; California (Wallack & Barrows, 1981)	2 years, 1978–80	1. Modify drinking behavior 2. Reduce alcohol problems	1. "Winners Quit While They're Ahead" 2. Rewards of moderate drinking	1. Males, 18–35 2. Females, 25–40 3. Adolescents and parents 4. Hispanics 5. Blacks	1. TV 2. Radio 3. Mass transit cards 4. Billboards 5. Other print	Yes
15	"Moderation Rules O.K." Campaign; Finland (Holmila et al., 1980)	Length not specified, but no longer than 3 months, 1979	1. Promote moderate drinking 2. Reduce excessive drinking	1. "Moderation Rules O.K." 2. More restrained hospitality norms	1. General population 2. "Influential People"	1. Newspaper 2. Other print	No

(continued)

Table 1. (Continued)

Campaign number	Title, location, reference	Length, dates of implementation	Objectives	Messages	Audience	Media mix	Community mobilization
16	California Women's Council on Alcoholism; California (Wittman, 1980)[b]	Current; length, dates unknown	Prevent Fetal Alcohol Syndrome	Not specified	1. Females of childbearing age 2. Physicians	1. Media (not specified) 2. Print material	Yes
17	NIAAA 1982 Alcohol Abuse Prevention Campaign; United States (NIAAA new, 1980; URSA/Pacificon, 1981a,b)[b]	Length unknown, 1982–	1. Prevent Fetal Alcohol Syndrome 2. Reduce alcohol abuse in women and youth	1. "How To Say No" 2. Don't drink when pregnant 3. Don't drive when drunk 4. O.K. to refuse alcohol	1. Females of childbearing age 2. Females, 18–44 3. Males, 16–21	1. TV 2. Radio 3. Print	Yes

[a]Law enforcement component.
[b]Evaluation in process.

viewed (15 with completed evaluations, 2 with evaluations planned or in progress). Programs are listed in chronological order of program implementation and are categorized by length, objectives, messages, target audience, media mix, and presence of a community mobilization/interpersonal reinforcement component.

LENGTH AND DATES

Campaigns are spaced fairly evenly by date over the 12-year period; that is to say, there has been little increase in the rate with which evaluated campaigns have been initiated. This observation appears to run counter to the belief that more and more mass media campaigns to reduce alcohol abuse are being mounted. Of course, it may well be that more campaigns are being started but have not been reported and evaluated.

Campaigns are either short or long in duration. Of 15 completed campaigns, 6 were three months or shorter and 6 were a year and a half or longer. Although short campaigns tend to be intensive and to occur around holidays (Farmer, 1975; Pierce, Hieatt, Goodstadt, Lonero, Cunliffe, & Pang, 1975), campaign length for the most part varies little with other program factors. The rather extreme variation in program duration fails to take into account findings that message repetition reaches a point of diminishing returns with regard to acceptance of a message. This is nowhere more evident than in findings that long-term repetition during the 1950s and 1960s of the message "If you drink, don't drive; if you drive, don't drink," was well remembered during the mid-1970s, but with no evidence that it was accepted (Rappeport, Labaw, & Williams, 1975).

OBJECTIVES

Responsible use of alcohol and drunk-driving countermeasures are the two most predominant themes in alcohol-related mass media campaigns. Recent campaigns have begun to stress reduction or moderation in drinking habits. Although moderation has always been implicit in the responsible use philosophy, more recent campaigns focus on it specifically (e.g., Holmila, Partanen, Piispa, & Virtanen, 1980; NIAAA, 1980; Wallack & Barrows, 1981). Also, the early tendency to emphasize consciousness raising and agenda setting oriented toward alcoholics and problem drinkers is giving way to a trend toward moderating abusive drinking that increases the risks of problem occurrence (e.g., fetal alcohol effects, accidents) as well as to moderation for its own sake. In some instances, alcohol-specific objectives

are part of a broader set of objectives as, for example, in the health promotion series, "Feeling Good" (Mielke & Swinehart, 1976) and drug abuse
campaigns (Hanneman, Eisenstock, Hunt, & Weinbeck, 1977; Hanneman,
Weinbeck, Goldman, Svenning, Nicol, Quattlebaum, & Scoredos, 1978;
Wotring, Heald, Carpenter, & Schmeling, 1979). The objectives of at least
two campaign reports were essentially methodological in nature. Hanneman *et al.* (1977, 1978) and King and Anderson (1981) replicated the
design of the Stanford Heart Disease Study by comparing the effects of
mass media alone against mass media complemented by community mobilization. Hanneman *et al.* compared the effects of purchased and nonpurchased mass media space.

MESSAGES

Of 17 campaigns, 10 had a tag line or image that integrated specific
messages. Most tag lines had negative connotations (e.g., "You Are Your
Own Liquor Control Board," "Think About Your Drug Habits. If You
Don't It'll Cost You," "How To Say No") not calculated to engage the
audience toward whom they were directed. Only two campaigns managed
positive tag lines: "Feeling Good" and "Winners Quit While They're
Ahead."

With regard to specific messages,the negative connotations of prevention, namely, reducing behaviors that for many are pleasurable and not
hazardous, again predominated. Eight programs dealt directly with the
negative consequences of drinking, most often in drunk-driving countermeasures campaigns. Eight presented messages of a more neutral informational or responsible use position. All these messages also are negative by
implication (e.g., how to ask for a nonalcoholic beverage; a drink has to be
alcoholic to be good; drink by drink, different alcoholic beverages are
equivalent). The five campaigns that included messages on how to identify
problem drinking (in oneself or others) and how to obtain help were also
negatively toned even though these messages have potential utility. Only
one program clearly had positive messages with a positive tag line, based on
the rewards of moderate drinking: the "Winners" campaign (Wallack &
Barrows, 1981). Inevitably, perhaps, the bottom line for this campaign, like
many others, was to reduce problems by lessening drinking.

Although the predominant emphasis in the campaigns was on giving
something up, several showed great sophistication from a media and/or
program standpoint in making relinquishment pleasurable. The Feeling
Good Series and the Winners Campaign are examples. Another is Project
CRASH (Worden *et al.,* 1975), one of the more carefully thought-out and

articulated campaigns under review. Targeted at male, beer-drinking drivers, 16 to 29 years old, its messages, with a tag line "Beer and Consequences," focused on the legal consequences of drunk driving (fear induction) and how to avoid these consequences by pacing drinks, waiting before driving after heavy drinking, and so on (fear reduction). The notion behind this approach was that fear-reducing behaviors would be more potent than pleasure-enhancing behaviors that did not reduce fear.

Relatively few campaigns (7) made direct appeals to modify behavior and these tended to be associated with drinking–driving campaigns. There does appear to be a trend toward more direct appeals to reducing or otherwise modifying drinking behavior in general alcohol problems prevention campaigns. For example, the "How To Say No" campaign (URSA/Pacificon, 1981a,b) messages are do not drink when pregnant and do not drive when drunk; it also gives witty and explicit ways of refusing alcoholic beverages.

TARGET AUDIENCE

A trend toward increasing segmentation of target audiences may be noted over the 12-year period, a trend consistent with good marketing and advertising practices. Although target audiences vary widely, adolescents, young adults, and females have been favorite groups lately, whereas the general population and problem drinkers were more popular targets until the mid-1970s. This shift parallels earlier interest in consciousness raising and agenda setting with regard to alcohol problems and creating an accepting climate for provision of treatment services and more recent interest in prevention and early intervention accompanied by increasing awareness of frequent heavy drinking among young adults (Blane, 1979) and new knowledge concerning the effects of drinking during pregnancy on fetal development.

MEDIA MIX

Most campaigns have a broad media mix that typically emphasizes television spots or films, backed up by parallel radio spots, and a wide variety of printed materials. The three campaigns that did not use television included a college-based program and two foreign programs where television capability might not have been as great as in the United States. Two campaigns were designed for and aired only on public television networks, sharply reducing penetration in the intended market.

Several campaigns showed considerable ingenuity in their use of media. Project CRASH (Worden *et al.*, 1975) developed short films to be shown during intermission at drive-in theaters and had special displays at stock-car races, particularly apposite uses of media for young, beer-drinking, male drivers. The California Medicine Show (Hanneman *et al.*, 1977, 1978) and Winners campaigns (Wallack & Barrows, 1981) used mass transit cards, a cost-effective means of reaching working class audiences without having to be concerned about articulating peak viewing and listening times on television and radio with the airing of messages. Several programs used billboards (Farmer, 1975; Hanneman *et al.*, 1977, 1978; Wallack & Barrows, 1981), which have advantages similar to those of mass transit cards. Findings indicate that billboards reach more adults and youth than radio, though fewer than television, and the point of contact through mass transit cards is higher for youth than adults (Hanneman *et al.*, 1978; Wallack & Barrows, 1981). In one study (Hanneman *et al.*, 1978), a billboard message achieved 22% recall, considerably higher than the highest recall (6%) attained by any other media message.

COMMUNITY MOBILIZATION

Community mobilization refers to follow-through activities during and following a mass media campaign that take place as community organization operations or interpersonal interactions to reinforce campaign objectives and to stimulate desired behavioral changes. Two types of community development activities have occurred in alcohol abuse prevention campaigns: a law enforcement component in drunk-driving countermeasures campaigns and a broader community organization component in general prevention campaigns. The former has long been a feature of drunk-driving campaigns, while the latter is a relatively new development stimulated by the Stanford Heart Disease Prevention Program (Meyer, Nash, McAlister, Maccoby, & Farquhar, 1980), frequently cited as a model for health education campaigns and the only recent prevention program to claim major behavioral effects. In addition to media, the program combined supportive services and face-to-face instruction. Community development also draws heavily on marketing principles, technology transfer processes, knowledge utilization, and diffusion of innovations theory. Blane (1981) reviewed this literature as it applies to prevention programming in the alcohol problems area.

Excluding law enforcement components from consideration, there has been a distinct move since 1977 toward incorporating interpersonal communication components in alcohol-related media campaigns (25% prior to 1977 vs. 83% since 1977). Although such components are costly, the evidence from research and practice in communications, advertising and marketing, knowledge utilization, and diffusion of innovations uniformly supports their use. Thus the relatively recent addition of community development components represents a salutary change, with the caveat that marketing prevention by interpersonal communications involves highly technical sets of operations and methods that can be used effectively only by trained and experienced practitioners. This implies that effective campaigns and programs require careful thought and planning, the involvement of specialists from a variety of areas, and a management system that can integrate the necessary parts into a totality greater than the sum of its parts.

EVALUATION CHARACTERISTICS OF ALCOHOL-RELATED MASS MEDIA CAMPAIGNS

Evaluation characteristics of the 15 campaigns that completed their evaluations are summarized in Table 2. The evaluation characteristics considered in this section include evaluation design, sampling, data collection techniques, air play, and exposure. The campaigns in Table 2 are listed in the same order as in Table 1 and are identified by the number assigned in Table 1.

EVALUATION DESIGN

Three basic designs have been employed to evaluate the outcomes of alcohol-related media campaigns: (1) posttest with no control (comparison) site; (2) pre-posttest with no control site; and (3) pre-posttest with control site design. Five campaigns used (or plan to use) the first design, four used (or plan to use) the second, and nine used the third design (one evaluation employed both the first and third designs).

All evaluations studied cross-sectional samples, although one also included an additional panel design and a repeated-measure experimental design (Mielke & Swinehart, 1976). Short campaigns that used a pre-posttest design typically had two data collection points. Longer pre-posttest campaigns, on the other hand, had multiple data collection points, in one instance as many as six (Mielke & Swinehart, 1976). One posttest-only evaluation (Harris, 1974; Rappeport *et al.,* 1975) had six data collection points to "monitor" ongoing campaign activities over a three-year period.

Evaluations containing control or comparison sites typically selected a city, county, or region that was not exposed to the media campaigns. In the case of four campaigns including a community mobilization component, the

Table 2.
Evaluation Characteristics of Evaluated Alcohol-Related Mass Media Campaigns, 1971–1982

Campaign number	Evaluation design				Sample		Data collection technique	Airings/week	Air play	Exposure percent	
	Pre-posttest	Control	Posttest	Type[a]	n	Response rate percent			Purchased	Recall	Recognition
1	Roadside samples	Yes	No	NP	2,162–3,122	NI[b]	Roadside survey. BAC test	NI	No	NI	NI
2	Roadside samples	2 graded exposure regions, 1 nonexposed region	No	NP	377–567	98	Roadside survey. BAC test	TV: 2 Radio: 14	No	Recall source of messages: Test: 27–34 TV 14–23 Radio Control: 17 TV 7 Radio	NI
3	Cross-sectional samples	9 exposed, 9 nonexposed	No	P	1,053–1,112	NI	Telephone survey	NI	No	NI	NI
4	Cross-sectional samples	Yes	Yes[c]	P	1,594–2,157	NI	Personal interview	NI	No	57–68 recall some TV ads; 2–12 recall some program messages	51–58 recognize one or more ads; 7–35 recognize specific ads
5	Cross-sectional and repeated measure samples	2 graded incentive samples, 1 nonincentive sample	No	Study 1: P Study 2: P	96–237 411–5,063	83–91 72–91	Personal/telephone interviews; Telephone screening/mail survey	1 hour. Nielsen ratings: 1.0–1.4. 1–3% viewed	No; prime time airing	NI	NI
6	No	None	Yes	P	1,200	NI	Telephone interview	1½ hours; 2.3% viewed	No	NI	NI
7	No	None	Yes	P	1,000	NI	Personal interview	TV: 2 Radio: 5–10	Yes	85 recall some radio/TV ads; 61 recall fictitious ads; 16 recall TV program	80 recognize punch line; 36 recognize fictitious punch line

messages; 13
recall radio
program mes-
sages; 9 recall
theme

No.		Control			Sample	%	Method	Exposure		Result	Result
8	Cross-sectional samples	None	No	P	467–555	68–73	Personal interview	3–4 Test: 66 viewed Control: 19 viewed	NI	Test: 52–67 recall some film details Control: 10	NI
9	No	None	Yes	P	960	NI	Telephone interview	16	No	51 recall[d] seeing one ad; 37–53 recall punch line	NI
10	Cross-sectional samples	None	Some	P	738–927	57–70	Mail survey	NI	No	15–16 recall radio ads	NI
11	Cross-sectional samples	3 graded exposure cities	No	P-NP	400–500	NI	Personal interview	TV: 17–22 Radio: 13	Yes	Recall theme Test 1: 40 Test 2: 30 Control: 17 Recall specific messages 1–6	6–56 recognize specific spots, with significant difference between sites for one spot
12	Cross-sectional samples	1 exposed, 4 nonexposed districts in one city	No	P	150–150	NI	Telephone interview	NI	No	NI	NI
13	Cross-sectional samples	3 graded exposure, 1 nonexposed county	No	P	377–401	30–31	Telephone interview	NI	No	NI	Recognize program ads: Test 1: 41–45 Test 2: 36 Control: 34
14	Cross-sectional samples	2 graded exposure sites, 1 nonexposed site	No	P	Adults: 447–528 Adolescents: 78–111	69–76 70–86	Personal interview	TV: 17–23 Radio: 26–64	No	NI	Recognize program theme: Test: 72–86 Control: 19–21 Recognize fictitious theme: Test: 19–34 Control: 22–40 Recognize specific ads:

(continued)

Table 2. (Continued)

| Campaign number | Evaluation design | | | Sample | | | Data collection technique | Air play | | Exposure percent | |
	Pre-posttest	Control	Posttest	Type[a]	n	Response rate percent		Airings/week	Purchased	Recall	Recognition
15	Cross-sectional samples	None	No	NI	1,000	NI	Personal interview	NI	NI	Recall theme: 18	Test: 14–67 Control: 2–14 Recognize theme: 50 Recognize fictitious theme: 17–28

[a] P = probability; NP = nonprobability.
[b] NI = no information in source document.
[c] One pre-post evaluation included a control site in 1975; most evaluations were posttests only without control sites.
[d] Not clear whether recall or recognition.

model popularized by the Stanford project was followed (i.e., a site exposed to media plus community development, a site exposed to media, and a site exposed to neither). It is of interest to note that Project CRASH (Worden *et al.,* 1975), which used this model, was completed about the time the Stanford project began. Evaluations comparing exposed to nonexposed sites compared several exposed to several nonexposed sites (Pierce *et al.,* 1975), one exposed to several nonexposed sites (Vingilis, Salutin, & Chan, 1979), or one exposed to one nonexposed community (Rappeport *et al.,* 1975).

An interesting and unique approach was Mielke and Swinehart's (1976) assignment of randomly selected community members to three conditions: an incentive to watch all programs in the "Feeling Good" series and participate in interviews, an incentive to participate in interviews without any viewing incentive, and a nonincentive condition to participate in interviews. Subjects were interviewed at pretest, interim, and two posttests, with overall retention rates of 83% to 91%.

The pre-posttest with control, the strongest design, was used by over half of the evaluations. However, comparing localities raises a number of problems, perhaps largely unavoidable in evaluations of community-directed interventions, that few of the investigations address. The absence of random selection from a population of sites and the failure to assign exposure conditions randomly to sites are two key issues. Given the methodological and sociopolitical difficulties in attaining random selection and treatment assignment, it is at least helpful to know the distribution of characteristics in target and comparison sites that are likely to be related to outcome variables. Such data were available in only two reports (King & Anderson, 1981; Wallack & Barrows, 1981), which unfortunately demonstrated clearly that the three communities were not comparable on a number of key variables. Another problem is exposure contamination in the nonexposed site from media spillover, travel in the exposed site by members of the nonexposed site, or communication between members of both sites. This issue is discussed in some of the evaluations and, more important, empirically examined by a few. Finally, even though the comparison-site design is strong, the manner in which it is carried out in detail, including sampling, measures, analysis, and other methodological procedures are crucial in evaluating outcomes.

SAMPLING

Most studies (86%) used probability techniques for selecting samples. Only two used nonrandom samples, each involving roadside surveys in which automobiles were stopped at a checkpoint for interview and blood alcohol concentration (BAC) determination. Random selection of vehicles is difficult, if not impossible, given the circumstances. In both studies, care was taken to randomize location of checkpoints and the periods of time during which vehicle selection was conducted.

Studies employing household interviews tended to have the most rigorous and sophisticated sampling designs and appear to have obtained samples most representative of the populations in question. Samples based on telephone directory listings, however, overrepresent high socioeconomic status groups and underrepresent lower socioeconomic status in direct proportion to the percentage of households in a locality that do not have telephone service. This factor was not addressed by any of the evaluations that used telephone directories to define the population.

Sample sizes tended to be large, with more than half ranging from 900 to over 5,000 subjects. Most samples of this size do not provide sufficient additional information over smaller samples to justify the increase in costs for sample selection, data collection, and other contingent efforts. Most of the evaluations provided no rationale for the particular sample size selected, although some indicated the need to include sex, age, and other strata. As noted earlier, all studies used cross-sectional samples, often with three or more data collection points. The reliance on large samples and a cross-sectional approach suggests that most evaluations paid insufficient attention to sampling issues in relation to costs, efficiency, and evaluation objectives. Several alternatives are available. Given fixed resources, for instance, one might reduce sample size, but allow for the use of more powerful, but more expensive data collection techniques (e.g., personal interviews as contrasted to telephone interviews or mail surveys). Panel designs can reduce the need for the repeated selection of a sample needed for multiple data collection points in a cross-sectional approach. Further, the use of panel designs permits the use of repeated measures statistical tests (the lack of appropriate statistical tests for analyzing repeated cross-sectional designs that do not meet criteria for time-series analyses is discussed below).

Less than half (40%) of the evaluations reported the response rates reached in their sampling procedures. What is surprising is that evaluations in which sampling was conducted by large survey firms were more likely to be the ones that failed to report response rates. For studies reporting response rates the range was 30% to 98%. Household interviewing response rates ranged from 68% to 91%, with an average percentage for four samples of 77%. Two mail surveys range from 57% to 91%; that is, from rather low to suspiciously high. One telephone survey reports response rates of 30% to 31%, an extremely low figure apparently based on the percentage of interviews completed to all telephone numbers to which a call was made; when number of completed calls is the base, response rate rises to 57% to

60%. The 98% response is reported in a drunk-driving campaign that used a roadside survey; of cars stopped, very few refused to be interviewed, an unsurprising occurrence for those flagged down by the police at night.

The general failure to report response rates or adequate information regarding response rates is consistent. Although this particular omission may not be serious in and of itself, it appears to be symptomatic of a more general failure to report procedures, measures, analyses, and findings in a systematic, comprehensible, and scientific manner.

Another question of interest is the extent to which samples reflected the target audiences toward which mass media campaigns were directed. Only two evaluations had a major incongruence between sample and target audience characteristics. Dickman and Keil (1977) and Wotring *et al.* (1979) each studied general population samples; in the first case, the target audiences were alcoholics and their relatives, friends, and employers, and, in the second, the audience was middle and upper class adults. Evaluations with multiple target audiences often used general population samples from which target subsets could be but were not drawn; others specifically sampled specific target audiences, especially adolescents and young adults.

DATA COLLECTION TECHNIQUES

Data collection techniques were evenly divided between personal interviews and telephone interviews (40% each). Two evaluations used mail surveys and two had roadside interviews complemented by BAC determinations. In the panel study (Mielke & Swinehart, 1976), initial personal interviews were followed in subsequent data collection phases by telephone interviews. For their cross-sectional surveys, these investigators also screened potential respondents by telephone and then conducted a mail survey with the final sample. The other mail survey was conducted through the campus mail of a large university (Duston, Hornik, & Kraft, 1980).

Although interview schedules or questionnaires were not usually reproduced in the reports, they appeared to be highly structured, consisting mainly of closed questions and limited open-ended items. Descriptions of measurement domains and specific variables were generally lacking and psychometric properties of measures, where relevant, were infrequently stated.

AIR PLAY

The opportunity for audience exposure to a mass media campaign is a critical precondition for actual exposure that is in turn linked to campaign effects. Opportunity for exposure may be conceived as the degree of potential linkage between media distribution and members of the target audience. Media that are known to be highly utilized by the target audience are ideally the ones selected for intensive distribution. With regard to television and radio, two elements may be examined: the frequency with which a spot or ad is shown or aired and the time at which it is shown or aired. In order to assess opportunity for exposure, air play was examined according to these two variables. The first was operationally defined as the number of airings per week and the second as purchased time. The latter was selected because purchase of time on television will at least permit a specified number of showings during prime time (8 to 11 P.M.). Without purchase of time, stations may or may not air a public service announcement and if they do there is no control over the time of airing. Other types of opportunity for exposure, either for electronic media (e.g., selecting a particular radio station because a high percentage of its listeners are in the target audience) or other media (e.g., billboard placement, newspaper or magazine placement relative to demographic characteristics of the readership) are also important. They are considered here selectively because their coverage is generally low in the evaluations.

Of the 14 campaigns utilizing television/radio, 7 reported sufficient information to make an estimate of airings per week. For television, the range was 2 to 23 spots per week, and for radio it was 5 to 64 spots per week. The two public television network campaigns did not air spots or ads, but a series of full-length shows. For the Pennsylvania campaign (Dickman & Keil, 1977) there was a five-part series of 90-minute programs, with each program shown once a week. The Feeling Good series (Mielke & Swinehart, 1976) contained four 60-minute programs dealing largely with alcohol abuse prevention. These were shown weekly, but interspersed throughout the entire series of 24 health promotion programs. The Scottish campaign (Plant, Pirie, & Kreitman, 1979) also consisted of four films rather than spots; during the campaign, the films were shown 3 or 4 times per week.

For the campaigns on which information is available, only two showed high opportunity for exposure with regard to electronic media. The California Medicine Show (Hanneman *et al.,* 1977, 1978), which purchased time, showed TV spots 17 to 22 times per week and radio spots 13 times per week. The Winners campaign had respective figures of 17 to 23 and 26 to 64. Three other campaigns had relatively high opportunity for exposure: (1) The Scottish campaign, with only 3 or 4 shows per week, may be regarded as high because there are only two television networks that operate on limited hours, so that penetration is apt to be high; (2) Project CRASH had only 2 television spots per week, but 14 radio spots on stations targeted toward its audience; and (3) Drug Abuse campaign in Florida (Wotring *et al.,* 1979) showed 16 spots per week, but without control over timing. The Canadian Campaign (Goodstadt, 1977), despite purchased time (2 TV spots, 5 to 10 radio spots) was not intensive. The Feeling Good series was shown on public television during prime time and it is likely that the Pennsylvania series was also shown on prime time.

A few campaigns report viewing figures. In the Scottish campaign, 66% in the exposed sample reported viewing one or more of the films; this contrasted to 19% in the nonexposed sample (these figures may be due to media spillover). The two public television series each report viewer percentages of one to three percent of a general population sample, thereby showing extremely low penetration rates. This observation is reinforced by Nielsen ratings on the Feeling Good series of 1.0–1.4 (by contrast, major network prime time ratings range from 15 to 30).

EXPOSURE

Exposure is usually measured by obtaining data concerning the proportion of the target audience that reports having seen or heard campaign messages. Recall, the spontaneous recollection of messages, is considered the soundest indicator of actual exposure. Recognition, the selection of campaign messages embedded in a series of other messages, is another commonly used measure of exposure, but is considered to be less sound an indicator than recall because of greater opportunities for response bias. In order to control for bias, fictitious messages are sometimes introduced into a recognition list. Table 2 summarizes exposure findings by recall and recognition. In several instances, it was necessary to make arbitrary decisions as to whether recall or recognition was the technique used because the manner in which data were obtained varied widely and were sometimes imprecisely described. Five evaluations provided no information on recall or recognition. Of the remaining 10 studies, 8 provided data on recall and six on recognition.

Recall

Recall of the campaign's main theme was available in three evaluations, ranging from 9% for the "You Are Your Own Liquor Control Board" campaign to 40% for the California Medicine Show. The Finnish campaign's theme (Holmila *et al.,* 1980), which used newspapers and other print materials, was recalled by 18%. The California Medicine Show, which had a graded-exposure design of public service announcements (PSA) only, purchased PSAs, and purchased PSAs plus community development, reported recall of 17%, 32%, and 40%, respectively. These differences indicate the effectiveness of purchased time (32%) and the effectiveness of the combination of purchased media and community mobilization (40%). The 9% recall of the Liquor Control Board theme (Goodstadt, 1977) also occurred in a campaign that purchased time, but as noted above, the intensity of the campaign was not high; further, the campaign theme itself is not compelling. It would appear that without special efforts exposure as assessed by recall of the campaign theme will not be more than 20%. This figure probably can be doubled by purchased media, community development, and an intensive campaign that includes billboards.

Recall of specific messages of a campaign was provided in four evaluations. Recall of television messages ranged from 1 to 16%; for radio messages recall ranged from 13 to 16%. The lowest percentages of recall (1% to 6%), were, interestingly enough, for the California Medicine Show, which had the highest recall for campaign theme. A billboard message, the purchased PSAs plus community development site, achieved 22% recall, which may have been due to the fact that it appeared for two months longer than other media messages.

Recognition

Findings concerning recognition of the main theme of the campaign were provided in three evaluations that also controlled for response bias by including fictitious themes. Recognition of the theme ranged from 50% to 86% for four samples, but recognition of the fictitious themes was also relatively high, from 17% to 44%. Subtracting fictitious recognition from campaign recognition nets a "true" recognition rate of 22% to 44% for three adult samples and 63% to 67% for one adolescent sample.

Recognition of specific messages was studied in three evaluations, only one (Wallack & Barrows, 1981) of which attempted to control for fictitious messages. Recognition of specific messages ranged from 6% to 67% for four samples. Recognition of a fictitious message was 2% or less in the one study that controlled for it. However, the fictitious message was so different from the four campaign messages that it may have stood out as one not to be recognized or it may have inflated recognition of actual messages by contrast. Well-designed controls for response bias would in all likelihood have resulted in lower net recognition percentages. As with theme recognition, message recognition was higher for an adolescent sample (20% to 67%) than adult samples (6% to 56%).

There were also considerable differences in recognition of different messages from the same campaign. In the Winners campaign (Wallack & Barrow, 1981), for example, one message was recognized over twice as frequently (43% to 50% among adults) as the least recognized message (14% to 20%). The same ordering was also observed among adolescents. The California Medicine Show campaign (Hanneman *et al.*, 1978) had similar findings: the most recognized PSA ranged from 23% to 56% and the least recognized from 11% to 18%. These differences in recognition of messages have to do with variables involving opportunity for exposure as well as differences in the intrinsic appeal of messages.

It may also be noted that purchased media and purchased media plus community mobilization had successively higher recognition rates over nonpurchased media (Hanneman *et al.*, 1978), reinforcing the previously mentioned findings on recall of the campaign theme. The percentages for nonpurchased media were 6% to 23%, for purchased media they were 18% to 40%, and for purchased media plus community mobilization they rose to 11% to 56%.

In summary, exposure as judged by recognition is considerably higher than exposure judged by recall. It is probably important to use both measures in evaluating penetration and exposure. Latent memories that are triggered into consciousness by a mnemonic cue may be just as important as free recall in terms of attaining campaign objectives, although the question is an empirical one at this time. Recall is greater for the campaign theme than for specific messages within a campaign; this tends to be true for recognition, too, although failure to use fictitious messages to control for response bias in recognizing specific messages precludes definite conclusions.

A variety of programmatic variables may affect the exposure achieved by media campaigns. Programs that are able to purchase media time achieve control over the frequency with which messages appear and the general times (e.g., prime, fringe) when they appear. Of course, funds must be sufficient if purchased time is to equal or exceed the air play that would otherwise be achieved. Figures on air play from the California Medicine Show, which purchased time, and other campaigns indicate that the total air play achieved under purchased time conditions may not be appreciably different from that achieved under conditions of donated time. However, the same amount of air play can be more effective when media time is purchased since, for example, some control can be achieved over the time of day when messages appear in order to reach a wider general audience or a particular target group. Buying segments of prime time will increase the potential audience considerably.

Television has been cited as the most effective medium for the achievement of maximum exposure. Campaigns that used other media in addition to television report greater exposure with television. However, the Winners and California Medicine Show programs achieved nearly as much or greater exposure through the use of billboards as through television and radio (Hanneman *et al.,* 1978; Wallack & Barrows, 1981). Thus, billboards may be a very cost-effective media choice. If television is the choice, commercial television is preferable to public television, unless the target audience is similar to the select population of public television viewers. Campaigns that utilized public television programs achieved very low exposure rates and one did not reach the major target group.

Characteristics of the audience may be the most crucial variable in determining exposure achieved by a mass media campaign. Evaluations that have analyzed exposure in relation to audience characteristics have obtained a variety of often contradictory results. Comparison of results is further complicated by the fact that measures of audience characteristics differ across campaign evaluation studies. One fairly consistent finding is that the audience must first have the opportunity to be exposed to the campaign. Thus, several campaigns using television have found greater exposure among those who watch television more frequently (Hanneman *et al.,* 1978; Wotring *et al.,* 1979), and a university-based program found more exposure among students who lived on campus and more recall of radio ads among radio listeners (Duston *et al.,* 1980).

Several programs have found no consistently significant differences in exposure by sex (Dickman & Keil, 1977; Duston *et al.,* 1980; Plant, Pirie, & Kreitman, 1979; Wotring *et al.,* 1979). Age has been found to be related to exposure in some campaign evaluations, with young adults or adolescents having higher rates of recognition and recall (Dickman & Keil, 1977; Duston *et al.,* 1980; Goodstadt, 1977; Hanneman *et al.,* 1978; Wallack & Barrows, 1981).

In reviewing the results of evaluations of public campaigns concerning alcohol conducted in the mid 1970s, Whitehead (1979) concluded that evidence that campaign messages ever reach the audience is "thin," adding that campaign awareness that is evaluated is of a superficial nature, often indicating only that an individual has seen a PSA and not measuring comprehension, impact, and so forth. More recent campaign evaluations have provided additional evidence that campaign messages reach at least some portions of the audience. However, due to problems such as lack of data on comprehension and interpretation of ads, intensity of exposure and attention to them, and results that indicate that people recall nonexistent messages, our understanding of the extent and depth of campaign exposure and of variables related to exposure remains superficial.

OUTCOMES OF ALCOHOL-RELATED MASS MEDIA CAMPAIGNS

Systematic review of the outcomes of the campaigns reviewed is complicated by measurement factors, issues of statistical analysis, and issues in attribution of findings to campaign effects. Measurement of knowledge and attitudes was typically based on responses to single items; rarely was a scale or test composed of a number of items used. When multi-item measures were utilized their reliability and validity were unknown or not reported. Further, many items showed pretest ceiling effects that made positive assessment of change more difficult than necessary to achieve. Measurement of behavior was mostly indirect, based on self-report, and not susceptible to independent measurement. However, some drunk-driving countermeasure campaign evaluations did measure alcohol crash statistics or BACs. Finally, measurement was usually based on the nominal scale; even when ordinal or interval scale measures had been used, they were most often treated in analysis as nominal. This sharply reduced the potential for statistical analysis.

Statistical analysis was also complicated by the kinds of research designs generally employed in the evaluations. The use of cross-sectional samples over time makes statistical comparisons that take change into account difficult. The relatively low number of assessment points did not permit the use of statistics appropriate to time series designs, while the use of a cross-sectional rather than a longitudinal design did not permit the use of repeated measures statistics. In any event, few evaluations used more than a two variable chi-square approach that precluded partitioning of higher order tables or examination of interactions. Because sample sizes were often large, attaining statistical significance was maximized so that trivial percentage differences were often accorded practical meaning.

Despite design and measurement problems, data in many of the evaluations lent themselves to more sophisticated statistical treatment than was used. Analysis of variance and/or log linear analysis were appropriate in several instances but were not performed. Although a few evaluations used a more sophisticated analytic scheme (Duston *et al.,* 1980; Goodstadt, 1977; Hanneman *et al.,* 1978; Mielke & Swinehart, 1976), in some instances, no statistical analysis was performed.

The attribution of findings to the effects of the campaign was rendered difficult due to spillover effects, absence of control conditions, inability to control historical effects, the aforementioned problems with statistical analysis, and other methodological difficulties. Many evaluations based their findings on the total sample rather than examining it according to viewer, recall, or recognition status. Given the fact that campaigns rarely reached more than 50% of the population, it would seem overly conservative to include individuals never exposed to a campaign in an assessment of its impact.

The effects on conclusions of problems in measurement, analysis, and interpretation are complex. In some instances, they converge to find effects where none exist, while in others they operate to obscure the presence of

Table 3.
Outcomes of Evaluated Alcohol-Related Mass Media Campaigns, 1971–1982

Campaign number	Knowledge	Attitudes	Behavior
1	+	NS	NC
2	±	NC	+
3	+	NS	+
4	NC	NC	NS
5	+	+	NC
6	NC	NS	NC
7	NS	NS	NC
8	+	NS	NC
9	NS	+	NS
10	+	NC	±
11	+	±	+
12	+	NS	NC
13	NC	±	NC
14	NC	NC	NC
15	NS	NC	NS

Key: + = some findings in desired direction; ± = both positive and negative findings; NC = no change; NS = not studied.

true effects. Although it is tempting to say that these tendencies probably cancel each other, there is little evidence that this is the case. Within one evaluation (Worden *et al.,* 1975) we conducted two re-analyses of data. In one, a reportedly significant knowledge effect turned out to be nonsignificant and, in the other, a finding that was discussed but not analyzed was significant.

Table 3 summarizes findings of knowledge, attitude, and behavior domains: (1) Positive (and negative) findings were based on statistically significant differences; (2) Findings could be attributed to campaign activities on a reasonably possible basis (i.e., findings were not due to the passage of time or occurrences over which the campaign had no control and did distinguish exposed from nonexposed sites or viewers from nonviewers); and (3) Significant findings occurring in a context of many nonsignificant comparisons were not included, but patterns of significant and nonsignificant effects that made sense in terms of campaign objectives were.

KNOWLEDGE

Of the 15 evaluations, 12 contained an assessment of knowledge outcomes. Seven found changes in the desired direction, four reported no change, and one reported both positive and negative findings. Studies that analyzed knowledge variables by exposure status tended to report positive findings (4 out of 5 evaluations) slightly more often than studies that did not (4 out of 7 evaluations). All four of the drunk-driving campaigns found knowledge gains consistent with Smart's (1979) conclusion that drinking–driving countermeasure programs have generally been successful in imparting knowledge. None of these studies analyzed knowledge by exposure, suggesting that the effects obtained were relatively widespread. The success of drinking–driving campaigns in the knowledge area may be due to the fact that the knowledge imparted is specific and factual with minimal ambiguity, including items such as the BAC level that legally defines intoxication, the average number of drinks to reach that level, and the penalties for driving while intoxicated.

Although several campaigns found knowledge effects, gains were modest at best. Among programs reporting large effects, Vingilis, Salutin, and Chan (1979) found significant gains by analysis of variance on a seven-point knowledge scale, but gains were less than one point, with baseline scores low (about 1.5). Significant effects reported by Mielke and Swinehart (1976) were in the range of 11% to 17%, among the largest obtained in any study. In several evaluations, knowledge levels were initially high, making small knowledge gains even less impressive.

One evaluation (Worden *et al.*, 1975) reported a pattern of mixed knowledge effects (e.g., no gains, positive effects at treated but not comparison sites, positive effects at comparison but not treated sites, and gains at all sites). Findings were, for the most part, fairly impressive for the site that received the campaign plus countermeasures, although their interpretation is limited due to the findings for the other sites, the type of analysis employed (simple χ^2), and the presence of media spillover between treated and untreated sites. The campaign itself was extremely well conceived and generally well conducted. Findings might be considered positive in light of the fact that viewing status was not used as a variable in the analysis. Reanalysis of data with more powerful techniques would aid in clarifying findings for this evaluation.

ATTITUDES

Nine of the 15 evaluations assessed attitudes, two of the nine reported changes in the desired direction, five reported no change, and two reported a pattern of mixed positive and negative findings. As was observed for knowledge, studies that analyzed data by exposure status tended to report positive findings (3 out of 4 evaluations) more often than studies that did not (1 out of 5 evaluations). Campaigns with a primary drunk-driving thrust tended to examine attitudes less often (1 out of 4 evaluations) than campaigns with a more general focus (8 out of 11).

The evaluations reporting positive attitudinal changes only (Mielke & Swinehart, 1976; Wotring *et al.*, 1979) found moderately higher subscription to a small series of attitudinal items among viewers than nonviewers. Statistical significance of association was inflated in the Wotring study as a consequence of its large sample size ($N = 960$), with percentage differences of less than 15% reaching probability values of less than .001. Small percentage differences present in the Mielke and Swinehart study also reached significance, but this is due more to use of a one-tailed test rather than to sample size.

The two evaluations that reported both positive and negative findings (Hanneman *et al.*, 1978; King & Anderson, 1981) analyzed attitudinal data both as scales and by individual items within the scale (since neither reports on the internal consistency of the scales, it is not known whether they measure a single domain or have a multifactor structure). Findings for the attitude scales shows no differences for either study across time or across sites. The Medicine Man evaluation (Hanneman *et al.*, 1978) reported results for the total sample and also by exposure status (awareness of the campaign). There were no differences for the total sample, but in the exposure status analysis, respondents from the least exposed site who were *not* aware of the campaign showed a significant change in the desired direction. Although this difference reached significance, the group mean difference was only 0.9 of a point on a 30-point scale.

Both evaluations also analyzed attitudinal data for each item in the scale. In the Medicine Man evaluation, analysis produced statistically significant but contradictory findings with small absolute differences. As noted earlier, each of the three sites received graded exposure to the campaign. The site that received paid PSAs and community mobilization showed positive item changes over time in 4 out of 15 comparisons. The sites that received either PSAs or paid PSAs each showed 4 changes out of 15 comparisons, but in both instances 2 comparisons were in the desired direction and 2 were opposite to the desired direction. Also, when items were analyzed by exposure status, the only significant effects, all positive, occurred among respondents *not* aware of the campaign. Further, 3 of the 5 effects occurred in the least treated site. This mixture of results, given their small absolute values and the fact that they may have occurred by chance in a context of numerous comparisons, suggests that attitude change objectives were probably not reached in this campaign, even though the high intensity site tended to show more positive change. It should be noted, however, that ceiling effects may have prevented the detection of real changes. Although the range of the scale was 5 to 35, with a theoretical mean of 20, since the average pretest score for all groups was about 30, there remained very little room to go higher. In fact, the item-by-item analysis shows that pre- posttest scores for the first posttest decreased absolutely for 12 out of 15 possible comparisons.

A similar pattern of mixed item-by-item results held for the King and Anderson (1981) evaluation, but the study was not subject to ceiling effects. The distribution of scale means was flat across time and sites, with the difference between the highest and lowest of 16 means being less than one point (0.78) for a 28-point scale. Numerous differences, however, were observed in the analysis of items, most of which were not more than 10 percentage points and were inflated by large sample sizes. There were two sites that received mass media plus community development activities. One showed no change over time for any of the attitude items, while the other showed modest but consistent changes for all items. A third site, which received media only, showed positive effects on some items and negative effects on others. Finally, a control site that received no treatment nevertheless showed positive effects on 3 of 7 items. There were also several nonscale items, which showed either no effects, effects in the preferred direction, or effects against the preferred direction. Desired effects, though absolutely small, tended to cluster as with the other attitude items in one of the intensively exposed sites.

It would appear that the intensive campaign did have a slight differential positive impact on one of the intensive treatment sites but no impact on the other. The difference between the two intensive treatment sites may have been due to differential delivery of the campaign (no information is available concerning this), demographic differences among sites, demographic differences between pretest and posttest samples within sites, or a combination of the three. Positive effects in the control site may have been a function of media spillover or other noncampaign-related factors. This is the only evaluation obtaining attitudinal effects in which exposure status is not an analytic variable. It is possible that effects would have been greater had exposure to the campaign been assessed and used as an analytic variable. Also, exposure status might permit more understanding of positive and negative effects.

Overall, evidence for attitudinal change is not strong. The majority of evaluations found no change in attitudes as a consequence of exposure to mass media campaigns. Since most of the studies did not use exposure status as an analytic variable, it is possible that real effects were not detected. Nevertheless, in studies where change did occur, the magnitude of change was not great, results were sometimes mixed, and interpretation was rendered difficult by a number of methodological problems.

BEHAVIOR

Twelve of the 15 evaluations included an assessment of behavioral change; 3 found changes in the desired direction, 8 found no change, and 1 showed both positive and negative changes. In contrast to the trend observed for knowledge and attitudes, none of the evaluations showing positive behavioral change analyzed behavioral data by exposure status, except the evaluation that showed mixed effects. Two studies that used exposure status as an analytic variable found no behavioral change. The campaigns showing behavioral effects included two drunk-driving countermeasure programs, a university-based program, and the California Medicine Man campaign which was oriented primarily toward preventing drug misuse. It should be noted that several of the evaluations claimed behavioral effects, but their findings did not meet the criteria of statistical significance and consistency required to demonstrate change.

The findings for the two drunk-driving campaigns were weak but consistent in one instance (Pierce *et al.,* 1975) and somewhat stronger but not as consistent in the other (Worden *et al.,* 1975). Responses to three behavioral questions in the Pierce study each showed small but significant changes in the desired direction after the campaign. Similar changes were also noted in the comparison site and were significant in one instance. As the authors noted: "Although the number of persons who changed their behavior seems trivially small we feel encouraged that apparently we were able to make some inroads in this very difficult area of changing behavior." The findings of the CRASH campaign (Worden *et al.,* 1975) are of interest because they deal with actual behavioral data (i.e., BACs and accident statistics). With regard to BACs, the site that received the campaign showed a significant reduction in the percentage of drivers with BACs over 0.05 from pretest to posttest. The difference, 14 percentage points, is not large and represents a relatively small number of cases, but is consistent with knowledge gains found in the study. The more intensively treated site and the untreated site showed no change. The data for alcohol-related fatal crashes were based on even fewer cases, but showed a reduction for the intensively treated site midway during the campaign; however, posttest rates rose to baseline levels. No other changes were noted at other sites over time.

The Medicine Man campaign (Hanneman *et al.,* 1978) examined self-reported use of three classes of drugs (including alcohol), information-seeking behavior, and communication behavior with health providers. No effects were found for drug use and insufficient information was provided to assess communication behavior. However, a strong effect was found for information-seeking behavior in the intensive treatment site, with a continued increase after the campaign's termination. Information seeking concerning drugs increased from a baseline 49% to 74% at final posttest. Similar increases were not detected at either of the other sites. This finding may have been stronger had data been analyzed by exposure status.

The University of Massachusetts program (Duston *et al.,* 1980; Kraft, 1980) showed mixed findings with regard to behavior. (This program is reviewed in detail in Chapter 9.) For the most part there were no changes reported for community indicators of alcohol-related problems, although a "dramatic" increase in the costs of dormitory damages occurred, one-third of which was attributed to alcohol use. Positive changes were observed in dormitory behavior around alcohol and participants in alcohol education courses reported entering fewer drinking situations and a lower frequency of getting drunk. However, annual surveys of the student body over four years showed significant increases in amount of alcohol consumed, entry into drinking situations, negative consequences of drinking, and problem outcomes. Although significant, absolute increases were small and have little practical significance. Although Duston *et al.* (1980) present several alternative hypotheses to explain the latter negative behavioral effects, the possibility that they may in part be attributed to the program cannot be ruled out.

In summary, few evaluations obtained behavioral effects. Those that did found relatively weak positive changes that might have occurred by chance or as a result of noncampaign-related factors. Some negative findings were also reported, but these, too, can be explained in ways unrelated to campaign effects.

CONCLUSIONS

A number of positive suggestions emerge from the present review both for the construction of campaigns and the conduct of their evaluation. An examination of program characteristics in relation to outcome reinforces already existing trends and suggests new emphasis in campaign planning, organization, and strategy; targeting; audience; penetration; and media mix.

CAMPAIGN PLANNING, ORGANIZATION, AND STRATEGY

Campaigns that proceed from a strong communications base, have considerable time to plan, integrate an evaluation component from the outset, and are well-grounded in the alcohol studies and prevention area will mount the most organized and conceptualized efforts. The programs under review had difficulty in meeting all of these conditions. Interestingly, of the three campaigns that showed promise, two (Hanneman *et al.,* 1977, 1978; Mielke & Swinehart, 1976) did not have a primary alcohol focus, and the third (Worden *et al.,* 1975) was a drunk-driving countermeasure program. But even here practical, conceptual, and methodological difficulties marred the execution and evaluation of the campaigns. In order to anticipate difficulties and to take into account as many aspects as possible, a careful planning and management scheme has to be developed that integrates principles and practices from communications, marketing, prevention, evaluation, and alcohol studies. Further, thorough pretesting, not simply of messages but of measures used for formative and summative evaluation, has to be included.

One trend that will undoubtedly continue and which receives support in this review is that mass media is simply a starting point in the process of behavior change. Recent programs almost uniformly include a community mobilization/interpersonal communication follow-through. This may be conceptualized as an extension service (e.g., in agriculture or education) or as a marketing and distribution system based on commercial principles. In either case, an up-front intensive media campaign will inform and sensitize the intended audience and a less intensive but continuing campaign will serve to reinforce community mobilization activities. Campaigns that utilize mass media alone appear to have minimal impact.

TARGETING

The trend away from targeting the general population is salutary and again borrows from marketing principles. Market segmentation is an extremely important principle that has not been carefully followed. Only the CRASH campaign (Worden *et al.,* 1975) followed the procedure of identifying the segment of the population that showed the highest incidence of the behavior for which change was desired (i.e., drunk driving that resulted in high crash involvement). Samples of this population were then studied and on the basis of the findings a campaign directed at the segment was constructed. Other campaigns have used several segments and have addressed them simultaneously with different messages integrated under a common theme; examples include the Winners campaign (Wallack & Barrows, 1981) and the current NIAAA campaign (URSA/Pacificon, 1981a,b). This strategy is likely to diffuse the impact of a campaign. Commercial marketing initially addresses a clearly defined market or population segment; when that has proved successful adjacent or other segments then become additional markets. Campaigns aimed at specific targets that show low incidence of desired behaviors or high incidences of undesired behaviors should be encouraged.

AUDIENCE PENETRATION

Exclusive use of public television networks for television portions of a campaign results in extremely low penetration and should be discouraged. The results of the two campaigns that used public television (Dickman & Keil, 1977; Mielke & Swinehart, 1976) provide clear-cut evidence for this conclusion, even though campaign materials were shown in prime time. On the other hand, paid PSAs for prime or fringe time can substantially increase penetration, provided resources are sufficient for reasonably frequent air play. Another avenue for increasing penetration is the use of billboards, which, if carefully placed, provide a means for frequent viewing by substantial proportions of an audience; billboards have the added advantage of being relatively economical. There is little evidence to suggest that use of printed materials, however intensive, substantially increases audience exposure.

MEDIA MIX

Media mix is dependent on media use by the target audience. For most audiences, prime time television is the first choice. Possible exceptions include late adolescents, college-aged persons, and housewives. Particular radio stations should be selected on the basis of listening habits in the target audience, and radio may be required for some audiences. Again, paid PSAs for radio will increase penetration. Billboards, as noted, are generally useful, but especially so if the audience has a high proportion of drivers. For those who use public transportation, mass transit cards would be a choice. Printed materials may be useful in community mobilization phases of a campaign, but have generally low penetration value for most audiences. Ingenious as matchbook covers, napkins, and stickers with printed messages are, they do not represent efficient use of resources.

EVALUATION FACTORS

Needed improvements in evaluation have been described throughout the chapter. These primarily include (1) defining objectives in measurable terms and matching measurement techniques to these definitions; (2) concentrating more on longitudinal than cross-sectional approaches, or perhaps combining them as Mielke and Swinehart (1976) did; and (3) sampling target populations rather than general populations (e.g., Hanneman *et al.*, 1978, sampled only the target population; Worden *et al.*, 1975, used a sampling technique calculated to obtain a high proportion of members of the target audience and then analyzed separately for target audience members).

Although the aim of most campaigns is to effect change in a population, analyses should be conducted for both the population and the proportion of the population actually exposed to the campaign. Much useful information may have been lost by failure to analyze by exposure status. Re-analysis of data may be indicated for some evaluations that had strong campaigns and evaluations (e.g., Wallack & Barrows, 1981).

Measures are rarely pretested and basic measurement properties are not assessed, which results in skewed distributions and ceiling effects. Preventive activities in this area are simple and economical, with long-range benefits. The use of statistical techniques appropriate to the design of an evaluation and the scale properties of its measures is needed. Also, the design of the evaluation should be planned with specific statistical analyses in mind. Many of the reviewed evaluations used designs for which there are no ready-made, directly appropriate statistical techniques. Measures, procedures, and analyses often were not described. In a few studies, nonsignificant findings were accorded significance and vice versa. Finally, the reporting of evaluation needs to meet standards of scientific reporting accepted by the most professional and refereed social science periodicals. None of the evaluations reviewed here met such standards, ranging from the overly concise to the verbose.

REFERENCES

Ajzen, I., & Fishbein, M. Attitude-behavior relations: A theoretical analysis and review of empirical research. *Psychological Bulletin,* 1977, *84,* 888–918.

Alcohol Abuse Prevention Project. *Comparison impact of two approaches to primary alcoholism prevention in Florida, 1978.* Unpublished manuscript, Department of Health and Rehabilitative Services, State of Florida, 1978.

Atkin, C. K. Research evidence on mass mediated health communication campaigns. In D. Nimmo (Ed.), *Communication Yearbook 3.* New Brunswick, N.J.: International Communications Association, 1979.

Blane, H. T. Education and the prevention of alcoholism. In B. Kissin & H. Begleiter (Eds.), *The biology of alcoholism: The social aspects of alcoholism* (Vol. 4). New York: Plenum Press, 1976.

Blane, H. T. Middle-aged alcoholics and young drinkers. In H. T. Blane & M. E. Chafetz (Eds.), *Youth, alcohol, and social policy.* New York: Plenum Press, 1979.

Blane, H. T. *Methods of technology transfer applicable to the prevention of alcohol abuse and alcoholism* (Final Report, Purchase Order 81MO58010901D). Pittsburgh: Author, 1981.

Blane, H. T., & Hewitt, L. E. *Mass media, public education and alcohol: A state-of-the-art review* (Final Report, Purchase Order NIA–76–12). Pittsburgh: University of Pittsburgh, 1977.

Brown, L. Perspectives on innovation diffusion. In I. M. Newman (Ed.), *Dissemination and utilization of alcohol information: A conference proceedings*. Lincoln: Nebraska Alcohol and Drug Information Clearinghouse, 1981.

Cameron, T. The impact of drinking-driving countermeasures: A review and evaluation. *Contemporary Drug Problems,* 1979, *8,* 495–565.

Chaffee, S. H. Mass media effects: New research perspectives. In D. Lerner & L. M. Nelson (Eds.), *Communication research: A half-century appraisal.* Honolulu: University Press of Hawaii, 1977.

Cialdini, R. B., Petty, R. E., & Cacioppo, J. T. Attitude and attitude change. *Annual Review of Psychology,* 1981, *32,* 357–404.

Comstock, G., Chaffee, S., Katzman, N., McCombs, M., & Roberts, D. *Television and human behavior.* New York: Columbia University Press, 1978.

Dickman, F., & Keil, T. Public television and public health: The case of alcoholism. *Journal of Studies on Alcohol,* 1977, *38*(3), 584–592.

Douglas, J. D. *The effects of mass media and education programs on problems of drinking and driving.* La Jolla, Calif.: University of California at San Diego, 1976.

Driessen, G. J., & Bryk, J. A. Alcohol countermeasures: Solid rock and shifting sands. *Journal of Safety Research,* 1973, *5,* 108–129.

Duston, E., Hornik, J., & Kraft, D. (Eds.). *Evaluation report for the University Model.* Amherst: Demonstration Alcohol Education Project, University Health Services, University of Massachusetts, 1980.

Farmer, P. J. The Edmonton study: A pilot project to demonstrate the effectiveness of a public information campaign on the subject of drinking and driving. In S. Israelstam & S. Lambert (Eds.), *Alcohol, drugs, and traffic safety.* Toronto: Addiction Research Foundation of Ontario, 1975.

Florida study looks at effect of media messages. *NIAAA Information and Feature Service,* March 3, 1981, 5.

Gans, H. J. The audience for television—and in television research. In S. B. Withey & R. P. Abeles (Eds.), *Television and social behavior: Beyond violence and children.* Hillsdale, N.J.: Lawrence Erlbaum, 1980.

Goodstadt, M. S. *An evaluation of the Ontario (1975–1976) Alcohol Education Program: TV and radio exposure and initial impact* (Substudy 847). Toronto: Addiction Research Foundation, 1977.

Goodstadt, M. S., & Kronitz, R. Public service radio: Development and evaluation of a campaign. *Journal of Drug Education,* 1977, *7*(2), 149–161.

Grunig, J. E. Time budgets, level of involvement and use of the mass media. *Journalism Quarterly,* 1979, *56,* 248–261.

Hanneman, G. J., Eisenstock, B. A., Hunt, M. F., & Weinbeck, W. L. *The medicine man message: Executive summary.* Los Angeles: Center for Communications Policy Research of the Annenberg School of Communications, University of Southern California, 1977.

Hanneman, G. J., Weinbeck, W. L., Goldman, R., Svenning, L., Nicol, J., Quattlebaum, C. T., & Scoredos, J. *The medicine man message* (Vol. 3): *Methods and results.* Los Angeles: Center for Communications Policy Research of the Annenberg School of Communications, University of Southern California, 1978.

Harris, L., & Associates, Inc. *Public awareness and the NIAAA advertising campaign and public attitudes toward drinking and alcohol abuse. Phase Four: Winter, 1974, and overall summary.* New York: Louis Harris, February, 1974.

Haskins, J. B. Effects of safety communications campaigns: A review of the research evidence. *Journal of Safety Research,* 1969, *1,* 58–66.

Hirsch, P. M. An organizational perspective on television (aided and abetted by models from economics, marketing, and the humanities). In S. B. Withey & R. P. Abeles (Eds.), *Television and social behavior: Beyond violence and children.* Hillsdale, N.J.: Lawrence Erlbaum, 1980.

Hochheimer, J. L. Reducing alcohol abuse: A critical review of educational strategies. In M. H. Moore & D. R. Gerstein (Eds.), *Alcohol and public policy: Beyond the shadow of Prohibition.* Washington, D.C.: National Academy Press, 1981.

Holmila, M., Partanen, N., Piispa, M., & Virtanen, M. *Alcohol education and alcohol policy* (Report No. 139). Helsinki: Social Research Institute of Alcohol Studies, 1980.

Holz, J. R., & Wright, C. R. Sociology of mass communications. *Annual Review of Sociology,* 1979, *5,* 193–217.

Jowett, G., & Linton, J. M. *Movies as mass communication* (Vol. 4. The Sage COMMTEXT Series). Beverly Hills: Sage, 1980.

King, T. R., & Anderson, D. S. *A comparative analysis of the baseline and final surveys of attitudes toward alcohol abuse for the Alcohol Prevention Project.* Communication Research Center, College of Communication, The Florida State University, January 1981.

Kohn, P. M., Goodstadt, M. S., Cook, G. M., Sheppard, M., & Chan, G. *Ineffectiveness of threat appeals about drinking and driving.* Unpublished manuscript, Addiction Research Foundation, 1981.

Kraft, D. P. *Summary report—September 1975 to August 1980.* Amherst: Demonstration Alcohol Education Project, University Health Services, University of Massachusetts, 1980.

McLeod, J. M., & Reeves, B. On the nature of mass media effects. In S. B. Withey & R. P. Abeles (Eds.), *Television and social behavior: Beyond violence and children.* Hillsdale, N.J.: Lawrence Erlbaum, 1980.

McQuail, D. The influence and effects of mass media. In J. Curran, M. Gurevitch, & J. Woollacott (Eds.), *Mass communication and society.* London: Edward Arnold, 1977.

Meyer, A. J., Nash, J. D., McAlister, A. L., Maccoby, N., & Farquhar, J. W. Skills training in a cardiovascular health education campaign. *Journal of Consulting and Clinical Psychology,* 1980, *48,* 129–142.

Mielke, K. W., & Swinehart, J. W. *Evaluation of the Feeling Good television series.* New York: Children's Television Workshop, 1976.

Morrison, A. J., Kline, F. G., & Miller, P. V. Aspects of adolescent information acquisition about drugs and alcohol topics. In R. E. Ostman (Ed.), *Communication research and drug education.* Beverly Hills: Sage, 1976.

NIAAA new public education campaign targets women and youth. *Alcohol, Health, and Research World,* 1980, *5*(1), 14–16.

Pierce, J., Hieatt, D., Goodstadt, M., Lonero, L., Cunliffe, A., & Pang, H. Experimental evaluation of a community-based campaign against drinking and driving. In S. Israelstam & S. Lambert (Eds.), *Alcohol, drugs, and traffic safety.* Toronto: Addiction Research Foundation of Ontario, 1975.

Plant, M. A., Pirie, F., & Kreitman, N. Evaluation of the Scottish Health Education Unit's 1976 campaign on alcoholism. *Social Psychiatry* (Berlin), 1979, *14,* 11–24.

Rappeport, M., Labaw, P., & Williams, J. *The public evaluates the NIAAA Public Education Campaign: A study for the U.S. Department of Health, Education, and Welfare* (Vol. 1). Princeton, N.J.: Opinion Research Corporation, July 1975.

Roberts, D. F., & Bachen, C. M. Mass communication effects. *Annual Review of Psychology,* 1981, *32,* 307–356.

Rogers, E. M., & Shoemaker, F. F. *Communication of innovations* (2nd ed.). New York: Free Press, 1971.

Shoemaker, F. Communication of alcohol information and behavior change. In I. M. Newman (Ed.), *Dissemination and utilization of alcohol information: A conference proceedings.* Lincoln: Nebraska Alcohol and Drug Information Clearinghouse, 1981.

Swinehart, J. W. Designing effective communications concerning alcohol. In I. M. Newman (Ed.), *Dissemination and utilization of alcohol information: A conference proceedings.* Lincoln: Nebraska Alcohol and Drug Information Clearinghouse, 1981.

Tudor, A. On alcohol and the mystique of media effects. In J. Cook & M. Lewington (Eds.), *Images of alcoholism.* London: British Film Institute, 1979.

URSA/Pacificon. *Memorandum concerning NIAAA public education campaign.* June 1, 1981. (a)

URSA/Pacificon. *Memorandum to colleagues interested in the NIAAA public education campaign.* December 15, 1981. (b)

Vingilis, E., Salutin, L., & Chan, G. *R.I.D.E. (Reduce Impaired Driving in Etobicoke): A driving-while-impaired countermeasure programme.* One-year evaluation. Toronto: Addiction Research Foundation, 1979.

Wallack, L. M. Mass media and drinking, smoking, and drug-taking. *Contemporary Drug Problems,* 1980, 9, 49–83.

Wallack, L. M., & Barrows, D. C. *Preventing alcohol problems in California: Evaluation of the three year "Winners" program.* Berkeley: Social Research Group, University of California, January 1981.

Watt, J. H. Television form, content attributes, and viewer behavior. In M. J. Voigt & G. J. Hanneman (Eds.), *Progress in communication sciences* (Vol. 1). Norwood, N.J.: Ablex, 1979.

Whitehead, P. C. Public policy and alcohol related damage: Media campaigns or social controls. *Addictive Behavior,* 1979, 4, 83–89.

Wilde, G. J. S. Evaluation of effectiveness of public education and information programmes related to alcohol, drugs, and traffic safety. In S. Israelstam & S. Lambert (Eds.), *Alcohol, drugs, and traffic safety.* Toronto: Addiction Research Foundation of Ontario, 1975.

Withey, S. B. An aerial view of television and social behavior. In S. B. Withey & R. P. Abeles (Eds.), *Television and social behavior: Beyond violence and children.* Hillsdale, N.J.: Lawrence Erlbaum, 1980. (a)

Withey, S. B. An ecological, cultural, and scripting view of television and social behavior. In S. B. Withey & R. P. Abeles (Eds.), *Television and social behavior: Beyond violence and children.* Hillsdale, N.J.: Lawrence Erlbaum, 1980. (b)

Wittman, F. D. *Current status of research demonstration projects in the primary prevention of alcohol problems.* Social Research Group, School of Public Health, University of California, Berkeley, June 1980.

Worden, J. K., Waller, J. A., & Riley, T. J. *The Vermont public education campaign in alcohol and highway safety: A final review and evaluation* (CRASH Report I–5). Montpelier, Vermont, 1975.

Wotring, C. E., Heald, G., Carpenter, C. T., & Schmeling, D. Attacking the drug norm: Effects of the 1976–77 Florida drug abuse TV campaign. *Journal of Drug Education,* 1979, 9, 255–261.

Zanna, M., Olson, J., & Fazio, R. Attitude-behavior consistency: An individual perspective. *Journal of Personality and Social Psychology,* 1980, 38(3), 431–440.

IV
Practical Applications of Prevention Strategies

Each chapter thus far has made it explicitly clear that the field of prevention is in its infancy. It seems to be the rule of the authors to temper their conclusions, pointing out the fact that previous research is plagued with methodological deficits and that therefore future research is needed. Investigators are just beginning to examine the actual utility of prevention strategies.

The present section addresses practical applications of prevention. Since each of the chapter authors has been actively involved in the particular program(s) they review, their insights are both revealing and critical to our understanding of these programs. They pinpoint the difficulty of evaluation and implementation and the necessity of gaining community support and funding. The programs reviewed are conducted in a variety of settings.

David Kraft (Chapter 9) describes his broad spectrum prevention program conducted since 1975 at the University of Massachusetts (Amherst). The program has received national attention and support. Although its utility has received only tenuous evaluative support, the comprehensiveness of its procedures and assessments warrant careful attention.

William Miller (Chapter 10) discusses the effectiveness of strategies that attempt to teach clients how to drink responsibly. In contrast to many prevention programs that present only factual information regarding the evils of drinking, the proponents of the responsible drinking model assume that the individuals who choose to drink will benefit from learning the components of nonproblem drinking.

The recent documentation of the devastating cost alcohol abuse places on business (e.g., absenteeism, loss of employees, lost production) has produced interest in prevention at the workplace. Peter Nathan (Chapter 11) reviews three worksite assistance programs that address alcohol abuse. Although evaluations of such programs have only recently begun, the use of the worksite as a prevention setting appears very promising.

Ronald Schlegel *et al.* (Chapter 12) examine the efficacy of three prevention programs for eighth-grade students. Since the use of alcohol is very prevalent among elementary school students, the evaluation of prevention efforts aimed at these youngsters is important. The researchers were not only able to identify an effective strategy but also elements of intervention that may actually detract from the overall effectiveness of prevention programs.

There have been numerous reports establishing a strong direct relationship between the level of alcohol intoxication of automobile drivers and their auto accident potential. For instance, a driver with a blood alcohol level of .10 (the legal intoxication limit in many states) is four times as likely to cause an auto crash as a driver at a blood alcohol level of .03. Felix Klajner *et al.* (Chapter 13) provide a critical review of the recent programs that attempt to reduce the incidence of drunk driving. They also discuss future policy issues and recommendations.

John Killeen (Chapter 14) examines the alcohol and drug prevention programs in the military. His thorough review reveals alcohol abuse to be a significant problem in the armed forces, which is being addressed aggressively by the Department of Defense. His analysis of the need to establish support by all personnel is especially noteworthy.

In the final chapter the editors synthesize the major chapter conclusions to pinpoint future concerns and directions in prevention.

9

A Comprehensive Prevention
Program for College Students

DAVID P. KRAFT

Drinking by young adults, especially college youth, has been an area of intense interest for many years. Ever since the classic study of college drinking by Strauss and Bacon in 1953, numerous investigators have documented the high prevalence of beverage alcohol consumption and its attendant problems at colleges and universities in the United States (Blane & Hewitt, 1977; Kraft, 1976). Recent reports have focused more directly on the adverse consequences of heavy drinking among college youth (DeLuca, 1981; DHEW, 1976; Noble, 1978) and have led to a large variety of prevention and intervention activities supported by federal, state, local community, and campus efforts (Kraft, 1977, 1979b).

In 1975, the Division of Prevention of the National Institute on Alcohol Abuse and Alcoholism (NIAAA) funded a grant to the University of Massachusetts at Amherst to develop a comprehensive alcohol abuse prevention program for institutions of higher education. The grant, titled "A University Demonstration Alcohol Education Project" (DAEP), received $585,195 in federal funds and $42,000 in university funds during its five years of operation between September 1975 and August 1980. The present chapter will review the major features of DAEP and summarize evaluation studies of its effectiveness. The University Model developed by DAEP was also adapted for use at four other campuses involved in NIAAA's Demon-

DAVID P. KRAFT • Mental Health Division, University Health Services, University of Massachusetts, Amherst, Massachusetts 01003.

stration Grant Replication Project between 1979 and 1981. Future comparisons of the results at the "parent" University of Massachusetts site and the four replication sites may lead to an effective program model that can be adapted to a variety of campuses.

The overall goal of the University Model was to create a campus environment that encouraged responsible use of beverage alcohol and discouraged irresponsible drinking behaviors. Program efforts attempted to influence all levels of the campus community. *Extensive educational approaches* utilized extensive media efforts to make all students and some staff and faculty aware of various alcohol-related problems and issues. *Intensive educational approaches* were developed to help some students (5% to 10% each year) examine their own and others' alcohol-related attitudes and behaviors, chiefly through student-led small discussion groups (workshops) and staff-led academic courses. The extensive and intensive educational efforts were augmented by persistent *community development efforts* with student leaders, staff, faculty, and administrative groups that intended to produce modifications in campus practices and regulations that influenced alcohol use and abuse.

PROGRAM RATIONALE

The University Model assumed that alcohol must be viewed not only as a food or beverage but as a drug if people are to avoid problems associated with its excessive use (Kraft, 1979b). The program was designed to prevent alcohol problems from occurring (primary prevention) by educating all levels of the community before clinical interventions became necessary. Individual, group, and institutional levels of intervention were used not only to change the drinking behaviors of individuals but also the reactions of others to drinking behaviors and the opportunities and settings for alcohol consumption.

A basic premise of the University Model is that most college students are at risk for a number of alcohol-related problems in addition to alcoholism. As a result, interventions and evaluation were focused on the distinct ("disaggregated") problems that posed the greatest risk for the population (Room, 1974). For university students, common alcohol-related problems include driving while intoxicated, accidental physical injuries, impaired academic performance, property damage, and broken social relationships.

The main techniques employed were educational in nature, based on an assumption that a series of planned, integrated educational inputs would result in positive health behavior. Values clarification techniques were designed and utilized in the small group education sessions, wherever possible, to help participants increase their knowledge and modify their attitudes, beliefs, and intentions to change behaviors. Although educational strategies based primarily on attitude or values changes have been of questionable effectiveness in earlier studies (Blane, 1976), the University Model utilized attitude change and values clarification methods focused on specific alcohol-related attitudes, beliefs, intentions to act, and behaviors, consistent with the model of behavior change proposed by Ajzen and Fishbein (Ajzen & Fishbein, 1974; Fishbein & Ajzen, 1975). The educational interventions were augmented by concomitant changes in campus norms, reflected in *regulations* and *practices* related to drinking.

The University Model adapted a comprehensive program-planning scheme titled PRECEDE, developed by Green (Green, Wang, Deeds, Fisher, Windsor, Bennett, & Rogers, 1978; Green, Kreuter, Deeds, & Partridge, 1980). The PRECEDE program-planning model was also used in certain evaluation studies reported below, to test the "path" of influence for certain behavioral variables (Duston, Kraft, & Jaworski, 1981).

Briefly, the PRECEDE model (Figure 1) postulates that a given health or social problem, such as a drunken driving accident, is preceded by one or more behavioral problems, such as drinking heavily at an off-campus party and then driving home. Each behavioral problem is, in turn, influenced by a combination of predisposing, enabling, and reinforcing factors. Predisposing factors include knowledge, attitudes, beliefs, and values that influence people's behaviors, such as the belief that a person can drive home safely despite excess alcohol consumption. Enabling factors include the availability and accessibility of services or skills that influence whether or not the person could prevent the problem behavior, such as the availability of public transportation or the assertiveness to ask someone else to take oneself home. Reinforcing factors include the attitudes or climate of support of service providers, families, community groups, and so forth, which influence the behavior of the individual, as, for example, peer group norms about driving after drinking.

Alcohol education interventions were targeted to change many of the predisposing, enabling, or reinforcing factors in a desired direction. For example, media and workshop efforts alerted both individuals and groups to the risks from driving while intoxicated in an attempt to change predisposing factors in persons at risk for driving after excess consumption and to change reinforcing factors among friends of the intoxicated person to take him or her home with them. Community development efforts encourage the continuation of public transportation schedules at late hours, to change an enabling factor in the desired direction.

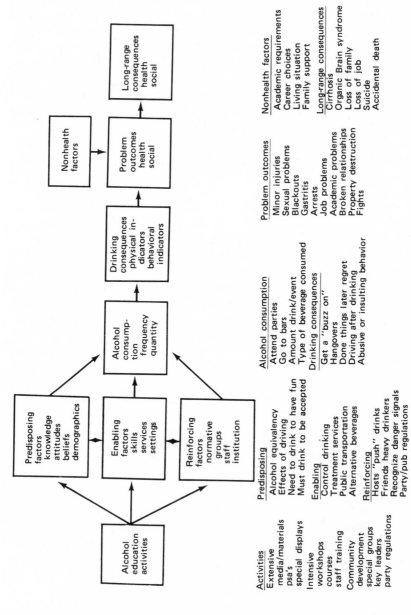

Figure 1. University model of drinking behavior, adapted from PRECEDE model developed by Green *et al.*, 1980, with representative samples of items.

PROGRAM DESCRIPTION

SETTING

The University of Massachusetts at Amherst is located in a semirural setting in western Massachusetts and enrolls a total of about 22,000 full-time undergraduate and graduate students and 3,000 additional part-time students. Over 11,500 students live in university dormitories, 900 in fraternity or sorority houses, and over 12,000 in various apartment complexes. One of the supporting services on campus is a large and active University Health Services (UHS), which employs over 250 staff including 15 full-time physicians, 12 full-time nurse practitioners, 13 full-time mental health professionals, and 9 full-time health educators. The UHS clinical staff provides over 70,000 medical and 9,000 mental health outpatient visits per year. Persons with alcohol problems are usually treated by staff of UHS and some are referred to area Alcoholics Anonymous groups.

Substance abuse services have existed in a major way since 1969, when a peer-counseling and education service called Room-to-Move (RTM) was established to help deal with problems of illicit drug abuse, especially "bad trips" and overdoses. By 1973, both Room-to-Move and the Community Health Education Division of the UHS began to shift focus to increased problems related to alcohol abuse. A campus-wide Alcohol Task Force was convened in 1974 and recommended that prevention-oriented educational efforts be developed to complement the adequate treatment resources available for students with alcohol problems. Three members of the task force subsequently developed and submitted a grant to the National Institute on Alcohol Abuse and Alcoholism (NIAAA) titled "A University Demonstration Alcohol Education Project" (DAEP). The grant was approved and funded beginning in September 1975.

DAEP federal funding involved between $90,000 to $139,000 per year for each of five years. DAEP staffing included one part-time physician and three full-time professional health education staff; between 6 to 8 half-time peer educators; one full-time evaluation assistant; two evaluation consultants; three half-time students to help with evaluation tasks; and a full-time secretary. In addition, funds were available for the purchase or production of various media and materials and for rental of computer facilities to assist evaluation efforts.

PROGRAM METHODS

The University Model developed by DAEP combined extensive educational approaches, intensive educational approaches, and community development efforts to accomplish its overall goal. Most community development efforts focused on the alcohol-related needs of special populations of students and led to the development of successful interventions, usually educational workshops, to address those needs. Some community development efforts also involved key decision makers and leaders. DAEP staff met regularly with the dean of students, director of public safety (the campus police force), director of the Student Development and Counseling Center (in charge of residence halls and vocational/educational counseling), heads of the three residential (dormitory) areas, the manager of the main campus pub (the Bluewall), the director of University Health Services, and key student leaders. In each case, the administrators and student leaders were kept informed of DAEP activities and were asked to assist in specific ways that involved their areas of responsibility.

Extensive approaches were used to raise awareness about alcohol use and abuse (Kelly, 1978). Methods included posters, pamphlets, newspaper articles, newspaper advertisements, radio announcements, radio shows, and special displays. One extensive approach involved the wide distribution of educational posters. For example, one poster had "Don't be afraid to ask. . ." in large letters, followed in small letters by, ". . . for soda, for juice, for tea, for coffee." Another asked, "What's in a drink?" followed by six recipes, three with an alcohol base and three without. A third poster described "Anstie's law of safe drinking."

A second extensive approach involved special displays in prominent places on campus, such as a breathalyzer display outside the campus pub on different evenings. This display included attractive posters and signs on the wall explaining the relationship between the blood-alcohol concentration (BAC), the amount of alcohol consumed by a given person, and the legally safe limit for driving.

A third extensive effort used the campus radio station. Student-produced public service announcements were played frequently between spring 1977 and spring 1980 to attract the attention of students. A disc jockey radio show, called the Salsa–Soul Medicine Show, was also aired from one to three hours per week from the fall of 1976 to the fall of 1977. Interspersed between popular, soul, and salsa (i.e., Latino) music were quizzes, poems, skits, and so forth, with messages about alcohol-related topics, such as drinking and driving, planning a safe party, and drinking myths.

Intensive approaches were designed not only to provide basic information about alcohol but also to help individuals and groups modify their attitudes and behaviors involving alcohol. The main intensive approach with students was the small discussion group or "workshop," using 1 of 13 designs. The most frequently used workshop design was a general "overview about alcohol" where major facts about alcohol, its use, and some problems related to drinking were covered. Other workshops focused on women and alcohol, "Sex with Ethyl," and alcohol and values. The student peer alcohol educators generally presented these workshops and combined values clarification techniques with alcohol-specific information.

Another intensive approach involved multiple-session courses for academic credit. For example, one three-credit seminar held in a residential area that housed 5,500 students was run by a DAEP professional staff member for about 20 participants for 3 successive fall semesters. During the fall semesters, students were presented factual information about alcohol and various educational techniques, helped distribute posters and pamphlets, and helped plan a workshop led by one of the peer alcohol educators. During the following spring semesters, some of the fall semester students prepared and led their own one-credit colloquia for 5 to 15 other students, with assistance from project staff.

The final intensive approach involved in-service training programs for various university staff. Most of these opportunities involved a combined lecture and small or large group discussion tailored to the needs of the specific group. In-service training was provided for heads of residence; residence assistants; health service physicians, nurses, and mental health professionals; campus police; and campus pub personnel.

PROGRAM EFFORT

During the five years of DAEP, a large number of students, staff, and faculty were contacted through various efforts. Community development activities resulted in regular contacts with students who lived in residence halls, who were Blacks or Latinos, or who belonged to women's groups. Less frequent contacts were made with fraternity and sorority members, Asian students, students who are parents, gay and lesbian students, students who lived off-campus, children of alcoholic parents, and veterans.

Periodic meetings between 1975 and 1977 with the dean of students, director of public safety, and the directors of the three residential areas (i.e., dormitories) led to the appointment of an Alcoholic Beverages Policy Task Force in 1977–78, which completely revised the policy in a manner that encouraged safe party practices. Meetings with the manager of the on-campus pub (the "Bluewall") resulted in staff training for pub personnel and the advertisement and provision of nonalcoholic food and beverages at the pub. Regular meetings with the director of public safety and division heads of the University Health Services led to periodic in-service training sessions with the campus police and with medical, nursing, and mental health staff.

Occasional contacts with the editorial staff of the campus newspaper (the *Collegian*) helped encourage the paper to examine its advertising policies, especially involving alcoholic beverage ads, and to eliminate ads that promote poor nutritional or extremely sexist views.

Community development efforts both led to and resulted from extensive and intensive educational activities. For example, as various community groups and individuals learned about responsible drinking behaviors, pressure increased on campus to revise the largely ineffective alcoholic beverages policy mentioned above, assisting a major community development activity. In return, the revised beverage policy required that party organizers attend educational sessions about planning and conducting safe events, which increased educational opportunities.

Media and materials were utilized extensively to raise awareness, increase knowledge, and reinforce other project activities. As a result

- An average of 4,300 posters and 2,700 pamphlets developed by DAEP were distributed on campus each year.
- The campus newspaper published an average of 7 educational "advertisements" and 4 articles about alcohol topics each year.
- An average of 3 articles written by DAEP staff were published in special newsletters each year.
- During two years, 700 automobile bumper stickers and 15,000 bookmarks were distributed with special alcohol-specific messages.
- An average of 3 radio interviews were conducted and 6 radio PSAs were produced and used by the campus radio station (WMUA) each year.
- During the first 2½ years of the project, a total of 23 hour-long segments on alcohol-related topics were produced and aired over the campus radio station (WMUA) during prime time.
- About 5 display tables were conducted in the campus center each year, for an average of 200 students per display.

Intensive approaches were designed not only to provide basic information and knowledge but also to help individuals and groups examine and modify alcohol-related attitudes, beliefs, and behaviors. Intensive approaches resulted in the following efforts:

- An estimated 14% of students each year were exposed to one or more intensive approaches. Virtually all students participating in intensive approaches were exposed to mass media and materials.
- Single-session workshops were conducted an average of 95 times each year, involving 1,616 students for over 2,800 hours of contact annually.

- Multiple-session academic courses were conducted an average of 6 times each year, involving 45 students and over 2,500 contact hours annually.
- Guest lectures in existing academic courses were given an average of 15 times each year, reaching 1,125 students for over 1,250 contact hours.
- Student-run colloquia occurred an average of 4 times each year, reaching 59 students for almost 950 contact hours.
- Staff training was conducted an average of 11 times each year, involving 377 participants for over 550 contact hours.

EVALUATION OF PROGRAM

The evaluation design included a variety of strategies sensitive to changes produced by DAEP activities. Evaluation was not limited to the measurement of outcome variables but included intervening variables predicted by the PRECEDE model described in Section 1.

Program effects were studied in three separate areas: program theory, community-wide indicators, and special investigations of alcohol education efforts. The major findings are summarized based on the *Evaluation Report for the University Model* (Duston, Kraft, & Hornik, 1980).

PROGRAM THEORY

Although the PRECEDE model was used to guide the overall planning from the beginning of DAEP, it was not rigorously adapted as an evaluation scheme until the fourth year of the project. As a result, most survey instruments did not adequately assess all of the intervening variables predicted by the model as thoroughly as initially envisioned.

Method of Evaluation

The PRECEDE model was evaluated to determine those specific variables most predictive of problem drinking behaviors. Data were used from a 56-item survey (the Consumer Survey) mailed each fall to a stratified random sample of between 1,200 and 1,450 students, with one or two follow-up mailings. Responses were obtained from an average of 61% of the sample each year (range 57% to 70%). Data analyses controlled for any significant differences found between the respondents and the university population.

Demographic comparisons between respondents and nonrespondents were not statistically significant. In general, no systematic biases seemed evident in the Consumer Survey samples (Table 1). Because extensive revisions were made on many survey items between Years 1 and 2, most analyses rely on data collected in Years 2–5.

Survey items were used to construct a number of indices under the major headings proposed by the model in order to analyze the validity of the PRECEDE model. Exposure to DAEP activities was assessed by items that recorded the number of respondents who recognized various DAEP extensive educational efforts and/or participated in DAEP intensive efforts. Predisposing factors were measured by two separate indices. An "attitudes toward drinking" index was constructed by averaging the responses to six questions ranging from attitudes toward getting drunk to beliefs that drinking will increase confidence with "the opposite sex." A "responsibility for self and others" index utilized responses to two items concerning driving after drinking. In addition, key demographic variables were considered important predisposing factors. Enabling factors were assessed by responses to an open-ended question assessing "knowledge of helping agencies" on campus for problem drinkers. Reinforcing factors were measured by responses to three items: with whom a respondent usually drinks (i.e., family, friends, and/or acquaintances); the number of close friends suspected of having a drinking problem; and the number of students whom one or more friends urged to seek help for a drinking problem.

Alcohol use behaviors were assessed by three sets of variables. First, the frequency of attendance at drinking establishments, including the frequency of party attendance and the frequency of bar attendance, was measured. Second, the frequency of entry into any drinking contexts per month by respondents was assessed. Third, the average amount of alcohol consumed per occasion by respondents was measured.

Four separate categories of undesirable results of drinking were used. Physical consequences were measured by the number of times a student reported getting "a buzz on" (i.e., high and/or drunk) in the past year. Negative behaviors were assessed by responses to four questions assessing whether respondents in the past year had done things they later regretted: driven a car after drinking excessively, been in a car with friends after all had been drinking, and/or become abusive or insulting after drinking. Problem outcomes included six items: academic problems, job-related problems, trouble with the police, property destruction, minor physical injuries, and adverse sexual performance. The final category assessed whether or not a respondent ever worried about the long-range consequences of his or her drinking.

The combination of items and indices were used to test the validity of

Table 1.

Selected Characteristics of Random Samples of Students Completing Annual Consumer Survey

| | Year 1 | Year 2 | Year 3 | Year 4 | Year 5 | |
| | Fall 1975 | Fall 1976 | Fall 1977 | Fall 1978 | Fall 1979 | Total |
Characteristics	(N = 794)	(N = 695)	(N = 837)	(N = 738)	(N = 926)	(N = 3990)
Sex						
Male	55	55	50	51	48	52
Female	45	45	50	49	52	48
Age						
17–18	13	14	17	22	19	17
19–21	35	44	45	45	48	43
22–24	22	20	15	16	15	18
25 plus	30	22	23	17	18	22
Marital status						
Never married	74	80	85	87	87	83
Married	22	16	11	9	10	13
Divorced, separated, widowed	4	4	4	4	3	4
Class Level						
Freshperson	13	15	20	25	20	18
Sophomore	13	16	17	18	21	17
Junior	16	21	18	17	19	18
Senior	19	25	21	19	19	21
Graduate	34	17	18	17	15	20
Other	5	6	6	4	6	6
Residence						
Same sex dorm	11	10	12	12	11	12
Coed dorm	25	31	42	43	39	36
Greek house	2	3	1	2	2	2
Off-campus with relatives	8	9	8	7	5	7
Off-campus, other	54	47	37	36	43	43

Proportion of respondents

the PRECEDE model, as modified by DAEP (Figure 1). Two major questions were asked: Is the causal order of the variables accurate for predicting drinking behaviors? How well does the model account for drinking and its associated behaviors? The main procedure used was step-wise regression in order to determine which independent variables were the strongest predictors of important dependent variables. Analyses were computed separately for Consumer Survey data from years 2–5. In addition, associations between certain key variables were tested using analyses of variance.

Results of Evaluation

Exposure to DAEP activities was analyzed in relation to other key alcohol-related variables (Table 2). Results showed that in all four years, significantly more younger students, students who were single and/or without children, and students living on campus reported greater exposure to DAEP media efforts ($p < 0.01$); no significant differences based on gender or grade point average (GPA) were found. Workshops were attended primarily by younger students and on-campus students, but none of the variables consistently reached a significant level.

Correlations between media exposure or workshop participation and key alcohol variables revealed few significant results. One exception was that persons exposed to media or to workshops had a significantly greater knowledge of helping agencies ($p < 0.01$) than those who did not report exposure. Correlations of media exposure and drinking behaviors also showed a tendency for those who drink more and who experience negative outcomes to have reported greater exposure to DAEP media efforts.

Drinking behaviors were analyzed according to the quantity (average amount) consumed per occasion and the frequency of entry into drinking occasions. In general, predisposing factors were the strongest predictors of drinking behaviors, compared to enabling and reinforcing ones, even though predisposing factors only accounted for between 15% and 25% of the variance. The "attitude toward drinking" and "attitude toward responsibility" indices were the strongest predictors of drinking behavior, with sex, age, and location of residence moderately strong factors. Due to the limited number of items on the Consumer Survey measuring enabling and reinforcing factors, extreme caution must be used in interpreting these results. In general, younger, single, male students living on campus are heavier drinkers than older students, students living with spouse and/or children and students living off campus. One exception is that older students reported drinking more frequently than younger students but drank less per occasion.

Drinking consequences involved two classes of variables: physical con-

Table 2.
Exposure to DAEP and Predisposing, Enabling, and Reinforcing Factors Reported by Students on Annual Consumer Survey

Variable	Proportion of respondents					
	Year 1 Fall 1975 (N = 794)	Year 2 Fall 1976 (N = 695)	Year 3 Fall 1977 (N = 837)	Year 4 Fall 1978 (N = 738)	Year 5 Fall 1979 (N = 926)	Total (N = 3990)
Exposure to DAEP						
Media; one or more, past year	NA	69	73	70	67	69
Workshop, past year	NA	4	6	5	4	5
Predisposing factors						
Index of drinking attitudes						
Strongly agree/agree	NA	17	22	20	22	21
Neutral	NA	56	58	59	59	58
Strongly disagree/disagree	NA	27	20	21	19	21
Index of responsibility						
Strongly agree/agree	NA	87	81	81	80	82
Neutral	NA	12	15	16	16	15
Strongly disagree/disagree	NA	1	4	3	4	3
Enabling factors						
Knowledge of helping agencies; one or more	33	NA	42	31	32	34
Reinforcing factors						
Usually drink with						
Alone	1	NA	1	1	1	1
Family	8	NA	6	6	6	7
Friends	60	NA	72	73	71	69
Acquaintances	18	NA	12	12	12	13
Whomever	4	NA	3	2	4	3
Do not drink	9	NA	6	6	6	7
Close friends with drinking problems; one or more	42	NA	35	29	31	34
Anyone urged you to get help in past year; one or more	NA	2	2	3	2	3

Note: "NA" = Information "Not Asked" in the year in question.

sequences and negative behaviors. Physical consequences (number of times "get a buzz on" in the past year) were strongly correlated with quantity per occasion and frequency of drinking occasions, which together explained roughly 50% of the variance. Negative behaviors were most strongly predicted by the quantity consumed per occasion and less strongly by the frequency of drinking. Quantity and frequency together explained between 19% and 37% of the variance, with the predisposing, enabling, and reinforcing factors accounting for very little of the residual variation (combined R^2 between 0.04 and 0.06).

Problem outcomes were assessed in relation to the other variables. In each year either "negative behaviors" or "physical consequences" was the strongest predictor with the other factor the second strongest variable. Combined, the two items explained between 35% and 42% of the variance. Predisposing factors and drinking behavior accounted for very little of the residual variation (combined R^2 of 0.03 to 0.04).

Anxiety about long-range consequences of drinking was assessed in relation to the preceding variables. In general, problem outcomes were the strongest consistent predictors of long-range consequences, although negative behaviors and physical consequences were also significant contributors. However, even combining all three variables only explained from 17% to 22% of the variance. The remaining variables accounted for 2% to 10% of the residual variation.

The results of these analyses, in general, confirm the causal ordering implied by the PRECEDE model of drinking behaviors. As might be expected, associations between drinking behavior, physical consequences, negative behaviors, and problem outcomes were most strongly confirmed. Links between predisposing, enabling, and reinforcing factors and drinking behavior were relatively weak, partly as a result of the limited number of survey items that measured enabling and reinforcing factors.

UNIVERSITY COMMUNITY INDICATORS

A number of studies attempted to measure changes in alcohol-related behaviors at an aggregate level. Consumer Survey data were examined for any trends that could be found. Structured interviews of key dormitory personnel were conducted to determine any systematic changes in alcohol-related behaviors. A combination of so-called archival data and special studies was used to determine the extent of alcohol-related health and social problems on campus. Finally, records of officially sanctioned alcohol use on campus were examined for trends.

Self-Reported Changes: Trends on Consumer Survey

The Consumer Survey data were examined for trends in drinking-related behaviors. The responses of students to key items during each year of the survey are displayed in Tables 1, 2, 3, and 4. In addition, time trends were examined for significance by using one-way analyses of covariance controlling for variations in sample characteristics from year to year.

Over the years, the sample of Consumer Survey respondents shifted from a higher proportion of males, older students, married students, and off-campus students than is present in the university to a sample with a higher proportion of females, younger students, single, and on-campus students than in previous years and in the university (Table 1). Although the shifts in age, on- or off-campus residence, and presence or absence of spouse and/or children were significant ($p < 0.001$), the magnitudes of the differences were small. These sample differences must be kept in mind in order to lead to accurate interpretations of the remaining data.

Results showed that an average of 69% of students recalled seeing one or more media presentation in Years 2–5 (Table 2) and that 5% reported participating in workshops or colloquia sponsored by DAEP. Responses to the various predisposing, enabling, and reinforcing factors displayed in Table 2 showed few trends that could not be attributed to variations in the sample of respondents.

Alcohol use behaviors and the negative consequences of drinking increased in most instances over the five years of the project, contrary to what was anticipated by project staff. Alcoholic beverage consumption increased each year in both quantity consumed per occasion and the frequency of drinking occasions (Table 3). The proportion of students regularly getting a "buzz on" and experiencing negative behaviors also increased (Table 3). Similarly, the number of students reporting problem outcomes of drinking increased during the five years of the project (Table 4), especially problems related to work and to minor injuries.

The drinking behavior variables were examined for significant trends (Table 5). In general, increases between 1976 and 1979 in average drinks per event, entry into drinking contexts, number of negative behaviors, and number of problem outcomes were statistically significant ($p < 0.001$) with the increase in negative physical consequences less significant ($p < 0.038$). Alcohol project activities seemed to have had little effect on such variables.

Examination of the various drinking variables revealed that sex, age, and GPA were stronger predictors of higher drinking and various problems related to drinking (physical consequences, negative behaviors, and problem outcomes) than was the year of the survey: younger, male students with

Table 3.

Drinking Behaviors and Immediate Consequences Reported by Students on Annual Consumer Survey

Variable	Proportion of respondents					
	Year 1 Fall 1975 (N = 794)	Year 2 Fall 1976 (N = 695)	Year 3 Fall 1977 (N = 837)	Year 4 Fall 1978 (N = 738)	Year 5 Fall 1979 (N = 926)	Total (N = 3990)
Alcohol-use behavior						
Average drinks per week	NA	6.2	6.4	6.6	7.0	6.6
Frequency of entering drinking events per week						
None/less than once	NA	28	22	23	21	23
Once per week	NA	30	27	24	28	27
Two–three times per week	NA	28	32	37	31	32
Four or more times	NA	14	19	16	20	18
Quantity consumed per event						
None	8	9	5	5	5	6
One drink	23	10	14	15	15	16
Two–three drinks	51	60	65	64	61	60
Four or more drinks	18	21	16	16	19	18
Drinking consequences						
Physical number of times got "a buzz on" in past year						
Do not drink/never	NA	22	17	16	14	17
Less than once a month	NA	43	43	39	41	42
More than once a month	NA	35	40	45	45	41
Negative behaviors, past year						
Number (1) None	NA	38	24	25	21	26
(2) One	NA	30	27	26	25	27
(3) Two or more	NA	32	49	49	54	47
Item (1) Done things later regretted	NA	44	50	49	54	50
(2) Driven car after too much to drink	12	24	33	32	42	29
(3) Been in car after all had been drinking	NA	42	60	62	66	58
(4) Became abusive or insulting after drinking	NA	15	17	16	16	16

Note: "NA" = Information "Not Asked" in the year in question.

Table 4.

Problem Outcomes and Worries about Long-range Consequences of Drinking Reported by Students on Annual Consumer Survey

Variable	Proportion of respondents					
	Year 1 Fall 1975 (N = 794)	Year 2 Fall 1976 (N = 695)	Year 3 Fall 1977 (N = 837)	Year 4 Fall 1978 (N = 738)	Year 5 Fall 1979 (N = 926)	Total (N = 3990)
Problem outcomes of drinking						
Number in past year						
Nondrinker/none	NA	NA	65	62	56	60
One	NA	NA	16	18	19	18
Two	NA	NA	9	10	13	11
Three or more	NA	NA	10	10	12	11
Item: Trouble in past year with						
Academic work	NA	NA	21	23	24	23
Job	NA	NA	11	12	18	14
Police	3	5	3	4	6	4
Destroyed property	NA	8	7	8	7	7
Minor injury	NA	13	15	19	20	17
Negative sexual performance	NA	23	14	16	16	17
Someone else ended relationship	NA	1	1	1	1	1
Worried about long-range consequences of drinking in past year						
Never	NA	NA	71	72	72	72
Seldom	NA	NA	15	15	17	15
Ocasionally/frequently	NA	NA	14	13	11	13

Note: "NA" = Information "not asked" in the year in question.

Table 5.

Analyses of Covariance of Key Alcohol-related Variables for Consumer Survey Subjects
by Year Controlling for Demographic Sampling Differences

Key alcohol variable[a]	Adjusted means				F test	df	Significance
	1976	1977	1978	1979			
Average drinks per event[b]	3.9	4.2	4.5	4.8	9.24	3, 2945	$p < .001$
Entry into a drinking context (times per week)[c]	1.69	2.10	1.95	2.15	8.54	3, 3120	$p < .001$
Number of negative behaviors[d]	1.10	1.57	1.58	1.75	38.37	3, 3116	$p < .001$
Number of negative physical consequences[e]	.55	.57	.66	.69	2.81	3, 3120	$p < .038$
Number of problem outcomes[f]	—	.68	.75	.90	7.62	3, 2433	$p < .001$

[a]Refer to text for detailed definitions of each key variable.
[b]Other significant F-ratios were: sex, $F = 104.92$; residence, $F = 21.73$; age, $F = 35.52$; and GPA, $F = 52.32$.
[c]Other significant F-ratios were: sex, $F = 86.76$; and age, $F = 16.20$.
[d]Other significant F-ratios were: sex, $F = 88.87$; family status, $F = 24.82$; age, $F = 18.54$; and GPA, $F = 30.24$.
[e]Other significant F = ratios were: sex, $F = 53.27$; age, $F = 25.41$; and GPA, $F = 34.03$.
[f]Other significant F-ratios were: sex, $F = 51.25$; age, $F = 14.40$; and GPA, $F = 31.10$.

lower grade point averages were more likely to drink heavier amounts and experience adverse problems than older, female, and higher GPA students. The only exception was the frequency-of-drinking variable, where older students actually reported drinking more frequently than younger students.

Residence Hall Staff Interviews: Trends of Observed Behaviors

The residential hall system at the University of Massachusetts houses over 11,500 students in 52 dormitory units. Much student drinking takes place in or around the dormitories and at formal and informal parties sponsored by dormitory residents. Each year DAEP staff interviewed a representative sample of heads of residence (HRs) to assess the perceived usefulness and effectiveness of alcohol education efforts with dormitory residents.

At the end of the spring semester, a random sample of between 12 and 20 "experimental" dormitories that had sponsored one or more DAEP workshops that year were chosen, along with between 6 and 14 "control" dormitories. Face-to-face interviews with the HRs were conducted by project staff for an average of 40 minutes per interview, using a detailed interview schedule.

Program effects were assessed by a series of questions focused on three areas: knowledge of referral agencies, changes in students' behavior regarding alcohol, and changes in party behaviors. Responses of HRs in experimental dorms were compared to control dorms.

No differences were found each year between experimental and control HRs regarding their knowledge of campus referral resources. Over the five years, however, both experimental and control dorm HRs increased their knowledge of referral agencies. When questioned about changes in student behaviors, a gradual increase in discussions of alcohol-related issues was noted in experimental dorms compared to control dorms, with a significant difference in 1980. Confrontations of problem drinkers by students occurred at about the same level for both groups, except in 1980 when experimental dorms reportedly confronted alcohol abusers significantly more often than control dorms. When responses by experimental and control HRs are combined, a trend toward increased confrontations over the years approached significance, $\chi^2(4) = 6.12$, $p = 0.2$.

Party behaviors were assessed by a series of three questions. Comparisons between experimental and control dorms each year from 1976 to 1980 showed no significant differences in the search for alternative forms of entertainment, the inclusion of nonalcoholic beverages at parties, or the presence of food at parties. However, when experimental and control dorm responses each year were combined to determine any trends, the cross-years analysis showed a highly significant increase in the search for alternative activities, $\chi^2(4) = 38.8$, $p < 0.0005$, with most change occurring between the 1977 and 1978 surveys when a new campus alcoholic beverage policy went into effect. A highly significant increase in the offering of food at parties also occurred over the five years, $\chi^2(4) = 23.607$, $p < 0.005$. Although there was an increase in the presence of nonalcoholic beverages between 1976 and 1980, the trend was not statistically significant.

Overall, dormitories that sponsored more workshops each year and sponsored workshops in successive years reported greater changes on the behavioral indicators enumerated above than those who sponsored fewer regular workshops. It appeared that the cumulative effect of continued educational interventions rather than one-time efforts was more effective in producing desired changes. No tests of significance were attempted because of the small numbers of dormitories with cumulative contacts.

Health Service Alcohol-Related Medical and Mental Health Contacts

Data were collected from both medical and mental health outpatient clinics of the UHS to determine the prevalence of alcohol-related health problems among students. Due to the rural nature of the Amherst campus and the comprehensive prepaid services of its University Health Services, most students receive all their health care at the UHS whenever they reside in the area, making it unnecessary to collect data from other providers.

Medical Clinic Contacts. For each medical clinic visit at the UHS, a separate encounter form is filled out by the patient and completed by the nurse and/or physician, including the problem for which the patient was seen. One of the 60 or 70 "most common problems" listed on the form is "Alcohol Problem." However, an analysis of the data recorded by clinicians on the encounter form between 1975 and 1977 revealed that only 0.10% of outpatient contacts for a two-year period were reportedly alcohol-related (169 out of 174,684 contacts).

To correct for such an apparent underreporting of alcohol-related contacts, a special week-long survey was conducted each semester beginning in the fall of 1976. In fall 1976 and spring 1977, clinicians were asked to complete an extra form for every outpatient visit during the sample weeks (Kraft, 1979a). Beginning in fall 1977, the actual medical clinic encounter form was modified with a special question to be completed for *every* visit during the survey week, indicating whether or not the problem for which the patient was seen was related to his or her own or someone else's drinking problem. Due to excellent cooperation from the clinical staff and careful review by medical records staff, the special alcohol-related question was completed for 88.6% of an average 2,053 contacts per survey week between fall 1976 and spring 1980.

Analyses of data from the week-long surveys for consecutive semesters between fall 1976 and spring 1980 revealed that 1.4% of the contacts were alcohol-related (range 0.7 to 2.2%). Most alcohol-related contacts occurred afterhours (3.6% of contacts occurring between 5:00 P.M. and 8:00 A.M., Monday through Thursday), or on weekends (8.2% of contacts occurring between 5:00 P.M. Friday and 8:00 A.M. Monday). Most contacts were related to the patient's own drinking (71%), with fewer related to someone else's drinking (12%), or to both the patient's own and another's drinking (17%). Most contacts (60%) involved minor injuries. Diagnostic categories with a high proportion of alcohol-related contacts included 9.3% of all forms of injuries, including lacerations (15%), head injuries (12%), abrasions/bruises (8%) and fractures (7%). Other categories that included alcohol-related problems were: adverse effect of medication (7%), gastrointestinal difficulties (6%), mental health problems (5%), and obesity (5%).

When trends were examined for the six semesters between fall 1977 and spring 1980, no significant differences between fall and spring semesters were discovered. However, the number of alcohol-related contacts in 1979–80 (84) was significantly higher than in 1977–78 (40) and 1978–79

Table 6.
Community-Wide Alcohol-Related Indicators, Extrapolated for a Campus of 100,000 Students[a]

	July–December 1975	January–June 1976	July–December 1976	January–June 1977	July–December 1977	January–June 1978	July–December 1978	January–June 1979	July–December 1979	January–June 1980
Incidents per 100,000 enrolled students on selected community variables										
Medical visits[b]										
Routine reports	54	197	207	238	—	—	—	—	—	—
Estimated from special surveys of MDs and nurses	—	—	1634	2946	1879	1019	1612	966	3083	3123
Mental health visits										
Estimated from special surveys of therapists	—	—	2531	2632	1969	1691	2343	2338	2556	2314
Public safety citations										
Driving under influence	139	121	75	77	100	197	279	156	54	90
Protective custody	267	355	431	140	326	498	641	519	587	464
Disturbing the peace	31	40	79	102	33	131	146	221	221	34
Malicious destruction and vandalism	637	614	568	515	514	507	720	814	600	464
Community-wide indirect indicators per 100,000 student enrollment										
Dormitory damages										
Total costs	$301,792	$592,290	$422,699	$514,450	$389,892	$633,553	$580,593	$496,127	$860,608	$369,745
Average cost per resident	$6.71		$8.83	$8.83	$8.82		$12.92		$19.24	
Bluewall alcoholic beverage sales	$575,371		$578,467		$593,575		$623,961		$216,775	
Special one-day licenses for alcoholic beverage sales	178	166	95	132	117	140	37	30	4	4

[a] To control for variations in headcount enrollment each year (average 23,950), rates were calculated on a population base of 100,000.
[b] Medical and mental health visits were based on week-long surveys each semester, then extrapolated to total clinic visits per 100,000 population.

(38), $\chi^2(2) = 29.05$, $p < 0.001$. Finally, the number of alcohol-related contacts occurring afterhours and on weekends was significantly higher than those occurring on weekdays, $\chi^2(2) = 311$, $p < 0.001$. Survey results were used to estimate the number of alcohol-related medical outpatient visits per year for a campus of 100,000 students (Table 6).

Mental Health Clinic Contacts. In order to determine the frequency and type of alcohol-related problems among students counseled at the Mental Health Clinic (MHC), a special week-long survey was conducted each semester beginning in fall 1976. Mental health clinicians were asked to complete a separate form for every MHC visit during one sample week each semester (the same survey week as the medical clinic survey described above). The special forms recorded identifying data for patient and therapist, diagnostic information, and impressions about whether or not the visit was alcohol-related. Due to excellent cooperation from the MHC clinical and support staff, forms were completed for virtually all of the average 229 individual, couple, or family contacts recorded for each of the 8 survey weeks. (Group therapy visits were excluded from the survey.)

Survey results showed that 13.9% of MHC visits during the sample weeks were alcohol-related, including 16.1% of visits by males and 12.6% by females. Contacts related to the patient's own drinking accounted for 7.2% of all visits, related to someone else's drinking for 5.5%, and related both to the patient's own and someone else's drinking 1.2% of visits. Significantly more women than men were likely to seek help for problems related to someone else's alcohol use, $\chi^2(1) = 39.02$, $p < 0.001$. No significant trends were evident in the number of alcohol-related contacts that occurred each semester. Survey results were used to estimate the number of MHC visits for a campus of 100,000 (Table 6).

MHC patients with alcohol-related problems were younger than other MHC patients and frequently were either undergraduates or special students. Patients with alcohol-related problems formed a high proportion of patients with mood disorders (17.2%), family difficulties (19.5%), self-destructive behaviors (16.7%), low self-esteem (14.3%), general isolation (14%), academic problems (12.9%), romantic relationship problems (12.9%), and identity problems (12.9%). Examination of representative charts also revealed that patients with a history of parental alcoholism frequently presented difficulties in therapeutic management, especially trouble establishing a working relationship with the therapist.

Campus Police Alcohol-Related Arrests

Statistics have been collected routinely from the Department of Public Safety (i.e., the campus police department) concerning the occurrence of various incidents and crimes associated with alcohol use. Pilot studies determined that four categories had high alcohol-related associations: driving under the influence (virtually 100% alcohol-related); protective custody (between 80% and 90% alcohol-related); malicious destruction and vandalism (between 60% and 70% alcohol-related); and disturbing the peace (about two-thirds alcohol-related, although quite variable). Data for these four arrest categories were analyzed to determine any trends for the university campus during the five years of DAEP.

The four main alcohol-related arrest categories did not show significant trends over the time of DAEP (Table 6). Changes in the data were neither systematic nor attributable to program efforts. Although an average of 62 driving while intoxicated (DWI) arrests, 189 protective custody (PC) arrests, 292 malicious destruction and vandalism (MD/V) arrests, and 47 disturbing the peace (DP) arrests occurred each year, the actual number of arrests in each category varied widely over the five years.

When police records are compared to student self-reports, it is clear that most alcohol-related high risk behavior is not detected. For example, MD/V arrests averaged 1.2% of the student body each year, compared to an average of 7% of students who reported destroying property after drinking in the past 12 months (Table 4). Review of the arrest data with personnel from the campus police also revealed that changes in the data seem more reflective of shifts in priorities of the campus police rather than true shifts in the occurrence of problem behaviors. The usefulness of such data to measure program effects on a campus the size of the University of Massachusetts seems minimal.

Dormitory Damage Statistics

A strong association between alcohol abuse and property damage in the dormitories has repeatedly been reported by staff and students. To supplement campus police arrests for malicious destruction and vandalism, separate data were compiled by dormitory personnel to determine damages attributable to alcohol use.

Dormitory damage costs for the university are available on a yearly basis and reflect the actual costs of completed repairs rather than estimates of costs at the time of the damage (Table 6). During the five years of the project, dormitory damage costs rose from an average of $6.71 per resident in 1975–76 to $19.24 per resident in 1979–80. Highest damages were recorded in the most densely populated residential area on campus (Southwest) which has five high-rise dormitories and 5,500 residents.

Separate studies were conducted in various dormitories to determine the proportion of alcohol-related damages. In an eight-month study in the

Southwest area during 1976–77, an average of 14 damage reports occurred per 100 residents, with only 12% of the reports indicating the damage was related to alcohol use. The highest damage costs occurred in dorms with a high proportion of male residents. Costs varied from $27.44 per resident in one high-rise dorm where 93% of residents were male, to two all-female, small, low-rise dorms where damages were less than $1.50 per resident.

Two smaller studies were conducted in other residential areas. A year-long study in 1977–78 in three dormitories revealed that 39% of 143 damage incidents were alcohol-related, and occurred more commonly in dorms with a high proportion of males. A three-month study in 1978 in four dormitories revealed that 36% of the 76 damage incidents were not witnessed. For damage incidents that were witnessed, over 45% were alcohol-related, caused most often by dorm residents, by males, and occurring during or after dorm parties.

In general, a significant proportion of dormitory damage seems related to drinking, varying from 12% to 48% of damage incidents in the three studies reviewed. However, because of the gross nature of the estimates, no measurement of the possible effects of DAEP activities on dormitory damages was possible. The data did confirm that dormitories with a high proportion of males and with a high density population (e.g., high-rise dorms) had the highest damage rates.

Licensed Alcohol Use on Campus

The sale of alcoholic beverages on campus was studied in two ways: sales at the campus pub (the Bluewall) and sales at specially licensed parties or events.

Bluewall Sales. Gross sales of alcoholic beverages at the Bluewall were compiled for six-month intervals (Table 6). In general, the sales remained fairly stable between July 1975 and December 1978. Due to the raising of the minimum drinking age in Massachusetts in April 1979, from 18 to 20 years of age, Bluewall alcoholic beverage sales dropped dramatically between January 1979 and June 1980.

When spot-surveys of Bluewall sales were conducted on three separate dates in 1976 and 1977, it was found that each patron consumed an average of 1.5 to 2.0 drinks (mainly beer). Heaviest drinking occurred between 3:00 and 6:00 P.M., which coincided with "Happy Hour" at the Bluewall.

Party Licenses. Sponsors of parties or events often sought special "one-day malt and wine licenses" in order to purchase beer or wine at wholesale prices and/or sell alcoholic beverages on campus. Such licenses required the approval of both the dean of students and the Board of Selectmen of the Town of Amherst (or Hadley). Records showed that the number of licenses issued varied between 54 and 97 licenses per year between fall 1974 and spring 1978. Beginning in fall 1978, however, the number of licenses was drastically reduced, initially due to a revised alcoholic beverages policy which took effect in September 1978, and subsequently a result of the raising of the legal drinking age in April 1979. Although drinking on campus continued at a high level, less occurred at officially sanctioned large parties or events.

Effects of Changing the Minimum Drinking Age

The legal minimum drinking age in Massachusetts was raised from 18 to 20 years toward the end of the fourth year of DAEP (April 16, 1979). Although the long-term effects will not be known for some time, DAEP evaluation data were used to determine immediate effects. Data were used primarily from the yearly Consumer Survey and secondarily from the annual interviews with heads of residence.

Consumer Survey Data. Self-reported items on the Consumer Survey questionnaire sent to a random sample of between 1,200 and 1,450 students each year were analyzed to determine any changes in drinking behaviors by 18- and 19-year-old students before and after the legal minimum drinking age was raised.

Examination of key drinking variables revealed that 18- and 19-year-olds in the autumn of 1974, six months after the age change, drank more frequently and in greater quantity per occasion than 18- and 19-year-olds in the two previous years. The increase in average consumption per occasion was moderately significant ($p = 0.041$) although the slight increase in the reported frequency of drinking was not significant. An increase in the frequency of "getting a buzz on" by 18- and 19-year-olds was also significant ($p = 0.048$), but occurred the year *prior* to the age change. Although the increase in the number of negative behaviors was not significant, an increase in the number of problem outcomes was significant ($p = 0.026$). No significant increase in party attendance was reported, but there was a significant decrease in bar attendance between 1978 and 1979 ($p < 0.001$). In general, 18- and 19-year-olds drank slightly more than before the legal age change but shifted the site of drinking to parties and private locations, away from public bars.

Heads of Residence Reports. Responses of heads of residence to structured interviews in spring 1979 were compared to similar interviews in spring 1980. Although most HRs had expected favorable changes from the new law in the 1979 interviews, by the spring of 1980 interview, they reported increased levels of drunkenness, alcohol abuse, and property destruction in the dorms. It seemed that the location of much drinking by underaged students had shifted almost entirely to private dormitory rooms after the minimum age was raised. The legal change also reduced the effectiveness of the newly revised campus Alcoholic Beverage Policy, since most dorm parties were "BYOB" (Bring Your Own Bottle) affairs, rather than events where the amount of alcohol distributed was closely regulated.

Special Investigations of Alcohol Education Efforts

A number of detailed studies were conducted on various activities or populations to determine the effects of certain segments of the program. They sought to demonstrate which efforts were more successful than others and why.

Effectiveness of Public Awareness Efforts

During April of 1977, 1978, and 1979, a random sample of students were questioned by a telephone survey to determine the extensiveness and effectiveness of DAEP public awareness efforts. Data collection and analysis were performed by the staff of the Student Affairs Research and Evaluation Organization (SAREO). Out of a random sample of between 700 and 1,000 students, 35% to 38% each year participated in the survey. (Separate SAREO studies suggest that respondents and nonrespondents do not differ significantly on major demographic characteristics, but merely were not home when the telephone call(s) was attempted.) Students surveyed each year represented about the same male/female ratio present at the university and a higher proportion of underclasspersons than is present.

Survey results showed that recall of a specific poster on alcohol equivalency varied between 66% and 75%. A higher proportion of moderate and heavier drinkers recalled the poster than other students (the difference was significant, $p < .05$, in 1977). Similarly, students who drank heavier amounts were more likely to answer questions about alcoholic beverage equivalencies correctly.

The recall of other specific DAEP posters varied from 30% to 63% over the three years. Differences in recall seemed due to varying levels of distribution of posters across campus and poorer recall for detailed, complicated poster designs.

Recall of specific pamphlets varied between 18% and 29% of survey participants each year. More women and on-campus students recalled each specific pamphlet. Slightly more than half of the students who recalled a specific pamphlet reported that they read the material.

About 49% of students surveyed listened to the campus radio station

(WMUA). When listeners were asked their recall of a specific radio PSA (public service announcement), the proportions varied from 37.9% in 1977, to 4.5% in 1978, and 4.1% in 1979 (or between 24.8% and 1.2% of the entire sample). Much of the variation seemed due to the frequency with which the PSAs were played by radio station staff during the three years.

A special radio program called the Salsa–Soul Medicine Show gave significant attention to ways drinking can be done safely and was aired every Wednesday night from 7 to 10 P.M. in 1976 and 1977 and fall 1977. In 1977, about 13% of the sample reported hearing the program while in 1978, about 9% of the sample heard the show.

Survey results suggest that media and materials can be effective in raising awareness about alcohol-related problems and about educational activities to counteract such problems. However, in order to be effective, media efforts must be actively marketed.

Evaluation of a Bookmark as a Medium for Alcohol Education

A special study was conducted during the fourth year of the project to determine the effectiveness of a special bookmark placed in each new book sold at the Textbook Annex in February 1979. The bookmark presented information about the relationship between alcohol consumption and blood alcohol content.

Students in five classes from different departments whose textbooks were sold at the Textbook Annex were given a short questionnaire at the end of class one day about two months after the start of the semester. The questionnaire included a few demographic items and 13 questions about general alcohol knowledge, specific alcohol knowledge contained in the bookmark, and exposure to other DAEP efforts. Out of 160 surveys distributed, 154 were completed and returned.

Results revealed that 38% remembered having seen the bookmark, with 28% reportedly reading the bookmark. A slightly higher proportion of students who read the bookmark lived on campus (58%) and/or were sophomores (47%) compared to the total sample.

Four questions assessed bookmark-relevant alcohol knowledge (BRAK). Respondents who recalled reading the bookmark were more likely to have higher BRAK scores than those who did not read it, $\chi^2(3) = 4.104$, $p < 0.10$. In contrast, student responses to one five-part question assessing general alcohol knowledge (GAK) were not significantly correlated with either reading of the bookmark, $\chi^2(3) = 0.198$, NS, or the BRAK score, $\chi^2(4) = 2.537$, NS. The lack of correlation between the BRAK and GAK scores makes it unlikely that students' scores were due to chance guessing rather than actual knowledge.

Students who rated themselves moderate to heavy drinkers knew more correct BRAK responses than light drinkers or nondrinkers ($\chi^2(6) = 13.1409$, $p < 0.05$). Students who lived on campus also had higher BRAK scores than off-campus students ($\chi^2(3) = 11.4471$, $p < 0.01$). No significant relationships between BRAK scores and gender or student class were found.

No significant relationship was found between DAEP exposure and BRAK scores ($\chi^2(6) = 6.153$, NS). However, the correlation between DAEP exposure and the GAK score was significant ($\chi^2(2) = 8.127$, $p < 0.025$). Students exposed to other DAEP efforts scored higher on the GAK item.

In general, the bookmark appeared to be a useful form of media to catch the attention of students. Although the relationship between reading the bookmark and answering bookmark-relevant alcohol knowledge questions correctly was not highly significant, the fact that a higher proportion of moderate and heavier drinkers actually read the bookmark indicates that the desired audience was being exposed to the information.

Training for Residence Hall Assistants in Alcohol Problem Management

Resident assistants (RAs) are students who help oversee an average of 30 other students in their dorm and are, in turn, supervised by the head of residence. Throughout the five years of DAEP, many RAs have received special training in handling alcohol- and drug-related issues. Training involved either a one-hour or two-hour workshop focusing on ways to intervene effectively in problem-drinking situations, to help other students plan and conduct safer parties in the dorms, and to learn about their own drinking patterns and the consequences of those patterns.

Dormitories were randomly selected to participate in the study. All RAs in a given experimental or control dorm were invited to participate. Overall, 59% of those asked to participate in the study agreed to do so, resulting in an initial sample of 89 experimental and 27 control subjects. Subjects were representative of the overall composition of RAs by gender, academic class, and living area. A total of 80% of the experimental subjects and 59% of the control subjects completed all of the study questionnaires.

Experimental and control subjects completed a pretest prior to the training session, a posttest immediately after the session (Post I) and a delayed posttest 5 months after training (Post II). A few RAs also were deliberately excluded from completing one or more of the tests in order to examine test/retest effects. Test items included: (1) knowledge about helping agencies, elements of responsible party planning, and emergency medical procedures; (2) attitudes about problem drinking in the dorm; (3) intention to confront a problem drinker, measured by responses to six anecdotal situations; and (4) the frequency of actual prevention and intervention behaviors.

On pretest, no significant differences were found between experimental and control subjects, except that those RAs who did not complete the study were less concerned about alcohol issues than completers, $F(1, 77) = 4.85$; $p < 0.05$. Posttest scores revealed that new RAs had increased their knowledge of helping agencies as measured at both Post I and Post II, although experienced RAs did not. Experimental subjects also increased their medical knowledge at Post I and retained that knowledge at Post II, which was significantly different from control group subjects at Post II, $F(1, 73) = 7.53$; $p < 0.01$. No significant increases in knowledge of responsible party planning elements or intentions to confront problem drinkers resulted from the training.

On the Post II instrument, subjects were asked if they had participated in any additional DAEP training activities. Results showed that RAs who attended additional DAEP training sessions had a significantly higher knowledge of helping agencies, knowledge of responsible party planning components, and had intervened more often with problem situations, compared to RAs with little or no additional training.

When RA interventions with alcohol problem situations were compared to key predictor variables at Post II, a moderately significant correlation was found between the number of interventions in the past month and an RA's knowledge of responsible party components ($p < 0.01$) and of medical intervention procedures ($p < 0.05$). Correlations between RA interventions and knowledge of helping agencies, degree of alcohol concern, or intention to confront problem drinkers were not significant. Finally, RAs who reported higher problem rates in their dorms were more apt to intervene with problem situations ($p < 0.05$).

In general, the single-session workshop for RAs increased RAs' levels of knowledge on certain items. However, unless the session was augmented by other training opportunities, actual RA interventions occurred less often than seemed indicated by the level of alcohol problem behaviors reported by RAs.

Single-Session Workshop for Students on "Alcohol and Values"

The main intensive educational intervention used by DAEP was single-session workshops. To assess their effectiveness, a popular workshop design on "alcohol and values" was systematically evaluated. The design relied heavily on values clarification techniques to help students find ways of enjoying themselves without drinking excessively.

The "alcohol and values" workshop used a two-hour small discussion group format and included four values clarification exercises. The workshop was designed to help participants develop more moderate attitudes toward alcohol use, to increase awareness of attractive settings in which to enjoy oneself whether or not drinking is involved, and to learn more about factors that influenced their own drinking patterns, such as friends, patterns of stress, and settings. Its effects were evaluated using a quasi-experimental, multigroup pretest–posttest design.

Study participants were recruited in February 1980 from either residence halls or an undergraduate public health class. The experimental group had 79 subjects, including 45 assigned to the no-pretest condition, and the control group involved 98 students, including 70 assigned to the no-pretest condition. Pretests were given prior to the workshop, a Post I test assessing qualitative impressions was given to experimental subjects directly following the workshop, and a Post II survey was conducted 2 months later. A total of 69 experimental subjects (87%) and 60 control subjects (61%) completed all the required questionnaires.

The experimental group had a significantly higher proportion of females (76%) than the control group (50%) ($\chi^2(1) = 9.34$, $p < 0.001$). Experimental and control group subjects did not differ significantly according to age, academic class, or grade point average.

Items on the questionnaires were used to construct four variable classes: drinking behavior variables, cognitive-affective variables, social influence variables, and environmental factors. A series of regression analyses were performed to discover those factors that influenced students' decisions about drinking. Consistently, attitudes toward drinking and "the number of friends who would support you if you drank less" were high predictors of the average number of drinks per event, frequency of entry into a drinking context, and the number of drinks consumed on the last occasion. Thirty three percent of subjects consumed four or more drinks per sitting compared to 19% of 1979 Consumer Survey subjects (Table 3).

Comparisons of pretest results for experimental and control subjects revealed only two moderately significant differences: workshop participants had significantly "wetter" attitudes toward drinking, $t(51) = -2.51$, $p = 0.02$, and workshop participants could name slightly more attractions of various drinking settings than could control subjects, $t(51) = 1.80$, $p = 0.08$. Comparisons of changes from pretest to posttest revealed only one significant difference: compared to control subjects, workshop participants were more likely to identify heavy drinking as an average of three or more drinks per day after the workshop than before.

The effects of taking the pretest produced changes independent of workshop attendance. At the time of Post II test, subjects who had taken the pretest reported entering drinking contexts less frequently ($F(1, 107) =$ 17.62; $p < 0.001$) and consuming less per occasion ($F(1, 107) = 7.26, p =$ 0.008) than subjects who had not taken the pretest. Pretested subjects, compared to the no-pretest subjects, also reported fewer friends with whom they got drunk ($F(1, 107) = 4.82, p < 0.03$), and that fewer friends would oppose them if they stopped drinking ($F(1, 107) = 3.22, p < 0.075$).

Interaction effects for taking the pretest and attending a workshop were found for one variable. Subjects in the pretest workshop group reported having more friends who would support them if they stopped drinking than the other test conditions ($F(1, 107) = 4.98, p < .028$). No other significant interaction effects were found.

In general, "the alcohol and values" workshop was extremely well received by participants (97% good or outstanding ratings) and effective in modifying some knowledge and attitude variables for a group composed of a high proportion of heavy drinkers. It had little effect on drinking behaviors, however. Ironically, subjects who took the pretest moderated their reported consumption of alcohol, without reference to workshop attendance.

Longitudinal Study of a Sample of Students

In the fall of 1977, a sample of first-year students was randomly selected and invited to participate in a prospective longitudinal study. Initially, participants were randomly assigned to an experimental and control group to assess the effects of participation in a DAEP workshop during the fall 1977 semester. Subsequently, all subjects were combined into one group to be evaluated for a total of three years between 1977 and 1980 for any changes on alcohol-related variables

Study of Workshop Effects. A list of 300 first-year students was chosen at random during summer and fall 1977, with one-third designated the experimental group (workshop attendees), one-third a standard control group (Control-1), and the final third, a second control group (Control-2), who would receive no pretest. Invitations to participate were sent to the new students in August and September 1977.

Students in the experimental and Control-1 groups were contacted by telephone and times were arranged for completion of the pretest questionnaire, which consisted of the 1977 Consumer Survey and an addendum. Subjects were tested in small groups, with testing completed by early November 1977. The 48 experimental subjects were given a list of workshops scheduled for the following few weeks and urged to attend; periodic reminders were also given to them over the next few months of additional workshops that had been scheduled. A total of 51 students formed the

Control-1 group. In addition, 53 students were contacted by letter in November, informed of the status of the project, and asked to participate as the Control-2 group at the end of spring 1978 semester. In mid-March all 152 students were recontacted to schedule the Post I test, administered in April and May 1978. Because some students in the experimental group never attended a workshop, they were added to the Control-1 group. At Post I test, 88% of subjects responded to give a final sample of 31 experimental subjects, 60 subjects in the Control-1 group, and 45 subjects in the Control-2 group.

Based on pretest responses, no significant differences were shown on key dependent variables based on age, residence, and family type. However, gender seemed to show enough variability that it was examined more thoroughly. It was found that at pretest, males were significantly more knowledgeable ($F(1, 105) = 9.46$; $p < .002$), averaged more drinks per occasion ($F(1, 105) = 7.57$; $p < 0.007$) and experienced more negative physical consequences ($F(1, 105) = 7.65$; $p < 0.006$) than women. No significant differences were found at pretest for experimental and Control-1 group subjects.

At Post I test, data was analyzed to determine whether or not the two control groups were comparable. In general, only marginally significant differences were found, with the Control-2 group exhibiting a greater knowledge of helping agencies ($F(1, 103) = 4.23$; $p < 0.05$) and reporting fewer physical consequences ($F(1, 103) = 2.94$; $p < 0.01$) than the Control-1 group.

Comparisons of the pretest and posttest responses revealed no significant differences between the experimental and control groups as a result of workshop participation. In addition, the Post I test data did not demonstrate any significant differences based on gender.

In general, the data showed no significant effect of the workshop intervention on experimental subjects, although some nonsignificant trends suggested that the knowledge and attitudes of workshop participants had been modified in the desired direction.

Study of Longitudinal Changes. The total sample of 134 students who responded to the Post I test (described above) formed the sample for the longitudinal study (LS). The second or Post II follow-up occurred in April 1979, and revealed that only 103 of the sample were still on campus, all of whom completed the Post II test. The third and final follow-up occurred in April 1980. Further attrition had occurred so that only 86 students were still on campus; 67 completed the Post III survey, including 42 who had completed all four surveys. Instruments were similar to those described earlier to evaluate the workshop effects.

Initial comparisons were made between the nonreturning student groups at Post I, Post II, and Post III and the final sample of 67 students, to determine whether or not alcohol-related attitudes or behavior could explain the "mortality" of the nonreturning students. Results revealed no significant differences on alcohol-related variables between the final longitudinal study sample and those who did not complete it.

The longitudinal sample of 134 students who completed the Post I test had essentially the same demographic characteristics as Consumer Survey respondents in 1977, except that the longitudinal sample of first-year students tended to be slightly, but not significantly, older than first-year students on the Consumer Survey. The LS sample included 44% males, 97% with no spouse and/or children, 92.5% residing on campus, and 95.5% aged 18 or 19 years.

Responses from LS participants who returned all four surveys ($N = 42$) were analyzed to determine if any alcohol-related knowledge, attitude, or behavior changes occurred between the first year and the junior year of college. Analyses of covariance revealed no significant differences in reported variables at the four survey points (Table 7). Although certain changes in mean values were consistent with earlier findings in the Consumer Survey, such as a decrease over the three years in the average number of drinks consumed per event and an increase over the years in average number of drinking events attended, the changes were not statistically significant. No changes were apparent for physical consequences, negative behaviors, and problem outcomes.

In general, the alcohol-related knowledge, attitudes, and behaviors of a

Table 7.

Analyses of Covariance or Longitudinal Study Subjects with Time (4 Data Points) as a Repeated Measure of Key Dependent Variables and Sex as a Covariate

Dependent variable	Adjusted means				F Ratio	df	Significance
	$\bar{X}$ Time 1	$\bar{X}$ Time 2	$\bar{X}$ Time 3	$\bar{X}$ Time 4			
Attitudes toward drinking	2.7	2.9	2.9	2.8	1.33	3, 123	NS
Knowledge inventory	10.8	10.8	11.7	10.8	1.6	3, 123	NS
Average per event	3.3	3.3	3.0	3.1	1.21	3, 123	NS
Entry into a drinking context	1.7	1.6	1.8	2.0	.71	3, 123	NS
Physical consequences	4.4	4.4	4.4	4.4	.06	3, 123	NS
Negative behaviors	1.8	1.7	1.7	1.8	.44	3, 123	NS
Problem outcomes	.9	.8	.9	1.1	1.4	3, 123	NS

$N = 42$: The number of experimental and control-1 study participants who returned all 4 surveys.

small sample of college students did not change significantly over their first three years of college. In fact, the responses of LS subjects showed far fewer fluctuations in reported averages than the cross-sectional survey data reviewed earlier, partly due to the small sample size of the LS. Although those students who moved off campus by the end of their second year of college appeared to be heavier drinkers who experienced a slightly greater number of problem outcomes, by the end of the third year students living on or off campus were indistinguishable on the two variables.

Seminar for Students: How to Run an Alcohol Colloquium

A special one-semester seminar for three academic credits was developed in 1977 to instruct student participants on how to plan and conduct an alcohol education colloquium. The seminar was offered for three successive years in the fall semester of 1977, 1978, and 1979. Although the emphasis each year varied to some extent, 32 hours of instruction were provided each year, including between 9 and 17 hours of direct lectures about content, 7 to 10 hours of focused experiential (values clarification) exercises, 3 to 4 hours on constructing a syllabus for a colloquium, and 5 to 10 hours practicing various skills. Those students who wished to use the seminar training to conduct a one-credit colloquium for between 5 to 15 other students in the spring semester were encouraged to do so. Students who led the colloquia were supervised individually and in small group sessions by DAEP professional staff and received two academic credits for their efforts.

Seminar participants were administered the Consumer Survey and an additional set of knowledge questions both prior to the beginning of the fall semester course and at the conclusion of the course each year. Out of the 22 participants in 1977, 17 participants in 1978, and 11 participants in 1979, pretest and posttest data were completed by 78%. For most analyses of the data, the three sample years were combined.

Participants included: 20 males and 19 females; 26 on-campus residents, and 13 off-campus residents; and 15 students aged 18 to 19, 18 aged 20 to 21, and 6 aged 22. Results were analyzed using repeated measures analysis of variance on nine constructed variables, with sex as a covariant.

Significant differences between pretest and posttest were found for six of the nine variables. The adjusted cell means on pretests and posttests were analyzed to determine the direction of the significance. Seminar participants entered less often into drinking contexts at posttest ($F(1, 36) = 5.12$; $p = 0.03$) compared to pretest; the overall trend reflected significant changes in 1977 and 1978, even though a small reverse tendency was true in 1979. Attitudes toward drinking shifted significantly between pre and posttest ($F(1, 36) = 4.16$; $p = 0.05$). Shifts were made from an extremely "dry" to a more "moderate" position in 1978 and 1979, although the shift in 1977 was in the opposite direction. Physical consequences (i.e., number of times "get a buzz on") showed a moderately significant decrease all three years between pre- and posttests ($F(1, 36) = 4.73; p = 0.036$). Party attendance decreased between pre- and posttest all three years ($F(1, 36) = 12.01; p < 0.001$). Bar attendance also decreased all three years ($F(1, 36) = 4.49; p = 0.041$). Knowledge scores showed a significant interaction effect between pre- and posttest differences and year ($F(2, 36) = 14.69; p < 0.001$), which involved a significant increase in knowledge in 1977 and 1978 and a significant decrease in knowledge in 1979. No significant differences were found for average consumed per occasion, negative behaviors, or problem outcomes.

In general, seminar participants were heavier drinkers than the average student and reported a significant moderation in their alcohol-related behaviors at the conclusion of the seminar, to a level that approximated the "average" student. The effects reported by participants at the end of the seminar were quite supportive of the value of multisession workshops given for credit and their effectiveness in producing significant changes in attitudes and behavior in students who were regular drinkers.

DISCUSSION AND RECOMMENDATIONS

The University Model developed and tested by the DAEP at the University of Massachusetts provides an integrated approach to the prevention of alcohol problems in a small community using widely available techniques. Probably the strongest feature of the program was its use of both education and regulation methods. Mass media, group, and individual techniques were used simultaneously and repeatedly to influence the community norms and contextual factors as well as the voluntary behavior of individuals. The adoption of a "disaggregated approach" to alcohol problems demonstrates how program planners can design and evaluate primary prevention efforts in a way that is accepted by community members. The extensive evaluation design also shows possible ways to measure the effectiveness of such a program using both simple and complex methods.

The basic program approach, concepts, and staff remained constant throughout the five years of the project, which ensured continuity for project efforts. Unfortunately, program constancy was not matched by sufficient attention to the evaluation design until the fourth year. Many of the evaluation studies were limited by survey instruments that did not contain sufficient items to test for enabling and reinforcing factors but focused too heavily on behavioral outcomes. In particular, although program methods focused heavily on altering peer norms and pressures, drinking settings, and contexts (Kraft, 1981), and the responses of key persons and helpers, the main evaluation instrument (the Consumer Survey) contained very few items that assessed those intervening factors. By the time the problem was recognized, it was too late to redesign the basic instrument without sacrificing needs for comparable data across years. Evaluation efforts in the final two years (47% to 66% of the budget, compared to 26% to 32% in the first three years) were at least able to use data gathered in the first three years to analyze the effectiveness of the intervention. Strategies in the final two years were also developed to test for knowledge, attitude, and belief changes among smaller groups of students even when behavioral changes might not have been demonstrated.

The adaptation and final application of PRECEDE as the framework for the University Model proved extremely useful. Although other theoretical schemes certainly exist, such as the Fishbein and Azjen model of behavior change (1975) and the Jessor and Jessor theory of problem behavior (1977), the PRECEDE model encompassed more factors that were important for changing a university environment at multiple levels. The PRECEDE model proved to be adequate both for program planning and evaluation purposes. Although DAEP's attempts to validate the causal relationships suggested by the PRECEDE model were encouraging, future studies need to evaluate the relative importance of predisposing, enabling, and reinforcing factors on producing changes in drinking behaviors more rigorously.

The University Model relies heavily on mass media approaches to pique the interest of all community residents to ways of preventing alcohol problems. DAEPs implementation demonstrated that significant levels of awareness could be raised using media approaches and that some changes in knowledge could also be produced. It further demonstrated that media that were unfocused or too complicated were less often recalled and were less effective even in changing knowledge. The finding lends support to the use of simple themes to create effective media presentations. Such media must be focused, attractive, and easy to understand. Media approaches must also be distributed widely and regularly to be effective. One of the most difficult tasks of DAEP staff was to make sure that posters, pamphlets, and radio PSAs were regularly distributed at an adequate level. The "marketing" of education materials was certainly as important as the production of attractive and effective media/materials.

One extensive approach that should receive further evaluation involves "special displays." Although one of the more successful displays by DAEP involved a breathalyzer outside a campus pub, other displays were conducted in widely frequented campus locations. Tables were set up in the

Student Union, for example, to distribute literature, show short films, and give information. Campus environments can make extremely successful use of such special displays but also need to evaluate their effectiveness.

A major disappointment for DAEP staff was the limited effectiveness of the single-session workshop. Although knowledge, attitudes, and beliefs could be modified, behavior changes were not evident at follow-up. The result may be due to the relatively small amount of time (2 hours) spent influencing a normal group of students with few drinking problems. Future efforts might either develop ways to attract and retain the same student participants in a series of workshops or make attempts to attract a higher proportion of problem drinkers to various single-session workshops, especially younger, male, undergraduates.

The most dramatic effects of the intensive approaches were found for participants in the semester-long Seminar in Alcohol Education course in two of the three years it was offered by DAEP staff. Participants in the course showed evidence of decreased drinking and associated changes in attitude. In the two most successful semesters, students were also likely to organize alcohol colloquia for other students in their residences during the following term.

The use of values clarification techniques to augment the alcohol-specific content of workshops was well received by students and seemed to assist in the education process. In fact, the seminar on "How to Teach an Alcohol Colloquium" in 1979 when the content was altered to include more didactic presentations and fewer experiential and practice sessions (about one-third of the time instead of one-half), resulted in the least amount of behavioral changes by participants at posttest. Certain changes observed the previous two years did not occur at all (e.g., increased knowledge) and others occurred in an undesired direction (e.g., entry into drinking contexts). Unfortunately, no evaluations were conducted on the effects of single-session didactic presentations in existing courses to allow a more direct comparison between traditional educational lectures and the combined information and experiential approach used in most workshops by the University Model.

Clearly, the most effective and lasting influences in the community occurred in relation to party planning. Students interested in learning how to plan safe parties learned about alcohol use and abuse in the process and actually adopted some of the principles of responsible drinking. Other campus environments should capitalize on this focus, since it is one positive approach to alcohol use that can involve students in preventing alcohol problems among peers.

The development and adoption of a revised Alcoholic Beverage Policy in September 1978 was an important accomplishment of DAEP. However, the policy change was preceded by years of education of the community regarding the complex factors involved in preventing alcohol problems. Without such preparation, it is doubtful that a reasonable, enforceable policy would have been accepted by both the regulators and the regulated. The revised policy contained a strong emphasis on planning and required that organizers of medium-sized and large parties learn to conduct safe events. As a result, the policy created educational opportunities with students who otherwise would not have participated in DAEP activities. Unfortunately, the raising of the minimum drinking age in Massachusetts from 18 to 20 years occured barely seven months after the revised beverage policy had taken effect. This prevented long-term evaluation of the effectiveness of a regulatory approach on campus since alcohol had now been legally prohibited for most on-campus students. Although drinking by 18- and 19-year-old students continued after the age change, and even increased, events during which alcoholic beverages were served to minors were strictly forbidden. Most parties became "BYOB" affairs making planning and the regulation of the amount of alcohol available per person extremely difficult.

The failure to demonstrate community-wide decreases in the occurrence of alcohol-related problems is probably related to a combination of factors in program design, program implementation, and program evaluation. Based on the theory that affecting 5% to 10% of a cross-section of students would "ripple" to other students the program design relied too heavily on one-session workshops voluntarily attended by interested students. Although a cross-section of students attended workshops, many of the students and student groups at highest risk for heavy drinking and negative consequences (i.e., 18- or 19-year-old males living in all-male dorms or fraternities) did not participate in significant numbers in the intensive efforts. Efforts to work with these groups were not consistent but varied from year to year, depending on staff interests.

Program implementation suffered from the relatively small size of program staff trying to influence an extremely transient community, in which 33% of the student population and 40% of the residential hall staff change every year. The transience limited the carryover of program effects from year to year at an aggregate level. Since few other programs can probably afford as large a staff as DAEP supported, future implementation efforts would do well to focus intensive efforts on high-risk populations wherever possible.

Program evaluation also contributed to the apparent lack of success in decreasing the occurrence of alcohol problems. Data on which community-wide changes are based are very unreliable even when augmented by special survey methods. The time that the major self-report Consumer Survey was conducted (the fall) may have limited the accurate reflection of short-term behavioral effects that a survey administered in the spring might have detected given the high turnover of the student body each year. In addition, most evaluation instruments were not sensitive enough to detect changes in predisposing, enabling, and reinforcing factors as well as the drinking behaviors and problem outcome measures.

Several specific questions for future research in alcohol education and alcohol problem prevention have emerged from the present study: What is the optimal level of exposure to intensive efforts required to produce change? How effective are specific workshops in producing change and what features make them effective? What is the reinforcing function of mass media efforts? How effective are peer versus professional staff in different program efforts? How can the effects of pretesting be used either alone or in combination with a workshop to produce desired changes? What are the independent and interactive effects of the multimodality program efforts? And what is an appropriate combination of educational and regulatory strategies to effect community-wide changes over time? One approach to doing research on many of these issues would be to use residence halls as treatment units, systematically varying the types and levels of efforts in order to disentangle their effects experimentally.

A number of recommendations can be offered to other programs that might attempt to use the University Model or similar approaches.

1. A specific theoretical framework should form the basis of a comprehensive program from its inception, especially to guide evaluation tasks. The PRECEDE model for planning effective community health programs served as the framework for the University Model and bears further testing.
2. Alcohol education efforts in a community should pay particular attention to modifying enabling and reinforcing factors, in addition to predisposing factors, in order to change undesirable behaviors.
3. A disaggregated approach to alcohol problems needs to be applied more rigorously in community-based programs, defining separate strategies to combat each identified alcohol problem rather than using a scattered approach to all problems.
4. The combined and phased use of educational and regulatory approaches to changing drinking practices must be utilized more extensively, with evaluative research to determine the most effective mixtures.
5. Media and materials must present a single, simple message in a clear and attractive manner to be effective.
6. Well-designed media and materials, including radio PSAs, must be distributed regularly and widely in order to have some effect on the intended audience.
7. The development of party planning guidelines and materials pro-

vides a useful way to focus on more "positive" aspects of alcohol use in a university community and can lead to increased interest in preventing alcohol-related problems.

8. Pamphlets were most useful when developed for a target audience, for example, heads of residence and resident assistants, or a specific problem, such as "How to Help a Problem Drinker," rather than for the general population. Pamphlets should be developed on single themes and should be clear in presentation.

9. Higher proportions of "high-risk" (heavier drinking) groups must be involved in intensive educational efforts, such as fraternity members, all-male dormitory residents, first-year student dormitory residents, and residents of high-rise dormitories. Attempts to involve such groups might include the use of educational "gimmicks" to increase interest, such as the use of a breathalyzer at a party.

10. Multiple-session workshop designs must be developed and tested if behavioral changes as well as changes in knowledge, attitudes, and beliefs are desired.

11. The training of residence assistants should involve more than one session in order to provide adequate experience in dealing with alcohol-related problems. Training should be as practical as possible in order to emphasize the day-to-day utility of the approaches developed.

12. Alcoholic beverage policies on campus should be clear, reasonable, and enforceable in order to be effective and acceptable to both the regulated and the regulators.

13. Alcohol education activities should use existing campus facilities and resources as much as possible in order to integrate the program into the community and to begin to influence community practices and norms.

14. The collection and interpretation of archival data must proceed with extreme caution due to the highly variable accuracy of such data.

15. Evaluation instruments should be constructed carefully according to the objectives of the study and tested for validity and reliability before use. Large randomized surveys may not be as useful as simpler techniques, depending on the resources available and the aims of the study.

The University Model seems feasible for adaptation by most colleges and universities, especially where a high proportion of students are in residence. The knowledge, methods, and techniques employed by the program model are widely available.

The program costs, when separated from the costs of elaborate evaluation studies required by the demonstration grant, seem reasonable, given the ultimate expense of various alcohol-problem behaviors (e.g., dormitory damage, automobile accidents, and personal injuries). For example, the estimated cost of mass media per exposed student averaged $0.21 per year. The estimated cost of intensive educational efforts per participant was $20.00 per year, which amounted to $8.00 per hour of actual contact, since most sessions were longer than one hour and some participants attended multiple sessions. In particular, the teaming of mass media approaches for the raising of awareness with approaches designed to educate smaller groups of students is a cost-effective prevention strategy.

CONCLUSIONS

The University Model developed by the Demonstration Alcohol Education Project at the University of Massachusetts at Amherst showed that concentrated primary prevention efforts could be successful in changing knowledge, attitudes, and behaviors of students. However, such efforts required multiple exposures of a small proportion of the target population. Less intensive efforts aimed at community norms showed changes in practices at the dormitory level without significant changes in individual drinking practices. Certain regulatory efforts were successful in changing community-wide norms, although insufficient time had elapsed to measure the effects on individual drinking behaviors. Few desired effects were demonstrated on the drinking behaviors of a random sample of students attending the university.

Mass media approaches were effective in reaching large proportions of campus students with simple messages. Some students, on follow-up, even planned to change behaviors, although no evaluation of such changes was attempted. Intensive educational approaches were more successful in changing knowledge and reported attitudes than in actually modifying drinking practices. Only educational approaches where students participated in multiple-session efforts resulted in actual changes in drinking behaviors. Community development efforts led to changes in party planning behaviors in dorms, so that nonalcoholic food and beverages were consistently available. Efforts to revise the campus-wide alcoholic beverage policies succeeded in 1978, with some preliminary positive effects, only to be cut short by the raising of the legal drinking age in April 1979 from 18 to 20 years. The emphasis on party planning and control of alcoholic-beverage purchases was severely affected by the age change, since most students living on campus were legally under age.

The results of program efforts and their subsequent evaluation suggested a number of modifications for alcohol education efforts aimed at the primary prevention of alcohol problems in a small community. The modifications should lead to more effective program interventions at colleges, universities, and similar communities. The discussion includes specific recommendations for future programs.

REFERENCES

Ajzen, I., & Fishbein, M. Factors influencing intentions and the intention–behavior relationship. *Human Relations,* 1974, *27,* 1–15.

Blane, H. T. Education and the prevention of alcoholism. In B. Kissin & H. Begleiter (Eds.), *The biology of alcoholism: The social aspects of alcoholism* (Vol. 4). New York: Plenum Press, 1976.

Blane, H. T., & Hewitt, L. E. *Alcohol and youth: An analysis of the literature 1960–75.* Final report prepared for the National Institute on Alcohol Abuse and Alcoholism under Contract No. ADM 281–75–0026, March 1977.

DeLuca, J. R. (Ed.). *Fourth special report to the U.S. Congress on alcohol and health.* Washington, D.C.: Superintendent of Documents, U.S. Government Printing Office, 1981.

Duston, E. K., Kraft, D. P., & Hornik, J. (Eds.). *Evaluation report for the university model.* Final report prepared for the National Institute on Alcohol Abuse and Alcoholism under Grant No. ADAMHA–AA–02331, 1980.

Duston, E. K., Kraft, D. P., & Jaworski, B. Alcohol education project: Preliminary answers. *Journal of the American College Health Association,* 1981, *29,* 272–278.

Fishbein, M., & Ajzen, I. *Belief, attitudes, intention and behavior: An introuction to theory and research.* Reading, Mass.: Addison Wesley, 1975.

Green, L. W., Kreuter, M. S., Deeds, S. G., & Partridge, K. B. *Health education planning: A diagnostic approach.* Palo Alto, Calif.: Mayfield, 1980.

Green, L. W., Wang, U. L., Deeds, S., Fisher, A., Windsor, R., Bennett, A., & Rogers, C. Guidelines for health education in maternal and child health. *International Journal of Health Education,* 1978, Supplement, 21(3), July–September, 1–33.

Jessor, R., & Jessor, S. L. *Problem behavior and psychosocial development: A longitudinal study of youth.* New York: Academic, 1977.

Kelly, N. B. Health education through entertainment: A multimedia campaign. *Journal of the American College Health Association,* 1978, *26,* 248–252.

Kraft, D. P. College students and alcohol: The 50 plus 12 project. *Alcohol, Health and Research World,* 1976, Summer, 10–14.

Kraft, D. P. Follow-up of a federal effort to encourage campus alcohol abuse prevention programs. *Journal of the American College Health Association,* 1977, *26,* 150–153.

Kraft, D. P. Alcohol-related problems seen at the student health services. *Journal of the American College Health Association,* 1979a, *27,* 190–194.

Kraft, D. P. Strategies for reducing drinking problems among youth: College programs. In H. T. Blane & M. E. Chafetz (Eds.), *Youth, alcohol and social policy.* New York: Plenum, 1979b.

Kraft, D. P. Public drinking patterns of college youths: Implications for prevention programs. In T. Harford (Ed.), *Conceptual and methodological aspects of drinking contexts.* Washington, D.C.: U.S. Department of Health and Human Services, 1981.

Noble, E. P. (Ed.). *Third special report to the U.S. Congress on alcohol and health.* Washington, D.C.: Superintendent of Documents, U.S. Government Printing Office, 1978.

Room, R. Governing images and the prevention of alcohol problems. *Preventive Medicine,* 1974, *3,* 11–23.

Straus, R., & Bacon, S. E. *Drinking in college.* New Haven: Yale University Press, 1953.

United States Department of Health, Education, & Welfare. *The whole college catalog about drinking: A guide to alcohol abuse prevention.* Washington, D.C.: Superintendent of Documents, U.S. Government Printing Office, 1976.

10

Teaching Responsible Drinking Skills

WILLIAM R. MILLER

TEACHING RESPONSIBLE DRINKING: FIVE PHILOSOPHIES

AN ANALOGY TEST

Prevent alcoholism by teaching responsible drinking? Is that a sensible idea? Consider the following multiple choice analogy. There is no one right or wrong answer, but probably one analogy will fit best or seem most true to you.

> Trying to prevent alcoholism by teaching people how to drink is like trying to:

1. Prevent fire by striking matches
2. Prevent diabetes by giving people candy
3. Prevent gunshot wounds by teaching safe use of firearms
4. Prevent unwanted pregnancy by teaching about birth control
5. Prevent drowning by teaching swimming

Which analogy rings true for you?

Each of these analogies corresponds to an underlying philosophy regarding the teaching of responsible drinking as a preventive approach.

WILLIAM R. MILLER • Department of Psychology, University of New Mexico, Albuquerque, New Mexico 87131.

THE PROHIBITIONIST POSITION

"Trying to prevent alcoholism by teaching people how to drink is like trying to prevent fire by striking matches." This view regards alcohol as a volatile and destructive agent. To expose individuals to alcohol is to risk their becoming drawn into the abyss of alcoholism. From this vantage point, teaching "responsible" drinking is an anomaly (if not anathema), as senseless as lighting matches to prevent fires.

There are some things to be said for this view. Certainly people who never drink will never become alcoholic. The damage and suffering that can occur in relation to alcohol are undeniable and those who have been closest to such pain understandably can develop a total revulsion to alcohol and its use in any form.

The problem, of course, is that total prohibition has been found to be unfeasible as social policy in our society. Most people will be exposed to alcohol, probably before leaving their teen years. Although an "all or none" stance on alcohol may reduce the probability of drinking, it does not seem to prevent alcoholism and problem drinking. Like children of alcoholic parents, children from abstinent families have a higher risk of developing drinking problems if they drink.

THE DISEASE MODEL

"Trying to prevent alcoholism by teaching people how to drink is like trying to prevent diabetes by giving people candy." Here the analogy is drawn to the disease diabetes. Most people will not be affected in major adverse ways by candy. It may increase tooth decay or cause mood swings, but in most cases it is not dangerous. For the person with this disease, however, candy can be life threatening. By analogy, alcohol may not be very hazardous for most people, but for those with the disease of alcoholism, exposure can be harmful or fatal. This view is most often attributed to Jellinek (1960), who described "gamma alcoholism" as one of several different subtypes of alcoholism.

Again, there is support for this view. There is increasing evidence that genetic factors play an important role in certain kinds of alcoholism. There may be an inherited type of alcoholism associated with a more rapid development of the disease, with childhood history of hyperactivity or antisocial behavior, and with family history of alcoholism or affective disorders. Some people seem to be unable to drink alcohol in moderation and are best advised to abstain totally.

Yet it is clear that the disease model with its assumptions of irreversibility and permanent loss of control cannot account for *all* or even most problem drinkers. A minority of people treated in alcoholism centers show signs of addiction serious enough to require detoxification (Feldman, Pattison, Sobell, Graham, & Sobell, 1975). Within the total spectrum of problem drinkers, many of whom have never sought treatment, the incidence of addiction and loss of control is still lower. The disease analogy can be extended to assert that problem drinkers without addiction or loss of control are merely alcoholics in early stages of development, but no empirical evidence exists to support this assertion, which also departs substantially from Jellinek's original type theory that viewed only certain kinds of alcoholism as disease. Further, research has raised serious questions about the integrity of the assumptions of automatic loss of control (e.g., Marlatt, Demming, & Reid, 1973) and irreversibility (e.g., Polich, Armor, & Braiker, 1981). As a preventive or general alcohol education model, then, the disease position appears to be limited.

THE PREPARATORY VIEW

"Trying to prevent alcoholism by teaching people how to drink is like trying to prevent gunshot wounds by teaching safe use of firearms." The proponent of this view might acknowledge that the world would probably be a better place if there were no guns (or alcohol) but would assert that people need to know how to use them because they are a part of the reality of our world. There may be an intense ambivalence here: On the one hand, guns (and alcohol) are not necessary to live a happy life and can pose serious dangers; yet proponents may jealously protect the right of people to have and use them in spite of their dangerousness. "Guns (alcoholic beverages) don't hurt people, people do." This "preparatory" position is that if you are going to live in a world of firearms (and firewater) you had better know how to use them and to protect yourself from their dangers.

THE SOCIAL LEARNING POSITION

"Trying to prevent alcoholism by teaching people how to drink is like trying to prevent unwanted pregnancy by teaching about birth control." This approach takes a more neutral view. Exposure to alcohol (like sex) is nearly inevitable. If we teach responsible behavior and methods of preventing harmful outcomes, then the person will be prepared to deal with—or abstain from—this aspect of life. This position emphasizes choice. People are encouraged to have a responsible attitude toward the use, meaning, and potential dangers involved.

THE ADVOCACY STANCE

"Trying to prevent alcoholism by teaching people how to drink is like trying to prevent drowning by teaching swimming." When I arrived at college, never having learned how to swim, I was horrified to hear the instructor of my mandatory freshman gym class say, "No one graduates from this college without knowing how to swim. You *will* learn. We're not about to spend years educating you only to have you drown in a lake or a ditch somewhere." I learned.

In analogy, this position is the precise opposite pole from the prohibitionist sentiment. Here drinking is seen as so ubiquitous that everyone should be required to learn how to stay afloat. If a person is suddenly cast into the water (alcohol) without having learned survival skills, the outcome may be unfortunate.

These latter three positions have in common their emphasis on the high probability of being exposed to alcohol, and this is their strength. Current evidence suggests that 80% to 90% of teenagers have consumed alcohol by the time they graduate from high school, and many of them have already become regular drinkers (Rachal, Maisto, Guess, & Hubbard, 1981).

The danger in these views is that they may cast abstinence as an invalid or undesirable choice. Certainly "responsible drinking" programs should also enable people to choose abstinence as a legitimate and responsible decision. A further and related danger is that these positions may encourage alcohol use in individuals who would otherwise abstain. That this is a possibility is demonstrated by Stuart's (1974) evaluation of a public school alcohol and drug abuse "prevention" program that increased the use, favorable attitudes toward, and selling of certain drugs and alcohol relative to a control group not receiving the program.

MODERATION AS A TERTIARY PREVENTION STRATEGY

The above represent five alternative philosophic positions on teaching responsible drinking as a preventive strategy, but what are the data regarding this approach? We will first consider research on moderation training programs for people who have *already* developed drinking problems. These represent tertiary prevention efforts in that they attempt to arrest the development of the problem and to prevent further deterioration.

THE GREAT CONTROLLED DRINKING CONTROVERSY

The Davies Study

The first evidence of a heated controversy around the issue of "controlled drinking" appeared in 1962 in a series of letters and responses protesting the publication of an article in the *Quarterly Journal of Studies on Alcohol*. In this article Davies (1962) reported that 7 of 93 "alcohol addicts" whom he had been following for a period of 7 to 11 years after treatment had resumed a pattern of "normal drinking" and were not experiencing problems with it. It is curious that this particular article should provoke such polemic, because reports of moderation outcomes from alcoholism treatment had appeared during the preceding decade. Perhaps it was related to the formalization of Jellinek's (1960) disease model of alcoholism, although Jellinek himself recognized the existence of nonaddictive types of alcoholism and thereby should not have been surprised by such outcomes. The substance of the protest, however, was the claim that alcoholics can never again resume drinking safely and that the article was mistaken and misleading.

The Rand Reports

Fourteen years later the issue flared again over press coverage of what came to be called "the Rand Report" (Armor, Polich, & Stambul, 1976). The controversy centered on the finding that a small percentage of people treated in alcoholism centers were drinking moderately and without problems at an 18-month follow-up. It is interesting that this particular study should evoke an emotional debate, because the years between 1962 and 1976 were filled with similar reports of moderation outcomes (Pattison, Sobell, & Sobell, 1977). In this case the flames were probably fanned most by the press coverage it received and by the press's mistaken conclusion that because of this finding abstinent alcoholics could safely resume drinking. The finding of stable long-term moderation outcomes has been reaffirmed recently by the 4-year follow-up of the original Rand study (Polich *et al.,* 1981).

The Rand reports and most others documenting moderation outcomes, however, are not true tests of the validity of teaching "responsible drinking" in that those who became controlled drinkers in these studies did so in spite of, rather than because of, treatment advice. These studies documented moderation outcomes from programs where total and lifelong *abstinence* was the dominant philosophy. What happens when one adopts *moderation* as a treatment goal and teaches specific skills for attaining it?

Controlled Drinking Treatment Programs

The first researchers to report such a program were Lovibond and Caddy in 1970. Since their initial work at least 20 other studies have been published and the results, reviewed elsewhere in detail (Miller & Hester, 1980), have been encouragingly consistent. The average rate of successful outcomes in these studies has been about 64% at 12-month follow-up, with roughly half of these being fully controlled drinkers and the other half being abstainers or improved cases. No other treatment approach for problem drinkers has received this volume of experimental scrutiny, nor has any other approach consistently achieved a higher success rate at 1-year follow-up (Miller, 1983; Miller & Hester, 1980).

The most frequently used approach for teaching moderation has been a varying set of strategies collectively called behavioral self-control training (BSCT). These include (1) setting specific limits and goals for drinking behavior, (2) learning how to discriminate blood alcohol concentration (BAC) either through biofeedback or through the use of BAC estimation rules or tables, (3) self-monitoring of alcohol consumption, (4) using rate control methods to slow down drinking, (5) applying operant principles such as self-reinforcement and self-contracting, (6) conducting functional analysis of drinking behavior to identify frequent antecedents or consequences that influence alcohol consumption, (7) applying stimulus control procedures to alter antecedent situations, and (8) learning behavioral alternatives to drinking so that psychological dependence is broken by providing new coping strategies for situations in which drinking has been the primary response. These and other BSCT procedures have been described in detail by Miller and Muñoz (1982).

Our own research on BSCT provides some hopeful directions for future preventive efforts based on moderation training. BSCT is basically an educational approach. It does not normally require extensive training and experience in psychotherapy, although basic counseling skills such as accurate empathy may increase effectiveness of the therapist (Miller, Taylor, & West, 1980). In comparing BSCT with alternative controlled drinking training strategies involving electrical aversion therapy or extensive practice drinking in the clinic, we found no significant differences in long-term effectiveness (Miller, 1978). This suggests that there may be little advantage in the use of aversive procedures or in the more extensive training procedures that require drinking within the treatment setting (cf. Vogler, Weissbach, Compton, & Martin, 1977). Research to date has found, at best, a modest advantage for broad-spectrum or multimodal training approaches relative to basic BSCT (Alden, 1978; Miller & Hester, 1980; Miller *et al.,* 1980). In other research the effectiveness of BSCT has compared favorably with aversion therapy (Hedberg & Campbell, 1974), psychotherapy (Pomerleau, Pertschuk, Adkins, & d'Aquili, 1978), and untreated control groups (Buck & Miller, 1981; Miller, 1983; Miller & Hester, 1980; Lovibond, 1975).

Our research also suggests that BSCT is very amenable to presentation within standard educational formats. We have found that group presentation is at least as effective as an individual therapy format (Miller & Taylor, 1980). Perhaps more surprising has been our finding in four controlled studies that clients working on their own with self-help BSCT materials have been as successful in learning moderation as were those working under the direction of an individual therapist (Buck & Miller, 1981; Miller, Gribskov, & Mortell, 1981; Miller & Taylor, 1980; Miller *et al.,* 1980).

In all of these studies the clients were outpatient problem drinkers seeking help for an already developed drinking problem. The outcome data suggest that such individuals can, in a majority of cases, attain and maintain successful outcomes through behavioral self-control training with a goal of moderation. Thus BSCT appears to be a successful tertiary prevention measure for problem drinking.

PREDICTING MODERATION OUTCOMES

What kind of person is likely to succeed in learning moderation? This is a crucial question for the professional in helping clients to select appropriate and effective treatment goals. Fortunately, there are now data to aid us in this decision process, and the direction of findings has been encouragingly consistent.

The first criteria for selecting appropriate candidates for controlled drinking were proposed by Miller and Caddy (1977). These were rationally based rather than empirically based criteria, and focused on a contraindications approach. Moderation was contraindicated for the more advanced alcoholic with signs of addiction, physical deterioration, or other medical or psychological condition that would render moderate drinking hazardous. Abstinence, on the other hand, was contraindicated for the early stage problem drinker without addiction or physical deterioration, particularly if the individual refused to consider abstinence or had previously failed to respond to an abstinence approach.

Subsequent empirical findings have supported these general criteria. In studies of moderation-oriented treatment programs, clients who have achieved and maintained controlled drinking (relative to successful abstainers) have been found to be younger (under 40), have shorter histories of problem drinking (less than 10 years), have fewer symptoms of alcoholism and fewer alcohol-related life problems, be drinking less, be less likely to regard themselves as alcoholics, and have fewer alcoholic relatives (Miller & Joyce, 1979; Popham & Schmidt, 1976; Vogler, Weissbach, & Comptom, 1977). Interestingly, the list of discriminating factors is nearly identical when controlled drinkers versus abstainers are differentiated following abstinence-oriented treatment (Armor, Polich, & Stambul, 1978; Levinson, 1977; Orford, 1973; Orford, Oppenheimer, & Edwards, 1976; Polich *et al.,* 1981; Smart, 1978).

In the 4-year Rand follow-up, Polich *et al.* (1981) found an important interaction effect. They contrasted clients who had been alcohol dependent at intake with those who did not show symptoms of dependence, then compared these two groups on outcome status at 18 months versus 4 years. Those who had been alcohol dependent were found to be more likely to relapse (by 4 years) from moderation than from abstinence (at 18 months); that is, abstinence was a more stable outcome for this group. For the nondependent clients, however, the reverse was true. Those who had been abstinent at 18 months were more likely to have relapsed by 4 years than were those who had been drinking moderately; that is, moderation was the more stable outcome for nondependent problem drinkers.

The implications for prevention seem clear. Given that earlier intervention is more effective in general (Miller & Hester, 1980) and that moderation strategies appear to be differentially effective for early stage problem drinkers in particular, these methods would seem to be deserving of further application and investigation in tertiary, secondary, and perhaps primary prevention efforts.

MODERATION AS A SECONDARY PREVENTION STRATEGY

Secondary prevention consists of the early identification of high-risk individuals and of interventions designed to decrease the risk of future problem development. If one differentiates alcoholism (alcohol dependence) from a more general category of problem drinking (alcohol abuse) as is done in the DSM-III (American Psychiatric Association, 1980), then the secondary prevention of alcoholism could consist of intervening at earlier stages of problem drinking to prevent the development of dependence (alcoholism). This is precisely what has been discussed above, and in this sense controlled drinking programs are "preventive" interventions (Alden, 1978).

It would be conceivable, however, to identify potential problem drinkers still earlier, either at the first sign of trouble or even before problems emerge. Certain situations commonly bring the problem drinker to society's attention at early stages, but unfortunately little is done in many cases to identify and treat the person at these points. They would include events such as arrest for drunk driving, emergency room visits (which are often due to alcohol-related incidents), and modest elevations in liver function values or blood alcohol level on routine medical examinations. Further, because we know some of the precursors of alcohol abuse it may be possible to identify individuals at high risk of developing drinking problems years before they begin to do so. Likely candidates would include blood relatives of alcoholics, children with diagnosed hyperkinesis or with a pattern of antisocial behaviors, felons, children or employees with marked performance decrements at school or work, and individuals in high-risk age groups or occupations.

Having identified high-risk individuals, however, what does one do? The most frequent answer has been "alcohol education," but data supporting traditional educational approaches are less than encouraging and even point to detrimental effects in some cases (e.g., Michelson, 1979; Stuart, 1974).

Would specific training in responsible drinking, found to be effective as a tertiary prevention measure, also be beneficial in secondary prevention efforts? To date there have been few applications of moderation methods in secondary prevention, but two such efforts will be examined: controlled drinking training as an early intervention with drinking drivers and as a preventive program in a high-risk population of Native American adolescents.

MODERATION TRAINING FOR DRINKING DRIVERS

Driving while intoxicated (DWI) is a punishable offense in all 50 states and in most other countries, although requisite BAC level for conviction varies considerably, as does the consistency of prosecution. Recent changes in DWI laws of many states have required harsher penalties and have decreased the minimum presumptive BAC level to limits as low as 50 mg% (as compared with prior limits of 100 or even 150 mg%). These minimum presumptive levels, however, understate the actual BAC of individuals *ar-*

rested for DWI. In Albuquerque, for example, although the legal limit has been 100 mg% (.100), the mean BAC of DWI offenders at arrest has been 200 mg%.

There is a general consensus that DWI offenders represent a population with high risk and incidence of problem drinking. Yet many DWI offenders, particularly first offenders, show few signs of alcohol dependence or addiction. Here is a population where potential and early stage problem drinkers can be identified and treated if the court system provides an adequate evaluation, referral, and treatment network combined with the motivational aspects of alternative sentencing.

Several researchers have evaluated the effectiveness of controlled drinking programs for drinking drivers. Lovibond (1975) used a multimodal program to teach controlled drinking to DWI offenders and reported an overall success rate of 85% (59% controlled + 26% improved), as compared with a 12% success rate in a matched group of untreated controls. Miller (1978) found comparable success rates for voluntary self-referred and involuntary court-referred individuals in a moderation training program. Brown (1980) contrasted controlled drinking training with a conventional education program and an untreated control. Only the controlled drinking group showed a reduction in number of days intoxicated at the 12-month follow-up, and although both education groups evidenced a reduction in days of drinking and driving relative to the control group, the controlled drinking group showed a greater reduction than did the conventional education group.

These data are encouraging with regard to the efficacy of controlled drinking as a strategy with DWI offenders. What would be more sensible than a wholesale prescription of BSCT for drinking drivers, however, would be a differential diagnostic screening program that would place DWI offenders into the treatment modality most likely to succeed in each case. Criteria for selecting optimal candidates for moderation have been described earlier, and differential predictors of success in other approaches have been identified in the clinical literature (Miller & Hester, 1980). This matching of individuals with optimal interventions would seem to hold the greatest promise for impact.

TEACHING MODERATION TO NATIVE AMERICAN ADOLESCENTS

Moderation training can also be applied to high-risk populations where a high incidence of alcoholism at a future point would be predicted but where present problem development may be minimal.

Such an application of BSCT in prevention was introduced by Carpenter (1981) who evaluated a program designed to teach controlled drinking skills to 30 Native American students living at a residential high school. The self-control training was conducted by older Native American students working as paraprofessional/peer counselors. Over the course of the training program, significant reductions were observed in frequency and volume of alcohol consumption, BAC levels, and disciplinary infractions among students involved in the program. Modest increases in a psychometric index of self-esteem were also reported. A year follow-up of these students generally supported maintenance of these changes (Lyons, 1981).

MODERATION AS A PRIMARY PREVENTION STRATEGY

In primary prevention programming, an entire population is targeted for intervention without any attempt to identify or focus on high-risk individuals. The hope is that this general intervention will ultimately lower the incidence of the problem in the population.

It is in this area that we have fewest empirical data from which to proceed. The reasons for this are understandable. The full evaluation of a primary prevention effort requires that the individuals under study be followed over the period of time during which the disease or problem would be expected to emerge. In the case of problem drinking this means following people at least through age 30 or 40, and even then many people would be expected to develop drinking problems later in life (Cahalan, 1970). Shorter-term follow-ups may give indications of whether signs of problem development have been changed relative to control populations, but the truest test of primary prevention efforts would be in long-term patterns of alcohol use and abuse.

Consequently we have very little knowledge at present regarding the efficacy or advisability of primary prevention efforts in general or of moderation training in particular. As indicated earlier, the benevolent effects of "preventive" interventions cannot be assumed (Michelson, 1979; Stuart, 1974). Thus the implementation of any intervention aimed at a general population (e.g., school district, church, city) should be appropriately cautious, tempering enthusiasm with a skepticism that waits for at least short-term data to reveal initial beneficial or detrimental changes.

Given this caveat, one could proceed to extrapolate primary prevention interventions based upon BSCT. Encouragement for so doing is to be found in the apparently successful extrapolation of moderation training from tertiary to secondary prevention applications and in the finding that the earlier in problem development one encounters BSCT, the more likely one is to succeed in learning moderate and nonproblematic drinking.

As an example, a module on how to drink moderately could be incorporated into standard alcohol education curricula. Support for this can be found in Brown's (1980) report that the addition of controlled drinking training to conventional education increased its efficacy as a secondary prevention measure.

One such integrated approach was developed at the University of Oregon in the mini-curriculum "The Psychology of Drinking," prepared by Edward Lichtenstein and his colleagues (Muñoz, 1976). Designed for use in the public school system, it consists of 10 50-minute sessions appropriate for inclusion in regular health curricula:

1. Introduction: Alcohol in Our Society
2. What is Alcohol?
3. Short-Term Effects of Alcohol: Intoxication and Hangover
4. Values Clarification About Drinking Decisions
5. Reasons for Drinking
6. Reasons for Not Drinking: Long-Term Risks
7. Controlling Your Drinking
8. Alternatives to Drinking
9. Recognizing and Treating Drinking Problems
10. Final Discussion and Evaluation

This embeds moderate drinking material within several important contexts. Abstinence is legitimized as a responsible choice. Safe and reasonable limits for drinking are discussed in light of the information about short-term (e.g., driving impairment) and long-term (e.g., medical problems) effects of drinking as they relate to volume and pattern of consumption. Drinking is not accepted as a given, but is examined in relation to values about drinking decisions, reasons why people drink, and alternatives to the use of alcohol for coping. Finally information is provided about how to recognize and deal with the signs of a developing drinking problem, so that the limits of moderate and nonproblem drinking are defined. A similar curriculum appropriate for more advanced audiences (e.g., college and professional) has been developed by Miller, Rozynko, and Hamburg (in press).

CONCLUSIONS

Controlled drinking strategies in general and behavioral self-control training in particular have been well supported by research as effective tertiary prevention interventions. These strategies appear to be differentially effective with the early stage problem drinker, who often is unreceptive and unresponsive to traditional treatment approaches emphasizing a disease model and lifelong abstinence. Initial research with secondary prevention applications of moderation training also has produced promising results. Controlled drinking training appears to be effective with DWI offenders and may be useful in other high-risk populations. Primary prevention applications can be extrapolated logically from other research, but these require the verdict of "unproved" until more substantial data become available.

REFERENCES

Alden, L. Evaluation of a preventive self-management programme for problem drinkers. *Canadian Journal of Behavioural Science,* 1978, *10,* 258–263.

American Psychiatric Association. *Diagnostic and statistical manual of mental disorders* (3rd ed.). Washington, D.C.: Author, 1980.

Armor, D. J., Polich, J. M., & Stambul, H. B. *Alcoholism and treatment.* Santa Monica, Calif.: Rand Corporation, 1976.

Armor, D. J., Polich, J. M., & Stambul, H. B. *Alcoholism and treatment.* New York: Wiley, 1978.

Brown, R. A. Conventional education and controlled drinking education courses with convicted drunken drivers. *Behavior Therapy,* 1980, *11,* 632–642.

Buck, K., & Miller, W. R. *Why does bibliotherapy work? A controlled study.* Paper presented at the annual meeting of the Association for Advancement of Behavior Therapy, Toronto, November 1981.

Cahalan, D. *Problem drinkers: A national survey.* San Francisco: Jossey-Bass, 1970.

Carpenter, R. *Native American peer alcohol abuse prevention program.* Unpublished doctoral dissertation, Utah State University, 1981.

Davies, D. L. Normal drinking by recovered alcohol addicts. *Quarterly Journal of Studies on Alcohol,* 1962, *23,* 94–104.

Feldman, D. J., Pattison, E. M., Sobell, L. C., Graham, T., & Sobell, M. B. Outpatient alcohol detoxification: Initial findings on 564 patients. *American Journal of Psychiatry,* 1975, *132,* 407–412.

Hedberg, A. G., & Campbell, L. M. A comparison of four behavioral treatment approaches to alcoholism. *Journal of Behaviour Therapy and Experimental Psychiatry,* 1974, *5,* 251–256.

Jellinek, E. M. *The disease concept of alcoholism.* Highland Park, N.J.: Hillhouse, 1960.

Levinson, T. Controlled drinking in the alcoholic: A search for common features. In J. S. Madden, R. Walker, & W. H. Kenyon (Eds.), *Alcoholism and drug dependence: A multidisciplinary approach.* New York: Plenum Press, 1977.

Lovibond, S. H. Use of behavior modification in the reduction of alcohol-related road accidents. In T. Thompson & W. S. Dockens 3rd. (Eds.), *Applications of behavior modification.* New York: Academic, 1975.

Lovibond, S. H., & Caddy, G. Discriminated aversive control in the moderation of alcoholics' drinking beavior. *Behavior Therapy,* 1970, *1,* 437–444.

Lyons, C. A. *One year follow-up of a Native American peer counseling alcohol abuse prevention project.* Paper presented at the Grand Canyon International Conference on Treatment of Addictive Behaviors, Grand Canyon, November 1981.

Marlatt, G. A., Demming, B., & Reid, J. B. Loss of control drinking in alcoholics: An experimental analogue. *Journal of Abnormal Psychology,* 1973, *81,* 233–241.

Michelson, L. The effectiveness of an alcohol safety school in reducing recidivism of drinking drivers. *Journal of Studies on Alcohol,* 1979, *40,* 1060–1064.

Miller, W. R. Behavioral treatment of problem drinkers: A comparative outcome study of three controlled drinking therapies. *Journal of Consulting and Clinical Psychology,* 1978, *46,* 74–86.

Miller, W. R. Controlled drinking: A history and critical review. *Journal of Studies on Alcohol,* 1983, *44,* 68–83.

Miller, W. R., & Caddy, G. R. Abstinence and controlled drinking in the treatment of problem drinkers. *Journal of Studies on Alcohol,* 1977, *38,* 986–1003.

Miller, W. R., & Hester, R. K. Treating the problem drinker: Modern approaches. In W. R. Miller (Ed.), *The addictive behaviors: Treatment of alcoholism, drug abuse, smoking, and obesity.* Oxford: Pergamon, 1980.

Miller, W. R., & Joyce, M. A. Prediction of abstinence, controlled drinking, and heavy drinking outcomes following behavioral self-control training. *Journal of Consulting and Clinical Psychology,* 1979, *47,* 773–775.

Miller, W. R., & Muñoz, R. F. *How to control your drinking.* (Rev. ed.) Albuquerque, N. M.: University of New Mexico Press, 1982.

Miller, W. R., & Taylor, C. A. Relative effectiveness of bibliotherapy, individual and group self-control training in the treatment of problem drinkers. *Addictive Behaviors,* 1980, *5,* 13–24.

Miller, W. R., Taylor, C. A., & West, J. C. Focused versus broad-spectrum behavior therapy for problem drinkers. *Journal of Consulting and Clinical Psychology,* 1980, *48,* 590–601.

Miller, W. R., Gribskov, C. J., & Mortell, R. L. Effectiveness of a self-control manual for problem drinkers with and without therapist contact. *International Journal of the Addictions,* 1981, *116,* 1247–1252.

Miller, W. R., Rozynko, V., & Hamburg, S. R. *Understanding alcoholism and problem drinking.* Davis, Calif: International Dialogue Press, in press.

Muñoz, R. F. The prevention of problem drinking. In W. R. Miller & R. F. Muñoz, *How to control your drinking.* Englewood Cliffs, N.J.: Prentice-Hall, 1976.

Orford, J. A comparison of alcoholics whose drinking is totally uncontrolled and those whose drinking is mainly controlled. *Behaviour Research and Therapy,* 1973, *11,* 565–576.

Orford, J., Oppenheimer, E., & Edwards, G. Abstinence or control: The outcome for excessive drinkers two years after consultation. *Behavior Research and Therapy,* 1976, *14,* 409–418.

Pattison, E. M., Sobell, M. B., & Sobell, L. C. *Emerging concepts of alcohol dependence.* New York: Springer, 1977.

Polich, J. M., Armor, D. J., & Braiker, H. B. *The course of alcoholism: Four years after treatment.* New York: Wiley, 1981.

Pomerleau, O., Pertschuk, M., Adkins, D., & d'Aquili, E. Treatment for middle income problem drinkers. In P. E. Nathan, G. A. Marlatt, & T. Loberg (Eds.), *Alcoholism: New directions in behavioral research and treatment.* New York: Plenum Press, 1978.

Popham, R. E., & Schmidt, W. Some factors affecting the likelihood of moderate drinking by treated alcoholics. *Journal of Studies on Alcohol,* 1976, *37,* 868–882.

Rachal, J. V., Maisto, S. A., Guess, L. L., & Hubbard, R. L. Alcohol use among adolescents. In National Institute on Alcohol Abuse and Alcoholism, *Alcohol consumption and related problems.* Rockville, Md.: NIAAA, 1981.

Smart, R. G. Characteristics of alcoholics who drink socially after treatment. *Alcoholism: Clinical and Experimental Research,* 1978, *2,* 49–52.

Stuart, R. B. Teaching facts about drugs: Pushing or preventing? *Journal of Educational Psychology,* 1974, *66,* 189–201.

Vogler, R. E., Weissbach, T. A., & Compton, J. V. Learning techniques for alcohol abuse. *Behaviour Research and Therapy,* 1977, *15,* 31–38.

Vogler, R. E., Weissbach, T. A., Compton, J. V., & Martin, G. T. Integrated behavior change techniques for problem drinkers in the community. *Journal of Consulting and Clinical Psychology,* 1977, *45,* 267–279.

11

Alcoholism Prevention in the Workplace
Three Examples

PETER E. NATHAN

WHY PREVENTION IN THE WORKPLACE?

Few readers will question the cost benefits of prevention of alcoholism as compared to its treatment costs. Many, however, might ask why prevention should take place in the workplace. After all, abusive drinking is not a common accompaniment of work (though some employees do drink on the job) and employers are understandably chary of intruding on employees' rights to privacy. In addition, prevention costs money and businesspeople do not part readily with funds that do not contribute directly to production, distribution, or sale of products. Why prevention in the workplace, then?

In theory, prevention of alcoholism at the worksite makes a great deal of sense. In fact, the benefits of prevention in the workplace, as we must acknowledge repeatedly in this paper, remain only prospective; hard data confirming the superiority of prevention in the workplace over other prevention sites are not easy to find (Schramm, 1977, 1980). The presumed advantages of worksite prevention are several, however. They include the clear advantages of working with persons likely to be functioning at adequate vocational, emotional, and interpersonal levels or better (since they

PETER E. NATHAN • Rutgers, The State University, New Brunswick, New Jersey 08903.

are members of the active work force), persons likely to be healthy physically and psychologically, to possess greater financial and familial resources, and to recognize the hazards to life, health, and happiness of a developing alcohol problem. Other reasons for locating prevention programs in the workplace include the existence of a "captive audience," which cannot avoid reading well-placed announcements of programs and activities or listening to enthusiastic co-workers who are participants in the program. Peer enthusiasm—and management support—are particularly facilitative in worksite prevention settings. Of course, the convenience of a worksite program, which does not require the employee to travel a distance to participate in prevention activities, is also an advantage. A final "plus" for these programs is the positive impact on employees' morale of their recognition that their employer is willing to fund a program that is clearly for their benefit.

There are also problems associated with prevention programs in the workplace. Foremost is the issue of confidentality—fear of disclosure—that onsite prevention programs present. The first questions virtually every potential client of an in-house alcoholism prevention (or treatment) program asks are whether any company manager will know he or she has sought help and whether the company will have access to the program's records. Although participation in a prevention program can be assumed to be less significant to both the individual and his or her employer than involvement in treatment, the risk nonetheless exists that many potential participants in a company-based, onsite prevention program will choose not to attend simply because of the threat they attach to their participation in terms of its effect on future opportunities for promotion. Even though steps can be taken to minimize the chilling effect of this concern on participation (some of which are discussed later), the effect nonetheless remains a potent one. An associated problem derives from the confidentiality issue: Being an acknowledged participant in a prevention program could conflict with the "macho" image that many who drink consciously or unconsciously foster.

Many prevention programs in the workplace—like many treatment programs—do not offer services to the families of the employees they serve, making it more difficult for the employee whose spouse or family is part of his or her drinking problem to get the kind of comprehensive help necessary for full effectiveness. In addition, even in companies whose officers wholeheartedly support prevention efforts as cost-effective, humane, or both, some managers and supervisors will believe that prevention programs could interfere with productivity, affect morale, or diminish their authority. These views accordingly affect willingness to permit or encourage employees to take advantage of these programs.

PREVENTION IN THE WORKPLACE: SCOPE AND FOCUS

Attention to alcohol problems in the workplace can take one of several forms. Programs range from those that are exclusively treatment-oriented and focus only on the employee's alcoholism to treatment programs that provide intervention services for familial, interpersonal, and behavioral problems as well as alcohol and drug problems, to programs that provide both treatment and prevention services centering only on alcohol and drug problems, to programs that conceptualize prevention very broadly and foster efforts by essentially healthy individuals to bring about "positive lifestyle change." In other words, a worksite focus on employees' alcohol problems can involve treatment services alone, only prevention efforts, or the two in one program. Programs can also focus exclusively on alcohol and/or drug problems or they can consider those problems along with other behavioral and emotional problems. Decisions on program scope and focus carry clear financial ramifications, of course; the broader the program, the greater its cost.

The three programs described in this chapter differ markedly in the scope and focus of services they provide employees in the workplace.

The most common kind of industrial program is oriented to treatment rather than prevention and is exclusively focused on alcoholism. Euphemistically termed "employee assistance programs" (EAPs), these programs typically employ an alcoholism counselor, often a recovering alcoholic, who announces his or her availability for counseling and referral to the problem drinker or alcoholic via both formal and informal networks. If hospitalization for detoxification or more intensive treatment is called for, the EAP counselor can make that arrangement as well. Few or no prevention services are offered on a formal basis, though the counselor may make alcohol education materials available on request and may provide consultation on prevention if asked. For the most part, however, because most EAP counselors are recovering alcoholics whose sobriety resulted from active involvement in a treatment program, they strive to maximize the reach of the treatment and referral services they provide at the expense of prevention.

The strength of the EAP model lies in the energy and enthusiasm of the recovering alcoholic EAP counselor, who may regard it as his or her mission to reach every alcoholic, admitted or hidden, with the promise of sobriety and the power of the self-help group. A weakness lies in exclusive reliance on a single treatment modality, which cannot be equally viable for all potential clients. Another weakness actually derives from the model's principal source of strength; in his or her missionary zeal, the counselor may "turn off" potential clients by demanding immediate change in consumption pattern from a person who may not be ready for it. In addition, the usual EAP may not enjoy full support from the company's senior managers, who may see in it an overly simplistic approach to but one of their employees' problems.

Many managers have concluded that traditional employee assistance programs, those that focus only on alcoholism detection, referral, and treatment, may not be as effective as programs that extend their purview to a broader range of problems, including familial, vocational and financial, interpersonal, behavioral, and psychological/psychiatric ones. Often, this realization comes when the manager observes that many of the alcohol problems that come to his or her attention are either caused or exacerbated by problems from emotional, behavioral, or familial areas. Yet the traditional EAP counselor is rarely equipped to offer broad-spectrum counseling. When this realization comes, or when a broad-spectrum EAP is planned from the start, both alcoholism counselors and mental health workers are included as staff. Number, kind, and level of staff must be decided at this time. To be decided, as well, is whether staff will be full-time employees of the company or whether an outside firm will be engaged to staff the facility. There are advantages to each alternative. An in-house facility is easier to manage, its costs can be better controlled, company policies will be fully implemented, and the loyalties of the staff are more likely to be to their employer. These advantages notwithstanding, many firms call on outside firms to develop EAPs because in-house programs can never provide the assurances of confidentiality that outside firms can. Because confidentiality is such an important matter to the employee who wishes to confront a drinking, financial, or marital problem, an outside firm may be most effective in mounting an EAP.

Prevention efforts are more likely to be a part of the activities of a broad-spectrum EAP than one that focuses exclusively on employees' alcoholism problems. Parent training groups, stress management programs, or communication enhancement efforts, all of which can be part of a broad-spectrum EAP, frequently turn up persons who are concerned about alcohol problems in others or their own potential to develop them. When that kind of case-finding occurs, the knowledgeable and experienced EAP person can provide individualized prevention services.

Positive life-style change programs, a new prevention model, combine the breadth of broad-spectrum EAPs with an explicitly prevention- (rather than treatment-) oriented activity package. These programs typically seek to interest essentially healthy employees in altering life-style practices that represent health risks, most often cardiovascular ones, at some point later in life. These programs are new because the impact of life-style on health risks has only been demonstrated clearly during the past several years (Davidson

& Davidson, 1980) and because the potential cost-effectiveness of such programs has only recently been recognized (Davidson, 1980). These programs are also, however, more expensive than either traditional or broad-spectrum EAPs and, for that reason, more difficult to justify on a cost basis alone. Because they focus on healthy persons who would not otherwise consider treatment for a "life-style problem," they epitomize prevention. Although most aim to prevent cardiovascular diseases by altering life-style factors that increase those risks, they may also include efforts to prevent development of alcohol abuse, which itself impacts on risk of cardiovascular disease.

Positive life-style change programs make a great deal of sense and hold great promise. They also have the potential, however, to conflict with efforts to treat or prevent alcoholism, drug dependence, and other psychological/psychiatric problems. Their emphasis on reduction of cardiovascular risk factors leads, naturally, to devaluation of other potential problems including those that, like alcoholism, do not relate so directly to cardiovascular fitness and do not present such a ready opportunity for improvement in risk status. Their focus on prevention also may interfere with employees' clear perception of where the life-style change program ends and an EAP that focuses on alcohol begins (the two programs are offered concurrently by some companies).

Prevention of alcohol problems can also take place, of course, in other contexts. Programs designed to teach employees how to care for or deal with potential customers or clients, for example, may include an alcohol education component that serves a preventive as well as educational function for the employee.

Every one of the diverse models for prevention identified above offers significant positives and important negatives to the decision maker who must choose among them. We propose to make this task easier for those readers faced with it by sharing our experiences developing three programs that included an alcoholism prevention component. One, a broad-spectrum employee assistance program currently providing services to 11 federal agencies in Atlanta, focuses on treatment and referral but includes an alcoholism prevention component. The second, a positive life-style change program, is as strongly prevention-oriented as the Atlanta EAP is treatment-oriented. The third program, designed to train a large and diverse group of specialized service workers to deal with heavy-drinking clients, was neither directly treatment-oriented nor particularly prevention-oriented; it had the potential, though, to be either or both, depending on client and employee.

Consideration of the three programs will include, for each, (1) a historical retrospective; (2) focus on the program's prevention aspects and on its relative success or failure, in the context of the major thrust of the program;

and (3) a comparison among the three programs—and with others—of prevention effectiveness, cost-effectiveness, and cost benefit.

A BROAD-SPECTRUM EMPLOYEE ASSISTANCE PROGRAM: THE ATLANTA FEDERAL CONSORTIUM

The federal government has become increasingly aware in recent years of the problems alcoholism, drug dependence, and other behavioral and psychosocial problems cause its employees and their mission. As a consequence, federal agencies in Washington and elsewhere have begun to develop employee assistance programs. Some of these focus exclusively on alcohol and drugs; others, including the one described here, are broad-spectrum programs. (Focus is often a function of the person who organizes and directs the program.)

In late spring 1979, the Atlanta Region of the federal Office of Personnel Management advertised for bids for an EAP to be provided for a consortium of federal agencies in the metropolitan Atlanta area. The agencies were heterogeneous in mission, in staffing, and in size. Ranging from two large agencies, the Center for Disease Control and the Federal Aviation Administration, each with close to 2,000 Atlanta-based employees, many highly skilled and highly trained, to agencies with fewer than 50 employees, most of whom are clerical and secretarial, the agencies presented formidable programmatic problems for the successful bidder. When this diversity was coupled with geographic dispersion throughout metropolitan Atlanta, the novelty of an EAP operated for a consortium of federal agencies, the plethora of rules and regulations governing federal personnel policies, and differences among the agencies in their motivation to join the consortium and their perception of its functions and potential benefits, the several contract bidders had a difficult time outlining programs that showed sufficient promise to merit serious consideration.

The successful bidder was a small New Jersey firm to which I had consulted for two years. Besides myself and two other clinical psychologist colleagues as consultants, the firm offered potential clients its executive director, a masters-level behavioral scientist with extensive experience with EAPs in the military environment, and one other full-time professional employee, a master of social work (MSW) whose principal clinical experience had been as a caseworker in a local community mental health center. The consultants provided treatment and prevention expertise in stress management, alcohol and drug problems, and weight control, as well as in psychosocial treatment from the behavioral perspective conceived more broadly. Notwithstanding limited direct experience in the operation of a civilian employee assistance program, the staff and consultants of this firm also represented a broader array of talents, experience, and background in relevant clinical and managerial skills than could be found among staff of the firms that competed for the award. I have since observed, in fact, that the EAP field is overpopulated with persons who have relatively little formal professional or clinical schooling and whose primary qualification for work in an EAP is either personal or family involvement with alcoholism or drugs, time spent as a lay counselor, and a strong desire to share with others their own personal formula for shedding the burden of the bottle or the needle. Few doctoral-level mental health professionals work in EAPs; fewer stay with them for long. Reasons are varied. They include the stigma associated with having to "market" oneself and one's services, however legitimate they may be, the hassles of working with alcoholic and drug dependent persons, the drawbacks of working within a bureaucracy (in this case, a consortium of bureaucracies), and the comparative facility with which competing activities, including lucrative private psychotherapy practice, offer viable competition.

In part because our proposal was carefully, completely, and thoughtfully written, in part because its authors knew what they were writing about, in part because of the experience of the principals in the consulting group, in part because our proposal showed clear knowledge of the intricacies of the federal personnel management system—but largely because we promised adequate service for the lowest price—our firm was awarded the contract. Services were to begin less than 30 days after the award was announced.

The proposal detailed treatment plans for alcohol and drug problems, family discord, financial problems, job dissatisfaction, the psychological and behavioral consequences of medical conditions, consequences of organizational change, and the usual range of functional psychological, psychiatric, and behavioral problems. Other problems anticipated included legal and familial difficulties and interpersonal problems in the work environment. The proposal was also successful in stressing our understanding of the crucial importance of guarantees of confidentiality for employees.

The program outlined—and followed—offered four elements: training, referral and treatment, prevention, and follow-up. Training was the first task begun as soon as the contract began. It required separate three-hour meetings with each agency's management team to orient them to the program and enlist their support and cooperation and with each agency's training and personnel staff, to enlist their support, explain the program, and agree on their complementary roles in the program; four-hour meetings with groups of each agency's supervisors to enlist their support, explain the program, and train them how to make referrals to the program and the bases on which referrals were to be made (e.g., they were not to function as junior psychologists but, instead, were to be alert to decrements in job performance that might signal personal problems); and one-hour meetings with each agency's workers to explain the program and its guarantees of confidentiality. In addition, an informational packet was sent to each employee, describing the program fully and giving telephone numbers and hours of availability.

Shortly after the orientation meetings began, a local staff was hired and an office established at a central location in Atlanta. Auxiliary offices in the two largest agencies were also provided for. A staff of three persons—an MSW with extensive alcoholism and family therapy experience, a pre-Ph.D. clinical psychologist with considerable family and individual therapy experience, and a secretary—were hired. Later, when it became clear that fewer problem drinkers and alcoholics were coming for help than had been expected, a part-time recovering alcoholic was also engaged. The program itself was straightforward in its services to employees in need of help. A person could call during business hours and arrange to see a counselor almost immediately, either at his or her place of work or, more commonly, at the EAP office away from the worksite. Or the person could call a 24-hour "hotline" outside business hours and speak directly to a counselor (one was always on "hotline" duty). In fact, almost all clients called during business hours; about half of them followed through with a visit to the office. On doing so, they saw a counselor, often for several sessions, until the counselor felt he or she could make an adequate assessment and arrange an appropriate disposition. Disposition might include continuation of counseling by EAP staff if resolution of the problem appeared likely within a few more sessions. If it appeared that resolution would take longer, referral to a carefully chosen public or private treatment resource was arranged and follow-up contacts with that agency were continued as long as the client remained in treatment. Both outpatient and inpatient referral resources had been identified. Most inpatient referrals were for alcoholics in need of detoxification.

The program was funded initially at a rate that was approximately break-even for the consulting firm. Several thousand employees were served at a cost of less than ten dollars per employee per year, a rate of return that covered the costs of leasing suitable office space, purchasing furniture, and hiring necessary staff. Because the program has been in operation less than two years, no data on cost-effectiveness are available. Utilization rates, however, have been very high for some segments of the employee population, surprisingly low for others. On balance, the program seems to have provided a service to one group that had not before been recognized as in need but to have failed to provide suitable service to another group whose need is widely recognized. Specifically, individuals with family and marital problems called and came for counseling and referral at unexpectedly high rates (approximately 2% of the employee pool during the first year); by contrast, and disappointingly, fewer than 1% of the same pool came for alcohol problems, despite our conviction that between 5% and 10% of employees were having problems with alcohol. Reasons for this unexpected first-year outcome are several; the major one may well have been that the first two counselors were not alcoholism oriented and, as a result, spent too much time developing employee awareness of available counseling for other than alcohol problems. The addition of a third counselor, a recovering alcoholic, appears to have altered this balance somewhat. The percentage of alcoholics and problem drinkers coming for treatment, still lower than expected, does appear to be rising. It is possible, however, that the EAP will continue to serve fewer alcoholics than expected, largely because the largest agency served, the FAA, has chosen, understandably, to be quite rigid about drinking on the job and serious drug or alcohol problems that affect job performance. It is likely that many FAA employees have not made use of the EAP for fear of public disclosure of their alcohol problems, despite all efforts to make clear the program's independence from usual governmental reporting requirements.

Much of what goes by the banner of treatment in the Atlanta employee assistance program also serves the purposes of prevention. The very extensive series of orientation sessions to every segment of each agency's work force, for example, clearly served important prevention functions by informing managers, supervisors, and employees of the scope of the problems confronting them and their co-workers and by outlining an approach to solution of those problems. The training/orientation programs for supervisors, designed to enhance supervisory skills but also to teach supervisors how to make referrals for service and when to do so (as early and effectively as possible), also met important prevention goals.

More explicitly prevention-oriented were a series of activities that began shortly after the training sessions concluded. These included preparation of articles on a regular basis for publication in each agency's newsletter on the services provided by the EAP, on causes and treatment of alcoholism and the other behavioral disorders dealt with by the program, and on such matters as the demographics and distribution of alcoholism and drug dependence nationally and locally. Articles on related topics were also published in a monthly newsletter distributed by the EAP to all employees as part of its informational and promotional activities. An Alcoholism Prevention Week campaign was also organized, with posters, press releases, and informational brochures prepared and distributed to all employees. EAP staff also arranged poster and booklet displays for each agency, with materials supplied by NIAAA, NIMH, and NIDA. Special materials on early detection and referral and on more effective management skills were supplied to agency newsletters prepared specifically for supervisors and managers. Special mailings to employees at their homes, designed for family consumption, were prepared on alcoholism and drug abuse prevention and education topics. Finally, regular, widely advertised "Brown-Bag Rap Sessions" on alcoholism and mental health topics were held at lunchtime at most of the agencies in the consortium. These proved especially popular, perhaps because they gave employees who might not otherwise have called on the services of the program the opportunity to meet program staff and talk, informally, about substance abuse and mental health issues about which they might be concerned. Most of the individuals who attended these sessions were not themselves currently experiencing a problem but were concerned about a friend or family member and/or wanted to prevent development of a personal problem at a later time.

A COMPREHENSIVE POSITIVE LIFE-STYLE CHANGE PROGRAM: LIVE FOR LIFE

Many forward-looking corporations now offer regular exercise programs and smoking and weight control clinics, in addition to the traditional alcoholism treatment programs incorporated in EAPs, to help their employees deal with life-style problems that have the potential to cause health problems at a later date (e.g., Keir & Lauzon, 1980; Milsum, 1980; Roskies, 1980). These life-style change approaches are typically fragmented and uncoordinated largely because the persons responsible for them are located most often in personnel or medical departments and usually see their primary responsibilities as something very different.

A few firms, however, have given comprehensive positive life-style change programs for their employees sufficiently high priority to fund coordinating teams to organize and administer broadly conceived programs. Justification for the expenditure of substantial funds for these programs include enhanced employee morale, improved productivity, and greater employee loyalty to the corporation, as well as potential cost savings in health insurance and hospitalization costs.

The Live for Life Program sponsored by Johnson & Johnson, the nation's largest health care products company, is one of the largest, best funded, and most effective positive life-style program yet developed, in large part because of the strong support given the program by the company's chief executive officer. The program has been in operation for more than three years and is currently offered to almost 10,000 employees. Plans are in the works gradually to offer the program to all 60,000 Johnson & Johnson employees worldwide. Those now participating in Live for Life live and work in the central New Jersey and eastern Pennsylvania region that is the location of Johnson & Johnson's corporate headquarters.

The staff of the Live for Life program are full-time employees of Johnson & Johnson who report to a corporation vice-president. The staff, which numbers about 10, is supplemented by several consultants from the ranks of academia, including the author of this chapter, and by a larger number of graduate students, most of them studying clinical psychology at Rutgers, who conduct the action groups, described below, which are at the heart of the program.

Live for Life is conceived as the means to make Johnson & Johnson employees the healthiest in the world; that is the explicit aim of the program as envisioned by Johnson & Johnson's chairman, who saw to it that the concept was implemented within his company. The program is predicated on the assumption that daily life-style decisions employees make on exercise, eating, smoking, and stress management have a direct impact on health, the quality of their lives, and their job performance. The program is also based on the conviction that a company-sponsored positive life-style change program, administered and organized by full-time personnel but voluntary and open to all employees, will be utilized sufficiently by employees to lead to significant positive life-style changes that will affect both employee health and quality of life. A promotional piece prepared for Live for Life puts it this way: "Our objectives include *measurable, sustained* life-style improvements among the *greatest number of employees possible* in regular exercise, smoking cessation, weight control, stress management, health knowledge, and awareness of medical intervention programs."

A company whose success has derived both from the quality of its products and finely honed marketing efforts, Johnson & Johnson has imbued Live for Life with both philosophies. Not only must the product— programs to alter life-styles in positive directions—be sustainable and effective, the product also must be marketed successfully to the widest possible potential clientele among employees of the company. Three philosophical positions characterize this marketing stance: (1) The positive approach: Since the Live for Life program competes for the attention of employees in an environment full of powerful alternatives, it must strive to attract participants by emphasizing the positive—the immediate benefits of the program, including better relationships, more energy, greater productivity—rather than the negative—the delayed benefits of avoiding premature death from cardiovascular disorders and cancer. (2) The program's focus on healthy people: Those employees who require medical or professional attention are served by the company's medical department and its employee assistance programs. (3) The program's practicality: Participants learn how to lose weight, stop smoking, manage stress, and start an exercise program; the emphasis is on action.

The core elements of Live for Life, in the sequence with which employees come in contact with them, include the following:

1. Health Screen: Each participating employee's current health and life-style status are evaluated by questionnaire and biometric measurement. Items evaluated include health knowledge, nutrition practices, physical activity, stress management, dental health, blood lipids, blood pressure, body fat, percent above ideal weight, and estimated maximum oxygen uptake.

2. Life-Style Seminar: The employee's current health and life-style status are fed back to him or her, via a confidential life-style profile, at the life-style seminar, that is also designed to promote the Live for Life Program as a means of altering life-style practices that affect current and future health and quality of life negatively.

3. Action Groups: These multi-session education/intervention/prevention programs are professionally led (for the most part, by advanced graduate students in clinical psychology with special interests and training in behavioral medicine) and action oriented. They are designed to teach employees how to alter life-styles and maintain the changes on a permanent basis. Action groups on smoking cessation, weight control, exercise, applied stress management, yoga, personal power, nutrition, and alcohol and drug education are offered.

4. Feedback and Follow-Up: Each employee is provided a quarterly summary of "life-style points" earned during the previous quarter for participation in Live for Life's diverse activities, for life-style improvements, and for fitness achievement. Participants are contacted 1, 3, 6, 9, and 12 months after the end of a life-style improvement program, either by letter or telephone, for information on their progress and reactions to the program.

5. Epidemiological Study: During a two-year period, health and life-style improvements among all employees at four "test" companies, each with an active Live for Life program, will be contrasted with health and life-style changes among employees at four Johnson & Johnson companies that have not yet begun their Live for Life programs. Unique among similar epidemiologic studies in terms both of goals and comprehensiveness, the Live for Life epidemiologic study will yield important data on both the overall effectiveness of the program in altering life-styles and changing medical utilization

patterns and the determinants of participation in a positive life-style change program. Results attained at the end of the first year of the survey indicate trends in improvement in physical activity, smoking prevalence, reduction in cigarettes, reduction in ideal weight, improvement in maximum oxygen consumption, and positive change in employee attitudes toward health and the goals of Live for Life.

The Live for Life program in 1981 differs in interesting ways from the program that began in 1978. (I have worked with the program from its start as principal behavioral sciences consultant.) At its beginning in 1978, the general view among those responsible for Live for Life was that it should be almost entirely volunteer organized and run, with few professionals and administrators involved and the major responsibility for the success or failure of the program on volunteers at each site who would organize and manage their company's program themselves. Despite some doubts about whether this plan would work—whether very busy Johnson & Johnson employees would find the time to run a complex positive life-style change operation along with demanding full-time jobs—the plan was implemented. A year's test, however, indicated that the volunteer concept generally was impractical and that ultimate responsibility for administering the program ought to be in the hands of an on-site coordinator hired and trained by Live for Life and that the action groups ought to be led by paid professionals who had the expertise to do so.

Another difference in the current program from the original plan relates to its alcoholism/alcohol problems component. Original planning for Live for Life envisioned an alcohol problems action group that would involve both an intervention mode (for those whose drinking had already caused them concern) and a prevention component (for those with an interest in alcohol problems, perhaps alcoholism in their families, but no pressing individual concerns about alcoholism themselves). When this plan was reviewed by a representative of one of the corporation's employee assistance programs (some of the Johnson & Johnson companies have EAPs, others do not), it was strongly attacked on "turf" issues. EAPs provide treatment for alcoholism. Live for Life could offer prevention services. It could not provide treatment. Hence, the action group on alcohol was changed to an alcohol education program; as such, it is only marginally interesting to most of the participants in Live for Life. Unfortunately, the EAP at the site of the Live for Life program in question also appears only marginally effective, largely because it is so strongly AA-oriented and so condemnatory of other approaches to prevention and treatment that many more less serious alcohol abusers in that company choose to go elsewhere for help with their alcohol problems.

Efforts at prevention of alcohol problems in Live for Life do not consist only of the occasional action group on alcohol that is adequately subscribed. Posters, informational pamphlets, speakers, and alcohol and drug education programs are regularly programmed, as are materials and speakers on weight control, smoking cessation, stress management, and exercise. Unfortunately, the effects of this prevention effort cannot be viewed in isolation since the epidemiologic survey will provide data on the overall effectiveness of the Live for Life program, not on its separate elements. Since reasons for hospitalization (one possible index of serious alcohol problems) are not separately analyzed either before initiation of Live for Life or during it, the separate contributions of alcohol problems to the corporation's employee health care costs (estimated at over $2,000 per employee in a recent year) will not be known.

A TRAINING PROGRAM IN THE MANAGEMENT OF THE INTOXICATED PATRON: THE NEW JERSEY CASINO CONTROL COMMISSION PROJECT

Following the repeal of Prohibition in the United States in 1933, control of alcoholic beverages was invested in the individual states. Most state legislatures have since provided for civil or criminal penalties or both to purveyors of alcoholic beverages who knowingly serve alcohol to intoxicated patrons. New Jersey purveyors who continue to serve alcohol to patrons when they "knew or should have known" that these patrons were "actually or apparently intoxicated" are subject to license revocation, fine, and other criminal penalties. Civil damages may also be levied if intoxicated patrons served illegally cause subsequent property damage or personal injury either to themselves or to other persons.

The legal terms *knew or should have known* and *actually or apparently intoxicated* assume that bartenders, waitresses or waiters, and private hosts can reliably distinguish intoxicated from nonintoxicated patrons and that they will do so in order to avoid legal penalties and preserve their livelihoods. Our own research suggests, however, that it is difficult for untrained persons reliably to distinguish among sober persons, those who are only moderately intoxicated, and those who are legally intoxicated (Nathan & Langenbucher, 1982; Langenbucher, Nathan, Hay, & Wainer, 1982).

Sellers and servers of alcoholic beverages in New Jersey, as in many other states, are caught in a double bind between the economic need to provide service to patrons and the legal responsibility to deny service to intoxicated persons. The problem may be greater in New Jersey than in most other states, moreover, in view of the large quantities of alcohol served by the casino hotels of Atlantic City. All casinos, for example, serve free drinks on request to patrons of their gaming tables. Many of these patrons, on leaving the casinos at their 4:00 A.M. or 6:00 A.M. closings, must drive long distances to their homes in the dark of the night, thereby exposing themselves and the casinos to legal sanctions if accidents occur. Some estimates are that over half of all persons at the gaming tables in the early hours of the morning are legally intoxicated—at or beyond 100 mg% in New Jersey.

Following discussions with representatives of the New Jersey State Casino Control Commission initiated by the commission, two colleagues and I developed a training program for Casino Control Commission inspectors (who are responsible for ensuring that the casinos observe all commission regulations) and casino employees, including cocktail waitresses, food and beverage supervisors, floor persons, pit bosses, and casino and hotel security people. Groups of between 16 and 24 persons, usually including Casino Control Commission inspectors and the employees of several casinos, attended the three-hour training sessions we developed.

The sessions were designed around a multi-media format. They began, typically, with a presentation by a Casino Control Commission attorney on the enabling legislation that makes the casinos responsible to the New Jersey State Casino Control Commission for their beverage licenses, governs the serving of alcoholic beverages, and sets civil and criminal penalties for providing alcoholic beverages to intoxicated persons. A representative of the State Division of Alcoholism then spoke briefly on legislation affecting public policy toward alcohol abuse. This legislation, the State Alcoholic Treatment and Rehabilitation Act (ATRA), recognized alcoholism as a treatable disorder rather than a moral depravity, committed public and private resources to the identification, treatment, and prevention of alcohol abuse, and repealed existing laws defining alcohol abuse as a legal offense. The significance of this legislation so far as treatment of intoxicated or aggressive patrons was also discussed. Participants were freely encouraged to engage speakers in discussion of practical issues raised by these brief presentations.

Participants were then asked to complete an 11-item alcohol/alcoholism knowledge quiz designed to reveal gaps in knowledge about alcohol and alcoholism, to motivate the filling of these gaps, and to encourage discussion of alcohol's drug and behavioral effects, the time-course of intoxication and methods of sobering up, legal limits on intoxication, and the epidemiology of drinking and of alcoholism. Following discussion of the quiz, an in-depth alcohol information presentation, complete with audiovisual aids and handouts took place. The physical and psychological effects of intoxication and alcoholism, factors responsible for these effects, and etiologic research on alcoholism received special attention.

Participants then viewed a videotape made at our laboratory that is designed to illustrate the range of common behavioral cues to intoxication. A young man and a young woman were portrayed sober, after they had achieved moderate blood alcohol levels (approximately 50 mg%) and at peak blood alcohol levels (over 100 mg%). Standard tests for intoxication were demonstrated, as were changes in speech pattern, articulation, and content associated with intoxication. At its conclusion, the tape was discussed and parallels were drawn between participants' experience with intoxicated patrons and the behavior of the subjects of the tape.

After a break, participants and seminar leaders role-played typical casino scenarios. They generally involved drunken, stuporous, angry, or aggressive patrons who demanded more drinks and wanted to continue their gaming, or retribution for a real or imagined theft, error, or insult at the hands of a dealer, waitress, or fellow patron. Stress was placed on the importance of ceasing to serve intoxicated patrons earlier rather than later in this sequence and on ways to handle drunken patrons in order to minimize disruption at the table and aggravation to the patron. Participants joined in the role-playing with enthusiasm. Particularly valuable to participants was the chance to observe more experienced casino personnel dealing more effectively with (role-played) troublesome patrons. The role-played scenarios completed the seminar.

The entire seminar can be viewed as prevention since it involved presentation and discussion of alcohol and alcoholism-related material to persons who were, for the most part, not alcoholics but who had the potential to develop an alcohol problem themselves and worked with persons who had such potential. However, certain components of the program almost certainly carried forward prevention more effectively than others. These likely included consideration of etiologic issues, of the physiology and psychology of addiction, and of the behavioral differences between the intoxicated nonalcoholic and the intoxicated alcoholic, material that would inform participants of their own potential problems with alcohol or of problems within their family or circle of co-workers. More important than the direct effect of the seminar on its participants from the prevention standpoint, however, was the indirect effect of an educational program that carried the imprimatur of the Casino Control Commission on employees of the commission and of the casinos. Alcoholism and drug dependence among employees are rarely mentioned as problems by managers of the casinos, in part because they are already subjected to considerable state regulation and wish to avoid more; in part because of understandable reluctance to confront a difficult, unpleasant, and costly problem; and in part because of ignorance about the costs of these conditions to them and to their employees. Hence, development of a program reaching large numbers of casino employees was bound to alert several layers of casino employees and managers to a problem among not only patrons, but also among co-workers, employees, and managers. Several participants in the program spontaneously alluded to the training program's sensitizing effect. In the absence of harder data, the belief that intoxicated patrons were being handled more effectively by casino personnel and that employees were talking among themselves about alcoholism sustained us in this endeavor.

ALCOHOLISM PREVENTION FOR INDUSTRY: AN ASSESSMENT

None of the three programs described above was established specifically to prevent alcoholism. And, in fact, none did so directly. All accomplished their prevention activities indirectly and discreetly, with varying effectiveness. Is this roundabout approach to prevention an accurate reflection of these efforts in industry or have I simply described three atypical programs, ones with which I happen to have worked?

I know of virtually no prevention programs in the workplace that focus exclusively—or even largely—on prevention activities. Instead, programs that are strongly alcoholism treatment oriented—as are conventional employee assistance programs—may offer public alcohol education opportunities on occasion; their major commitments, however, remain to treatment, not prevention. Broad-spectrum employee assistance programs, such as the Atlanta Consortium, somehow find it easier to expend a portion of their energies on alcoholism prevention, though their treatment purview extends beyond alcoholism to the full range of personal, vocational, and financial problems typically fostered by our society. Part of the reason for this concern is a generally broader view of mission. Instead of seeing themselves as running only an alcoholism treatment program, staff at the Atlanta Consortium feel responsibility for whatever interferes with the federal employees' ability to function effectively. Accordingly, their interest in prevention—prevention of alcoholism and prevention of interpersonal, behavioral, and psychological dysfunctions—comes more naturally. In addition, access to employees more interested in participating in prevention activities is made easier because much less stigma is attached to attending informational meetings of broad-spectrum EAPs than traditional EAPs. Because the traditional EAP has a single mission, everyone involved in any part of its activities identifies himself or herself as a problem drinker or alcoholic. By contrast, those who attend prevention-oriented programs offered by the

Atlanta Consortium may be experiencing family or financial problems—
benign by comparison with alcoholism—or, even better, may simply be
interested in doing something about job-related stress or learning how to be
a better supervisor.

Positive life-style change problems—such as Johnson & Johnson's Live
for Life—seem to offer the best chances for effective alcoholism prevention
in industry. Not only do they lack the stigma attached to involvement in
even a broad-spectrum EAP, but they take a positive, optimistic stance
toward life-style problems and make few value judgments beyond the importance of increasing quality of life and decreasing the risk of future health
problems. Their emphasis on behaviors that are related directly to quality of
life makes prevention more attractive as a concept and elicits more general
enthusiasm from a wider segment of the employee population. The fact that
alcoholism prevention is but one component of a very broad program that is
exclusively prevention oriented, moreover, makes it easier to "sell" persons
on involvement in formal alcoholism prevention efforts. Finally, the commitment of a corporation to a life-style change program usually is greater
than to an EAP, largely because these programs are more expensive and,
hence, require more enlightened management and more effective organization and administration. This being so, one can also expect a more sustained
willingness to expend funds on behalf of the prevention program, a necessary prerequisite to effective prevention.

The promise of the Live for Life effort notwithstanding, it cannot be
denied that alcoholism prevention efforts in the workplace are still modest,
imperfect, and variable in quality. Many or most corporations have moved
no farther than recognition that the alcoholism problems of their employees
may be costing them money; some have progressed a bit farther, to the
point where employee assistance programs of one sort or another have been
funded. But treatment, despite its problems, still seems far more cost-
effective than prevention to most managers. In other words, to this time,
industry has failed to recognize the dollars and cents value of alcoholism
prevention; as a consequence, when prevention efforts are undertaken,
they are usually a small, ineffective afterthought grafted onto a treatment
program. It is clear that data on the cost-effectiveness of prevention *per se*
are essential before hardheaded managers will heed appeals to heighten
efforts at prevention of alcoholism.

Compounding the problem of effective "marketing" of prevention
programs is the question of the optimal medium for conveying the prevention message. Conventional means—including booklets, informational
packets, public lectures, and demonstrations—can be provided as easily
outside as within the industrial setting. What is unique to the workplace is
the opportunity it provides to build employee commitment and enthusiasm

for a program that will heighten the program's appeal and increase its "market penetration." Such programs as Live for Life, which incorporate low-key alcoholism prevention messages in a comprehensive program that is exclusively prevention oriented and presented positively and with great corporate enthusiasm, would seem to hold the greatest promise because they represent a total prevention package that proclaims the imminence of an improved quality of life, rather than the uncertain benefits, simply, of an alcohol-free future.

If the medium is the message in prevention as in so many other aspects of our lives, the process by which the prevention message is conveyed is fully as important as the content of that message. We believe the message benefits from incorporation in programs that are largely or exclusively prevention oriented, rather than largely treatment oriented, because of the optimism and enthusiasm the former generate and the relative ease with which interest among employees can be elicited. But if a treatment program is the only one available for delivery of the prevention message, we recommend comprehensive treatment programs rather than traditional, exclusively alcoholism-focused employee assistance programs, which reach only persons whose alcohol problems have progressed far beyond the point where prevention has any meaning.

REFERENCES

Davidson, P. Evaluating lifestyle change programs. In P. O. Davidson & S. M. Davidson (Eds.), *Behavioral medicine: Changing health lifestyles.* New York: Brunner/Mazel, 1980.

Davidson, P. O., & Davidson, S. M. (Eds.). *Behavioral medicine: Changing health lifestyles.* New York: Brunner/Mazel, 1980.

Keir, S., & Lauzon, R. Physical activity in a healthy lifestyle. In P. O. Davidson & S. M. Davidson (Eds.), *Behavioral medicine: Changing health lifestyles.* New York: Brunner/Mazel, 1980.

Langenbucher, J., Nathan, P. E., Hay, W. M., & Wainer, D. *Police officers' determination of inebriety.* Unpublished manuscript, Rutgers, The State University, 1982.

Milsum, J. H. Lifestyle changes for the whole person: Stimulation through health hazard appraisal. In P. O. Davidson & S. M. Davidson (Eds.), *Behavioral medicine: Changing health lifestyles.* New York: Brunner/Mazel, 1980.

Nathan, P. E. & Langenbucher, J. *Are dramshop act penalties draconian?* Unpublished manuscript, Rutgers, The State University, 1982.

Roskies, E. Considerations in developing a treatment program for the coronary-prone (Type A) behavior pattern. In P. O. Davidson & S. M. Davidson (Eds.), *Behavioral medicine: Changing health lifestyles.* New York: Brunner/Mazel, 1980.

Schramm, C. J. (Ed.). *Alcoholism and its treatment in industry.* Baltimore: Johns Hopkins University Press, 1977.

Schramm, C. J. Evaluating industrial alcoholism programs: A human-capital approach. *Journal of Studies on Alcohol,* 1980, *41,* 702–713.

12

A Guided Decision-Making Program for Elementary School Students
A *Field Experiment in Alcohol Education*

RONALD P. SCHLEGEL, STEPHEN R. MANSKE, AND
ANDREA PAGE

INTRODUCTION

The illicit use of beverage alcohol by adolescents has long been acknowledged as the primary drug problem among young people (Braucht, Brakarsh, Follingstad, & Berry, 1973; Wechsler & Thum, 1973). One report (U.S. Department of Health, Education, & Welfare, 1974) found that 7% of seventh grade students drank beer at least once a week, while 42% drank weekly by Grade 12. An Addiction Research Foundation of Ontario survey in 1974 found that alcohol use among Grade 7 students in a major metropolitan area had increased to 51.1% from the 1968 level of 22.9% (Smart & Fejer, 1974). Among a representative sample of 4,734 students in Ontario in 1979, alcohol use in the past year among Grade 7 students was reported

RONALD P. SCHLEGEL, STEPHEN R. MANSKE, and ANDREA PAGE • University of Waterloo, Waterloo, Ontario, Canada. The research reported in this study was supported by Grant No. 1213–5–17 from Non-Medical Use of Drugs Directorate, Health and Welfare Canada.

by 57% (Smart, Goodstadt, Sheppard, & LeBain, 1980). An in-depth study of a smaller sample representative of Ontario revealed 24% of 15- to 17-year-olds have had at least one symptom of dependent drinking (Smart, Blair, & Brown, 1978). Another study (Ennis, 1978) found that 23% of auto collisions among students 16 to 18 years of age involved alcohol despite alcohol use being illegal below age 18. Sixty percent of this same sample had driven a car within an hour of consuming two drinks and 20% had done so 10 or more times. Since alcohol use is increasingly prevalent by the eighth grade and significant problem drinking appears to occur soon thereafter, Grade 8 students would be an appropriate age group to target for alcohol intervention programs.

Considering the accessibility and acceptability of alcohol in today's society, what is a realistic goal for alcohol intervention programs? Social realities point toward the establishment of moderate or controlled alcohol use by the majority of people. Primary prevention of problem drinking therefore can be viewed in at least three ways. One aspect focuses on abstinence. It is not expected that a majority of young adolescents will adopt abstinence as their choice of drinking behavior but it is important that they recognize it as one alternative. A second aspect pertains to delaying the age of drinking onset. This is important since problem drinking is more likely to occur for persons starting to drink earlier in life (Rosenberg, 1969; Terris, 1975). A third aspect involves the prevention of abusive drinking among those already initiated. Given the increased prevalence of alcohol use by young adolescents, it is not surprising to discover a corresponding increase in problem behaviors associated with alcohol use (Ennis, 1978; Smart, 1980). Therefore it would appear worthwhile to target all aspects of primary prevention in this critical period of drinking initiation and experimentation. In cases where problem drinking has already developed, alcohol intervention programs even for young adolescents need to be viewed as secondary preventive efforts as well, that is, attempts to "modify for the better, a disorder, process or problem at the earliest possible moment" (World Health Organization, 1979).

In response to the problem of alcohol use and abuse in young adolescents, a multitude of interventions has evolved (Milgram, 1980). It is not surprising that the school system is the setting for a majority of these programs. Alcohol education programs in the schools vary widely in their theoretical basis, content, and pedagogical approach, and ultimately in their effectiveness. Some are based on sound psychological and educational principles while others are "trendy," often with little underlying theoretical justification. Some typical program approaches include information giving, small group encounters stressing a clarification of values, peer counseling by adolescents, experiential approaches (which give field experience to the students) and various combinations of these approaches (Seliske, 1977).

There has been particular widespread usage of two types of program methodology in alcohol education. Information giving or facts exposure is by far the most popular of the educational approaches (Milgram, 1980). This approach has been presented in a number of different forms. The use of sensationalism, distortions, and exaggerations have represented alcohol education programs at their worst. At their best, programs based on truthfulness and frankness provide factual information derived from scientific evidence regarding physiology, pharmacology, psychology, sociology, and legality of alcohol use. Facts can be presented didactically in a lecture-type format or with the use of persuasive techniques. The coercive imposition of particular attitudinal positions, however, may result in a reaction that is in the opposite direction intended by the instructor (Schlegel & Norris, 1980).

A discovery learning approach can also be used to increase factual knowledge regarding alcohol. In this method the students seek out information on alcohol use and become actively involved in the learning process. It is felt that facts that are discovered by one's self have a greater impact on learning than those presented in a more passive lecture environment. A review (Goodstadt, 1974) of the research literature on programs using the factual or information-giving approach indicates that significant improvements in knowledge can usually be obtained, but the findings are mixed with respect to attitude and behavior change. Stuart (1974), for instance, found that a 10-week factually or cognitively oriented curriculum increased not only drug knowledge, but also actual (self-reported) use of alcohol, marijuana, and LSD. Conversely, Swisher and Horman (1970) reported the results of their program to be more uniformly positive, especially, with respect to knowledge and attitudes.

The second program approach that has been given widespread usage is values clarification. The popularity of values-oriented educational approaches (Swisher, 1974) has resulted in the use of this technique in alcohol education programs. It stresses values exposition, values clarification, and the achievement of values consonance (Harmon, Kirschenbaum, & Simon, 1973). Active participation within a comfortable setting fosters an examination of personal feelings about alcohol use and abuse. Using a variety of exercises, students learn to identify the role of values in their lives as well as to appreciate values held by others. They can recognize discrepancies between what they value and how they behave and determine ways of resolving these discrepancies in future behavior. The emphasis on values appears to have developed in response to a dissatisfaction with traditional methods of education in their dealings with human behavior (Goodstadt, 1974).

A review of the effectiveness of programs using a values clarification approach is no less confusing than that for the information-giving approach. The Coronado School District Program (Carney, 1972) was an educational program including both cognitive and affective content, the latter concentrating on "values" training especially related to risk taking. The authors concluded that the actual frequency of drug use tended to be less in experimental values classes than in control groups. However, a careful scrutiny of these findings points out many methodological inadequacies of the study as well as some contradictory findings. A study by Swisher and Piniuk (no date) found that a more structured mental health approach was superior at the elementary level whereas values clarification was better for secondary school students. Those students experiencing the values clarification program demonstrated a significant reduction in reported drug use. Again, however, these conclusions were weakened by contradictory statements in presenting the results as well as an ambiguous presentation of the methodology. Therefore, despite the popularity of the values clarification approach, the paucity of evaluation research and ambiguity of reported results have led to confusion as to its effectiveness in drug and alcohol education programs. The relationship between value change and drug-related behavior change requires further clarification.

One of the main problems in the literature on alcohol education is that many programs are very naively conceived, especially with respect to the theoretical relationship of knowledge, attitudes, intentions, and behavior. It is often assumed that the simple giving of facts will not only improve knowledge but also change attitudes. Once changes in knowledge and attitudes have been brought about, it is then further assumed that changes in intentions and behavior will automatically follow. Flay, DiTecco, and Schlegel (1980) have recently reformulated McGuire's classic information-processing model (McGuire, 1972) of general attitude and behavior change as shown in Figure 1. The arrows from one dependent variable to another suggest a causal chain where (1) exposure will lead to awareness, *but only* when the message is attended to; (2) awareness will lead to changes in knowledge, *but only* when the message is comprehended; (3) changes in knowledge will lead to changes in beliefs, *but only* if the arguments or conclusions of the message are accepted or yielded to; (4) changes in beliefs will lead to changes in attitudes (i.e., an affective response), *but only* if this response is based on an underlying set of beliefs where each is weighted by the value placed upon the associated attribute (in relation to an object) or expected outcome (in relation to an action); and (5) changes in attitude *might* (hence the dashed arrows) lead to changes in intentions and ultimately perhaps behavior.

The informational approach in alcohol education is designed to provide facts to the individual regarding alcohol use and abuse. This should increase knowledge regarding the effects of alcohol (in a classroom setting which assumes presentation and exposure) provided students attend to and com-

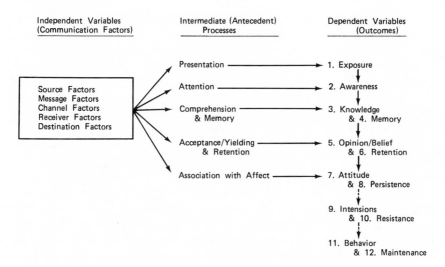

Figure 1. A reconceptualization of McGuire's information-processing model.

prehend the material. According to the model, however, this does not necessarily ensure that belief and attitude change will result. Harmon *et al.* (1973) support these arguments and suggest that although a primarily factual and conceptual approach may lead to increased ability for rational and abstract thought, this capacity does not necessarily enable people to make value decisions.

A belief can be defined as the degree to which one subjectively accepts an association between some object or behavior (e.g., excessive alcohol drinking) and an attribute or consequence (e.g., cirrhosis of the liver). To the extent that these attributes or consequences have either a negative or positive value associated with them, this set of evaluative beliefs generates an affective response (i.e., an attitude) toward some object or action (Fishbein & Ajzen, 1975). The values clarification strategies outlined by Harmon *et al.* (1973) attempt to relate facts and concepts pertaining to alcohol use to the students' own feelings and values. Unlike the informational approach, an evaluative component is added which could be expected to result in an attitudinal impact.

A further presumption of many values programs is that clarification of general values will lead to specific decisions that in turn will result in overt behavior. The model in Figure 1 indicates that changes in attitude *might* lead to changes in intentions and/or behavior. It would seem advisable that a more deliberate and theoretically based effort be made to translate attitudes into actual behavior. Can students be assisted in some systematic manner to make decisions about their intentions and behavior so that these decisions may serve as guidelines for future behavior? A strategy that may satisfy at least in part this requirement has been outlined by Janis and co-workers. Hoyt and Janis (1975) developed a motivational balance sheet procedure whereby a person analyzes the consequences of a decision. The anticipated gains or benefits and the anticipated losses or costs can be exhaustively categorized into four major types of consequences: (1) utilitarian gains or losses to self; (2) utilitarian gains or losses to significant others; (3) self-approval or disapproval; and (4) approval or disapproval from significant others. This procedure has been found helpful to persons adhering to decisions with respect to college choice, career choice, weight reduction, and physical activity (Hoyt & Janis, 1975; Wankel & Thompson, 1976). It is suggested that the mediating process that accounted for the positive effects of the balance sheet procedure seems to have been self-persuasion, whereby subjects became more aware of the facts and values supporting a given course of action.

The decisional balance sheet can be used as a guided decision-making procedure in the area of alcohol use. After the facts have been identified and the values clarified, the individual can then use this information in order to categorize the positive and negative consequences of alcohol use from both the individual and significant others perspectives. This decision-making procedure maps out "a structure for action" which helps to translate facts and values into an actual decision concerning alcohol use. Thus it could be expected that this process would lead to a change in at least intentions to perform the behavior and perhaps even overt behavior itself. At a minimum it is anticipated that the individual develops guidelines for future behavior based upon personal reasoning in terms of facts, beliefs, and values. The possibility of simultaneously using values clarification and more direct behavior change procedures has been recognized previously (Greenberg, 1975), but no attempt has been made to date to implement and evaluate this combined educational method.

The present alcohol education project was proposed to examine the effectiveness of three educational approaches for the prevention of adolescent alcohol use and abuse. The three approaches comprised (1) a primarily factually oriented exposure, (2) a facts exposure plus experience in values clarification, and (3) a facts exposure plus values clarification plus a guided decision-making procedure using the Janis balance sheet technique. A control group was included for comparison purposes. The first two groups were included because of the widespread use of these approaches. It was expected that the facts exposure would affect student knowledge about alcohol use. Further, it was expected that facts exposure combined with values clarification (thereby adding the affective component) would affect student attitudes in addition to the knowledge effects. Finally, it was expected that the addition of a guided decision-making process would affect intentions and actual behavior as well. The third group in the study presents a possible innovative option for future programs in the area of alcohol education and, as noted previously, has already been used successfully in weight control and exercise programs.

DESCRIPTION OF PROGRAMS

A curriculum encompassing seven class periods was developed for each of the educational methods. This curriculum was then offered within the context of the regular ongoing school health education program. Exposure time for each component across treatment conditions was standardized (e.g., same amount of facts to each group). At the same time, overall teacher attention was equalized across conditions by teaching nonalcohol-related "filler" topics from the regular health curriculum when necessary. The three educational approaches and the control group are described in turn.

FACTS ONLY

The facts components totalled approximately three class periods: Week 1 and half of each class in Weeks 3, 4, 5, and 6. The primary purpose of the facts exposure was an explanation of alcohol and its physical and social effects. In the initial class the teacher distributed booklets of newspaper articles on youth and drinking. Following a discussion of the articles and alcohol generally, students generated "research" questions about alcohol. Teachers placed them into predetermined categories common to all groups, including:

1. What is alcohol?
2. The path of alcohol through the body; the organs affected
3. The effect of alcohol on various body organs, especially the brain
4. What would alcohol do if substituted in the diet?
5. Alcoholism and problem drinking
6. Teenage drinking
7. Where to go for help
8. Social drinking; how does alcohol affect social interaction?

Groups of three to five students were formed to select and research one of the topics above as well as specific questions generated by the class. Subsequently, groups made a five-minute presentation, the content and format of which was approved by the teacher prior to class. The groups distributed a one-page summary of their research to each class member. As an index of student involvement all groups were marked based on information presented, thoroughness of research, and effort shown.

Students were provided with guides as to sources from which information could be obtained. These sources included the school library, which we had supplemented with additional books and materials, and various social agencies in the community (e.g., Addiction Research Foundation) dealing with alcohol-related problems. In addition, groups presenting social drinking were directed to carry out mini-research surveys. The first involved watching specific types of television programs and recording on a form provided all instances of alcohol use, references to drinking, and visible signs of drinking. After the programs, students summarized the reasons for drinking during the show. Second, if possible, they were to interview several adults about their reasons for drinking or not drinking alcohol. Results were summarized in their presentation.

Students were instructed to make notes on any questions concerning the presentations. If time was available, questions were allowed during the class. Otherwise, teachers collected the questions for Week 6, which was set aside for a review and summary of the facts learned. Teachers ensured a reasonably uniform exposure to factual information by supplementing presentations as necessary from a guide developed for that purpose.

Facts plus Values Clarification

This condition included all of the procedures and material for the "facts only" approach, plus selected values clarification procedures. The strategies based on values clarification used approximately $2\frac{1}{2}$ class periods beyond the time used for facts exposure during Weeks 2 to 5. The initial emphasis in this approach was aimed at discerning basic values that an individual esteems and then discerning values specific to alcohol.

One week prior to the values clarification class, students were given instructions for an activity diary. Diary entries consisted of type of activities (e.g., eating, school, hockey, TV) and time spent in each activity. After recording for one week, students completed a summary sheet listing the 10 activities done most often and consuming the most time. In the first values class the students generated another list, "10 things in life I love to do," and compared it to "10 things I really do" as reflected by their activity diary. The lists were coded for characteristics that described the activity, such as monetary cost, risk involved, and whether it is performed alone or with others. Students identified the three most important activities on each list.

After completion of this exercise students were instructed to reflect on what they had learned. Are they doing what they want with their lives? What parts can be changed? Students were asked to respect the opinions of others in order to facilitate a personal and honest exchange. Discussion was kept fast paced and continued only as long as general interest was shown.

Teachers followed the discussion by listing seven criteria used in recognizing a value (Harmon *et al.*, 1973). The list included (1) making a choice freely, (2) choosing from among alternatives, (3) choosing after thinking about the good and bad outcomes of each alternative, (4) cherishing or being happy with the choice of values made, (5) being willing to affirm the choice in public, (6) acting on the choice, and (7) acting with consistency. Students were instructed to choose one or more items from their lists and see how closely it came to reflecting a value. It was pointed out that not all entries on the lists meet each of the standards required for a value.

In order to summarize, clarify, and reinforce the day's class activities, students ended this first values exposure by completing "I learned" statements. They were given time to complete one or more of the prepared sentence stems (e.g., I learned that . . . , I discovered that . . . , I was surprised that . . .). Groups of three or four were formed and students were given the opportunity to share one or more of their "I learned" statements. It was stressed that the statements should be personal, not about people in general.

In the second class the teachers reviewed the value criteria using honesty as one example. Students were asked to think of a time when they were not honest and to determine what they were valuing above honesty in the situations. Consequently, they learned that people have conflicting values. This is something to be aware of, but not necessarily worry about, so long as the alternatives have been considered.

This strategy allowed the teacher to introduce alternatives in a particular topic area without appearing to favor any one. It was emphasized that often people do not identify all the alternatives available. She indicated that people have many alternatives to consider for drinking alcohol and, due to individual beliefs and values about alcohol use, each will choose the alternative he or she wants. The teacher drew a long line on the blackboard to represent a drinking/nondrinking continuum. Several factors, including how much and where alcohol is consumed, were used to place drinking alternatives suggested by students along the continuum. Discussion of the consequences of each behavior included good/bad outcomes, long-term/short-term outcomes, and outcomes for self/friends/family/society. Following this discussion students were referred back to their "I learned" statement stems from the first values class. Several minutes were alloted to complete new "I learned" statements resulting from the class activities.

The last class on values clarification was designed to give practice to seeking out alternative behaviors that serve the same functions as drinking alcohol. Students who completed the television survey were asked to contribute a list of reasons for drinking alcohol. These reasons were listed under the four general categories of rebellion, social, physical, and personal. Students then brainstormed possible alternative actions or behaviors for each of the reasons for drinking alcohol. At the end of the day's activities "I learned" statements were completed and volunteers shared their statements with the class.

FACTS PLUS VALUES CLARIFICATION PLUS DECISION-MAKING

This method included all procedures in "facts plus values clarification" as well as a decision-making phase. The decision-making strategies took approximately $1\frac{1}{2}$ class periods beyond the time taken for the facts and values exposure. The purpose of this approach was to facilitate an actual decision regarding alcohol use while considering the alternatives and consequences of this behavior.

In the first class on decision making the teachers introduced the decisional balance sheet procedure (Hoyt & Janis, 1975). This procedure allows students to consider a particular decision by listing the advantages and disadvantages that will result. The balance sheets were kept personal and were to be completed as if one were actually engaged in the behavior. Teachers did not grade the sheets and did not ask to see their contents. Separate decisional balance sheets were completed for three levels of personal alcohol consumption. The class decided on definitions of drinking levels that were similar to the following:

1. Heavy drinking: any drinking over a period of time that causes problems for the drinker and his or her environment
2. Abstaining or nondrinking: may include limited ceremonial drinking (i.e., wine at church, toasting at a wedding)
3. Moderate drinking: any alcohol consumption patterns between nondrinking and heavy drinking

The first balance sheet was completed for heavy drinking. A sheet of paper was divided into four equal sections on each side. At the top left students wrote "Gains to Self" and listed all the personal benefits that could potentially result from their drinking alcohol heavily. Students were encouraged to be frank and honest and keep entries personal. Other sections of the balance sheet were completed in a similar fashion, with headings designated as follows: "Losses to Self," "Gains to Important Others," "Losses to

Important Others," "Approval from Self," "Disapproval from Self," "Approval from Important Others." Example entries in a decisional balance sheet for not drinking alcohol are shown in Figure 2.

Students were instructed to complete a balance sheet as homework before the next health class for each of the other two alternatives, namely nondrinking and moderate drinking.

The last decision-making class focused on the introduction and completion of a self-contract. The teacher explained that a self-contract can be used to confirm a decision that has been thought out carefully in order to help a person act consistently with the decision. In order to arrive at a personal decision, students used their three balance sheets pertaining to nondrinking, moderate drinking, and heavy drinking. After reviewing the respective entries, students were encouraged to make a clear decision based on their perceived consequences (positive and negative) of drinking (at the various levels) in relation to what they had learned about their values and life. For example, a student may have determined that a change was needed in his or her present behavior with respect to the use or nonuse of alcohol. On the other hand, he or she may have simply wanted to confirm a decision already made and being followed. The importance of setting realistic goals that were attainable and likely to be followed was emphasized. Based on these guidelines, students were instructed to complete a self-contract for their own decision concerning the use or nonuse of alcohol. In addition to recording their decision, they also were asked to write down the steps that would be involved in order to implement this decision. The self-contract was dated to terminate at the end of the school year (i.e., about six months later). At that time each student was to open his or her contract and examine it to see how well he or she had done.

After signing the self-contract, students found a partner with similar behavioral intentions for alcohol. Each person read to his or her partner the balance sheet weighing the pros and cons of the particular decision as declared in the self-contract. The purposes of reviewing the balance sheet were to review and add further entries, and secondly, to help students anticipate difficulties they may encounter that could work against their holding to their decision. Partners were to assist further by making suggestions of what to do about problems that might arise. Privacy was respected in this disclosure. Partners were encouraged to act as positive listeners, responding only in a helpful manner. Finally, the pairs brainstormed about alternative behaviors they could engage in instead of using alcohol. These alternative behaviors were to fulfill the same reasons the individual would have for using alcohol.

Plain envelopes were distributed and the self-contracts were placed inside and sealed. Contracts were identified with birth dates instead of

Gains to Self	Losses to Self
-I won't get hangovers - -	-may feel excluded from groups of friends who do drink - -
Gains to Others -the rest of society won't have to pay for problems caused by alcohol (car accidents, hospital) - -	**Losses to Others** -friends who drink won't include me when they are drinking - -
Approval from Self -I am able to save more money - -	**Disapproval from Self** - -
Approval from Others -parents happy that I am obedient - -	**Disapproval from Others** -some friends may think I should drink - -

Figure 2. Example decisional balance sheet for not drinking alcohol.

names as a reassurance of confidentiality. A safe storage place was agreed on by students and teacher and the contracts were kept intact until the end of the school year.

CONTROL GROUP

This group continued to receive regular topics in the health education curriculum minus the alcohol education component. Therefore, while time exposure to the teacher was constant, time spent on the specific topic of alcohol varied across the groups.[1]

EVALUATION STRATEGY TO ASSESS PROGRAM IMPACT

SAMPLE

Three schools participated in the study providing a total of 16 eighth-grade classes. A total of 324 students completed the initial questionnaire prior to the treatment programs. At the same time that parents gave consent for their child's participation in the study, the student countersigned the form with a statement of commitment to participate throughout the entire survey. This procedure has been found helpful in prior research as a means of ensuring a high response rate. Attrition reduced this total to 312 after the 6-month follow-up survey. There were approximately equal numbers of each sex, with a mean age of 13.2 years. All schools came from an urban area where the socioeconomic status (Blishen & McRoberts, 1976) of the students ranged from 34.1% lower, 50.7% middle, to 15.2% upper class. Thus the sample was somewhat skewed toward lower and middle class.

DESIGN

Two of the schools provided 14 classes and the third added two classes that were assigned to the control group. The 14 classes were randomly assigned to the four conditions with the restraint that only two more be designated as control. The design approximated an hierarchical analysis of variance with repeated measures (Myers, 1972) where subjects were nested within classes that in turn were nested in the educational treatment. This hierarchical design allows partitioning of variance due to subject interaction

---

[1]The detailed guides (39 pages) for these various educational curricula are available for others wishing to develop and evaluate similar programs.

within the classroom unit. A fundamental assumption of the hierarchical design is that an individual's score is in part influenced by the social unit of which he or she is a member.

The two main independent variables in the design then were "Educational Method" and "Effects of Educational Methods over Time" (i.e., a repeated measures factor). The repeated testing consisted of questionnaires administered 1 week and 6 months after the program. Prior to delivery of the treatment protocol, measures were also administered to determine if initial differences existed. In order to provide the student with confidentiality, a number code was assigned to each subject for follow-up matching purposes.[2]

PROCEDURES

The four experimental conditions were incorporated into the ongoing Grade 8 health curriculum and were delivered by the regular teacher in health education. Training sessions demonstrating the prepared lesson plans were conducted for the teachers to ensure uniformity of program delivery. Weekly contact with teachers through the duration of the intervention also helped to reduce variability within programs and increase experimental control. A total of four teachers (two male and two female) was involved and every teacher taught each of the different educational interventions. The teacher thus was another independent factor completely crossed with educational method (provided no class effects were significant).

The experimental interventions were incorporated into the regular health education curriculum so that students would be blind with respect to their involvement in an experiment. Minimizing student perceptions of involvement in research was important in order to reduce the following:

1. Demand expectancies that could affect responses on the dependent measures.
2. Hawthorne effects; that is, had an outsider delivered the program instead it no doubt would have been regarded as something special and student interest aroused unnecessarily.
3. Communication between students from different treatment conditions (which would confound the separate treatments).

Since the regular teachers in these schools typically varied their health topics and the manner in which they were taught, our checks indicated that

---

[2]A more detailed description of the methodological procedures and study design can be found in Schlegel (1977).

the different alcohol education approaches for different classes within the same school did not produce any discernible suspicions.

Data collection procedures employed two further techniques to minimize student perceptions of participating in a study on alcohol education. First, data collection was entirely dissociated from program delivery. Students were asked to complete a "Questionnaire on Health Knowledge and Practices" as part of a longitudinal research project conducted by an ostensibly independent research team.[3] Secondly, the alcohol-specific items were embedded in similar types of questions concerned with nutrition and exercise. It was hoped that these respective precautions would reduce (1) response bias (e.g., not wanting to report illegal behavior to a teacher) and (2) pretest sensitizing or posttest by treatment interactions (Campbell & Stanley, 1963).

Dependent Variables

The dependent variables included knowledge, attitudes, intentions, and behavior. It was considered important that the level of specificity of these variables correspond to the actual content in the educational programs(Schlegel, Crawford, & Sanborn, 1977). That is, three behavioral alternatives regarding alcohol consumption (i.e., abstinence, moderate drinking, heavy drinking) were explicity addressed in both the values clarification and decision-making procedures. It is logical, therefore, that program outcomes be examined specific to these alternative behaviors. The measures included the following:

1. Knowledge about the effects of beer and liquor, assessed by 10 multiple-choice items.
2. Attitudes toward drinking beer and liquor at both moderate and high levels of consumption, as well as towards abstinence. An example semantic differential measure is: Drinking *just enough* beer to feel the effects (without getting drunk) is
    Good __:__:__:__:__:__:__ Bad
    Unpleasant __:__:__:__:__:__:__Pleasant
    Foolish __:__:__:__:__:__:__Wise
    Helpful __:__:__:__:__:__:__Harmful
3. Intentions toward drinking beer and liquor at both moderate and high levels of consumption, as well as towards abstinence. Students

---

[3]Parental consent had been obtained only for the survey part of the overall study and not for their child's participation in the different curricula, as teachers had full legislative discretion over the latter.

were asked, for example, "In the next six months, how likely is it that you will drink *just enough* beer to feel the effects (without getting drunk)?" They rated their intention on a seven-point scale from very unlikely to very likely.

4. Behavior was measured in several ways. Frequency of beer, liquor, and wine consumption at moderate and high levels in the last four weeks was assessed. The reason students had for drinking each of these substance/level combinations was also requested. The average quantity consumed in one sitting in the last four weeks was measured in bottles for beer, drinks or shots (1½ oz.) for liquor, and 4-ounce glasses for wine. Finally, the frequency of negative consequences of alcohol use in the past six months (e.g., My drinking led to me picking a fight for no reason) was assessed.

A secondary dependent variable, normative beliefs, was also included, since the Fishbein behavior prediction model (Fishbein & Ajzen, 1975) includes this factor as a predictor of behavior. The Fishbein model asserts that a person's overt behavior is a function of one's intention to perform the behavior, which in turn can be predicted by one's (1) attitudes and (2) normative beliefs toward the behavior. This model has received extensive theoretical development and empirical testing, and consequently its full measurement was included so that relationships among the dependent variables could be studied within a known theoretical context. Normative beliefs toward drinking beer and liquor at both moderate and high levels of consumption, as well as toward abstinence, were assessed for each of two social referents (best friends and two significant adults). For example: My best friend(s) think I should drink *just enough* beer to feel the effects (without getting drunk).

Strongly   Strongly
agree __:__:__:__:__:__:__disagree

A criticism can be made with respect to assessment of behavior in terms of self-report. Realistically, it must be acknowledged, however, that self-report is essentially the only way to obtain these data.[4] Nonetheless, accuracy of response was a considered factor for establishing the protocol for data collection (i.e., administration of survey independent from school personnel, procedures for confidentiality), as well as embedding the critical measures within a questionnaire with an ostensibly broader purpose. There is no reason in any case (especially given these procedures) to expect differ-

---

[4]Various options can be considered for validating self-report. Of these, the use of confederate reports is not practical for a variety of reasons. Nor is checking alcohol sales a feasible method for this particular age group.

ential reporting bias across the four treatment conditions that, of course, are being compared for their relative effects.

Data Analysis

Data were analyzed as an hierarchical ANOVA design with repeated measures. The first treatment factor, type of educational intervention, consisted of four levels, and there were four classes nested within each treatment. Difference scores were analyzed where the pretest score (T_0) was subtracted from the immediate posttest score (T_1) to reflect short-term changes in the dependent measures. The pretest score was subtracted from the 6-month posttest score (T_2) in order to assess the longer-term impact of the program. Thus, two levels of treatment effects over time were analyzed as a repeated measures factor.

RESULTS

Participants in the study can be characterized in terms of their knowledge, attitudes and normative beliefs, and alcohol use behavior from responses to the initial pretreatment (i.e., T_0) questionnaire. Scores on the knowledge test for alcohol were generally low at pretest. The mean score out of 10 questions was 2.7. Only 16% had 5 or more correct on the alcohol items.[5] In general the affective responses of students reflected attitudes and social norms strongly opposed to alcohol. At T_0 attitudes scores could range from 4 to 28, a lower score reflecting a less favorable attitude. The mean response for drinking beer and liquor to get drunk were 7.5 and 7.1 respectively. Moderate drinking was viewed somewhat less negatively with mean scores of 13.1 and 10.9 for beer and liquor. The normative belief scale ranged from 1 to 7 with a higher score reflecting a more favorable perceived social norm for drinking. Whether drinking beer or liquor at moderate or high levels, the mean response in all cases was less than 2.3 for friends and 1.7 for adults as the social referents respectively.

Reports of behavior at T_0 indicated 27% of students had consumed some form of alcohol in the last four weeks. Drinking to feel the effects was more common than getting drunk, but up to 10% reported getting drunk on one or more types of alcohol. The quantity measures generally reflected moderate drinking. Only 8% of all subjects consumed more than two bottles of beer in an average sitting. Negative consequences resulting from

[5]Students fared better on the exercise and nutrition scores with 46% of students scoring better than 50%.

alcohol use were reported as occurring 296 times in the past six months (some students had more than one consequence occur more than once). Hangovers and sickness were most often mentioned (16% or 50 subjects), followed by mental anguish and conflict (7% or 23 subjects), and overt aggressive behavior (6% or 20 subjects). Drinking occurred most frequently with friends, although drinking alone was admitted in eight cases. The five most frequently reported reasons for drinking were taste, feels good, for fun, special occasion, and to be part of the crowd.

Table 1 shows a comparison of changes in alcohol knowledge following the three educational interventions. An analysis of variance indicated a significant difference ($p < .05$) existed between the treatment conditions with the largest increase in knowledge occurring in the facts group. Newman-Keuls post hoc analyses (all post hoc testing in this report used this procedure) indicated it was significantly different from the control condition ($p < .01$). Although no other differences between groups were significant, there was a trend for the values and decision-making groups to also have larger knowledge increases than the control group. Although not shown in Table 1, further knowledge improvements occurred over the follow-up 6-month period ($p < .01$).

Table 1.
A Comparison of Changes in Alcohol Knowledge and Attitudes Following Three Educational Interventions

| | | Means for educational interventions | | |
Variable	Control (77)[a]	Facts (59)	Values (81)	Decision making (79)
Knowledge	.51[b]	1.27	1.20	1.04[e]
Attitudes				
Abstaining	1.38	−.03	.64	1.33
Drinking beer to feel effects	1.11	.88	−.98	1.19[d]
Drinking beer to get drunk	.82	.42	−.22	.49
Drinking liquor to feel effects	.37	1.36	−.40	1.00[c]
Drinking liquor to get drunk	1.24	.42	−.37	−.03[d]

[a]Sample sizes vary slightly for analyses on the different variables.
[b]Scores reflect the change from pretreatment values.
[c]Significant Time × Treatment interaction ($p < .05$).
[d]$p < .10$.
[e]$p < .05$.

Table 1 also shows a comparison of changes in attitudes following the three educational interventions. Although no measures tapping the affective dimension (i.e., attitudes toward alcohol) exhibited main effects for educational methods at the generally accepted significance level of alpha = .05, an overall pattern and some specific trends were apparent. The overall pattern shows that the values clarification group became more negative in their attitudes toward drinking alcohol. On the more specific level, trends ($p < .10$) were found for the variables "attitude toward drinking beer to feel the effects" and "attitude toward drinking liquor to get drunk." For the first case, the values group changed to a more negative attitude as compared to the other groups which became more positive. In the second case, both the values and decision-making groups differed especially from the control group by becoming more negative in their attitudes. A third affective variable, "attitude toward drinking liquor to feel the effects," also showed significance—a method by time interaction ($p < .05$). The interaction could be accounted for again by the values group where post hoc tests indicated that this group differed significantly from each other group at the 6-month follow-up ($p < .05$). Not infrequently the values procedure group actually increased in its impact on attitude change over time. In summary, the values clarification intervention did affect attitudes as was predicted, although these effects were not strong from a strict statistical significance viewpoint. The decision-making group, however, did not show a similar impact even though they had also received the same values clarification intervention.

The most dramatic results from the study occurred with respect to actual behavior change. Table 2 reports both the marginal means (reflecting the overall effect across both the immediate posttest and the 6-month follow-up) as well as the cell means where one can directly observe the immediate behavioral change as compared to follow-up impact. Students in the facts group exhibited a consistent pattern of reduced alcohol use as compared to the other groups. Not only did the facts group drink less immediately after the alcohol education intervention, but also this effect generally persisted in the 6-month follow-up point. Results are reported in Table 2 for those variables where the effects were significant for either the educational or time conditions. The facts group less frequently drank liquor to feel the effects ($p < .01$), liquor to get drunk ($p < .10$), and wine to get drunk ($p < .10$). These students also consumed a lower quantity of beer ($p < .05$) and liquor ($p < .05$) per occasion. The variables not shown in Table 2, while nonsignificant, showed an entirely consistent pattern with that reported. That is, the facts group showed a reduced frequency of drinking beer to get drunk and a reduced quantity level of wine per drinking occasion. In summary, the facts group tended to drink less frequently

Table 2.
A Comparison of Changes in Alcohol Use Following Three Educational Interventions

		Means for educational intervention			
Variable	Control (78)[a]	Facts (60)	Values (75)	Decision making (75)	Time effects
Frequency of drinking					
Beer to feel effects					
T_1-T_0	-1.27[b]	-2.21	.19	$-$ .99	-1.07
T_2-T_0	.21	$-$ .25	.28	1.48	.43[f]
$\overline{X}$	$-$ .53	-1.23	.24	.25	
Liquor to feel effects					
T_1-T_0	.72	-2.33	-1.19	1.10	$-$ .42
T_2-T_0	.67	-1.78	$-$ 05	2.04	.22[c]
$\overline{X}$	.69	-2.05	$-$ .62	1.57[e]	
Liquor to get drunk					
T_1-T_0	1.01	$-$ .64	.01	$-$ .18	.05
T_2-T_0	.99	-2.63	.91	1.11	.10
$\overline{X}$	1.00	-1.63	.46	.46[c]	
Wine to feel effects					
T_1-T_0	$-$ .01	-1.98	.09	$-$ .12	$-$ .50
T_2-T_0	.26	.01	1.86	.17	.58[e]
$\overline{X}$	.13	$-$ .99	.98	.02	
Wine to get drunk					
T_1-T_0	$-$ .68	-1.94	$-$ .19	$-$ .12	$-$ .74
T_2-T_0	$-$ .62	-1.72	.26	$-$ .01	$-$ .52
$\overline{X}$	$-$ .65	-1.83	.03	$-$ .06[c]	
Quantity					
Bottles of beer					
T_1-T_0	.40	$-$ .39	$-$ .02	.08	.02
T_2-T_0	.40	.02	.18	.41	.25[e]
$\overline{X}$	.40	$-$ .19	.08	.24[d]	
Drinks of liquor					
T_1-T_0	$-$ .12	$-$ .54	$-$ .25	.08	$-$ .21
T_2-T_0	.05	$-$ .29	.45	.33	.13[e]
$\overline{X}$	$-$ .04	$-$ .41	.09	.20[d]	
Total quantity– frequency (average grams absolute alcohol/person/ day)					
T_1-T_0	.07	-1.14	$-$ .13	$-$ .20	$-$ .35
T_2-T_0	$-$ .16	-1.14	$-$ .15	$-$ .04	$-$ .37
$\overline{X}$	$-$ .05	-1.14	$-$ .14	$-$ .12[f]	

[a]Sample sizes vary slightly for analyses on the different variables.
[b]Scores reflect the change from pretreatment values.
[c]$p < .10$.
[d]$p < .05$.
[e]$p < .01$.
[f]$p < .001$.

and with reduced quantity as compared to the other two treatment groups as well as the control group. In no instances did the values clarification or decision-making groups differ significantly from the control group.

This general behavioral result can be illustrated further by creating a quantity–frequency index that assesses the group's average total daily intake of alcohol in terms of grams of absolute alcohol per person per day. The facts group showed the lowest daily intake of alcohol ($p < .001$) whereas none of the other groups differed significantly from each other. These results are quite surprising in terms of our initial predictions in that the facts group was expected to affect knowledge only. The decision-making group was expected to affect behavior but this group did not differ significantly from the (no intervention) control group. The particular effects of the facts group are even more dramatic given that impact endured for the full six-month follow-up; that is, the facts group drank at below pretreatment baseline levels for all six frequency measures and two out of three quantity measures still at the 6-month point.

Also of interest in Table 2 are the analyses of the main effects for time. The various programs appear to have caused in general an initial depressing effect for behavior measures at the immediate follow-up as compared to pretreatment. However, six months later the trend is reversed. For example, students report drinking beer to feel the effects 1.07 times less often per month immediately after the alcohol education intervention as compared to before. After six months, however, they have increased frequency of consumption beyond pretreatment levels by .043 times per month ($p < .001$). In general, Table 2 indicates that alcohol consumption increased over the 6-month period.

Normative belief measures and behavioral intentions demonstrated a pattern consistent with the time changes for behavior. Table 3 reveals that normative beliefs of friends to drink alcohol were perceived as being more favorable at T_2 than at T_1. Immediately after the educational program all groups revealed favorable normative beliefs concerning not drinking. At T_2, this trend was reversed. All groups reflected a change by the students to believe their friends to be more negative about not drinking ($p < .05$). In conjunction with this, normative beliefs for friends became more favorable over time toward drinking beer and liquor at both moderate (i.e., to feel the effects) and high (i.e., to get drunk) levels. This increasingly favorable perceived social environment for drinking was restricted to peers as none of the normative beliefs pertaining to parents were significant. Thus the results for normative beliefs provide both convergent and divergent validity for the influence of one's social environment as it pertains primarily to peers. Table 3 also indicates a pattern of increased intentions over time to drink alcohol, with this effect being most pronounced for liquor both to feel

Table 3.
Changes in Normative Beliefs and Behavioral Intentions across Time

Variable	Time means[a]	
	T_1	T_2
Normative beliefs of		
Friends to abstain	.38	−.09[c]
Friends to drink beer to feel the effects	.31	.51[b]
Friends to get drunk on beer	.09	.29[b]
Friends to drink liquor to feel the effects	−.05	.34[e]
Friends to get drunk on liquor	.00	.23[c]
Adults to abstain	.23	.05
Adults to drink beer to feel the effects	.11	.24
Adults to get drunk on beer	.19	.22
Adults to drink liquor to feel the effects	.17	.09
Adults to get drunk on liquor	.12	.14
Behavioral intentions to		
Abstain from alcohol	−.36	−.27
Drink beer to feel effects	.20	.39
Drink beer to get drunk	.02	.24[b]
Drink liquor to feel effects	.03	.36[c]
Drink liquor to get drunk	.07	.40[d]

[a] Scores reflect the change from pretreatment values.
[b] $p < .10$.
[c] $p < .05$.
[d] $p < .01$.
[e] $p < .001$.

the effects and to get drunk. This pattern coincides rather closely with that for perceived peer norms and thus suggests that this aspect of the adolescent's social environment is crucially related to decisions in the realm of drinking behavior. In contrast to normative beliefs, none of the five personal attitude measures showed any changes across time and instead remained rather stable (except for the values clarification group as noted earlier).

DISCUSSION

The various alcohol education programs in the present study were designed to differentially affect alcohol knowledge, attitudes, and behavior. The three treatment groups did not differ substantively in the type and amount of alcohol facts that they received and thus were expected to show approximately equal improvements in knowledge scores. This expectation was generally upheld with all groups reflecting increased knowledge levels from pretreatment. The control group, as expected, showed the least knowledge improvement. Although the groups providing factual information did improve knowledge, it must be acknowledged that the gains were not large. At pretest students scored only 2.7 correct responses out of 10 questions, and this improved only by approximately one additional correct response at immediate posttest. Of course our posttest was not a classical examination situation for which students would have deliberately studied; rather, knowledge was assessed as part of an ostensibly independent research study by personnel and an organization (i.e., Health & Welfare Canada) not especially associated with these schools in general or these classrooms (and teachers) in particular. In any event, the ability to improve alcohol knowledge is not a unique finding. A review of the current literature (Goodstadt, 1974) reveals that this is one component that most programs are able to affect.

Of further interest is the increase in knowledge over time. This may reflect a general increase in awareness of alcohol as a result of personal or peer consumption of alcohol among 13-year-olds. Alternatively, it may be simply a result of repeated testing, that is, improved responses on the follow-up resulted from a greater familiarity with test items.

Attitudes appeared relatively more resistant to change. The value clarification group did demonstrate a modest, although consistent, pattern of inducing a negative attitudinal shift. Further, it was quite unexpected to observe in several instances evidence of further impact over the 6-month follow-up period. These results stand in distinct contrast to the typical decay effects found in the persuasion literature (Cialdini, Levy, Herman, Kozlowski, & Petty, 1976; Cook & Flay, 1978).

Although the values group showed the expected knowledge and attitudinal effects, the decision-making group demonstrated only knowledge changes. These results are surprising since the latter group received the identical values clarification curriculum as did the values group. Thus it had been expected that the decision-making group would reflect a similar effect on attitudes. The guided decision-making strategies appear to have cancelled out (in some unexplainable way) the values clarification strategies and their effects in the affective realm. A lesson to be learned from this result is that components within a program may interact to produce effects that cannot be predicted from the singular effects of each constituent component. It cannot be safely assumed, therefore, that the addition or deletion of a further element will produce any simple and straightforward effect. The combining of two or more "good" components may not produce the desired positive results. Educators thus must be aware of the potential interacting effects of various elements within a given curriculum. Furthermore, program evaluators need to assess the specific impact of a complete curriculum as defined by all its elements. Schlegel, d'Avernas, and Best (1979) had previously noted this point for the area of smoking cessation and argued that "the treatment package should be defined as a curriculum that is treated as a single independent variable. . . . Because the elements of the treatment programs interact and thus cannot be isolated . . . the independent variable should be conceptualized as a 'curriculum' rather than a series of separate elements or independent variables" (p. 26).

With regard to behavioral results, our initial arguments held that a more systematic and theoretically based effort was needed to translate knowledge and attitudes into overt behavior. Thus a balance sheet procedure developed by Janis (Hoyt & Janis, 1975) was adapted as a guided decision-making strategy in order to develop "a structure for action" whereby one's facts and values could be translated into an actual decision concerning alcohol use. It was predicted that the decision-making group would show effects for behavioral intentions and possibly overt behavior itself. It was somewhat unanticipated that actual behavior would be so strongly influenced. However, most surprising was the finding that the "facts only" group demonstrated the most favorable results on every single behavior (and intentions) measure. It was the only group to consistently decrease intentions and consumption of alcohol immediately subsequent to the educational program. At 6-month follow-up, the facts group also retained its advantage over the other educational methods.

The decision-making group did not show any significant differences as compared to the control group except for one variable "proportion of new drinkers." Table 4 shows that the groups differed significantly ($p < .05$) in terms of proportion of new drinkers. The marginal means for time effects indicate that in general the prevalence of drinking increased among the eighth grade students over the six-month period ($p < .05$). However, the most dramatic increase occurred for the decision-making groups. It reported 41% who started drinking after the beginning of the educational program (to the six-month point) as compared to 13% in the facts group, again the lowest group with respect to alcohol involvement. The control group also showed a substantially lower percentage of new drinkers (23%) as compared to the decision-making group. In essence, then, the decision-making group demonstrated a counterproductive effect, given that our program objectives were to delay the onset of drinking and to prevent the abuse of alcohol among individuals already drinking.

As these results were unexpected, the behavioral intentions variables were further examined since they reflect volitional choices or decisions to perform a behavior. The facts group again exhibited a consistent pattern where behavioral intentions coincided with that seen in the behavioral measures. For instance, analyses for the variable "intentions to drink beer to get

Table 4.

A Comparison in Proportion of New Drinkers Following Three Educational Interventions

Variable	Control (83)	Facts (60)	Values (77)	Decision making (79)	Time effects
			Means for educational intervention		
T_1-T_0	.17[a]	.13	.15	.26	.18
T_2-T_0	.23	.13	.21	.41	.24[b]
$\overline{X}$	.20	.13	.18	.34[b]	

[a] Scores reflect the change from pretreatment values.
[b] $p < .05$.

drunk" indicated the groups differed significantly ($p < .05$) with the facts group demonstrating more negative intentions (relative to the pretreatment baseline) at both T_1 and T_2. In contrast, all other groups held more positive intentions relative to their pretreatment levels with these intentions becoming increasingly more positive at the 6-month follow-up. A finding of particular interest pertains to their intentions to abstain from alcohol. Again the groups differed significantly ($p < .05$) and, most interestingly, the decision-making group held the most negative intentions with respect to abstaining. That is, the guided decision-making procedure appears to have had the effect of precipitating a volitional choice *not to abstain*. This decision then seems to have been translated into actual behavior as reflected by the increased incidence of new drinking. It would appear that the decision-making group "guided" students to make a decision to begin drinking. Recall that students employed the Janis balance sheets in order to consider three alternatives with respect to drinking: abstaining, moderate drinking, and heavy drinking. Students were then instructed to choose from these alternatives. (The teacher did not endorse nor promote any particular one.) This procedure obviously had the effect of precipitating decisions in the direction of beginning to drink.

From the behavioral intentions data, it is apparent that the facts group can be viewed de facto as a decision-making group as well. That is, it made volitional choices (i.e., their intentions) to drink less often. The pedagogy of this group involved a discovery learning method whereby students generated their own questions about alcohol and then actively proceeded to research answers from a variety of sources. During the process of reading library materials, visiting alcohol-related social agencies, analyzing television programs for drinking, interviewing adults about their drinking, and so forth, students obviously were formulating personal decisions either to not drink at all or to do so with reduced frequency. It also should be noted that students were not forced with this educational procedure to make a decision from a range of alternatives. This may have had two results; first, they may simply have reaffirmed their current status vis-à-vis drinking (which for most at that time was nondrinking), and second, they were not faced as explicitly with the choice to drink including its positive consequence (and perhaps thereby making it more attractive to try drinking).

As a further way of interpreting the possible dynamics that occurred in the facts group, correlations between behavioral intentions (BI) and behavior (B) were completed for the control and facts groups separately. It was thought that if students had made a rational decision to perform a given behavior, then one should observe greater consistency between stated intentions and actual behavior. Consequently correlations were computed for four BI–B sets of variables within each treatment condition, these variables being (1) drinking beer to feel the effects, (2) drinking beer to get drunk, (3) drinking liquor to feel the effects, and (4) drinking liquor to get drunk. For the control group, the average BI–B correlation at T_0 was .49, at T_1 .43, and at T_2 .46. Thus the correlations across data waves remained quite constant. For the facts group, the average BI–B correlation at T_0 was .49, at T_1 .69, and at T_2 .69. There existed a clear pattern of increased consistency between intentions and actual behavior subsequent to the educational intervention. A further correlation was done within each group where intentions at T_1 were correlated with behavior six months later (i.e., T_2). This correlation was .29 for the control group as compared to .49 for the facts group, again demonstrating greater consistency within the latter. These correlations provide further plausibility to the interpretation that the facts group actually experienced a curriculum in which students made rational decisions about their drinking behavior. This intervention could thus be viewed as a decision-making procedure that would appear more appropriate for this target age group.

Although it seems that "forcing" 13-year-olds to make a decision concerning alcohol use from a range of alternatives can precipitate earlier onset of drinking, further analyses indicated that the decision-making group was drinking in a more controlled manner. Additional hierarchical ANOVAs were completed using only drinkers in the analyses. As dependent variables, analyses involved the various frequency and quantity measures for beer, liquor, and wine, as well as the overall quantity–frequency index and a measure of negative consequences. Although few effects were significant, results, especially at T_1 indicated a consistent overall pattern for the decision-making group to be drinking alcohol less problematically. Students in the decision-making group reported getting drunk on beer an average of

1.5 times per 4-week period as compared to students in the control condition who reported 4.1 times per 4-week period. The pattern was similar for the variable getting drunk on liquor (1.3 times versus 4.0 times). The decision-making group also reported only about one-half the number of negative consequences as the controls. Although more students started drinking in the decision-making group, these supplementary analyses suggest that they were drinking more responsibly.

It would be remiss, however, to pretend lack of concern for the results pertaining to the decision-making group. It did induce early onset of alcohol use by some students. The concern for early drinking was outlined in the introduction as being one indicator of future problematic drinking behavior. This finding presents serious limitations for using decision-making procedures with this age-level population.

Goodstadt, Sheppard, Crawford, Cook, McCready, and Leonard (1979) conducted an alcohol education program for Grade 9 students in an attempt to evaluate the same three components as the present study. The three treatment methods (information/cognitive, values clarification, and decision-making) were presented separately, however, rather than in combination. The study found significant improvement in knowledge and intentions for the "facts" group at both immediate posttest and 6-month follow-up, effects that were greater than those for the other experimental or control groups. Also, as with our study, they found no significant effects on attitudes. With respect to behavior, they found at the 6-month follow-up that the groups were ordered in terms of lowest to highest frequency of alcohol use as follows: control, decision-making, facts, and values clarification. The control group differed significantly from the values group, and, values was the only group to significantly increase its frequency from pretest to 6-month follow-up. Thus, their results also displayed boomerang as did our study, except that this result pertained to the values clarification rather than decision-making group.

A more detailed review of the values clarification procedures used by Goodstadt *et al.* indicated that students completed a self-contract regarding a behavior they wished to change. Students were to identify achievable goals, complete step-by-step planning, and specify a time limit. They were also to share the contents of the contract with another student. This procedure is very similar to that used as part of the decision-making protocol in our study. The self-contract demands that a decision be made and the specific details of how the decision is to be translated into actual behavior and carefully outlined. It may be speculated, therefore, that this was one of the critical elements common to both studies that induced adolescents to begin drinking.

In general, their predictions for the decision-making group with respect to behavioral effects were not met either. The nature and purpose of the decision-making skills program were described as follows:

> Students will be provided with a model of decision-making which will include exposure to elements involved in arriving at a decision. Through the use of decision-making exercises, knowledge of facts, social influence and behavioral options will be considered and demonstrated as elements in decision-making. Decision-making components will be considered individually, but, more importantly, their interdependence and influence on decision outcomes will be stressed. Within the process of decision-making, students will be exposed to information regarding alcohol. The information will be integrated into the process rather than being dealt with separately. At least one of the exercises will be based on decision-making and the use of alcohol. (Goodstadt *et al.*, 1979, p. 5)

Essentially, students used a problem-solving approach in which a problem was identified, alternative solutions were generated, and the consequences of each alternative were projected in terms of short- and long-term outcomes as these may pertain to both self and others. This procedure is not unlike the Janis decisional balance sheet. However, their application of the model was more general in nature and less specific to an actual personal decision as we had operationalized it. They applied the model to student problems in general which were not necessarily in the realm of alcohol. In the one case where the model was applied specifically to alcohol, it pertained to an adult faced with a decision about whether to accept an offer for a drink. Goodstadt *et al.* (1979) commented that students were unaccustomed to the nondidactic teaching style and were, therefore, unable to assimilate the program content.

From the experience and results obtained in our study, as well as those from Goodstadt and others, one can suggest some implications for future programming in the alcohol education area. One area that would warrant more attention in alcohol curricula is the role of social pressure and influence. Results of the present study indicate a definite need to deal with the effects of social influence. Table 3 showed that the perceived social environment vis-à-vis alcohol use became significantly more positive over the 6-month follow-up period, with these changes being delimited principally to the peer group. The increased (peer) normative beliefs were matched by increased intentions to consume alcohol and consumption of alcohol over the six months. This parallel change, together with the lack of attitude change over time, suggests that behavior change was mediated by normative beliefs rather than personal attitudes. The Fishbein model for behavior prediction can be used to determine the actual role of normative beliefs relative to attitudes in determining intentions and behavior. Stepwise regression analyses were computed within each treatment group respectively for each of T_0, T_1, and T_2 data points. Four criterion variables were predicted for each group at each particular data point—drink beer to feel the effects, drink beer to get drunk, drink liquor to feel the effects, and drink liquor to get drunk. Results of these analyses indicated that attitudes and normative beliefs were selected first in the stepwise regressions an equal number of times at the T_0 and T_1 data points. In contrast, normative beliefs were selected first for 15 out of 16 regressions at the T_2 data point, thereby confirming the increased role of social influence as the primary determinant of intentions and behavior. In all 15 cases, normative beliefs pertaining to peers rather than adults were selected.[6] It would appear, therefore, that programs of prevention in alcohol use and abuse should incorporate more carefully defined strategies for dealing with the role of social influence. Social influence "inoculation" techniques have been evaluated experimentally for smoking initiation in adolescents and have been found to reduce the incidence of new smoking by about one-half (Evans, Rozelle, Maxwell, Ralnes, Dill, Guthrie, Henderson, & Hill, 1981; Hurd, Johnson, Pechacek, Bast, Jacobs, & Luepker, 1980; McAlister, Perry, & Maccoby, 1979). These programs attempt to provide skills for coping with peer pressure to smoke by using techniques such as modeling using students of similar age (as shown on videotape), personal role-playing, covert rehearsal of counterarguing, guided practice, and positive reinforcement. The present study did not incorporate such direct techniques for dealing with peer influence and thus, quite predictably, no program effects with respect to normative beliefs were observed.

Another implication for future programming concerns the notion of sequencing a set of strategies from Grade 8 (and perhaps earlier) through Grade 12 in which each strategy is targeted to the appropriate developmental level of the student. The present study suggests that the decision-making procedure (as we had operationalized it at least) was premature and not appropriate for the Grade 8 student. It would appear that a facts/informational type of intervention is more appropriately suited to this level student, possibly because it is less abstract in nature and thus less complex for them to assimilate.

This method is also more likely to accept the students' present position vis-à-vis alcohol use (which most often is nonuse for this age group) rather than forcing him or her to evaluate and choose from other possibilities that the student may not yet have explicitly considered at this stage. This method required also that students become actively involved in a discovery learning process and this may have contributed to the observed persistence of the behavioral change. In Grades 9 and 10, when many students begin to

---

[6]The multiple Rs, when intentions were regressed on attitudes and normative beliefs were .57, .67, .60, and .64 for the control, facts, values, and decision-making groups respectively as averaged across 12 analyses in each group.

drink alcohol anyhow, the present guided decision-making procedures may be more suitable. These procedures require the student to explicitly examine various drinking options with respect to their reasons and consequences and then to make a conscious choice. Although many students no doubt will make the choice to drink at this time, this more conscious and deliberate decision may result in more responsible drinking (i.e., with fewer problem consequences). This may be contrasted with an essentially de facto drinking "decision" that results from social pressure from one's peers where more problem-oriented drinking could be the normative expectation. Thus, social inoculation techniques may also be appropriate at this age level in order to counter peer influence. This strategy would be expected to shift the relative weights in the Fishbein model from the normative to the attitudinal component. When students begin to drink then, it should be more for their own personal reasons than due to peer influence. Having shifted the locus of the decision from the social to the personal realm, the decisional balance sheet technique can then be useful to assist the student to make a more rational decision as well as to adhere to that decision (Hoyt & Janis, 1975).

Having effected the appropriate behavior, specific techniques can subsequently be deployed to facilitate attitude and value change consonant with either abstinence or moderate alcohol consumption in order to maintain that behavior over the longer term. Values clarification thus can be introduced at Grades 11 and 12 since the level of abstraction required by these techniques is more appropriate to the cognitive development of students at this age. Values clarification does not seem appropriate at an earlier stage (e.g., Grade 9) where Goodstadt *et al.,* (1979) found counterproductive effects for behavior. Another technique that may be useful is Rokeach's values self-confrontation (Rokeach, 1973, 1979) where he outlines some techniques to shift values in a direction consistent with one's desired self-concept vis-à-vis a given social role (e.g., being a nondrinker or moderate drinker). Given that values are more enduring and assuming value-behavior consistency, behavior change should consequently be more persistent and enduring as well. Manske (1980) used the Rokeach model to demonstrate that smoking cessation can be maintained more effectively if nonsmoking-related values can be effected by the self-confrontation technique.

The predominant task in alcohol education today is to assist individuals to make intelligent and rational choices concerning their use of alcohol. Although the decisional balance sheet procedure as used in the present study proved (at best) ineffective for Grade 8 students, the general area of guided decision making does appear to offer promise and deserves further thought and attention. In general, it should not prove especially difficult to improve knowledge levels by any program that includes a factual/informational component. The main challenge will be to systematically influence behavior, consistent with either abstinence or moderate consumption, which persists across time. Having attitudinal and value change consonant with this behavior may have an important role to play with this persistence. It would seem imperative, therefore, that sound theoretical bases be identified for future alcohol education interventions so that the processes of knowledge, attitude, and behavior change may become better understood. It should also be emphasized that program development in the area of guided decision making continue to be subjected to rigorous scientific evaluation.

REFERENCES

Blishen, B., & McRoberts, H. A socioeconomic index for occupations in Canada. *Canadian Review of Sociology and Anthropology,* 1976, *13,* 71–79.

Braucht, G. N., Brakarsh, C., Follingstad, D., & Berry, K. L. Deviant drug use in adolescence: A review of psychosocial correlates. *Psychological Bulletin,* 1973, *79,* 92–106.

Campbell, D. T., & Stanley, J. C. *Experimental and quasi-experimental designs for research.* Chicago: Rand McNally, 1963.

Carney, R. E. *An evaluation of the effect of a values-oriented drug abuse education program using the risk taking attitude questionnaire.* Coronado Unified School District, Coronado, Calif., 1972. (Mimeograph)

Cialdini, R. B., Levy, A., Herman, C. P., Kozlowski, L. T., & Petty, R. E. Elastic shifts of opinion: Determinants of direction and durability. *Journal of Personality and Social Psychology,* 1976, *34,* 663–672.

Cook, T. D., & Flay, B. R. The persistence of experimentally induced attitude change. In L. Berkowitz (Ed.), *Advances in experimental social psychology* (Vol. 11). New York: Academic Press, 1978.

Ennis, P. *Drinking and driving among Ontario students in 1977.* Substudy No. 938, Addiction Research Foundation, Toronto, 1978.

Evans, R. I., Rozelle, R. M., Maxwell, S. E., Raines, B. E., Dill, C. A., Guthrie, T. J., Henderson, A. H., & Hill, P. C. Social modeling films to deter smoking in adolescents: Results of a three year field investigation. *Journal of Applied Psychology,* 1981, *66,* 399–414.

Fishbein, M., & Ajzen, A. *Belief, attitude, intention and behavior: An introduction to theory and research.* Don Mills, Ontario: Addison-Wesley, 1975.

Flay, B. R., DiTecco, D. A., & Schlegel, R. P. Mass media in health promotion: An analysis using an extended information-processing model. *Health Education Quarterly,* 1980, *7,* 127–147.

Goodstadt, M. S. *Research on methods and programs of drug education.* Toronto: Addiction Research Foundation of Ontario, 1974.

Goodstadt, M. S., Sheppard, M., & Crawford, S. H. *Development and evaluation of two alcohol education programs for the Toronto Board of Education.* Toronto: Addiction Research Foundation, Substudy 941, 1978.

Goodstadt, M. S., Sheppard, M. A., Crawford, S. H., Cook, G., Mc Cready, J., & Leonard, J. *Alcohol education: A comparison of three alternative approaches.* Toronto: Addiction Research Foundation of Ontario, 1979.

Greenberg, J. S. Behavior modification and values clarification and their research implications. *The Journal of School Health,* 1975, *45,* 91–95.

Harmon, M., Kirschenbaum, H., & Simon, S. B. *Clarifying values through subject matter.* Minneapolis: Winston, 1973.

Hoyt, M. F., & Janis, I. L. Increasing adherence to a stressful decision via a motivational balance-sheet procedure: A field experiment. *Journal of Personality and Social Psychology,* 1975, *31,* 5, 833–839.

Hurd, P. D., Johnson, C. A., Pechacek, T., Bast, L. P., Jacobs, D. R., & Luepker, R. V. Prevention of cigarette smoking in seventh grade students. *Journal of Behavioural Medicine,* 1980, *3,* 15–28.

Manske, S. R. *Rokeach's self-confrontation theory and smoking cessation: The role of self-concept.* Unpublished Masters Thesis, University of Waterloo, 1980.

McAlister, A., Perry, C., & Maccoby, N. Adolescent smoking: Onset and prevention. *Pediatrics,* 1979, *63,* 650–658.

McGuire, W. J. Attitude change: The information processing paradigm. In C. G. McClintock (Ed.), *Experimental social psychology,* New York: Holt, Rinehart, 1972.

Milgram, G. G. A descriptive analysis of alcohol education materials, 1973–1979. *Journal of Studies on Alcohol,* 1980, *41,* 1209–1216.

Myers, J. L. *Fundamentals of experimental design.* (2nd ed.). Boston: Allyn & Bacon, 1972.

Rokeach, M. *The nature of human values.* New York: Free Press, 1973.

Rokeach, M. *Understanding human values.* New York: Free Press, 1979.

Rosenberg, C. M. Young alcoholics. *British Journal of Psychiatry,* 1969, *115,* 181–188.

Schlegel, R. P. Some methodological procedures for the evaluation of educational programs for prevention of adolescent alcohol use and abuse. *Evaluation Quarterly,* 1977, *1,* 657–672.

Schlegel, R. P., Crawford, C. A., & Sanborn, M. D. Correspondence and mediational properties of the Fishbein model: An application of adolescent alcohol use. *Journal of Experimental Social Psychology,* 1977, *13,* 421–430.

Schlegel, R. P., d'Avernas, J., & Best, J. A. *Self-management and smoking cessation: A critical analysis and integrative model.* Health & Welfare Canada, Health Services and Promotion Branch, 1979.

Schlegel, R. P., & Norris, J. E. Effects of attitude change on behavior for highly involving issues: The case of marijuana smoking. *Addictive Behaviors,* 1980, *5,* 113–124.

Seliske, P. *Implications of current research for alcohol and drug related programming in schools.* Report to the Non-Medical Use of Drugs Directorate, University of Waterloo, Waterloo, Ontario, 1977.

Smart, R. G. *The new drinkers: Teenage use and abuse of alcohol* (2nd ed.). Toronto: Addiction Research Foundation of Ontario, 1980.

Smart, R. G., & Fejer, D. *Changes in drug use in Toronto high school students between 1972 and 1974.* Toronto: Addiction Research Foundation, 1974.

Smart, R. G., Blair, N. L., & Brown, G. *Drinking problems and treatment for them among young teenagers: A study of a general sample in Durham region in Ontario.* Substudy No. 999, Toronto: Addiction Research Foundation of Ontario, 1978.

Smart, R. G., Goodstadt, M. S., Sheppard, M. B., & LeBain, M. E. *Alcohol and drug use among Ontario students in 1979 and changes from 1977: Preliminary findings.* Substudy No. 1070, Toronto: Addiction Research Foundation of Ontario, 1980.

Stuart, R. B. Teaching facts about drugs: Pushing or preventing? *Journal of Educational Psychology,* 1974, *66,* 189–201.

Swisher, J. The effectiveness of drug education: Conclusions based on experimental evaluations. In M. Goodstadt (Ed.), *Research methods and programs of drug education.* Toronto: Addiction Research Foundation of Ontario, 1974.

Swisher, J. D., & Horman, R. E. Drug abuse prevention. *Journal of College Student Personnel,* 1970, *11,* 337–341.

Swisher, J. D., & Piniuk, A. J. *An evaluation of Keystone Central School District's Drug Education program.* The Pennsylvania State University. No date. (mimeograph).

Terris, M. Breaking the barriers of prevention: Legislative approaches. *Bulletin of New York Academy of Medicine,* 1975, *51,* 242–257.

United States Department of Health Education and Welfare: National Institute of Alcohol Abuse and Alcoholism. Second Special Report to the U.S. Congress on Alcohol and Health. Washington, D.C.: Government Printing Office, 1974.

Wankel, L. M., & Thompson, C. Motivating people to be physically active: Self-persuasion versus balanced decision-making. *Journal of Applied Social Psychology,* 1976, *7,* 332–340.

Wechsler, H., & Thum, D. Teenage drinking, drug use and social correlates. *Quarterly Journal of Studies on Alcohol,* 1973, *34,* 1220–1227.

World Health Organization. *Prevention of alcohol-related problems: Measures, policies, programs. An international review and evaluation.* Complied by Jay Moser, Division of Mental Health, World Health Organization, Geneva, 1979.

13

Prevention of Drunk Driving

FELIX KLAJNER, LINDA C. SOBELL, AND MARK B. SOBELL

Casualties resulting from drunk driving extract an enormous toll from society. At least 30%, and up to 50%, of highway fatalities are related to excessive drinking (Cimburra, Warren, Bennett, Lucas, & Simpson, 1981; Filkins, Clark, Rosenblatt, Carlson, Kerlan, & Manson, 1970; Perrine, Waller, & Harris, 1971; Transport Canada, 1975; Waller, King, Nielson, & Turkel, 1970; Zylman, 1974), as are 9% to 13% of nonfatal traffic injuries and 5% of property-damage crashes (Borkenstein, Crowther, Shumate, Ziel, & Zylmand, 1964; Farris, Malone, & Lilliefors, 1976). The relatively low proportion of nonfatal and property-damage accidents should not obscure the fact that the actual number of such accidents is staggering. In the United States in 1975 there were an estimated 765,000 property-damage and 120,000 personal-injury accidents involving drivers with blood alcohol concentrations (BACs) of at least 100 mg ethanol/100 ml blood volume (.10%), as compared to 15,200 fatal crashes (Jones & Joscelyn, 1978). Jones and Joscelyn (1978) estimated that if these alcohol-related collisions could have been prevented, a cost savings of approximately 6.5 billion dollars would have resulted. When the composite costs of drunk driving to both individuals and society are considered (e.g., loss of income and property, medical care, legal proceedings, insurance, productivity, disfigurement, trauma, and death), there can be little argument that prevention of drunk

FELIX KLAJNER, LINDA C. SOBELL, and MARK B. SOBELL • Addiction Research Foundation and University of Toronto, 33 Russell Street, Toronto, Canada M5S 2S1.

driving should be a priority for legal and social planners. Yet, the prevention of drunk driving has persistently defied the efforts of highway safety planners, researchers, and clinicians alike, despite a sizeable expenditure of resources.

The two major approaches to the prevention of driving while intoxicated (DWI), primary and secondary prevention, differ in their stated aims and their intended target populations. Technically, *primary prevention* of drunk driving refers to precluding the initial occurrence of *any* drunk driving by an individual who has never engaged in this act, and *secondary prevention* refers to preventing the recurrence of drunk driving episodes by persons who have driven at least one time while legally intoxicated. Unfortunately, definitions and intentions of prevention programs have not been consistent. While the objective of some drunk driving countermeasure programs (e.g., education of juveniles and other not yet licensed drivers) has been primary prevention, more often the intended objective is the prevention of drunk driving offenses (i.e., lowering the incidence of alcohol-related arrests and accidents). Thus, primary prevention, as commonly defined, refers to preventing a first drunk driving arrest while secondary prevention concerns preventing further arrests for once-convicted drinking drivers.

Although it is implicitly assumed that prevention of arrests will be associated with decreased incidence of drunk driving, the assumption may be erroneous. Arrests might decrease simply because of lessened enforcement or better avoidance strategies employed by drunk drivers to escape detection. The definitional confusion related to DWI prevention is so pervasive that, in some cases, it is difficult to determine whether the objective of a program is prevention of drunk driving, prevention of drunk driving arrests, or both. Thus, in the following review our classification of programs by objectives is sometimes arbitrary. Since the bulk of the countermeasure programs are aimed at preventing drunk driving offenses, the reader should assume that unless otherwise noted, this is the intended objective of these programs. Furthermore, it seems self-evident that many of these programs might also have an effect in terms of preventing drunk driving *per se*. Although this chapter focuses on secondary prevention, most of the recent prevention efforts have been oriented toward primary prevention; thus, the primary prevention literature will also be briefly reviewed.

PRIMARY PREVENTION

Primary prevention of drunk driving can be viewed from several perspectives. Although most prevention efforts have focused on reducing drunk driving, some have been focused on making the driving environment safer and less susceptible to the deleterious effects of drunk driving through environmental engineering (e.g., devices that prevent the impaired driver from entering or operating a vehicle and passive restraint systems such as air bags. See Jones & Joscelyn, 1978). Although such environmental engineering is technologically achievable, its use in the near future seems unlikely, as both car manufacturers and the government argue that these devices are too costly.

The most salient primary prevention effort has involved attempts to dissuade people from drunk driving by providing them with information about its legal and personal consequences. Such efforts have been most apparent in deterrence programs sponsored by government agencies involved in the legislation and enforcement of laws and penalties for DWI offenses (e.g., increased police visibility and surveillance, in-field spot checks involving alcohol breath tests for intoxication, direct media campaigns aimed at informing the public of both increased enforcement and legal penalties). A few information campaigns, notably the Lackland project (Barmack & Payne, 1964) and a press campaign in Australia (Australia's Unique Press Campaign, 1974), have also stressed the negative social consequences of DWI.

The effectiveness of disseminating information in reducing drunk driving has not been demonstrated due to either methodological flaws in evaluation research or simply its ineffectiveness (cf. Jones & Joscelyn, 1978). These disheartening findings are related to many factors. For example, if the public is to be convinced of the serious nature of drunk driving, then severe penalties for the offense are needed. However, penalties for DWI are usually low fines, a short license suspension, or, much less commonly, a few days or weeks in jail (cf. Joscelyn & Jones, 1971). In this regard, enforcement is usually weak and sporadic; the probability of being apprehended for drunk driving is low, ranging from 1 in 200 (0.5%; Beitel, Sharp, & Glauz, 1975) to 1 in 2,000 (.05%; Borkenstein, 1975; Marshall, 1974), and police officers are generally not eager to administer roadside breath tests (Borkenstein, 1977; Hurst, 1980). Thus, it should not be surprising that deterrent information campaigns that are not associated with increased DWI enforcement and severe penalties produce little long-term reduction in DWI offenses despite occasional short-term gains (e.g., Noordzij, 1977; Carr, Goldberg, & Farber, 1975; Ross, 1973).

Those programs that have increased enforcement without a concomitant increase in penalties have found that such a strategy does not alter the number of drunk-driving accidents (Department of Transportation, 1975) or even the average driver's perception of "personal" risk of apprehension (Vingilis & Salutin, 1980). However, the increase in DWI arrests needed to demonstrate an effect is astronomical: In a typical American community of one million people, it is estimated that in one year this group will collectively drive legally drunk four million times and be involved in 60 alcohol-related traffic fatalities. A reduction of 66,600 DWI arrests is needed per year just to prevent one fatality. (The present rate is 2,000 arrests per year cf. Borkenstein, 1975; Zylman, 1975.) This analysis, however, is simply concerned with increased DWI law enforcement and assumes that penalties do not change. The issue of whether increased enforcement coupled with more severe penalties would produce better results has also been examined and the results are largely negative (e.g., Buikhuisen, 1972; Ross, 1974, 1975; Wilde, 1974). However, even in these cases, the severity of the sanctions (see Organization for Economic Cooperation and Development, 1978) has not approached the punishment meted out for other crimes against person and property; drunk driving seems to be viewed as a "social nuisance" rather than a serious criminal act.

Information and legal-disincentive programs often focus on factors that increase the risk of driving while intoxicated, (e.g., effects of various types of beverages on driving performance; maximum hourly rate of consumption before the legal intoxication level is reached; threats posed to the driver and others by DWI; the role of social pressures in encouraging excess drinking before driving). Although this information is primarily disseminated by the media (newspapers, television, billboards), it has been also provided through driver license examinations; pamphlets given to the general public (e.g., RIDE Program; Vingilis & Salutin, 1980); the use of self-test devices (in bars and at private parties) for determining one's blood alcohol levels (Oates, 1978); and lectures in high school driver education courses. The immediate goals of these programs are to encourage individuals to (1) avoid excessive drinking before driving, (2) use public transportation if excessive drinking is anticipated or has occurred, and (3) resist social pressure to drink if driving is planned. Since this information is generally coupled with information about the legal consequences of DWI, any effects that it may have are conceptually confounded. Although the major impact of these programs has been to increase the public's knowledge about the risks of drinking and driving, change in knowledge has *not* been accompanied by either changes in attitudes toward drunk driving or fewer drunk-driving arrests (see Jones & Joscelyn, 1978). In fact, the effect of a conviction for drunk driving on the attitudes of offenders may actually be negative; some evidence suggests that after people are arrested for DWI they may consider this offense as less serious than does someone who has never been arrested for DWI (Pocock & Landauer, 1980).

Important reasons for and solutions to the dismal effectiveness of DWI primary prevention programs may relate more to the characteristics of drinking drivers than the actual programs themselves. It is well established that individuals with chronic drinking problems are overrepresented in road accidents, DWI arrests, and serious or fatal alcohol-related collisions (e.g., Fine, Scoles, & Mulligan, 1974; Schmidt & Smart, 1959; Waller, 1965; Zelhart, Schurr, & Brown, 1975). Since this is true for first as well as multiple DWI offenders, and since such persons may have a "compulsion" to drink, threats of legal sanctions and educational campaigns would be expected *a priori* to have little, if any, deterrent effect (Fine *et al.*, 1974), at least as regards drinking. A possible solution might be to screen problem drinkers at the time of licensing and at regular intervals thereafter, and to make the issuance of renewal of the driver's license contingent upon participation in treatment when indicated. Although such an approach may prevent some DWI incidents, it would not be a total solution since many (up to 50%) drinking drivers are neither problem drinkers nor alcoholics (e.g., Fine *et al.*, 1974; Zylman, 1975) and many alcoholics are not problem drivers (e.g., Clay, 1972; Filkins *et al.*, 1970). For example, Zelhart (1972) found that *only* those alcoholics described as "unsocialized and aggressive" had high-risk driving records. Other personality characteristics related to drinking and high-risk driving include impulsivity and risk taking (e.g., Clay, 1972; Perrine, 1974; Selzer & Chapman, 1971; Sterling-Smith, 1976). If these factors are important, then primary prevention efforts focusing on the risks of drunk driving would be ineffective. If predictively valid screening instruments existed, then an alternative approach might again include periodic screening. However, it is difficult to envision the development of a fool-proof screening method. It is also questionable, both legally and ethically, whether licenses could be denied based on correlative data suggesting that one person *may* be at greater risk of drunk driving than another.

Age is another characteristic frequently associated with DWI offenses. The risk of an alcohol-related crash or fatality decreases with age and is the greatest for drivers aged 15 to 17, (e.g., Borkenstein *et al.*, 1964; Farris *et al.*, 1976; Warren, 1976). This, of course, is probably related to young drivers' lack of experience with driving in general, driving after drinking in particular, and to a life-style of nocturnal recreational driving (Carlson, 1973; Zylman, 1975). Whatever the explanation, legislation raising the legal driving age as a means of lowering the frequency of alcohol-related accidents is another way of approaching primary prevention (cf. Douglass, 1979). Its utility, however, is rather limited, since the youngest drivers constitute the smallest proportion of drinking drivers involved in crashes, despite their high crash risk *when* impaired (e.g., Borkenstein *et al.*, 1964; Filkins *et al.*, 1970; Perrine *et al.*, 1971). In other words, raising the drinking age would affect only the tip of the iceberg of the drinking driver population.

As stated earlier, most primary prevention programs are aimed at deterring drunk driving by disseminating information about the negative consequences of DWI and risk factors associated with those consequences. An alternative, but largely neglected, approach is to provide reinforcement for low-risk nonimpaired driving behavior. Admittedly, this approach will not be easily implemented. It has been attempted on a limited basis by reducing car insurance premiums for nondrinkers and for drivers with accident-free records although its effectiveness as a primary prevention measure has not yet been empirically evaluated. In any case, the delay between safe driving behavior and the receipt of reinforcement is unlikely to make it optimally effective.

Indirect evidence exists to support the potential effectiveness of a primary prevention program based on reinforcement of safe, nonimpaired driving; specifically, multiple DWI offenders who have lost their driver's license as a result of a DWI conviction have signifiantly better driving records *after* regaining their license as compared to DWI offenders who manage to avoid losing their license (Hagen, McConnell, & Williams, 1980; Hurst, 1980). Hurst (1980) has postulated that loss of one's license could lead to the long-term acquisition of safe and cautious driving behavior in order to avoid detection. This can be contrasted with the lack of a positive effect on subsequent driving behavior as a result of jail incarceration (Homel, 1977).

SECONDARY PREVENTION

As noted earlier, the only distinction between primary and secondary prevention is in terms of their *stated* aims: primary prevention is aimed at preventing the initial occurrence of a DWI arrest, while secondary prevention is aimed at preventing the recurrence of a DWI arrest. In this regard, prevention of the recurrence of drunk driving and its consequences is the focus of this chapter.

Although the development of effective secondary prevention programs for DWI offenders is a worthwhile enterprise, it should be noted that even successful efforts will not solve this problem. Unfortunately, the potential impact of secondary prevention measures is limited, since the majority of DWI offenders in any given year are first offenders. Whether one considers a short evaluation period (2 to $2\frac{1}{2}$ years; Spielman, Knupp, & Holden, 1976; Zelhart & Schurr, 1977) or a person's entire driving career (Whitehead, 1975), recidivism rates for first DWI offenders range from 20% to 25%. Thus, even if a perfectly effective secondary prevention program existed, no more than one-fourth of all subsequent DWI *convic-*

tions would be prevented. Furthermore, assuming that the odds of apprehension for DWI may be as low as 1 in 2,000 (e.g., Borkenstein, 1975), the number of actual DWI *occurrences* prevented would be negligible (cf. Whitehead, 1975).

Effective DWI secondary prevention programs, however, should not be dismissed as inconsequential. They could, in fact, be quite useful in reducing traffic accidents and deaths, as DWI offenders are grossly over-represented in fatal and nonfatal traffic accidents (Filkins *et al.*, 1970; Perrine *et al.*, 1971; Sterling-Smith, 1976; Zylman, 1974), in alcohol-related accidents (e.g., Lacey, Stewart, & Council, 1977), and in moving traffic violations (Maisto, Sobell, Zelhart, Connors, & Cooper, 1979). Repeat offenders also have a markedly higher probability of incurring additional DWI convictions as compared to the probability of a first offense for the general population of drivers (Maisto *et al.*, 1979). Nonetheless, demonstrated effectiveness of these programs has been elusive for two reasons. First, since the DWI recidivism rate is already low, this leaves little room for further reduction. Consequently, only highly effective secondary prevention programs can be expected to significantly decrease recidivism. Second, most programs have suffered from flaws in basic design, conflicting treatment goals, and arbitrary assignment of clients to treatments.

DIFFERING OBJECTIVES OF SECONDARY PREVENTION PROGRAMS

Two basic approaches to secondary prevention can be identified. The first approach involves increasing the magnitude of legal sanctions applied to multiple DWI offenders. It is assumed that punishment will act as a specific deterrent to subsequent DWI violations. The overall goal is to reduce the recidivism rate, as indicated by a decrease in further arrests and convictions. The second approach attempts to change the behavior of DWI offenders through education programs about drinking and driving or by specific treatment strategies aimed at problem drinking or alcoholism. Since most people in education programs are court-referred, the primary goal is the reduction of further DWI offenses (e.g., Ellingstad & Struckman-Johnson, 1978; Malfetti & Simon, 1974; Zelhart, 1973; Poudrier, Mulligan, & Gray, 1975; Preusser, Ulmer, & Adams, 1976). The goal of treatment programs, however, is more ambiguous. Most treatment programs assume that DWI offenders are problem drinkers or alcoholics. The primary goal of these programs (as viewed by the treatment agencies and staff) is to remediate drinking problems and poor social adjustment, with decreased DWI recidivism often being an indirect or less emphasized consequence of treatment (Ellingstad & Struckman-Johnson, 1978).

Nature and Effectiveness of Current Secondary Prevention Programs

There are three types of countermeasures aimed at secondary prevention of drunk driving: legal, educational, and treatment. Although the nature and effectiveness of each will be discussed individually in this section, these measures can be used in combination. Legal countermeasures aim at changing the behavior of DWI offenders through punitive means (e.g., fines, incarceration). Educational programs aim at changing behavior by providing offenders with information about drinking and driving and the potential consequences associated with such behavior. Treatment programs, although primarily designed to ameliorate an offender's drinking problem, if successful will also prevent recidivism (i.e., if people no longer drink or drink in a nonproblem manner, then drunk driving will not occur).

Both educational and treatment countermeasures are regarded by the judicial/legal system as nonpunitive. There has been an increasing trend in Western society toward viewing deviant and illicit behaviors as treatable problems. This shift is apparent in the entire sociological system where "maladjustment" and "rehabilitation" often replace "accountability" and "punishment," and it has had a marked impact on the ways in which we deal with drinking drivers. Specifically, the courts are increasingly viewed as referral systems to channel DWI offenders to appropriate treatment and/or educational programs, rather than as judicial systems to pass judgment and dispense legal sanctions for the DWI offense. This situation may stem from the prevailing attitude on the part of the public and the legal system that the crime of drunk driving is a social nuisance rather than a criminal act.

Legal Countermeasures

Control of drunk driving by means of legal sanctions has two distinct aims: (1) *general deterrence* (primary prevention) of the initial offense in the driving population and (2) *specific deterrence* (secondary prevention) of subsequent offenses by DWI offenders. Effectiveness in meeting the first objective hinges on demonstrating a general reduction in DWI offenses and alcohol-related traffic accidents in the driving population following increased enforcement and/or imposition of severe penalties. As noted earlier, there is little evidence supporting the effectiveness of primary prevention efforts. Demonstrating the effectiveness of the second objective requires a specific reduction of subsequent DWI offenses by previous DWI offenders as a result of a specific prevention strategy.

Although specific legal consequences (penalties) vary considerably, three major types can be identified: monetary fines, jail sentences, and driver's license suspension or revocation. Despite legislation in some states that increases the fine as a function of repeated DWI violations, fines are generally small or nonexistent (Organization for Economic Cooperation and Development, 1978). Also, fines are not related to severity of an accident (Blumenthal & Ross, 1973).

In the United States, jail terms are relatively rare for first offenders, and although mandated for repeat offenders in many states, the average sentence is as low as 10 days (e.g., Joscelyn & Jones, 1971; Spielman *et al.,* 1976). Although two countries (the Netherlands and Sweden) impose jail sentences for many drunk drivers (Farmer, 1973), the maximum terms are three and six months, respectively. Finally, there is little evidence that the severity of fines or jail sentences is related to lower recidivism rates (Homel, 1977; Organization for Economic Cooperation and Development, 1978). This is not surprising given the minimal to nonexistent consequences for offenders and the low recidivism rate against which further reductions are compared.

Of the three major legal sanctions, license suspension or revocation may be by far the most effective. In the United States, the average suspension period for a first DWI conviction is 6 to 10 months (Joscelyn & Jones, 1971); this period increases for subsequent convictions, with the duration usually specified by law rather than being left to judicial discretion. For example, a second and a third DWI violation in California incurrs a 12-month and 36-month suspension, respectively. An interesting and perhaps surprising finding is that DWI offenders who receive license suspensions show better driving records and lower recidivism rates for up to four years after regaining their license as compared to those who receive only fines and jail terms (Hagen *et al.,* 1980; Hagen, Williams, & McConnell, 1979; Homel, 1977). Hurst (1980) argues that this may simply occur because many people continue to drive despite their loss of license, but that they do so safely and cautiously in order to avoid detection and that these safe driving habits appear to persist when licenses are reinstated. It may also be that license loss for a substantial period of time is a more severe punishment than a small fine and/or a very short jail term. For those who do not drive during the suspension period, loss of their license obviously can create serious transportation problems in an automobile-oriented society. On the other hand, loss of license is not effective for everyone or forever. Of those who are charged with the same offense after license suspension, 25% to 50% do so while their licenses are suspended (Zelhart & Schurr, 1975, 1977). Many multiple DWI offenders (up to 60%) have had at least one prior license suspension (Perrine *et al.,* 1971).

Besides the above sanctions, other punishments have either been proposed or used sparingly (cf. Organization for Economic Cooperation and

Development, 1978). Almost all insurance companies raise rates or cancel insurance policies on convicted drunk drivers. However, the effectiveness of this sanction, in terms of DWI recidivism, has not been established by a sound empirical test. The utility of monetary fines is similarly questionable. Other possible countermeasures include periodic interviews and warning letters by the government agencies that regulate the licensing of drivers. The effectiveness of periodic interviews has not been tested, and the effectiveness of warning letters is equivocal in the case of traffic violations and is unknown in the case of DWI violations (Organization for Economic Cooperation and Development, 1978). More drastic sanctions include impounding drunk drivers' cars and requiring convicted drunk drivers to have special licenses or license plates. Such measures may have primary prevention potential in dissuading the general public from drunk driving, but their utility in rehabilitating DWI offenders is questionable. In fact, such measures could easily result in elaborate avoidance strategies, pose legal and ethical problems (should any criminal be made to "go public"?), or even impede the prosecution of DWI cases (see Jones & Joscelyn, 1978).

When legal sanctions for drunk driving are examined, the evidence suggests that, with the exception of license suspension, they are inconsistently enforced, reluctantly applied, and far from optimally effective. However, despite such shortcomings, one undeniable fact persistently emerges: the recidivism rate for first DWI offenders is low (20% to 25%). One plausible reason may be that a simple encounter with the criminal justice system is, for many people, a sufficient deterrent from future violations. An alternative explanation also exists. The enforcement–apprehension system for drunk driving is inefficient and ineffective; the chance that any driver will be caught for DWI more than once is very low, especially in contrast with other crimes (e.g., bank robbery) where the odds of apprehension and punishment are reportedly higher. Unfortunately, this may falsely impart the impression that legal countermeasures are effective as well as obscure the fact that recidivism rates (in terms of further incidents of drunk driving) among convicted DWI offenders are high. In essence, an illusion of effectiveness may be fostered by inadequate law enforcement.

Educational Countermeasures

In recent years, by far the most popular alternative to legal sanctions has been to refer drunk drivers to DWI "schools," a course of action that is based on the assumptions that (1) drunk driving results from a lack of knowledge about the effects of alcohol on driving, the circumstances leading to and the consequences of drunk driving, the actual nature of the individual's drinking habits, and ways of modifying drinking practices to decrease drinking driving and (2) the delivery of such information will increase an individual's knowledge and produce a positive attitude change, which will result in a lower probability of recurrence of drunk driving and, ultimately, in a reduction in alcohol-related traffic accidents. The archetype of DWI schools is the Phoenix DWI program (Stewart & Malfetti, 1970), which has served as the model for hundreds of similar schools throughout North America. In this approach DWI offenders attend a series of two- to three-hour group meetings which include lectures and/or films designed to provide information on the issues mentioned above, discussion of the group members' specific drinking and driving problems, oral and written exercises requiring self-analysis of drinking habits, and assignments of relevant reading material. Although some variation exists among schools with respect to number and spacing of sessions, nature of the didactic material, and extent of personal contact with the instructors, the overall structure has been remarkably similar.

Following the Phoenix program, over 500 DWI schools have been established in various parts of the United States and Canada and many more were created as part of the now defunct Alcohol Safety Action Projects (ASAPs) sponsored by the Department of Transportation (1975) during 1971–73. The ASAPs have processed over 250,000 DWI offenders and have provided most of the evaluation data, while non-ASAPs have yielded few outcome evaluation studies (Organization for Economic Cooperation and Development, 1978). However, evaluation of DWI schools within the ASAP program is complicated by the fact that ASAPs have used additional countermeasures (most notably, increased police enforcement and changes in the judicial processing system) which potentially confound effects of the schools themselves.

Virtually all clients entering the DWI schools are referred by the courts as a condition of probation and/or in exchange for a reduced charge and sentence (cf. Jones & Joscelyn, 1978). Since the primary concern of the legal system is road safety, the ultimate goal of the schools is a reduction of alcohol-related traffic accidents. However, automobile crashes do not occur frequently enough to provide an adequate measure of success and their causes are often undocumented (Organization of Economic Cooperation and Development, 1978; Zylman, 1974). A more popular goal is reduction in alcohol-related driving violations. Although this can be measured in terms of either DWI arrests or convictions, both indices can be problematic. For example, if the educational program is accompanied by an increase in enforcement (as in the ASAPs), the resulting increase in arrests may mask any reduction in drunk driving produced by the school. This problem can be overcome by random assignment to a school or no-treatment group within a given jurisdiction. However, random assignment has met with

considerable opposition from both the legal system and treatment personnel and is the exception rather than the rule (e.g., Ellingstad & Springer,
1976; Malfetti & Simon, 1974; Preusser *et al.,* 1976). Moreover, DWI
convictions may not reflect violations or arrests, since participation in the
program may be accompanied by a reduction of the convicted charge to
reckless driving (e.g., Maisto *et al.,* 1979). Since the frequency of recidivism
for drunk drivers is low, arrest and conviction criteria do not provide adequately sensitive outcome measures, especially if small sample sizes are
used (e.g., Brown, 1980). Finally, many studies do not employ a sufficiently
long follow-up period. Since the average interval between first and second
DWI convictions is about two years, a follow-up period of at least three
years is needed for optimal assessment of recidivism (Maisto *et al.,* 1979).
Unfortunately, many studies fail to use even a two-year period.

Aside from traffic accidents and recidivism, most DWI schools have
two other goals: to increase clients' knowledge and to produce a "positive"
change in attitudes concerning drunk driving. However, merely changing
DWI offenders' knowledge and attitudes is not a sufficient demonstration
of overall success; changes in alcohol-related driving behavior must be demonstrated. Many programs have failed in this respect despite showing
knowledge and attitudinal changes (e.g., Ellingstad & Springer, 1976).

The various educational countermeasure programs have yielded little
evidence of their efficacy in reducing drunk driving. For example, although
the original Phoenix DWI program produced a decrease in recidivism as
well as changes in knowledge and attitudes when compared with a no treatment control population, there was no attendant decrease in alcohol-related
crashes (Crabb, Gettys, Malfetti, & Stewart, 1971). Unfortunately, assignment to the school or the control group was not random and a baseline
difference in prior driving records between the two groups makes these
data inconclusive. As with the Phoenix program, published evaluations of
Phoenix-type programs are wrought with similar methodological problems.
For example, a Phoenix-type program in New York State (Malfetti & Simon, 1974) also found desirable changes in knowledge and attitude, but
failed to evaluate accidents or recidivism rates. In this program, both problem and nonproblem drinkers showed increased knowledge and improved
attitudes, but nonproblem drinkers showed greater gains. The lack of a
control group again precludes definitive statements about effectiveness. In
another study, Zelhart and Schurr (1975) found no difference in DWI
recidivism rates between school (Alberta Impaired Drivers' Program) and
control subjects, although the former had better driving records following
the program. Once again, lack of random assignment makes this effect
ambiguous. Finally, in a $3\frac{1}{2}$ year follow-up study of the Oshawa Impaired
Drivers' Program (Vingilis, Adlaf, & Chung, 1981), where subjects (multi-

ple DWI offenders, most of whom were diagnosed as problem drinkers) were randomly assigned to either a school or a control (probation only) condition, the results indicated gains by the school subjects in knowledge and attitudes, but no effects were found on recidivism or driving offense measures.

Overall, the results of the Phoenix and Phoenix-type programs that have been evaluated are not encouraging. It appears that methodological rigor is inversely related to the claimed effectiveness of the DWI schools. The programs are able to convey information on drunk driving and to induce positive attitude changes, and these effects seem greater for non-problem than for problem drinker DWI offenders (Hayslip, Kapusinski, Darbes, & Zeh, 1976). However, even the attitude change effect is suspect. Since attitude changes are measured immediately after program completion, a time when most offenders are still on probation, the attitudes expressed toward drunk driving may be confounded with the demand characteristics of being on probation rather than being an accurate reflection of opinion (Organization of Economic Cooperation and Development, 1978). The schools have demonstrated little impact on DWI recidivism and alcohol-related accidents.

Recently, two novel educational programs have been reported. One is the "3-D" (three-day) program in California (McGuire, 1978), that is aimed at DWI offenders who do not have diagnosable drinking problems other than their arrests. Besides the standard Phoenix procedures, subjects consumed alcohol and drove on a course while being videotaped. When sober, they viewed the videotape and discussed the effects of even small quantities of alcohol on their driving as well as ways of interrupting the drink–drive sequence. The program markedly reduced recidivism, accidents, moving-traffic violations, and license suspensions relative to a control group. However, subjects were not randomly assigned to groups and follow-up was only one year in length. Thus, the 3-D program, while promising, needs further evaluation.

The second educational program was conducted in New Zealand by Brown (1980). Clients (predominantly problem drinkers) were randomly assigned to one of three groups: a Phoenix-type course, a no treatment control, or a controlled-drinking educational course. The latter included drinking under *ad libitum* conditions in an experimental bar, an assessment of baseline drinking behavior, practice in reducing drinking by lessening drink strength and sip size and increasing spacing between drinks, videotape reply of the client's intoxicated behavior, and homework assignments to record daily alcohol intake and the benefits of controlled drinking. The controlled-drinking education was predicated on the assumption that drunk driving by problem drinkers could be reduced if they learned to moderate their drinking. The program was evaluated after one year on the basis of subjects' self-reports about their drinking and drinking/driving behaviors. The controlled-drinking education group showed the greatest reduction in drunk driving and was the only group that reported a reduction in drinking *per se.* Brown (1980) acknowledged the shortcomings of using clients' self-reports as outcome data, but argued that since actual DWI recidivism has a low frequency of occurence (only two clients were reconvicted), recidivism would not have been an adequately sensitive measure given the small number of clients per group ($n = 20$). Obviously, before it can be said that this potentially valuable approach is effective it must be replicated on a larger scale and for longer follow-up periods using drunk driving as an outcome measure.

As stated previously, the Phoenix DWI school has not only served as a model for a great number of subsequent programs but was also adopted by the ASAP programs. Within the comprehensive ASAP system, this model has been subjected to intensive evaluation efforts. Many of these evaluations, however, have been flawed by methodological problems. The outcome data from a large number of such studies have been summarized and reported by Ellingstad and Springer (1976) as follows: (1) *increased knowledge*—the ASAP schools appeared to be effective; (2) *changing attitudes*— the schools were again effective, although the demand characteristic of concomitant probation makes this effect questionable; (3) *DWI recidivism*— little evidence was found of the schools' overall efficacy, but nonproblem drinkers recidivated less than controls and problem drinkers and the latter did better in small group "interactive" schools than in larger group lecture-format schools; and (4) *alcohol-related traffic accidents*—the schools had no beneficial effect. The outcomes for problem drinkers were also evaluated in 1975–77 for 11 of the 35 ASAP projects, using random assignment to the school and control conditions (cf. Ellingstad & Struckman-Johnson, 1978). As before, the schools were found to have no effect on either recidivism or accidents (see also Levy, Voos, Johnson, & Klein, 1978), and only a slight effect on drinking *per se.*

A particularly illustrative example of the effects of a DWI school is provided in the evaluation of an ASAP educational program in New York State (Preusser *et al.,* 1976). In this well-controlled study, 2,805 DWI offenders were randomly assigned to the school, which incorporated the conventional didactic program plus a one-to-one interactive component. An additional 2,660 subjects were randomly assigned to serve as controls and received only a fine and license suspension. Preliminary data indicated the usual positive changes in knowledge and attitudes for the school subjects (Ulmer & Preusser, 1973). However, when DWI recidivism and other driving data were examined 15 to 17 months after the subjects' convictions, a different story emerged. Whereas the school program did not reduce either recidivism or blood alcohol concentrations for those arrested, attendance at the school (as compared to assignment to the control group) was associated with an *increase* in accident involvement, presumably because the school subjects retained their driver's license while the control subjects lost their license for 60 days as a result of their conviction (and probably drove on fewer occasions).

Until the DWI school approach can be modified and shown to be effective, it does not seem advisable to suspend legal sanctions in exchange for attendance at a DWI school. Thus far, such programs have not lived up to their initial expectations.

Alcohol Treatment Countermeasures

Treatment, the other nonpunitive form of DWI secondary prevention, gained marked popularity with the advent of the ASAP programs in the United States. A major aim of the ASAP programs was to refer clients to *appropriate* treatment modalities based on an assessment of their actual problems (e.g., Department of Transportation, 1975). In many cases (e.g., multiple DWI offenders; Zelhart & Schurr, 1977) the primary problem was alcohol abuse rather than drunk driving and, consequently, these individuals were referred to alcohol treatment programs rather than or in addition to DWI schools. As a result, treatment became a common way of dealing with the problem of drunk drivers.

The use of treatment alternatives by the legal system is predicated on two assumptions (which differ from those underlying the DWI schools): (1) For some people, their abuse of alcohol (primary problem) is the cause of drunk driving (a secondary effect), and (2) Successfully dealing with these individuals' alcohol problems will produce a subsequent decrease in drunk driving and alcohol-related accidents. The latter assumption is of prime concern to the courts and government transportation agencies, since their ultimate goal is the reduction of drunk driving and promotion of traffic safety. However, this goal may not be of cardinal importance for the treatment agencies. Most alcohol treatment programs were established to deal with alcohol abuse and its attendant life-functioning problems, and thus, most programs view this as their mission and criterion for success. Many programs, then, might see the goal of secondary prevention of drunk driving as being imposed on them by the courts. Despite potential conflicts between the legal system and treatment agencies working with DWI offenders (e.g., Zelhart & Schurr, 1977), it is the goal of the courts (i.e., preventing recidivism) that is of prime importance when evaluating any DWI secondary prevention program. Therefore, the treatment approaches described below will be evaluated primarily in terms of their effects on recidivism and accidents, and beneficial changes in drinking and related life problems will be viewed as only ancillary criteria of success. It should be added that for those programs that aim at abstinence (and are successful), assessment of drunk driving behavior is superfluous, as abstinence, by definition, precludes drunk driving.

If successful treatment programs for the drunk driver are to emerge, they must take into account the characteristics of DWI offenders. To date, there is little evidence that this has happened, despite much research on the characteristics of DWI offenders. The typical drunk driver is male, neither very young nor very old, usually not presently married, has a low socioeconomic status (e.g., Perrine, Waller, & Harris, 1971; Pollack, 1973; Wolfe, 1975), and a prior history of driving problems (e.g., Clark, 1972; Filkins *et al.*, 1970; Perrine *et al.*, 1971). The drinking practices of DWI offenders are quite complex. Generally, there is evidence of heavier drinking and of overrepresentation of those with chronic drinking problems in accidents, fatalities, and both single and multiple DWI arrests (e.g., Filkins *et al.*, 1970; Fine *et al.*, 1974; Sterling-Smith, 1976; Zelhart *et al.*, 1975). However, although many people (perhaps up to 50%) exhibit some patterns of alcohol abuse (Filkins *et al.*, 1970; Selzer & Barton, 1977), many drunk drivers are not problem drinkers or alcoholics (Fine *et al.*, 1974; Zylman, 1975). In fact, not all alcohol abusers are high-risk drivers or even drive when drinking (Clay, 1972; Filkins *et al.*, 1970).

Psychological variables that interact with drinking problems to produce the high-risk driver are aggression and hostility, interpersonal problems, depression, low self-esteem, low stress tolerance, overall psychopathology, poor emotional adjustment, risk taking, and impulsivity (Clay, 1972; Perrine, 1974; Selzer & Barton, 1977; Selzer & Chapman, 1971; Selzer, Vinoken, & Wilson, 1977; Sterling-Smith, 1976; Zelhart, 1972). However, such variables, as well as the characteristics described previously, cannot predict with any certainty which individuals are at high risk for drunk driving (e.g., Organization for Economic Cooperation and Development, 1978; Zelhart *et al.*, 1975). In the words of Jones and Joscelyn (1978):

> No characteristic described above or any combination of such characteristics can identify any given individual as a sure-fire perpetuator of future alcohol-related crashes. In no instance can it be said that all persons possessing certain characteristics are high-risk drivers (e.g., alcoholics, young males). The data can help determine the gross alcohol-crash risk of entire groups of drivers, but are far more difficult to apply to individual drivers. (p. 46)

The above limitation may be one reason why alcohol treatment programs for DWI offenders typically ignore the characteristics of these clients when determining the type of treatment to be provided. It also may be that these programs generally are geared to serve alcohol abusers and tend to offer only one type of treatment, regardless of individual client differences (Armor, Polich, & Stambul, 1978). Also, even if programs were designed to serve the needs of individual DWI offenders, decisions regarding treatment assignment are usually dictated by the courts rather than the treatment facility or professional service providers (Jones & Joscelyn, 1978). Unfortunately, such decisions are often based on the availability of treatment rather than the characteristics or treatment needs of the drunk driver.

The types of treatments used with DWI offenders, the way these clients are assigned to treatment, and the effectiveness of these programs are important issues. In general, treatments are largely of a traditional nature: individual and group psychotherapy, referral to Alcoholics Anonymous, and the use of disulfiram, an anti-alcohol drug. Some programs also combine these approaches in various ways for different lengths of time. Assignment of clients is usually dictated by the courts and is based on practical (availability) rather than rational considerations. There is seldom random assignment to groups when programs are being formally evaluated. Overall, there has been a paucity of evaluation studies and the available evidence is largely negative with respect to decreasing drunk driving (e.g., Blumenthal & Ross, 1973; Didenko, McEachern, & Berger, 1972; Hagen *et al.,* 1979; Jones & Joscelyn, 1978).

A systematic approach to the DWI problem was undertaken by the various ASAP programs. Efforts were focused on multiple DWI offenders, who, unlike first offenders, often have marked alcohol problems and a high probability of being diagnosed as alcoholic (e.g., Kelleher, 1971; Zelhart & Schurr, 1977). Among the goals of the ASAP system were the identification of problem drinkers from among the DWI population and referral of such individuals to alcohol treatment facilities, usually in lieu of legal sanctions or referral to a DWI school. The stated assessment and referral criteria included checks of driving and criminal records for alcohol-related convictions, checks of previous contacts with health and social service agencies, pre-sentence interviews with the offender and family members, diagnostic tests for problem drinking (notably the Mortimer-Filkins test), and medical and psychological evaluations. However, as noted by Jones and Joscelyn (1978), the referral system ultimately reflected the *subjective* judgment of the legal system rather than that of the treatment staff and, thus, it is not surprising that the ASAP system worked imperfectly. Although problem drinkers were more likely than nonproblem drinkers to be referred to alcohol treatment facilities, 46% of problem drinkers were referred to DWI schools, with 17% referred to group psychotherapy, 17% to Alcoholics Anonymous, 1% to chemotherapy, and the remaining 19% to other modes, including inpatient treatment and individual psychotherapy (Department of Transportation, 1975).

Evaluations of the ASAP approach have been negative. For example, Levy *et al.* (1978) evaluated the 35 ASAP sites with respect to impact on nighttime fatal crashes and found that only 12 sites reported significant reductions. The authors primarily attributed the successes that occurred to deterrence rather than to the rehabilitation of problem drinkers. Similarly, Swenson and Clay (1977) found no difference in recidivism between no-treatment subjects and those attending alcohol prevention workshops, alcohol therapy, or power motivation training.

The most comprehensive evaluation of alcohol treatment programs for DWI problem drinkers was done by Ellingstad and Struckman-Johnson (1978). They evaluated 11 ASAP sites where DWI offenders were randomly assigned to either a treatment program or a control condition. The treatments included group therapy, power motivation training, and individual therapy, as well as a DWI school, and various combinations of these modalities depending on the ASAP site. However, the average number of available treatment modalities per site was only slightly over two, virtually precluding any matching of clients with treatments. The results were clearly negative: none of the treatments, either alone or in combination, had a marked impact on drunk driving behavior, drinking, or social adjustment measures. It has been suggested that in view of the lack of impact of alcohol treatment programs on drunk driving behavior, a *raison d'être* for their continued use might be their success in other areas, notably drinking and social functioning (Organization for Economic Cooperation and Development, 1978). However, considering the above evidence, this justification seems premised on tenuous grounds. Moreover, it is doubtful that the legal system could retain its mandate for referring DWI offenders to treatment if the goal of treatment were not related to the offense in question.

Despite frequent acknowledgments that differential assessment and treatment planning are prerequisites for successful alcohol treatment, differential assessment of DWI offenders is restricted to classifying individuals as nonproblem versus problem drinkers. Differential treatment planning is virtually nonexistent. At the very least, it may prove useful to differentiate the DWI population into subtypes rather than simply dichotomizing drinking practices into problem and nonproblem. A particularly good example of this approach is found in a recent report by Donovan and Marlatt (1982). They measured a number of personality traits, hostility characteristics, and accident-related driving attitudes in convicted DWI offenders and identified subtypes within the DWI population by means of cluster analysis. The subtypes were then externally validated by assessing additional differences among them in terms of demographic variables, drinking practices, and driving records. Finally, different secondary prevention strategies were suggested for each subtype, based on its unique constellation of characteristics.

For example, the most popular subtype was characterized by the least frequent and lightest drinking, best emotional adjustment, lowest hostility and driving-related aggression, and best driving attitudes and driving record. For this group, the authors suggested use of a behavioral controlled drinking program (cf. Sobell & Sobell, 1978) stressing identification of high-risk DWI situations and ways of coping with them. Perhaps an educational program, especially a "fortified" one such as that used by Brown (1980) and McGuire (1978), might also prove effective for this group. Another subtype was characterized by depression, resentment, and lack of assertiveness. Donovan and Marlatt (1982) suggested that these individuals might benefit from an intervention involving self-management training, the expectation being that the increased self-control skills and self-efficacy would decrease both drinking and drunk driving.

The above classification of DWI offenders into distinct subtypes is an example of an approach that may lead to better assessment and, consequently, more rational assignment of individuals to particular treatments. Matching clients to alcohol treatments is not a new idea (see Glaser, 1980). This approach, however, has not been used with DWI offenders, and this may be an important reason for the lack of treatment success with this population. Nevertheless, the use of subtypes should not be accepted and implemented on logical, theoretical, or intuitive grounds. The rapid establishment and overwhelming failure of DWI schools and ASAP projects should serve as a reminder of the consequences of such impetuous actions. Until treatment approaches for DWI offenders are empirically validated, we must conclude that, at present, treatment is not an effective way of dealing with the DWI problem.

POLICY ISSUES AND RECOMMENDATIONS

As evident in the preceding review, the state-of-the-art in secondary prevention of drunk driving paints a bleak picture. Simply put, the problem of drunk driving continues to plague society without any obvious remedies. Despite the lack of evidence showing marked effects, DWI schools undoubtably will continue to be a popular countermeasure for two reasons. First, they are often entrepreneurial enterprises that depend on court referrals for their existence. Second, they constitute an expeditious alternative to certain legal sanctions (e.g., jail terms) and to treatment. The legal system can only incarcerate a limited number of individuals without precipitating overcrowding in already crowded jails. Treatment programs are also faced with a conflict created by court referrals: since the treatment programs are usually intended to serve voluntary clients, they can only serve a limited number of court-referred DWIs before voluntary clients will, by necessity, be denied ready access to services.

On logical grounds, it seems sensible to differentially assign DWI offenders to countermeasures that are determined to be most effective. Considerable research is necessary, however, before such assignments can be empirically determined. The treatment alternative, although obviously appropriate in some cases, raises perplexing legal, social, and ethical issues. One concern is the impact of the social consequences of entering alcohol treatment, and specifically the stigmatization that can result from being labelled an "alcohol abuser" or "alcoholic." Although social views are changing toward viewing alcohol abuse as a public health problem rather than a reflection of moral corruption and lack of will power (Beauchamp, 1980), the moralistic view has not disappeared (Orcutt, Cairl, & Miller, 1980) and causes great concern for people seeking treatment for drinking problems. Individuals are often reluctant to enter treatment for fear that it will become known to significant others or employers. Employers are especially likely to gain such information in cases that involve reimbursement for treatment from insurance plans contracted by and reporting to the employer (see Sobell & Sobell, 1981). In view of such possible "side effects" of treatment, it is hardly surprising that many drunk drivers who are court-referred into treatment are frightened or angered at the prospect of being labeled as alcoholics by virtue of their admission to an alcohol treatment center. This often leads to antagonism and deception during the assessment process. Such individuals may also functionally drop out of the program by participating in only a perfunctory manner.

An obvious way to minimize the problem of stigmatization is to ensure the confidentiality of treatment information and records. Whereas recent legislation has provided a measure of such protection, some problems, especially for drunk drivers, still remain (Sobell & Sobell, 1981). The threat to a client's legal rights posed by breach of confidentiality regarding treatment can be addressed and minimized if the individual is informed in advance of the situations under which information will be released and agrees to these conditions. It would be deceptive to consider this a truly "voluntary" consent, however. Although most alcohol treatment programs are legally obligated to serve only those who voluntarily request treatment, the consent obtained from court-referred clients can be considered only "technically" voluntary. The individual often grants consent under coercion since the court has threatened legal sanctions if he or she does not enter treatment. A more detailed consideration of the ethical problems associated with providing services to legally coerced clients is beyond the scope of this chapter. The important point, however, is that the imposition of such conditions is likely to cloud or obscure treatment success.

Considering the above, one wonders why the courts continue to coerce DWI offenders into treatment instead of applying legal sanctions. Although it can be argued that incarceration would result in overcrowded jails, especially given the frequency of this offense, jail terms are exceedingly rare for first offenders, who constitute the majority (at least 75%) of convicted drunk drivers. Furthermore, when jail terms are imposed, they are exceedingly short. Consequently, given present sentencing practices, the specter of jails teeming with DWI offenders is unlikely.

An alternative explanation for the lack of stern legal consequences is that judicial actions reflect societal attitudes whereby drunk driving, in relation to other serious crimes, is viewed as "social crime" or social nuisance. An obvious recommendation, therefore, is to enforce the existing laws and punish the DWI offender with the same vigor as is applied to other crimes. A sanction that seems particularly suitable on the basis of available evidence is prolonged license suspension coupled with increased enforcement efforts to detect individuals who drive without a valid license. This would obviously remove many drunk drivers from the roads and those who continue to drive despite loss of license might do so safely and cautiously (cf. Hurst, 1980), resulting in an overall decrease in DWI offenses and their consequences. These changes seem unlikely, however, unless there is greater popular acceptance of the belief that drunk driving is a serious offense. In this regard, large scale efforts to solidify public opinion seem a logical and necessary prerequisite to achieving enhanced enforcement.

If effective treatments can be developed, the use of this type of countermeasure for some individuals could become desirable and justifiable. A direction that seems particularly promising involves individualized assessment, treatment planning, and goal setting (cf. Sobell & Sobell, 1978). We have already noted that DWI offenders are not a homogeneous group. Although they can be dichotomized as having or not having serious drinking problems, this traditional classification, which was prominent in ASAP programs, has not been helpful in designing effective treatments. Perhaps a better approach is to develop a DWI typology based on personality characteristics related to driving risk (see Donovan & Marlatt, 1982); this approach may provide a more rational and efficient way of matching clients and treatments. However, the special nonvoluntary nature of the DWI client in treatment necessitates further individualization of treatment to minimize the problems of resistance and noncompliance with a program that is imposed rather than chosen. Specifically, the individual should be involved in the process of assessment and the selection of treatment goals as well as in the development of the particular treatment strategies (Zelhart & Schurr, 1977). Although subtyping DWI offenders may delineate the range of objectives and strategies that might be considered, the specific ones chosen should reflect the specific needs and characteristics of the individual in question.

A final treatment consideration is that many DWI offenders do not show serious alcohol problems. These individuals seem to be excellent candidates for a nonproblem drinking outcome (Sobell, 1978) with a treatment emphasis on avoiding driving when legally intoxicated. For DWI offenders without marked alcohol problems this alternative can be considered as potentially the most effective and the least restrictive treatment (Sobell, Sobell, & Nirenberg, 1982). This alternative might be seen as enhancing the chances of obtaining cooperation from the nonvoluntary client. A final caveat is also in order: Until evidence shows that treatment of any sort is an effective means of dealing with DWI offenders, treatment must be viewed as a *potential* solution that deserves empirical inquiry rather than acceptance. Meanwhile, we must rely on primary prevention, with an emphasis on changing the attitudes of lawmakers and society toward the seriousness of the crime of drunk driving, as well as on the need for consistent enforcement and application of those sanctions that appear most effective. At present, the "sentencing" of the drunk driver to treatment is a premature countermeasure that has few benefits but many risks and costs.

AN OVERLOOKED WAY OF INCREASING PUBLIC SUPPORT OF COUNTERMEASURES

Shortly after this chapter was completed, it came to our attention that a series of events in California might be the harbinger of a changing public attitude toward drunk drivers. These new initiatives emanated neither from any scientific development nor from the efforts of traffic safety activists, but rather from the personal lobbying of citizens previously victimized by drunk drivers. Specifically, a woman whose child was killed by a drunk driver (the driver had had several previous drunk-driving arrests) was outraged by the flaccid, almost nonexistent legal consequences for drunk drivers. This led her to form an organization of concerned citizens, Mothers Against Drunk Drivers (MADD). The lobbying of this group recently (1981) resulted in a significant stiffening of California's laws aimed at drunk drivers. A *Newsweek* article ("Curbing Drunk Drivers," 1982) reporting these events noted that in California and in other states (e.g., Maryland, New York, Arizona, Connecticut) grassroots lobbying has resulted in the proposal or passage of new laws making prosecution and punishment for drunk-driving offenses much more likely than in the past. Among the main features of these new laws are: "A blood-alcohol content of .10 . . . is no longer just evidence, but a crime in itself; certain offenses carry mandatory jail sentences—and drunk-driving incidents stay on a driver's record" ("Curbing Drunk Drivers," 1982, p. 30). The *Newsweek* article also noted that similar legislation was enacted in Oregon in 1971, legislation that can be looked to as setting a precedent. In fact, over the last decade, the number of fatalities in Oregon has decreased by 6% despite a concurrent 46% increase in drivers and a 62% increase in vehicles, resulting in a 35% drop in fatality rate.

The above events identify one obvious course of action that might be expected to have considerable societal impact, but that has received little attention by those involved in the field of alcohol and public policy. Statistics surrounding drunk driving suggest that a large pool of individuals related to victims of drunk drivers must exist. Many of these relatives and friends are likely to have strong feelings about the need to deal forcefully with such drivers. The concerted efforts of such individuals probably represent one of the most effective means of implementing social change and of changing public attitudes toward drunk driving. Although this amalgamated concern has arisen spontaneously, there is no *a priori* reason why the formation of similar groups could not be officially encouraged by governmental agencies and by others in a position to influence public opinion.

REFERENCES

Armor, D. J., Polich, J. M., & Stambul, H. B. *Alcoholism and treatment.* New York: Wiley, 1978.

Australia's unique press campaign to combat the drinking driver. *California Highway Patrolman,* 1974, *38,* 10–11.

Barmack, J. E., & Payne, D. E. The Lackland accident countermeasure experiment. In W. Hadden, E. Suchman, & D. Klein (Eds.), *Accident research: Methods and approaches.* New York: Harper & Row, 1964.

Beauchamp, D. E. *Beyond alcoholism: Alcohol and public health policy.* Philadelphia: Temple University Press, 1980.

Beitel, G. A., Sharp, M. C., & Glauz, W. D. Probability of arrest while driving under the influence of alcohol. *Journal of Studies on Alcohol,* 1975, *36,* 109–116.

Blumenthal, M., & Ross, H. L. *Two experimental studies of traffic law* (Vol. 1): *The effects of legal sanctions on DWI offenders.* Prepared for Department of Transportation, National Highway Safety Administration. (Report No. PB 220–467). Springfield, Va.: National Technical Information Service, 1973.

Borkenstein, R. F. Problems of enforcement, adjudication and sanctioning. In S. Israelstam & S. Lambert (Eds.), *Alcohol, drugs, and traffic safety.* Toronto: Addiction Research Foundation, 1975.

Borkenstein, R. F. An overview of the problem of alcohol, drugs, and traffic safety. Presidential Address. *Proceedings of the 7th International Conference on Alcohol, Drugs, and Traffic Safety,* Melbourne: Australian Government Publishing Service, 1977.

Borkenstein, R. F., Crowther, R. F., Shumate, R. P., Ziel, W. B., & Zylman, R. *The role of the drinking driver in traffic accidents.* Bloomington, Ind.: Indiana Union Press, 1964.

Brown, R. A. Conventional education and controlled drinking education courses with convicted drunken driver. *Behavior Therapy,* 1980, *11,* 632–642.

Buikhuisen, W. *General deterrence: Research and theory.* The Netherlands: Groningen University, 1972.

Carlson, W. L. Age, exposure, and alcohol involvement in night crashes. *Journal of Safety Research,* 1973, *5,* 247–259.

Carr, B. R., Goldberg, H., & Farbar, C. M. The Canadian breathalyzer legislation: An inferential evaluation. In S. Israelstam & S. Lambert (Eds.), *Alcohol, drugs, and safety.* Toronto: Addiction Research Foundation, 1975.

Cimburra, G., Warren, R. A., Bennett, R. C., Lucas, D. M., & Simpson, H. M. Drugs detected in fatally injured drivers and pedestrians in the Province of Ontario. *Traffic Injury Research Foundation of Canada,* 1981.

Clark, C. D. A comparison of the driving records and other characteristics of three alcohol-involved populations and random sample drivers. *HIT Lab Report 2,* (No. 10) 1972, 1–5.

Clay, M. L. *Which drunks shall we dodge?* Selected Papers, 23rd Annual Meeting of the Alcohol and Drug Problems Association, Atlanta, Georgia, 1972.

Crabb, D., Gettys, T. R., Malfetti, J. L., & Stewart, E. I. *Development and preliminary try-out of evaluation measures for the Phoenix Driving-While-Intoxicated Reeducation Program.* Temple, Ariz.: Arizona State University, 1971.

Curbing drunk drivers. *Newsweek,* January 25, 1982, p. 30.

Department of Transportation, *Alcohol safety action programs. Evaluation of operations–1974.* Prepared by Department of Transportation, National Highway Traffic Safety Administration. (Report No. DOT–HS–801–709) Springfield, Va.: National Technical Information Service, 1975.

Didenko, O. R., McEachen, E. W., & Berger, R. M. *Drinking driver traffic safety project: Final report* (Vol. 1). Prepared for Department of Transportation, National Highway Traffic Safety Administration. (Report No. DOT–HS–800–699) Springfield, Va.: National Technical Information Services, 1972.

Donovan, D. M., & Marlatt, G. A. Personality subtypes among driving-while-intoxicated offenders: Relationship to driving behavior, driving risk, and treatment implications. *Journal of Consulting and Clinical Psychology,* 1982, *50,* 241–249.

Douglass, R. L. The legal drinking age and traffic casualties: A special case of changing alcohol availability in a public health context. *Alcohol Health and Research World,* 1979–1980 (Winter), 18–25.

Ellingstad, V. S., & Springer, T. J. *Programme level evaluation of ASAP diagnosis, referral and rehabilitation efforts* (Vol. 3): *Analysis of rehabilitation countermeasure effectiveness.* Prepared for Department of Transportation, National Highway Traffic Safety Administration. (Report No. DOT–HS–802–044) Springfield, Va.: National Technical Information Service, 1976.

Ellingstad, V. S., & Struckman-Johnson, D. L. *Short-term rehabilitation (STR) study, interim analysis of STR performance and effectiveness.* Prepared for Department of Transportation, National Highway Traffic Safety Administration. (Report No. DOT–HS–803–285) Springfield, Va.: National Technical Information Service, 1978.

Farmer, P. J. Review and evaluation of legislative and enforcement programs related to the use of alcohol and other drugs. *Proceedings of the Conference on Medical, Human, and Related Factors Causing Traffic Accidents, Including Alcohol and Other Drugs.* Ottawa: Traffic Injury Research Foundation of Canada, 1973.

Farris, R., Malone, T. B., & Lilliefors, H. *A comparison of alcohol involvement in exposed and injured drivers. Phase I and II.* Prepared for Department of Transportation, National

Highway Traffic Safety Administration. (Report No. DOT–HS–801–826). Springfield, Va.: National Technical Information Service, 1976.

Filkins, L. D., Clark, C. D., Rosenblatt, C. A., Carlson, W. L., Kerlan, M. W. & Manson, H. *Alcohol abuse and traffic safety: A study of fatalities, DWI offenders, alcoholics, and court-related treatment approaches.* Prepared for Department of Transportation, National Highway Traffic Safety Administration. (Contract No. FH–11–6555 and FH–11–7129). Springfield, Va.: National Technical Information Service, 1970.

Fine, E. W., Scoles, P., & Mulligan, M. J. Alcohol abuse in first offenders arrested for driving while intoxicated. In S. Israelstam & S. Lambert (Eds.), *Proceedings of the Sixth International Conference on Alcohol, Drugs, and Traffic Safety.* Toronto: Addiction Research Foundation, 1974.

Glaser, F. B. Anybody got a match? Treatment research and the matching hypothesis. In G. Edwards & M. Grant (Eds.), *Alcoholism treatment: Finding new directions.* London: Croom Helm, 1980.

Hagen, R. E., McConnell, E. J., & Williams, R. L. *Supervision and revocation effects on the DWI offender.* Sacramento: California Department of Motor Vehicles, Report No. 75, 1980.

Hagen, R. E., Williams, R. L., & McConnell, E. J. The traffic safety impact of alcohol abuse treatment as an alternative to mandated licensing controls. *Accident Analysis and Prevention,* 1979, *11,* 275–291.

Hayslip, B., Kapusinski, D., Darbes, A., & Zeh, R. Evaluation of driving-while-intoxicated programmes: Some methodological considerations. *Journal of Studies on Alcohol,* 1976, *37,* 1742–1746.

Homel, R. *Sanctions for drinking and driving.* Paper presented at the 7th International Conference on Alcohol, Drugs, and Traffic Safety, Melbourne January, 1977.

Hurst, P. M. Traffic officers' attitudes toward blood alcohol law enforcement. *Accident Analysis and Prevention,* 1980, *12,* 259–266.

Hurst, P. M. Can anyone reward safe driving? *Accident Analysis and Prevention,* 1980, *12,* 217–220.

Jones, R. K., & Joscelyn, K. B. *Alcohol and highway safety 1978: A review of the state of the knowledge.* Prepared for Department of Transportation, National Highway Traffic Safety Administration. (Report No. UM–HSRI–78–9). Springfield, Va.: National Technical Information Service, 1978.

Joscelyn, K. B., & Jones, R. K. *A system approach to the analysis of the drinking driver control system.* Prepared for Department of Transportation, National Highway Traffic Safety Administration. (Contract No. FH–11–7270). Springfield, Va.: National Technical Information Service, 1971.

Kelleher, E. J. A diagnostic evaluation of 400 drinking drivers. *Journal of Safety Research,* 1971, *3,* 52–55.

Lacey, J. H., Stewart, J. R., & Council, F. M. Development of predictive models to identify persons at high risk of alcohol related crash involvement. *Proceedings of the 7th International Conference on Alcohol, Drugs, and Traffic Safety,* Melbourne: Australian Government Publishing Service, 1977.

Levy, P., Voos, R., Johnson, P., & Klein, T. M. An evaluation of the Department of Transportation's alcohol safety action projects. *Journal of Safety Research,* 1978, *10,* 162–176.

Maisto, S. A., Sobell, L. C., Zelhart, P. F., Connors, G. J., & Cooper, T. Driving records of persons convicted of driving under the influence of alcohol. *Journal of Studies on Alcohol,* 1979, *40,* 70–77.

Malfetti, J. L., & Simon, K. J. Evaluation of a program to rehabilitate drunken drivers. *Traffic Quarterly,* 1974, *28,* 49–59.

Marshall, J. Level of alcohol in motorists being tested. *The Globe and Mail,* June 24, 1974, Toronto, Canada.

McGuire, F. L. The effectiveness of a treatment program for the alcohol-involved driver. *American Journal of Drug and Alcohol Abuse,* 1978, 5, 517–525.

Noordzij, P. C. *The introduction of an 0.05 percent limit in the Netherlands: The effect on drinking and driving.* Paper presented at the 7th International Conference on Alcohol, Drugs, and Traffic Safety, Melbourne, January 1977.

Oates, J. F., Jr. *Study of self-test devices.* Prepared for Department of Transportation, National Highway Traffic Safety Administration. (Report No. DOT–HS–803–400). Springfield, Va.: National Technical Information Service, 1978.

Organization for Economic Cooperation and Development, Road Research Group. *New research on the role of alcohol and drugs in road accidents.* Paris: Organization for Economic Cooperation and Development, 1978.

Orcutt, J. D., Cairl, R. E., & Miller, E. T. Professional and public conceptions of alcoholism. *Journal of Studies on Alcohol,* 1980, 41, 652–661.

Perrine, M. W. The Vermont driver profile: A psychometric approach to early identification of potential high-risk drivers. In S. Israelstam & S. Lambert (Eds.), *Proceedings of the 6th International Conference on Alcohol, Drugs, and Traffic Safety.* Toronto: Addiction Research Foundation, 1974.

Perrine, M. W., Waller, J. A., & Harris, L. S. *Alcohol and highway safety: Behavioral and medical aspects.* Prepared for Department of Transportation, National Highway Traffic Safety Administration. (Report No. DOT–HS–800–599). Springfield, Va.: National Technical Information Service, 1971.

Pocock, D. A., & Landauer, A. A. The severity of drunken driving as perceived by drunken drivers. *Accident Analysis and Prevention,* 1980, 12, 105–111.

Pollack, S. *Drinking driver and traffic safety: Final report.* Los Angeles: University of Southern California, 1973.

Poudrier, L. M., Mulligan, E., & Grady, R. H. Driving while impaired: Description of an educational program for second and subsequent offenders as an alternative to incarceration. (Addiction Research Foundation Substudy No. 647.) Toronto: Addiction Research Foundation, 1975.

Preusser, D. F., Ulmer, R. G., & Adams, J. R. Driver record evaluation of a drinking driver rehabilitation program. *Journal of Safety Research,* 1976, 8, 98–105.

Ross, H. L. Law science and accidents: The British Road Safety Act of 1967. *Journal of Legal Studies,* 1973, 2, 1–78.

Ross, H. L. The effectiveness of drinking-and-driving laws in Sweden and Great Britain. *Proceedings of the 6th International Conference on Alcohol, Drugs, and Traffic Safety.* Toronto: Addiction Research Foundation, 1974.

Ross, H. L. The Scandinavian myth: The effectiveness of drinking and driving legislation in Sweden and Norway. *Journal of Legal Studies,* 1975, 4, 285–310.

Schmidt, W. S., & Smart, R. G. Alcoholics, drinking, and traffic accidents. *Quarterly Journal of Studies on Alcohol,* 1959, 20, 631–644.

Selzer, M. L., & Barton, E. The drunken driver: A psychosocial study. *Drug and Alcohol Dependence,* 1977, 2, 239–253.

Selzer, M. L., & Chapman, M. Differential risk among alcoholic drivers. *Proceedings of the 14th Annual Conference of the American Association for Automotive Medicine.* New York: Society of Automotive Engineers, 1971.

Selzer, M. L., Vinoken, A., & Wilson, T. D. A psychosocial comparison of drunken drivers and alcoholics. *Journal of Studies on Alcohol,* 1977, 38, 1294–1312.

Sobell, L. C., & Sobell, M. B. Client rights in alcohol treatment programs. In J. T. Hannah, W. P. Christian, & H. B. Clark (Eds.), *Preservation of client rights: A handbook for practitioners providing therapeutic, educational, and rehabilitative services.* New York: Macmillan, 1981.

Sobell, L. C., Sobell, M. B., & Nirenberg, T. D. Differential treatment planning for alcohol abusers. In E. M. Pattison & E. Kaufman (Eds.), *Encyclopedic handbook fo alcoholism.* New York: Gardner, 1982.

Sobell, M. B. Alternatives to abstinence: Evidence, issues and some proposals. In P. E. Nathan, G. A. Marlatt, & T. Løberg (Eds.), *Alcoholism: New directions in behavioral research and treatment.* New York: Plenum Press, 1978.

Sobell, M. B., & Sobell, L. C. *Behavioral treatment of alcohol problems: Individualized therapy and controlled drinking.* New York: Plenum Press, 1978.

Spielman, E., Knupp, R. T., & Holden, R. T. Offenses and sanctions: DUI arrests and adjudications in Metropolitan Nashville, 1973–1975. *Report of the Alcohol Safety Project of the Urban Observatory of Metropolitan Nashville,* 1976.

Sterling-Smith, R. S. *Psychosocial identification of drivers responsible for vehicular accidents in Boston.* Prepared for Department of Transportation. (Report No. DOT–HS–801–915). Springfield, Va.: National Technical Information Service, 1976.

Stewart, E. I., & Malfetti, J. L. *Rehabilitation of the drunken driver: A corrective course in Phoenix, Arizona, for persons convicted of driving under the influence of alcohol.* New York: Teachers College Press, 1970.

Swenson, P., & Clay, T. R. *An analysis of drinker diagnosis, referral, and rehabilitation activity—Analytical study VI.* Prepared for Department of Transport, National Highway Traffic Safety Administration. (Report No. DOT–HS–0521–068). Springfield, Va.: National Technical Information Service, 1977

Transport Canada. *Draft report on an initial exchange of information on alcohol and highway safety.* Ottawa, Canada: Ministry of Transport, 1975.

Ulmer, R. G., & Preusser, D. R. *Nassau County Alcohol Safety Action Project annual report for the year 1972.* Minnesota, N.Y.: Nassau County Traffic Safety Board, 1973.

Vingilis, E., & Salutin, L. A prevention programme for drinking driving. *Accident Analysis and Prevention,* 1980, *12,* 267–274.

Vingilis, E., Adlaf, E., & Chung, L. The Oshawa Impaired Drivers Programme: An evaluation of a rehabilitation programme. *Canadian Journal of Criminology,* 1981, *23,* 93–102.

Waller, J. A. Chronic medical conditions and traffic safety. *New England Journal of Medicine,* 1965, *273,* 1413–1420.

Waller, J. A., King, E. M., Nielson, G., & Turkel, H. W. Alcohol and other factors in California highway fatalities. *Proceedings of the 11th Annual Meeting of the American Association for Automotive Medicine,* New York: Society of Automotive Engineers, 1970.

Warren, R. A. *Total risk impairment factors.* Ottawa, Canada: Traffic Injury Research Foundation of Canada, 1976.

Whitehead, P. C. DWI programs: Doing what's in or dodging what's indicated. *Journal of Safety Research,* 1975, *7,* 127–134.

Wilde, G. J. S. *Alcohol and highway safety: A review in quest of remedies.* Ottawa, Canada: Transport Canada (Report CTS–la–74), 1974.

Wolfe, A. C. Characteristics of late-night weekend drivers: Results of the U.S. national roadside breath-testing survey and several local surveys. In S. Israelstam & S. Lambert (Eds.), *Alcohol, drugs, and traffic safety.* Toronto: Addiction Research Foundation, 1975.

Zelhart, P. F. Types of alcoholics and their relationship to traffic violations. *Quarterly Journal of Studies on Alcohol,* 1972, *33,* 811–813.

Zelhart, P. F. *The Alberta Impaired Drivers Programme: Final Report, Phase I.* Edmonton: University of Alberta, 1973.

Zelhart, P. F., & Schurr, B. *The Alberta Impaired Drivers' Programme: Final report on evaluation.* Ottawa: Ministry of Transportation (Report CR7505), 1975.

Zelhart, P. F., & Schurr, B. People who drive while impaired: Issues in treating the drinking driver. In N. Ester & E. Heinemann (Eds.), *Alcoholism: Development consequences and interventions.* St. Louis, Mo.: Mosby, 1977.

Zelhart, P. F., Schurr, B. C., Jr., & Brown, P. A. The drinking driver. In S. Israelstam & S. Lambert (Eds.), *Alcohol, drugs and traffic safety.* Toronto: Addiction Research Foundation, 1975.

Zylman, R. A critical evaluation of the literature on "alcohol involvement" in highway deaths. *Accident Analysis and Prevention,* 1974, 6, 163–204.

Zylman, R. DWI enforcement programs: Why are they not more effective? *Accident Analysis and Prevention,* 1975, 7, 179–190.

14

Military Intervention Programs

JOHN E. KILLEEN

The armed forces of the United States have acquired years of experience in coping with the problems caused by alcohol abuse. The surgeon general of the army reported to the secretary of war in 1890 that

> Little is said . . . concerning the habits of the men, but a good deal may be learned by considering the statistics of alcoholism. The admission rate on account of the effects of intoxicating liquors was 41.43 per thousand of strength, as compared with 3.22 in the British, .35 in the German, and .04 in the Italian army. Among our colored troops the rate was 2.07; among the white troops, 45.64. With these figures before us showing the abuse of intoxicating liquors in the Army, the desirability of lessening the evil is manifest. Prohibition on the military reservation has been suggested and tried, but this has immediately invited the establishment of dens of dissipation and disease just beyond the jurisdiction of the commanding officer. License on the reservation, in the opinion of our medical officers, is infinitely preferable to unbridled license outside of it. It is believed that the canteen system will have a greater effect in reducing the statistics of alcoholism than any measure that has yet been tried. (War Department, 1890)

Interventions were innovative even then. One physician, who was reported to have had the worst alcoholism rate in the army at his post in 1892, reported the following procedure to the surgeon general in 1895:

> I am confident that mistaken kindness has done a great deal in the past to encourage drunkenness. Now each man who has reported at the hospital in any

---

JOHN E. KILLEEN • Lieutenant Colonel, United States Army, Office of Drug and Alcohol Abuse Prevention, Department of Defense, Washington, D.C. 20301.

stage of simple alcoholism is treated as a case of alcoholic poisoning, taken immediately to the operating room, his stomach emptied by the use of the stomach pump, and thoroughly washed out with warm 2 percent soda solution. After this, he is given a bowl of hot beef extract, with cayenne pepper, allowed an hour's rest, after which he is generally able, however unwilling, to do his duty. . . . Occasionally some resistance is met with, but two, or at most three, able-bodied hospital corps men and a perforated wooden gag . . . will, with patience and determination, overcome almost any ordinary opposition.

The effect of this treatment has been uniformly excellent. . . . (I)n almost all cases the craving for liquor is very much diminished. Of course cases may occur which are too serious for such summary treatment. . . . These cases, of course, are promptly taken into the hospital and treated as dangerously sick men.

The deterrent effect of this treatment is excellent. It is, of course, not agreeable, though no one can deny that it is perfectly rational and merciful. In the past ten months but one man has been admitted to hospital for alcoholism. There are no doubt other factors that enter into the production of this marked change in the Post in two years, but I am confident that this method of treating simple alcoholism as poisoning has been a very important, if not the principal one. I may add that in but one case has it been necessary to use this treatment on the same man more than once. (War Department, 1895)

In more recent years, Department of Defense (DoD) policymakers have been committed to a bit more comprehensive approach, based on rigorous analysis of the nature of the alcohol problem coupled with systematic evaluation of program results. Such a comprehensive approach is certainly warranted, as DoD expects to spend over $100 million in Fiscal Year 1982 in direct efforts to prevent and treat alcohol and drug abuse problems in the armed forces. DoD has focused efforts around a number of critical questions and has sought data-based answers to those questions.

In the present chapter six key topics regarding military intervention programs are discussed. These include (1) the target of prevention; (2) the characteristics of alcohol abuse in the military; (3) why the problem is the way it is; (4) why alcohol abuse is so difficult to attack; (5) review of current programs; and (6) evaluation of current programs.

THE TARGET OF PREVENTION

Military alcohol and drug abuse programs seek to reduce the negative impact of alcohol and drug abuse on the national defense, on the health and behavior of military members, on military families, and on society. Therefore, the decided focus of DoD prevention programs is on measurable adverse consequences of abuse rather than upon more peripheral aspects of alcohol and drug use. This clear-eyed focus on specific adverse consequences has not always existed. A brief history of the evolution of this concept will show why it has become the cornerstone of DoD policy and programs.

EARLY PROGRAMS AND PROBLEMS

The first contemporary military alcohol programs began in a small way in the navy in Long Beach, California, and the air force in Dayton, Ohio, in the mid-60s. These early programs were exclusively oriented toward providing hospital care for serious alcoholics. Until 1970, relatively few persons were treated in these facilities (Killeen, 1979).

The 1970s, the latter years of our involvement in Viet Nam, brought social upheaval in American society including increased use of marijuana and other illicit drugs. The most dramatic evidence of this drug usage was provided by television coverage of encamped front-line combat troops "stoned" on heroin and marijuana. In 1971, President Nixon launched the "War on Drugs" and the response by the DoD was massive. Drug detection, treatment, and rehabilitation programs requiring thousands of full-time workers were established around the world.

Before long, perceptive individuals working in these programs began to see that Southeast Asian heroin, which provided public fear and funding, was not even a close contender for the most serious drug abuse problem. Alcohol, the ubiquitous social lubricant, was the number one problem. Alcohol was used by private and colonel alike and resulted in the most damage to the greatest number of service members. The programs formed to cope with the illicit drug threat slowly but perceptively shifted emphasis toward alcohol abuse.

By 1972, over 350 military programs for the prevention, treatment, and rehabilitation of alcohol and drug abuse were in operation. This rapid growth had its drawbacks. The experience base in the armed forces with social programs of this nature was very low. For the most part, line military officers and noncommissioned officers were drafted into the effort. Their primary qualification was a concern for people who were having problems, although a good number of the enlisted program workers were recovered alcoholics or former drug users. Few program workers were previously trained or experienced. No common conceptual theme united the field. It was a time of wide-ranging experimentation, with each program sending workers to civilian training that suited their fancy. Transactional analysis, Rogerian nondirective counseling, gestalt, short-term psychotherapy, aversion therapy, group process, rational-emotive therapy, primal scream, transcendental meditation, reality therapy, Antabuse, scare films, auditorium lectures, hospital treatment, sensitivity training, physical conditioning, and other techniques were tried—primarily without evaluation of results. Needless to say, this explosion of prevention and treatment efforts was perceived to be somewhat unusual by many conservative military line officers and noncommissioned officers.

The initial focus of generally inexperienced program workers was on treating clients. This orientation often resulted in excessive protection and attempts to provide long-term treatment to recidivists, manipulators, and malingerers. These actions alienated line commanders who were short-handed and pressed to get their jobs done. The commanders resented the large amount of time they were required to spend with the 10% who were their worst performers. Commanders preferred to discharge their non-producers and obtain better replacements. Some estrangement developed between the line "hardnosers" and the drug and alcohol program "do gooders." Support for the programs slowly began to erode.

EARLY ASSESSMENT EFFORTS

During this period, recognizing the confusion in the field, military alcohol and drug abuse program policymakers were attempting to assess the scope of the problem and to evaluate program results more systematically. Some of these efforts were very well done and proved necessary steps in program evolution (A. D. Little Co., 1975; Cahalan, Cisin, Gardner, & Smith, 1972; Cahalan & Cisin, 1975; Fisher, 1972, 1973). However, the findings still did not lend themselves to integration into a common conceptual scheme for military programs.

In the alcohol problem area, the results appeared startling. The authors defined problem drinking in terms of personal problems experienced within the three years prior to the survey (Cahalan *et al.,* 1972; Cahalan & Cisin, 1975). The range of problems included was broad, making it possible to classify a person as a problem drinker even though the problems were not too serious. For example, a person indicating that his or her drinking was "very displeasing to a relative" and that he or she had any other problem (such as "spent too much money on drinks or after drinking") at any time during the last three years would be classified as a problem drinker. The studies classified 35 to 40% of the enlisted men in the army and navy as problem drinkers.

EROSION OF SUPPORT

Alcohol and drug abuse program workers accepted and promulgated the findings. The studies corresponded with their perceptions since the majority of the people they dealt with each day were having trouble with alcohol and drugs. The extent of the problem also made their jobs—often accused of being "soft-core"—appear much more critical to the national defense. However, commanders simply did not believe the assessments and most dismissed them from their active list of concerns.

The concept of 40% problem drinkers simply did not describe reality for line officers and senior sergeants who were supervising soldiers and sailors every day and were getting difficult and complex jobs done with them. In fact, many of the behaviors defined as problems did not appear to many officers to be of any significance to the services. These problems were seen as purely the personal business of the individuals involved. Career military were angered by the negative media attention to problem drinking in the armed forces. Enthusiastic campaigns by program workers—often regarded as zealots—were seen as infringements on the privacy of the individual. Particularly in the alcohol area, prevention messages based on "everybody has a problem" did not sell and program support eroded.

In 1975 and 1976, the House Appropriations Committee (HAC) became troubled by the profusion of counselors in the military. At a time of reduced funding for the armed forces, the HAC was scrutinizing the "teeth-to-tail ratio," that is, the proportion of fighting forces to support forces. They directed a cut in the number of military counselors, and some services chose to reduce alcohol and drug abuse programs substantially.

RENEWAL

As an unintended counterpoint to the program reductions, the General Accounting Office (GAO) published a report entitled "Alcohol Abuse Is More Prevalent in the Military than Drug Abuse" (April 1976). The basic finding of this investigation was that the $16.7 million expended by the services in fiscal 1976 to cope with military alcohol problems may not have been enough, given the magnitude of the problem. The report was controversial and responses to it were mixed. However, General David C. Jones, then chief of staff of the air force, agreed with the findings and authorized his staff to launch a comprehensive alcohol abuse prevention program in the air force.

One critical element of this renewal of emphasis was the decision to develop an operational definition of alcohol abuse and alcoholism that would be persuasive to all who would play a role in coping with the problem. Most importantly, the concept had to make sense to line commanders because, whether program specialists liked it or not, in the military services commanders set priorities and make programs either succeed or fail.

A review of concepts used by civilians in the field at the time revealed nearly universal lack of unanimity. Loud and long debates persisted at work-shops, conferences, and universities concerning such concepts as alcohol abuse versus problem drinking, alcoholism versus alcohol dependence, al-coholism as disease versus alcoholism as learned behavior, single-distribu-tion theory versus genetic predisposition theory, and controlled drinking versus abstinence. None could agree how misuse of prescription drugs or use of illicit drugs should be factored into alcohol abuse concepts. Alcohol and drug programs in the United States seemed bifurcated between alco-hol-only and illicit-drug-only approaches, partly because of the manner in which the federal effort was organized (i.e., the National Institute on Drug Abuse separate from the National Institute on Alcohol Abuse and Alcohol-ism) and partly because of significant demographic differences between the national alcoholism and the national drug abuse constituencies. (As of late 1981, this unwarranted bifurcation still persisted in both the executive and legislative components of the federal alcohol and drug abuse effort.)

After assessing the confusion in the field, the air force chose to develop its own operational definitions of abuse based on one clear question: "At what point should the military intervene to change a member's alcohol or drug consuming behavior?" The answer decided upon was, "The military will intervene when the member's behavior has, or can reasonably be ex-pected to have, an adverse impact on the air force." Given this focus, it became necessary to flesh out specific policy-relevant criteria that balanced the needs and obligations of the servicemember with the needs and obliga-tions of the military institution.

TOUGH-MINDED ASSESSMENT

In 1977, the air force chartered Rand Corporation to conduct a com-prehensive study of air force alcohol programs. The first step in the study required a thorough assessment of the number of active duty personnel affected by specific alcohol problems that could both be measured and clearly be seen to warrant formal intervention. This assessment component of the larger study was begun in 1977 and was published in 1979 (Polich & Orvis, 1979). The focus on specific behaviors that warranted institutional intervention opened the possibility of establishing a new coherence and credibility to military alcohol and drug abuse prevention programs.

The concepts developed in the Rand study of the air force generally were adopted by the Office of the Secretary of Defense, were expanded to apply to illicit drugs, and were incorporated into a worldwide prevalence assessment effort. The definitional and assessment groundwork laid by Rand and the air force culminated in a *Worldwide Survey of Nonmedical Drug*

Use and Alcohol Use Among Military Personnel: 1980 (Burt & Biegel, 1980). This seminal work provided for all services a realistic and persuasive appraisal of the prevalence of alcohol use, of heavy drinking, of those at risk of experiencing adverse physiological effects, and of those who are alcohol dependent. It also detailed specific consequences of alcohol abuse to the individual and to the military, with special emphasis on work impairment. Finally, it provided a similar appraisal for illicit drug abuse and laid the groundwork for analyzing the relationship between alcohol abuse and drug abuse in the military population.

This comprehensive appraisal is assisting the military services to progressively evolve systematic, data-based programs to reduce the adverse effects of alcohol and drug abuse on the national defense and on servicemembers. Before outlining these military programs in some detail, the characteristics of alcohol use and abuse in the armed forces as revealed by the 1980 Worldwide Survey (Burt & Biegel, 1980) are described.

THE CHARACTERISTICS OF ALCOHOL ABUSE IN THE MILITARY

WHO DRINKS?

The percentage of the active military population that drank any alcohol beverage during the 30 days preceding the survey is shown in Table 1. Most military members (83%) drank at least occasionally. The highest prevalence

Table 1.
Population Using Alcohol during Past 30 Days (Percentage)[a]

Pay grade group	Total DoD	Service			
		Army	Navy	Marine Corps	Air Force
Total worldwide	83	80	86	86	82
E1–E5	83	81	88	86	82
E6–E9	77	75	78	83	78
W1–W4	76	76	80	–	*
O1–O3	83	80	88	91	82
O4–O6	91	92	94	84	90

[a]$n = 15,268$.
–Less than 30 respondents.
*Not applicable.

of drinking any alcohol was reported by senior officers; the lowest was reported by senior enlisted and warrant officers. Beer was the most commonly consumed beverage (73%). Hard liquor was next (51%). Only 35% drank wine during the past 30 days.

WHO DRINKS HEAVILY?

The Worldwide Survey defined heavy drinking in two ways. First, consumption of 8 or more drinks on a typical drinking day during the past 30 days was considered to be heavy drinking. Second, consumption of 8 or more drinks in a single day at least once a week during the past 12 months also was considered heavy drinking. It should be noted that these categories were not created to be problem categories in themselves. They were designed as an intermediate step to permit analysis of the relationship of heavy drinking to alcohol dependence and adverse consequences of use.

The percent of population consuming 8 or more drinks on a typical drinking day is shown in Table 2. Overall, 8% regularly drank 8 or more drinks per drinking day. Heavy drinking was reported largely by junior enlisted personnel. Twelve percent of junior enlisted and 4% of senior enlisted reported heavy drinking of beer. Eight percent of junior enlisted and 3% of senior enlisted reported heavy use of hard liquor. Only 1% of each enlisted group reported heavy drinking of wine. Only 1% or less of each officer group reported any heavy drinking during the past 30 days.

Table 2.
Quantity Consumed on a Typical Drinking Day during Past 30 Days—Worldwide Total (Percentage of Population)[a]

Beverage/frequency	Total DoD	Service			
		Army	Navy	Marine Corps	Air Force
Beer					
8–11 drinks	5	5	7	7	3
12 or more drinks	3	3	5	4	1
Wine					
8–11 drinks	+	+	+	+	+
12 or more drinks	1	1	1	1	1
Hard liquor					
8–11 drinks	4	3	5	6	2
12 or more drinks	2	2	3	2	1

[a] $n = 15,268$.
+ Less than half of one percent.

Table 3.
Heavy drinkers[a]*—Worldwide Total (Percentage of Population)*

		Service			
Beverage	Total DoD	Army	Navy	Marine Corps	Air Force
Beer	21	22	25	28	13–14
Wine	5–6	8	5–6	7	3–4
Hard liquor	11	12	14	13	7–8

[a]Defined as a person who drank eight or more cans, glasses, or drinks in a single day at least once a week during the past 12 months.
[b]N = 15,268

Table 3 depicts heavy drinking during a 12-month period. Twenty-one percent of those surveyed indicated that they had consumed beer heavily at least once a week during the past 12 months. The heavy drinking patterns were similar to those described for typical drinking during the last 30 days, although the percentages naturally were higher for the 12-month period. Twenty-eight percent of junior enlisted and 10% of senior enlisted reported heavy drinking of beer; 14% junior enlisted and 5% senior enlisted drank hard liquor heavily; 8% and 1%, respectively, reported heavy use of wine. Drinking of this intensity was rarely reported by officers.

WHO RISKS SEVERE MEDICAL PROBLEMS?

The review of the literature by Rand in the air force study (Polich & Orvis, 1979) found compelling evidence that persons regularly consuming over five ounces of ethanol (about 10 drinks) a day were at great risk of developing severe medical problems, especially cirrhotic or precirrhotic conditions. Table 4 shows the results of the special analysis using this five ounce limit as the point where risk of severe medical problems could be presumed. Again, the high-risk drinking group clusters in the junior enlisted population.

WHO IS DEPENDENT ON ALCOHOL?

Based on the constructs developed by Rand for the air force (Polich & Orvis, 1979), a conservative but realistic definition of alcohol dependence was employed. A person was defined as alcohol dependent who, during the preceding 12-month period, experienced one or more of the following

Table 4.
Population at High Risk for Severe Medical Problems (Percentage)[a]

| Pay grade group | Total DoD | Service | | | |
		Army	Navy	Marine Corps	Air Force
Total	7.9	9.2	9.9	10.1	3.6
E1–E5	10.9	12.2	13.9	12.9	5.3
E6–E9	3.1	4.9	2.7	2.6	1.3
W1–W4	0.2	0	1.0	–	*
O1–O3	0.7	1.5	0.1	0.9	0.4
O4–O6	0.6	0	0	2.4	1.0

[a]n = 15,268.
–Less than 30 respondents.
*Not applicable.

symptoms during at least 48 of the 52 weeks: (1) tremors (shakes); (2) morning drinking; (3) impaired control; and (4) blackouts. The specific definitions provided to respondents for each symptom were

- Tremors (shakes): "I had the 'shakes' because of drinking."
- Morning drinking: "I took a drink the first thing when I got up in the morning."
- Impaired control: "I could not stop drinking before becoming drunk."
- Blackouts: "I awakened the next day unable to remember what I had done while drinking the day before."

The results of this analysis are shown in Table 5. Seven percent of all military personnel were found to be alcohol dependent during the 12 months prior to the survey. Again, alcohol dependence clustered in the junior enlisted population (10%). The senior enlisted rate was 3%, and alcohol dependency was rare among warrant officers and commissioned officers. These patterns of alcohol dependency were consistent with the patterns of heavy drinking and medical risks due to alcohol.

WHAT ARE THE CONSEQUENCES?

Given the DoD focus on reducing the adverse effects of alcohol abuse on the military, the data on consequences of alcohol use were of particular concern. Respondents were asked to report whether specific consequences had occurred because of their use of alcohol during the preceding 12

Table 5.
Alcohol Dependence during Past 12 Months (Percentage of Population)[a]

Region/pay grade	Total DoD	Service			
		Army	Navy	Marine Corps	Air Force
Conus					
Total	7	8	10	11	4
E1–E5	10	11	13	14	5
E6–E9	4	4	5	4	2
O1–O3	1	1	+	3	0
O4–O6	+	0	0	1	1
Europe					
Total	6	8	5	*	3
E1–E5	9	11	7	*	4
E6–E9	1	2	1	*	1
O1–O3	+	0	1	*	0
O4–O6	1	–	3	*	0
Pacific					
Total	7	5	7	11	6
E1–E5	10	8	12	13	7
E6–E9	3	4	3	2	4
O1–O3	3	2	1	–	1
O4–O6	0	0	–	0	2
Other locations					
Total	4	5	4	*	4
E1–E5	5	6	4	*	6
E6–E9	3	3	3	*	3
O1–O3	0	–	–	*	–
O4–O6	4	–	–	*	–
Total worldwide					
Total	7	8	9	11	4
E1–E5	10	11	12	14	5
E6–E9	3	3	5	4	2
W1–W4	+	0	0	–	*
O1–O3	1	1	+	5	+
O4–O6	+	0	1	1	1

Note: A person is defined as "alcohol dependent" who, during the preceding 12-month period, experienced one or more of the following symptoms during at least 48 weeks: (1) tremors (shakes), (2) morning drinking, (3) impaired control, and (4) blackouts.
[a] $n = 15,268$.
*Not applicable.
–Less than 30 respondents.
+Less than half of one percent.

months. Table 6 details the percentages of respondents who reported that at least one of 15 physical, social, or work consequences of alcohol use had occurred during the preceding 12 months. A significant number of respondents indicated that they had experienced more than one negative consequence. The "total with any consequence" figures, reflecting an unduplicated count, show that 11% of all respondents reported suffering at least one consequence. As is indicated by the data in Table 7, these adverse consequences again clustered in the junior enlisted force.

Table 6.
Consequences of Alcohol Use during Past 12 Months—Total DOD (Percentage of Population)[a]

| Consequence | Total DoD | Service | | | |
		Army	Navy	Marine Corps	Air Force
Illness kept from duty 1 week or longer	2	2	2	2	1
Did not get promoted	2	2	1	3	1
Got lower score on efficiency or performance report	2	2	3	4	1
Received judicial or article 15 punishment	2	3	2	3	1
Arrested for driving after drinking	3	3	3	5	2
Arrested for nondriving drinking incident	2	3	3	4	1
Incarcerated due to drinking	3	2	4	5	1
Hurt in accident connected with drinking	2	2	4	4	1
Drinking caused accident where others hurt or property damaged	2	2	3	3	1
Spouse threatened to leave	2	2	2	2	1
Hit spouse or children	1	1	1	2	1
Spouse left	1	1	+	1	+
Entered rehabilitation or treatment program	2	2	2	2	1
Attended training or education program	2	2	2	3	1
Detoxified	1	1	1	1	+
Total with any consequence[b]	11	11	14	17	6

[a] n = 15,268.
[b] Percentage of population with at least one of the consequences during the past 12 months.
+ Less than half of one percent.

Table 7.
Total with Any Consequence of Alcohol Use during Past 12 Months
(Percentage by Grade)[a]

Pay grade group	Total DoD	Service			
		Army	Navy	Marine Corps	Air Force
E1–E5	14	15	18	21	8
E6–E9	7	6	8	11	5
W1–W4	1	0	3	–	*
O1–O3	1	2	3	2	+
O4–O6	3	1	7	2	1

[a]*n* = 15,268.
–Less than 30 respondents.
*Not applicable.
+Less than half of one percent.

These data provided, for the first time, a persuasive prevalence assessment of the extent of significant adverse consequences due to alcohol that occur in the military services. They provided a basis for developing clear, behaviorally oriented indicators that commanders could look for in deciding whether or not formal intervention is appropriate. Although each of the consequences already discussed is clearly significant, it was anticipated that commanders and supervisors would be most concerned about work-related consequences of abuse. For that reason, a special analysis of work impairment was performed.

HOW IS WORK AFFECTED?

Table 8 reflects the percentages of all respondents who reported suffering work impairment because of alcohol use during the preceding 12 months. Of those reporting, 22% reported lowered performance, 13% reported that they were late for work or left early, 11% were drunk or "high" while working, and 5% did not come to work. A considerable number reported more than one of these categories of impairment. The total percentage of persons suffering at least one instance of work impairment is 27%.

Table 9 indicates, again, that the adverse consequences are greatest in the junior enlisted population. However, this tendency was less pronounced in this work impairment category than it was in some of the earlier categories. The higher percentage of officers and senior noncommissioned officers who

Table 8.
Work Impairment Due to Alcohol Use during Past 12 Months—Total DoD[c]
(Percentage of Population)[a]

Impairment/number of days happened	Total DoD	Service			
		Army	Navy	Marine Corps	Air Force
Lowered performance					
total	100	100	100	100	100
0	78	81	70	71	83
1	5	5	6	7	5
2–3	7	5	10	9	6
4–11	6	5	8	8	4
12–39	2	2	4	3	1
40 or more	2	2	3	2	1
Late for work/left early					
total	100	100	100	100	100
0	87	87	83	84	90
1	4	4	4	4	4
2–3	4	4	6	6	3
4–11	3	2	4	3	2
12–39	1	1	1	1	+
40 or more	1	2	2	2	+
Did not come to work					
total	100	100	100	100	100
0	95	94	95	95	98
1	1	1	2	2	1
2–3	1	1	2	1	1
4–11	1	1	1	1	+
12–39	+	+	+	+	+
40 or more	1	2	a1	1	+
Drunk/high while working					
total	100	100	100	100	100
0	89	89	84	85	94
1	2	2	3	3	2
2–3	3	3	4	4	2
4–11	3	2	4	3	1
12–39	1	1	2	2	+
40 or more	2	3	3	3	+
Total with any impairment[b]	27	24	35	34	20

[a] n = 15,268.
[b] Percentage of population with any impairment at least once during past 12 months.
[c] Less than half of one percent. Percents may not add to 100 due to rounding.

Table 9.

Total with Any Impairment Due to Alcohol Use during Past 12 Months (Percentage by Grade)[a]

Pay grade group	Total DoD	Service			
		Army	Navy	Marine Corps	Air Force
E1–E5	31	29	40	38	24
E6–E9	19	16	25	25	16
W1–W4	9	4	12	–	*
O1–O3	17	15	29	21	12
O4–O6	12	7	14	15	15

[a]$n = 15,268.$
–Less than 30 respondents.
*Not applicable.

reported work impairment primarily reported lowered performance on the job or late for work/left early. Missing work or being drunk/high while working was rarely reported by the senior grades. These more serious aspects of work impairment were most frequently reported by junior enlisted personnel.

What about Illicit Drugs?

The prevalence and consequences data presented above address alcohol abuse behavior in a manner unrelated to other drug abuse behavior. Secondary analyses of the survey data have shown this approach to be unrealistic. As has been noted, the greatest amount of alcohol abuse occurs among the junior enlisted population—the same age group that abuses drugs. However, with incorporation of the prevalence and consequences of the use of illicit drugs as well as alcohol into the analysis, the description begins to grow complex. Although use patterns are relatively easy to outline, disentangling alcohol-caused consequences from illicit drug-caused consequences is virtually impossible. The complications inherent in such an analysis inexorably push one toward adoption of the concept of substance abuse rather than toward distinguishing alcohol abuse from drug abuse. A young military person who has trouble with alcohol can be most accurately described as a substance abuser.

As Table 10 indicates, 48% of the E1–E5s stated they had used marijuana or hashish at least once together with alcohol. Twenty percent re-

Table 10.
Combined Use of Drugs and Alcohol (Percentage of E1–E5 Population)[a]

Drug type/frequency	Total DoD	Army	Navy	Marine Corps	Air Force
			Service		
Marijuana/hashish					
Total	100	100	100	100	100
Never	52	50	45	40	67
Once	6	6	5	8	6
Sometimes	22	24	24	25	17
Very often	13	12	17	17	7
Always	7	9	9	10	3
Phencyclidine					
Total	100	100	100	100	100
Never	92	93	89	87	98
Once	3	3	5	4	1
Sometimes	3	3	5	6	1
Very often	1	1	1	2	+
Always	1	1	1	1	+
Other hallucinogens					
Total	100	100	100	100	100
Never	88	91	82	80	94
Once	2	2	4	3	1
Sometimes	6	5	10	11	3
Very often	2	1	2	3	1
Always	1	2	2	3	1
Cocaine					
Total	100	100	100	100	100
Never	84	85	77	75	92
Once	3	3	4	5	2
Sometimes	9	8	12	13	4
Very often	3	2	4	5	1
Always	2	2	2	3	1
Amphetamines/ other uppers					
Total	100	100	100	100	100
Never	84	86	76	78	91
Once	3	3	3	3	2
Sometimes	9	8	14	12	5
Very often	3	2	5	4	1
Always	2	2	2	3	1
Tranquilizers					
Total	100	100	100	100	100
Never	93	94	89	90	97
Once	2	2	3	2	1
Sometimes	4	3	6	5	2
Very often	1	1	2	1	+
Always	1	1	1	1	+

[a]Percents may not add to 100 due to rounding.
+Less than half of one percent.

ported combined use frequently. Sixteen percent had used cocaine with alcohol, and 16% used amphetamines with alcohol. Other illicit drugs were much less frequently used with alcohol (i.e., heroin, other opiates, and barbiturates).

Even more compelling evidence supporting the concept of substance abuse, especially among the young, is provided in Table 11.

Of those junior enlisted personnel who drank three ounces or more of ethanol (about 6 drinks) a day, 62% used marijuana at least weekly. Forty-two percent were daily users. On the other hand, of those junior enlisted who used no alcohol in the past 30 days, 90% also used no marijuana. Senior enlisted personnel who had not used alcohol during the past 30 days also did not use marijuana. No significant marijuana use by senior enlisted is reported until ethanol use rates reach three ounces or more. These same relationships held for use of other illicit drugs, specifically, heavy alcohol use correlated with heavier illicit drug use, although the prevalence of use of the other drugs was much lower.

Evidence is becoming increasingly clear that young military members who drink heavily often have more than alcohol problems alone. It can be reasonably assumed that a military person under the age of 25 who is having difficulty with a mood-altering chemical such as alcohol also may be having a problem with other illicit drugs.

Table 11.
Current Alcohol Use Compared to Current Marijuana Use (Percentage)

Marijuana use (By grade)	Average daily alcohol consumption (Last 30 Days)[a]		
	None	0.1 to 2.9 oz. ethanol	3 oz. or more ethanol
Nonuser			
E1–E5	90	62	29
E6–E9	99	95	86
Monthly user			
E1–E5	3	10	9
E6–E9	+	2	5
Weekly user			
E1–E5	2	15	20
E6–E9	+	2	1
Daily user			
E1–E5	5	13	42
E6–E9	+	1	8

[a]n = 15,268.
+Less than half of one percent.

Summary

What then are the main characteristics of alcohol use and abuse in the military? Most military members drink. However, less than one in four drinks heavily. Heavy drinking occurs most frequently among the junior enlisted population. About 8% of the population regularly consumes a sufficient amount of alcohol to be considered at high risk for severe medical problems. About 7% of the population is dependent on alcohol. About 11% of military members experience at least one serious adverse consequence each year due to alcohol abuse. About 22% experience at least some impairment on the job. Eleven percent have been drunk or high while working; 3% were drunk or high on the job 12 or more times during a year. Overwhelmingly, the high consumption and the negative consequences cluster in the junior enlisted population. When the complicating factor of illicit drug use by the young is added to the analysis of alcohol abusing behavior, one is impelled toward acceptance of the concept of substance abuse, at least for this segment of the population. Heavy drinkers of alcohol among the junior enlisted members of the armed forces tend to also be heavy users of marijuana and, to a lesser extent, other illicit drugs.

WHY IS THE PROBLEM THE WAY IT IS?

The common perception, even among professional alcohol abuse and alcoholism researchers, is that alcohol and drug abuse problems in the United States armed forces are significantly worse than the problems in the general society (Blane, 1979; Cahalan & Cisin, 1975; Chafetz, 1979). This perception is both true and false.

Relative Rates of Use

In relative terms, especially when key demographic variables are standardized for the military and for the civilian population, the perception is false. The first comprehensive analysis of this phenomenon was performed by Rand (Polich & Orvis, 1979). They standardized the variables age, sex, education, marital status, and location and concluded that "the available data strongly imply that the differences among military and civilian groups are in large measure attributable to the different demographic characteristics of these groups."

This line of analysis was continued in the DoD Worldwide Survey (Burt & Biegel, 1980). The subpopulation at highest risk (i.e., persons 18 to

25 years old) for nonmedical drug and alcohol abuse in both military and civilian populations was compared. The data were standardized for sex, age, marital status, and education. This standardization provided prevalence rates that are not biased by the differences in occurrence of the significant characteristics in the two populations. Results are displayed in Table 12. As can be seen, there is no general pattern of drug or alcohol use being more prevalent for military or civilian populations. Current nonmedical drug use for military personnel and civilians is about the same for all drug types analyzed. The same pattern holds true for annual rates of use. However, this evidence that substance abuse problems are relatively no worse in the military leaves little room for comfort.

Table 12.
Prevalence of Nonmedical Drug Use and Alcohol Use Among Military Personnel and Comparable Civilians—Ages 18–25 (Percentage of 18–25 Year-Old Population)

Type	Military ($n = 8224$)	Comparable civilians[a] ($n = 2022$)
Marijuana/hashish		
Past 30 days	40	42
Past 12 months	52	54
Amphetamines or other uppers		
Past 30 days	10	4
Past 12 months	21	12
Cocaine		
Past 30 days	7	10
Past 12 months	18	23
Hallucinogens		
Past 30 days	5	5
Past 12 months	13	12
Barbiturates or other downers		
Past 30 days	4	4
Past 12 months	9	10
Tranquilizers		
Past 30 days	3	3
Past 12 months	9	12
Heroin		
Past 30 days	1	1
Past 12 months	3	1
Alcohol		
Past 30 days	84	82
Past 12 months	93	90

[a]Data standardized with respect to sex, age, marital status, and education. Based on special tabulations from the 1979 national survey on drug abuse.

ABSOLUTE RATES OF USE

In absolute terms, the common perception is true that the military has a more serious problem than do civilian institutions. Per capita, the problem is worse in the military. If random groups of civilians and military personnel were studied (without standardizing for demographic variables), a greater percentage of substance abusers would be found in the military. Higher-risk persons populate the military; they are largely male, young, single, somewhat less educated, and more likely to be at least temporarily living in remote locations without families. These factors are known to predispose all people to alcohol and drug abuse problems.

It is the absolute scope of the problem that the military must confront and manage. The captain of a ship can take no comfort in the fact that his crew is comparable to their civilian contemporaries in their substance abusing habits. He must confront and deal with the adverse consequences of their use as they occur in his environment and as they impede his mission accomplishment.

In summary, the problem of alcohol and drug abuse in the military is the way it is largely because of the demographic characteristics of the persons who comprise the armed forces. They are young, single, somewhat less educated males who serve under challenging conditions, often in remote locations. The army surgeon general's report noted earlier indicated that the military has been attacking at least the alcohol problem for a very long time. Why hasn't the problem been solved?

WHY IS ALCOHOL ABUSE SO DIFFICULT TO ATTACK?

Alcohol and drug abuse are very difficult problems to solve. Both the evidence and my thinking concerning the nature of the difficulty with alcohol are clear. I will, therefore, focus primarily on alcohol, but I will briefly address the drug question in a theoretical vein.

ALCOHOL ABUSE

The problems associated with alcohol are difficult to attack because the use of alcohol, for the most part, is traditional and beneficial to the military and to its people. Some history will clarify this point.

The origins of alcohol are lost in the mists of prehistory, but some clues to the nature of its early use can be gathered from studies of more contemporary preliterate societies. Most preliterate societies make beer and wine and accord its use a central place in their cultures. The social importance of this alcohol use can be inferred from the nature of the events and ceremonies to which its use has become attached. These events and ceremonies include, for example, births, religious initiations, worship services, marriages, treatment of illness and pain, social gatherings, and funerals.

Historical evidence for the social importance of alcohol abounds. Rules for drinking are included in Hammurabi's Laws, the oldest known legal code (circa 1770 B.C.). Sumerian and Egyptian doctors included beer and wine in their prescriptions (circa 1500 B.C.) (Alcohol Consumption, 1977).

Alcohol served a key role in early religious rites both as an offering to the gods and as a drink. Although they counsel moderation, both the Old and New Testament clearly regarded wine as a gift of God. The use of red wine to symbolize the blood of life still persists in the Christian Eucharist.

Military history extensively records the social importance of alcohol consumption to military forces. To soldiers of Rome (Windrow & Wilkinson, 1971), medieval knights (Windrow & Wilkinson, 1971), fifteenth-century French and English soldiers at Agincourt (Keegan, 1976), Civil War soldiers of the Sixth Pennsylvania Cavalry (Windrow & Wilkinson, 1971), and soldiers of the modern U.S. Army (Ingraham, 1978), alcohol consumption served important individual and group functions.

Moderate alcohol use in the military continues to serve important functions, primarily by enhancing group cohesion. Ceremonies associated with alcohol, such as launching of ships, dining-ins (formal military dinners in dress uniform), military weddings, and Christmas parties provide shared traditions. Promotion celebrations, change of command parties, reassignment parties, and "wetting-down" parties on graduation from flight school or completion of 100 combat missions provide rites of passage. Liberties in port and nights on the town provide shared experiences that frequently are recounted as "war stories" and enhance small group bonds (Ingraham, 1978). Happy hours and beer busts after periods of particularly hard work or on completion of major inspections aid informal interaction, coordination, and cohesion of work units.

Most military leaders strive to reinforce the belief among military members that they are part of a special institution and are not just employees (Janowitz & 1979). In this regard, dining-outs (formal military dinners in full dress uniform, with spouses), happy hours, picnics, cocktail parties, and formal holidy parties provide important social interaction among military co-workers, leaders, and their family members. This interaction often helps to impress upon family members the special nature of the military calling and to provide a tangible sense of being part of a larger community.

Additionally, for both individuals and groups, alcohol serves its centuries-old function of relieving tension. A few beers at the club after a hazardous mission ease combat tension. A tranquilizing cocktail before dinner eases the transition from the pressured work environment to family interaction. Work units relax after the inspector leaves by holding a beer bust.

From a budgetary viewpoint, alcohol also serves a vital function. Alcohol sales in military clubs and package stores provide substantial funds that are used to support other popular morale, welfare, and recreation activities that cannot be self-supporting (U.S. Congress, 1979).

It is clear that alcohol consumption serves useful, socially integrative purposes in the DoD. Most members are moderate drinkers who experience no harm from their use of alcoholic beverages. Nevertheless, it also is clear that a substantial number of persons do suffer adverse consequences from the consumption of alcohol, and that these consequences impact negatively on mission accomplishment and operational costs.

Drug Abuse

Basically, the problems associated with alcohol are difficult to attack because use of the drug is both beneficial and destructive. Striking a proper balance is the challenge. On the other hand, illicit drug use, particularly marijuana use, does not have any beneficial effects on the military services. Many users will argue that use of marijuana benefits them personally, but few observers—including the users—maintain that marijuana use is helpful to the military institution. In fact, it is the second most serious drug problem in the military services. Its use appears to persist because of youth custom, peer pressure, availability, profitability, and the pleasure individuals perceive from its use. However, the continual violation of military standards, conflict between "lifers" and "first-termers" over the issue, legal and law enforcement costs, premature separations for refusal or inability to stop using, shoddy work, accidents, and lost productivity compound into very costly adverse consequences.

One of the adverse consequences most difficult to quantify is the impact of marijuana use on unit cohesion. Most young soldiers will drink a beer with all other military members, often enhancing communication and cohesion. However, the characteristics of marijuana use tend to create small in-groups whose cohesion often is directed *against* the "straights" and the "lifers." Discipline, trust, and unit cohesion are all negatively affected (Ingraham, 1978).

Use of marijuana is difficult to attack both because its use is well concealed and because personal profits from illegal sales are enormous. Increasing use of drug detector dogs and recently developed urine testing systems, coupled with recent research information about the negative impact of marijuana on health, are expected to reduce the amount of marijuana use in the next several years. However, this divisive problem can be expected to persist for the forseeable future and will continue to add to the cost of national defense.

REVIEW OF CURRENT PROGRAMS

The Department of Defense is progressively developing a substance abuse control system. This system is designed to be realistic, data-based, and cybernated (i.e., able to provide self-correcting feedback). It is operationally decentralized but monitored from a central point of authority. It strives to properly balance the needs of the individual with the needs of the military institution. Significantly, the substance abuse control system focuses on specific consequences or potential consequences of abuse. It is organized so that it can be continually evaluated and improved in light of new knowledge and experience.

Although this comprehensive substance abuse control system is not yet fully established in all military departments, significant progress has been made. The current state of development is discussed below. The primary functional components are assessment, prevention, treatment/rehabilitation, and program evaluation.

ASSESSMENT

The assessment component is chartered to define accurately the nature, extent, and consequences of the substance abuse threat to the DoD. Assessment occurs at each level of military command: base, major command, service headquarters, and the office of the Secretary of Defense.

At the local base or post, the Drug and Alcohol Abuse Control Committee (sometimes called the Drug and Alcohol Abuse Review Board) is the key element in both problem assessment and program oversight. This committee, chaired by the senior installation commander or his deputy, is basically a board of advisors concerned with the scope, efficiency, and quality of the community effort to reduce the negative effects of substance abuse. The membership consists of drug and alcohol abuse prevention, medical, law enforcement, investigative chaplain, public information, recreation, legal, safety, and other appropriate officers. They are responsible for:

1. The analysis of the nature, extent, and effect of the substance abuse threat to the installation community and organizational missions,
2. The development of a comprehensive installation plan responding to all aspects of the substance abuse threat,

3. The qualitative evaluation of existing programs to provide guidance for systematic change; and
4. The maintenance of installation-wide support for the substance abuse programs. (U.S. Air Force, 1979)

Assessments of the local threat are updated at least every three months. These assessments are provided from each base to the major command responsible for that base.

Major commands are established, with some exceptions in the navy and Marine Corps, to command bases and posts with similar missions. Normally, each major command controls between 5 and 30 bases. At each of these commands, there is a drug and alochol abuse control staff and a drug and alcohol abuse control committee. These agencies gather and assess the information provided from each installation. Coupling this information with data gathered through other methods (intelligence, law enforcement trends, treatment information, etc.), each major command develops a regional or command assessment. These assessments are provided to the headquarters of the services in Washington, D.C.

The services' headquarters gather assessments from each of the major commands and integrate them into a service-wide assessment of the substance abuse problem. Based on these assessments, the headquarters establish service-unique policies and operate drug and alcohol abuse prevention programs. Historically, each service also conducted independent surveys to assess the drug and alcohol abuse problem in its organization. Now, however, each relies primarily on the worldwide surveys conducted by the Office of Drug and Alcohol Abuse Prevention (ODAAP) in the office of the Secretary of Defense.

The Office of Drug and Alcohol Abuse Prevention (ODAAP) has designed and implemented an epidemiological assessment system. This worldwide assessment system consists of a point prevalence assessment (i.e., survey of the nature, extent, and consequences at a given point in time) coupled with a trend assessment (i.e., analysis of indicators to identify trends occurring between surveys).

The current point prevalence assessment (Burt & Biegel, 1980), summarized earlier in this chapter, will be administered again in 1982. Additionally, point prevalence assessments are being prepared for the DoD civilian employee population and for military high school students.

The continuous trend assessment between the two-year surveys consists of assessments from the services (the equivalent of a drug and alcohol abuse control committee also functions at this level) and a series of required quarterly reports. (DoDI 1010.3, 1981). These include reports of rejections of recruits for drug or alcohol reasons; identifications of servicemembers as drug or alcohol abusers; drug testing (urinalysis) results; treatment/rehabilitation entries and dispositions; law enforcement trends; accident and injury trends; and reports of drug and alcohol related deaths. Additionally, information obtained from other federal agencies such as the State Department, the Drug Enforcement Administration, the National Institute on Alcohol Abuse and Alcoholism, the National Institute on Drug Abuse, the Office of Personnel Management, and others is integrated into the assessment.

The goal of this comprehensive assessment system is to enable DoD to assess the nature of substance abuse problems in the military continually and accurately in order to rapidly adjust policy and program responses to reduce the impact of substance abuse on our forces.

PREVENTION

The prevention component of the DoD program consists of two elements: deterrence/detection and education/training. Deterrence and detection programs are intended to suppress drug use and alcohol misuse in the military. Education and training programs provide information and skills to help members avoid drug and alcohol abuse and to deal effectively with these problems in their subordinates.

Deterrence and Detection

Deterrence and detection efforts begin before induction. Recruiters screen potential enlistees and reject those who are drug or alcohol dependent or who have a record of serious drug or alcohol abuse. After induction, background checks performed on the individual insure that no history of recent or serious substance abuse exists. At the armed forces entrance and examining stations (AFEES) recruits are medically evaluated and screened. Urine tests for illicit drugs frequently are accomplished. At basic training the individual is taught military standards of behavior and performance. Recruits sign documents acknowledging that they understand DoD drug and alcohol abuse policy and the consequences for violating that policy.

At all bases, drug testing through urinalysis is accomplished. Individuals are required to provide urine samples in all stiuations in which suspicion of drug abuse arises, for example, upon return from or apprehension after an unauthorized absence; failure to obey lawful orders; deteriorating, abnormal, or bizarre behavior; assault; violations of safety provisions; and apprehension or investigation for drug offenses. Additionally, when commanders suspect that a drug abuse problem exists in a unit, a urine test of that entire unit may be ordered. These urine tests are analyzed at one of eight DoD drug testing laboratories around the world. They are analyzed for the presence of opiates, amphetamines, barbiturates, cocaine, methaqualone, and phencyclidine. The capability to screen for cannabis was added in late 1981. Results are used to place service members in rehabilitation, if necessary. Under appropriate circumstances, disciplinary action also is taken based on urine test results.

Law enforcement efforts are intense, particularly in areas with high drug availability. To reduce alcohol problems, driving-while-intoxicated, driving-under-the-influence, and alcohol incident laws are strictly enforced. These efforts are backed up by breath analyzers and blood tests. In drug law enforcement, undercover investigators, narcotic detector dogs (dogs trained to smell the presence of marijuana, heroin, and cocaine), searches at the gates entering the base, barracks inspections, and stringent customs procedures are widely used. The goal of all of these efforts is to make drug use and alcohol misuse in the military a high-risk behavior that can be expected to result in identification, disciplinary action, and rehabilitation or, if appropriate, separation from the service.

Education and Training

The second critical element of the DoD prevention effort is the education and training program (DoDI 1010.5, 1980). The program requires that specific learning objectives be accomplished by specific target groups. Upon entry into the military, classes for enlisted personnel emphasize both the positive and the negative aspects of the preventive program. Desired behaviors are specified, credible role models are provided, and participation in healthy alternatives to drug and alcohol abuse is encouraged. New enlistees also are made aware of the legal, health, and career consequences of substance abuse.

For young officer and warrant officer candidates, emphasis is placed on the role, duties, and responsibilities of junior leaders in the prevention and control of alcohol and drug problems. Although the consequences of personal substance abuse are addressed, most focus is on the role of the junior officer in creating and maintaining military discipline. The prevalence, causes, and symptoms of substance abuse are discussed along with the programs that exist to cope with the problem. Intervention and supervisory counseling techniques are demonstrated.

Each time servicemembers are reassigned, continued alcohol and drug abuse education is required. For junior enlisted, emphasis is placed on the consequences of abuse, the local drug/alcohol situation (including local penalties for violations and alternatives available in the local environment), and standards of expected behavior and performance. Officers and noncommissioned officers are taught local prevalence rates, policies, resources, consequences, and program responsibilities.

Probably the most critical portion of the education program is that which is embedded into the system of professional military education. Officers and noncommissioned officers are required to continue their professional education; promotion hinges on their efforts. Alcohol and drug abuse education is one requirement in that educational program. For junior officers and noncommissioned officers, methods of deterrence and detection, coordination of law enforcement and legal efforts, and counseling and motivation skills are stressed. Middle and senior grade officers address the impact of their attitudes about alcohol and drug abuse on subordinates, the reasons for and benefits of a strong prevention program, how the military response to substance abuse fits into the federal effort, and intervention techniques for senior personnel who develop alcohol problems.

The training aspect of DoD programs focuses primarily on continuing education for alcohol and drug abuse program staff and associated health care professionals. Four military schools train alcohol and drug program staff. This training is supplemented by formal on-the-job training, civilian schools, workshops, conferences, and in-service training.

Even with all of this effort, however, a large number of DoD personnel experience problems with alcohol and drugs. These persons may enter the treatment and rehabilitation component of the DoD substance abuse control system (DoD 1010.6, 1981).

Treatment and Rehabilitation

The DoD operates the largest alcohol and drug abuse rehabilitation program in the world. In 1981, there were 56 inpatient facilities and 422 nonresidential and referral centers. During fiscal 1981, over 100,000 servicemembers were treated for alcohol or drug abuse problems; over 20,000 were cared for in residential facilities as inpatients. Operational costs for the treatment, rehabilitation, and referral component approximated $60 million.

Rehabilitation programs are tailored to the needs of the individual and range from intensive education seminars to inpatient hospital care. A general sequence of events for a person entering treatment would be as follows. First, the individual is identified in some manner as a person having problems with chemicals. This identification can be made by a commander, a supervisor, a medical doctor, a urine test (illicit drugs only), or a law enforcement official or can be a self-referral. If the person is using illicit drugs, disciplinary as well as rehabilitative action may be taken (except for self-referrals). Each entrant receives an intake interview and is evaluated. If detoxification is required, it is accomplished at the hospital. Working together, appropriate drug/alcohol staff, medical authorities, and the commander determine the appropriate rehabilitative regimen for each person.

If the member is not deeply involved in substance abuse, he or she is sent to a remedial education program. There are two separate remedial education programs, one for drug and one for alcohol involvement. If the member is judged to have a more serious problem, the education program is supplemented by a formal nonresidential program of rehabilitation that includes individual and group counseling; special supervision on the job; medical, legal, financial, or other assistance; recreational and fitness programs; spiritual assistance by the chaplain; and participation in an appropriate organization such as Alcoholics Anonymous. Each participant's progress is formally evaluated regularly and the regimen is adjusted accordingly.

If the person's alcohol problem is considered too serious for nonresidential care, he or she is sent to one of the 56 inpatient facilities for care. If the person is addicted to illicit drugs, he or she normally is provided 30 days of drug free treatment, is discharged from the military, and is transferred to a Veterans Administration hospital for further care. Only the navy continues to run as inpatient program for drug-dependent persons. All other services separate addicts based on the history of poor results and high costs of such long-term treatment programs.

When servicemembers return from inpatient care, they generally are provided formal follow-up support, including participation in Alcoholics Anonymous. Those who succeed in returning to military standards of performance and behavior are retained and continue their careers. Those who do not meet standards are separated from the military and referred to the Veterans Administration.

Rehabilitation success rates average about 60% for drug abusers and 70% for alcohol abusers. However, there is wide and complex variance based on the nature of the substance; the degree of involvement; the age, job, career, and family status of the abuser; and the military service. For example, young first-term enlisted who are single and are both heavy drinkers and drug users have low rates of success (i.e., 40% and less, depending on degree of drug involvement). On the other hand, married career noncommissioned officers and officers have very high rates of success (i.e., 85+% successful completion).

PROGRAM EVALUATION

The program evaluation component of the DoD substance abuse control system is the least developed. A great deal of effort has gone into program evaluation, both by the individual services and by the Office of Drug and Alcohol Abuse Prevention. Some noteworthy accomplishments have come out of these efforts, but progress is slow. It is inherently difficult to quantify and measure things that have been prevented from happening. It is almost as difficult to measure changes in drug or alcohol consumption patterns. It is impossible to quantify the human worth of increased organizational cohesion, recovered servicemembers, stronger families, more contented base communities, and other similar factors related to an environment with lower levels of substance abuse. An ideal program evaluation system has not yet evolved.

However, some evaluations have done much to shape current programs. Arthur D. Little Company (A.D. Little Co., 1975) completed a thorough study of the drug abuse control programs that resulted in significant management improvement. Presearch, Inc. performed cost-benefit analyses of navy (Borthwick, 1977) and army (Adamson & Borthwick, 1978) programs that clarified costs and benefits of the substance abuse programs and advanced the conceptualization of how to measure the problem. Rand Corporation performed a series of evaluations for the air force that played a large role in the current emphasis on consequences of abuse, education program modifications, and present efforts to assess cost-benefit elements of the programs (Carpenter-Huffman *et al.,* 1981; Orvis *et al.,* 1981; Polich, 1979). Army human readiness reports also have been useful (Department of the Army, 1975, 1978).

A recently completed evaluation of the DoD drug and alcohol treatment program performed by the DoD staff culminated in the publication of a new DoD instruction (DoD I.1010.6, 1981). A continual double-blind urine testing quality control evaluation has been instituted. With this, laboratory effectiveness in identifying illicit drugs is monitored. An evaluation scheme for comparing urine testing rates by region of the world with the drug threat for that region has been developed. Portable urine testing kits for use in drug screening in the field have been tested and evaluated. A theoretical model for evaluating costs and benefits of the programs has been developed and plans are going forward for testing the model. However, no comprehensive and completely satisfactory program evaluation system has been developed.

Given the present inability to design a truly satisfactory scientific evaluation system, one of the most important existing evaluation techniques remains the field visit. The Office of Drug and Alcohol Abuse Prevention visited over 150 installations, commands, and programs during late 1980 and 1981 to evaluate program effectiveness subjectively. This direct observation by knowledgeable professionals remains one of the more effective evaluation tools.

EVALUATION OF CURRENT PROGRAMS

Clear, unequivocal scientific evidence of overall program efficacy does not yet exist. However, persuasive, persistent, and significant pieces of evidence from several quarters suggest that the stronger DoD programs are working and working well. Table 13 summarizes drug program trends from 1974 to 1980. Prevalence of hard drug use by junior enlisted (E1–E5) declined in all areas of the world. Prevalence of cannabis use declined in the air force (26% to 20%) and the army (46% to 40%) but increased in the navy (35% to 47%) and Marine Corps (43% to 47%), resulting in a stable rate of use in DoD as a whole. However, these results are only suggestive, not conclusive. A wide range of variables other than program effectiveness may have contributed to these changes over a six-year period and the exact causes of the variance cannot be accounted for in retrospect.

Another suggestive but not conclusive piece of evidence of the effectiveness of the DoD program as it is presently being developed is provided by comparing air force prevalence rates to those of other serivces. The prevalence of alcohol and drug abuse in the air force is significantly lower than in the other services (less than half the rate of current illicit drug use; one-fourth the drug dependence rate; less than half the work impairment; less than half the alcohol dependence rate). However, some of this variance is attributable to differences in the demography of the services' populations. A study was conducted to identify precisely how much of the variance was attributable to these demographic factors (Booz-Allen & Hamilton, 1981). The conclusion reached was that, even with the demographic variables, age, sex, marital status, and education controlled for, the air force has statistically significant lower rates of illicit drug usage. These lower rates of use appear to be attributable to program effectiveness. Since all military programs are now being generally shaped in the direction of the air force

Table 13.
Comparison: 1974 and 1980 Drug Use E1–E5 During Past 30 Days
(Percentage of Population)

Prevalence worldwide	1974[a]	1980[b]	Change
Cannabis	37	37	Same
Stimulants	15	12	Down 3
Depressants	11	5	Down 6
Hallucinogens	14	5	Down 9
Narcotics	7	2	Down 5

[a]A. D. Little Co., 1975.
[b]Burt and Biegel, 1980.

program, significant prevalence rate reductions are expected by the time the 1982 DoD Worldwide Survey is taken.

With regard to alcohol rehabilitation programs, a Rand study for the air force provides the most compelling evidence of effectiveness (Orvis, Armor, Williams, Barras, & Schwarzback, 1981). A treatment follow-up survey indicated that clients experienced substantial improvement after treatment. A significant reduction in the overall problem rate of more than 50 percentage points occurred during the follow-up assessment period when contrasted with the year prior to admission. Both alcohol dependence symptoms and adverse consequences occurring to nondependent drinkers decreased ($p < .001$ by chi-square test in both cases).

Two other pieces of the puzzle came from independent studies unassociated with the DoD. The first piece was supplied by Dr. Lloyd Johnston of the Institute for Social Research in the course of his national study of drug using patterns of high school seniors. He found that for marijuana smokers overall there is a 2.6% *increase* in the prevalence of daily marijuana use after graduation from high school. However, daily use *declined* for two categories of people, those who had children (down 1.5%) and those entering the military (down 1%) (Johnston, 1980).

A second piece of evidence was found in a study of drug abuse in rural America by Harrell and Cisin (Harrell & Cisin, 1981). The researchers expected rural drug use to be consistently higher in areas where visitors or temporary residents were able to bring in drug use experience, such as near colleges, near military bases, and near resort areas. The expectation of higher rates of drug use held true in the cases of resorts and colleges. However, the researchers consistently failed to find proximity to military bases to predict higher than average rural drug use.

As indicated, these pieces of evidence do not provide scientific proof that DoD alcohol and drug abuse prevention programs are working. However, the preponderence of evidence suggests that those that are functioning properly are having a positive impact on alcohol and drug problems. As current program evaluation and assessment efforts mature, and as all programs achieve the quality of the best, the exact nature of the impact of military intervention programs can be scientifically documented.

Several key aspects of military intervention programs seem to be most essential. First, at the macrolevel, a systems approach to organization is critical. All levels and all components of the organization must be thoughtfully integrated and focused to reduce alcohol and drug abuse as part of the course of daily business. Although development of such a system takes longer than creating a special interest office, a program "stovepiped" or grafted onto the exterior of the organization will not work. A special interest program cannot sustain support.

The system must be data based (i.e., based on measurable facts that can be agreed upon by most observers) and must be linked by a policy-relevant assessment and evaluation system that is capable of detecting intrasystem and external changes. The intervention system must be decentralized in operation to insure ownership and responsiveness to local needs, but must be centrally monitored to insure consistency and high standards.

At the micro level, community organization is essential. A key ingredient in air force program success has been the use of the Drug and Alcohol Abuse Control Committee as a means to organize major community leaders, to focus them on the problem, and to hold them accountable for producing positive results in their areas of responsibility. Knowledgeable and committed involvement by community leaders is absolutely essential, even though it takes much time and effort to develop such involvement.

The spectrum of alcohol and drug problems runs the gamut from occasional unwise use to life-threatening dependence. The organizational response must accommodate all parts of that spectrum, including setting clear standards of expected behavior and providing prevention education, deterrence, detection, remedial education, outpatient counseling, medical care, inpatient treatment, follow-up systems to reintegrate recovering persons back into the organization, and disposition programs for those who cannot or will not recover.

SUMMARY

The Department of Defense has been coping with alcohol and other drug problems for many years. The effectiveness of that coping has waxed and waned depending on the severity of the problem, on command perceptions, and on public concern. In the final analysis, the department has sought to reduce the adverse impact of alcohol and drug abuse on the national defense and on the health and behavior of military members and their families. In recent years, with the unprecedented explosion of illicit drug use by the youth of American society, substance abuse prevention in the military has become both more important and more difficult to achieve.

During the late 1970s, a common concept for preventing alcohol and drug abuse began to evolve. The core elements of this concept are (1) a systems approach to organization; (2) comprehensive assessment of the nature, extent, and consequences of abuse expressed in scientifically valid but policy-relevant terms; (3) application of most prevention and intervention resources to the aspects of the problem that cause the most serious negative effects; (4) local community organization monitored from central points of authority; (5) continued evaluation of cost-effectiveness and program results; and (6) thematic emphasis on manpower conservation and mission accomplishment.

This unifying concept requires time to translate into programs. The core elements have been incorporated in Department of Defense directives. The air force has largely translated the ideas into program structure and it appears to be working well. The other services are at varying stages of implementation. Initial program evaluations and research efforts suggest that the approach is having substantial positive impact. However, accurate measurement of results of prevention programs is difficult to achieve.

The major challenge, other than bringing all military programs to a common level of effectiveness, faced by the Office of Drug and Alcohol Abuse Prevention is to develop improved scientific methods of program evaluation in order to better close the feedback loop and develop a truly balanced alcohol and drug abuse prevention and intervention system.

REFERENCES

A. D. Little Co., *A study of Department of Defense drug abuse prevention and control programs.* Washington, D.C.: OASD/HA. January 1975. (Reprint)

Adamson, G. A., & R. B. Borthwick. *Cost-benefit analysis of the army's alcohol and drug abuse prevention and control programs, 1978.* Arlington, Va.: Presearch, 1978.

Alcohol Consumption. *Encyclopaedia Britannica, 1977.*

Blane, H. T. Middle-aged alcoholics and young drinkers. In H. T. Blane & M. E. Chafetz (Eds.), *Youth, alcohol, and social policy.* New York: Plenum Press, 1979.

Booz-Allen & Hamilton. *Intra service comparative analysis of 1980 DoD drug prevalence and consequence data: Enlisted personnel in pay grades E1 through E5.* Washington, D.C.: Naval Military Personnel Command, March 1981.

Borthwick, R. B. *Summary of cost benefit study results for navy alcoholism rehabilitation programs, July 1977.* Arlington, Va.: Presearch, 1977.

Burt, M. R., & Biegel, M. M. *Worldwide survey on nonmedical drug use and alcohol use among military personnel: 1980.* Bethesda, MD: Burt Associates, 1980.

Cahalan, D., & Cisin, I. *Final report on a servicewide survey of attitudes and behavior of naval personnel concerning alcohol and problem drinking.* Washington, D.C.: Bureau of Social Science Research, 1975.

Cahalan, D., Cisin, I., Gardner, G., & Smith, G. C. *Drinking practices and problems in the U. S. Army, 1972.* Washington, D.C.: Information Concepts, 1972.

Carpenter-Huffman, P., Orvis, B. R., Armor, D., & Burkholz, G. *The effectiveness of air force alcohol education seminars.* Santa Monica, Calif.: The Rand Corporation, 1981.

Chafetz, M. E. Epidemiology of drinking practices among adolescents and young adults. In H. T. Blane & M. E. Chafetz (Eds.), *Youth, alcohol, and social policy.* New York: Plenum Press, 1979.

Department of the Army. *Human readiness report No. 2, January 1975.* Washington, D.C.: Office of Deputy Chief of Staff for Personnel, 1975.

Department of the Army. *Human readiness report No. 4, March 1978.* Washington, D. C.: Office of Deputy Chief of Staff for Personnel, 1978.

DoD Instruction 1010.3, *Drug and alcohol abuse reports.* Washington, D. C.: OASD/HA, 1981.

DoD Directive 1010.4, *Alcohol and drug abuse by DoD personnel*. Washington, D. C.: OASD/HA, August 25, 1980.

DoD Instruction 1010.5, *Education and training in alcohol and drug abuse prevention*. Washington, D. C.: OASD/HA, December 5, 1980.

DoD Instruction 1010.6, *Rehabilitation and referral services for alcohol and drug abusers*. Washington, D. C.: OASD/HA, August 12, 1981.

Fisher, A. H., Jr. *Preliminary findings from the 1971 DoD survey of drug use*. Washington, D. C.: HumRRo, TR 72–8, March 1972.

Fisher, A. H., Jr. *Major findings from the 1972 DoD survey on drug use*. Washington, D. C.: HumRRo, TR 73, May 1973.

General Accounting Office. *Alcohol abuse is more prevalent in the military than drug abuse*. Washington, D. C.: Report to the Congress, MWD–76–99, April 8, 1976.

Harrell, A. V., & Cisin, I. H. *Drug abuse in rural America*. Washington, D. C.: U. S. Department of Health and Human Services, 1981.

Ingraham, L. H. *The boys in the barracks: Observations on American common soldiers in garrison*. Washington, D. C.: Walter Reed Army Institute of Research, 1978.

Janowitz, M., & Moscos, C. C., Jr. Five years of the all-volunteer force: 1973–1978. *Armed Forces and Society*, 1979, 5(2), 171–217.

Johnston, L. D. *The daily marijuana user*. Paper for National Alcohol and Drug Coalition. Ann Arbor, Mich.: Institute for Social Research, September 18, 1980.

Keegan, J. *The face of battle*. New York: Viking, 1976.

Killeen, J. E. U. S. military alcohol abuse prevention and rehabilitation programs. In H. T. Blane & M. E. Chafetz (Eds.), *Youth, alcohol, and social policy*. New York: Plenum Press, 1979.

Orvis, B. R., Armor, D. J., Williams, C. E., Barras, A., & Schwarzbach, D. S. *Cost and effectiveness of alcohol rehabilitation in the United States Air Force*. Santa Monica, Calif.: The Rand Corporation, 1981.

Polich, J. M., & Orvis, B. R. *Alcohol problems: Patterns and prevalence in the U. S. Air Force*. Santa Monica, Calif.: The Rand Corporation, 1979.

U. S. Air Force, *Drug and alcohol abuse control committee management guide*. Washington, D. C.: HQ USAF, 1979.

U. S. Air Force Regulation 30–2. Social actions program. Washington, D. C.: HQ USAF, June 22, 1981.

U. S. Congress. House Committee on Armed Services. *Review of military clubs and package beverage stores*. Hearings. Washington, D. C.: GPO. October 16–19, 1979.

War Department. *Report of the surgeon-general of the army to the Secretary of War for the fiscal year ending June 30, 1890*. Washington, D. C.: Government Printing Office, 1890.

War Department. *Report of the surgeon-general of the army to the Secretary of War for the fiscal year ending June 30, 1895*. Washington, D. C.: Government Printing Office, 1895.

Windrow, M., & Wilkinson, F. *The universal soldier: Fourteen studies in campaign life, A. D. 43–1944*. Garden City, N.Y.: Doubleday, 1971.

15

Alcohol Abuse Prevention
Conclusions and Future Directions

PETER M. MILLER AND TED D. NIRENBERG

Throughout this volume the contributors have provided a thorough over-view of current thinking regarding alcohol abuse prevention. Available techniques and a state-of-the-art summary of policies, programs, and prac-tices have been reviewed. It is apparent that prevention of alcohol problems is in its infancy from both a technological and a methodological standpoint. The information presented in this book, therefore, can serve as an excellent base upon which to build future prevention efforts.

METHODOLOGICAL CONCERNS

A major problem discussed most notably by Cellucci (Chapter 2), Hewitt and Blane (Chapter 8), Braucht and Braucht (Chapter 7), and Kill-een (Chapter 14) is the inadequate evaluation of prevention projects. Spe-cific methodological concerns involve either the total absence of evaluation or poorly designed experimental studies. There is a need to go beyond simple case studies and correlational data and to use more basic experimen-

PETER M. MILLER • Sea Pines Behavioral Institute, Sea Pines Plantation, Hilton Head, South Carolina 29928. TED D. NIRENBERG • Alcohol Dependence Treatment Program, Veterans Administration Medical Center and Section of Psychiatry and Human Behavior, Brown University, Providence, Rhode Island 02908.

tal procedures including control groups and the random assignment of subjects to groups.

A better description of intervention approaches used is also needed. Unfortunately, many reports of projects in the prevention literature omit essential details regarding assessment, procedures, and statistical analyses. Investigators too often report, for example, the use of "values clarification" or "controlled drinking training" without describing exactly what such interventions involve.

More comprehensive evaluation measures must also be used. Multiple measures are usually needed to assess the full impact of a prevention strategy. For example, drunken-driver programs must address not only recidivism but also more sensitive measures such as job performance, marital satisfaction, and emotional adjustment. Recidivism is not sensitive enough to measure outcome since the arrest rate for such driving offenses is very low (approximately 1 in 2,000). Measures must also assess changes in several dimensions including knowledge, attitudes, and behavior.

Subjects chosen to participate in prevention research projects often are part of a unique population. For instance, since the probability of being arrested for a drunken-driving offense is so low, those arrested may represent a small and unique subset of drinkers on the highways. Prevention efforts that are effective for them may not be appropriate or effective for others.

One of the most glaring deficiencies in the prevention literature is the absence of long-term follow-up studies. Most investigators simply evaluate the immediate short-term effects of their prevention programs. The long-term effects may be quite different. For example, a strong correlation seems to exist between lowering the legal drinking age and increases in alcohol problems among 18- to 20-year-old youth. More recently, however, Douglass and Freedman (1977) and Whitehead (1977) report that this relationship declines and stabilizes over time. Likewise, some forms of alcohol education may increase an individual's interest in and experimentation with alcohol but, in the long run, may reduce his or her potential for developing an alcohol problem.

EARLY PREDICTORS OF ABUSE

More information is needed on the developmental trends and situational determinants of problem drinking. Although several extensive long-term studies have been reported, a more refined analysis is necessary to pinpoint individuals who are most susceptible to alcohol abuse problems. For example, Goodwin (Chapter 4) makes a strong case for a hereditary component to at least some alcohol problems. More evidence along these lines could allow for very early intervention with children of close alcoholic relatives. Cellucci (Chapter 2) also reviews evidence suggesting the importance of such variables as broken homes and delinquent behaviors as being predictive of heavy drinking. Harford (Chapter 5) stresses the role of situational variables (e.g., physical location, intent of drinking) that initiate and maintain appropriate and inappropriate drinking.

The most sensible and comprehensive approach would seem to be to search out clusters of genetic, individual, and situational variables that correlate highly with future alcohol abuse. Then prevention efforts could be more specially matched with unique population groups.

GOAL CLARIFICATION

The goals of prevention efforts should be relatively straightforward. In actuality, the aims of alcohol abuse prevention represent a complex and sometimes controversial issue.

Two specific goals for prevention exist. First, some investigators insist that total and complete abstinence is the only reasonable goal. That is, if no one drank alcohol, no alcohol problems would exist. Although this may be true theoretically, attempts at prohibition have shown that such a goal is both unpopular and difficult, if not impossible, to enforce.

Second, others argue that the goal of prevention is to prevent problem drinking. That is, the assumption is that alcohol *per se* is not inherently evil, only its excessive use. Although this is the more accepted of the two goals, it is often challenged on theoretical and conceptual grounds by many proponents of Alcoholics Anonymous.

Braucht and Braucht (Chapter 7) note that prevention goals are often so vague as to be meaningless. For example, many projects propose to increase "positive self-concepts," "rational choices," or "healthy values." From a scientific standpoint, these goals must be operationally defined if they are to be evaluated and if the projects are to be replicated.

DIFFERENTIAL TREATMENT PLANNING

It would not be surprising to learn that one type of prevention program is not suitable for all individuals. However, from a historical prospective, prevention programs have been provided in a blanket or "shot-gun" fashion to widely diverse populations. Alcohol abuse prevention has grown to the point where specific interventions must be matched up with specific populations.

Several authors in this volume note the importance of targeting intervention to certain groups. Schlegel *et al.* (Chapter 12) found that the "decision-making" component of his prevention package was not appropriate for use with eighth graders. In fact, its inclusion reduced the benefits of the program to this age group. He emphasized the importance of sequencing and timing of these interventions based on grade levels.

Braucht and Braucht (Chapter 7) also stress the need for tailoring educational programs to different populations of youth. The question is not "Is alcohol education effective?" but "What kinds of educational strategies have what kinds of effects with what kinds of people?" In fact, in the analysis of three distinct populations—women, blacks, and American Indians—Noel and McCrady (Chapter 3) note several important group differences that are crucial to prevention efforts.

Nowhere are these individual differences so evident as in prevention projects utilizing the mass media. Hewitt and Blane (Chapter 8) discuss the ways in which different target groups respond differently to mass media messages. For instance, many target groups are most influenced by television messages during the prime-time evening hours. However, if adolescents, college students, or housewives are the targets, these prime-time hours are not the most appropriate for intervention.

ETHICAL CONSIDERATIONS

Prevention programs raise some very important ethical issues that must be addressed by present and future investigators. One of the foremost problems is that of confidentiality. Nathan (Chapter 11) notes that this is a particularly important issue in employee assistance programs. The employee has the right to privacy and participation in such programs may result in stigmatization based on labeling participants as problem drinkers or potential alcoholics. Confidentiality is also subject to abuse when a person is referred into treatment by the courts (Klajner *et al.,* Chapter 13). Those needing prevention services the most may avoid it due to fear of such labeling.

PROGRAM COMPONENT ANALYSIS

Future investigations must not only determine the most effective approaches but, more importantly, the most effective components of those approaches. Benefits to the participant must be weighed against the cost-effectiveness, in terms of time and money, of the program. More intervention is not necessarily better intervention. As noted earlier, Schlegel *et al.* (Chapter 12) found that the addition of a "decision-making" procedure to his prevention package did not significantly improve the results. In fact, it actually detracted from the total program. Students receiving the added component benefited less from the total package than those not receiving it.

From both a clinical and ethical viewpoint effective prevention strategies that are the least restrictive and disruptive to an individual's life must be determined (Nirenberg, 1983). It is not sufficient for prevention to be effective, that is, to accomplish the intended goal. The goal must be accomplished with minimum side effects. For example, suppose that a prevention program based on the notion of total lifelong abstinence from alcohol were found to be effective in terms of preventing alcoholism. However, also suppose that to maintain a life of total abstinence, some individuals find that they must alter their social and recreational habits so drastically that total abstinence is not worth the cost. Alternatively, an effective but less restrictive program may involve social skills training in which individuals learn to restrict their alcohol intake.

ACCESS TO "HIDDEN POPULATIONS"

One major area of need in the prevention field is to identify population groups that are most in need of intervention. Unfortunately, these groups are often "hidden" and not easily accessible. By *hidden* is meant that either society or the group members themselves ignore the potential of alcoholism in such groups(i.e., American Indians, blacks, the elderly, and housewives).

Specific strategies must be devised to reach these groups. A general pamphlet or media message may completely miss these target individuals. Rather than waiting for them to "get the message," educational efforts must be implemented on a grassroots level.

For example, Nathan (Chapter 11) describes the use of the workplace as an excellent "penetration" point for prevention efforts. Not only can all levels of employees be exposed to the program, but the focus of the intervention can be broadly based. Alcohol use is usually only one element of these employee assistance programs, which aim to teach social/emotional problem-solving skills and to change inappropriate habits to establish healthier life-style patterns.

Possible future sites for these broad-based intervention programs include schools, daytime television programming (to reach the housewife group), parent–teacher organizations, professional meetings, and group housing projects.

OUTCOME STUDIES

A glaring deficit in the alcoholism prevention literature is the absence of well-controlled outcome studies. Since future problems with alcohol are the targets of intervention, long-term follow-up assessments must be conducted. Unfortunately, the current literature lacks even short-term evaluation of results. Prevention projects without a built-in measure of effectiveness should be considered a thing of the past. The state-of-the-art demands more experimental sophistication.

The studies presented by Kraft (Chapter 9) and Schlegel *et al.* (Chapter 12) provide excellent examples of the evaluation of prevention programs. However, such evaluations should be the rule rather than the exception.

An example of a multifaceted evaluation is provided by a currently ongoing prevention study by Nirenberg, Miller, and McClure (1982). This study examines the effects of different prevention strategies with moderate to heavy drinking college students. Subjects participated in one of five prevention programs, each consisting of four two-hour group sessions. Based on differing prevention strategies, the programs included (1) behavioral self-control training using assertiveness, relaxation, problem solving, responsible drinking, self-management training, and alcohol education; (2) behavioral self-control training and alcohol education with practice at estimating different blood alcohol levels; (3) alcohol education consisting of information and attitude change messages based on a responsible drinking model; (4) alcohol education consisting of information and attitude change messages based on the Alcoholics Anonymous model; and (5) a no-intervention control group.

A comprehensive assessment conducted prior to and during training will be followed by similar assessments at one, three, and five-year follow-ups. The assessment includes self-monitoring of alcohol-related behaviors, self-report of measures of alcohol use and life functioning, biochemical determinants of alcohol use (liver function studies), health profile analyses, and reports from family and friends.

Researchers in the health education field who are establishing programs to prevent cardiovascular disease are well ahead of alcohol researchers in terms of methodological and evaluation procedures. A prime example is the Stanford Heart Disease Prevention Program (Meyer, Nash, McAlister, Maccoby, & Farquhar, 1980). These researchers examined the efficacy of programs designed to reduce the risk of heart disease by modifying dietary, smoking, and exercise patterns in an attempt to change such factors as blood pressure and cholesterol levels.

Four groups of subjects, preselected to have a higher than average risk for cardiovascular disease, received either (1) mass media instructions alone or (2) mass media instructions together with group meetings focusing on risk factors and using social learning techniques and behavioral self-control principles. The researchers found that while mass media alone led to changes in behavior that lowered the risk of heart disease, subjects receiving the group meetings showed the greatest overall improvement.

COMMUNITY SUPPORT AND ORGANIZATION

The prevention of alcohol abuse must involve several elements of the community at large. Researchers must be realistic about the fact that alcohol education programs are not necessarily popular with all groups. The distilled spirits industry, although it has endorsed some of these efforts, remains skeptical about the negative influence of prevention approaches on alcohol sales. Some abstinence-oriented treatment groups may oppose any prevention program that attempts to teach responsible drinking since they view *any* drinking as a problem or potential problem.

Without community wide support, certain forms of alcohol abuse prevention are not possible. For instance, legislative penalties for driving while intoxicated have little meaning unless they are enforced by law enforcement officers and judges. The recent decriminalization of public drunkeness in many states led to much opposition. Although the number of public drunkeness arrests declined (since it was no longer considered a crime), law enforcers in many states continued to arrest public drunks under the guise of other criminal charges (e.g., protective custody detention, disorderly conduct charges). Instituting new laws, especially in the absence of sufficient explanations for their use, frequently leads to a reluctance of these enforcers to put these laws into practice.

Along the same lines, Killeen (Chapter 14) notes that the support of military commanders is essential for military prevention programs to be successful. Nathan (Chapter 11) also describes the importance of upper-level management in implementing employee health education programs.

In addition, government and professional support for prevention efforts is needed. Government research funds for alcoholism prevention are increasing and, it is hoped, will continue to grow. Several authors of the international chapters in this volume note that worldwide organizations such as the World Health Organization and the European Common Market may provide financial support for such projects in the future.

REFERENCES

Douglass, R. L., & Freedman, J. A. A study of alcohol-related casualties and alcohol beverage availability policies in Michigan. Ann Arbor, Mich.: Highway Safety Research Institute, Ann Arbor, 1977.

Meyer, A. J., Nash, J. D., McAlister, A. L., Maccoby, N., & Farquhar, J. Skills training in a cardiovascular health education campaign. *Journal of Consulting and Clinical Psychology,* 1980, *48*(2), 129–142.

Nirenberg, T. D. Treatment of substance abuse. In C. E. Walker (Ed.), *Handbook of clinical psychology.* New York: Dorsey, 1983.

Nirenberg, T. D., Miller, P. M., & McClure, G. *Comparative efficacy of alcohol abuse prevention strategies.* Unpublished manuscript, 1982.

Whitehead, P. C. Alcohol and young drivers: Impact and implications of lowering the drinking age. Ottawa: Department of National Health and Welfare, Monograph Series No. 1, 1977.

Index